COMPREHENSIVE ASPECTS OF TAXATION

37th Edition
DAVID BERTRAM, F.C.A., A.T.I.I.
and
STEPHEN EDWARDS, F.C.A., F.T.I.I.

Part 1
Income tax, corporation tax,
anti-avoidance provisions, value added tax

HOLT, RINEHART AND WINSTON
LONDON · NEW YORK · SYDNEY · TORONTO

Holt, Rinehart and Winston Ltd: 1 St Anne's Road,
Eastbourne, East Sussex BN21 3UN

British Library Cataloguing in Publication Data

Bertram, A. D. W.
    Comprehensive aspects of taxation.—37th ed.
    1. Taxation—Great Britain
    I. Title   II. _Edwards, S. G.
    336.2'00941   HJ2619

ISBN 0–03–910606–3

Printed in Great Britain by A. Wheaton & Co. Ltd, Exeter

37th edition 1985

Last digit is print no: 9 8 7 6 5 4 3 2 1

Preface

Our aim, in writing this book, is to provide those studying taxation and indeed the practitioner with a thorough understanding of the framework of the law and practice of taxation.

Wherever possible we have tried to avoid legal phraseology, and have sought to explain the statutes and relevant case law in clear and simple language. However, we believe that it is essential that students and practitioners should be familiar with the law itself. Accordingly, statutory references have been included to enable them to turn to the appropriate legislation for further study or research.

Another feature of the book is the large number of examples setting out the practical application of the legislation. These are considered to be a vital ingredient, not only in preparing students for examinations and in assisting practitioners to prepare computations but also as an easy and straightforward means towards an understanding of the complexities of tax law.

This edition of the book has been revised and updated to include the Finance Act 1985, and relevant case law up to 31st July 1985. Additionally, we have included for the first time (in Appendix 3) the current rates of National Insurance contributions.

David Bertram
Stephen Edwards

Abbreviations

C.A.A.	Capital Allowances Act
C.G.T.	Capital gains tax
C.G.T.A.	Capital Gains Tax Act
C.T.T.	Capital transfer tax
C.T.T.A.	Capital Transfer Tax Act
D.L.T.	Development land tax
D.L.T.A.	Development Land Tax Act
F.A.	Finance Act
I.C.T.A.	Income and Corporation Taxes Act
T.M.A.	Taxes Management Act
V.A.T.	Value added tax
V.A.T.A.	Value Added Tax Act

Contents

1. Income Tax—Scope and Administration

§ 1.—THE TAXES ACTS

Income Tax was first introduced in 1799, and was repealed in 1816. In 1842 Income Tax was re-imposed, and has been continued in force ever since. The Income and Corporation Taxes Act 1970, consolidated the provisions contained in the Income Tax Act 1952, and Finance Acts up to 1970 inclusive. Subsequent Finance Acts have not been consolidated. The 1970 Act does not purport to be a codification of Tax law, that is, it does not attempt to incorporate the results of decided cases or to give statutory effect to Inland Revenue practice where it differs from the strict law, or to correct anomalies or remove ambiguities.

The Capital Gains Tax legislation has been consolidated into the Capital Gains Tax Act 1979, and the Development Land Tax provisions are to be found in the Development Land Tax Act 1976.

The Income and Corporation Taxes Act 1970, and other Acts that relate to Income Tax, Capital Gains Tax, Development Land Tax (see Chapter 32) and Corporation Tax, are known collectively as "The Taxes Acts."

Provisions relating to the administration of Taxes have been consolidated in the Taxes Management Act 1970.

In addition, regulations are made under the Taxes Acts, known as "Statutory Instruments." Having statutory force, these must be construed in conjunction with the statute under which they were made. One example is the "Pay As You Earn Regulations" (see Chapter 8, §12).

The rate of tax is suggested by the Government, which endeavours to match its financial requirements with its revenue. Variations in the tax laws are also suggested by the Government, either as a matter of policy or as a result of the experience of those officials whose duty it is to administer taxes.

Such variations in the tax code are often the result of case law, where the Courts have held against the Inland Revenue and the statutory provisions in question have failed to have the effect originally planned, and must therefore be modified (e.g. Section 478 I.C.T.A. 1970 following the decision in *Vestey* v. *C.I.R.* (1980)).

§ 2.—THE INCOME TAX YEAR (s. 2(2), I.C.T.A. 1970)

The "Income Tax year" (or year of assessment) runs from the 6th April to the following 5th April; for example, the year of assessment 1985–86 runs from 6th April 1985 to 5th April 1986.

§ 3.—PROVISIONAL COLLECTION OF TAX

Although Income Tax is re-imposed from year to year, the machinery for assessment and collection of the tax is kept alive from one year to another by the Provisional Collection of Taxes Act 1968. Shortly before or after the commencement of each year of assessment, a resolution of the Ways and Means Committee of the House of Commons renews the tax for the current year.

In the case of a resolution passed in March or April in any year, the Provisional Collection of Taxes Act 1968, gives this resolution (which is, of course, based upon the Chancellor's Budget) statutory effect until 5th August in the same calendar year. In the case of any other resolution, the Act gives the resolution statutory effect for four months from the date on which it is expressed to take effect. Any deduction of income tax within one month after the end of any Income Tax year, pending the resolution of the Ways and Means Committee, is also legalised by the Provisional Collection of Taxes Act 1968. The Finance Act 1985 extends this Act to include reduced and composite rate tax, deducted by banks, building societies and others deducting tax at source on deposits (see Chapter 9).

It will thus be seen that although Income Tax is a "temporary" tax imposed for each year, the machinery for assessment and collection is kept alive from one year to another, and for all practical purposes Income Tax may be regarded as a permanent source of revenue to the Government.

§ 4.—RATE OF INCOME TAX (s. 32, F.A. 1971)

(*a*) BASIC RATE
The basic rate of income tax for 1985–86 is 30%. The rates of income tax for earlier years are set out in the Appendix to this work.

(*b*) HIGHER RATES
Individual taxpayers, whose income, after deducting specified allowances, exceeds a certain limit (fixed annually by the Finance Act) are subject to rates of tax in excess of the basic rate known as higher rate tax.

(*c*) YEARS PRIOR TO 1984–85: INVESTMENT INCOME SURCHARGE
Investment income in excess of a certain limit was subject to an additional tax charge known as the *investment income surcharge*. (See Appendix I).

§ 5.—ADMINISTRATION OF INCOME TAX

The chief officials concerned with the administration of Income Tax, etc. are:

(*a*) THE COMMISSIONERS OF INLAND REVENUE ("the Board") (s. 1, T.M.A., 1970), senior permanent civil servants in whose hands rests the care and management of income tax. This means they have the ultimate responsibility for the general administration of the tax, although the work of assessment and collection is delegated to Inspectors of Taxes and Collectors of Taxes.

The Board acts in an advisory capacity to the Treasury regarding the introduction of amendments to the tax laws, and in the preparation of Budget estimates, etc.

(*b*) H.M. INSPECTORS OF TAXES, civil servants appointed by the Board. They issue return forms, examine them and make assessments on behalf of the Board and have power to amend assessments where necessary. In practice, they are the officials with whom the taxpayer or his representative deals, and all returns and notices of appeal must be sent to them. For convenience, their work is allocated to Districts throughout the country.

(*c*) THE COLLECTORS OF TAXES collect the assessed tax for districts in respect of which they are appointed. They are full-time officials who work in conjunction with the Inspectors of Taxes.

(*d*) THE SPECIAL COMMISSIONERS (s. 4, T.M.A. 1970), full-time civil servants whose main function is the hearing of appeals against assessments. These are now to be under the control of the Lord Chancellor.

(*e*) THE GENERAL COMMISSIONERS (ss. 2 and 3, T.M.A. 1970), members of the public appointed for the various divisions except in Northern Ireland, where their function is discharged by the Special Commissioners and the County Court.

Except in exceptional circumstances, all appeals, unless the taxpayer elects for the appeal to be heard by the Special Commissioners, are heard by the General Commissioners.

The General Commissioners are unpaid, other than for travelling and subsistence allowance. In addition, the General Commissioners appoint the Clerk (whose remuneration is paid by the Treasury), to act as legal adviser and perform the secretarial work in connection with the hearing of appeals. However, he does not take part in their deliberations. The age limit for General Commissioners is 75 and the retirement age for their Clerk is 70 (this can be extended by the General Commissioners concerned, if thought appropriate).

(*f*) THE BOARD OF REFEREES. The board of referees was dissolved by s. 156 F.A. 1982 and its functions transferred to the tribunal mentioned below.

(*g*) THE TRIBUNAL (s. 463, I.C.T.A. 1970, s. 80(3)), a body which has judicial functions on anti-avoidance provisions connected with "transactions in securities" (s. 460, I.C.T.A. 1970), and for *inter alia*—determining and reviewing the percentage rates on wear and tear allowances for plant and machinery (now rare following the introduction of "standard" capital allowances in F.A. 1971), and determining the tax charge on nonresidents as a percentage of turnover. (s. 80(3) T.M.A. 1970).

All the above persons are required, on taking office, to make a declaration of secrecy in a form appropriate to their appointment (s. 6 and Schedule 1, T.M.A. 1970). This declaration requires that information received by such persons in the course of their duties will not be disclosed except in so far as required for the purposes of carrying out such duties, in prosecutions for tax offences and in certain other instances, where so required and authorised by law, to:

(i) the Revenue authorities of other countries under double taxation treaties;
(ii) Customs and Excise officers;
(iii) Social Security Departments;
(iv) the Occupational Pensions Board;
(v) the Departments of Industry and of Employment;
(vi) the Charity Commissioners;
(vii) the Police, in respect of investigations into murder or treason.

General and Special Commissioners, except with the express consent of all parties to the proceedings, are debarred from acting in respect of any matter in which they have a personal interest, or in which they are interested on behalf of another person (e.g. as the taxpayer's agent) (s. 5, T.M.A. 1970).

The General and Special Commissioners, along with the Tribunal, all come under the jurisdiction of the Council of Tribunals.

§ 6.—CONSTRUCTION OF TAXING ACTS

Liability to tax depends entirely upon the provisions of the Acts in force. In interpreting the Taxes Acts and regulations, reference must, of course, be made to a considerable volume of case law, i.e., to decisions of the Courts on points of law. Before the cases of *W. T. Ramsay* v. *C.I.R.* (1981), *Eilbeck* v. *Rawling* (1981), *C.I.R.* v. *Burmah Oil Co. Ltd* (1981) and *Furniss* v. *Dawson* (1984) it had been held that if a person came within the letter of the law he must be taxed, however great the hardship may appear to be; and that on the other hand, if the Crown, in seeking to recover the tax charged, could not bring the subject within the letter of the law, then he was relieved of the obligation to pay, however apparently within the spirit of the law the case might otherwise appear. This principle now needs to be closely scrutinised following the *Ramsay*, *Burmah* and

Furniss and Dawson decisions since these cases establish that a review of the transaction as a whole will also be made in determining the taxation treatment of particular steps within the transaction. These cases have effectively curtailed blatant anti-avoidance schemes that previously were becoming a market in themselves, but it remains to be seen how far reaching their effect will be. *Avoidance* of taxation must not be confused with *evasion* of taxation, for the former relates to the arranging of affairs for the purpose of avoiding tax on purely legal grounds (e.g., taking out additional retirement annuity policies to ensure maximum relief from taxation, as explained in Chapter 2, § 13), whereas the latter relates to the wilful evasion of liability to tax (e.g., by non-disclosure of taxable income or gains). Evasion of tax may result in heavy penalties (and even imprisonment) being incurred by the culprit.

§ 7.—PERSONS LIABLE TO INCOME TAX

The liability to tax extends, in general, to:

> (*a*) All persons resident in the United Kingdom, whether or not British subjects and whether or not their income is derived from inside or outside the United Kingdom; and
>
> (*b*) All persons not resident in the United Kingdom, whether British subjects or not, in so far as they derive income from any property, trade, profession, vocation, or employment in the United Kingdom.

The word "person" does not necessarily refer to an individual and can include trustees, partnerships and companies (although companies normally pay corporation tax).

"United Kingdom" for income tax purposes includes Great Britain (England, Wales and Scotland) and Northern Ireland, but not the Isle of Man or the Channel Islands. The tax area is extended (by s. 38, F.A. 1973) to include the territorial sea of the United Kingdom and designated areas of the United Kingdom sector of the continental shelf.

Put another way, a person resident in the United Kingdom is liable upon his "world income," except in certain circumstances, to be dealt with later in this work, whereas one not resident in the United Kingdom is liable only upon that income arising in the United Kingdom.

Exactly what constitutes residence is considered in Chapter 8.

§ 8.—THE SCHEDULES

Although Income Tax is a tax on "income," "profits" or "gains," none of these terms is easy to define and the Taxing Statutes deliberately avoid concise and exact definitions thereof. Nevertheless some rules must be prescribed for measuring income (or profits or gains) and it is logical that these rules should vary according to the type of income, etc., i.e., the source from which the income, etc., arises, as will be seen below.

The various forms of income, etc., are divided for purposes of assessment to Income Tax and Corporation Tax into the following Schedules:

SCHEDULE A (s. 67(1), I.C.T.A. 1979).—Annual profits or gains arising from rents or receipts from land or buildings in the United Kingdom. The basis of assessment is the income to which the taxpayer becomes entitled in the year of assessment (see Chapter 2).

SCHEDULE B (ss. 91 and 92, I.C.T.A. 1970).—Income arising from the occupation of woodlands in the United Kingdom managed on a commercial basis and with a view to profit. The basis of assessment is one third of the annual value (see Chapter 2).

SCHEDULE C (s. 93, I.C.T.A. 1970).—Interest, annuities or dividends payable under deduction of tax out of any public revenue, whether of the United Kingdom, the Commonwealth or any foreign State, where payment is made through an agent resident in the United Kingdom. The assessment is on the agent and is the actual amount of the interest, etc., paid in the year of assessment (see Chapter 10).

SCHEDULE D (s. 108, I.C.T.A. 1970).—The profits of trades and professions, and any other form of income which does not fall under any of the other Schedules. This Schedule is sub-divided into six Cases, under which different classes of income are assessed (see Chapter 3, § 1).

SCHEDULE E (s. 181(1), I.C.T.A. 1970).—Wages, salaries, fees and pensions arising from any office or employment (except pensions from overseas assessed under Case V of Schedule D). Schedule E is sub-divided into three Cases, under which different categories of individuals are assessed (see Chapter 8, § 1). The basis of assessment is normally the salary, etc., for the actual year of assessment.

SCHEDULE F (s. 232(1), I.C.T.A. 1970).—This Schedule prior to the imputation system applied income tax to dividends and other distributions paid by companies, etc., chargeable to Corporation Tax. Under the "imputation system" companies account for advance corporation tax (A.C.T.) (see Chapter 15). Individuals are treated as receiving a gross amount equal to the aggregate of the dividend etc. paid, together with a "tax credit" in respect of the A.C.T. paid by the company. The tax credit is deemed to be income tax paid on behalf of the recipient.

§ 9.—TOTAL INCOME (ss. 3 and 528, I.C.T.A. 1970)

Except in certain cases, which will be referred to later (of these perhaps the most important is Schedule E income, on which tax is collected on the "Pay As You Earn" principle, as explained in Chapter 8, § 12), Income Tax is not levied upon the actual income received by the taxpayer from a source of income during the year of assessment, *but upon a hypothetical or "statutory" income which he is deemed to have received during that period* in accordance with the rules applying under the various Schedules of income tax. Any income received under deduction of income tax, as well as dividends (plus the tax credit) are also included.

Once this "statutory income" has been arrived at, it is taken to represent the income of the person concerned for the year of assessment in question, quite irrespective of the method adopted in arriving thereat. For example, assume that a sole trader has profits from his business for the year ended 31st December 1984, of £7,000. As will be seen later, the trader will be assessed for the year of assessment 1985–86 on the profits of the business year ending within the *preceding* year of assessment, i.e., £7,000. Thus his *statutory* income from this source for the purposes of assessment of Income Tax from 6th April 1985 to 5th April 1986, is £7,000, and upon this amount he will be assessed. During the period in question he may, in fact, have *actual* profits of £10,000, but except in certain special circumstances, e.g., the discontinuance of the business (see Chapter 3, § 5), he cannot be assessed at more than £7,000 for the year of assessment 1985–86 in respect of income from this particular source.

From this "statutory income" are deducted annuities, interest and other annual payments (collectively known as *annual charges*) in so far as such amounts are *paid* during the year in question, even though they may accrue wholly or partly before or after that year. Total income is therefore statutory income *less* annual charges.

§ 10.—MINORS (s. 73 T.M.A. 1970)

A minor is liable to Income Tax in the same way as any other individual, and in default of payment by him, his parent, guardian or tutor is liable for any tax payable. (See Chapter 2, § 3 regarding the treatment of a minor's unearned income).

The age of majority for tax purposes is 18 (s. 16, F.A. 1969).

§ 11.—OTHER PERSONS CHARGEABLE IN A REPRESENTATIVE CAPACITY (ss. 71, 72 to 76, T.M.A. 1970)

A "body of persons" is chargeable to income tax in the same way as an individual. Thus for every such body an officer acting as Treasurer etc. is chargeable to tax and answerable for fulfilling the duties imposed upon an individual in relation to his tax. Such a person is indemnified under s. 71(3) for any tax which he pays on its behalf.

The position is similar for trustees, guardians, etc. of incapacitated persons (e.g. infants, lunatics) and for receivers appointed by the Court.

The personal representatives (executors or administrators) of a deceased person are liable for any tax charged upon such a person, but can deduct any tax payments so made from the assets of the deceased.

Where such persons make the appropriate return (under s. 13, T.M.A. 1970), their responsibility for payment of tax, etc. ceases.

§ 12.—TAXATION AT SOURCE*

INTRODUCTION (s. 3, I.C.T.A. 1970; s. 86, F.A. 1972)

Whenever practicable, the Inland Revenue endeavour to collect Income Tax at source, i.e., where the income first arises, since:

(a) it ensures that tax is properly accounted for in many cases in which evasion would be an extremely easy matter, and

(b) it undoubtedly reduces considerably the work of the Revenue authorities.

Under this method many forms of income which are "unearned" in the hands of the recipients come to them already taxed at the basic rate, and consequently there is no necessity for a direct assessment on the taxpayer in respect of such income, unless he is liable to higher rates of tax.

In the event of the recipient not being liable to tax, in respect of the income so received, he will be able to claim repayment of the appropriate amount of the tax deducted at the source. But as it is a general rule that tax cannot be reclaimed from the Revenue authorities unless they have already received the tax, it is obvious that the person paying the income must account to the Revenue authorities for the tax deducted by him. The method of accounting to the Revenue authorities for such tax is apt to cause confusion, but if it is remembered that the payer of the income is in the position of a collecting agent for the Inland Revenue and must hand over any tax deducted, either along with his own Income Tax or separately, little difficulty should be experienced.

The classes of income concerned are:

(a) annuities and other annual payments (but *not* interest, for which special rules apply—see below);

---

* Income which is assessed under Schedule E is also taxed at source, on the "Pay As You Earn" principle, but in view of the fairly detailed regulations which are involved, an explanation of this subject is deferred until Chapter 8, § 12.
Similarly interest paid to U.K. residents by banks etc. is from 6th April 1985 subject to tax at source (but see Chapter 9).

(b) royalties, etc. for the use of patents;
(c) mineral royalties (if properly subject to deduction of income tax).

In similar manner, dividends and other distributions made by United Kingdom companies are deemed to have suffered income tax (at the basic rate on the gross amount thereof) equal to the A.C.T. paid by the company. In general, the rate of tax deducted in the case of annual payments, interest etc. is that in force at the time the payment is made (s. 36, F.A. 1971).

ANNUAL PAYMENTS (EXCLUDING INTEREST) (ss. 52 and 53, I.C.T.A. 1970). The tax on annual payments is collected, not from the recipient, but from the payer. The payments falling under these provisions include annuities, mineral rents and royalties but not loan or mortgage interest (except where paid to a non-resident) or interest paid to a bank or building society.

Annual payments (often termed "annual charges") fall into two classes:

(A) Those paid out of profits or gains brought into charge to income tax (s. 52).
(B) Those *not* paid out of profits or gains brought into charge to income tax (ss. 53 and 56, I.C.T.A. 1970). The term "profits or gains" simply means "income."

(A) *Where an annual payment is made wholly out of profits or gains brought into charge to income tax*, no deduction is allowed on account of such payment when computing the assessment on the profits or income out of which it is paid, in spite of the fact that it reduces the income of the payer and becomes the income of the recipient. Thus if Albert receives a salary of £10,000 for the year ended 5th April 1986, but pays an annuity of £200, his assessment for the year 1985–86 will be on £10,000. But since the person paying the interest is *entitled* under s. 52, I.C.T.A. 1970 to deduct and retain a sum representing Income Tax thereon at the basic rate in force when the payment *became due*, he is left in the same position as if he had only been assessed on his net income, leaving the recipient to be assessed direct.

Annual payments are regarded as having been made out of profits or gains brought into charge to tax when the total assessments raised on the taxpayer (inclusive of income taxed at the source, such as dividends from a company) are equal to or greater than the amount of the annual payment.†

(B) *Where annual payments are not paid—or wholly paid—out of profits or gains brought into charge to income tax* (that is to say, where the annual payment exceeds the payer's income for the year of assessment) then under s. 53, I.C.T.A. 1970, the payer *must* deduct Income Tax at the basic rate in force *when the payment is made*, and must account to the Commissioners of Inland Revenue for the tax so deducted. In practice, a separate assessment is raised by the Special Commissioners in respect thereof under s. 53, I.C.T.A. 1970.

Example

If Charles, having made a loss of £750 for the year ended 31st December 1984, and having therefore a "nil" assessment for the year 1985–86, pays an annuity of £60 on 31st December 1985, deducting tax therefrom, he must account for such tax to the Revenue authorities. Assessment will therefore be made under s. 53 on the annuity of £60. Similarly, if Ernest made an adjusted profit of £100 which formed the subject of his 1985–86 assessment, but pays an annuity of £120 on 31st December 1985, he will be assessed under Schedule D on £100, and under s. 53 on £20, so that he will account for tax on £120.

---

† It will be seen from Chapter 4 § 5, that in the case of an individual the allowances and reliefs are restricted where necessary in order to ensure that sufficient tax is recovered at the basic rate to cover the amount of the annual payment.

It will be seen, therefore, that the person paying the annuity merely acts as an agent in collecting the tax for the Inland Revenue and must, either by direct assessment or otherwise, account for the tax deducted.

Companies are specifically provided for under s. 53, although the collection of tax from payments made by Companies is contained in Schedule 20 F.A. 1972 (see Chapter 15).

If a person entitled to deduct tax from an annual payment fails to do so he cannot, as a general rule, deduct it from later payments, though he is liable to account for the tax that should have been deducted. The recipient cannot claim any repayment of tax in such circumstances, as he has not borne any tax.

Where tax should have been, but has not been, deducted under s. 53, the recipient of the payment can be assessed under Case III, Schedule D. The Revenue can, however, assess the payer, though in practice the claim is only enforced for any balance remaining due after payment has been claimed from the payee.

Where both the payer and recipient of an annuity, etc. are not liable to tax in view of their small incomes, the Commissioners of Inland Revenue may allow annual payments to be made without deduction of tax to avoid undue hardship to the recipient and the work and expense in making unnecessary assessments and repayment claims.

By concession (A16) the Revenue will allow payments made to be related back to the year in which payment should have been made and the taxpayer may then, if there were sufficient profits or gains in charge to tax for that year, deduct and retain the appropriate income tax and not pay it over to the Revenue.

ANNUAL INTEREST (s. 54, I.C.T.A. 1970). Income tax at the basic rate is deducted from annual interest when *paid* by a company, by a partnership of which a company is a member, or by any person (company or individual) to a person whose usual place of abode is outside the United Kingdom. Thus in most cases individuals pay interest gross. Payments of interest, whether by a company or an individual, in respect of an advance from a bank carrying on a *bona fide* banking business in the U.K. are, however, made gross.

Section 242, I.C.T.A. 1970 requires that a company making a payment of interest from which tax is deducted must accompany such payment by a statement showing the gross amount, tax deducted and net amount.

CERTIFICATES OF DEDUCTION (s. 55, I.C.T.A. 1970). A person making an annual payment etc. subject to deduction of income tax may be required to supply a certificate (on Form R 185) of the amounts so paid and deducted.

DIVIDENDS FROM UNITED KINGDOM COMPANIES (ss. 86 and 87, F.A. 1972). A tax credit (equivalent to tax at the basic rate of income tax) attaches to dividends paid by United Kingdom companies.

The cash dividend is received by the shareholder and he is entitled to the appropriate tax credit—thus:

	£
Cash Dividend	70.00
Tax Credit (Basic Rate 30%).........................	30.00
"Deemed" Gross Dividend...........................	£100.00

A shareholder who is not liable to Income Tax could claim repayment of the £30 tax credit, while a shareholder liable to tax at higher rates or to investment income surcharge would have further tax to pay.

The shareholder must enter both the cash dividend received and the tax credit in his annual return of total income.

Section 242, I.C.T.A. 1970 requires that every warrant or cheque drawn by a company in payment of any dividend or interest must be accompanied by a statement showing:

1. The cash payment;
2. The appropriate tax credit.

The tax credit attaching to such dividends is equivalent to the A.C.T. paid (see Chapter 15) by the company paying the dividend, the rate of A.C.T. being that in force for the financial year (for corporation tax purposes) in which the dividend is actually paid (s. 86, F.A. 1972).

§ 13.—RETURNS OF INCOME (ss. 7–9, T.M.A. 1970)

Every person who is chargeable to income tax for any year of assessment must deliver a return of his profits or gains or total income for that year to the Inspector of Taxes. A return is usually made upon the form provided by the Inspector of Taxes' office, so that, on receipt of such a form, the recipient is legally bound to make a return of his income, any failure to do so rendering the recipient of the form liable to penalties. If no such form is received from the Inspector of Taxes' office, any person who is chargeable for income tax for any year of assessment must give notice to the Inspector of Taxes that he is so chargeable in the period not later than one year after the end of the year of assessment in which the income was received. Any failure to give such notice will render the recipient of the income liable to a penalty of £100.

Normally the Inspector issues a return form which must be completed by the recipient in accordance with the terms of the Income Tax Acts, specifying each separate source of income and the amount from each source. If the source is income chargeable under Case I or II of Schedule D or any other income which may be computed by reference to the profits or gains of a period which is not a year of assessment, the notice requires that a return of such profits or gains, computed in accordance with the Income Tax Acts for a period for which accounts are made up or for a period by reference to which income is to be computed, should be filed with the return of income. There is also in every return a declaration which has to be completed by the person making the return to the effect that the return is correct and complete.

There are return forms designed to meet the particular needs of partnerships whereby the "precedent acting partner" makes the return on behalf of himself and his partners.

§ 14.—OTHER RETURNS

TAXABLE INCOME OF OTHERS (s. 13, T.M.A. 1970)

Every person, who is in receipt of any money or value, profits or gains belonging to another person (e.g. a bank acting as trustee; an underwriting agent) who is chargeable to income tax in respect thereof must, whenever required to do so, submit a return in the prescribed form stating the amount of such money, the name and address of every person to whom the money belongs and a declaration of whether the recipient is of full age or is a married woman, is resident in the United Kingdom or is an incapacitated person.

LODGERS AND INMATES (s. 14, T.M.A. 1970)

An Inspector may require a return from any person regarding the name of any lodger or inmate resident in his dwelling house and the name and ordinary place of residence of such lodger who has a place of residence elsewhere at which he can be assessed.

RETURNS BY EMPLOYERS ETC.

(i) An employer can be required to deliver to the Inspector a return containing the names and places of residence of all persons employed by him and the amount of payments made to those persons in respect of that employment. Payments made to the persons employed include payments made, in respect of expenses or on behalf of employed persons, which are not repaid and any payments made for services rendered in connection with the trade or business, whether the services were rendered in the course of their employment or not; some returns required relate to all employees; others to "higher-paid employees" only. Returns can also be required in respect of workers on contract to employment agencies (s. 15, T.M.A. 1970; s. 38 F(No. 2)A 1975).

(ii) A U.K. trader is also required to give details of persons performing duties, in the U.K. for a non-resident employer but for the benefit of the U.K. trader, during a period in the U.K. of not less than 30 days (s. 24, F.A. 1974).

(iii) Various returns are required under the PAYE regulations (s. 204, I.C.T.A. 1970).

(iv) Various returns are required in respect of retirement benefit schemes, pension schemes, etc. (ss. 20 to 26, F.A. 1970).

(v) If a payment is made to any holder of an office or employment by way of compensation on retirement or removal from the office or employment in such circumstances that the payment is taxable, a return thereof to the Inspector is required. (s. 187, I.C.T.A. 1970).

(vi) Information concerning any grant to directors or employees of rights to acquire shares must be provided for the Inspector (s. 186, I.C.T.A. 1970).

FEES AND COMMISSIONS (s. 16, T.M.A. 1970)

The Inspector may require any person carrying on a trade or business to make a return of payments made in the course of the trade or business for services rendered for persons not employed in the trade or business and of payments by way of periodical or lump-sum payments made in respect of a copyright. Payments which do not need to be returned are those from which income tax is deductible or where the amount does not exceed £15 to any one person or any payments made in a year of assessment ending more than three years before the date on which the notice was served. Failure to make a return can incur a penalty of £50 plus £50 per day after judgement is given.

BANK INTEREST (s. 17, T.M.A. 1970)

An Inspector may require details of interest paid or credited to any person exceeding £15 in a year of assessment where tax is not deducted at source. In practice a much higher threshold (currently £150) is applied. A recipient of interest who gives notice to the payer that the person beneficially entitled to the interest is ordinarily resident abroad, and has asked to be excluded, may be omitted from the return. From 6th April 1985 this will have limited effect since banks are required to deduct tax from deposit interest paid.

OTHER INTEREST (s. 18, T.M.A. 1970)

A return of other interest paid without deduction of income tax, or received on behalf of another person may be required by asking for details of interest paid and the names and addresses of the persons concerned.

Details of interest paid by Industrial and Provident Societies: Societies may be required to make a return of interest in excess of £15 paid without deduction of tax giving the names and addresses of the recipients (s. 340, I.C.T.A. 1970).

SCHEDULE A (s. 19, T.M.A. 1970, s. 87, I.C.T.A. 1970)
The Inspector may require certain details concerning leases, from past or present lessees or occupiers of premises. The recovery of rent previously treated as irrecoverable must be notified to the Inspector.

ANNUAL PAYMENTS (ss. 53 and 54, I.C.T.A. 1970)
An account is required under ss. 53 and 54, I.C.T.A. 1970 of any payment, in excess of amounts brought into charge to tax, of any annuity or annual payment charged under Schedule D, Case III, patent royalties, royalties paid on copyright held be persons not having a usual abode within the U.K., and rents where the recipient is resident abroad (s. 89, I.C.T.A. 1970).

SETTLEMENTS (ss. 443 and 453, I.C.T.A. 1970)
The Inspector has power to require the provision by any party to a settlement of information relative thereto.

DECEASED'S ESTATES (s. 431, I.C.T.A. 1970)
Returns may be required from personal representatives, or persons having an interest in the residue of an estate.

HERD BASIS FOR FARM ANIMALS (Schedule 6, I.C.T.A. 1970)
Returns of information with respect to the herd may be required by the Inspector under I.C.T.A. 1970, Schedule 6, para 10.

PAYING AGENTS FOR FOREIGN DIVIDENDS (Schedule 5, I.C.T.A. 1970)
The Inspector may require the provision of accounts and other information by paying agents.

§ 15.—POWER TO OBTAIN DOCUMENTS (ss. 20, 20A–D, 22–24, T.M.A. 1970)

The Revenue are empowered to require the delivery of documents which contain or may contain information relevant to any tax liability from either:

(*a*) the taxpayer.
(*b*) the taxpayer's spouse and any son or daughter of the taxpayer.
(*c*) any business associate (past or present) of the taxpayer.

A notice requiring delivery of such documentation can be made by the Inspector of Taxes only if authorised by the Board *and* after obtaining the consent of the General or Special Commissioners.
The Revenue are further empowered to require documentation from a *tax accountant* which contains information relevant to tax liability to which any client of his may have been subject.
This requirement *only* relates to a tax accountant who:

(*a*) is convicted of an offence in relation to tax (excluding V.A.T.) by or before a U.K. court; or
(*b*) has awarded against him a penalty for assisting in preparing a return which he knows to be incorrect (i.e. a penalty under s. 99, T.M.A. 1970).

For a notice however to be served to such an accountant it is necessary for the Inspector to obtain the consent of the appropriate *judicial authority*, and that consent will only be given by the judge (or sheriff in Scotland) if he is satisfied that in the circumstances the Inspector is justified in so proceeding.

The appropriate *judicial authority* is:

(*a*) In England and Wales, a Circuit Judge.

(*b*) in Scotland, a Sheriff.
(*c*) in Northern Ireland, a County Court Judge.

A *tax accountant* is a person who assists another person in the preparation of returns or accounts to be made or delivered by the other for any purpose of tax, and his clients are those to whom he stands or has stood in that relationship. In the case of both the above notices (i.e. to the taxpayer etc. or the tax accountant), reasonable opportunity must have been given for delivery of the documentation before the notice can be served.

Furthermore, the notices *do not* apply in documentation relating to a taxpayer's pending appeal.

FRAUD

In the case where any offence involving any form of fraud in connection with, or in relation to, tax is suspected of having been committed; and that evidence is to be found on specified premises (see below); an officer of the Board is empowered to enter by force if necessary those premises and search, seize and remove any things which he considers appropriate to the fraud.

The entering of premises can only be effected by the production of a warrant which is only issued by the appropriate judicial authority (see definition above) who must be satisfied that, on information given on oath by an officer of the Board, there are reasonable grounds for suspecting that a tax fraud has been committed, and that evidence is to be found on the premises specified in the information (i.e. that given on oath).

The officer of the Board is not authorised to remove any documents from a barrister, advocate or solicitor where professional privilege could be maintained.

In cases where documents have been seized, the officer shall afford reasonable access to these where they are required to facilitate the continued conduct of the business.

A recent illustration of the force given to this power by the courts can be seen from the case of *R. v. Commissioners of I.R. ex parte Rossminster Ltd* and others (1980), where the House of Lords decided in favour of the Inland Revenue. The extent of these powers in 1983 were the subject of a report (the Keith report) and alterations by legislation are anticipated in the Finance Act 1986 (those relating to VAT have been implemented in the Finance Act 1985—see Chapter 25).

MISCELLANEOUS

Section 22, T.M.A. 1970 gives the Revenue a general power to obtain any relevant information from the taxpayer concerning his income and deductions therefrom. This was previously a return required for the purposes of the now defunct surtax. However, it is now of general application.

Because of the specialised nature of their business, s. 21, T.M.A. 1970 gives the Revenue authority to require information from stock-jobbers relating to transactions made in the course of their trading, including receipt and payment of interest on securities passing through their hands.

Under s. 23, T.M.A. 1970 the Revenue may require any body corporate to deliver to them within a specified time (not less than 21 days) a certified copy of any register (or of extracts therefrom) containing the names of the holders of any shares, stock, debentures or other securities for a payment at the rate of 25p per 100 entries.

Section 24, T.M.A. 1970 provides that the registered or inscribed holder (including banking companies) of stocks and shares who has received on behalf of any other person the income arising from such securities, must furnish the Revenue with details of the amounts received (in excess of £15 per annum in respect of any one person) and the names and address of the person(s) entitled to the income. The provisions of the Section also enable the Revenue to demand information from secretaries of companies and from the present or previous holders of bearer bonds regarding the name and address of the person(s) beneficially interested in such bearer bonds. The required information must be supplied within a specified time (not less than 28 days) from receipt of written notice from the Commissioners. The provisions of Section 24 are of particular value to the revenue authorities in enabling them to trace schemes directed at avoidance of income tax, particularly where securities are registered or inscribed in the names of nominees or where they have been issued in bearer form.

§ 16.—SUBMISSION OF ACCOUNTS

The usual practice is to submit a copy of the Balance Sheet and Trading and Profit and Loss Accounts, duly prepared or audited by a professional accountant, to the Inspector of Taxes. Frequently these will be accompanied by the taxation computations and supporting schedules (giving details of certain items in the accounts, etc.) prepared by the professional adviser. The taxpayer, acting through his professional adviser—usually his accountant—is thus able to "agree" the forthcoming assessment in respect of his business with the Inspector of Taxes before he makes out his Return for the year. In the case of a trade, a certificate as to the basis on which stock has been taken is often required from the proprietor of the business.

§ 17.—THE NOTICE OF ASSESSMENT (ss. 29, 30, 34–38 T.M.A. 1970; s. 2(1) I.C.T.A. 1970)

During the year Notices of Assessment are sent out, showing the amount of the assessment, any allowances and reliefs granted and the net tax payable. In order to facilitate the administration of Income Tax, a "Notice of Pay" is attached to the Notice of Assessment wherever possible, and, if no appeal is made against the assessment, the amount of tax shown on the Notice to Pay should be paid to the Collector in accordance with the directions on the Notice to Pay. The dates of payment of the tax under the various Schedules are set out in § 23 below. The normal time-limit for assessment is 6 years.

The tax under Schedule E, however, is deducted by employers from the wages and salaries of employees and the Notice of Assessment is sent out *after* the end of the year of assessment (i.e., after 5th April 1986, in the case of the year 1985–86), showing how much tax was due for the year and how much tax has been deducted from the wages or salary during the year and the amount of tax over-paid (or under-paid, as the case may be). Notices of Assessment are not normally sent out except:

(*a*) at the tax-payer's request, or
(*b*) where the tax deducted differs materially from that due for the year.

An assessment, or additional assessment, may be made in respect of any emoluments, expense allowances, benefits in kind, etc., paid in respect of any year earlier than the year of receipt, at any time up to six years after the year of receipt. Thus an assessment in respect of emoluments for the year to 5th April 1985, paid during the year to 5th April 1986, can be made at any time before 6th April 1992.

In the case of a deceased person, however, any assessment must be made within *three* years after the end of the year of assessment in which such person died, and is subject to the limitation of six years mentioned above. Thus an assessment in respect of a person dying in the year of assessment 1985–86 must be made before 6th April 1989.

Section 36, T.M.A., 1970, extends the time within which an assessment or an additional assessment can be made, in cases where there has been *fraud or wilful default.*

Assessments are "rounded down" to the nearest pound below. However, the tax charged by an assessment is calculated to the nearest penny (s. 2, I.C.T.A. 1970).

An assessment is normally based on the information supplied by the returns of the person assessed. If, however, the Inspector is dissatisfied with the return, he may make an assessment to tax to the best of his judgment. Notices of all assessments to tax must be served on the person assessed. The notice must state the date on which it is issued and the time within which an appeal against the assessment may be made.

If an Inspector (or the Board) discovers that any profits or other income that ought to have been assessed has not been assessed, that an assessment is insufficient, or that excessive relief has been given, an assessment (or further assessment) can be made to bring into assessment the amount which, in his opinion, should be charged.

The term "discover" has been the subject of considerable legal argument but, arising out of the dicta in the House of Lords in *R. v. Kensington Commissioners ex parte Aramayo* (1916), a "discovery" arises whenever it newly appears that the taxpayer has been undercharged. From this it will be seen that the word "discover" has a very wide meaning.

§ 18.—APPEALS AGAINST ASSESSMENTS

RIGHT OF APPEAL (ss. 31 and 49, T.M.A. 1970)

An assessment can only be amended through the appeals procedure. Upon an assessment being made, the person upon whom the tax is assessed (or his agent) has the right to appeal against the assessment. Notice of appeal must be given to the Inspector (or officer of the Board) who made the assessment within thirty days of the date of issue of the assessment. Late appeals may be allowed in cases where the appellant has been prevented from making an appeal within the statutory time owing to absence, sickness or other reasonable cause.

The appellant must, in the notice of appeal, specify the grounds of the appeal. This does not, however, prevent further grounds from being raised at the actual hearing of the appeal. Pending the determination of the appeal, such part of the tax as appears to the Commissioners not to be in dispute must be paid in the normal course, an adjustment being made as may be necessary when the appeal is finally determined.

The appeal will always be made to the General Commissioners unless the taxpayer elects or exceptionally the provisions of s. 31(3), T.M.A. 1970 apply, when the appeal will be to the Special Commissioners.

JURISDICTION (ss. 44 and 46, Schedule 3, T.M.A. 1970)

The rules for determining which body of General Commissioners will hear an appeal are summarised below.

Case I, Schedule D	Place where business carried on, or where head office or principal place of business situated
Schedule E	Place of residence (if so elected by employee), place of employment or (if so elected by the Inspector) place of assessment
Schedule B	Where property lies
Schedule A and other Cases of Schedule D	Place of residence (if so elected by taxpayer), place where trade etc. carried on, or where head office or principal place of business situated. If no trade carried on, place of residence (if so elected by taxpayer) or place of employment (if any). In other cases, where the appellant normally resides
"Pooled cars" (benefits in kind)	Place where majority of employees concerned are employed
Other appeals	Place where appellant ordinarily resides

Although the notice to have an appeal heard before the Special Commissioners instead of the General Commissioners is required to be given on the appeal notice or by a separate notice, in any event within the normal period within which to make appeals, it is nonetheless possible, if the parties agree, to transfer proceedings from the General Commissioners to the Special Commissioners. Additionally, following the Finance Act 1984 matters of complexity may be passed by the General Commissioners to the Special Commissioners without the consent of the parties, but having taken account of any representations made by the parties.

PROCEDURE (ss. 44, 45, 48, 50 and 56, T.M.A. 1970, as amended by s. 127 and Schedule 22, F.A. 1984)
The onus of proof that the assessment under appeal is erroneous rests with the appellant unless the Revenue have made some basic assumption in raising the assessment which the appellant requires substantiating. If the subject of the appeal is the amount of the gain or profits on which the assessment has been raised and no proof of the profits or gains to the satisfaction of the Inspector has been produced, and if, after the case has been adjourned for further evidence to be produced by the appellant he fails to produce it at the adjourned hearing, the Commissioners are entitled to confirm the assessment. If the Commissioners decline to accept accounts, they must substantiate their reason for doing so. The Commissioners may discharge, increase, reduce or confirm any assessment under appeal, but they have no power to go into any matters not raised by the appeal.

Every appellant is entitled to notice of the day for the hearing, as is the Inspector. The Commissioners may agree to postpone a hearing in cases of absence, sickness or other reasonable cause on the allotted day. Alternatively they may agree to the appeal being made by the taxpayer's agent, servant, etc.

On appeal, the General and Special Commissioners are required to hear any barrister, solicitor or member of any incorporated body of accountants who may appear on behalf of the appellant.

The procedure at an appeal before the Commissioners follows that at judicial proceedings and, although in theory the procedure is the same before any body of Commissioners, in actual practice it is subject to variation as between one district and another. In general, the formal procedure follows the sequence set out below, although in a simple case the procedure is more informal:

(*a*) The appellant (whether taxpayer or Inspector) opens his case and explains the matter under appeal upon which he requires a decision from the Commissioners.
(*b*) The appellant calls and examines his witnesses.
(*c*) The respondent cross-examines the appellant's witnesses.
(*d*) The respondent (whether taxpayer or Inspector) opens his case as in (*a*).
(*e*) The respondent calls and examines his witnesses.
(*f*) The appellant cross-examines the respondent's witnesses.
(*g*) The respondent closes his case.
(*h*) The appellant replies and then closes his case.

The appellant and the respondent then retire while the Commissioners consider their decision and the appellant and respondent are then recalled and informed of the Commissioners' decision. In certain cases an immediate decision may not be given, the appellant and respondent being informed in writing at a later date of the decision.

The Commissioners' decision may be arrived at on the basis of a majority but when only two Commissioners sit, it is usual in the case of disagreement for the junior Commissioner to withdraw his opinion.

On a question of *fact*, the finding of the General Commissioners is final; unless it can be shown by the Court that, on the evidence available, the Commissioners were not entitled to reach that conclusion (*Edwards* v. *Bairstow and Harrison* (1955)). If the Crown or the taxpayer wishes to appeal on a point of *law*, the Commissioners may be required to state a case for the opinion of the High Court, whose ruling is subject to an appeal to the Court of Appeal and thence, if leave is given, to the House of Lords. In Scotland, appeal is made to the Court of Session and thence to the House of Lords. Subsequent to the Finance Act 1984 by order from the Lord Chancellor appeals from the Special Commissioners may be direct to the Court of Appeal.

Immediately after the determination of an appeal by the General Commissioners, or by the Special Commissioners, the appellant or the Inspector of Taxes, if dissatisfied with the determination as being erroneous on a point of law, may declare dissatisfaction to the Commissioners who heard the appeal, and within 30 days after the determination by notice in writing to the clerk to the Commissioners require them to state and sign a case for the opinion of the High Court. A fee of £25 must be paid to the clerk to the Commissioners before the party concerned can have the case stated.

The case, which must set out the facts and the determination of the Commissioners, must be transmitted to the High Court by the party concerned within 30 days of receipt, and notice in writing of the fact that the case has been stated, together with a copy of the case, must be sent to the other party.

Although a case is to be stated or is pending before the High Court, tax must be paid in accordance with the determination of the Commissioners. If the amount of the assessment is altered by order or judgment of the High Court, the amount of tax overpaid will be refunded together with any interest allowed by the High Court, or the amount of tax unpaid will be treated as arrears of tax, and will be paid and recovered accordingly.

It is not permissible, when a case is remitted to the High Court, for fresh evidence to be called on a point which could have been raised before unless the order making the remission permits the calling of fresh evidence.

Where an appeal has been brought before the General Commissioners it may, because of the complexity of a case or the length of time it is likely to take, be transferred by those Commissioners to the Special Commissioners. This can only be done with the consent of the Special Commissioners and after having considered the representations of the parties involved.

EVIDENCE (ss. 51 to 53, T.M.A. 1970)
The Commissioners have power to order the production of relevant books, accounts and other documents having a bearing on the appeal. The Revenue are entitled to inspect such documents. Failure to comply with a precept may result in penalties (see § 24).

A party to an appeal can adduce any lawful evidence and, as indicated above, produce witnesses. Subject to certain exceptions, any witness who refuses or neglects to appear, or refuses to be sworn, or refuses to answer a lawful and relevant question, can be fined up to £50.

SETTLEMENT OF APPEALS BEFORE HEARING. Section 54, T.M.A. 1970 gives statutory recognition to settlements reached between the Inland Revenue and taxpayers who have given notice of appeal to the General or Special Commissioners, thereby avoiding the appeal going forward for formal hearing. The vast majority of appeals are settled in this manner. The main provisions of s. 54 are as follows:

(*a*) Any agreement reached, whether in writing or not, is treated as if it were a determination of the appeal.
(*b*) After the agreement has been reached, the appellant or claimant has 30 days during which he may, by written notice, revoke it.

(c) Any agreement so made is effective only after it has been communicated by the Inland Revenue to the taxpayer or *vice versa*, in writing, the period of 30 days mentioned in (b) above running from the date of such confirmation.

(d) Notices of appeal may be withdrawn, either orally or in writing, in which event the proceedings are regarded as determined by rejection of the claim or contention involved, unless the Inland Revenue give written notice requiring that they should proceed despite the proposed withdrawal.

(e) Where notice of agreement is made by, to or with an agent (e.g., the accountant) of the taxpayer, it has effect as though made by, to or with the taxpayer, as the case may be.

NORTHERN IRELAND (ss. 58 and 59, T.M.A. 1970)

As there are no General Commissioners in Northern Ireland, appeals are made to the Special Commissioners (subject to a right to elect for the hearing to be before the County Court). From there further appeal lies to the Court of Appeal in Northern Ireland and thence to the House of Lords.

§ 19.—ERROR OR MISTAKE (s. 33, T.M.A. 1970)

Where tax has been paid on an assessment, and it is subsequently found that the assessment was excessive owing to some error or mistake in any return or statement made for the purposes of such assessment (e.g., omission to claim capital allowances in respect of machinery or plant—see Chapter 5, § 5), an application for relief may be made to the Commissioners of Inland Revenue within *six* years after the end of the year or accounting period during which the assessment was made. Thus any such application for relief in respect of the year of assessment 1985–86 must be made not later than 5th April 1992. No relief will be granted in the case of any error as to the basis on which the liability ought to have been computed, where the return was in fact made on the basis, or in accordance with the general practice, obtaining at the time of making the return. The Inland Revenue may refuse a claim where a return has not been made within the time limit.

§ 20.—CLAIMS (ss. 42 and 43, Schedule 2, T.M.A. 1970)

Certain reliefs can only be given if the taxpayer concerned makes a claim. Most claims are made to an Inspector of Taxes, but certain claims have to be made direct to "the Board". If a taxpayer is dissatisfied with an Inspector's decision on a claim, an appeal must be lodged within, in most cases, 30 days following receipt of written notice of the decision. The time limit for appeals against the Board's decision is three months in the following cases:

(a) Personal reliefs for non-residents (s. 27, I.C.T.A. 1970—see Chapter 11, § 3);

(b) Residence, ordinary residence or domicile (See Chapter 7, § 9);

(c) Pension funds for service abroad (s. 218, I.C.T.A. 1970).

In most cases appeals against a decision by an Inspector on a claim are made to the General Commissioners, although the taxpayer can elect to have the appeal heard by the Special Commissioners.

Where there is already an outstanding appeal against an assessment concerning the same source of income as that to which the claim relates, the appeal is to the same body of Commissioners as the one which will hear the appeal against the assessment.

Appeals against a decision by an Inspector on the following claims can only be made to the General Commissioners:

(*a*) Personal reliefs and allowances (Chapter II, Part I, I.C.T.A. 1970—see Chapter 2, § 3);

(*b*) Deductibility of small maintenance payments (s. 65, I.C.T.A. 1970);

(*c*) "Top-slicing" relief for lease premiums taxable under Schedule A (Schedule 3, I.C.T.A. 1970).

In the undernoted cases, appeals against decisions or claims by an Inspector must be made to the Special Commissioners only:

(*a*) Management expenses of owners of mineral rights (s. 158, I.C.T.A. 1970);

(*b*) Various claims by insurance companies (ss. 310, 311 and 315, I.C.T.A. 1970);

(*c*) Various claims by friendly societies and trade unions in respect of pension and life assurance business (ss. 331, 332 and 338, I.C.T.A. 1970);

(*d*) Claims for tax exemption by Savings Banks (other than TSBs) (s. 339, I.C.T.A. 1970);

(*e*) Spreading of patent royalties (s. 384, I.C.T.A. 1970);

(*f*) Copyright payments (ss. 389 and 391, I.C.T.A. 1970);

(*g*) Spreading of payments to painters, sculptors etc, (s. 392, I.C.T.A. 1970);

(*h*) Double taxation relief (ss. 497 and 498, I.C.T.A. 1970).

Appeals against a decision on a claim by "the Board" can only be made to the Special Commissioners.

The general time-limit for claims is six years from the end of the year of assessment concerned, but certain claims specify a shorter period. Where a claim arises following the making of an assessment and would not otherwise have been made, it must be lodged before the end of the year of assessment next following that in which the assessment is made.

See also Chapter 11.

§ 21.—TIME LIMITS (ss. 34 to 38, 40 and 41, T.M.A. 1970)

Section 34, T.M.A. 1970 provides that an assessment to tax may not be made after the expiry of six years from the end of the chargeable period to which the assessment relates. This means for example that, during the year 1985–86 assessment may be made for years of assessment back to 1979–80.

FRAUD

In the case of fraud or wilful default an assessment may be raised *at any time* on the person guilty of the fraud or wilful default with a view of recovering the tax lost by their actions. Such an assessment may only be made with the leave of the General or Special Commissioners which is given on their being satisfied by an Inspector or other Officer of the Board that there are reasonable grounds for believing that tax has been lost by the Crown owing to the fraud or default of the taxpayer.

NEGLECT

Section 37, T.M.A. 1970 extends the time limit for making assessments to recover any tax loss attributable to a person's neglect. Neglect is defined as negligence or a failure to give any notice, make any return, or produce or furnish any document or other information required by the Taxes Acts. An additional assessment under this section may be raised in respect of any of the six years of assessment preceding any year of assessment for which an assessment has been made within the normal six year limit on the person concerned for tax lost, wholly or partly on account of his neglect. Such assessment must be made before the end of the year of assessment following that in which the tax lost in the normal year has been finally determined. Such additional assessment may only be made with the leave of the General or Special Commissioners.

There is also provision for an additional assessment to be raised with the leave of the General or Special Commissioners for any year, even though more than six years has expired since the end of that year, provided that the Commissioners are satisfied that there are reasonable grounds for believing that tax for a year ending not earlier than six years before the end of the year for which an assessment is now to be raised was or may have been lost to the Crown owing to the neglect of the person concerned.

Partnership assessments can be made upon any person who was a partner for the year concerned. However such an assessment can exclude the share of a partner who can prove that he was not, himself, guilty of neglect.

Assessments following fraud, wilful default or neglect can be made on the personal representative of a deceased person only for the six years prior to his death, and must be made within three years thereafter.

Assessments under Schedule E are valid up to six years after the income concerned was received. This applies even if the amount received is assessed for an earlier year.

§ 22.—DOUBLE ASSESSMENT (s. 32, T.M.A. 1970)

Where by error a double assessment has been made on the same income, relief may be claimed and the tax paid in excess will be repaid. An example of a double assessment would arise where a professional accountant acting as secretary to a limited company includes his secretarial fee as part of his professional earnings for assessment under Schedule D, and is also assessed in respect thereof under Schedule E as an officer of the company.

The claim must be made within six years after the end of the year of assessment to which it relates.

§ 23.—PAYMENT OF INCOME TAX

The provisions relating to the payment of tax, interest chargeable on unpaid tax and repayment supplement are described below.

DUE DATE OF PAYMENT

Tax not under appeal (s. 4, I.C.T.A. 1970).
Payment of tax not under appeal is due 30 days after the issue of the assessment, or the normal due date, whichever is the later.

The normal due dates for payment of tax are as follows:

Schedule A—Tax in respect of income from property is payable on 1st January within the year of assessment.

Schedule B—Tax on woodlands managed on a commercial basis is payable in full on 1st January within the year of assessment.

Schedule C—Tax is payable by deduction at source.

Schedule D—Tax in respect of Case I and II profits from any trade, profession or vocation is payable in two equal instalments on 1st January within, and 1st July following, the year of assessment. Tax in respect of Case III, IV, V, and VI income etc. assessable under this Schedule is payable in full on 1st January within the year of assessment, except for income from a foreign trade, profession or vocation, or for foreign pensions, assessed under Case V, when the tax is payable in two equal instalments on 1st January within, and 1st July following, the year of assessment.

Schedule E—Tax in respect of wages, salaries, etc., under this Schedule is payable under what are popularly known as the "Pay As You Earn" provisions, which are dealt with in detail in Chapter 8, § 12.

Higher rate tax—Tax is payable on the 1st of December following the year of assessment (for years prior to 1984–85 tax on Investment Income Surcharge was due on 1st December following the year of assessment.)

Tax under appeal (s. 55, T.M.A. 1970)

The above position is altered where an appeal has been made to the Commissioners to postpone part, or all, of the tax payable. The tax not postponed is then due at the *later* of:

(*a*) The normal due date.
(*b*) 30 days after the date of the assessment.
(*c*) 30 days after the Commissioners' determination.

Whilst the balance of the tax is payable 30 days after the determination of the appeal (or the normal due date, if later), it should be noted that:

(*a*) The agreement of tax to be paid on appeal is normally made between the taxpayer and the Inspector direct. The Commissioners act only in extreme or contentious cases;
(*b*) An appeal against an assessment takes two forms: firstly, the appeal against the amount charged to taxation; and secondly, the amount of tax charged (technically an application to postpone).
Thus, to make an appeal to postpone part or all of the tax payable an appeal must be made specifically to this end as an appeal simply against the assessment will not suffice.

The 30-day time limit for application is extended (with no time limit) if there is a change of circumstances giving the taxpayer grounds for believing the tax charged is excessive.

INTEREST ON UNPAID TAX (ss. 86, 89, 90 to 92, T.M.A. 1970)

Interest on unpaid tax is due from the reckonable date, and the reckonable date is the date from which interest begins to be charged. The rate was increased to 11% from 1st May 1985; previously it was 8% (from 1st December 1982).

In determining the reckonable date, it is necessary to split the tax payable into cases as follows:

(1) Tax not under appeal.
(2) Tax under appeal:
    (*a*) Tax determined as payable (i.e. not postponed) following appeal;
    (*b*) Balance of tax payable (including that, if any, not originally assessed) being the difference between the ultimate liability and the tax paid following determination, e.g. Olivia receives an assessment to income tax for 1985–86 in respect of her Schedule D earnings in the sum of £15,000. Olivia appeals against the assessment, and the tax is determined at £8,000. When Olivia's accounts have finally been agreed, the agreed, revised assessment is £10,000. The balance of tax payable is then £2,000.

The reckonable date is then:

(1) *Tax not under appeal.* The later of:
    (*a*) Normal due date.
    (*b*) 30 days after the issue of the assessment (either the original or revised assessment).

(2) *Tax under appeal.*
  (*a*) *Determined as payable.* The later of:
    (i) Normal due date.
    (ii) 30 days after the issue of the assessment.
    (iii) 30 days after the Commissioners' determination (or agreement with H.M. Inspector of Taxes).
  (*b*) *Balance of tax* (including that, if any, not originally assessed—see below). The later of:
    (i) the due date as if there had been no appeal *and*
    (ii) the earlier of:
      (1) The date on which the tax finally becomes due and payable (normally following the revised assessment or the determination of the appeal); and
      (2) The date in the following table.

Description of tax	*Date applicable*
1. Tax charged by an assessment to income tax under Schedule A or an assessment to income tax under Schedule D other than public revenue, or foreign dividends paid via a paying agent.	1. The 1st July following the end of the year of assessment.
2. Tax charged in public revenue and foreign dividend paid via a paying agent.	2. The last day of the six months following the end of the thirty days after the issue of an assessment.
3. Higher and additional rate tax on taxed investment income.	3. The 1st June next but one following the year of assessment (i.e. 1st June 1987 for 1985–86).

Tax under appeal—effect of further assessment
Where an assessment has been appealed and the final revised assessment is greater than the original assessment, the final revised assessment is treated as issued at the date of the original assessment. *This only applies where an appeal has been lodged.* In other cases interest on the excess tax charged by the final revised assessment will run from the later of:

  (*a*) the normal due date.
  (*b*) 30 days from the issue of the revised assessment.

In view of the possible "retrospective" interest charge it is therefore essential to review the amount of tax ultimately payable in cases where tax has been postponed, at the dates shown in the table to ensure that the final tax liability will not be greater than that already paid.

Example

Delta receives an assessment to Higher Rate Tax for 1985–86 in the sum of £25,000 on 5th July 1986. Delta appeals against the assessment, applying for postponement of £10,000 tax. The Inspector of Taxes agrees this postponement on 7 August 1986, and Delta pays £15,000 on 1st December 1986.

The final agreed determination shows tax payable of £18,000 and this is issued on 12th June 1987. The balance of tax (£3,000) is paid by Delta on 10th July 1987. The interest situation is as follows:

  (a) The reckonable date in respect of tax determined (i.e. £15,000) is the later of:
    (i) Normal Due Date (1.12.86)

(ii) 30 days after the issue of the assessment (4.8.86)

(iii) 30 days after Commissioners' determination (6.9.86)

As Delta paid the tax on 1st December, no interest falls due, as the reckonable date is 1st December.

(b) The reckonable date in respect of the balance of tax (i.e. £3,000) is the later of:

    (i) the due date as if there had been no appeal (1st December 1986) *or*

    (ii) the *earlier* of:

        (a) the date on which the tax finally became due and payable (12th July 1987—30 days after the issue of the revised assessment) *or*

        (b) the date shown in the table (item 3) (i.e. 1st June 1987)

The reckonable date is therefore 1st June 1987. Delta is therefore liable to interest at 11% from 1st June to 10th July on the tax outstanding—i.e. £3,000, even though the tax is not payable until 12th July 1987 (i.e. 30 days after issue of the final determination).

The interest payable is:

$$11\% \times \frac{40}{365} \times £3{,}000 = £36.16$$

[N.B. If the final agreed assessment had been £30,000 interest would have been due on the whole of the tax unpaid of £15,000 (£30,000 − £15,000) from 1st June 1987 notwithstanding the original assessment was only for £25,000 since the assessment was under appeal. Interest would have been payable as follows:

	£
Final assessment	30,000
Less Amount paid on account.................	15,000
Tax outstanding	£15,000

Interest thereon (1.6.87–10.7.87)

$$11\% \times \frac{40}{365} \times £15{,}000 = £180.82$$

If Delta had not appealed against the original assessment the excess tax charged by the final assessment (or determination) i.e. £5,000 would have been due 30 days after the issue of the final assessment.]

Sundry points

(1) The reckonable date need not be an ordinary business day.

(2) Interest if the Board thinks fit will be waived provided that it does not exceed £30 (£10 for assessments prior to 1st August 1981).

(3) By concession (A17), in the case of a deceased taxpayer the reckonable date is postponed to 30 days after grant of probate or letters of administration if that date is later than the table date.

(4) If funds are blocked by exchange restrictions, interest runs only from the date when such funds are freed.

(5) Interest on unpaid tax is not eligible for tax relief.

REPAYMENT SUPPLEMENT

Individuals (s. 47 F(No. 2)A 1975)

A repayment of income tax, surtax, or capital gains tax made to an individual for a year of assessment for which he was resident in the U.K. shall be supplemented by an interest element equal to 11% per annum for the period between the relevant time and the end of the tax month in which the order for repayment is issued. (Before 6th May 1985 interest was at 8% from 1st December 1982 and 9% prior to that.)

The repayment must be:

(1) greater than £25 and
(2) after 31st July 1975.

—otherwise interest will not accrue.

Relevant time
This depends upon the circumstances in which the tax was paid:

(1) If the repayment is in respect of tax paid *after* the end of the 12 months following the year of assessment, *the relevant time is the end of the year of assessment in which the payment was made.*

e.g.		Tax paid	Relevant time
	Year of assessment 1984/85	6.4.86	5.4.87
		4.4.87	5.4.87
		6.5.87	5.4.88

(2) In any other case *the relevant time is twelve months following the year of assessment,*

e.g.		Tax paid	Relevant time
	Year of assessment 1984/85	6.6.85	5.4.86
		6.12.85	5.4.86
		6.3.86	5.4.86

(3) If the repayment is of the special charge (i.e. a premium on investment income for 1967–68 payable 1.1.69) which is paid before the end of the year 1969–70, *the relevant time is the end of that year.*
If it is paid after that year, it is *the end of the year in which it is paid.*

Sundry points
(1) Tax credits are to be treated as tax paid.
(2) Repayments of tax under s. 228 I.T.A. 1952 (personal allowances of minors) are to be treated as tax paid in the year in which the contingency occurred. The repayment was only available up to the year 1968–69, although, of course, the contingency may be later.
(3) Tax deducted under P.A.Y.E. is to be treated as being paid in that year only.
(4) A Schedule E repayment of not less than £25, which takes into account over- and under-payments in previous years, is to be apportioned to those years in accordance with Regulations made by the Board.
(5) "Tax Month" has the usual meaning for P.A.Y.E., i.e. counted from 6th April to the following 5th April.
(6) *The repayment supplement is exempt from all forms of tax.*

CERTIFICATES OF TAX DEPOSIT
Certificates of Tax Deposit, available to individuals, partnerships and companies, are evidence of deposits made by the taxpayer for payment of tax. It is not necessary for the deposit to be specifically set against a tax liability, although deposits *cannot* be made against P.A.Y.E. or be deducted from payments to subcontractors. The minimum initial deposit is £2,000, with minimum investments of £500. Interest is payable gross on the deposit but is subject to tax. Interest is payable up to a maximum period of 6 years from the date of deposit

to the date of payment of the tax. The rate of interest is governed by the rate ruling at the date of deposit for the first two years; for the next two years, by the rate ruling on the second anniversary of the deposit; and for the final two years, by the rate ruling on the fourth anniversary of deposit.

Withdrawals may be made at any time, although interest is then reduced.

Collection of tax in cases of official error
Some relief is given to taxpayers who find that they have large unpaid tax liabilities because tax arrears have built up owing to failure of the Revenue to make proper and timely use of the information supplied. Collection is accordingly due to "official error".

Depending on the taxpayer's income, the Revenue will refrain from collecting some or all of the tax otherwise due. For notifications after 23rd July 1985, the amount not collected is as follows:

Gross income	Fraction of Arrears Collected	Remitted
Not above £8,500	None	All
Above £8,500 but not above £10,500	$\frac{1}{4}$	$\frac{3}{4}$
Above £10,500 but not above £13,500	$\frac{1}{2}$	$\frac{1}{2}$
Above £13,500 but not above £16,000	$\frac{3}{4}$	$\frac{1}{4}$
Above £16,000 but not above £23,000	$\frac{9}{10}$	$\frac{1}{10}$
Above £23,000	All	None

The limits are increased for taxpayers aged 65 or over at the date of notification, by £2,500 for each band.

Special consideration will be given to the exceptional case of a taxpayer with large family responsibilities whose income is just above the normal limits for full or partial remission.

This practice of remission of tax in cases of official error stems from a White Paper issued by the Government in July 1971. The scale has been altered several times.

§ 24.—PENALTIES

FAILURE TO INFORM OF LIABILITY TO CHARGE (s. 7, T.M.A. 1970)
Every person who is chargeable to Income Tax for any year of assessment and who has not delivered a statement of profits or gains or of his total income for that year shall, not later than one year after the end of that year of assessment, given notice that he is so chargeable. Such notice must ordinarily be given to the Inspector of Taxes. The penalty for failure to give such a notice is not to exceed £100. This is a maximum penalty, and the Commissioners of Inland Revenue have power to mitigate it.

FAILURE TO DELIVER STATEMENTS, ETC. (ss. 93 and 98, T.M.A. 1970)
Where a person has been required by a notice (under ss. 8 or 9, T.M.A. 1970, or s. 39(3) I.C.T.A. 1970) to deliver any return, statement, declaration, list or other document, to furnish any particulars, to produce any document, or to make anything available for inspection, and fails to do so, he will normally be liable to a penalty not exceeding £50. If failure continues after it has been declared by the Court or Commissioners before whom proceedings were commenced, the person is liable to a further penalty not exceeding £10 for each day during which failure continues. The penalty mentioned in this paragraph is not chargeable if the failure is remedied before proceedings for recovery of the penalty are commenced.

Where the failure referred to in the preceding paragraph relates to a return by an individual of his previous year's income, or to a return of the current year's chargeable income under the respective schedules, or to a return (under s. 8, T.M.A. 1970) on behalf of an incapacitated person or a non-resident, or to a partnership total return, or to a return required in regard to a claim for separate assessment and that failure continues after the end of the year of assessment following that during which the notice was served, the maximum penalty is £50 plus the total amount of tax with which the person is charged (whether for one or for more than one year of assessment) in assessments based wholly or partly on any income that ought to have been included in the return required by the notice, and made after the end of the year next following the year of assessment in which the notice was served.

In both these instances the penalty is restricted to £5 if for each offence the taxpayer shows that there was no income to be included in the tax return for the year concerned.

FRAUDULENT OR NEGLIGENT RETURNS (SS. 95, 97, 98 and 99, T.M.A. 1970)
Where a person negligently delivers an incorrect return or statement of the type mentioned in the preceding paragraph; or makes any incorrect return, statement or declaration in connection with any claim for any allowance, deduction or relief; or submits incorrect accounts; he is liable to a penalty not exceeding £50 plus the amount of the difference between the correct tax chargeable and that chargeable on the basis of the returns, etc., actually made. In the case of fraud, the penalty for doing these things is £50 plus twice the amount of the difference computed as above.

For negligence in relation to other returns, statements, certificates, etc., the penalty is a fine not exceeding £250. In the case of fraud, the penalty is a fine not exceeding £500. Any person who assists in, or induces, the making or delivery for any purposes of Income Tax of any return, accounts, statement or declaration which he knows to be incorrect is liable to a penalty not exceeding £500.

Furthermore, if having made a return which he subsequently discovers to have been incorrect, a taxpayer fails to notify the Inspector of the error, he is guilty of negligence. In the case of death this will apply to the personal representatives.

REFUSAL TO DEDUCT TAX (s. 106, T.M.A. 1970)
If a person refuses to allow a deduction of income tax, a penalty of £50 will be incurred. Any agreement to pay interest, rent or other annual payments gross is void.

PROCEDURE FOR RECOVERY (s. 100, T.M.A. 1970)
An Inspector of Taxes may, without an order of the Commissioners of Inland Revenue, commence before the General Commissioners proceedings for the recovery of the penalties, for the lesser type of failure to deliver a return, statement, but the penalty recoverable is then limited to £50.

In all other cases, no proceedings can be commenced for the recovery of a penalty except by order of the Commissioners of Inland Revenue. Proceedings may be commenced either before the General or Special Commissioners, or in the High Court.

TIME LIMIT FOR RECOVERY (s. 103, T.M.A. 1970)
Where an assessment has been made within the normal six year time limit for the purpose of making good to the Crown a loss of tax wholly or partly attributable to fraud, wilful default or neglect, provision is made for the making of assessments for earlier years notwithstanding that they would normally be out of time. The sole purpose of any such assessment must be the making good to the Crown of a loss attributable to neglect. Normally, assessments can be made only in respect

of the six years immediately preceding the earliest assessment which is still in date and which relates to a loss attributable to fraud, etc., though the Inspector may apply for leave to make assessments in certain cases to the General or Special Commissioners.

If the Inland Revenue prove the existence of fraud, they will not need to rely on the above provision, for ss. 34 and 36, T.M.A. 1970, gives them power to amend or make assessments for the purpose of making good to the Crown losses attributable to fraud or wilful default at any time.

PARTNERSHIPS (s. 38, T.M.A. 1970)
Special provisions apply regarding the treatment of persons in partnership, some of whom were guilty of a default and some of whom were not, whereby the share of an innocent partner is exempt from penalties.

TIME LIMIT FOR RECOVERY OF TAX LOST THROUGH DEFAULT OF A DECEASED PERSON (s. 40, T.M.A. 1970)
For the purpose of making good to the Crown any loss of tax attributable to the fraud, wilful default or neglect of a person who has died, an assessment on his personal representative may be made for any year of assessment ending not earlier than six years before his death, provided it is made before the end of the third year next following the year of assessment in which he died.

INTEREST ON TAX RECOVERED (ss. 88 and 89, T.M.A. 1970)
Where an assessment is made for the purpose of making good to the Crown a loss of tax wholly or partly attributable to the fraud, wilful default or neglect of any person, the additional tax charged by the assessment carries interest at the rate of 8 per cent per annum (12 per cent before 1st December 1982) from the date on which the tax ought to have been paid until payment. The Commissioners of Inland Revenue have power to mitigate any interest so due, at their discretion.

CRIMINAL PROCEEDINGS (s. 104, T.M.A. 1970)
It is also open to the Revenue to instigate criminal proceedings for fraud and perjury in addition to the penalties described above.

MITIGATION OF PENALTIES (s. 102, T.M.A. 1970)
The Board have a discretion to reduce these penalties in appropriate cases (e.g. if the taxpayer co-operates in the enquiry).

§ 25.—BACK DUTY

The term "back duty" has been coined to indicate arrears of tax in respect of sources of income upon which the taxpayer has not been assessed or has been under-assessed for past years, by reason of non-disclosure on the part of the taxpayer. Such non-disclosure may be due to ignorance or carelessness on the part of the taxpayer, or it may be due to wilful evasion or fraud. Although, strictly speaking, the Inland Revenue authorities have no legal right (apart from the provisions cited in this Chapter) to raise assessments for any year earlier than six years prior to the current year of assessment, the penalty provisions for rendering an incorrect return are so severe (e.g. in the case of fraud, £50 plus double the tax lost for the six years) that the taxpayer may prefer to compromise by paying all arrears of tax and interest thereon together with a sum to cover mitigated penalties. The total amount which the taxpayer is required to pay is largely dependent on the degree of his guilt (e.g., as to whether non-disclosure was accidental, and whether he made a voluntary disclosure immediately on becoming aware of the facts).

The Inland Revenue procedure in back duty cases has been based to a great extent on what is termed the "White Paper" statement, made in 1923, under which the Inland Revenue authorities were able to accept a pecuniary settlement from a defaulting taxpayer instead of taking proceedings against him. It has not been the practice of the Commissioners of Inland Revenue to give a definite undertaking to accept such a settlement, but it has been understood that in coming to their decision they have been influenced by the fact that the taxpayer has made a full confession of any fraud or default to which he has been a party, and has given full facilities for investigation. Moreover, in affording these facilities, the taxpayer may have been induced to make certain statements or to produce certain documents to the Commissioners, or to have statements made or documents produced on his behalf. Section 105, T.M.A. 1970, provides that such statements or documents shall not be inadmissible in evidence, by reason only of the fact that their making or production may have been induced in accordance with the above-mentioned "White Paper" procedure, against any person in (*a*) any criminal proceedings against him for any form of fraud or wilful default in connection with Income Tax, or (*b*) any proceedings against him for the recovery of any sum due from him, whether by way of tax or penalty, in connection with Income Tax.

CAPITAL STATEMENTS

The ascertainment of the tax under-paid in a "back-duty" case is frequently a complicated matter, owing to the paucity of data to work from. In such circumstances, capital statements are prepared, in which the taxpayer's net worth at the beginning and end of the years under review are set out, to arrive at the increase in his net worth over that period. Estimated living expenses, Stock Exchange losses, etc., must then be added, and such items as legacies and capital profits on the sale of assets, deducted, the result being the total estimated taxable profits over the period. Deduction of the assessments already made leaves the unexplained surplus upon which tax has not been paid. This sum must then be apportioned over the period concerned, but each year does not necessarily bear an equal amount, as the taxpayer's capital may have increased more in some years than in others.

Example

C. Daniels, a retail draper, keeps his books by single entry and shows profits as follows:

	£
Year ended 31st December 1980.	735
Year ended 31st December 1981.	740
Year ended 31st December 1982.	787
Year ended 31st December 1983.	1,375
Year ended 31st December 1984.	1,214
Year ended 31st December 1985.	926
	£5,777

The Inspector of Taxes refuses to accept these accounts and you are asked to prepare a statement showing the increase in capital over the period and the relation of such increase to the accounts. You are given the following information:

	31st December 1979	31st December 1985
	£	£
Creditors.	732	840
Debtors.	145	592
Cash	947	1,945
Stock	542	674

C. Daniels owed his brother £400 on 31st December 1979. This was repaid on 15th February 1983. On 1st January 1985, C Daniels lent his brother £300.

C. Daniels purchased the following:

	£
1968—House costing................................	2,000
1981—Car costing....................................	450
1984—£1,000 $3\frac{1}{2}$% Conversion Loan	1,050

In 1984, £300 in cash was stolen from his house. His living expenses are estimated at—1980, £650; 1981, £700; 1982, £800; 1983, £1,000; 1984, £1,100; 1985, £1,200. He received a legacy of £125 in August 1982, from the estate of his father.

Capital Statement

	£	£	£
Business capital, 31st December 1979:			
Debtors..........................	145		
Cash.............................	947		
Stock............................	542		
	1,634		
Less: Creditors....................	732		
		902	
Personal capital, 31st December 1979:			
House...........................	2,000		
Less: Loan......................	400		
		1,600	
			2,502
Business capital, 31st December 1985:			
Debtors..........................	592		
Cash.............................	1,945		
Stock............................	674		
	3,211		
Less: Creditors....................	840		
		2,371	
Personal capital, 31st December 1985:			
House...........................	2,000		
Car.............................	450		
Investment	1,050		
Loan............................	300		
		3,800	
			6,171
Increase in capital			3,669
Add: Living expenses...............			5,450
Amount stolen................			300
Total estimated profits...			9,419
Deduct: Profits per accounts		5,777	
Legacy		125	
			5,902
Unexplained surplus (undisclosed profits)			£3,517

This surplus must be apportioned equitably over the period, and the total tax payable computed. This will then form a basis on which negotiations for a settlement can commence.

§ 26.—NON-RESIDENTS (ss. 78 to 83, T.M.A. 1970)

Subject to s. 89, I.C.T.A. 1970, a non-resident to whom income arises in the United Kingdom which is under the control or management of a trustee, guardian etc. (see § 11) resident in the U.K. is assessable in the name of such a person as though the non-resident were in fact resident in the U.K. Where the non-resident has a branch or agency in the U.K., the branch or agent will be assessed, notwithstanding that the branch or agent has not actually received the income. The profits from the branch or agency itself are of course assessed and charged on the branch or agency.

In cases where the profits of a branch or agency are not otherwise determinable, the Inspector can estimate the profits on the basis of a percentage of turnover. A decision on this point by the Inspector can be subject to appeal to the General or Special Commissioners.

Where a non-resident has manufactured goods outside the U.K. but sells them in the U.K. through a branch or agency, he has the right to elect that he is taxed on the basis of the profits that a merchant buying or selling (but not manufacturing) the goods could reasonably expect.

These rules do not apply where the agent in the U.K. is carrying on a brokerage or general commission business on normal commercial terms and is not otherwise connected with the non-resident (i.e. the non-resident is "trading with" the U.K. rather than "trading in" the U.K.)

By concession (B13) interest (e.g. bank interest) is not assessed on the non-resident unless connected with a branch or agency that the resident has in the U.K.

§ 27.—COLLECTION AND RECOVERY (ss. 60 to 70, T.M.A. 1970)

The Collector of Taxes will, when tax becomes due and payable, issue a demand to the last known abode of the taxpayer concerned, or the premises covered by the assessment (e.g. Schedule A). On payment, the Collector must issue a receipt if requested to do so.

If tax due and payable is not paid, the Collector can distrain on the taxpayer's goods and chattels, and if, after holding them five days, the tax is still unpaid, he can sell them by public auction. Any surplus remaining after payment of tax and related costs is returned to the taxpayer. In order to carry out the distraint, after the Collector has obtained a warrant signed by the General Commissioners, he can break into the taxpayer's premises, with the assistance of the police if necessary.

Unpaid tax liabilities for one year only rank as a preferential debt in bankruptcy or liquidation. Any other unpaid tax liabilities rank as non-preferential debts along with those of unsecured creditors.

Similar rules apply in Scotland, with necessary modifications.

Recovery proceedings can be started in the Magistrates' Court for sums up to £50, in the County Court for sums up to £750, and in the High Court for larger amounts.

Interest on overdue tax ranks along with the assessment to which it relates. In practice this is not enforced in the case of insolvent taxpayers.

§ 28.—MISCELLANEOUS

VALUATION (ss. 110 and 111, T.M.A. 1970)
The Revenue have power to inspect premises for valuation purposes and to enter premises to inspect assets for such purposes.

DOCUMENTS (ss. 112 to 115, T.M.A. 1970)
The Revenue have authority to prescribe the form of various returns and other documents. If an assessment or a return is lost or destroyed, the Revenue may issue or make new ones, but not so as to require the taxpayer to pay the tax due more than once. Minor errors in assessments do not render them invalid.

Tax returns, assessments etc. can be sent to taxpayers through the post to their last known address, place of business or place of employment. If a taxpayer submits Form 64–8 to the Inspector, copies of assessments can be sent to the taxpayer's accountant or other agent.

2. Personal Allowances and Reliefs

§ 1.—THE RETURN FORM

In order that an individual taxpayer may receive the allowances and reliefs due to him, his total income from all sources must be ascertained.

A Return is required of all income, both taxed and untaxed, for the preceding year, together with a statement of any annual charges payable during the preceding year and of any changes in either the sources of untaxed income or the annual charges since the commencement of the preceding year. This Return is made to the Inspector of Taxes. The statutory income for the year concerned is computed by the Inspector from the information supplied by the taxpayer in his Return of income, as explained in § 2 of this chapter. The Return contains spaces for details of the allowances which may be applicable.

Return Year

Difficulty is sometimes encountered in establishing the year to which the Return relates. This can perhaps be simplified if it can be remembered that the Return is for the tax year in which it is *returned* which relates to details of income for the immediately preceding tax year.

The Return completed in, say, May 1986, is headed as follows:

RETURN OF INCOME FOR THE YEAR 1985–86, ENDED 5TH APRIL 1986.

AND

CLAIM FOR ALLOWANCES FOR THE YEAR 1986–87, ENDING 5TH APRIL 1987.

This return would normally be referred to as the 1986–87 Return.

The income of a married woman living with her husband must be included with that of her husband, unless an application for separate assessment has been made (see § 10 of this chapter).

The statement of income *not taxed at the source* for the preceding year will be as follows:

From Trade, Profession or Vocation.
From Interest, Dividends, Annuities and other Annual Payments, and Commonwealth and Foreign Securities and Possessions, not subjected to United Kingdom Income Tax at the source.
From other Profits or Income not taxed at the source (e.g., letting a furnished house, or rents).
Wife's Untaxed Income, if not included above.

In each case the actual income for the preceding year should be entered (i.e. the income in the year to 5th April 1986 would be entered in the 1986–87 Tax Return).
Space is provided for a deduction for capital allowances claimed in the case of a Trade, Profession or Vocation.

If there have been any changes in the sources of untaxed income (i.e. either through the acquisition of a new source of income or the cessation of a source of income since the preceding 5th April) of the taxpayer or his wife during the year covered by the Return, these must be stated.

The statement of income *taxed at the source* for the preceding year will be as follows:

From Partnership Income.	A partner should enter his share of the net total income of the firm in one sum. The firm will, of course, be assessed in respect of the untaxed income.
From any Office, Employment or Pension.	The actual income for the preceding year should be entered.
From Land, Houses, etc.	The gross income, including premiums, less expenses, should be entered.
From Occupation of Woodlands.	The Schedule B assessment should be entered unless election has been made to be assessed under Schedule D.
From Dividends, Interest, Annuities etc., taxed at source.	The gross amount receivable in the preceding year should be entered. (N.B. For building society and bank interest the "gross" is that received grossed at the basic rate (30%) notwithstanding the fact that tax is deducted at a composite rate.) In the case of dividends the cash dividend and the tax credit will be entered.
Wife's Taxed Income, if not included above.	As above.

A statement of Annual Charges payable in the preceding year will be included in the Return form, and if there has been any alteration in the amount of any charge, or any new charge has become payable, since the preceding 5th April, particulars thereof must be stated.

Any income from which tax is deducted at the source at the basic rate in force for any year is to be deemed to be income of that year, and any deductions on account of annual charges are allowed for the year in which the payment becomes due.

Any chargeable gain or allowable loss for Capital Gains Tax purposes must be entered on the Return form, and also details of Chargeable Assets acquired in the year (refer to Chapter 26, § 4 for non-reporting requirements of "small gains").

The Return must be signed by the taxpayer and certain penalties are provided by the Income Tax Acts if incorrect returns are submitted (see Chapter 1). Returns relating to Capital Transfer Tax must be made separately. Details of lifetime transfers are returned on form C.5. See Chapter 36.

§ 2.—TOTAL INCOME AND TAXABLE INCOME

The Return form having been completed, it is possible to arrive at the total income.

Total income is an individual's (including normally his wife's) statutory income from all sources *less* charges. Charges include mortgage interest, certain bank interest, etc.

Taxable Income is the total income *after* deducting personal allowances (see § 3 below).

It is important to arrive at a figure of total income as certain allowances (e.g. Age allowance) are dependent thereon. In arriving at total income, income from various sources will be included "net" of allowable deductions. Thus for example

Schedule E emoluments will be net of expenses wholly exclusively and necessarily incurred (refer to Chapter 8).

Similarly retirement annuity premiums (see § 6) and approved pension payments will be deducted from the income to be brought into total income.

Charges on income may be deducted from investment income in priority to other income if this is advantageous to the taxpayer (s. 34 (2) F.A. 1971) (only effective up to 1983–84 as investment income surcharge is abolished for 1984–85 onwards).

The total income of a taxpayer for, say, 1985–86 is assessed under the preceding year basis (Schedule D, Case I, II or III etc.) from his 1985–86 Return and by adding to this his income assessed currently (Schedule A, Schedule E, etc.) from his 1986–87 Return. (N.B. It will be necessary to look to the later Return year where income normally assessed on the preceding year basis is assessed currently, e.g. in the opening year.)

Capital Gains do not form part of Total Statutory Income.

The following example illustrates the method of ascertaining net total income of a taxpayer for the purpose of a claim for allowances.

Example

John Green is the proprietor of a cycle business established many years, the adjusted profits of which for the year ended 30th September 1984, were £15,000.

He receives an annual fee of £1,000 as a Director of Milk Supplies Ltd, and dividends (taxed at source) from various companies in England, amounting in 1985–86 to £300 (including tax credit).

For the year ended 5th April 1986, he received bank interest amounting to £7 (gross £10) from the Midland Bank and £80 on a National Savings Bank Ordinary Account opened in 1957.

His wife owns their house on which there is a mortgage of £20,000 at 12 per cent, and receives an annual fee of £750 as a Director of Needlework Ltd.

It is desired to show Green's net total income for Income Tax purposes for 1985–86.

John Green: Statement of net total income, 1985–86.

		£
Business Profits	—Case I, Sch. D	15,000
Director's Fee (Milk Supplies Ltd)	—Sch. E	1,000
Dividends (including tax credit)	—Taxed at source	300
Taxed Interest		10
Untaxed Interest (£80 less £70)	—Case III, Sch. D	10
Wife's Director's Fee (Needlework Ltd)	—Sch. E	750
Total Statutory Income		17,070
Less: Annual Charges—		
Mortgage Interest (see note)		2,400
Net Total Income		£14,670

Note. Relief for mortgage interest would normally be given under MIRAS (see Chapter 11) but it would still be necessary to show the deduction as above to arrive at total income. The interest can therefore be considered an annual charge on which tax has been deducted. National Savings Bank interest is not subject to interest deduction at source (see Chapter 9).

§ 3.—PERSONAL ALLOWANCES (s. 5, I.C.T.A. 1970)

The allowances which may be claimed by an individual taxpayer *resident in the United Kingdom*, irrespective of the amount of his net total income, are as follows:
- (*a*) Personal Reliefs;
- (*b*) Relief for Widows, etc., in respect of children;
- (*c*) Age Allowance;
- (*d*) Allowance for Dependent Relative;
- (*e*) Allowance for Daughter's or Son's Services;
- (*f*) Allowance for Relative or other person acting in the capacity of a House-keeper;
- (*g*) Relief for Blind Persons.
- (*h*) Allowance for Children; (limited application for 1979–80 onwards) abolished after 1981–82.

Relief was also granted up to 14th March 1984 in respect of Life Assurance premiums paid, but this was deducted from the premium payable, and did not form part of the individual's tax computation (see § 15).

These allowances will be dealt with in detail in the following pages. The allowances applicable prior to 1984–85 are set out in Appendix 1.

The position of non-residents (who are not normally entitled to the above allowances) is dealt with in Chapter 11, § 3.

(a) PERSONAL RELIEFS (s. 8 I.C.T.A. 1970)
For 1984–85 and 1985–86 the personal reliefs in respect of the various classes of taxpayer are as follows:

TAXPAYER	RELIEF	
	1985–86	1984–85
Single person	£2,205	£2,005
Wife's earned income (maximum)	£2,205	£2,005
Married man whose wife is living with him, or is wholly maintained by him, during the year of assessment	£3,455	£3,155

In the year of marriage, the allowance is reduced, by £104 ($\frac{1}{12} \times$ £1,250) for each complete month which has elapsed between 6th April and the date of marriage, but a man may elect to retain allowances under ss. 12, 13 and 14, I.C.T.A. 1970 (housekeeper, etc. relief), and will then not be entitled to the married allowance for the year of assessment in which he marries.

Married man, whose wife has any earned income — £3,455 (1984–85: £3,155) plus amount of wife's earned income to a maximum of £2,205 (1984–85: £2,005)

(b) RELIEF FOR WIDOWS IN RESPECT OF CHILDREN (ss. 14 to 15, I.C.T.A. 1970)
A person who proves in the case of a year of assessment that a "qualifying child" is resident with him or her for the whole or part of a year of assessment is entitled to an allowance of the difference between the ordinary married and single person's allowance i.e. £1,250 (£1,150 for 1984–85), provided that he or she is:
- (*a*) A widow or widower,
- (*b*) Not entitled to the married rate of personal allowance.
- (*c*) A married man entitled to the married rate of personal allowance, if his wife has been totally incapacitated by physical or mental infirmity throughout the year.

A claimant is only entitled to one deduction, irrespective of the number of qualifying children resident with her or him.

A "qualifying child" means a child who:

(1) Is born in, or is under the age of 16 at the beginning of, the year of assessment, or, if over 16, is receiving full-time instruction at any university, college, school or other educational establishment; *and*

(2) Is a child of the claimant *or* (if not) is under the age of 18 at the beginning of the year of assessment and is maintained by the claimant at his own expense for the whole or part of that year.

"Child of the claimant" includes any step-child, an illegitimate child if the claimant has married the natural parent after the child's birth, and an adopted child provided that the child was under 18 when adopted.

A child whose birthday falls on 6th April will be considered over 16 or 18 in the year of assessment in which that birthday falls.

Where more than one individual is entitled to relief under this heading in connection with the same child, the allowance of £1,250 is to be apportioned between such individuals in such proportions as may be agreed between them; in default of agreement, it is to be apportioned between them in the same proportion as the time for which the child is resident with them during the year.

A man who marries during the year may elect to claim housekeeper allowance or additional child relief instead of married persons' allowance if more beneficial (s. 15 I.C.T.A. 1970).

Widow's Bereavement Allowance (s. 15A I.C.T.A. 1970)

In the year of death *and the year following death* of her husband a widow is entitled to a "bereavement allowance" equivalent to the difference between ordinary married and single person's allowance i.e. £1,250 (£1,150 for 1984–85). This allowance is given in addition to the personal allowance and both will be available to offset against the widow's income arising in that part of the year of assessment remaining following the death.

Example

Taylor dies on 25th August 1983 leaving a widow. The widow will be entitled to bereavement allowance of £1,150 for 1984–85 (i.e. in respect of the period of assessment 26th August 1984 to 5th April 1985) and £1,250 for 1985–86.

(c) AGE ALLOWANCE (s. 8, I.C.T.A. 1970)

For individuals who are aged 65 or more at any time in a year of assessment, an age allowance (subject to an income limit—see below) is given instead of the ordinary single or married allowance.

The allowances for 1985–86 are as follows:

	£
Single	2,690
Married	4,255

For the married allowance to apply, it is only necessary for one of the spouses to be aged 65 or more in the year of claim.

An income limit applies where the total income from all sources exceeds £8,800. In these cases the age allowance is reduced by two-thirds of the excess over £8,800 until the ordinary single or married personal allowance is reached, whereupon that allowance is used and no further reduction is made.

Example 1

Lightfoot, a married man aged 66, has the following income for the year ended 5th April 1986:

	£
Salary	8,000
Dividends (including tax credit)	1,300

His taxable income for 1985–86 is as follows:

	£
Salary	8,000
Dividends	1,300
Total statutory income	9,300
Less Age allowance (see below)	3,922
Taxable income	£5,378

Note. The age allowance is calculated thus:

	£
Total allowance	4,255
Less $\frac{2}{3}$ (£9,300–£8,800) $= \frac{2}{3} \times$ £500 $=$	333
	£3,922

Since this is greater than the ordinary married allowance (£3,455), this will be the relief claimed.

Example 2

Heavyhand, a married man aged 65 on 10th March 1986, has the following income for the year ended 5th April 1986:

	£
Dividends (including tax credit)	9,000
Untaxed interest	1,300

Heavyhand's wife is aged 62.

His taxable income for 1985–86 is as follows:

	£
Dividends	9,000
Untaxed interest	1,300
Total statutory income	10,300
Less Personal allowance (see note)	3,455
Taxable income	£6,845

Note. The age allowance is available in this case, since the taxpayer reached the age of 65 during the year of claim, but the income limitation reduces the claim to the ordinary married allowance as follows:

	£
Age allowance	4,255
Less $\frac{2}{3}$ (£10,300 − £8,800) $= \frac{2}{3} \times$ £1,500 $=$	1,000
	£3,255

Since this is less than the married allowance (£3,455), the ordinary married allowance will prevail.

During the year of marriage (provided that either spouse is 65 or over), the allowance is reduced by 1/12 of the difference between the *married* age allowance and the applicable *single* allowance [i.e. either ordinary (£2,205) or age (£2,690)] for each complete month of the tax year before the marriage took place.

Example 3

Smith, aged 66, marries Miss Jones, aged 63, on 17th May 1985. The age allowance available to Smith (subject to income limitation) for 1985–86 is as follows:

	£
Maximum allowance	4,255
Less Reduction: 1/12 × (£4,255 − £2,690)	130
Allowance available	£4,125

Notes.

  (1) Smith is over 65, so the reduction is by relation to the single age allowance.
  (2) There is only one *complete* month of non-marriage in the year, and accordingly the reduction is 1/12 only.

A claim for age allowance is not available to either the husband or wife where a wife's earnings election is in force (see below).

(d) ALLOWANCE FOR DEPENDENT RELATIVE (s. 16 I.C.T.A. 1970)
The amount of the allowance is (i) £100 or (ii) £145 where the claimant is a single woman or one electing for wife's earnings.
This allowance may be claimed where a taxpayer maintains at his own expense
  (*a*) Any relative of his or of his wife who is incapacitated by old age or infirmity from maintaining himself or herself, and whose total income from all sources for the year 1985–86 (exclusive of voluntary allowances) does not exceed the basic retirement pension plus the amount of the allowance.
  (*b*) His or his wife's widowed mother (whether or not she is incapacitated by old age or infirmity) whose total income from all sources for the year 1985–86 (exclusive of voluntary allowances) does not exceed the basic retirement pension plus the amount of the allowance.
The taxpayer's contribution to the relative's maintenance is treated as a voluntary allowance, and is not regarded as part of the relative's total income for Income Tax purposes.
The above provisions apply to a female taxpayer with the substitution of "husband" for "wife", but it will be noted that an increased allowance is granted where a female claimant satisfies the conditions above.
The expression "relative" includes any person of whom the taxpayer had the custody and whom he maintained at his own expense while such person was under 16 years of age.
Where the relative's income exceeds the basic retirement pension applicable for the year, the allowance is reduced pound-for-pound on the excess. For instance, where the relative of a male taxpayer has an income £75 over the basic retirement pension, the allowance will be £25 (£100 − £75).
The allowance is restricted, however, to the amount of the taxpayer's contribution, whatever the amount of the relative's income. Thus, if the contribution is £50 and the dependent relative is not living with the claimant, so that there is no question of accommodation and maintenance being provided in addition, even if the relative has no income, the allowance cannot exceed £50.

If two or more persons maintain the dependent the relief given to each is a proportionate part of the allowance based upon the contributions of each or the amount contributed if less.

(e) ALLOWANCE FOR DAUGHTER'S OR SON'S SERVICES (s. 17, I.C.T.A. 1970)
Where a taxpayer, by reason of old age or infirmity, is compelled to depend upon the services of a daughter or son resident with and maintained by him or her, an allowance of £55 may be claimed. This allowance cannot be claimed in addition to Blind Persons Relief (see (g) below).

(f) WIDOW'S OR WIDOWER'S HOUSEKEEPER (s. 12, I.C.T.A. 1970)
A widow or widower who has resident with her or him, for the year of assessment, a relative or a relative of the deceased spouse acting in the capacity of housekeeper, or, if no such relative is available, employs some other person to reside with her for this purpose, may claim an allowance of £100 provided that:

(1) No other person is claiming an allowance for the relative, unless such person has relinquished his claim.
(2) Where the relative is a married woman living with her husband and a claim for married allowance has been made, no relief is available—but a claimant who marries during a year of assessment may elect to retain the housekeeper's allowance and will not then be entitled to the married relief.
(3) Not more than one deduction is allowed to any one claimant for any year.
(4) No relief will be allowed where a claim for additional relief in respect of children (see next section) has been made.

No allowance, however, is made where any other individual is entitled to claim an allowance as housekeeper, child, dependent or daughter attending infirm or aged parent, in respect of the same person, unless such individual has relinquished his claim. No allowance is given if the housekeeper is a relative, whose husband claims married allowance but if the housekeeper is not a relative, the fact that her husband claims the married personal relief does not bar the housekeeper relief. Not more than one deduction of £100 is allowed to a claimant in any one year, and married and housekeeper allowance are not given in the same year to a claimant.

(g) RELIEF FOR BLIND PERSONS (s. 18 I.C.T.A. 1970)
If   (a) A married man who has a wife living with him for the year of assessment and either (but not both) of them were registered blind persons throughout the year; or
    (b) not being married the person was registered as a blind person throughout the year; and
    (c) any tax free disability payments receivable in the year do not exceed £360,
relief from income tax is £360 reduced by any payments under (c).
    If (a) above applies but both husband and wife are blind the sum of £360 is increased to £720 throughout.
    A claim for this relief will not be allowed if relief for the same year is claimed in respect of the services of a daughter, unless such a claim is relinquished.
    If a person is a registered blind person during part only of a year, the sum of £360 (or £720) shall be apportioned accordingly, and only disability payments received during the period from date of registration as a blind person shall be taken into account.

(h) ALLOWANCE FOR CHILDREN—*up to 1981–82* only (ss. 10 and 11, I.C.T.A. 1970; ss. 25 and 26 F.A. 1977; s. 25, F.A. 1980)

From 1979–80 onwards child allowances (apart from those for certain students and children living abroad) *were abolished* and replaced by a *non-taxable* child benefit payable in cash.

In the case of certain children living abroad and students over 19 child benefit is not available. To compensate for this situation, a special allowance was available, up to and including *1981–82* only.

The allowance is as follows:

		Child	
	Under 11	*11–15*	*16 or over*
	£	£	£
1980–81	300	335	365
1981–82	100	135	165
1982–83	None	None	None

Aggregation of Child's Income—where income from settlement made by parents (see Chapter 12).

Income of a child which is settled on or provided for the child by the parents is treated as income of the father (or the parent having custody of the child). This situation does not apply where the child is over 18 *or* married, in which case the income is that of the child.

RATES OF TAX AND METHOD OF CHARGING (S. 32, F.A. 1971)

(*a*) *Rates of tax*
For 1985–86 these are as follows:

Taxable income (after allowable deductions and personal reliefs) £	*Rate of tax* %	*Remarks*
1–16,200	30	Basic rate
16,201–19,200	40	⎫
19,201–24,400	45	⎪
24,401–32,300	50	⎬ Higher rate bands
32,301–40,200	55	⎪
over 40,200	60	⎭

Note. The additional rate on investment income (Investment Income Surcharge) no longer applies for the year 1984–85 and subsequent years. See Appendix 1 for earlier years' charge.

Example 1

H. Brown is a married man with income for 1985–86 as follows:

Salary £12,500
Dividends £7,500 (including tax credit)
Net income from property £1,600

He pays interest of £1,500 p.a. on a mortgage. Show the tax payable for 1985–86.

Taxable income:		£
Salary		12,500
Dividends		7,500
Schedule A		1,600
		21,600
Less Mortgage interest		1,500
		20,100
Less Personal allowance		3,455
		£16,645

Tax payable:	£		£
	16,200 at 30%		4,860.00
	445 at 40%		178.00
	£16,645		5,038.00

Example 2

J. Wood is a married man, his wife being employed by him in his business at a salary of £500 per annum. His business profits assessable for the year 1985–86 (after deduction of the salary paid to his wife) are agreed at £14,150.

STATEMENT OF TAXABLE INCOME 1985–86

		£
Business Profits—Schedule D Case I		14,150
Salary (wife)—Schedule E		500
Total income	£	14,650
Less: Personal allowance	3,455	
Wife's earnings allowance	500	
		3,955
Taxable Income		£10,695

Tax payable £10,695 at 30% = £3,208.50

Note. The effect of the additional personal allowance is that no tax is paid on the salary of Mrs. Wood.

For the purposes of this additional personal allowance, any income of the wife arising in respect of any pension, superannuation or other allowance, deferred pay, or compensation for loss of office, given in respect of past services of the husband in any office or employment of profit, is *not* deemed to be earned income of the wife, and therefore the allowance cannot be claimed in respect of such income.

(*b*) *Method of charging Income Tax*

According to statutory provisions, as set out in the Income Tax Acts, Income Tax is charged at the basic and higher rates on the Total Statutory Income, the allowances being deducted in terms of tax.

The following example shows the strictly legal method of ascertaining the tax payable by an individual for 1985–86.

Example

A. Davies is a married man. His total statutory income for 1985–86 is as follows:

	£
Business profits—Case I, Schedule D [Profits of trading year ended in 1984–85]	4,550
Director's fees—Schedule E [Fees earned in year 1985–86]	2,500
Taxed Dividends (including tax credit) [Received in 1985–86]	300

STATEMENT OF INCOME TAX PAYABLE 1985–86.

	£
Business profits	4,550
Directors fees	2,500
Taxed dividends (gross)	300
Total Statutory Income	£7,350

	£
Tax thereon: £7,350 at 30%	2,205.00
Less Tax on personal allowance £3,455 at 30%	1,036.50
	1,168.50
Deduct Tax borne at source £300 at 30%	90.00
Tax payable direct	£1,078.50

Note. The tax on Directors' Fees will be deducted at source under "Pay As You Earn" (see Chapter 8, § 12), thus the amount of tax payable direct will be reduced by the amount of tax deducted under Schedule E.

When the tax charged on the income liable to direct assessment is insufficient to cover the relief due in respect of allowances, a repayment claim in respect of the tax deducted from income taxed at source will of course be necessary (see § 12 of this Chapter).

(*c*) *Alternative Method of Computing the Tax Payable* (used in practice)

Although the method of ascertaining the tax payable by an individual shown in the above example is strictly correct, the Board of Inland Revenue still retain the pre-existing practice of calculating the Assessable Income (i.e. the Total Income) and then calculating the tax payable on the Taxable Income (i.e. the Assessable Income as further reduced by personal allowances). This is also the method normally employed by practising accountants. In these circumstances, the method is adopted in this book, the term "Taxable Income" being retained to describe the total income after deduction of the allowances.

Example 1

Mrs. R. Jackson is employed as a secretary at a salary of £5,900 per annum. Disregarding the liability for tax on Mrs. Jackson's unearned income and the income (whether earned or unearned) of her husband, the tax payable on her salary for 1985–86 is computed as follows:

STATEMENT OF INCOME TAX PAYABLE 1985–86

	£
Salary	5,900
Less: Additional personal allowance—	2,205
Taxable income	£3,695

TAX PAYABLE

	£
£3,695 at 30%	£1,108.50

The following is a further illustration of the method of ascertaining the tax payable by an individual for the year 1985–86.

Example 2

H. Hilton is a married man with four children aged 9, 10, 17 and 19 respectively on 6th April 1985. The youngest child is entitled to an unearned income in his own right of £15 per month (capital settled by parents).

For the year ended 31st December 1984, Hilton's business profits (as adjusted for Income Tax purposes) were £8,700. In the year ended 5th April 1986, his wife receives an annual fee of £2,750 as a director of Fashions Ltd, child benefit (for two qualifying children) and taxed dividends amounting to £50 gross.

STATEMENT OF INCOME TAX PAYABLE 1985–86

	£
Business profits: 1984	8,700
Director's fee (wife)	2,750
Youngest child's income	180
	11,630
Taxed dividends (wife)	50
Total income	£11,680

	Wife's Earned Income. £	Balance of Income. £
	2,750	8,930
Less Personal allowance		3,455
Additional personal allowance	2,205	
Taxable income	£545	£5,475

TAX PAYABLE

£6,020 (£545 + £5,475) at 30% = £1,806.00

Notes: (1) The income of the youngest child is regarded as that of the parent as it arises on capital settled by the parents.
(2) Child benefit is not subject to taxation.
(3) In practice, tax will be paid under the Schedules concerned as shown below.

		£
Schedule D—Business profits	......	8,700
Less Personal allowance	......	3,455
		£5,245

Tax thereon:	£	£
	5,245 at 30%	£1,573.50

Taxed dividends (taxed at source): £50 at 30%	£15.00

Child's income (Schedule D Case III, or taxed at source): £180 at 30%	£54.00

Wife's income

Fee	2,750
Less Personal allowance	2,205
	£545

Tax thereon
£545 at 30% = £163.50

Total tax borne:

Own income	1,573.50
Taxed dividends	15.00
Child's income	54.00
Wife's income	163.50
	£1,806.00

§ 4.—LIFE ASSURANCE RELIEF

LIFE POLICIES EFFECTED AFTER 13TH MARCH 1984

Abolition of relief in respect of life policies issued after 13th March 1984 and others where terms are varied (s. 72, F.A. 1984)
The 15% life assurance premium relief (L.A.P.R., see below) no longer applies for any policy effected after 13th March 1984 (Budget Day).
Additionally, any policy effected before this date whose terms are varied so as to increase the benefits secured (e.g. increase in sum assured, or conversion of term insurance to whole life assurance) or to extend the term of the insurance will be treated as a policy effected after 13th March 1984 *irrespective of when the*

alteration occurs. A change in a policy includes changes arising from the exercise of any option contained in the original policy. Any person thinking of altering the benefits of a pre-14.3.84 policy would therefore be advised to consider effecting a completely new policy, so as to retain the L.A.P.R. on the 'old' policy.

Policies issued in the course of industrial assurance business will be effective for relief provided a proposal form was completed prior to 14th March 1984 and before 31st March 1984 the policy was prepared for issue, and a record of the issue was made. See below for gains on qualifying policies which apply to policies issued after 13th March 1984.

LIFE POLICIES EFFECTED PRIOR TO 14TH MARCH 1984 (ss. 19 to 21, I.C.T.A. 1970)
An individual resident in the U.K. who is entitled to life assurance relief (see below) can deduct from the premium payment to the life insurance company an amount equal to 15% of the premium. The allowance was $17\frac{1}{2}\%$ for 1979–80 and 1980–81. (One of the effects of this deduction is that an allowance is now available where taxable income is nil—previously relief was given by reducing the tax payable and consequently, if no tax liability arose, no relief was available.)

Allowable deduction
The deduction is limited to one-sixth of total income or £1,500, whichever is the greater. If the policy does not secure a capital sum at death (e.g. a policy for a deferred annuity), the deduction is restricted to £15 (15% × £100).

The life office will recover the amount deducted from the Inland Revenue.

Husband and wife for these purposes are treated as one, although where an election for separate taxation of a wife's earned income is in force, premiums paid by one spouse for the other will be eligible for relief. Similarly premiums paid by one spouse for the other following divorce (provided that the divorce was after 6th April 1979) will also be eligible for relief.

Entitlement to relief
Subject to the qualifying policies rules (see below), premiums are allowed only if paid by an individual under a policy of insurance or contract for a deferred annuity where:

(1) The payments are made to:
  (*a*) Any insurance company legally established in the U.K., or any branch in the U.K. of an insurance company lawfully carrying on life assurance business in the U.K.;
  (*b*) Underwriters who are members of Lloyds or of any other association of underwriters approved by the Department of Trade (or the Ministry of Commerce in Northern Ireland) who comply with the requirements of s. 73 Insurance Companies Act 1974 (or Schedule 1 to the Insurance Companies Act (Northern Ireland) 1968);
  (*c*) A registered friendly society; or
  (*d*) In the case of a deferred annuity, the National Debt Commissioners; *and*
(2) The insurance or deferred annuity is on the life of the individual or his spouse.
(3) The insurance contract was made by him or by his spouse.
Personal accident insurance will not give rise to a deduction unless the policy also includes life insurance cover.

A premium is deemed to fall into the year of assessment in which it is due and *not* that in which it is paid.

CLAWBACK OF PREMIUM RELIEF ON SURRENDER OR CONVERSION OF LIFE POLICIES
(*a*) *Within Four Years of Issue of Policy*
A qualifying life assurance policy issued after 26th March 1974 is subject to a

"clawback" of relief granted if any of the following events have occurred within four years from the date of inception of the policy:
  (i) total or partial surrender of the policy;
  (ii) any payment by way of participation in profits on the policy (otherwise than on death);
  or
  (iii) conversion of the policy into a paid-up or partly paid-up policy;
(See above in relation to variation in life or lives assured)
In these circumstances the Life Office concerned is required to make a deduction (referred to hereafter as "clawback") from the proceeds arising. The Life Office is required to remit any amounts of clawback to the Inland Revenue.

The amount of the clawback will be the lesser of:
  (i) the "appropriate percentage" of all premiums paid on the policy prior to the surrender etc;
  and
  (ii) the surrender value of the policy at the time less the "complementary percentage" (i.e. 100 per cent less the appropriate percentage).
This latter provision has the effect of limiting the clawback to the tax relief due on an amount equal to the proceeds arising. The appropriate percentage is expressed as twice the percentage deduction, appropriate to the year in which the clawback occurs, for qualifying premiums paid to life offices in respect of policies taken out after 22nd June 1916 (i.e. $2 \times 15\%$ for 1984–85). The maximum "clawback" and ceiling for 1982–83 are set out below.

Time of surrender	*Maximum clawback*	*Ceiling*
1st or 2nd year	$\frac{1}{2} \times 30\% = 15\%$	Surrender value less 85% of premiums paid.
3rd year	$\frac{1}{3} \times 30\% = 10\%$	Surrender value less 90% of premiums paid.
4th year	$\frac{1}{6} \times 30\% = 5\%$	Surrender value less 95% of premiums paid.

Policies issued under a Sponsored Superannuation Scheme or an Approved Retirement Benefit Scheme are not subject to clawback.

The clawback provisions may apply to life policies issued before 26th March, 1974 if the premiums thereon are increased by more than 25 per cent of the first annual premium. Similarly an increase of more than 25 per cent of a policy issued after 26th March, 1974 is treated as relating to a new policy and a new four year period runs from the time of the increase.

(b) After initial four-year period
If, during the fifth or any later year after the issue of a life policy there occurs either of:
  (i) total or partial surrender of the policy; or
  (ii) any payment by way of participation in profits on the policy (otherwise than on death or maturity)
and this has happened before, then the Life Office concerned must make retention out of the proceeds arising by way of clawback to be paid over to the Revenue.

Thus there will be no clawback (after the initial four year period) in the case of the first partial surrender or profit participation on any policy.

The clawback under this provision is at one-half of the applicable fraction (i.e. the percentage deduction for life insurance premiums in the year in which the clawback occurs (15% for 1982–83)) of the lower of the total premiums payable in the year of surrender etc., or of the sum payable on surrender etc. If more than one surrender etc. occurs during the course of a year the sums payable thereon are aggregated and account is taken of clawbacks on earlier surrenders etc. in the year.

In general, this rule applies to qualifying policies issued after 26th March 1974. However, the rule may also apply to policies which are deemed to be new policies following an increase in premiums by more than 25 per cent.

The clawback in the fifth or later year does not apply in respect of industrial life policies.

(c) *Imputation of clawback to policyholders*

Any amount of clawback under either the rule applying to surrenders, etc. within four years of issue of a policy or that applying in respect of such an event in the fifth or later year is treated as income tax paid in satisfaction of the increase in tax liability arising from the reduction in premium relief. Normally, the two amounts will match, but where the clawback exceeds the increase in liability as would occur if the tax relief had been limited (e.g. due to an insufficiency of total income) the excess will be repaid to the policyholder by the Revenue following a claim. This claim must be made within six years of the end of the year of assessment in which the event which gave rise to the clawback occurred.

(d) *Loans on policies*

The provisions for clawback of premium relief, as well as the charging of basic rate tax on encashment of guaranteed income bonds and the levying of higher rate tax on gains from life policies, annuities etc. could be avoided by withdrawing funds under the guise of loans. It is therefore provided that, with the exception of bona fide loans of qualifying purposes, loans are treated as equivalent to surrenders and taxed accordingly. These provisions affect only loans arranged with the Life Office issuing the policy and do not apply to loans made by an independent third party on the security of an insurance policy.

Section 30 F.A. 1980 provides that certain life policies known as *income bonds* no longer qualify for the relief. The bonds combined two policies, a deferred annuity with another policy qualifying. The disqualification relates to a policy which is connected with another policy, which provides benefits which are greater than would reasonably be expected if any policy connected with it were disregarded. The disqualification is to affect all policies issued after 25th March 1980.

GAINS ON INSURANCE POLICIES (ss. 394 to 402 I.C.T.A. 1970 and s. 10 and Schedule 2, paras 8 to 20 F.A. 1975)

Introduction

Although the Finance Act 1984 removes the availability of Life Assurance Relief for post-13.3.84 policies, new policies will still need to be categorised into qualifying and non-qualifying in order to determine the taxation treatment of any proceeds arising from encashment or otherwise.

Gains realised on *non*-qualifying life insurance policies (i.e. those not complying with the qualifying provisions set out below) and certain qualifying policies (see below) are subject to higher rate tax and investment income surcharge.

Policies affected are those taken out after 19th March 1968 and include in addition to non-qualifying life policies qualifying life policies in certain circumstances, life annuity contracts and capital redemption policies. A charge to tax applies equally to gains on total or partial surrender although in the later case a charge will not arise until the sums withdrawn exceed certain limits.

Gains chargeable

The gain chargeable is:

    (a) the surrender value immediately prior to death plus any capital sums received prior to this date   *or*

(*b*) the amount received on maturity, surrender, or assignment for value
plus any previous capital sums received (e.g. bonuses, etc.)
less the premiums paid (see below for partial surrender).

Qualifying life policies affected
Policies chargeable (higher rate tax and investment income surcharge only) are
those on which the proceeds arise on death or maturity where the policy has been
converted into a paid up policy within 10 years or if a shorter period, within three
quarters of the policy's intended term.

A charge will also arise where the policy has been surrendered or assigned
within the "10 year three quarter time limit". This applies equally to partial
surrenders within this time limit where an "excess of reckonable aggregate value
over allowable aggregate amount" (see below) arises.

Life annuity contracts (Guaranteed income bonds) are chargeable on the total
amount received up to and including surrender or assignment less any premiums
paid. For contracts after 26 March 1974 gains are chargeable *at the basic rate* in
addition to higher rates and investment income surcharge.

A life annuity contract is one which provides for an annuity payable for a term
ending with (or ascertain only by reference to) the end of a human life, whether
or not there is provision for the annuity to end during the life at the end of a fixed
term, or on the occurrence of any event or otherwise, or to continue after the end
of the life in particular circumstances (s. 230 I.C.T.A. 1970).

Capital redemption policies are chargeable (to higher rate tax and investment
income surcharge) on the total amounts received up to and including maturity,
surrender or assignment less premiums paid. A capital redemption policy is any
policy issued in the course of the business (not being life assurance business or
industrial assurance business) of effecting and carrying out contracts of insurance,
whether effected by the issue of policies, bonds or endowment certificates or otherwise, whereby, in return for one or more premiums paid to the insurer, a sum or
a series of sums is to become payable to the insured in the future (s. 324 I.C.T.A.
1970).

Partial surrender
Gains arising on life policies, capital redemption policies and annuity contracts
are chargeable to income tax on partial surrender (or assignment) but only where
the *reckonable aggregate value* exceeds the *allowable aggregate amount*.

The calculation to determine whether an excess occurs is required after the
anniversary of each policy year (i.e. twelve months after the policy commencement).

Reckonable aggregate value—is the total of all surrenders or assignments of the
policy to date (but excluding policy years prior to 13th March 1975) less the
amounts already taken into charge.

Allowable aggregate amount—is the appropriate portion of all premiums and
lump sum payments made to date (i.e. to the end of the policy year in question)
less those which have been brought into account in earlier chargeable events.

The appropriate portion is:

$$\frac{\text{the years from the commencement of the policy to the end of the current year}}{20}$$

Top slicing relief
An individual may claim that any tax payable as a result of a gain arising as above
be calculated as follows:
(*a*) Divide the gain by the complete number of years the policy has run
(either from inception or from the previous chargeable occasion if later)
to calculate the appropriate fraction.

(*b*) Calculate the tax payable on this sum as if it represented the top slice of the individual's income in the chargeable tax year in question (i.e. the year of maturity etc.)

(*c*) Multiply the tax at (*b*) by the number of years the policy has run as in (*a*) above.

Where gains arise on more than one policy, the calculations are applied by reference to the aggregate of the gains and appropriate fractions. The average tax rate on the "appropriate fractions" is then calculated, and applied to the sum of the policy gains.

Example

Henry purchased two non-qualifying life policies for single lump-sum premiums. He encashed both policies on 10th November 1985. Details of the policies are as follows:

Purchase date	Premium paid	Proceeds
(1) 7th May 1975	£5,000	£8,000
(2) 12th August 1980	4,000	9,000

Henry is a single man whose only income in 1985–86 is a salary of £18,040.

The tax charge for 1985–86 in respect of the gains on the policies is as follows:

Gains chargeable		Total of whole years since policy commencement
	£	
(1)	3,000	10 (1975–1985)
(2)	5,000	5 (1980–1985)
	8,000	

Tax on income other than gains:

Salary		18,040
Less personal allowance		2,205
		15,835

Tax on policy gain (as the top slice):

Appropriate fraction

Policy 1	$\dfrac{3,000}{10}$		=	300
Policy 2	$\dfrac{5,000}{5}$		=	1,000
				£1,300

Tax thereon:

15,835 − 16,200 =	365 @ 30%	=	109.50
16,200 − 17,135 =	935 @ 40%	=	374.00
	1,300		£483.50

Average rate of tax $\dfrac{483.5}{1,300}$ = 37%

Total tax on the policy gains is therefore

8,000 at 37%   = £2,960

This may be calculated alternatively as:

Tax on policy (1)

         £300 @ 37% × 10 =   1,110

    on policy (2)

         £1,000 @ 37% × 5 =   1,850

Total tax on policy gains   =   £2,960

QUALIFYING POLICIES (Schedule 1, I.C.T.A. 1970; Schedule 2, Parts I to III, F.A. 1975 and s. 30 F.A. 1980)

Restrictions are included in s. 19, I.C.T.A. 1970, in respect of policies effected after 19th March, 1968. A policy effected after that date will qualify for life assurance relief only if benefits under the policy are confined to a capital sum payable on death (plus possible disability benefits or, in some cases, a subsequent series of capital sums), and the following conditions are fulfilled, in addition to the limitations previously mentioned.

(*a*) *Policies payable only on death within a specified period*
If the period is less than 10 years, any surrender value must not exceed the return of premiums paid. Where the specified period exceeds 10 years, premiums must be payable at yearly, or shorter, intervals during at least three-quarters of the period or until the assured's earlier death, and the premiums payable in any one year, excluding any loading for exceptional mortality risk, must not exceed (*i*) twice the amount of the premiums payable in any other year or (*ii*) one-eighth of the total premiums payable.
For policies issued on or after 1st April 1976 where the specified period ends after age 75, and provision is made for whole or partial surrender, then the capital sum, so far as it is payable on death, must not be less than 75% of the total premium that would have been payable if death had occurred at age 75.

(*b*) *Endowment assurance policies*
The term of such policies must be for at least 10 years or until the assured's earlier death, and must guarantee on death (or death after age 16) a sum at least equal to three-quarters of the total premiums which would be payable during the full term. Where the benefit is limited to death after age 16, the sum payable on earlier death must not exceed the return of premiums paid. Premiums must be payable annually, or at shorter intervals, for a period of for not less than 10 years, or until death. The limitations (*i*) and (*ii*) and (*a*) above apply.
For policies effected on or after 1st April 1976 in respect of a person aged over 55, the 75% standard can be reduced by 2% for each year the individual exceeds 55 (e.g. age 60—75% is reduced to 65%).

(*c*) *Whole life policies*
The premiums on such policies must be payable annually, or at shorter intervals, during the life of the assured, or for a specified period

of at least 10 years should the assured live longer. The premium limitations (*i*) and (*ii*) in (*a*) above are applicable, the total premiums under (*ii*) being those for the first 10 years, or for the specified period, as above, if longer.

The above restrictions are, however, not to apply to (*a*) policies solely for the payment on an individual's death of the balance of a mortgage (repayable by instalments) on his (or her) residence or business premises, or (*b*) to policies under a superannuation scheme where at least one-half of the cost of the scheme is borne by the employer.

Where a life policy does not fulfil the above requirements, any excess of the cumulative figure of proceeds of surrenders etc. taken under the policy over the cumulative figure of allowances for premiums paid, will be treated for higher rate purposes (but not for basic rate tax) as income of an individual owner, or as income, and distributable income, for Corporation Tax purposes, if the policy benefits a close company. Similar treatment applies if a policy which does qualify for relief as above is surrendered, assigned or converted to a paid-up policy before it has run 10 years. The allowances in this case being $\frac{1}{20}$ of premiums paid in a year together with $\frac{1}{20}$ of premiums paid in earlier years (up to a maximum of twenty years.)

Similar provisions are applicable to life annuity contracts and capital redemption policies.

In the case of a partnership where a "joint" policy (i.e. the sum assured being payable on the first death) has been taken out, no relief in respect of the premiums can be claimed, although, by concession, the Inland Revenue will grant relief in respect of premiums paid on a policy on the joint lives of a husband and wife.

Premiums paid on industrial life policies also qualify for relief but the aggregate of sums assured under policies issued to any one policyholder must not exceed certain monetary limits.

Certification of qualifying policies was taken over by the Revenue from the Life Offices with effect from the "appointed day" (1st April 1976). Also from the appointed day a number of new requirements were introduced:

(*a*) *Whole life or term policies*
Such policies must now assure a capital sum on death of not less than 75 per cent of all premiums payable up to the age of 75. However term policies which do not make provision for any payment on total or partial surrender, and where the term of the policy does not run beyond age 75 are excluded from the 75 per cent rule. Premiums are taken into account at the annual rate and any additional payments made to secure shorter periodic payments are ignored. In the case of industrial policies a standard 10 per cent of premiums is excluded for the purpose of the 75 per cent test. If the capital sum on death is payable either as a single sum or as a series of sums the 75 per cent rule applies to the smallest total sum which could be payable.

(*b*) *Endowment assurance policies*
An endowment policy is now required, if it is to be a qualifying policy to secure on death a capital sum of at least 75 per cent of the total premiums payable during its prospective term. The 75 per cent standard is reduced by 2 per cent for each year by which the age of the assured exceeds 55.

(*c*) *Substituted policies*
Where the initial premium on a policy issued in substitution for another is inflated because of the inclusion in it of the accumulated value of an old policy such value is left out of account in testing the substituted policy for qualification.

(*d*) *Policies providing options*

At the inception of a policy which includes options each hypothetical policy which would result from the exercising of the options is tested to ensure that each such policy would be a qualifying policy. Only if all of the hypothetical policies would qualify is the initial policy to be treated as a qualifying policy.

(*e*) *Connected policies* (s. 30, F.A. 1980)

A policy is non-qualifying if it is connected with another policy the terms of which provide benefits which are greater than would be expected if the policy were unconnected. Policies are connected for this purpose if they are at any time simultaneously in force and either of them is issued with reference to the other, or with a view to enabling the other to be issued on particular terms.

(*f*) *Variation in life or lives assured* (s. 34, F.A. 1982)

This section was introduced to take out of the anti-avoidance provisions (i.e. those dealing with chargeable events and clawback of relief—see below) changes in the life or lives assured where one qualifying life assurance policy is replaced by another. The anti-avoidance provisions are excluded where the later policy comes into existence on or after 25th March 1982.

(*g*) *Life assurance qualifying policies and policies on the lives of children* (s. 35, F.A. 1982)

As a result of certain amendments made to the Insurance Companies Act 1974 by the Insurance Companies Act 1981, certain amending provisions were required. The maximum annual premium for policies on the lives of children is increased from £52 to £64. These alterations affect policies made on or after 25th March 1982.

Anti-avoidance

(*i*) *Second-hand bonds* (s. 18, F.A. 1983)

Under the provisions of ss. 394 (4) and 396 (2) I.C.T.A. 1970 the assignment of a life policy or annuity contract precludes a subsequent event being a chargeable event if the assignment is for money's worth. As a result profits made on the policy or contract after the assignment are subject only to capital gains tax and not income tax.

To counter avoidance devices that were taking advantage of this loophole, i.e. simply assigning the policy through a broker, who had acquired the policy, rather than purchasing direct from the life company, legislation was introduced in the Finance Act 1983 (s. 18 and Schedule 4, F.A. 1983) with effect from 26th June 1982. The effect was:

(i) to charge to income tax chargeable events for all policies or contracts assigned *after* 25th June.

and

(ii) To charge to income tax chargeable events for policies or contracts assigned before 25th June if after 23rd August 1982:

(a) the rights of the policy or contract are again assigned *or*

(b) a payment is made by way of premium or a lump sum consideration to the policy or contract

(c) a sum is lent by arrangement with the body issuing the policy or contract (only affects policies/contracts issued after 26th March 1974).

(*ii*) *Capital and income bonds* (s. 74, F.A. 1984)

A policy that is connected with another policy under the provisions of s. 30, F.A.

1980 is not a qualifying policy if the other policy provides benefits that would not otherwise exist but for the connection.

To counter the device of linking a qualifying and a non-qualifying policy together (capital and income bonds) such that the qualifying policy provides the benefits and avoids the s. 30, F.A. 1980 charge, the above section was introduced effective for policies issued on or after 23rd August 1983 (with appropriate transitional provisions).

(iii) Roll-over policies (s. 75, F.A. 1984)
This section amends the provisions of s. 394(3), I.C.T.A 1970 to prevent the avoidance of tax by higher-rate tax payers extracting funds from non-qualifying life policies by rolling over only part of the proceeds from one policy to another.

(iv) Policies issued outside the U.K. (s. 76, F.A. 1984)
Policies issued after 22nd February 1984 outside the U.K. will no longer be treated as qualifying policies.

Policies effected on or before 22nd June 1916
Relief is available to an individual where, under any Act of Parliament or under the terms or conditions of his employment, he is liable for the payment of any sum, or for the deduction from his salary of any sum, for the purpose of securing a deferred annuity for his widow, or provision for his children after his death.

The allowance is given in terms of tax at a rate which depends upon the net total income, as follows:

Net total income	*Rate of relief (%) on allowable premiums*
Not exceeding £1,000	Half the basic rate
£1,001 – £2,000	Three-quarters of the basic rate
Over £2,000	The basic rate

The relief is given in terms at the appropriate rate on the premiums paid during the year of assessment and is deducted from the amount of income tax with which he is chargeable. (N.B. $\frac{1}{6}$ total income limit applying to post-1916 policies does *not* apply to pre-1916 policies from 1979–80 onwards.)

Marginal relief. Marginal relief may be claimed where the net total income just fails to exceed £1,000 or £2,000 as the case may be, and relief is obtainable in respect of policies effected on or before 22nd June, 1916.

Where the tax ultimately payable by any person after deducting life assurance relief is greater than the amount of tax which would be payable if the net total income exceeded £1,000 or £2,000, as the case may be, the life assurance relief is increased by a sum equal to tax at $\frac{1}{4}$ of the basic rate (i.e. for 1985–86 $\frac{1}{4} \times 30\%$) on the amount of the allowable premiums, less tax at the basic rate (i.e. for 1985–86, 30%) on the amount by which the net total income falls short of £1,000 or £2,000 as the case may be (s. 20 I.C.T.A. 1970).

§ 5.—RETIREMENT ANNUITIES (ss. 226 and 227 I.C.T.A. 1970 as amended by ss. 31–33 F.A. 1980)

GENERAL

Relief from income tax is available to an individual who pays a premium under an annuity contract approved by the Inland Revenue as having as its main object the provision of a life annuity in old age (generally starting at 60 but see below). The relief is available only against relevant earnings of any trade, profession or employment carried on by the individual.

Considerable discretionary power is given to the Inland Revenue in approving contracts which meet these general requirements (see s. 226(3) I.C.T.A. 1970). For example whilst the general rule is that annuities cannot commence before 60 (s. 226 (2) (b)) a contract may still be approved if the individual's occupation is one in which retirement normally occurs before 60 (e.g. sportsmen and women).

Any annuity received in due course will be treated as earned income, in so far as it is payable in return for an amount in respect of which relief has been given. Any excess ranks as unearned income.

The Inland Revenue will not approve an annuity contract unless it is made by the individual with a person carrying on a life assurance business and it includes provisions securing that no annuity payable under it is capable of surrender, commutation or assignment.

Power is, however, given to the Board of Inland Revenue to approve the transfer of annuity contracts. Thus an individual may (subject to Inland Revenue approval) transfer his accrued rights under a retirement annuity contract with one life office to another life office, in order to secure the most beneficial situation. The transferred rights must be applied as the premium under an annuity contract.

CONTRACTS FOR DEPENDANTS OR LIFE INSURANCE (s. 226A).
The Inland Revenue will also approve an annuity contract satisfying the conditions above if it provides:
   (i) an annuity for the spouse or for any one or more of the individual's dependants,
   (ii) a lump sum on the death of the individual before he reaches 75 years of age.

RELEVANT EARNINGS
The earnings to which relief is applicable, the *relevant earnings* are income from
   (i) non-pensionable employments,
   (ii) income chargeable under Schedule D from a trade, profession, etc., carried on by the individual personally or as an active partner and
   (iii) patent income treated as earned income (see Chapter 11 § 16).

Relevant earnings do not include remuneration of a controlling director of an investment company, nor the relevant earnings of the wife or husband of the individual.

In the case of the profits of a business assessed under Case I or II, Schedule D, the amount to be included is the Income Tax assessment before deducting capital allowances, but inclusive of any balancing charges. N.B. *relief is, however, granted by reference to net relevant earnings* (see below).

RELIEF AVAILABLE
The maximum relief available for 1985–86 onwards for individuals born after 1933* is $17\frac{1}{2}\%$ of *net relevant earnings*. These are relevant earnings as above before capital allowances (except those given by deduction) but after balancing charges, and as reduced by:
   (i) deductions for annuities, royalties for the user of a patent and mining rents or royalties under ss. 156, 157 I.C.T.A. which but for s. 130 I.C.T.A. would be trading deductions,
   (ii) stock relief under Schedule 5 F.A. 1976,
   (iii) capital allowances and losses arising from activities which would be included in computing relevant earnings.

---

* (For 1980–81 and 1981–82 maximum relief was $17\frac{1}{2}\%$ of net relevant earnings for individuals born after 1916).

The limit of $17\frac{1}{2}\%$ is increased where date of birth is before 1933 as follows:

Year of birth	Percentage
1916 to 1933	20
1914 or 1915	21
1912 or 1913	24
1910 or 1911	$26\frac{1}{2}$
1908 or 1909	$29\frac{1}{2}$
1907 or earlier	$32\frac{1}{2}$

The relevant maximum percentage applies irrespective of the number of premiums paid and whether or not inclusive of premiums paid under s. 226A (i.e. those for dependants or providing life assurance relief).

Where premiums are paid under s. 226A (see above) the overall maximum for such premiums is 5% of net relevant earnings.

Example

Rupert pays the following approved retirement annuity premiums in 1985–86:

For dependants	£ 750
For himself	£1,200

His net relevant earnings for the year were £10,000.
Relief is available for 1985–86 as follows:

Dependants (restricted to 5% × 10,000).........................	500
Himself	1,200
Relief available (not restricted since less than $17\frac{1}{2}\%$ × £10,000)	£1,700

CARRY FORWARD OF EXCESS RELIEF

Where in any year of assessment premiums paid fall short of the relief available, the excess relief can be carried forward for offset in any of the next six years of assessment, taking relief for an earlier year first. The excess relief can only be utilised when premiums paid exceed the normal annual limits. The relief applies for the year 1980–81 and subsequent years of assessment. This has the effect of allowing excess relief to be carried forward from at the earliest 1974–75.

Premiums paid are utilised first against the earliest years' unused relief, thus allowing maximum benefit.

Example

Theta makes retirement annuity premium payments as follows:

	Premiums	Net relevant earnings	Maximum relief	Unused relief	Latest date relief obtainable
	£	£	£	£	
1974–75	400	3,000 (15%)	450	50	5.4.81
1975–76	600	4,200 (15%)	630	30	5.4.82
1976–77	700	5,000 (15%)	750	50	5.4.83
1977–78	700	6,000 (15%)	900	200	5.4.84
1978–79	900	8,000 (15%)	1,200	300	5.4.85
1979–80	1,000	10,000 (15%)	1,500	500	5.4.86
1980–81	1,250	12,000 ($17\frac{1}{2}\%$)	2,100	850	5.4.87
1981–82	1,500	10,000 ($17\frac{1}{2}\%$)	1,750	250	5.4.88
1982–83	2,000	10,000 ($17\frac{1}{2}\%$)	1,750	(250)	N/A
1983–84	2,050	10,000 ($17\frac{1}{2}\%$)	1,750	(300)	N/A
1984–85	2,400	12,000 ($17\frac{1}{2}\%$)	2,100	(300)	N/A
1985–86	2,100	12,000 ($17\frac{1}{2}\%$)	2,100	—	N/A

Note: On the basis that Theta makes no other premium payments, the "over-payment" in 1982–83 would be absorbed by unused relief for 1976–77 (£50) and 1977–78 (£200), the overpayment for 1983–84 (£300) utilised by unused relief for 1978–79 (£300) and the overpayment for 1984–85 utilised by part of the unused relief for 1979–80. The earlier years' relief unused would be lost.

Transitional Arrangements

To allow relief for premiums carried forward prior to the alterations in the manner of granting relief effected by the F.A. 1980, transitional arrangements provide that unrelieved premiums paid up to 5 April 1980 are available for offset in 1980–81 and 1981–82. The effect is without regard to the maximum percentage allowable in those years and can be apportioned between the years as the individual requires.

Example

Casio paid the following retirement annuity premiums:

Year of assessment	Net relevant earnings	Maximum relief	Premium paid	Excess premium
1978–79	5,000	750 (15%)	1,000	250
1979–80	12,000	1,800 (15%)	2,000	200
1980–81	10,000	1,750 (17½%)	1,750	N/A
1981–82	10,000	1,750 (17½%)	1,750	N/A

Casio can elect for the unrelieved premiums at 5.4.1980 of £450 to be utilised in 1980–81 or 1981–82 or partly in each year regardless of the fact that the maximum premiums have been paid.

CARRY BACK OF PREMIUMS PAID

In any year of assessment after 1979–80 an individual can elect for premiums paid to be carried back and treated as paid:

    (*a*) in the preceding year *or*

    (*b*) if no relevant earnings in the preceding year, in the next preceding year.

Where an election is made to carry back premiums the premium for purposes of relief is treated as being paid in the earlier year. *The election must be made before the end of the year of assessment in which the premium is paid.* The Inland Revenue will accept that part of a premium may be carried back.

Example 1

Delta makes retirement annuity premiums payments as follows:

	£
1984–85	2,000 (2 premiums of £1,000)
1985–86	4,000 (4 premiums of £1,000)

His net relevant earnings in 1984–85 are £20,000 and in 1985–86 £18,000.
The maximum relief available to Delta is

1984–85	17½% × 20,000	=	3,500
1985–86	17½% × 18,000	=	3,150.

If Delta elects for one of the 1985–86 premiums to be treated as paid in 1984–85 he will obtain full relief for the payments (£3,000 in each year), £850 of which (i.e., £4,000–£3,150) would otherwise have been lost since excess premiums cannot be carried forward.

Detailed Example

The income of Mr Morris and his wife for 1985–86 is as follows:

	Mr Morris £	Mrs Morris £
Farm assessment (£6,000), less capital allowances (£600) plus balancing charge (£500)	5,900	
Salary from farm		450
Business assessment (after deducting capital allowances £450)		270
Directors' emoluments (not pensionable)	1,800	2,000
National Savings Bank interest:		
Ordinary account	75	50
Investment account		15
Bank deposit account (gross)	534	
Dividends (including tax credit)	2,000	1,800

Mr Morris pays the maximum allowable premium to obtain a self-employed retirement annuity. He was born in 1907. They have three children (no income), all at school, aged 10, 12 and 18 respectively.

STATEMENT OF INCOME TAX PAYABLE 1985–86

	Wife's Earned Income £	Other Income £
Business assessment	270	5,900
Salary from farm	450	
Director's emoluments	2,000	1,800
	2,720	7,700
Deduct: Retirement annuity premium (see Note)		2,502
	2,720	5,198
Savings bank interest (£75 − £70 + £50 − £50 + £15)		20
Bank deposit interest		534
Dividends (including tax credit)		3,800
Total statutory income	2,720	9,552
Less: Personal allowance		3,455
Additional personal allowance	2,205	
Taxable income	£515	£6,097

INCOME TAX PAYABLE

	£	£
On 6,612 at 30%		1,983.60

Note:

net relevant earnings are computed as follows:

	£
Farm assessment	6,000
Balancing charge	500
Directors' emoluments	1,800
Relevant earnings	8,300
Less: Capital allowances	600
	£7,700

The maximum allowable premium is thus $32\frac{1}{2}$ per cent of £7,700 (i.e. £2,502.50).

§ 6.—RELIEF FOR INVESTMENT IN CORPORATE TRADES—THE BUSINESS EXPANSION SCHEME (s. 26 and Schedule 5 F.A. 1983)

HISTORICAL BACKGROUND

In an attempt to encourage investment in new business ventures, a completely new form of relief ("start-up" relief) was introduced under provisions of ss. 52–67 of the Finance Act 1981. The relief was not only new but somewhat radical in that it created an income tax deduction for capital investment.

The start-up scheme was superseded by the business expansion scheme introduced in the Finance Act 1983 which applies for investments made from 6th April 1983 to 5th April 1987, although many of the original definitions of the start-up relief are retained. *The essential difference between the reliefs is that under the expansion scheme the venture need not be new*, although new ventures continue to qualify. (For the sake of completeness the start-up scheme provisions are outlined in Appendix 2.)

BUSINESS EXPANSION SCHEME RELIEF

APPLICATION

  (i) The relief applies for the years 1983–84 to 1986–87 to qualifying individuals subscribing for *eligible shares* in a qualifying company for the purpose of raising money for a qualifying trade which is carried on by the company wholly or mainly in the UK or which it intends to carry on within two years from the date of the issue of shares.
Eligible shares are new ordinary shares which throughout the period of five years from the date of issue carry no present or future preferential right to dividends, assets on a winding up, or redemption.

  (ii) The relief is given as a deduction (a personal allowance) against the individual's total income in the year of assessment in which the shares are issued.

  (iii) A claim for the relief must be made and is not available unless and until the company has carried on the trade for four months. If the company is not carrying on the trade when the shares are issued the relief will be denied unless the trade is commenced within twenty four months of the issue date. The earliest date on which a claim can be made was, however, 1st January 1984.

  (iv) The relief is granted after all other personal allowances, although the restriction as to the order of set-off (i.e. earned income first) does not apply.

(v) The conditions as to qualifications (see below) must be met throughout the relevant period. If the conditions are not satisfied the relief is withdrawn (or reduced in the case of sale within the five year relevant period).

RELEVANT PERIOD

The relevant period is the period throughout which the various conditions as to qualification must be met.

In the case of:
qualifying individual
disposal of shares
value received from company
replacement capital
value received by persons other than the claimant

the period is that beginning with the incorporation of the company (or two years prior to the share issue if later) and ending five years after the share issue.

In the case of:
qualifying companies
qualifying trades
application to subsidiaries

the period is that beginning with the date the shares are issued and ending three years after that date or where the company at the share issue date was not carrying on a qualifying trade, three years after the date it commences to trade.

RELIEF LIMITATION

The maximum relief available to an individual is £40,000 in any one year of assessment.

No relief is granted if investment in a company is less than £500 (unless investment is made via an approved investment fund).

Example 1

Horse, Bear and Dog subscribe in 1985–86 for shares in Nexos and Paxos Ltd as follows:

	Nexos Ltd	Paxos Ltd
	£	£
Horse	400	300
Bear	2,000	450
Dog	8,000	36,000

Assuming all qualifying conditions are satisfied relief will be granted:

Horse—Nil (since investment in each company is less than £500)
Bear—£2,000 (no relief for investment in Paxos Ltd since less than £500)
Dog—£40,000 (maximum claim available)

There is no restriction on the percentage of shares issued on which relief may be claimed (i.e. all shares issued may be shares qualifying for relief) although there is a restriction on the percentage each individual may hold (see below).

QUALIFYING CONDITIONS

Relief for investment will not qualify unless all the conditions attaching to the individual, company and trade are satisfied. These are as follows:

(1) INDIVIDUAL SUBSCRIBERS

An individual will only qualify for relief if he is resident and ordinarily resident in the U.K. in the year the shares are issued *and* he is *not* connected with the company at any time in the relevant period (five years). This broadly means the individual cannot receive income from the company or control more than 30% of the issued ordinary share capital. The detailed rules are as follows.

An individual is connected with a company if he *or an associate* of his is:
  (*a*) an employee of the company or an employee of a partner of the company;
  (*b*) a partner of the company;
  (*c*) a director of the company or of a company which is a partner of the company, *unless* no payment is received by the director.

Payment of the following sums to a director are ignored in considering whether payment is received:
  (*a*) any payment or reimbursement of travelling or other expenses wholly, exclusively and necessarily incurred by him or his associate in the performance of his duties as a director of the company;
  (*b*) any interest which represents no more than a reasonable commercial return on money lent to the company;
  (*c*) any dividend or other distribution which does not exceed a normal return on the investment;
  (*d*) any payment for the supply of goods which does not exceed their market value; and
  (*e*) any reasonable and necessary remuneration which:
    (i) is paid for services rendered to the company in the course of a trade or profession (not being secretarial or managerial services or services of a kind provided by the company itself); and
    (ii) is taken into account in computing the profits or gains of the trade or profession under Case I or II of Schedule D.

An individual is also connected with a company if:
  (i) he directly or indirectly possesses or is entitled to acquire more than 30% of:
    (*a*) the issued ordinary share capital of the company; or
    (*b*) the loan capital and issued share capital of the company; or
    (*c*) the voting power in the company.
  (ii) he directly or indirectly possesses or is entitled to acquire such rights which would in the event of a winding up of the company entitle him to receive more than 30% of the assets available to the equity holders (The percentage distribution and equity holders for this purpose are determined by reference to paragraphs 1 and 3 of Schedule 12 F.A. 1973).

(2) QUALIFYING COMPANIES

The requirements to be met for a company to be a qualifying company are that throughout the relevant period (in this case "three years"):
  (*a*) it must be incorporated, and resident in the U.K.;
  (*b*) it must be unquoted (this excludes companies listed on the Unlisted Securities Market)
  (*c*) it must exist wholly or substantially wholly for the purpose of carrying on wholly or mainly in the UK one or more qualifying trades:
  (*d*) all shares are fully paid up:
  (*e*) it is not controlled by another company or itself controls another company (other than a 100% subsidiary which itself would qualify for relief if available).
  (*f*) no individual must have a controlling interest in the company's trade after 5.4.1983 *if* that individual has, or has had, a controlling interest in another trade and that trade or a substantial part of it is concerned with similar activities or serves the same market outlets (the time scale

is two years before and three years after the share issue date, or if later the trade commencement date).

A controlling interest is deemed to be 30% where the company is a close company, otherwise the usual control rules apply (i.e. s. 302 (2) to (6), I.C.T.A. 1970).

A company ceases to be a qualifying company if during the relevant period a winding up commences *unless* the winding up is for bona fide commercial reasons (and not for tax avoidance purposes) and the assets are distributed before the end of the relevant period or within 3 years from the date of winding up if later.

(3) QUALIFYING TRADES

No definition as to a *qualifying trade* is given although the trade must during the relevant period ("3 years") be carried on with a view to profit and on a commercial basis.

If the trade consists substantially of any of the following activities or of *farming* (s. 37, F.A. 1984) *or property development* (from 19.3.85), however, it will *not* qualify:

(*a*) dealing in commodities, shares, securities, land or futures; or

(*b*) dealing in goods otherwise than in the course of an ordinary trade of wholesale or retail distribution; or

(*c*) banking, insurance, money-lending, debt-factoring, hire-purchase financing or other financial activities; or

(*d*) leasing (including letting ships on charter or other assets on hire) or receiving royalties or licence fees (but see below for films); or

(*e*) providing legal or accountancy services; or

(*f*) providing services or facilities for any trade carried on by another person which consists to any substantial extent of above activities and in which a controlling interest is held by a person who also has a controlling interest in the trade carried on by the company.

N.B. Property development means the development of land by a company which has or at any time has had an interest in the land with the sole or main object of realising a gain from disposing of the land when developed (hence *non*-land owning developers are not excluded).

Films. A company carrying on a trade of film production is *not* excluded by virtue of (*d*) above provided all royalties and licence fees in the relevant period are derived from the production of films or sound recordings.

Research and Development. From 6.4.85, shares issued by companies for research and development from which a qualifying trade will arise, qualify for relief. The issue can also include sums raised for the resultant trade as well as the R&D. (R&D means any activity which is intended to result in a patentable invention or in a computer program.)

Only an ordinary trade of wholesale or retail distribution is a qualifying trade. A trade of wholesale distribution is one in which the goods are offered for sale and sold to persons for resale by them or for processing and resale by them. A trade of retail distribution is one in which the goods are offered for sale and sold to members of the general public for their use or consumption.

In determining whether a trade is an ordinary trade of wholesale or retail distribution the following factors are relevant:

(1) The goods are bought by the trader in quantities larger than those in which he sells them.

(2) The goods are bought and sold by the trader in different markets.

(3) The trader employs staff and incurs expenses in the trade in addition to the cost of the goods and, in the case of a trade carried on by a company, in addition to any remuneration paid to any person connected with it.

Factors which indicate that an ordinary trade is *not* being carried on are:
(1) There are purchases or sales from or to persons who are connected with the trader.
(2) Purchases are matched with forward sales or vice versa.
(3) The goods are held by the trader for longer than is normal for goods of the kind in question.
(4) The trade is carried on otherwise than at a place or places commonly used for wholesale or retail trade.
(5) The trader does not take physical possession of the goods.

REDUCTION/WITHDRAWAL OF RELIEF
Apart from non-satisfaction of the qualifying criteria set out above, (and the anti-avoidance provisions—see below) relief can also be reduced or withdrawn in the following cases where in the relevant period:
(*a*) the shares are disposed of *or*
(*b*) value is received from the company.

(*a*) *Disposal of shares* (N.B. only within the relevant period)
Relief is totally withdrawn if the disposal is not at arm's length. In other cases the relief is reduced by the amount of the disposal proceeds.

Where shares on which relief has been given and other shares are held disposals are deemed to be made from "relief shares" first.

Example

Hamlet acquires the following shares in Shake Ltd:

	Shares	Amount £
1980–81	2,000	4,000
1984–85 (relief claimed)	3,000	7,000

If Hamlet sells 2,500 shares in Shake Ltd in 1986 (i.e. within the relevant period) for £4,000 in an arm's length transaction, the relief withdrawn will be £4,000 (N.B. The total relief claimed on 2,500 shares is £5,833 = 2,500/3,000 × £7,000.)

(*b*) *Value received from a company* (N.B. only in the relevant period)
Relief is reduced to the extent that value is obtained from the company. Value is received if the company:

	AMOUNT OF VALUE
(*a*) repays, redeems or repurchases any of its share capital or securities which belong to the individual or makes any payment to him for giving up his right to any of the company's share capital or any security on its cancellation or extinguishment;	The greater of the shares' market value or the amount received.
(*b*) repays any debt owed to the individual other than a debt which was incurred by the company (i) on or after the date on which he subscribed for the shares in respect of which the relief is claimed; and (ii) otherwise than in consideration of the extinguishment of a debt incurred before that date;	The greater of the market value of the debt or the amount received.

	AMOUNT OF VALUE
(*c*) makes to the individual any payment for giving up his right to any debt (other than a debt for travelling or other expenses incurred in the performance of the duties of a director or for professional etc. services rendered or an ordinary trade debt) on its extinguishment.	The greater of the market value of the debt or the amount received.
(*d*) releases or waives any liability of the individual to the company or discharges, or undertakes to discharge, any liability of his to a third person;	The amount of the liability.
(*e*) makes a loan in advance to the individual;	The amount of the loan.
(*f*) provides a benefit or facility for the individual;	The cost of providing the benefit less any amount made good.
(*g*) transfers an asset to the individual for no consideration or for consideration less than its market value or acquires an asset from him for consideration exceeding its market value; or	The market value of the asset less any consideration received.
(*h*) makes to him any other payment except a payment mentioned above as not being treated as a payment to a director (refer Qualifying Conditions above) or a payment in discharge of an ordinary trade debt.	The amount of the payment.

Additionally, value is received where the individual receives any distribution in the course of a winding up (and the winding up in itself does not deny relief: see above).

Relief is withdrawn for earlier share issues first.

Relief will also be reduced if at any time in the relevant period the company redeems or repays any of its share capital which belongs to a shareholder other than an individual claiming the relief. The reduction in the relief is the greater of the amount received the nominal value of the shares redeemed. Where value is received under these circumstances, adjustment is also made to the company's issued share capital for the purposes of calculating future applicability of the 30% test.

REPLACEMENT CAPITAL

Relief will also be withdrawn if an individual claiming relief can receive back capital from a person other than the company, if the company or any of its subsidiaries:

(*a*) begins to carry on a trade previously carried on by another person or
(*b*) acquires the whole a greater part of a trade previously carried on by another person AND either
   (i) the person(s) controlling the transferee company or
   (ii) the person(s) owning more than half the share in the previous business trade own such a share in the trade after transfer.

ANTI-AVOIDANCE

Expansion relief will not be granted unless the shares are issued for bona fide commercial reasons and not as part of a scheme or arrangement the main purpose of which is the avoidance of tax. (It is understood that the Commissioners of Inland Revenue do not interpret obtaining relief *per se* as "an arrangement the main . . .")

HUSBAND AND WIFE

A husband and wife living together are treated as one. Subscriptions are accordingly aggregated for limit purposes. Relief is given against the husband's total income (which includes the wife's income) unless an election to separate assessment (s. 38 I.C.T.A. 1970) or separate taxation of the wife's earnings (s. 23 F.A. 1971) applies.

In the case of separate assessment, relief due to the wife is set against her income and any excess set against her husband's income (i.e. as with personal allowances).

In the case of separate taxation of wife's earnings, relief is given to the spouse making the payment and set off as with other personal allowances. In both cases where the annual limit is exceeded, relief is apportioned according to the amount subscribed.

Where marriage occurs during the year, husband and wife are treated as separate individuals, so that the limits of £500 and £40,000 are applied separately. Excess relief in the year of marriage where an election under s. 36(7) F.A. 1976 is made can be set against the other's income. The husband can offset any surplus relief against the wife's income, but where the wife has excess relief only that relief applicable to the period after marriage is available for offset.

Where the marriage ends as a result of divorce, or the couple cease to live together or the husband dies, the wife is treated as a separate person from the date the marriage ends and is entitled to her own relief for this period to the end of the year of assessment.

Any assessment withdrawing relief as a result of a disposal by the spouse subscribing for the shares, following the ending of a marriage, is made on that spouse notwithstanding relief may have been granted to the other spouse.

Disposals of shares between spouses does not give rise to a withdrawal of relief and the relevant period is therefore not broken. Where however the shares are sold to a third party following a transfer *and* at that time the marriage has ended, the assessment for withdrawing relief is made on the spouse making the disposal.

CLAIMS AND ASSESSMENTS WITHDRAWING RELIEF

Claims for relief in respect of share issues cannot be made until four months after the company commences the qualifying trade.

The claims to be valid must then be made not later than two years from the end of the year of assessment in which the shares were issued or, if later, two years after the four months following trade commencement.

A claim must be accompanied by a statement by the company that the conditions as to the company and the trade are satisfied up to the date of the claim. The statement must contain a declaration that the information is correct to the best of the company's knowledge and belief. Any fraudulent or negligent statement is liable to a fine not exceeding £250 or £500 in the case of fraud.

Interest on overdue tax will run notwithstanding relief is subsequently given, but tax not paid (or due and payable later) will for interest purposes be regarded as paid on the date of making the claim.

Assessments for withdrawing relief are made under Case VI of Schedule D in the year in which the relief is granted. The assessment (subject to fraud, wilful default and neglect) can be made up to any time within six years of the end of the year of assessment in which the event giving rise to the withdrawal occurred.

No assessment can however be made for any event occurring after a person's death which would give rise to a relief withdrawal.

The reckonable date for interest purposes depends on the event giving rise to the relief withdrawal. In the case of a disposal the reckonable date is the date of disposal, in the case of value received the reckonable date is the date value is received. For other events it is the date of the event and where relief is not due as a result of tax avoidance it is the date the relief was given.

INFORMATION

Individuals or companies concerned with the expansion relief are required to notify the Inspector if certain events take place. The Inspector is also empowered to obtain information in certain circumstances.

An individual must within 60 days inform the Revenue where events take place which cause relief to be withdrawn, as a result of the following:
  (i) there is a disposal of shares (within the relevant period)
  (ii) the individual ceases to qualify
  (iii) value is received from the company
  (iv) following a spouse transfer and after the marriage ends there is a disposal to a third party.

The company is similarly required to inform the Inspector within 60 days of an event which causes relief to be withdrawn, as a result of the following:
  (i) the company ceases to be a qualifying company or the trade ceases to be a qualifying trade
  (ii) value is received from the company
  (iii) shares are issued as part of an avoidance scheme (in practice this will be difficult to determine), or shares are redeemed or a shareholder becomes entitled to receive value.

The Inspector is entitled to obtain information either from the individual or the company if he believes a scheme or arrangements is in existence such that:
  (i) the company can become a subsidiary of another company
  (ii) the issue of shares is part of a scheme the main purpose of which is the avoidance of tax
  (iii) the individual is connected with a company by virtue of any arrangement whereby he subscribes for shares through another person.

The Inspector is furthermore empowered to disclose to a company the number of shares on which relief has been granted notwithstanding an obligation to secrecy that may otherwise apply.

CAPITAL GAINS TAX

The sum deductible in computing any capital gains tax liability is reduced only to the extent a capital loss would otherwise arise (i.e. where cost exceeds proceeds). In this case the cost is reduced by the *lesser* of:
  (i) the whole amount of the relief *or*
  (ii) the difference between cost and proceeds.

Example

In 1985–86 Lear subscribed £12,000 for shares in Othello Ltd and obtained £10,000 of "expansion" relief.

Assuming he sells the shares six years later for:

	£
(a)	15,000
(b)	9,000
(c)	750

the gain will be as follows:

		£
(a) Proceeds		15,000
Cost (no restriction)		12,000
		Gain £3,000
(b) Proceeds		9,000
Cost..................................	12,000	
Less (cost excess £12,000 − £9,000)	3,000	9,000
		Gain £ Nil
(c) Proceeds		750
Cost..................................	12,000	
Less Relief granted.....................	10,000	2,000
Capital loss		£(1,250)

(In this case the relief granted (£10,000) is less than the difference between proceeds and cost (£11,250) and accordingly is used to reduce the original cost.)

Identification of shares

The pooling rules as to shares under s. 65, C.G.T.A. 1979 do not apply to shares on which relief has been granted. The shares are for the purposes of capital gains tax separately identified and where mixed holdings occur, "relief shares" are deemed to be disposed first: earlier acquisitions before later acquisitions.

MISCELLANEOUS

(1) Subsidiaries

As noted above, a company will not qualify for relief if it is a 51% subsidiary of another company or itself has 51% subsidiaries. This rule is relaxed so that a company will qualify if it has 100% subsidiaries which themselves would be qualifying companies or acquires a subsidiary during the relevant period which would be a qualifying company. The subsidiaries will *not* qualify. The relief also applies if the issue of shares was to provide funds for a new qualifying trade carried on or to be carried on by a subsidiary.

(2) Nominee Holdings

Shares subscribed, issued and held by or disposed of for an individual by a nominee are treated for relief purposes as shares of the individual.

(3) Approved Investment Funds

Relief is available to an individual who invests through an approved investment fund (approved for expansion relief purposes) given the fund merely acts as nominee. Furthermore the £500 *de minimis* limit does not apply where investment is channelled through a fund.

§ 7.—MARRIED WOMEN (s. 37, I.C.T.A. 1970; s. 36 F.A. 1976)

For Income Tax purposes, the income of a married woman living with her husband is deemed to be part of his income (except in the year of marriage) and must be included in any return of income made by him.

Year during which Marriage Takes Place

Where a woman marries during the year of assessment (except on 6th April) her income for that year is not aggregated with that of her husband and she is treated as if she were a single person throughout the year. The following provisions do, however, apply:

(1) The husband is entitled to the married personal allowance reduced by £104 (1/12 × (£3,455 − £2,205)) for each *complete* month from 6th April to the date of marriage.

(2) If either spouse has unutilised allowances, these may be set-off against the other spouse's income for the whole year if either of them makes a claim. The allowances available for the offset against the other spouse's income are:

(*a*) in the case of the husband,
(i) All personal reliefs, and
(ii) Allowable interest under s. 75 F.A. 1972.

(*b*) in the case of the wife,
(i) All personal reliefs, (except single personal relief, single age relief, housekeeper relief and additional relief for children) and
(ii) Allowable interest as above (though only since the date of marriage).

(3) For the purpose of the "1/6 restriction" relating to allowable life assurance premiums, the incomes of the spouses for the whole year may be aggregated.

(4) For the purposes of setting off against other income losses and capital allowances, the incomes are treated as aggregated following the date of marriage. Thus losses of the husband will be available for offset against the wife's income *after* marriage, and losses of the wife *after* marriage can be set off against the husband's income.

Example

Derby married Miss Joan on 26th June 1985. Their incomes during the year ended 5th April 1986 were as follows:

		£
Derby	—Salary	4,000
Mrs Derby	—Salary	2,000
	Bank deposit interest (gross)	1,000

During the year, Derby paid mortgage interest of £1,500 on a loan of £24,000 which was in respect of his principal private residence (not under MIRAS).

STATEMENT OF TAXABLE INCOME 1985–86

	Derby £	Mrs Derby £
Salary	4,000	2,000
Bank deposit interest	—	1,000
	4,000	3,000
Less Mortgage interest	1,500	—
	2,500	3,000
Less Personal allowance	3,247	2,205
	NIL	795
Claim to offset allowances unutilised by Mr Derby (£3,247 − £2,500)		747
Taxable income	NIL	£48

Note. Derby's personal allowance is calculated thus:

	£
Married personal allowance	3,455
Less 2 × 104(1/12 × (£3,455 − £2,205))	208
(The number of *complete* months of non-marriage is 2)	£3,247

N.B. (i) Mrs Derby will reclaim tax deducted on bank interest.
(ii) Although not relevant to the example, it would be preferable for Derby to obtain a MIRAS deduction (see Chapter 11, § 2).

Death/Divorce or Permanent Separation
Where a married woman becomes a widow during the year of assessment, only that portion of her statutory income arising between the date of her husband's death and the following 5th April is regarded as her income. From this she is entitled to deduct the full personal allowance for a single person, and additionally the widow's bereavement allowance (see § 7 above).

A woman who is divorced or permanently separated from her husband is treated as if she were unmarried, being separately assessed, and entitled to the full personal allowance for a single person. This also applies to the year in which the separation or divorce takes place.

Either spouse non-resident (s. 42 I.C.T.A. 1970)
Where a married woman is living with her husband and either:
(a) one of them is resident in the United Kingdom for the year of assessment and the other is not; or
(b) both are resident in the United Kingdom but one of them is, and the other is not, absent from the United Kingdom for the whole of the year of assessment,

the same consequences are to ensue as if they had been permanently separated for that year, i.e., there will be assessments as though each were unmarried. The foregoing provision, however, is not to increase the aggregate tax which would have been payable if no separate assessments had been made.

§ 8.—WIFE'S EARNINGS ELECTION (s. 23 and Schedule 4, F.A. 1971)

The broad effect of an election under above section is to separate the wife's *earned income* from that of her husband and to treat the husband and wife as separate single persons. The election is effective until revoked and has to be made within the period commencing 6 months before the year of assessment and ending 12 months after the year of assessment, i.e. the election for 1985–86 has to be made in the period 6th October 1984 to 5th April 1987.

The specific effects of the election are as follows:
(a) The husband is assessed only on his earned income and their combined unearned income.
(b) The wife is assessed on her earned income, but this does not include a retirement pension received by virtue of her husband's national insurance contributions. The assessment is made on the wife as if she were a single woman. Any repayment is made direct to the wife (Schedule 4 para. 5).
(c) The husband receives only the single person's allowance, as does the wife (age allowance cannot be claimed).
(d) All other reliefs are given as if they were single persons. (This has the effect of allowing the higher dependent relative claim (£145) where the relative is wholly maintained by the wife.)

(e) Any deductions, for payments, losses, or capital allowances, which in the first instance would be offset against the wife's earned income are treated as reducing that income, and not other income. In any other case, the deductions reduce other income (Schedule 4, para. 4).

✗   The effect of this provision needs to be carefully reviewed, where, for example, the wife pays mortgage interest which is available for tax relief. The election will result in an alteration of the tax payable (unlike separate assessment—see § 10 below), although the effects must be calculated each year to determine whether or not the alteration is beneficial.

Example

Mr and Mrs Smith have the following incomes for 1985–86:

Husband	Earnings £25,000	Dividends £200 (including tax credit)
Wife	Earnings £7,020	Income from lettings £750

Calculate the tax payable for 1985–86 (1) where no earnings election has been made (2) where the election has been made.

(1) **No election**

	£	£
Earnings (self and wife)............................		32,020
Unearned income................................		950
		32,970
Less: Personal allowance	3,455	
Additional personal allowance................	2,205	5,660
		£27,310

Liability:

	£	£
On 16,200 @ 30%.............................		4,860.00
3,000 @ 40%.............................		1,200.00
5,200 @ 45%.............................		2,340.00
2,910 @ 50%.............................		1,455.00
£27,310		£9,855.00

(2) **With election**

Husband:	£	*Wife:*	£
Earnings..........	25,000	Earnings..............	7,020
Unearned.........	950		
	25,950		7,020
Less Personal allowance....	2,205	*Less* Personal allowance	2,205
	£23,745		£4,815

Liability:

£	£	£	£
16,200 at 30%	4,860.00	4,815 at 30%	1,444.50
3,000 at 40%	1,200.00		
4,545 at 45%	2,045.25		
£23,745	£8,105.25		£1,444.50

	£
Total liability: Husband	8,105.25
Wife	1,444.50
	£9,549.75

In this case the election would result in a tax saving of £305.25 (£9,855.00 − £9,549.75).

Any deductions for payments, losses or capital allowances which in the first instance would be offset against the wife's earned income are treated as reducing that income and not other income. In any other case the deductions reduce other income (para. 4, Schedule 4).

The effect of this provision needs to be carefully reviewed, where for example the wife pays mortgage interest which is available for tax relief.

§ 9.—SEPARATE ASSESSMENT OF HUSBAND AND WIFE (ss. 38 to 40 I.C.T.A. 1970)

On an application made by either husband or wife within six months before 6th July in the year of assessment (e.g., an application in respect of 1985–86 must be made between 6th January and 6th July 1985), they may be separately assessed. Any such application will remain in force for subsequent years until revoked. No reduction in the tax payable, unlike the wife's earnings election, will, however, be effected, the various allowances being apportioned between them, on the following bases:

ALLOWANCES, ETC.	BASIS
Personal Allowance (and others than those below).	In proportion to the amount of tax which would have been payable by each if no personal reliefs had been allowed (N.B.: this will generally be in the proportion of total income).
Allowance for children, dependent relatives, son's or daughter's services.	To the person maintaining the relative or child. If both contribute, the allowance is apportioned on the basis of the contributions.

The amount of the reliefs in terms of tax allocated to the wife is not to be less than those which would accrue in respect of her earned income (provided an additional overall tax liability does not arise).

Example 1

R. Adams has the following statutory income for 1985–86:

	£
Business profits—Schedule D	2,000
Director's fees—Schedule E	450
Taxed dividends (including tax credit)	1,450

His wife's statutory income is as follows:

	£
Business profits—Schedule D	750
Taxed dividends (including tax credit)	530

They have two children aged 6 and 7 both in the U.K. and the wife supports her aunt (aged 70) whose total income is £200 per annum (exclusive of voluntary allowances).

It is required to show the Income Tax payable for 1985–86 and the apportionment thereof if an application is made for separate assessment.

STATEMENT OF INCOME TAX PAYABLE 1985–86

	Husband £	Wife £
Business profits—Schedule D	2,000	750
Director's fees—Schedule E	450	—
Taxed dividends (including tax credit)	1,450	530
Total income	3,900	1,280
(Personal allowance £3,455 + £750 = £4,205)		
$\dfrac{3,900}{5,180} \times £4,205$	3,166	
$\dfrac{1,280}{5,180} \times £4,205$		1,039
Allowance for dependent relative...................	—	100
Total allowances................................	3,166	1,139
Taxable income.................................	£734	£141

Tax payable:

Husband			Wife		
On £734 at 30%	=	£220.20	£141 at 30%	=	£42.30

Notes: (1) The amount of tax allocated to the wife is not to exceed the amount that would be due if allowances allocated were those in respect of her earned income. This notional amount is computed as follows:

No liability on business profits (covered by additional personal allowance, i.e. relief for earned income).

Liability on other income:

	£
Taxed dividends £530 at 30%.......................	£159.00

As the tax payable in respect of the wife's income (£42.30) on the claim for separate assessment is less than the amount of £159.00, the restriction does not apply.

(2) No restriction of dependent relative relief is necessary.

(3) The tax under Schedule E (i.e. on the director's fees of the husband) will be deducted at source under "Pay As You Earn".

(4) The total liability of £262.50 will be deducted at source (and a repayment will be made as appropriate).

Example 2

V. Wilkins has the following statutory income for 1985–86:

	£
Business Profits—Schedule D	8,200
Untaxed War Loan Interest—Schedule D	300
Taxed Dividends (including tax credit)	500

His wife's statutory income for 1985–86 is as follows:

	£
Salary as dress designer	1,505
Taxed dividends (including tax credit)	100

It is required to show the Income Tax payable for 1985–86 and the apportionment thereof if an application is made for separate assessment.

STATEMENT OF INCOME TAX PAYABLE 1985–86

On a claim for separate assessment, the total payable will be apportioned between husband and wife as follows:

	Husband £	Wife £
Business profits	8,200	
Salary		1,505
Untaxed interest	300	
Taxed dividends	500	100
Total statutory income	9,000	1,605

(Personal allowances £3,455 + £1,505 = £4,960)

$$\frac{9,000}{10,605} \times £4,960 \quad\quad 4,209$$

$$\frac{1,605}{10,605} \times £4,960 \quad\quad 751$$

	Husband	Wife
Taxable income	£4,791	£854

Tax payable:

Husband £		Wife £
On £4,791 at 30% 1,437.30	On £854 at 30%......	256.20
Adjustment for restriction on wife's earned income 226.20	*Less*................	226.20
£1,663.50		£30.00

Notes: (1) The apportionments of the earned income allowance between husband and wife are calculated to the nearest £.

(2) The amount of tax allocated to the wife is not to exceed the amount that would be due if allowances allocated were those in respect of her earned income. This notional amount is computed as follows:

	£
Wife's earned income (salary)	1,505
Less: Additional personal allowance	1,505
Balance of wife's earned income	Nil
Wife's taxed dividends	100
	£100

The tax charged thereon would be:

	£
On £100 at 30%	£30.00

If the result of allocating the various allowances is to absorb the whole of the taxable income of either spouse, the allowances of that spouse not so far given (because the income was insufficient) shall be given against the income of the other spouse.

COLLECTION OF TAX FROM WIFE

If in any year an assessment has been made on the husband and the Commissioners of Inland Revenue consider that, if separate assessments had been in force, an assessment in respect of all or part of the same income would have fallen on the wife, and the tax has not been paid by the twenty-eighth day after the due date, they may serve a notice on the wife (or her trustees or personal representatives) requiring payment of the tax appropriate to her income. The tax so recoverable from the wife will cease to be recoverable from the husband under the original assessment.

§ 10.—PARTNERSHIP CLAIMS (s. 26 I.C.T.A. 1970)

The assessment on the profits of a partnership is made on the firm in the firm name (as explained in Chapter 3, § 7), but each partner is entitled to claim such allowances as are due to him according to his particular circumstances.

Example 1

O. Peters and P. Orton, trading as Peters, Orton & Co., carry on business in partnership, sharing profits four-sevenths and three-sevenths respectively, after charging interest on capital and partners' salaries.

For 1985–86 their Schedule D assessment is £6,800 and they are credited with Interest on Capital: Peters, £200; Orton, £100, and partners' salaries of £400 each. The firm pays an annuity of £100 from which tax is deducted on payment.

Peters is married. Orton is a bachelor. Neither has any other income.

It is required to show the tax payable by the firm for 1985–86 and the division thereof between the partners.

The 1985–86 assessment is divisible as follows:

	£	£
Gross assessment.................................		6,800
Less: Annuity...................................		100
		———
		6,700
Less: Interest on capital.........................	300	
Partners' salaries	800	
	———	1,100
Leaving.......................		£5,600
		═══

to be divided—$\frac{4}{7}$ to Peters = £3,200; $\frac{3}{7}$ to Orton = £2,400.

The assessment is therefore apportioned thus:	£	£
Peters—Interest on capital.........................	200	
Salary......................................	400	
Share of balance.........................	3,200	
	———	3,800
Orton—Interest on capital	100	
Salary.....................................	400	
Share of balance	2,400	
	———	2,900
Peters, Orton & Co.—Annuity......................		100
		———
		£6,800
		═══

STATEMENT OF INCOME TAX PAYABLE 1985–86

	Peters £	Orton £
Business profits.................................	3,800	2,900
Less: Personal allowance	3,455	2,205
Taxable income.................................	345	695
Tax thereon at 30%.............................	£103.50	£208.50

In addition, the annuity will be included in the firm's assessment, i.e., £100 at 30% = £30.00. (This amount is recouped by the firm on payment of the interest.)
The total tax payable by the firm will therefore be:

	£
Peters	103.50
Orton..	208.50
Peters, Orton & Co.	30.00
	£342.00

If a firm has taxed income to an amount equal to or greater than the amount of its annual charges, the latter would be regarded as paid thereout, and would not, therefore, require separate treatment in the apportionment of the assessment.

Where a firm has taxed income not appropriated as a set-off against annual charges, and a partner pays personal charges not covered by personal taxed income, such charges may be treated as being paid out of his share of the firm's unappropriated taxed income.

Example 2

Morris and Richards are in partnership, sharing profits five-sevenths and two-sevenths respectively. Their Schedule D assessment for 1985–86 is £11,200, and the firm receives taxed dividends amounting to £70 (including tax credit.)

Morris is married and has other income as follows:

	£
War Loan Interest (untaxed)......................	50

Richards is single, and has no income outside the firm. He pays an annuity of £10 per annum, from which tax is deducted on payment.
It is required to show the Income Tax payable for 1985–86.

The Schedule D assessment of the firm is divisible:

	£
To Morris: five-sevenths...........................	8,000
To Richards: two-sevenths	3,200
	£11,200

The firm's dividends will be allocated in the same proportions—i.e. £50 to Morris and £20 to Richards.

The tax payable will therefore be calculated as follows:

	£	Morris £	Richards £
Share of firm's profits.....................		8,000	3,200
Share of firm's dividends (gross)............	50		20
War loan interest	50		
	—	100	
Total income.............................		8,100	3,220
Less Personal allowance....................		3,455	2,205
Taxable income...........................		4,645	1,015
Tax thereon at 30%.......................		1,393.50	304.50
Less Tax recouped on annuity (£10 at 30%)..		—	3.00
Tax payable..............................		1,393.50	301.50
Less Share of tax credit on dividends		15.00	6.00
Tax due		£1,378.50	£295.50

Note. In practice, the tax will be paid as follows:

	Morris £	Richards £
Case I, Schedule D, business profits................	8,000	3,200
Less Personal allowance.........................	3,455	2,205
	4,545	995
Tax thereon at 30%............................	1,363.50	298.50
Case III, Schedule D, War Loan interest, £50 at 30%....................................	15.00	—
Dividends taxed at source at 30% .... (£50)	15.00	(£20) 6.00
Tax payable...................................	1,393.50	304.50
Less Tax recouped on Annuity (£10 at 30%)...............................	—	3.00
Tax credit on dividends	15.00	6.00
Tax due	£1,378.50	£295.50

§ 11.—PERSONAL COMPUTATIONS

As far as possible, the various reliefs and allowances to which a taxpayer is entitled are set off against any direct assessments upon him, to avoid the inconvenience of the taxpayer first paying tax under the direct assessments and then having to reclaim tax on his reliefs and allowances. Where the direct assessments are not large enough to cover the whole of the reliefs and allowances and the taxpayer has already suffered tax at the source on other portions of his income (e.g. on dividends), then a claim may be made for repayment of tax on the balance of the reliefs and allowances not already set off against the direct assessments.

Such a claim may be made at any time within six years of the end of the year of assessment to which it relates. Thus, a claim in respect of 1985/86 can be made at any time before 6th April, 1992.

Example 1

James Norton possesses the following statutory income for the year 1985–86:

	£
Business profits..	2,000
Taxed dividends (including tax credit)....................	1,000
	£3,000

He is married and has three children, aged 6, 7 and 8. Norton is entitled to reclaim the sum of £300.00 in respect of reliefs and allowances not covered by direct assessment, made up as follows:

	£
Total statutory income (as above)	3,000
Deduct: Personal allowance............................	3,455
Taxable income..	Nil
Tax deducted from dividends, £1,000 at 30%	£300

Where any allowances to which an individual is entitled have not been claimed through ignorance or other cause, tax in respect thereof may be recovered at any time within six years after the end of the year of assessment to which the claim relates (s. 33, T.M.A. 1970).

In practice, if the claim is made in time, the relief will be granted where possible against the second instalment of tax, the necessity for repayment then being avoided.*

RELIEF FOR CHARGES ON INCOME (s. 25 I.C.T.A. 1970)

Where income tax on annual charges is payable by the taxpayer (e.g. on annuities or other annual payments (not being interest) which are not payable or wholly payable out of profits or gains brought into charge to tax), the tax thereon is collected at the source from the taxpayer, who deducts tax at the time of payment. *He must bear tax at the basic rate on an amount of income at least equal to the amount of the charges.* It will thus be seen that the person paying the annuity, etc., is in precisely the same position as if the annuity were paid in full (i.e., without deduction of tax) and allowed as a deduction when computing for Income Tax purposes the income out of which it is paid. In other words, reliefs and allowances cannot be given against that portion of a taxpayer's total income which is required to cover the annual charges from which tax has been deducted on payment.

---

* Special provisions apply in the case of Schedule E taxpayers (see Chapter 8, § 12).

Example 2

Richard Hogg, a bachelor, has the following statutory income for 1985–86:

	£
Business profits.	1,220
Taxed dividends (including tax credit)	3,000

He pays an annuity of £750 (gross) per annum, under deduction of tax. Hogg's liability to income tax for 1985–86 is as follows:

	£
Total income (as above).	4,220
Deduct: Personal allowance.	2,205
	£2,015

TAX PAYABLE

	£
On £2,015 at 30%	£604.50

Hogg has obtained his tax relief on the annuity by retaining the income tax deducted at the time of payment.

In the case where there is not enough income to cover the charges paid, tax on the "shortfall" will be assessed and must be repaid. Assessment is made under s. 53, I.C.T.A. 1970.

If Hogg had received income of only £450 he would be assessed to tax on £300 (£750 − £450), as this represents the unabsorbed amount of the annuity.

§ 12.—DEATH OF TAXPAYER

Where the taxpayer dies during the year of assessment the whole of the allowances and reliefs to which he was entitled for the year of assessment may be deducted from the statutory income for the period from the commencement of the year to the date of death. The income for the remainder of the year will be assessed in the hands of the trustees or beneficiaries according to circumstances, and in the latter case, allowances are deductible as applicable to the individual's circumstances.

Where a woman dies the husband may, by serving notice on the Inspector (and the wife's executors) disclaim responsibility for any unpaid income tax of the wife during which he was her husband and she was living with him (s. 41 I.C.T.A. 1970). In these circumstances the Revenue are obliged to collect tax under s. 40 I.C.T.A. 1970) (collection of tax from wife—see above).

In the case of a business carried on by a sole trader, his death brings about a discontinuance of his business for Income Tax purposes, and an adjustment of the assessment for the year in which death occurred becomes necessary, while the Inland Revenue have the right to increase the assessments of the pre-penultimate and penultimate years to the actual profits of those years (see Chapter 3, § 5).

By concession (A7 1980) the discontinuance provisions are not enforced (unless claimed) where the business of a sole trader passes on death to the spouse. In either case, however, losses and capital allowances unutilised cannot be carried forward.

This concession also applies where a business has been carried on by husband and wife in partnership and one succeeds to the whole business on the death of the other, and no election is made under s. 154(2) I.C.T.A. 1970 for "continuation". In these circumstances the losses carried forward are restricted to those of the surviving spouse.

The normal six year time limit for raising assessment by the Inland Revenue is reduced to three years.

3. Schedule D, Cases I and II

§ 1.—INCOME ASSESSABLE UNDER SCHEDULE D (ss. 108 and 109, I.C.T.A. 1970)

Tax is assessed under Schedule D on annual profits or gains arising or accruing to any person resident in the United Kingdom from any kind of property whatever, whether it is situated in the United Kingdom or elsewhere, or from any trade, profession or vocation, whether carried on in the United Kingdom or elsewhere.

Income derived by a person, whether a British subject or not, who is not resident in the United Kingdom, from property situated in the United Kingdom, or from a trade profession or vocation exercised within the United Kingdom is also assessed under Schedule D.

The Schedule also brings into charge to tax all interest, annuities and other annual profits or gains not charged under any other schedule and not specifically exempt from Income Tax.

In this context "*annual* profits or gains" means profits or gains of an income or revenue nature rather than of a capital nature.

Schedule D is divided into six Cases in order to facilitate the assessment to tax:

Case I.—Income arising from carrying on a trade in the U.K., or elsewhere, e.g., the profits of a retail draper or of a manufacturer.

Case II.—Income arising from carrying on a profession or vocation not included in any other Schedule, e.g. the profits of a chartered accountant.

Case III.—Income arising from untaxed interest (e.g. interest on War Loan paid, "gross"; interest credited by a bank;) and all discounts.

Case IV.—Income arising from any foreign securities (and not included in Schedule C.)

Case V.—Income from any foreign possessions (but not including emoluments of any office or employment.)

Case VI.—Any annual profits or gains not included in Cases I to V nor under any other Schedule. In general, this will include profits which although of an isolated or non-recurrent nature and outside any regular business activity still have the character of revenue or income, e.g. isolated commissions on sales or insurances; receipts for information supplied to newspapers (but not regular contributions); furnished lettings. Assessments raised to recover relief previously given, or to counter devices for the avoidance of tax, are usually made under Schedule D, Case VI.

§ 2.—TRADE, PROFESSION OR VOCATION

It has been shown (See Chapter 1) that all taxable income must be derived from a source specified in one or other of the Schedules. As noted above (See § 1 of this chapter) Schedule D is divided into six Cases. This Chapter is concerned with income assessable under Cases I and II, Schedule D, and, following the "source" principle, income can only be charged to tax if it is shown that the intended taxpayer is carrying on a trade (or, as the case may be, a profession or vocation) and the income concerned derives from that trade (or profession or vocation).

TRADE

Although "trade" is defined for the purposes of the Taxes Acts, the definition (in s. 526 (5), I.C.T.A., 1970), which states that

> ...."trade" includes every trade, manufacture, adventure or concern in the nature of trade...

is not a model of clarity, indeed over the years it has given rise to much litigation. The difficulty which is often encountered is to determine whether or not a trade exists, particularly in the marginal cases where casual profits arise from isolated transactions.

Although there is no fixed rule which can be applied to this question, and whilst every case must be decided upon its own facts and circumstances, the Courts (see below) have tended to review transactions to see if it bears any of the "badges of trade". These "badges of trade" were identified and summarised in 1955 in the Final Report of the Royal Commission on the *Taxation of Profits and Income*. Each of these badges is described below together with a summary of what the Royal Commission regarded as the major relevant criteria that have a bearing on whether a trade exists.

1. THE SUBJECT-MATTER OF THE REALISATION

Whilst almost any form of property can be acquired to be dealt in, those forms of property, such as commodities or manufactured articles, which are normally the subject of trading are only very exceptionally the subject of investment. Again property which does not yield to its owner an income or personal enjoyment merely by virtue of its ownership is more likely to have been acquired with the object of a deal than property that does. (*C.I.R.* v. *Fraser* (1942))

2. THE LENGTH OF THE PERIOD OF OWNERSHIP

Generally speaking, dealing transactions (and hence trading) anticipates realisation within a short time of acquisition. But there are many exceptions from this as a universal rule. (*Rutledge* v. *C.I.R.* (1929))

3. THE FREQUENCY OR NUMBER OF SIMILAR TRANSACTIONS BY THE SAME PERSON

If realisations of the same sort of property occur in succession over a period of years or there are several such realisations at about the same date a presumption arises that there has been dealing in respect of each. (*Pickford* v. *Quirke* (1929))

4. SUPPLEMENTARY WORK ON OR IN CONNECTION WITH THE PROPERTY REALISED

If the property is altered in any way during the ownership so as to bring it into a more marketable condition; or if any special exertions are made to find or attract purchasers, such as the opening of an office or large scale advertising, there is some evidence of dealing. For when there is an organised effort to obtain profit there is a source of taxable income. But if nothing at all is done, the suggestion turns the other way. (*C.I.R.* v. *Livingstone* (1926))

5. THE CIRCUMSTANCES THAT WERE RESPONSIBLE FOR THE REALISATION

There may be some explanation, such as a sudden emergency or opportunity calling for ready money, that negates the idea that any plan of dealing prompted the original purchase. (*Martin* v. *Lowry* (1926))

6. MOTIVE

There are cases in which the purpose of the transaction of purchase and sale is clearly discernable. Motive is never irrelevant in any of these cases. In particular it should be noted that whilst an intention to make a profit is a relevant factor in deciding whether or not there is a trade it is not of itself decisive. Indeed for tax purposes a trade may be carried on even though there is no intention to make a profit. The reverse is also true and the realisation and accumulation of a surplus of receipts over outgoings from carrying on an activity does not necessarily amount to a trade.

Other important decisions in determining whether or not a trade is being carried on are: *Wisdom* v. *Chamberlain* (1969) and *California Copper Syndicate* v. *Harris* (1904).

In general the destination of a surplus is irrelevant. If a trade is carried on then any profit derived therefrom is taxable unless provision has been made for it to be exempt e.g. a profit made by a charity as part of its charitable activities.

OCCUPATION OF LAND (ss. 110 and 112, I.C.T.A. 1970)

Although most income derived from land is charged to tax under Schedule A (Chapter 10, § 1–§ 18) or under Schedule B in the case of woodlands managed on a commercial basis (Chapter 10, § 19). There are however, three special provisions under which certain kinds of income from land are taxed under Schedule D Case I. Firstly all farming and market gardening in the United Kingdom is treated as the carrying on of a trade or as part of a trade, and all the farming carried on by any particular person is treated as one single trade. The occupation of land in the United Kingdom for any purpose other than farming or market gardening is also treated as the carrying on of a trade if the land is managed on a commercial basis and with a view to the realisation of profits. However this does not apply to woodlands managed on a commercial basis which are, primarily, taxable under Schedule B. Secondly there is provision for a person who occupies woodlands and manages them on a commercial basis to elect to be charged to tax in respect of those woodlands under Schedule D instead of under Schedule B. The purpose of this election is to allow relief for losses incurred during the planting and growing period on the estate concerned. However once this election has been made it applies for all future years of assessment whilst the woodlands remain in the same ownership. Finally profits or gains arising out of land from a number of miscellaneous, but specified, concerns are charged to tax under Case I, Schedule D:

(*a*) Mines and quarries (including gravel pits, sand pits and brickfields),
(*b*) Ironworks, gasworks, saltsprings or works, alum mines or works and waterworks and streams of water,
(*c*) Canals, inland navigations, docks, and drains or levels,
(*d*) Fishing rights,
(*e*) Rights of markets and fairs, tolls, bridges and ferries,
(*f*) Railways and other wayleaves, and
(*g*) Other concerns of the like nature as any of the concerns specified in paragraphs (*b*)–(*e*) above.

PROFESSIONS AND VOCATIONS

The Taxes Acts do not define "profession", but probably a "profession" can be said to be an occupation requiring either purely intellectual skill, or of any manual skill controlled, as in painting and sculpture or surgery, by the intellectual skill of the operator, as distinguished from an occupation which is substantially the production or sale of commodities.

Three further tests of a profession have been put forward:

(*a*) Its practice is based on preliminary study, training and, possibly, examination in the general principles of the pursuit
(*b*) The profits which may be made from its pursuit do not primarily depend upon the provision of great quantities of capital

(*c*) A profession is a pursuit which is followed not solely as a livelihood, but always subject to overriding duties, prescribed by a code of professional honour involving, in an especial degree, the strict observance of confidences, in which services must be rendered to the client without stint in proportion to the client's need rather than in proportion to the reward which is received.

A "vocation" has been said to mean the way in which someone passes their life. Except in a number of minor ways there is no difference between the basis of assessment under Case I, Schedule D, and Case II, Schedule D, so that the distinction between a "trade" on the one hand and a "profession" or "vocation" on the other is now of very limited importance.

§ 3.—BASIS OF ASSESSMENT (s. 115, I.C.T.A. 1970)

The normal basis of assessment on the profits arising from a trade, profession, or vocation carried on by a sole trader or a partnership assessed under Cases I and II, Schedule D, is *the profits of the business year ended within the preceding year of assessment* (e.g., the 1985–86 assessment upon a business, the accounts of which are made up annually to 31st December, would be upon the profits for the year ended 31st December 1984 while where the accounts are made up to 31st March the assessment would be upon the profits for the year ended 31st March 1985). The assessment on the preceding year basis stands, regardless of the actual profit made during the year of assessment, e.g., even if the latter is very much less than the assessment.

The preceding year basis is subject to modification:

(*a*) in the opening years of a new business (see § 4);
(*b*) on the discontinuation of a business (see § 5);
(*c*) where a change is made in the date to which accounts are made up (see § 6);
(*d*) where a change in partners occurs (see § 8).

§ 4.—NEW BUSINESS: ASSESSMENTS FOR FIRST THREE YEARS (ss. 116 and 117, I.C.T.A. 1970)

DATE OF COMMENCEMENT AND PRE-TRADING EXPENSES (s. 39, F.A. 1980)
It is of course important to determine when a trade, profession, or vocation is set up or commenced. Indeed a distinction must be drawn between setting up and commencing a trade, etc. as compared to preparing to commence a trade etc. The distinction was of considerable importance before 1st April 1980 because pre-trading expenses were not allowed as deductions in computing the profits of the trade, and the nature of the payments is such that they are unlikely to qualify as allowable expenditure under the capital gains rules. From 1980–81, however, such expenses are allowable provided that they would have been allowable if the business were trading, and that they were incurred *within three years* after commencement of trading.

In a typical case a trade might decide to set up in business and over a period of a few months construct works and instal plant. During the same period contracts for the purchase of raw materials and for the sale of the business's products might be entered into. However it is probable that the trade could not be said to have commenced until the business began to receive raw materials for manufacture and thus became able to fulfil its obligations under any sales contracts.

In a retail business it is probable that the trade be said to commence when the firm was first open for business. A similar rule would probably apply to a service business.

ASSESSMENT

In the year the business commences there are special rules to arrive at the *preceding year basis of assessment:*

—*For the first year of assessment: the basis will be the actual profits from the date of commencement to the next 5th April.*
—*For the second year of assessment: the basis will be the actual profits for the first twelve months from the date of commencement.*
—*For the third and subsequent years' assessments: the basis will be the profits of the accounting year ended in the preceding year of assessment.*

A taxpayer may elect to have his *second and third years of assessment based on his actual profits* of those years. Such a claim must be made within seven years after the end of the second year of assessment.

FIRST YEAR OF ASSESSMENT

Where a trade, profession or vocation is set up or commenced within the year of assessment, in practice no assessment is usually made until the first accounts of the business are available and the actual profits ascertained. An assessment is then made, on the actual profits arising within the year of assessment, i.e. from the date of commencement to the subsequent 5th April (inclusive).

SECOND YEAR OF ASSESSMENT

The assessment for the second year of assessment is based on the profits of the first twelve months' trading from the commencement of business.

THIRD YEAR OF ASSESSMENT

The assessment for the third year of assessment is on the normal basis (i.e. on the profits of the trading year ended within the preceding year of assessment.) Where profits in the preceding year are not for a twelve month period, the Inland Revenue have the right to decide which twelve month period shall form the basis of assessment. This will usually be equivalent to the first twelve months of trading (see Example 3), although the position may alter where a change in the date to which accounts are made up takes place (see Example 4 and § 6).

Example 1

A. Brown commenced business on 6th October 1984. The profits (as adjusted for income tax purposes) for the first year ended 5th October 1985 were £10,000.

FIRST YEAR OF ASSESSMENT
The assessment for 1984–85 (covering the period 6th October 1984 to 5th April 1985) will be 6/12 of £10,000 = £5,000.

SECOND YEAR OF ASSESSMENT
The assessment for 1985–86 the *second* year of assessment will be on £10,000 i.e. the profits of the first year's trading to 5th October 1985.

Where the first accounts are for a period of less than one year, a proportionate part of the second accounts must be taken in arriving at the profits of the twelve months from the date of commencement.

THIRD YEAR OF ASSESSMENT
The assessment for 1986–87, the *third* year of assessment, will be on £10,000, i.e. the profits of the trading year ended within the preceding year of assessment, 1985–86.

The assessments for the first, second and third years of assessment will be as follows:

		£
1984–85	Actual profits from 6th October 1984 to 5th April 1985 – 6/12 of £10,000	5,000
1985–86	Profits of first 12 months' trading	10,000
1986–87	Profits of preceding year	10,000

Where the first accounts are for a period of twelve months and commence after 6th April (i.e. they commence in the first year of assessment and finish in the second year of assessment), the assessment for the third year of assessment will be equal to the assessment for the second year of assessment.

Example 2

B. Green commenced business on 1st May 1985. The profits (as adjusted for income tax purposes) for the trading period of eight months ended 31st December 1985 and for the twelve months ended 31st December 1986 were £12,000 and £8,400 respectively.

FIRST YEAR OF ASSESSMENT
The assessment for 1985–86 covering the period from 1st May 1985 to 5th April 1986 will be computed as follows:

$$£12,000 + \frac{3}{12} \text{ of } £8,400 = £14,100$$

SECOND YEAR OF ASSESSMENT
The assessment for 1986–87, the *second* year of assessment, will be on £14,800 (£12,000 + $\frac{4}{12}$ of £8,400), i.e. the profits of the first 12 months' trading to 30th April 1986.
Where the first accounts are for a period of more than one year, an apportionment of the first accounts must be taken in arriving at the profits of the twelve months from the date of commencement.

THIRD YEAR OF ASSESSMENT
The assessment for 1987–88, the *third* year of assessment, will be on £8,400, i.e. the profits of the trading year ended within the preceding fiscal year, 1986–87.
Note. The normal assessments for the first, second and third fiscal years will be as follows:

		£
1985–86	Actual profits from 1st May 1985 to 5th April 1986—£12,000 + 3/12 of £8,400	14,100
1986–87	Profits of first 12 months' trading—£12,000 + $\frac{4}{12}$ of £8,400.	14,800
1987–88	Profits of preceding year	8,400

Where the first accounts are for a period of less than twelve months and terminate within the first year of assessment and subsequent accounts are prepared for periods of twelve months, the assessment for the third year of assessment will not usually be equal to the assessment for the second year of assessment.

Example 3

H. Gray commenced business on 1st June 1984. The profits (as adjusted for income tax purposes) for the trading period of sixteen months ended 30th September 1985 were £8,000.

FIRST YEAR OF ASSESSMENT
The assessment for 1984–85 (covering the period 1st June 1984 to 5th April 1985), will be computed as follows:

$$\frac{10}{16} \text{ of } £8,000 = £5,000$$

SECOND YEAR OF ASSESSMENT

The assessment for 1985–86 the *second* year of assessment will be on £6,000 ($\frac{12}{16}$ of £8,000), i.e. the profits of the first year's trading to 31st May 1985.

THIRD YEAR OF ASSESSMENT

The assessment for 1986–87, the *third* year of assessment, will be on £6,000 ($\frac{12}{16}$ of £8,000), i.e., the first twelve months' trading, since no period of twelve months ends in the preceding year.

The normal assessments for the first, second and third years of assessment will be as follows:

		£
1984–85	Actual profits from 1st June 1984 to 5th April 1985—($\frac{10}{16}$ of £8,000)	5,000
1985–86	Profits of first twelve months' trading—$\frac{12}{16}$ of £8,000	6,000
1986–87	Profits of preceding year—$\frac{12}{16}$ of £8,000.	6,000

Thus, where the first accounts are for a period of more than twelve months, the normal assessment for the third year of assessment will be equal to the normal assessment for the second year of assessment.

Example 4

J. White commenced business on 1st July 1984. The first accounts for the trading period of eighteen months ended 31st December 1985 show a profit (as adjusted for income tax purposes) of £12,000. Thereafter accounts were made up to 31st March, the adjusted profits for the three months ended 31st March 1986 amounting to £5,000.

The assessment for 1986–87 (the third year of assessment) will be based, at the discretion of the Commissioners of Inland Revenue, upon the profits of the year ended 31st December 1985 or the year ended 31st March 1986.

			£
Year ended 31st December 1985	$\frac{12}{18}$ of £12,000	=	8,000
Year ended 31st March 1986	$\frac{9}{18}$ of £12,000 + £5,000	=	11,000

In all probability the second alternative would be adopted by the Commissioners. Thus, where the first accounts are for a period of more than twelve months but the accounts for the second trading period cover more or less than twelve months, the normal assessment for the third fiscal year will not usually be equal to the normal assessment for the second fiscal year.

Note. The normal assessments for the first, second and third years of assessment will be as follows:

		£
1984–85	Actual profits from 1st July 1984 to 5th April 1985—$\frac{9}{18}$ of £12,000.	6,000
1985–86	Profits of first 12 months' trading—$\frac{12}{18}$ of £12,000	8,000
1986–87	Profits of preceding year to 31st March 1986—$\frac{9}{18}$ of £12,000 + £5,000.	11,000

TAXPAYER'S OPTION FOR SECOND AND THIRD YEARS OF ASSESSMENT

The taxpayer may, if he wishes, make a claim for the assessments for *both* the second *and* third years of assessment to be based on the actual profits of those years. The claim must be made within seven years after the end of the second year of assessment, but may be withdrawn within six years after the end of the third year of assessment, in which case the assessments for the second and third years will be made as if no such claim had ever been made.

Example 5

L. Pink commenced business on 6th October 1984, the adjusted profits for the first three years being as follows:

	£
Year ended 5th October 1985	15,000
Year ended 5th October 1986	14,000
Year ended 5th October 1987	8,000

If no claim is made, the assessments for the first three years will be:

		£
1984–85	Actual profits covering the period 6 October 1984 to 5 April 1985—$\frac{6}{12}$ of £15,000	7,500
1985–86	Profits of first 12 months' trading	15,000
1986–87	Profits of preceding year (equivalent to 1st twelve months)	15,000

On a claim being made before 6th April 1993 the assessments for the second and third years of assessment would be amended to the actual profits of those years, as follows:

		£
1985–86	$\frac{6}{12}$ of £15,000 + $\frac{6}{12}$ of £14,000	14,500
1986–87	$\frac{6}{12}$ of £14,000 + $\frac{6}{12}$ of £8,000	11,000

As a result of making the claim for these two years, a reduction of £4,500 in the total assessments is obtained.

The power to withdraw the claim makes it possible for a taxpayer to make the claim when it would be advantageous for the second year of assessment and subsequently to withdraw it if he finds that, owing to the amount of his profits in the third year, on the whole, the claim would not be beneficial.

Example 6

J. Black commenced business on 6th April 1984, the profits as adjusted for income tax purposes being:

	£
Year ended 5th April 1985	50,000
Year ended 5th April 1986	40,000
Year ended 5th April 1987	70,000

The normal assessments would, therefore, be:

		£
1984–85	Actual profits	50,000
1985–86	Profits of first 12 months' trading	50,000
1986–87	Profits of preceding year	40,000

The trader could claim before 6th April 1993, to be assessed on the actual profits for 1985–86 and 1986–87. He would not be aware of the amount of profits for the year ended 5th April 1987 until some time after that date, but nevertheless, he could make the claim say on 30th April 1986, so that his assessment for 1985–86 would be reduced to £40,000. His assessment for 1986–87 would then be on the actual profits of £70,000, i.e. a total of £110,000 for the two years concerned, but at any time before 6th April 1993, the claim could be withdrawn, the normal assessments of £50,000 and £40,000 for 1985–86 and 1986–87 (a total of £90,000 for the two years) being thereby revived.

In deciding whether a claim should be made (or withdrawn) for adjustment of the profits of a new business to the actual profits for the second and third years, the rates of tax, capital allowances (see Chapter 5) and the personal and other allowances (see Chapter 2) should be taken into consideration in addition to the amount of the assessments.

§ 5.—DISCONTINUED BUSINESS (s. 118, I.C.T.A. 1970)

It is important to determine when a trade, profession or vocation is permanently discontinued for two reasons. First if a trade, etc. has ceased, for *expenses* incurred after the cessation are not deductible, whilst, generally, post-cessation *receipts* are assessable. Second, the opportunities for obtaining relief for losses sustained in the trade, etc. will be severely restricted (See Chapter 7).

It appears probable that a trade can be said to have ceased permanently when there is no longer any likelihood that further sales or contracts will be made and when all effort to obtain sales or to make contracts has ceased. A distinction must be drawn between sales which are incidental to the cessation and sales which are incidental to the carrying on of a trade. Thus the sale of a complete business as a going concern would not amount to a trading transaction whereas the selling of goods in the ordinary way until no stock was left would represent a continuing trade which could not have been said to cease until all the stock was disposed of.

Death. Where an individual trader dies the cessation provisions automatically apply *unless* by concession (A7–1980) the business is passed to a spouse who then commences to carry it on, in which case the cessation rules are not insisted upon. However, if losses were sustained by the deceased these may not be carried forward against future profits made by the surviving spouse.

Partial retirement. On a partial retirement (i.e. where the scope of his duties are significantly reduced), a trader may, by concession (A20–1980) claim a notional cessation of his business and the commencement of a "new" one. The purpose of this is to avoid aggregation of pension income under Schedule E with, in the same year, a Schedule D assessment. The concession only applies where the scope of a business, hours of work or share of profit have been reduced in order to ensure qualification for the full National Insurance retirement pension.

CLOSING YEAR OF ASSESSMENT

Where a trade, profession or vocation is permanently discontinued, the assessment for the year of assessment in which the discontinuance takes place is based on the actual profits for the period from the preceding 6th April to the date on which the business is discontinued.

Example 1

F. Coin ceased his business on 31st July 1985. The adjusted profits for the last two trading years were:

	£
Year ended 31st July 1984	9,000
Year ended 31st July 1985	6,000

The normal assessment for 1985–86 (the closing year) would be on £9,000, but on the cessation of the business, the assessment would be reduced to the profits for the period from 6th April 1985 to 31st July 1985, i.e., four-twelfths of £6,000 or £2,000.

PENULTIMATE AND PRE-PENULTIMATE YEARS OF ASSESSMENT

Where a trade, profession or vocation is discontinued, the Inland Revenue have the power to raise an additional assessment or otherwise adjust a person's liability to tax if the *aggregate* profits of the years ending on 5th April in each of the two years preceding the year of assessment in which the discontinuance occurs exceed the *aggregate* of the assessments raised for those two years. The raising of an additional assessment is optional, but it is understood in practice that the option is always exercised, even though the ultimate tax charge (e.g. as a result of differing tax rates, stock relief, capital allowances) may be less. The decision is therefore based solely by reference to the profits.

It should be noted that it is the aggregate of the two years that applies. Thus, if the "actual" profits exceed the amount assessed in the penultimate year but the aggregate profits of that year and the preceding year do not exceed the aggregate profits for those two years as already assessed, no adjustment can be made to either of the two assessments already raised for those years.

Example 2

M. Dollar, who made up his accounts regularly to 30th June each year, ceased trading on 30th June 1985. His adjusted profits had been as follows:

		£
Year ended 30th June 1982	....	28,000
Year ended 30th June 1983	....	16,000
Year ended 30th June 1984	....	10,000
Year ended 30th June 1985	....	30,000

The normal assessments raised would be as follows:

		£	
1983–84	....	28,000	
1984–85	....	16,000	Aggregate £44,000
1985–86	....	10,000	

Upon cessation the assessments would be adjusted as follows:

	£	£	£
1985–86—$\frac{1}{4}$ × £30,000 =			7,500
1984–85—$\frac{3}{4}$ × £30,000 =	22,500		
$\frac{1}{4}$ × £10,000 =	2,500		
		25,000	
1983–84—$\frac{3}{4}$ × £10,000 =	7,500		
$\frac{1}{4}$ × £16,000 =	4,000		
		11,500	
		£36,500	

Although the actual profit for the penultimate year (£25,000) exceeds the amount assessed, the aggregate of the "actual" profits for 1983–84 and 1984–85 (£36,500) does not exceed the aggregate of the assessments made for those two years (£44,000) and, therefore, no additional assessments will be raised for those years.

Assuming that the profits in Example 1 were as follows:

		£
Year ended 30th June 1982	....	10,000
Year ended 30th June 1983	....	28,000
Year ended 30th June 1984	....	48,000
Year ended 30th June 1985	....	20,000

The normal assessments raised would be as follows:

		£	
1983–84	....	10,000	
1984–85	....	28,000	Aggregate £38,000
1985–86	....	48,000	

Upon cessation the assessments would be adjusted as follows:

	£	£	£
1985–86—$\frac{1}{4}$ × £20,000 =			5,000
1984–85—$\frac{3}{4}$ × £20,000 =	15,000		
$\frac{1}{4}$ × £48,000 =	12,000		
		27,000	
1983–84—$\frac{3}{4}$ × £48,000 =	36,000		
$\frac{1}{4}$ × £28,000 =	7,000		
		43,000	
		£70,000	

The aggregate of the "actual" profits for 1983–84 and 1984–85 (£70,000) exceeds the aggregate of the assessments made for those years (£38,000) and accordingly the adjustments to be made are:

	£
1983–84—Additional assessment	33,000
1984–85—Reduction	1,000
Net increase	£32,000

§ 6.—CHANGE OF ACCOUNTING DATE (s. 115, I.C.T.A. 1970)

Assessment on the "preceding year basis" is governed by s. 115, I.C.T.A. 1970, which provides that where, in the case of any trade, profession, or vocation, an account has (or accounts have) been made up to a date (or dates) within the three years immediately preceding the year of assessment, and one account only was made up to a date within the preceding year and was for a period of twelve months, beginning either at the commencement of the trade, etc., or at the end of the period on the profits of which the assessment for the preceding year was based, then the assessment is to be based on the profits of that year ended within the preceding year of assessment.

In any other case (i.e., if no account for a period of twelve months was made up to a date within the preceding year (see § 4 above), or if more than one set of accounts was made up to dates within that year), the Revenue have power to decide what period of twelve months ended within the preceding year shall be taken as the basis of the assessment. The decision of the Commissioners as to the period to be taken may involve "splitting" profits of the period for which accounts have actually been made up, any necessary apportionments being made on the basis of months or fractions of months. In practice, fractions of months are usually ignored unless their inclusion would make an appreciable difference to the amounts involved.

In cases in which such a decision is given by the Revenue, and they consider that the assessment for the preceding year should be based on the profits of a corresponding period, they may direct that the assessment for the preceding year shall be increased or decreased accordingly.

If no accounts have been made up to a date within a period of three years preceding the year of assessment, the Commissioners of Inland Revenue have no power to make assessments as described above, and estimated assessments will be made pending the submission of accounts.

Inland Revenue statement of practice
The Board of Inland Revenue have issued a statement as to the practice adopted in cases where a trader permanently changes his accounting date and the main

provisions of the official statement as to the application of s. 115, I.C.T.A. 1970 are summarised in the following paragraphs:

1. Where, in the normal case, there is only one account ending in the year preceding the year of assessment and that account is for a period of twelve months, the assessment is to be based on the profits of that period. In other cases, the Board of Inland Revenue will decide what period of twelve months ending on a date in the preceding year of assessment is to be the basis of assessment, i.e., the "basis year." Where the Board have determined the "basis year" they may direct that the assessment of the preceding year of assessment shall be adjusted to the profits of the "corresponding period" in the previous year, i.e., the year ending on the same date in the previous year.

2. In normal cases the Board will decide that the assessment is to be based on the profits of the period of twelve months ending on the new accounting date in the preceding year, i.e., the date to which it is proposed to make up accounts in future.

3. In deciding whether to adjust the assessment for the preceding year of assessment to the profits of the "corresponding period," where there is a permanent change in the accounting date then, whether or not adjustment is ordered, one of two things must, in the ordinary course, happen:
   (a) If the new date is later in the year of assessment than the old, the profits of some period will escape assessment.
   (b) If the new date is earlier in the year of assessment than the old, the profits of some period will be assessed twice.
   If the profits of the period omitted were relatively low, or the profits of the period coming in twice were relatively high, the Inland Revenue would gain; conversely, if the profits of the period omitted were relatively high, or the profits of the period coming in twice were relatively low, the taxpayer would gain. Thus the Board endeavour to secure that the profits to be omitted from assessment, or to be assessed twice, as the case may be, are "average" profits. This object, as a general rule, cannot be secured by straightforward revision or non-revision, but only by taking for the year to which s. 115 applies some figure intermediate between the revised and unrevised figures. Such intermediate figure is normally computed by consideration of:
   (i) the profits of all the accounting periods of which any part enters into the "basis year(s)" or the "corresponding period" (the "relevant accounting periods"); and
   (ii) the number of years for which the assessments are based in whole or in part on any of the profits of such accounting periods ("relevant years").
   The aggregate profits of the accounting periods falling within (a) are expanded or reduced on a time basis so as to give a proportionate figure for the number of years of assessment falling within (ii), and the assessment for the year to which s. 115 applies, is increased or decreased so that the total of the assessments for all the years falling within (ii) is precisely equal to the proportionate figure as explained above.

4. The taxpayer, if he does not accept the Board's proposal, has the right of appeal to the General or Special Commissioners against any direction made by the Board under s. 115 or against any omission to make such a direction, and the Commissioners are empowered on appeal to give such relief as is just.

5. Where the "average" computation brings out a figure for the adjusted preceding year assessment which exceeds, or falls short of, the unrevised figure for that year by a relatively small amount, it is not the Board's

normal practice to take any action by way of "average" adjustment. For this purpose the Board normally regard as relatively small a difference that does not exceed 10 per cent. of the average of the current and preceding years' assessments and is less than £1,000.

6. The practice outlined above is suitable for the majority of cases but it is subject to modification in certain special cases which are not capable of solution on the normal basis, e.g.:

(a) Cases where the "average" computation brings out a figure for the preceding year of assessment which is not intermediate between the unrevised figure and the profits of the corresponding period.

(b) Cases where there is a marked seasonal fluctuation in the rate of profit, e.g., seaside hotels.

(c) Cases where in some or all of the periods concerned losses were incurred.

(d) Cases where any one of the years concerned is affected by the commencement or cessation provisions (see §§ 4 and 5 of this chapter).

The general principle followed in such exceptional cases is that of equating the average rate of assessments over the years affected to the average rate of profits in the accounting periods that form the basis of those assessments. Such modifications are not described or illustrated in the official statement made by the Board of Inland Revenue as each case will be considered in relation to its own special circumstances.

EXAMPLES

Change less than one year over following 5th April

(a) Upward review
John Cain makes up his accounts annually to 30th September. In 1985 he decides to change this date to 30th June and accounts are consequently made up for the nine months to 30th June 1985.

The adjusted profits were:

	£
12 months to 30th September 1983	36,000
12 months to 30th September 1984	18,000
9 months to 30th June 1985	12,000

It is agreed that 30th June shall be the future accounting date. The assessments are computed as follows:

1986–87	The Board of Inland Revenue decide that the assessment shall be on the profits of the year to 30th June 1985, i.e., $\frac{3}{12}$ of £18,000 + £12,000 = £16,500.
1985–86	(i) *Aggregate profit.* The profit for the "relevant accounting periods (33 months to 30th June 1985) is £66,000. The "relevant years" are 1984–85, 1985–86 and 1986–87 (36 months). The aggregate profit is therefore $\frac{36}{33}$ × £66,000 = £72,000.
	(ii) *Sum of assessments for "relevant years" without revision.* £36,000 (1984–85) + £18,000 (1985–86) + £16,500 (1986–87) = £70,500.

Since the difference between (i) £72,000 and (ii) £70,500 is greater than £1,000, one proceeds to:

(iii) *Sum of assessments for "relevant years" with revision of 1985–86 to "corresponding period".*

"Relevant years"

	£	£
1984–85		36,000
1985–86 Year to 30.6.84: $\frac{1}{4} \times £36,000 = 9,000$		
$+\frac{3}{4} \times £18,000 = 13,500$		22,500
1986–87		16,500
Sum of assessments for "relevant years"		£75,000

The figure at (i) £72,000 is intermediate between (ii) £70,500 and (iii) £75,000. The assessment is therefore revised as follows:

	£	£
Figure at (i)		72,000
Assessed 1984–85	36,000	
Assessed 1986–87	16,500	
		52,500
Balance to be assessed for 1985–86		19,500
Deduct Original assessment		18,000
Additional assessment		£1,500

(b) Downward revision

W. Smith makes up accounts regularly to 30th September. In 1985 it is decided to make up accounts to 30th June in future.

The adjusted profits were:

	£
12 months to 30th September 1983	12,000
12 months to 30th September 1984	30,000
9 months to 30th June 1985	24,000

The assessments are computed as follows:

1986–87   The Board decide that the assessment shall be on the profits of the year to 30th June 1985, i.e., $\frac{3}{12}$ of £30,000 + £24,000 = £31,500.

1985–86   (i) *Aggregate profit.* The profit for the "relevant accounting period" (33 months to 30th June 1985) is £66,000. The "relevant years" are 1984–85, 1985–86 and 1986–87 (36 months). The aggregate profit is therefore $\frac{36}{33} \times £66,000 = £72,000$.

(ii) *Sum of assessments for "relevant years" without revision.*

	£
1984–85	12,000
1985–86	30,000
1986–87	31,500
	£73,500

Since the difference between (i) £72,000 and (ii) £73,500 is greater than £1,000, the calculation proceeds as follows.

(iii) *Sum of assessments for "relevant years" with revision of 1985–86 to "corresponding period".*

"Relevant years"

	£	£
1984–85.................		12,000
1985–86 Year to 30.6.84: $\frac{1}{4} \times £12,000 = 3,000$		
$+ \frac{3}{4} \times £30,000 = 22,500$		25,500
1986–87		31,500
Sum of assessments for "relevant years"		£69,000

The figure at (i) £72,000 is intermediate between (ii) £73,500 and (iii) £69,000. The 1985–86 assessment is therefore revised as follows:

		£
Profits for 36 months:		
$\frac{36}{33}$ of £66,000		72,000
	£	
Assessed 1984–85	12,000	
Assessed 1986–87	31,500	
		43,500
Balance to be assessed for 1985–86		28,500
Deduct Original assessment		30,000
Reduction in assessment		£1,500

Change less than one year prior to following 5th April
J. Richardson makes up accounts regularly to 30th September. In 1984 it is decided to make up accounts to 31st March in future.
The adjusted profits were:

	£
12 months to 30th September 1983	14,000
12 months to 30th September 1984	30,000
6 months to 31st March 1985	22,000

The assessments are computed as follows:

1985–86   The Board decide that the assessment shall be on the profits of the year to 31st March 1985, i.e., $\frac{6}{12}$ of £30,000 + £22,000 = £37,000.

1984–85   (i) *Aggregate profit*. The profit for the "relevant accounting period" (30 months to 31.3.85) is £66,000. The "relevant years" are 1984–85 and 1985–86 (24 months). The aggregate profit is therefore $\frac{24}{30} \times £66,000 = £52,800$.
(ii) *Sum of assessments for "relevant years" without revision.* £14,000 (1984–85) + £37,000 (1985–86) = £51,000.

Since the difference between (i) £52,800 and (ii) £51,000 is more than £1,000, the calculation proceeds as follows.

> (iii) *Sum of assessments for "relevant years" with revision of 1984–85 to "corresponding period".*

"Relevant years"		£	£
1984–85 Year to 31.3.84:	$\frac{1}{2} \times$ £14,000 =	7,000	
	$+ \frac{1}{2} \times$ £30,000 =	15,000	22,000
1985–86			£37,000
Sum of assessments for "relevant years"			£59,000

The figure at (i) £52,800 is intermediate between (ii) £51,000 and (iii) £59,000 and therefore the 1984–85 assessment must be revised as follows:

Profits for 24 months:	£
$\frac{24}{30}$ of £66,000	52,800
Assessed 1985–86	37,000
Balance to be assessed for 1984–85	15,800
Deduct Original assessment	14,000
Additional assessment	£1,800

Change of more than one year (covering two "5th Aprils")

C. Skinner makes up accounts regularly to 31st March. In 1984 it is decided to make up accounts to 30th June in future.

The adjusted profits were:

	£
12 months to 31st March 1982	16,000
12 months to 31st March 1983	32,000
15 months to 30th June 1984	24,000

The assessments are computed as follows:

1984–85 and 1985–86	In this case a decision under s. 115, I.C.T.A. 1970 has to be given for two years. The Board decide that the assessment for the year 1984–85 shall be on the profits of the year to 30th June 1983, and that the assessment for the year 1985–86 shall be on the profits of the year to 30th June 1984:

		£
1984–85	$\frac{9}{12}$ of £32,000 $+ \frac{3}{15}$ of £24,000	28,800
1985–86	$\frac{12}{15}$ of £24,000	19,200

1983–84	(i) *Aggregate profit.* The profit for the "relevant accounting periods" (39 months to 30.6.84) is £72,000. The "relevant years" are 1982–83, 1983–84, 1984–85 and 1985–86 (48 months). The aggregate profit is therefore $\frac{48}{39} \times$ £72,000 = £88,615.
	(ii) *Sum of assessments for "relevant years" without revision.* £16,000 (1982–83) + £32,000 (1983–84) + £28,800 (1984–85) + £19,200 (1985–86) = £96,000.

Since the difference between (i) £88,615 and (ii) £96,000 is more than £1,000, the calculation proceeds as follows.

(iii) *Sum of assessments for "relevant years" with revision of 1983–84 to "corresponding period".*

"Relevant years"

	£	£
1982–83		16,000
1983–84 Year to 30.6.82: $\frac{3}{4} \times £16,000 = 12,000$		
$+ \frac{1}{4} \times £32,000 = 8,000$		20,000
1984–85		28,800
1985–86		19,200
Sum of assessments for "relevant years"		£84,000

The figure at (i) £88,615 is intermediate between (ii) £96,000 and (iii) £84,000 and therefore the 1983–84 assessment must be revised as follows:

		£
Profits for 48 months:		
$\frac{48}{39}$ of £72,000		88,615

	£	
Assessed 1982–83	16,000	
Assessed 1984–85	28,800	
Assessed 1985–86	19,200	
		64,000
Balance to be assessed for 1983–84		24,615
Deduct Original assessment		32,000
Reduction in assessment		£7,385

§ 7.—PARTNERSHIPS

INTRODUCTION

A partnership is "The relationship which subsists between persons carrying on a business in common with a view to profit", and may be known collectively as a firm (Partnership Act 1890, ss. 1(1), 4(1)).

Where a trade or profession is carried on by two or more persons jointly *income tax* is computed and stated jointly and in one sum, separate from any tax chargeable upon the partners *per se* and a joint assessment is made in the name of "the firm" (s. 152, I.C.T.A. 1970).

By comparison, tax on chargeable gains accruing on the disposal of partnership assets is assessed and charged upon the partners separately and all dealings by the firm are treated as made by the partners individually and not by the firm as such.

The Partnership Act 1890, s. 2 sets out certain actions by or relationships between persons which do not *of themselves* create a partnership or make a person a partner therein:

(a) Joint tenancy, tenancy in common, joint property, common property, or part ownership do not *of themselves* create a partnership in relation to the property concerned irrespective of whether or not any profit therefrom is shared;

(*b*) The sharing of gross returns does not *of itself* create a partnership irrespective of whether the persons so sharing have a joint or common right or interest in the property concerned or not;

(*c*) Although the receipt by a person of a share in the profits is *prima facie* evidence that he is a partner in the business, the receipt of a share or payment varying with the profits of the business does not *of itself* make him a partner, e.g.

(i) payment of a debt, by instalments out of profits as they accrue

(ii) a contract whereby an employee is remunerated by a share of profits

(iii) the receipt by a widow or child of a deceased partner of part of the profits of a business by way of annuity

(iv) a loan whereby the lender receives a rate of interest varying with profits, or a share of the profits

(v) the receipt by a person who has sold the goodwill of a business by way of annuity.

It must, however, be noted that a "trade" is defined as including every trade, manufacture, adventure or concern in the nature of trade (s. 526 (5), I.C.T.A. 1970). In deciding if a partnership exists all the circumstances must be considered including the intentions and aspirations of the persons concerned.

The existence of a partnership deed is not conclusive evidence of the existence of a partnership, but neither is a deed stating that no partnership exists. A partnership can exist without there being any formal document. In the absence of a deed of partnership, the relationship between the partners is governed by the terms of Partnership Act 1890.

A formal agreement of partnership is not valid if it is ignored and the business carried on as before. In contrast the Revenue cannot be prevented from assessing a business as a partnership by stating in a deed that no partnership exists. A deed cannot backdate the commencement of a partnership unless the partnership relationship existed before the deed was drawn up and similar considerations apply in bringing a partnership to an end.

It is important to understand the different categories of "partner" which exist.

(*a*) A partner is a *full partner* unless under the arrangements within a firm he has any lesser status.

(*b*) A *salaried partner* is usually remunerated by means of a salary, although he may also receive a commission or share of profits. On occasion he may only receive a commission or profit share but no salary. Such salary, etc. is usually a prior charge on the profit before its division among the full partners.

To the outside world such a person has the appearance of being a partner. Within the partnership his income is limited as noted above, he does not normally share in goodwill, and has no right to direct the partnership, nor except as authorised to contract on its behalf. Normally his remuneration is assessed under Schedule E, although there may be circumstances where either Case I or II, Schedule D, is appropriate. He will not, however, be liable for any share of the firm's Schedule D assessment.

However a salaried partner, by holding himself out to the world at large as a partner may be liable for the debts of the firm in the event of default by all full partners.

(*c*) The so called *sleeping partner*, takes no active part in a business, but receives part of the profits, perhaps because he has provided the funds for the business (but in the absence of other factors this would not of itself necessarily make him a partner) or because he has retired and the share of profits is a form of pension. However, if he is not active in the business his share of profits may not be treated as *earned income* (see s. 530, I.C.T.A. 1970).

RETURNS AND ASSESSMENTS

Section 9, T.M.A. 1970 provides that the precedent acting partner of a firm should make the return of income required under s. 8, T.M.A. 1970 on behalf of the firm. Rules are laid down to determine which partner is the precedent acting partner. If there is a no partner who is resident in the UK, this return must be made by the firm's UK resident agent, or manager, etc. (s. 78, T.M.A. 1970).

The return must also give details of the names and residences of the partners, and of any disposal of any partnership property which is a chargeable asset for Capital Gains Tax purposes. The Inspector can require any partner to provide the like information.

The usual penalties apply for failure to make a required return or making an incorrect return except that those based on total income and total tax are limited to taxes chargeable in the partnership name. Likewise the provisions concerning tax lost by fraud, wilful default or neglect are effective in respect of partnerships although subject to certain appropriate modifications which in particular provide protection for a partner who is innocent of such conduct.

It should be noted that each partner is required to make a separate personal return of his own income in the normal manner.

Section 152, I.C.T.A., 1970 provides that an assessment in respect of profits of a trade, etc. carried on by a partnership is made upon the partnership and not upon individual partners. The partnership is therefore treated for this purpose as a separate person or as an 'entity of assessment'. Other sources of *income* of a partnership are similarly assessed, but it would appear that there is no statutory authority for such treatment. Chargeable gains arising on the disposal of partnership assets are, however, assessed upon the partners individually.

The liability of tax on partnership profits is a partnership debt and partners are *jointly liable* therefor. The Revenue can therefore claim the entire tax from any one or more partners irrespective of their actual sharing arrangements. Note that partners are jointly liable and not *severally liable* so that failure to sue one partner when others are sued may release that one from liability (so far as the Revenue is concerned) and a release of one partner may amount to a release of all.

A claim by a retiring partner to be indemnified against partnership taxation liabilities arising from the period prior to his retirement has been upheld by the courts.

The normal rules relating to date of payment, payment pending appeal, interest on overdue tax and repayment supplement on late repayment of tax, apply to assessments upon partnerships as they do for other assessments.

As will be seen later, the various allowances to which each partner is entitled are brought into account before calculating the actual tax payable, and for this purpose it is necessary that the firm's assessment be correctly allocated between the partners.

APPORTIONMENT OF ASSESSMENT AMONGST THE PARTNERS

The assessment upon the firm is based upon the adjusted profits of the preceding year, but the *apportionment* of the assessment is made according to the respective interests of the partners in the partnership profits *during the year of assessment*. Thus, if in a firm of 3 partners, profits were shared 3:2:1 during the period on the profits of which the assessment is based, and the ratio is altered to 2:2:1 for the whole of the year of assessment, then the firm's assessment for that year will be apportioned in the *new* profit-sharing ratio. If the profit-sharing ratio is varied *during* the year of assessment, effect will be given thereto in apportioning the assessment for that year. For instance, if A and B share profits equally during the first half of the year of assessment and in the ratio 3:2 during the second half, the assessment will be apportioned equally as to one half, and in the ratio 3:2 as to the other half.

Similar considerations apply to the treatment of partners' salaries and interest on capital. Where the salaries and interest on capital are fixed, no difficulty arises; but in cases where they vary from year to year and consequently the exact amounts are not known at the time of making the Return, it is usual in practice to take the figures for the year preceding the year of assessment; although an adjustment may be made at a later date if necessary. Of course, where the facts are known the correct treatment is applied at the outset (see Example 2).

Example 1—simple apportionment

Abbott, Beadle and Curate are in partnership sharing profits equally after charging Interest on Capital (Abbott £3,000, Beadle £2,000, Curate £1,500) and Partner's Salaries (Abbott £5,000, Curate £3,000). Both Interest on Capital and Partners' Salaries are fixed.

The Case I, Schedule D, assessment for 1985–86 which is based on the adjusted profits for the year ended 31st March 1985 is £59,500.

	£	£
Case I, Schedule D, Assessment, 1985–86		59,500
Deduct: Interest on capital	6,500	
Partners' salaries	8,000	
		14,500
Balance, divisible equally		£45,000

The 1985–86 assessment is divided between the partners as follows:

	Abbott £	Beadle £	Curate £	Total £
Interest on capital	3,000	2,000	1,500	6,500
Salaries	5,000	—	3,000	8,000
Balance of profits	15,000	15,000	15,000	45,000
	£23,000	£17,000	£19,500	£59,500

Example 2—change of profit sharing ratio for whole year

Abbott, Beadle and Curate (see previous example) decide that, as from 6th April 1985 Beadle shall be entitled to a salary of £3,000 per annum and that the profit-sharing ratio shall be altered to 2:2:1.

	£	£
Case I, Schedule D, Assessment, 1985–86		59,500
Deduct: Interest on capital (as before)	6,500	
Partners' salaries	11,000	
		17,500
Balance, divisible 2:2:1		£42,000

The 1985–86 assessment is divided between the partners as follows:

	Abbott £	Beadle £	Curate £	Total £
Interest on capital	3,000	2,000	1,500	6,500
Salaries	5,000	3,000	3,000	11,000
Balance of profits	16,800	16,800	8,400	42,000
	£24,800	£21,800	£12,900	£59,500

Note. In arriving at the assessment, i.e., £59,500 in the above case, the interest on capital and partners' salaries charged *in the accounts* to 31st March 1985 will have to be added back. Interest and salaries are taken into account only for the purpose of *dividing the assessment between the partners.*

Example 3—change of profit sharing ratio during year

Davis, Evans and Frank are in partnership sharing profits equally, after charging interest on capital (which is the same each year)—£3,000, £2,000 and £1,000 respectively. The 1985–86 assessment based on the profits for the year ended 31st December 1984, was £36,000.

As from 6th October 1985, it is decided to adjust the profit-sharing ratio to Davis: one-half; Evans: one-third; and Frank: one-sixth; interest on capital to remain unchanged.

	£
Case I, Schedule D, Assessment 1985–86	36,000
Less: Interest on capital	6,000
	£30,000

The balance of £30,000 is divisible into two parts in respect of the period of six months ended 5th October 1985, and the remaining six months of the year to 5th April 1986, respectively, the portion in respect of the former period being divided in the old profit-sharing ratio and the remaining portion in the new profit-sharing ratio.

The 1985–86 assessment is divided between the partners as follows:

	Davis £	Evans £	Frank £	Total £
Interest in capital	3,000	2,000	1,000	6,000
Share of profits (six months to 5th October 1985)	5,000	5,000	5,000	15,000
Share of profits (six months to 5th April 1986)	7,500	5,000	2,500	15,000
	£15,500	£12,000	£8,500	£36,000

Example 4—change of profit sharing ratios with salaried partner

Robin, Swallow and Thrush are in partnership, sharing profits equally. Interest on capital is credited at 5 per cent per annum, and Swallow receives a salary of £12,000 per annum.

The capital accounts of the partners are as follows: Robin, £100,000, Swallow, £60,000, and Thrush, £40,000.

The adjusted profits for the year ended 31st March 1985 were £127,000.

On 6th October 1985, Robin brought in a further £100,000 capital, the profit-sharing ratio being adjusted 5:2:3.

	£	£
Case I, Schedule D, Assessment 1985–86		127,000
Less: Partner's salary	12,000	
Interest on capital	12,500	
	———	24,500
		£102,500

The 1985–86 assessment is divided between the partners as follows:

	Robin £	Swallow £	Thrush £	Total £
Profit for the six months ended 5th October 1985	£63,500			
Less: Interest on capital (Half-year at 5 per cent on £200,000)...	5,000 2,500	1,500	1,000	5,000
Partner's salary	6,000	6,000		6,000
Balance divided 1:1:1	£52,500 17,500	17,500	17,500	52,500
Profit for the six months ended 5th April 1986	£63,500			
Less: Interest on capital (Half-year at 5 per cent on £300,000)...	7,500 5,000	1,500	1,000	7,500
Partner's salary	6,000	6,000		6,000
Balance divided 5:2:3	£50,000 25,000	10,000	15,000	50,000
	£50,000	£42,500	£34,500	£127,000

Sharing losses

Where the assessment on a partnership firm is less than the amount required to meet the salaries of partners and interest on capital, the apportionment must be made in accordance with the terms of the partnership agreement governing the partners' shares of profits and losses. Where, in such circumstances, a partner's adjusted share is a "loss", the assessment must be borne by those partners whose adjusted shares result in a "profit" in proportion to their adjusted shares.

Example 5

George, Harris and James are in partnership sharing profits and losses in the proportion of one-half, one-fifth and three-tenths respectively. George is entitled to a salary of £4,000, and interest on capital amounting to £800, £600 and £200 respectively is charged before division of profits. The 1985–86 assessment, before adjusting partner's salary and partners' interest on capital, is £4,500.

The assessment is divided between the partners as follows:

	£	£
Assessment		4,500
Less: Partner's salary.....................	4,000	
Interest on capital	1,600	
		5,600
Loss adjusted for division between the partners		£1,100

The 1985–86 assessment is divided between the partners as follows:

	George £	Harris £	James £	Total £
Salary	4,000	—	—	4,000
Interest on capital	800	600	200	1,600
	4,800	600	200	5,600
Less: Share of adjusted Loss	550	220	330	1,100
	Profit £4,250	Profit £380	Loss £130	£4,500
Apportionment of loss:				
George $\frac{4,250}{4,500} \times 130$	− (120)	—	120	—
Harris $\frac{380}{4,500} \times 130$	—	—(10)	10	—
	£4,130	£370	—	£4,500

No claim for relief for his "loss" can be made by James, since the *firm* has an adjusted profit but, in actual practice, it is probable that George and Harris may undertake to compensate James privately in respect of the benefit they derive from the utilisation of his "loss" of £130.

Where annual charges, from which income tax is deducted at the source, are payable during the year of assessment, and apart from its profits the firm has no taxed income against which such charges can be set, or the partners have no taxed income against which their respective shares of such charges can be set, the assessment will include the amount of such charges.

Example 6—Payment of annuity

Jones and Smith are in partnership, sharing profits equally after charging interest on capital (Jones £1,500, Smith £1,000) and a salary of £3,000 to Smith. They pay an annuity of a fixed amount of £2,500 (gross) per annum. Neither partner has any other source of income.

The 1985–86 assessment on the firm amounts to £17,000.

	£	£
Case I, Schedule D, Assessment 1985–86		17,000
Deduct: Annual charges		2,500
		14,500

		£	
Deduct: Interest on capital...............		2,500	
Partner's salary		3,000	
		———	5,500
Balance, divisible equally			£9,000

The 1985–86 assessment is divided between the partners as follows:

	Jones	Smith	Firm	Total
	£	£	£	£
Interest on capital	1,500	1,000	—	2,500
Salary	—	3,000	—	3,000
Annuity.................	—	—	2,500	2,500
Balance of profits........	4,500	4,500	—	9,000
	£6,000	£8,500	£2,500	£17,000

Note. Jones and Smith will include as taxed income £6,000 and £8,500 respectively in their statutory incomes for 1985–86. The firm will be assessed on £17,000 and the partners will be responsible for tax on this amount subject to any allowances to which they may be entitled. Tax on the annual charges is finally recouped by deducting tax when paying the annuity.

If the annual charges during the year 1985–86 increased to (say) £5,000 the assessment of £17,000 would be apportioned as follows:

	Jones	Smith	Firm	Total
	£	£	£	£
Interest on capital	1,500	1,000	—	2,500
Salary	—	3,000	—	3,000
Annuity.................	—	—	5,000	5,000
Balance of profits........	3,250	3,250	—	6,500
	£4,750	£7,250	£5,000	£17,000

Receipt of other income, effect on charges

Where, however, the *firm* has any other income which is taxed at source, e.g., dividends and interest, or taxed under another Schedule, e.g., rents assessed under Schedule A, the charges are treated as being paid primarily out of such income, and the balance of charges applicable to each partner is treated as paid out of his private unearned income, if any. Only the balance of the charges not covered by such income of the year of assessment will be included in the Schedule D assessment.

Example 7

Finch and Gamble are assessed under Schedule D for 1985–86 on £25,000. No provision is made for partners' salaries or interest on capital. The partnership receives regular taxed dividends amounting to £1,500 (gross)*. Finch and Gamble have no other sources of income.

For 1985–86 the firm will pay an annuity of £2,500 (gross) and patent royalties of £2,000 (gross).

———————————

* Cash dividend plus tax credit

	£	£
Case I, Schedule D, Assessment 1985–86......		25,000
Less: Annual charges—		
Annuity.........................	2,500	
Patent royalties..................	2,000	
	4,500	
Less: Other income—		
Taxed dividends.................	1,500	
		3,000
		£22,000

The balance of £22,000 is divided equally, i.e., £11,000 to each partner.
The 1985–86 assessment is divided between the partners as follows:

	£
Finch...	11,000
Gamble.......................................	11,000
Firm (balance of charges)	3,000
	£25,000

Note. As £1,500 of the charges are set off against the taxed dividends only the balance of £3,000 is included in the Schedule D assessment.

If Finch and Gamble had private investment incomes of, at least, £1,500 each, the assessment would be divided as follows:

	£
Finch.............................	12,500
Gamble............................	12,500
	£25,000

§ 8.—CHANGE OF OWNERSHIP OF BUSINESS (PARTNERSHIPS AND OTHERS)

Two distinct types of change in the proprietorship of a business are recognised for taxation purposes, a clear distinction being drawn between:
(*a*) a partial change in the constitution of a business, *and*
(*b*) a complete change of ownership of a business.

(*a*) PARTIAL CHANGE—PARTNERSHIPS

Discontinuance provisions (s. 47, FA 1985)
To avoid abuses that were considered to be taking place where partnership changes took place, the new business *commencement* rules as explained in §4 were altered with effect from 19th March 1985.

The general rule for partnership change is dealt with under s. 154, I.C.T.A. 1970. This provides that where there is a *partial* change in the constitution of a business (e.g. where, in the case of a partnership, *any* member of the new firm was a member of the old firm), the assessments will be made as if the business had been discontinued on the date of the change, and a new business commenced. For partnership changes taking place after 19th March 1985, whilst the cessation provisions remain (see §5 above) the commencement provisions are altered in cases where:

    (i) a person engaged in carrying on the business before the change carries it on after the change and

    (ii) *no* election is made under s. 154 (2) I.C.T.A. 1970 (below) for the continuance provisions to apply.

The change has the effect of extending the actual basis of assessment to the first *four* years. The taxpayer's right to elect for actual basis to apply (under s. 117, I.C.T.A. 1970) then arises in respect of the fifth and sixth years.

Example

Laura, Emma and Carole have been running a fashion business in partnership for many years, making up accounts to 31st January.

On 1st February 1985 it is decided to make Alison a partner. The profits indicate that the continuation provisions are not beneficial so no election under s. 154(2), I.C.T.A. is to be made.

The bases of assessment for the *new* partnership are as follows:

Year of assessment	Basis period
1984–85	1.2.85–5.4.85
1985–86	6.4.85–5.4.86
1986–87	6.4.86–5.4.87
1987–88	6.4.87–5.4.88
1988–89 (fifth year)	Year to 31.1.88
1989–90 (sixth year)	Year to 31.1.89

(N.B. The basis of assessment for 1988–89 and 1989–90 can be revised to actual, if this is beneficial.)

It should be noted that although the above is essentially anti-avoidance legislation it applies to all partnership changes where no election for "continuation" is made under s. 154(2), I.C.T.A. 1970 and there is one partner common to both the old and new partnership.

Loss offset

For the purpose of carrying forward losses under s. 171, I.C.T.A. 1970 (see Chapter 7, §4), a person who is a member of both the old and the new firms is to be treated as carrying on the same business and he may also set-off any loss incurred by him in the part of the year of assessment before the change, against any profit earned in the same year after the change. Similarly, a continuing partner may carry forward his share of any unexhausted capital allowances and stock relief for set-off against future profits of the new firm.

Election for continuation (s. 154 (2) I.C.T.A. 1970)

If, however, all the members of both firms (or their legal personal representatives, in the case of deceased partners) give notice in writing to the Inspector of Taxes within two years after the date of change that they do not wish the cessation and commencement provisions to be applied, the business will be treated as continuing. The amounts of the assessments will not be affected by the change but the assessment for the year of assessment in which the change takes place will be apportioned between the old and new firms on a time basis. This type of claim may be made, not only in the case of the retirement of one of several partners or the introduction of one or more new partners, but also where a sole trader takes a partner or where one of two partners retires and the business is continued by the other, i.e., there must be at least one individual who was interested in both the old and the new businesses.

If the claim should provide advantageous to the members of the new firm but disadvantageous to a retired or deceased partner, the latter (or his personal representative) will probably sign the notice of claim provided the members of the new firm compensate him (or his estate) for any additional tax suffered by him (or his estate) as a result of the claim. A converse arrangement may be come to where the making of the claim benefits the old firm at the expense of the new firm.

The claim can also extend to unrecovered stock appreciation relief existing at the date of change (see Chapter 6).

Example 1

Hook, Line and Sinker carry on business in partnership. On 31st December 1983 Hook retires and Carp and Pike are admitted into the firm.

Accounts are made up to 31st December in each year and profits (as adjusted for Income Tax purposes) are as follows:

	£
1980.	175,000
1981.	160,000
1982.	240,000
1983.	100,000
1984.	152,000
1985.	240,000

It is required to show the assessments for 1981–82 to 1986–87 on Hook, Line and Sinker (the old firm) and on Line, Sinker, Carp and Pike (the new firm).

The normal assessments will be as follows:

	£	
1981–82.	180,000	normally £175,000 but increased to the actual profits of £180,000 (i.e., 9/12 of £160,000 plus 3/12 of £240,000)—Hook, Line and Sinker
1982–83.	205,000	normally £160,000 but increased to the actual profits of £205,000 (i.e., 9/12 of £240,000 plus 3/12 of £100,000)—Hook, Line and Sinker
1983–84.	75,000	Actual Profits (i.e., 9/12 of £100,000)—Hook, Line and Sinker
	38,000	Actual Profits (i.e., 3/12 of £152,000)—Line, Sinker, Carp and Pike
1984–85.	152,000	Profits of first 12 months' trading—Line, Sinker, Carp and Pike
1985–86.	152,000	Preceding year—Line, Sinker, Carp and Pike
1986–87.	240,000	Do.—Line, Sinker, Carp and Pike
	1,042,000	

(N.B. The change takes place before 19.3.85, so the F.A. 1985 provisions are not effective.)

Since Line and Sinker are partners in both firms the change is only of a partial nature, a claim *may* be made by *all* the partners concerned before 31st December 1985 that the assessments shall be as follows:

		£
1981–82.	175,000	Hook, Line and Sinker
1982–83.	160,000	Hook, Line and Sinker
1983–84.	240,000	(9/12) £180,000—Hook, Line, and Sinker
		(3/12) £60,000—Line, Sinker, Carp and Pike
1984–85.	100,000	Do.
1985–86.	152,000	Do.
1986–87.	240,000	Do.
	1,067,000	

It will be noted that the normal assessments on the old firm amount to £460,000 and those on the new firm to £582,000 whereas the amended assessments on the old firm amount to £515,000 (i.e., an increase of £55,000), those on the new firm to £552,000 (i.e., a decrease of £30,000). Hence the overall disadvantage of the claim is £25,000 (£1,067,000–£1,042,000) although the personal, etc., allowances and the rates of tax payable in the various years of assessment must be taken into account before the desirability or otherwise of making a claim can be definitely ascertained.

(*b*) COMPLETE CHANGE—SOLE TRADERS AND PARTNERSHIPS

Where there is a *complete* change of ownership (e.g., where a sole trader's business is sold to a company or to another sole trader), the assessments are computed as if the business had been discontinued at the date of the change and a new business commenced. Where a business is sold to a limited company, the effective date for computing the assessments on the change of ownership is the *de facto* date of acquisition (which cannot be earlier than the date of incorporation) and not of necessity the date stated in the agreement. The vendor is liable for tax to that date and the company is then liable for tax from the same date. If, following the death of a trader, his widow carries on the business the cessation provisions are not applied unless insisted upon by the widow. However, losses, capital allowances and stock relief cannot be carried forward.

Example 2

Bill owns a business which he sells to Ben on 5th April 1984. The adjusted profits are as follows:

	£
Year ended 5th April 1981	8,000
Year ended 5th April 1982	10,000
Year ended 5th April 1983	14,000
Year ended 5th April 1984	8,000
Year ended 5th April 1985	12,000
Year ended 5th April 1986	16,000

It is required to show the assessments for the years from 1981–82 to 1986–87.

Bill will have been assessed for 1981–82 on £8,000, for 1982–83 on £10,000 and for 1983–84 on £14,000.

These assessments will be adjusted to the actual profits, i.e., £10,000 for 1981–82, £14,000 for 1982–83 (since these are higher than the original assessments) and £8,000 for 1983–84.

Ben will be assessed as a new business as follows:

		£
1984–85	Actual profits	12,000
1985–86	Profits of first 12 months' trading	12,000
1986–87	Preceding year	16,000

Where an employee is taken into partnership, the employee's salary is allowed as a charge against the profits of the previous period upon which the first assessment of the new firm is based assuming a claim is made for continuance. The salary is a proper trade expense of the business in the years during which the partner was an employee, and this fact cannot be altered by a subsequent change in the status of the individual concerned.

Effect of discontinuance on stock and capital allowances
Where a business is regarded as discontinued for Income Tax purposes, special rules apply for stock valuation (see Chapter 11, § 13), for work in progress (ss. 144, 145, 147, 148 and 149, I.C.T.A. 1970) and capital allowances (s. 44(6) F.A. 1971). See also Chapter 6 for the effects of stock relief.

§ 9.—DOUBLE CHANGE IN PARTNERSHIP

Where the constitution of a partnership is changed twice within a comparatively short period and notice has been given on the first change not to have the business treated as discontinued at the date of the change, and a new business commenced (see § 8 of this Chapter), but no such notice has been given on the second change, the assessments for the penultimate and pre-penultimate years will be increased to the actual profits for these years if they exceed the aggregate of the original assessments for those two years (s. 154, I.C.T.A., 1970). Note that the second new partnership will be subject to the provisions of s. 47, F.A. 1985 such that the first four years of assessment will be taxed on the actual basis.

Example—effect on first change

Roberts, Smith and Tompkins carried on business in partnership until 31st March 1985 (the normal date of preparation of the accounts) when Roberts retired. Smith and Tompkins, together with a new partner, Underwood, carried on the business until 31st March 1986 at which date Venables was admitted as a partner. Notice was given by Roberts, Smith, Tompkins and Underwood, on 31st March 1985 to treat the business as not discontinued at that date, but no such notice was given in respect of the second change of ownership. The adjusted profits are as follows:

	£
Year ended 31st March 1983	30,000
Year ended 31st March 1984	50,000
Year ended 31st March 1985	114,000
Year ended 31st March 1986	Nil (there being a loss in this year).

In view of notice being given in respect of the first change in ownership the assessments for 1983–84, 1984–85 and 1985–86 were as follows:

	£
1983–84	30,000
1984–85	50,000
1985–86	114,000

As no notice was given in relation to the second change in ownership on 31st March 1986, the assessment of £114,000 for 1985–86 will be reduced to "Nil" and additional assessments raised for the years 1984–85 (£64,000, i.e., £114,000 less £50,000) and 1983–84 (£20,000, i.e., £50,000 less £30,000) upon Roberts, Smith and Tompkins as they were the persons charged for those years.

§ 10.—SUNDRY PARTNERSHIP MATTERS

LOSS RELIEF—LIMITED PARTNERS (S. 48, F.A. 1985)

Losses incurred in chargeable periods beginning after 19th March 1985 are now limited to the capital at risk in the business.

This provision reverses the effect of the decision in *Read v Young* (1984) where it was held that the taxpayer (Mrs Young) was entitled to relief for the whole of her share of the partnership loss even though the sum involved was greater than the sum of money actually at risk in the partnership. (It is understood the Inland Revenue have appealed the case to the House of Lords.)

Example

Delta, a limited partner in Gamma, is entitled to 25% of the profits or losses of the business. His capital introduced is £10,000.

The partnership results for the year ended 31st March 1986 shared a loss of £60,000. Delta can only claim £10,000 as loss relief, even though under the partnership agreement his losses would be £15,000. The balance of the loss (£5,000) is available for offset against future partnership losses.

Note that this loss would reduce the capital of Delta and consequently reduce or eliminate loss relief for future years unless further injections of capital were made.

These anti-avoidance provisions apply also to capital allowances where a s. 169, I.C.T.A. 1970 claim (see Chapter 7) would apply.

PARTNERSHIPS CONTROLLED ABROAD (S. 153, I.C.T.A. 1970)

Where the control and management of a partnership is situated outside the U.K., the partnership is deemed to be resident outside the U.K. notwithstanding that some of the partners may be U.K. resident, and that part of the trading activity is carried on within the U.K.

If any part of the business is however conducted in the U.K., the non-resident partnership is chargeable to tax on the profits generated in the U.K., on the basis that a non-resident trading in the U.K. would be chargeable, irrespective of the fact that there may or may not be U.K. resident partners.

Assessments to tax for the U.K. trading activity of the firm can be made in the name of any U.K. resident partner.

PARTNERSHIPS INVOLVING COMPANIES (S. 155, I.C.T.A. 1970)

Introduction

The computation of assessable profits proceeds on the basis of a "corporation tax computation" (see Chapter 14) by reference to accounting periods and without regard to any changes in the partnership. The "corporation tax computation" is however amended so that:

(1) references to distributions do not apply;
(2) no deduction or addition is made for charges on income, capital allowances and charges, and losses arising in preceding or succeeding periods;
(3) a change in the persons carrying on the trade is treated as a transfer of the trade to a different company if a different company is engaged in the trade after the transfer.

The provisions of s. 154, I.C.T.A. 1970 do not apply unless the partnership change is the exclusion or addition of an individual.

Allocation and assessment of profits

The profits of the company partnership as calculated are apportioned between the partners in their profit-sharing ratio.

In the case of a company partner the profits/losses, together with the appropriate share of charges, capital allowances etc., are chargeable to corporation tax as if the trade were carried on separately. The profits are then assessed by reference to the company's own accounting period.

Example 1

Cass Ltd has an equal share in a partnership with Sell Ltd. The results of the partnership for the year ended 31 December 1985 are as follows:

	Total	Cass Ltd	Sell Ltd
	£	£	£
Adjusted profit	50,000	25,000	25,000
Capital allowances	15,000	7,500	7,500

Cass Ltd (whose accounting period is to 31st March) will be assessed as follows:

Year to 31st March 1985:	£
Profit (1.1.85–31.3.85) $\frac{1}{4} \times$ £25,000	6,250
Less Capital allowances: $\frac{1}{4} \times$ £7,500	1,875
Profits chargeable to corporation tax	£4,375

Year to 31st March 1986:	£
Profits (1.4.85–31.12.85) $\frac{3}{4} \times$ £25,000	18,750
Less Capital allowances $\frac{3}{4} \times$ £7,500	5,625
Profits chargeable to corporation tax	£13,125

Note. The profits chargeable will form part of Cass Ltd's total liability to corporation tax. Appropriate reliefs, e.g. other trading losses may therefore reduce the tax charge—see generally Chapter 14.

In the case of a partner who is an individual, the share of profits is assessed to income tax as if the partnership were a partnership comprising individuals (see § 7). Capital allowances, etc. *are given for the year of assessment to which the period relates* (apportioning where necessary).

Example 2

Assume that in Example 1 Cass Ltd was an individual, the assessment would be:

1986–87	£
Profits, year ended 31.12.1985	25,000
Capital allowances	Nil
	£25,000

NB: The capital allowances will be granted as follows:

1984–85 $\frac{1}{4} \times$ £7,500	=	£1,875

1985–86 $\frac{3}{4} \times$ £7,500	=	£5,625

Stock relief is treated as a deduction or increase to the trading profit and assessed accordingly (Schedule 9, Para. 18, F.A. 1981)

Where individual partners' interests have altered during any year of assessment, the amount assessable on the individuals cannot be less than the total amount of the individuals' share of the partnership income (s. 155(5) (a), I.C.T.A. 1970).

OTHER INCOME

There have been several cases over the years concerned with the receipt of interest by trades and professions in circumstances where it could be argued that the interest arose as part of the profits of a trade (e.g. in a banking partnership). Such income, if derived from a trade, etc. is not investment income if the proceeds of sale of the investment, would be taken into account in computing the profits of trade, etc.

Interest arising from loans and deposits by a firm of solicitors from clients' monies is not earned income, and indeed is properly income of the clients and not of the firm. Solicitors Act 1965, s. 8(3) provides that monies held *generally* on account of clients (e.g. as stakeholders in property sales, small balances held against fees, etc.) are regarded as the solicitor's income but other amounts remain the income of the client.

Interest earned by a partnership is assessed according to the normal rules of Case III Schedule D (i.e. except in the opening and closing years, on the income of the year preceding the year of assessment). Similarly if a partnership receives income taxed under Cases IV or V Schedule D, the basis will normally be income of the preceding year.

If rent is received on property owned by a partnership, a Schedule A assessment will ultimately be made based on the actual income of the year of assessment (although initially a provisional assessment will be based on the income of the previous year).

The tax due on an assessment on the above income will be due for payment in one amount on 1st January in the year of assessment except in the case of income, under Case V Schedule D, from a foreign trade which is due in two instalments as for Case I or II, Schedule D.

Partners in professional practices such as solicitors or accountants often receive directors' fees or similar income which in practice is often included as part of the partnership profits available for division among the partners. Strictly tax should be deducted under PAYE (and often it is) or a Schedule E assessment raised.

Where a partnership receives rent, or dividends or income taxed at source, or income assessed under Schedule E, or makes annual payments, such items are apportioned between the partners according to the profit sharing arrangements in the year of assessment. Income assessable under Cases I–III Schedule D, is divided between the partners in their profit sharing ratios in the year of assessment, irrespective of the sharing ratios applying in the basis period in which the profits were earned. It is not clear whether Case IV and V Schedule D income is divided in the ratio that the actual was shared rather than the ratio applying in the year of assessment.

§ 11.—FARMING AND MARKET GARDENING: RELIEF FOR FLUCTUATING PROFITS (s. 28, F.A. 1978)

Where profits earned by individuals, partnerships and trusts carrying on a trade of farming or market gardening in the United Kingdom fluctuate over two consecutive years of assessment, in order to avoid wide variations in the taxation burden upon profits, a system of averaging applies. The first two years of assessment for which an averaging claim can be made are 1979–80 and 1980–81.

Total relief
The basic rule is that, subject to certain limitations, the profits of two consecutive years are added together and only one half of the aggregate is assessed in each year. The relief is only available if, on a comparison of the profits of two such years the profits of one year do not exceed 70% of the profits of the other year (treating a loss, for this purpose, as a "nil" profit). Profits for this purpose are trading profits, as adjusted for taxation purposes *but before* capital allowances, balancing charges, stock relief claims or claw-back or any loss relief.

Once profits for a tax year have been averaged the revised assessment is taken into the calculation of the average profit for the next pair of years.

Example 1—total relief

	Original £	1st Revision £	2nd Revision £
1983–84	18,000	15,000	—
1984–85	12,000	15,000	19,500
1985–86	24,000	—	19,500

Example 2

	Original £	1st Revision £	2nd Revision £
1983–84	16,000	8,000	—
1984–85 (£4,000 loss)	Nil	8,000	10,000
1985–86	12,000	—	10,000

Partial relief
Marginal relief applies where the profits of one year exceed 70% of the profits of the other year but do not exceed 75% thereof. This is achieved in effect by a transfer of profits from one year to the other, the amount transferred being found by comparing the profits of the two years, multiplying the *higher* profit by 3 and taking 75% of the product (i.e. effectively multiplying by 2.25), and deducting therefrom 3 times the *lower* profit. The difference is then deducted from the higher profit and added to the lower profit, the effect of this transfer being to reduce the difference in the two profits without giving full averaging.

Example 3—partial relief

Original profits:	1984–85	£32,000
	1985–86	£23,000

	£
3 × 0.75 = 2.25 times higher profit	72,000
Less 3 times lower profit	69,000
Transfer	£3,000

	Original £	Transfer £	Revised £
1984–85	32,000	− (3,000)	29,000
1985–86	23,000	3,000	26,000

Effect of discontinuance
Averaging is not allowed for the profits of a year in which a trade is set up or discontinued nor where on a change of partnership, the change is treated as a

discontinuance. However, an election under s. 154, I.C.T.A. 1970, for a continuation allows the averaging provisions to apply. A claim for relief must be made within two years after the end of the second of the two years concerned. However, if after making a claim for averaging, the profits of either or both of the years are adjusted the averaging claim becomes invalid and, if appropriate, a new claim must be made. The new claim must be made within two years of the year of assessment in which the adjustment is made. Where a loss is taken into an averaging claim as a "nil" profit, the loss remains available for relief in all the usual ways. Furthermore claims already made for other relief may be amended as a result of an averaging claim. Provision is made for further claims, for revised claims, or for the withdrawal of claims provided action is taken within the time limit for the averaging claim and before the averaging claim has been determined.

Once an averaging claim has been made for a particular year, it is not possible to go back and make a claim for an earlier year.

Any adjustment of profits following an averaging claim is ignored by the Inland Revenue in deciding whether, on a discontinuance, the profits assessed for the two years of assessment preceding the year of cessation should be increased to the actual profits thereof. The adjustments are also ignored in computing relevant income for stock relief under the "old" system (see Chapter 6, § 2).

Definitions
Farming and market gardening are defined in s. 526(5), I.C.T.A. 1970 in relation to the activity undertaken on farm and market garden land respectively. "Farm land" is land in the U.K. wholly or mainly occupied for the purpose of husbandry, but *excluding*:
    (i) any dwelling or domestic offices;
    (ii) market garden land.
"Market garden land" is land in the U.K. occupied as a nursery or garden for the production or sale of produce (other than hops). The definition of "land" is all land in the U.K., so that a trade of market gardening or farming will include all land in the U.K. so utilised.

§ 12.—FARMERS—ANIMAL STOCKS

Animals kept by a farmer for the purpose of farming are treated as trading stock *unless* an election is made for the herd basis.

HERD BASIS (s. 139 and Schedule 6, I.C.T.A. 1970)

Introduction
An election for the herd basis applies to all *production herds* of a particular class including herds which the farmer first begins to keep after the election. The election, once made, is irrevocable.

An election must be made in writing to the Inspector stating the class of herds to which it relates and must be made within two years after the end of the *first* chargeable period whose profits are affected by the commencement of the production herd.

Example 1—election period

Bovine who has been farming for many years making up accounts to 30th April starts a sheep herd on 30th June 1985.

The herd commences during the year ended 30th April 1986. This forms the basis of assessment for 1987–88 so the election can be made any time up to *5th April 1990.*

This position may be altered where a loss arises in the year in which the herd commences (whether or not from the herd) and relief is claimed under s. 168, I.C.T.A. 1970. In this case the rules as to the election is the same (i.e. two years after the year first affected) but the time limit may well be shorter.

Example 2—effect of loss on election

Assume that in Example 1 Bovine incurred a loss during the year the sheep herd commenced and that relief under s. 168, I.C.T.A. 1970 is claimed.

The first chargeable period affected in this case is 1985–86, (i.e. the year of loss) and the election would therefore be required by *5th April 1988.*

The time limit for election is altered where the whole or substantial part of a herd is slaughtered by Government or local authority order, and compensation becomes payable. In these circumstances an election will be valid if made within two years of the chargeable period affected by the compensation *notwithstanding* that the normal time limit would have expired.

Following the abolition of stock relief as from 13th March 1984, an election for herd basis can now be made for the period of account beginning on or after 13th March 1984 and subsequent periods provided it is made within two years of the end of that period. The election is only valid for the profits in the period of account beginning after 13th March 1984 and subsequent periods.

The election applies to *all* species producing the same product (e.g. Jersey and Friesian milking cows) but separate elections will need to be made for herds of different species (e.g. cows, pigs, sheep etc.) *or* herds producing different products (e.g. dairy and beef herds).

Types of animals
(*a*) *Mature animals*
The herd basis election applies only to *mature* production herds. A female animal is mature when it produces its first young, laying birds are mature when they first lay.

An exception to the maturity rule is where the land on which the herd is kept is such that animals which cease to form part of the herd can only be replaced by animals bred on the same land (e.g. particular breeds of sheep—Romney Marsh sheep).

(*b*) *Production herd*
A production herd is a herd of the same species (irrespective of breed) which is kept for the sale of the products obtainable from the living animal. A product obtainable from the living animal is:
(i) The young of the animal;
(ii) Any other product, not being a product obtainable by slaughter.

(*c*) *Living creatures and animals kept singly*
Creatures other than animals and animals kept singly provided the criteria above are satisfied are also eligible for herd basis treatment.

(*d*) *Excluded animals*
No election can be made for working animals, or animals kept for public exhibition, racing or other competitive purposes.

Consequences of election
(*a*) *General*
The effect of a herd basis election is that the herd in general is treated as a fixed asset. The original cost of the herd and *additions* are ignored for trading purposes, and the disposal of the whole herd or a substantial reduction in the herd number is not treated as a trading receipt (see below for isolated sales).

Immature animals included in trading stock which on becoming mature are added to the herd are included as trading receipts (as a normal stock disposal) but the value to be included is:

(i) In the case of a home-bred animal, the cost of breeding and rearing;

(ii) In any other case, the original cost and rearing costs.

(*b*) *Replacement animals*

(i) *Partial replacement*

Where an animal dies or is sold *and* is replaced, any proceeds from the disposal are treated as a trading receipt, whilst the replacement animal is treated as a trading expense.

Where the replacement animal is of better quality than the animal it replaces, the trading expense is limited to the replacement value of the animal ceasing to belong to the herd. In the converse case (i.e. the replacement animal being of inferior quality) the trading receipt is *only* restricted where the animal ceasing to belong to the herd has been slaughtered by Government or local authority order.

Example 3

Farmer Rupert's dairy herd has the following transactions in 1985:

Disposals	£
Sales: 6 cows	420
Deaths: 2 cows (proceeds for carcasses)	100

Replacements:	
10 cows (same quality) @ £80	800

Rupert's adjustments to his trading account will be:

Trading receipts	£520
Trading expense 8 @ £80	£640

The additional 2 cows will simply be herd acquisitions for which no trading adjustment is required.

(ii) *Whole herd replacement*

Where the whole herd is sold *and replaced* by a similar production herd, the trading adjustments apply as above to the *smaller* herd; the balance of animals is ignored as a trading receipt or expense.

Example 4

Farmer Emu sells the whole of his beef herd consisting of 65 animals for £250 each and replaces them with 60 animals costing £300 each. The replacement animals cost £20 more than an animal of similar quality to those sold. The trading account adjustments are:

	£
Trading receipt	
60* @ £250	15,000

	£
Trading expenses	
60** @ £280	16,800

---

* Limited to the smaller herd.

** Limited to the replacement value of the herd sold.

(*c*) *Sales without replacement*
    (i) *Isolated sales*

Any profit or loss arising from the sale of a herd animal, or the sale of animals *not* amounting to a substantial herd reduction, is treated as a trading receipt (or expense if a loss). The profit/loss is the difference between the sale proceeds and the cost of sale; the latter is calculated:
    (1) In the case of a home-bred animal, as the cost of breeding and rearing to maturity.
    (2) In any other case, as the original cost together with the cost of bringing the animal to maturity.

Example 5

Farmer Cossack sells 14 sheep from his herd (not amounting to a substantial reduction) for £35 each.

Cossack bred the sheep himself and the estimated cost of breeding and rearing to maturity is £20 per sheep.

The profit to be added to the trading account is £210 as follows:

	£
Sale proceeds: 14 @ £35	490
Cost of sale (breeding and rearing) 14 @ £20	280
Profit to trading account	210

    (ii) *Sale of whole or substantial part of herd*

As previously mentioned the sale of the whole herd or substantial part (understood in practice to be 20%) does not give rise to any trading account adjustments.

The disposal will be of a wasting chattel so that no capital gains tax will apply.

If however within a period of five years from the sale date the seller acquires or begins to acquire a production herd of the same class, the replacement provisions apply. In the case of disposals outside the seller's control the amount to be included as a trading receipt, where animals of inferior quality are acquired, will be equal to the replacement cost of the inferior animal.

The date at which the sale proceeds are brought into account where replacement occurs in the five-year period is at the date of the corresponding acquisition.

A farmer ceasing to keep production herds of a particular class for five years shall for future periods be deemed never to have kept herds of that class.

Anti-avoidance

A transfer in whole or part of a production herd at a price lower than market value where either:
    (*a*) the transferor is a body of persons controlled by the transferee or the transferee is a body of persons controlled by the transferor, or both the transferor and transferee are bodies of persons controlled by another; or
    (*b*) it appears that the sole or main benefit accruing from the transfer was a benefit resulting from the obtaining of a right to make a herd basis election;
results in market value being substituted for the transfer price.

In this context "body of persons" includes a partnership.

Application to trades other than farming
The provisions as to election apply with the necessary adaptation equally to trades other than farming.

Accounting information
Detailed records of animals forming the production herd are necessary, since the Inspector of Taxes is at liberty to request such returns as to the animals and products of the animals (or other creatures) kept for the purposes of the trade. The Inland Revenue have produced forms for this purpose (refer to Revenue pamphlet IR9), although any reasonable form of recording and registry is likely to be accepted.

Stock relief (Schedule 9, Para. 25, F.A. 1981)
Animals forming part of the herd are *not* eligible for stock relief. In the case of an election taking place during a period of account, animals forming the herd are disregarded in ascertaining the trading stock at the end of the preceding year of account. Unrecovered stock relief is apportioned according to the respective values at the time the election is made (note that stock relief no longer applies for periods of account beginning after 12th March 1984—see Chapter 6).

§ 13.—DEALERS IN LAND (s. 142, I.C.T.A. 1970)

As dealers in land often sell land by granting a lease for a premium and reserving an annual rental, the premiums have been deemed a receipt of the trade and the unrealised freehold reversion has been included in stock at the lower of cost or market value.

In the case of leases requiring the straightforward payment of a premium, or where a premium becomes payable by reason of a surrender of the lease or a variation or waiver of any of the terms of the lease, the premium to be brought in as a trading receipt is reduced by the amount assessed under Case VI, Schedule D or Schedule A.

Example

A partnership which deals in land and buildings makes up its accounts annually to 31st March. On 30th June 1984, it granted a lease of land to Mac Ltd for 16 years in consideration of a premium of £20,000 in addition to a yearly rental.

For 1984–85 the Schedule A assessment will be:

	£
Premium...	20,000
Less: $\dfrac{16-1}{50} \times £20,000$	6,000
Schedule A assessment................................	£14,000

The amount that will be included as a trading receipt for the year ended 31 March 1985 will be as follows:

	£
Premium...	20,000
Less: Amount assessed under Schedule A	14,000
Trading receipt, Case I, Schedule D year 1985–86..........	£6,000

Where an amount is treated as a premium on the subsequent assignment of a lease at undervalue or on the sale of land with a right to reconveyance, the amount to be treated as a trading receipt is the amount treated as a premium less the part thereof which is assessed under Schedule A. Where the amount treated as a premium is adjusted at a later date under the provisions relating to the sale of land with a right to reconveyance, the adjusted amount shall be brought into account and an additional assessment will be raised or a repayment of tax will be made accordingly.

If a person is a dealer in land he will be entitled to relief under Schedule 3, I.C.T.A. 1970, in respect of the Schedule A assessment but this does not affect the amount to be brought in as a trading receipt. Because part of the premium is charged on an actual basis in the year of receipt and the remainder is charged in trading profits, normally on the preceding year basis, such a transaction will affect two years of assessment. It is quite probable that the property leased will have been bought just before the lease commences and the purchase must be brought into account.

§ 14.—AUTHORS AND ARTISTS (ss. 389 to 392, I.C.T.A. 1970)

AUTHORS' COPYRIGHTS

There are specific provisions relating to lump sums received by authors for the sale of copyrights assessable under Case II, Schedule D whereby it is possible for the amount received to be spread over a period not exceeding (depending on circumstances) three years (s. 389, I.C.T.A. 1970). For the spread to apply the author must:

    (1) assign the copyright or grant an interest by licence in the copyright; and

    (2) be engaged on the work for more than twelve months.

The income spread then follows that of artists (see below).

There is additional relief where the sum is received not less than ten years after the first publication of the work. This relief depends on whether the copyright is assigned or granted for a period greater or less than six years. Where it is for a period of, or exceeding, six years, the amount will be treated as receivable in six equal instalments, at yearly intervals, commencing on the date of receipt. If it is for less than six years, the receipt is spread over a number of instalments equal to the number of whole years. No relief is available if the copyright is assigned or granted for a period of less than two years (s. 390, I.C.T.A. 1970). In the case of copyright royalties paid to owners resident outside the U.K., tax must be deducted from the payment as if the payment fell within s. 53, I.C.T.A. 1970.

The term "copyright" does not include dramatic work incorporated in a cinematograph production or photographic artistic work (s. 391, I.C.T.A. 1970). The rate of withholding tax (currently 30%) is subject to reduction or elimination under the terms of any applicable double tax treaty (see Chapter 13).

ARTISTS' RECEIPTS

Where an artist receives a sum for the sale of a painting, sculpture or other work of art and he spent more than 12 months on making the work of art or it was one of a number of works of art made for an exhibition which required more than 12 months' work on them, he may spread the receipts as follows:

    (*a*) Where the time spent does not exceed 24 months, then, for tax purposes, one half of the payment shall be treated as having become receivable on the date it was actually due, the remaining half being treated as receivable 12 months preceding that date.

    (*b*) Where the period taken does exceed 24 months one third of the amount of the payment shall be regarded as being receivable on the actual date it was due, one third being treated as receivable 12 months earlier, and the other third, 24 months prior to the due date (s. 392, I.C.T.A. 1970).

§ 15.—DIVERS AND DIVING SUPERVISORS (s. 29 F.A. 1978)

Divers and diving supervisors, engaged in operations concerned with the exploration and exploitation of the seabed, its subsoil and their natural resources, within the territorial waters of the United Kingdom, or the designated areas of the continental shelf are taxed under Case I, Schedule D, as though carrying on a trade, and not, as might otherwise be the case as being employed and therefore taxed under Schedule E.

Schedule D liability only exists for 1978–79 onwards, so that where an individual has carried on diving operations before 6 April 1978 he is treated as setting up his deemed trade on that date (so that the commencement provisions will apply).

Persons making payments to divers have a duty to report such payments to the Revenue.

§ 16.—RELIEF FOR INDIVIDUALS TRADING PARTLY ABROAD (s. 27 F.A. 1978 and Part I, Schedule 4, F.A. 1978)

Following the Finance Act 1984, this relief, together with certain other overseas reliefs (see Chapter 7), is to be phased out.

The percentage relief (details below) is as follows:

Years prior to 1984–85	25%
1984–85	$12\frac{1}{2}\%$
1985–86 et seq.	Nil

Basis of claim

Relief can be claimed by self employed individuals (and members of partnerships) who whilst resident in the United Kingdom and carrying on a trade, profession or vocation within Schedule D, Cases I or II are absent from the United Kingdom in the course of that business on at least 30 *qualifying days*. The relief is $12\frac{1}{2}\%$ (see above) of the *relevant income* attributable to such qualifying days. Losses are similarly restricted. Note that these calculations are applied to the amount assessable for the year of assessment in which the absences from the United Kingdom occur and not to the profits generated by the overseas visits (i.e. the preceding year basis applies).

A qualifying day is either:

(*a*) a day on which an individual is absent from the United Kingdom and during which his time is substantially devoted to the activities of the trade, etc; or

(*b*) a day which is one of at least 7 consecutive days on which an individual is absent from the United Kingdom and during which period (taken as a whole), his time is substantially devoted to the activities of the trade; or

(*c*) a day on which the individual concerned is travelling wholly and exclusively for the purposes of the trade outside the U.K.

An individual is not regarded as absent from the United Kingdom on any day unless he is absent at the end of it. Time spent on board a ship or aircraft only constitutes absence to the extent that the journey begins or ends outside the United Kingdom. For this purpose the designated areas of the Continental Shelf are treated as being part of the United Kingdom. *For purposes of the computation of the relief relevant income is income from the trade etc. after taking account of capital allowances and balancing adjustments and of stock relief or claw-back but before taking account of loss reliefs.*

For any year of assessment the proportion of relevant income from a trade, etc. which is attributable to the qualifying days is the proportion which those days bear to 365 days. If the individual did not carry on the trade throughout the year the proportion is reduced rateably. If a day is a qualifying day for more than one trade it is, for the purpose of these calculations, divided equally between them.

Where an individual is a member of a partnership his relevant income is the share of the profits of the trade, calculated on the same basis as for a sole trader, attributed to him for the year of assessment concerned. If on a change of partners, a partnership is, for the purposes of computing tax discontinued that discontinuance is also effective for this relief, as is an election for continuation.

The $12\frac{1}{2}\%$ deduction is ignored in computing relevant income for stock relief purposes.

4. Schedule D, Cases I and II (continued)

§ 1.—PROFITS FOR INCOME TAX PURPOSES

INTRODUCTION

The general rule for the computation of profits for income tax purposes is to compute the full amount of the profits subject to certain allowances and to certain prohibitions of deductions.

In most cases where a trade is carried on accounts will be prepared. Usually these will take the form of a Profit and Loss Account and Balance Sheet, but other forms of account may be met, e.g. Receipts and Payments Accounts, Income and Expenditure Accounts.

The preparation of the Profit and Loss Account and Balance Sheet of a business is to some extent a matter of temperament, and is largely influenced by individual circumstances. For example, one firm may decide to provide for every doubtful debt or contingency, while another may aim at making provisions under these headings as small as possible. Again, one sole trader may charge against his business profits expenses which another would regard as personal.

In order, therefore, to obtain a reasonably equitable distribution of the burden of Income Tax, it has been necessary to make very definite rules as to the calculation of profits for Income Tax purposes. At first glance some of these rules appear to be arbitrary, but it must be realised that it is the intention of the legislature to treat every taxpayer on the same basis, and an appreciation of this fact will be of material assistance in obtaining a proper understanding of the principles upon which such rules are founded. _The general principle is that only revenue_ (as distinct from capital) _profits are assessable and only those expenses "wholly and exclusively laid out or expended for the purposes of the trade or profession" may be allowed._

Before proceeding to the consideration of particular adjustments it is important to understand the underlying legal principles involved. Thus in respect of a receipt it is necessary to consider whether the sum in question is of a capital or revenue (i.e. income) nature, and, if the latter whether it is a receipt of the trade. Similarly, an item of expenditure may be capital or revenue and if the latter consideration must be given to whether the amount is, following the ordinary rules of accountancy and in the absence of a specific statutory prohibition, a proper deduction in arriving at the taxable profits of the trade.

RECEIPTS

There is, unfortunately, no statutory definition of "capital" or "revenue". It can, however, be stated as a general rule that a receipt which is connected with the fixed capital (i.e. property acquired for retention and employment in a business with a view to profit) of a trade is not a trading receipt, but an item connected with the circulating capital (i.e. property acquired or produced with a view to sale at a profit) should be included in trading profits.

In most cases this distinction is not difficult to make. For example in a manufacturing business the factory, plant and machinery and goodwill of the business are clearly fixed capital which the trader will use for generating profits. Any receipt derived from the sale of such an asset would be a capital receipt. In contrast stock in trade, debtors and cash comprise the circulating capital of the trade in that raw materials would be bought, subjected to a process or otherwise worked-up and sold again within a relatively short time as completed goods.

There are, however, cases where it is not immediately clear as to whether a receipt is of a revenue (income) nature or of a capital nature. For these marginal cases it is necessary to look not only at the nature of the asset concerned but also at dealings with that asset in the context of the particular trade. For example in a manufacturing business an item of plant or machinery would usually be regarded as a capital asset and a sum received on the disposal thereof would be a capital receipt. But if the plant and machinery was itself manufactured by the trader and sold by him that sale would give rise to trading receipts.

It will be noted that a capital asset need not be tangible (e.g. a building or plant and machinery) but can be intangible (e.g. a lease).

(a) Receipts excluded from profits.

Examples

    (1) Dividends, and interest received under deduction of tax, should be excluded from the adjusted profit as they have already suffered tax. Such interest as is received gross is strictly assessable under Case III, Schedule D and should similarly be deducted, although in practice small amounts of untaxed interest may be allowed to remain in the Case I computation.

    (2) The letting of property is not an operation of trade so any rent received should normally be excluded. The liability in respect of rents received falls under Schedule A in the normal way. Where property is leased for the purposes of the trade and then sublet, it is common practice to include small amounts of rent receivable as a trading receipt, and deduct the rent payable. However this, as in the case of interest, is not strictly correct.

    (3) Capital profits upon the sale of fixed assets should be excluded as such a surplus is not assessable in the normal way but should be taken into account in the capital allowances computation or be subject to Capital Gains Tax.

    (4) Where insurance monies are quantified with reference to the diminished value of a capital asset, and not with reference to loss of profits, they are not a revenue receipt.

    (5) Any re-transfer from a reserve or provision which was disallowed at the time it was made, would also be deductible.

(b) Taxable receipts which may not appear in the accounts.

Sums may be received, which are "income" for tax purposes, but which are not credited in the Profit and Loss Account. Such amounts must be included in profits for taxation purposes.

Examples

    (1) Sums recovered in connection with stock destroyed by fire. However the cost of the lost stock would have been a deductible expense in computing profits.

    (2) Compensation received for cancelling an agency is assessable as trading income. (*Anglo-Persian Oil Co. Ltd* v. *Dale* (1932).)

EXPENDITURE

It has already been noted that for an item of revenue expenditure to be a proper deduction in computing the taxable profits of a trade that expenditure must be properly deductible in the accounts of the trade following ordinary commercial accounting principles provided that there is no specific statutory prohibition on the deduction of the expenditure concerned.

The general rule as to those deductions which are not allowable in computing taxable profits of a trade are contained in s. 130 I.C.T.A. 1970.

Section 130, I.C.T.A. 1970 lays down restrictions upon the items which may be deducted in computing profits. In particular it prohibits deduction in respect of:

(*a*) "*Any disbursements or expenses, not . . . wholly and exclusively laid out or expended for the purposes of the trade, etc. . .*"

Examples

(1) It was held that expenditure, incurred on an anti-nationalisation campaign, was wholly and exclusively for the purposes of the trade because it was, in effect, to ensure the survival of the company and therefore allowable for taxation purposes. (*Morgan* v. *Tate & Lyle* (1954))

(2) Payment by a company of a sum to a director as a compromise to prevent the director bringing an action against the company and certain staff members was held not to be deductible. (*Hammond Engineering Co. Ltd* v. *C.I.R.* (1975).

(3) A company ceased business on 31st March and paid its manager a sum representing the six months' notice to which he was entitled, to 30th September following. This was held not as payment to enable the company to carry on its business, and so not deductible. (*Godden* v. *A. Wilson's Stores* (*Holdings*) *Ltd* (1962))

(4) The costs of making an appeal to the Commissioners against a Schedule D assessment are not an allowable deduction for income tax purposes. (*Allen* v. *Farquharson Bros. & Co* (1932))

(5) Accountancy charges relating to a taxation appeal are not an admissible deduction, as they are not incurred for the purposes of earning the profits of the trade. (*Smith's Potato Estates Ltd* v. *Bolland* (1948))

(6) A colliery company which was required by the local Drainage Act to execute or pay for remedial works necessary to obviate or remedy loss of efficiency of a surface drainage system agreed to contribute a sum towards the cost of a comprehensive scheme devised by the Drainage Board which eliminated the need for remedial work. The contribution was paid by sixty half-yearly instalments and was held to be payments on account of capital which are not allowable deductions in computing the company's liability to income tax.

(7) Where a barrister practises in chambers in London and also at his private residence during the evenings and weekends, the expenses of travelling between residence and chambers are not allowable deductions for income tax purposes. (*Newson* v. *Robertson* (1953))

(8) Where a building sub-contractor travels from his home to the building site on which he is currently working the travelling expenses are an allowable deduction. The appellant's house is regarded as the location of the trade even though a minimal amount of business activity, e.g. the bookkeeping, may be carried on there. (*Horton* v. *Young* (1972))

(9) In return for a payment of £2,000 a company acquired the right to remove sand and gravel from certain land, but without acquiring any estate or interest in the land. It was held that the £2,000 was not a trading expense. The sand and gravel was not detached from the soil and was a natural deposit, and the transaction was not the acquisition of trading stock.

(*b*) *Losses not in connection with the trade.*

Examples

(1) Damages recovered by a guest whilst staying at an inn and who was injured by a chimney which fell in were not allowed, on the grounds that

the loss fell on the taxpayers in their capacity of "householder" and not that of "trader". (*Strong & Co of Romsey Ltd* v. *Woodifield* (1906))

(2) Where a man holds an office and also carries on a profession, the expenses of the office not allowed for purposes of Schedule E cannot be deducted from the assessment of the liability under Schedule D in respect of profits of his profession, as these Schedules are mutually exclusive.

(c) Capital expenditure

Examples

(1) A firm bought land for the purpose of open-cast mining, and covenanted to reconvey the land to the vendor after working and reinstatement. It was held that the amount paid was capital expenditure for taxation purposes.

(2) A timber merchant made payments under agreements to purchase timber, by which he had the right to enter the lands of the forest owners to fell and remove the trees at an unspecified future date, the property in the trees remaining with the sellers until that time. It was held that the payments were capital payments and not payments for stock in trade.

"Capital expenditure" has been defined as expenditure, "not only once and for all, but with a view to bringing into existence an asset or an advantage for the enduring benefit of trade." "Enduring" refers to a benefit which "endures in the way that fixed capital endures; not a benefit that endures in the sense that for a good number of years it relieves you of a revenue payment." (*Atherton* v. *British Insulated & Helsby Cables Ltd* (1926)—a leading case)

Abortive expenditure may be capital expenditure "if it be made 'with a view' to bringing an asset or advantage into existence. It is not necessary that it should have that result." (*McVeigh* v. *Arthur Sanderson & Sons* (1969))

(d) Expenditure on improvements to premises (specifically prohibited though "capital expenditure" in any event).

(e) Repairs to premises or for the renewal of implements or utensils except in so far as the sum is actually expended.

Example

A sum set aside to meet the cost of renewals under a contractual obligation will not be allowed if the renewals are not actually carried out. (*Merchant (Peter) Ltd* v. *Stedeford* (1948))

Disputes frequently arise between the Revenue and the taxpayer with regard to repairs to business premises, and whilst the principle involved is relatively simple, its practical application may be more difficult.

If expenses are incurred in erecting a new structure 'in its entirety' so that a new capital asset is created the expenses are clearly of a capital nature and are therefore not allowable deductions in arriving at trading profits. The replacement of an entirety (i.e. a distinguishable separate structure having no physical connection with any other part of an industrial plant) is a capital expenditure (*O'Grady* v. *Bullcroft Main Collieries Ltd* (1932)) but the renewal of a part of an existing structure is not (*Jones (Samuel) & Co.* v. *Devondale Ltd* (1951)). Expenses incurred in the maintenance or reconstruction of an existing asset are generally allowed as a revenue expense. There are, of course, borderline cases which depend on their own circumstances.

If repairs and improvements are mixed there is no provision for an apportionment of the total expenditure between repairs and improvements.

Repairs accumulated before use in the business are not allowable if the expenditure is necessary to bring the asset up to standard. Such expenditure is capital and therefore is disallowed as a charge on the profits of the trade (*C.I.R. v. Law Shipping* (1923)). Where the asset is capable of use before the expenditure is incurred, it is likely to be treated as a repair (*Odeon Associated Theatres Ltd v. Jones* (1972)). In this case some importance was placed on the accounting treatment, which had treated the expenditure as a repair. This importance was clarified in the case of *Heather* v. *P.E. Consulting Group Ltd* (1972), when the Court of Appeal made clear that whether expenditure is capital or revenue is a matter of fact for the Court to decide.

(*f*) *Business interest* is allowable, whether the interest is short or annual (ss. 130(6) and 519(1) I.C.T.A. 1970). A deduction will be available for interest paid on money used as capital in the business (s. 130(f) I.C.T.A. 1970 proviso). Hire Purchase interest is not really "interest", and the so-called "interest" element is really a hire charge for the use of the asset and may be deducted in the same way as such a hire charge.

(*g*) *Debts, other than bad debts or doubtful debts estimated to be bad.* A general bad debt provision to cover contingent bad debts is not allowed. A provision for discounts on debtors' accounts may be allowed, if it is reasonable and on a consistent basis from year to year.

As well as these general rules prohibiting the deduction of certain expenditure, specific prohibitions may also apply (e.g. entertaining United Kingdom customers) (s. 411, I.C.T.A. 1970). Likewise a number of deductions are specifically allowed to be made in computing the taxable profits of a trade, even though under the general rules outlined above the expenditure would not be allowable:

—Expense of obtaining a patent or registering a design or trade mark; (s. 132, I.C.T.A. 1970)

—Payments for technical education at a university, college etc., provided the technical education is related to the trade; (s. 133, I.C.T.A. 1970)

—Expenditure on scientific research of a kind related to the trade of a revenue rather than a capital nature. This also applies for payments to scientific research associations, universities etc.; (s. 90, C.A.A. 1968)

—An employer's ordinary contributions paid in the period concerned to an approved or partly approved superannuation fund. (s. 21, F.A. 1970)

—Statutory redundancy payments. (s. 412, I.C.T.A. 1970; s. 41, F.A. 1980)

—Payments to charities (s. 54, F.A. 1980)

—Relief for class 4 N.I. contributions (50%) (s. 42, F.A. 1985).

ADJUSTMENT OF PROFIT PER ACCOUNTS FOR TAX PURPOSES

In only the very simplest cases will the profits of a business, as disclosed by the Profit and Loss Account, coincide with the profits for Income Tax purposes. A number of adjustments will usually be found necessary.

These adjustments fall into four main classes:

1. ITEMS WHICH HAVE BEEN CHARGED AGAINST PROFITS BUT WHICH ARE NOT ALLOWED AS DEDUCTIONS FOR INCOME TAX PURPOSES

(*a*) Capital expenditure or capital losses.

(*b*) Personal expenses of the proprietor.

(*c*) Appropriations of profit.

(*d*) Any payment, from which tax is deducted at the time of payment (except for mortgage or loan interest paid to a non-resident by a partnership or sole trader).

(*e*) Expenses or losses not connected with the business.

(*f*) Contingent losses and reserves.

(*g*) Depreciation (since relief is given by way of capital allowances—see Chapter 5).

2. ITEMS WHICH HAVE BEEN CREDITED TO THE PROFIT AND LOSS ACCOUNT BUT WHICH MAY PROPERLY BE ELIMINATED FOR INCOME TAX PURPOSES.

(*a*) Capital profits or capital receipts.

(*b*) Dividends, royalties, etc., from which tax has been deducted at the source.

(*c*) Interest, etc., received "gross" but which is assessable separately under Case III, Schedule D.

(*d*) Transfers from reserves of undistributed profits.

(*e*) Profits not arising out of the business.

3. DEDUCTIONS WHICH, THOUGH ALLOWED FOR INCOME TAX PURPOSES, MAY NOT HAVE BEEN CHARGED IN THE PROFIT AND LOSS ACCOUNT, e.g., an allowance for a premium paid on a lease of premises used for business purposes (s. 134, I.C.T.A. 1970) or class 4 N.I. contributions.

4. ITEMS WHICH HAVE NOT BEEN CREDITED IN THE PROFIT AND LOSS ACCOUNT BUT WHICH SHOULD BE INCLUDED IN TRADING PROFITS FOR INCOME TAX PURPOSES, e.g., a profit which the company has regarded as a capital profit but which has to be treated as trading profits for income tax purposes.

The above points as to expenditure and receipts deductible or taxable respectively are now summarised in the following section.

§ 2.—SUMMARY OF ALLOWABLE AND NON-ALLOWABLE DEDUCTIONS AND RECEIPTS

DEDUCTIONS ALLOWED

Subject to the specific items enumerated below, which are not allowed as deductions from profits for Income Tax purposes, it may be stated that all disbursements and expenses *wholly and exclusively laid out or expended for the purposes of the trade or profession* may be deducted. What is money wholly and exclusively laid out for the purpose of the trade or profession is essentially a question of fact to be determined (by the Commissioners on appeal if necessary) from the precise circumstances of each case (see above).

The principal deductions allowed are as follows:

(1) Rent of premises occupied for business purposes, including rent in lieu of notice. (s. 130(c)) (Allowance is also given in respect of a premium paid on a lease of premises used for business purposes. (s. 134, I.C.T.A.)

(2) Local rates, lighting, etc., subject to apportionment where the proprietor resides on the premises

(3) Repairs to plant, buildings, tools, utensils, office machinery, fixtures and fittings, etc., but not expenditure upon the reconstruction of buildings even if undertaken in lieu of repairs; there being no provision for the allowance of a notional amount for repairs not done. (s. 130(d), I.C.T.A. 1970)

Any element of improvement is disallowed, and it is not permissible to deduct a provision (as against an accrued liability) for the cost of replacements to be made in the future.

(4) Renewals of plant, fixtures, etc., where no capital allowances have been or are claimed (see Chapter 5, § 5).

(5) Removal expenses (provided of a forced character, e.g., compulsory acquisition for road-widening purposes). In practice, the Inland Revenue frequently take a more lenient view and other expenses of this nature may be allowed. The expenses of removing plant and machinery, where not allowed as a deduction from profits, may be added to the cost of

the asset for the purpose of computing capital allowances (Chapter 5, § 5).

(6) Bad debts and doubtful debts to the extent that they are respectively estimated to be bad. (s. 130(i), I.C.T.A. 1970) (In practice, a specific provision against individual debts will be allowed, but not, as a general rule, a provision arrived at on an arbitrary basis as a percentage of the total debts.) An allowance will not be granted in respect of bad debts outside the usual course of business, e.g., certain loans made to employees which prove irrecoverable.

(7) Interest expended for business purposes (ss. 130(f) and 519(1), I.C.T.A. 1970).

Where the interest paid is expended for a qualifying purpose under s. 75 or Schedule 9, F.A. 1972 (as amended by s. 19 and Schedule 1, F.A. 1974), the payer may choose whether to claim relief as a business expense or against total income. The method chosen must be consistently followed.

(8) Interest paid abroad where tax has been deducted or the provisions of s. 131(2) I.C.T.A. 1970 satisfied.

(9) Instalments paid under hire-purchase agreements, to the extent that such payments represent a charge in respect of the "hire" of the asset (i.e., excluding the capital repayments). The hire charge is to be spread evenly over the period of the agreement.

(10) Legal expenses, if of a revenue nature, e.g., in connection with (i) collecting book debts, (ii) settling disputes with customers, (iii) defending existing trade rights, and (iv) preparing service agreements. Legal expenses in connection with the *renewal* of a lease are allowed, provided that the renewal is for a period of not more than 50 years.

(11) A payment to protect the title to land abroad, used for the purposes of the business.

(12) A payment to compromise an action regarding a revenue item.

(13) Patent renewal fees, and any fees paid or expenses incurred in obtaining the original grant of a patent (including the costs of an unsuccessful application for patent rights—s. 132, I.C.T.A. 1970), together with a writing-down allowance in respect of capital expenditure incurred on the purchase of patent rights, as explained in Chapter 5, § 9.

(14) Any fees paid or expenses incurred in obtaining the registration of a design or a trade mark, or the extension or renewal thereof (s. 132, I.C.T.A. 1970)

(15) Copyright royalties, paid or payable, unless taxed at source (see "Deductions not allowed," item (2)).

(16) Expenditure of a non-capital nature on scientific research (see Chapter 5, § 10).

(17) Payments for the purposes of technical education related to the particular trade at any university or other approved institution (s. 133, I.C.T.A. 1970)

(18) All remuneration paid to employees (provided that it is *bona fide* remuneration and assessed on the recipients) is deductible. This includes not only normal wages or salary but also any bonuses and benefits provided to the employee such as board and lodging, uniforms etc. Pensions paid to former employees are allowed.

Redundancy payments under the Redundancy Payments Acts, including payments in excess of the statutory redundancy scheme limit up to three times the statutory amount (s. 412, I.C.T.A. 1970), levies to Industrial Training Boards and other payments of like nature are allowable deductions for tax purposes but any rebates or refunds under those schemes are assessable. A deduction is allowed for the whole amount of an employer's social security contribution (but not for domestic servants etc. employed by householders in that capacity). Payments in respect of employee welfare including employee outings are an allowable deduction and not normally assessed on the employees.

(19) Compensation for loss of office provided the "wholly and exclusively" rule is satisfied.

(20) Ordinary annual contributions to superannuation funds, provided that the fund is approved by the Board of Inland Revenue.

(21) Advertising, unless of a capital nature, e.g., expenditure on a permanent sign (other than a renewal) would *not* be allowed.

(22) Premiums for insurance against fire, burglary, employers' liability, plateglass, etc., employers' social security, etc., contributions. Premiums for insurance against consequential loss of profits following a fire will be allowed but any sums which may be subsequently recovered under the policy must be brought into account.

Where an employer takes out a policy to cover the loss of profits consequent upon the injury or death of a key employee, the premiums are normally an allowable deduction, and receipts are trading profits, unless the policy is intended to cover a capital loss (e.g., goodwill), or, if the insurance is against death, unless the policy is a long-term one, or if the premiums are endowment and made for the directors by a family company (*Dracup (Samuel) & Sons Ltd* v. *Dakin* (1957)).

(23) Losses of cash and stock by fire, theft or embezzlement not covered by insurance, but not losses of fixed assets, e.g., plant and machinery (although a balancing allowance may be made in respect of these, see Chapter 5, § 5).

Defalcations by an employee are allowed but not those by a partner.

(24) Subscriptions to, or levied by, a Trade Association if the Association has agreed with the Board of Inland Revenue to be assessed on its own surplus income. If the Association has not entered into such an agreement, then the subscription is only deductible to the extent that it has been applied by the Association for purposes which if expended by the trader would have been deductible.

(25) Subscriptions and donations to institutions for the benefit of employees or their dependants, e.g., trade benevolent funds, or staff sports funds. Charitable donations also qualify if made wholly and exclusively for the purposes of the trade.

(26) Gratuities are allowable if they are a form of advertising, e.g., Christmas gifts, if the gift incorporates an advertisement for the donor, is not food, drink, or tobacco, or in the form of a token or voucher exchangeable for goods, and the total cost of all gifts by the donor to any one donee does not exceed £2 per annum (s. 411, I.C.T.A. 1970).

(27) Cost of raising loan finance (s. 38, F.A. 1980). The incidental costs of raising loan finance, such as fees, commissions, advertising etc., previously regarded as of a capital nature, qualify for tax relief. For a loan to qualify, the interest on it must rank as a trading deduction or, in the case of a company, be treated as a charge on income. The loan *must not* carry the right of conversion into or acquisition of shares or securities within a period of three years. Relief also extends to providing security for the loan and repaying it, as well as abortive expenditure. Any premium payable on repayment or any discount on issue, together with stamp duty and sums paid to protect against currency fluctuations, are specifically *excluded.*

(28) Pre-trading expenditure (s. 39, F.A. 1980). Business expenditure before

a trade commences, previously regarded as of a capital nature, now qualifies for relief (see Chapter 3, § 4).

(29) Contributions to "approved local enterprise agencies" (i.e. those approved by the Secretary of State), provided the contributor derives no benefit from the contribution (s. 48, F.A. 1982).

(30) Employee expenses where employee is seconded to a charity (s. 28, F.A. 1983). Applies to both corporate and non-corporate traders.

(31) Regional development grants, which would be treated as a revenue receipt (s. 54, F.A. 1984). This contrasts with interest relief grants, etc. under s. 7 or 8 of the Industry Act which are expressly subject to tax (s. 42, F.A. 1980).

(32) Class 4 National Insurance contributions. One half of the contribution is deductible for 1985–86 onwards.

DEDUCTIONS NOT ALLOWED

Various classes of deductions not allowed for Income Tax purposes are set out in general terms in s. 130, I.C.T.A. 1970. The more important items not allowed are as follows:

(1) Sums not wholly and exclusively laid out for the purposes of the trade, etc.

(2) Any annual payment from which Income Tax is deducted at the source other than interest e.g., annuities, patent royalties, mine royalties, etc. (This does not apply to copyright royalties, since these are not taxed at the source, unless paid to non-residents.) Mortgage or loan interest paid to a non-resident by a partnership or sole trader, from which income tax must still be deducted at source, unless the conditions of s. 131(2), I.C.T.A. 1970 are satisfied, or where withholding tax is excluded by a double tax treaty, is an allowable deduction.

(3) Appropriations of profit, e.g., sums transferred to reserve, interest on partners' capital, partners' salaries or drawings, Income Tax, Capital Gains Tax, etc.

(4) Sums invested or employed as capital in the trade or on account of capital withdrawn therefrom.

(5) Sums expended on improvements or additions to premises, plant, machinery, fixtures, etc., or amended fire precautions or exit arrangements to satisfy the local authority, or on the acquisition of know-how.

(6) Sums written off for depreciation of land, buildings, leases, plant, fixtures, exhaustion of mineral deposits, etc.

(7) Preliminary expenses; cost of raising finance (but see (28) above for deductions allowable in certain cases); bonus paid on the repayment of borrowed money, etc., but allowable if incurred after 1st April 1980 subject to certain conditions (see (27) above.)

(8) Any other expenditure of a capital nature which must be added back because it is not a proper charge against the income of the trade when computing the profits.

(9) Hypothetical rent-charges by an owner-occupier are disallowed.

(10) Legal expenses, if (i) of a capital nature, e.g., in respect of conveyancing or a deed of partnership, or (ii) incurred in defending a breach of the law, or (iii) incurred in connection with an appeal against an Income Tax assessment, whether successful or not. Legal charges in connection with an appeal against a rating assessment are, however, allowable. Fines and penalties for breaches of the law are disallowable as losses "not connected with or arising out of the trade." Costs of successfully refuting allegations of breaches of the law or contracts are, in general, allowable.

(11) Personal expenses of the proprietor of a business, or goods consumed from stock by the proprietor, e.g., living expenses of an hotel proprietor and his family.

(12) Travelling expenses of the proprietor of a business between residence and business premises. Other travelling expenses wholly and exclusively laid out for the purposes of the trade are allowable.

(13) Business entertaining expenses, unless for the entertainment of an overseas customer on a reasonable scale or for a business gift not exceeding £10 and displaying a conspicuous advertisement (food, drink and tobacco are not eligible).

(14) Rent of any dwelling-house or private accommodation; except such part thereof as is used for the purpose of the trade or profession.

(15) Losses of a capital nature, e.g. (i) losses incurred on the sale of investments by a manufacturing concern; (ii) or payment for the cancellation of a contract for the construction of a fixed asset; (iii) or those not arising out of the trade.

(16) Losses recoverable under an insurance or other contract of indemnity.

(17) Subscriptions and donations, other than those mentioned above under "Deductions Allowed".

(18) Life assurance premiums on the life of a sole proprietor or partner(s).

(19) United Kingdom Income Tax and Capital Gains Tax.

(20) Interest on arrears of Income Tax and Capital Gains Tax.

(21) Overseas tax for which a credit is allowable (see Chapter 13), but a deduction may be claimed for overseas tax for which credit is not available due to there being no equivalent amount assessed to tax in the United Kingdom. Overseas taxes not having the nature of a tax on income are normally allowed in deducting profits.

(22) A proportion of any payment for hire of an ordinary motor car if the retail price when new exceeds £8,000. The amount of such hire payments which is allowed is in the proportion which £8,000, together with one half of the excess, bears to the original retail price.

INCOME TO BE ELIMINATED

The following items, where credited to the Profit and Loss Account, should be eliminated in order to determine the balance of profit for taxation purposes under Cases I and II:

(1) Capital profits, e.g., a profit on the sale of land, buildings, investments, or other assets, *unless it is part of the business to deal in such assets*; a receipt for surrender of rights, receipts from the sale of know how (but see Chapter 5 § 11, as to the treatment for Income Tax purposes where certain categories of assets are sold for sums greater than the residual value). A capital profit, although excluded for Income Tax purposes, may fall within the scope of Capital Gains Tax.

(2) "Casual" profits or profits unconnected with the trade.

(3) Income from which tax has been deducted at source, e.g., debenture interest, dividends, etc.

(4) Building society interest (see Chapter 11, § 12).

(5) Interest which is received gross and which is separately assessable under Case III, Schedule D, e.g., bank deposit interest, interest on $3\frac{1}{2}$ per cent War Loan.

(6) Repayment supplement on overpayments of tax (see Chapter 1, § 23).

(7) Any other profits or gains which are assessable under another Schedule or another Case of Schedule D, e.g., profits from the letting of a furnished house, which are assessable under Case VI, Schedule D.

(8) Bad debts subsequently recovered and specific provisions for bad debts previously allowed and no longer required must be left in to the credit of the Profit and Loss Account as a profit for Income Tax purposes because they will have been allowed as a deduction for Income Tax purposes on their origin; but general provisions for bad debts previously disallowed and subsequently written back should be eliminated as they will not have been allowed as a deduction on their origin.

(9) Grants receivable under ss. 7 or 8 of the Industry Act 1972 or the corresponding Northern Ireland provisions made towards the cost of specified capital expenditure or as made by way of compensation for the loss of capital assets. Grants under these provisions and not designated as made towards the cost of specified capital expenditure or as made by way of compensation for the loss of capital assets are treated as taxable income.

ITEMS ASSESSABLE AS TRADING RECEIPTS

The adjustment of accounts for tax purposes may involve the addition of sums which are assessable as trading income but which have not been credited in the Trading and Profit and Loss Accounts. Amongst the items which may be involved are:

(1) Sums recovered under policies of insurance on items which are current assets (e.g. the full amount recovered from the insurer of stock destroyed by fire must be included as a trading receipt).

(2) Compensation, in so far as it goes to fill "a hole in the profits" rather than a "hole in the capital," e.g., compensation received upon the cancellation of an agency agreement.

(3) Sums recovered under insurance policies on the lives of employees where the premiums were allowed against profits.

(4) Subsidies, e.g., a ploughing-up grant, but not those on capital account (see Chapter 5 for effect on capital allowances).

(5) Copyright royalties, and, in the case of a person carrying on the profession of an author or writer, sales of copyright.

(6) Amounts received by a successor to a discontinued business which would have been taxable had the business not been discontinued are assessed as post-cessation receipts.

(7) Trade debts previously allowed as a charge for Income Tax purposes are assessed if they are released. If released after discontinuance they are treated as post-cessation receipts.

§ 3.—METHOD OF ADJUSTING ACCOUNTS FOR TAX PURPOSES

The usual method adopted in practice of adjusting the accounts of a business for Income Tax purposes is as follows:

(1) Take the *net profit* as shown by the Profit and Loss Account.

(2) *Add back* any items debited in the account which are *not allowed* to be charged. It is advisable to adopt a systematic approach, for example working *upwards* from the net profit, considering each item in turn.

(3) *Deduct* (i) any items credited in the account which may properly be eliminated, and (ii) any items which, though not charged in the account, may be deducted for Income Tax purposes.

(4) *Add* any items which have not been credited in the profit and loss account but which should be included in trading profits for Income Tax purposes.

Where a *net loss* is shown in the Profit and Loss Account the above procedure will be reversed.

The following example illustrates the method of arriving at the assessment.

Example

The Profit and Loss Account of Joan Smith, a retail shop-keeper, for the year ended 31st December 1984, was as follows:

PROFIT AND LOSS ACCOUNT FOR THE YEAR ENDED 31ST DECEMBER 1984

	£		£
Wages and salaries	5,600	Gross profit	15,560
Light and heat	330	Dividends	200
Travelling and enter-		War loan interest	
taining..................	700	(untaxed)	210
Rates....................	410	Profit on sale of shares	800
Bank interest	100		
Sundry expenses...........	1,930		
Bad debts................	230		
Advertising	720		
Repairs	140		
Mortgage interest	750		
Depreciation of lease	950		
Income tax*	360		
Net profit	4,550		
	£16,770		£16,770

Of the travelling and entertaining, £150 represents the cost of a season ticket from Smith's residence to her business and £200 is in respect of entertaining U.K. customers. The item of Sundry Expenses includes £200 for a life assurance premium.

Show Smith's assessment under Case I, Schedule D, for 1985–86.

JOAN SMITH: INCOME TAX COMPUTATION, 1985–86

	£	£
Net Profit as per profit and loss account for the Year ended 31st December 1984		4,550
Add: Income tax.....................	360	
Depreciation of lease.............	950	
Life assurance premium	200	
Travelling and entertaining	350	
	—	1,860
		6,410
Deduct: Dividends	200	
War loan interest (untaxed)	210	
Profit on sale of shares	800	
	—	1,210
Assessment, 1985–86.......		£5,200

---

* Income Tax would not normally be charged to the Profit and Loss Account of a sole trader, but direct to his Capital or Current Account. It is included in this case merely for illustrative purposes.

Notes.

Wages and salaries.   It is assumed that nothing is included in this item in respect of Smith's drawings.

Travelling and entertaining.   The cost of a season ticket from Smith's residence to her place of business will not be allowed, as it is an expense of a personal nature. Entertaining is only allowable in respect of overseas customers.

Sundry expenses.   It is assumed that, apart from the Life Assurance Premium added back, no inadmissible expenditure is included.

Life assurance premium.   No deduction from profits can be made in respect of this item.

Bad debts.   It is assumed that this represents debts actually written off as bad, or is a provision in respect of specific doubtful debts.

Advertising.   This item would be allowed unless capital items are included therein.

Mortgage interest.   Mortgage interest (assuming paid in connection with the business) is deductible. Relief if applicable can be claimed under s. 75 F.A. 1972 if more beneficial (a claim under s. 75 precludes a business relief claim, but any excess can be treated as a trading loss.)

Dividends.   Not assessable under Case I, Schedule D.

War loan interest (untaxed).   This interest is separately assessable under Case III, Schedule D, and must therefore be eliminated.

Profit on sale of shares.   As the business is not one dealing in shares, this is a capital profit and is therefore not assessable to Income Tax under Schedule D, Case I (although there may be a chargeable gain for the purposes of Capital Gains Tax).

§ 4.—SPECIAL CONSIDERATIONS

BUSINESS ENTERTAINING EXPENSES (s. 411 I.C.T.A. 1970)
Expenses incurred in providing business entertainment are not allowable as a deduction against profits charged under Schedule D. Similarly any asset for providing business entertainment shall be treated as used otherwise than for the purposes of a trade. This does not apply where an *overseas* customer is concerned. However, the entertainment must be of a kind and on a scale which is reasonable having regard to all circumstances.

Business entertainment is defined as entertainment (including hospitality of any kind) provided by a person or by a member of his staff in connection with a trade carried on by that person, but does not include anything provided by him for bona fide members of his staff unless its provision for them is incidental to its provision also for others.

Entertainment expenses are exempted from this provision where the cost of a gift does not exceed £10 (£2 prior to 5.4.85) per person per year and the gift incorporates a prominent advertisement for the donor. Such gifts must not be in the form of food, drink, tobacco or a token or voucher for goods.

Furthermore the provision by any person of anything which is provided by him in the ordinary course of his trade for payment, or with the object of advertising to the public generally gratuitously, is an allowable deduction. Thus the cost of samples is allowable as is, for example, the cost of providing music by a restaurateur.

LEGAL CHARGES
Legal expenses are normally allowed in the following circumstances:
  (*a*) Recovery of debts.
  (*b*) *Renewing* leases for less than fifty years.
  (*c*) Defending trade disputes, breaches of contracts, defending title to assets.
  (*d*) Obtaining business loan finance.
Legal expenses which are *not* allowable include:
  (*a*) Acquiring freehold or leasehold land and buildings.
  (*b*) Acquiring a fixed asset.
  (*c*) Penalties, fines and legal costs arising from breaches of the law.

SCIENTIFIC RESEARCH (s. 90. C.A.A. 1968)
Expenditure which is incurred by a person carrying on a trade, on scientific research, is normally allowable in full as a deduction against the profits of the trade.

SUBSCRIPTIONS
Subscriptions paid to a trade association are allowable provided the association is approved by the Board of Inland Revenue.

In certain cases, the subscription may be partly disallowed depending on the use the association makes of its funds (e.g. N.F.U.).

Before 1980–81, charitable subscriptions were allowed by concession (B7), but, provided wholly and exclusively incurred, are now statutorily deductible (s. 54 F.A. 1980).

RELIEF FOR LEASE PREMIUMS PAID (s. 134 I.C.T.A. 1970)
Where the payer of an amount, treated as a premium paid under the lease, uses the property acquired for the purposes of his trade he is given relief in addition to any rent paid under the terms of the lease in the following manner.

Relief is given each year on the amount chargeable appropriate to that year. For this purpose the amount chargeable is deemed to be the amount assessed on the recipient without taking into account any relief afforded by the 3rd Schedule, I.C.T.A. 1970. The period to be taken into account is that taken as the duration of the lease.

Example 1

Peacock acquired a leasehold interest in factory premises to be used for his trade, on 30th September 1984. The term of the lease was 30 years and Peacock paid a premium of £40,000. Accounts are made up annually to 31st December.

For the accounting year to 31st December 1984 and the next 29 accounting years Peacock will be able to deduct £560 from his chargeable profits in respect of the premium, computed as follows:

	£
Premium paid	40,000
Less: $\dfrac{30-1}{50} \times £\,40,000$.	23,200
Chargeable amount	£16,800
Period of lease	30 years
Annual deduction $\dfrac{£16,800}{30}$ = ...	£560

Partial usage

Where part only of the land acquired is for the purposes of the trade, the amount to be treated as additional rent will be reduced proportionately.

Example 2

Suppose that in Example 1 Peacock ceased to use one-quarter of the premises for the purpose of his trade on 1st January 1989. A like proportion of the annual deduction will be disallowed and accordingly from that accounting year the deduction will be limited to $\frac{3}{4} \times £560 = £420$. For the year 1990–91 therefore Peacock will only be entitled to deduct £420.

Improvement to lease

Where the cost of work carried out by a tenant is deemed to be a payment of a premium, it shall be disregarded for purposes of the above relief if a claim for capital allowances may be made for it.

Example 3

Assume that in Example 1, Peacock was required to install in the premises under the terms of the lease certain equipment that became the property of the owner on the expiry of the lease. The cost of such equipment was £10,000.

The owner would then be deemed to have received a premium of £50,000 in respect of the lease but as Peacock would claim capital allowances on the equipment, the deduction he could make is calculated only by reference to the part of the premium not qualifying for such allowances, namely £40,000, and the deduction will be £560 as in Example 1.

Alteration of lease premium

Where an alteration is made to the amount of any lease premium the original deduction must be recalculated.

Example 4

Rental Ltd sold factory premises and land to Stokes and Weeks (who traded in partnership) on 30th September 1981 for £100,000 and under the contract reserved the right to reacquire the premises for £70,000 on 1st December 1986. As Rental Ltd wished to reacquire the premises on 31st December 1984, the parties agreed to an amendment to the contract whereby Rental Ltd reacquired the premises and land for £80,000 on that date.

Under the original contract Stokes and Weeks can deduct £5,520 from their profits annually, as follows:

	£	£
Consideration on sale	100,000	
Price on reconveyance	70,000	
Amount taken as a premium		30,000
Less: $\dfrac{5-1}{50} \times £30,000$.		2,400
Chargeable amount		£27,600
Annual deduction for 5 years:		
$1/5 \times £27,600$		£5,520

Consequent upon the amendment, the annual deduction will be recomputed as follows:

	£	£
Consideration on sale	100,000	
Price on reconveyance	80,000	
Amount taken as premium		20,000
Less: $\dfrac{3-1}{50}$ × £20,000		800
Chargeable amount		£19,200
Annual deduction for 3 years:		
1/3 × £19,200		£6,400

The assessments on Stokes and Weeks for the years concerned would be amended to include a deduction of £6,400. Such an amendment can be made even though the years affected are outside the normal six year limit.

Salary paid by husband to wife

An additional personal allowance (see Chapter 2, § 3) is claimable in respect of any earned income of a wife, irrespective of whether the income is derived from a source connected with the husband. A *bona fide* salary paid to a wife in respect of services rendered to her husband in his business may therefore be allowed as a deduction from profits (but see *Copeman* v. *Flood* (1941)).

Satisfactory evidence of payment and particulars of the services rendered will usually be required in these circumstances before the above-mentioned additional allowance will be granted.

Rents received

The position as to rents received and credited in the Profit and Loss Account may be summarised as follows:

(1) If the property from which the rents are derived is separate from the property occupied by the business, and is accordingly separately assessed under Schedule A (or Case VI, Schedule D, if let furnished), from the business premises, both the rents credited and the expenses (e.g., repairs, rates, etc.) debited will be eliminated in adjusting the Profit and Loss Account for Case I, Schedule D, purposes. The rents received and the repairs, etc., are eliminated in order to prevent a double assessment.

(2) If a portion of the business property is sub-let unfurnished the rents received should be eliminated from the accounts and any expenses which relate to the sub-let premises such as repairs, rates, etc., should be added back. The deduction for rent will require to be restricted to the proportion occupied for business purposes. In practice, however, if the expenses cannot easily be separated, both the rents received and the expenses may be retained in the account, the total rent paid together with the total expenses in connection with the whole property, being allowed as deductions.

Example

The Profit and Loss Account of G Ellis for the year ended 31st August 1984, was as follows:

PROFIT AND LOSS ACCOUNT FOR THE YEAR ENDED 31ST AUGUST 1984

	£		£
Wages and salaries	15,000	Gross profit	28,450
Sundry expenses.	9,500	Rents received.	750
Annuity	1,000		
Net profit for year before			
taxation.	3,700		
	£29,200		£29,200

G. Ellis owns the property he occupies, a portion of which is sublet at £250 per annum. He also owns a house which is let at £500 per annum.

Included in sundry expenses is £300 for repairs, of which £100 is in respect of the house. It is required to show the Case I, Schedule D, Assessment for 1985–86.

G. ELLIS. INCOME TAX COMPUTATION: 1985–86

	£	£
Net profit as per Profit and Loss Account		
for the year ended 31st August 1984		3,700
Add: Annuity	1,000	
Repairs to property	100	
		1,100
		4,800
Deduct: Rents received (see note)		500
Case I, Schedule D, Assessment, 1985–86		£4,300

Note. The statutory income from the house will be the subject of a separate assessment under Schedule A, in the appropriate circumstances—see Chapter 10, § 7. The rent received (£500) and the repairs (£100) in respect thereof are therefore eliminated from the Profit and Loss Account for Case I, Schedule D, purposes.

Often owing to the lack of information as to the extent of the sub-let portion of the premises, the rents received (and expenses in connection therewith) are, in practice, retained in the Profit and Loss Account.

Residence on business premises

Where a portion of the business premises is occupied by the proprietor as living accommodation, only that portion of the rent which is attributable to that part of the premises used for business purposes may be deducted. In practice not more than two-thirds is usually allowed, but the allowance is not necessarily restricted to this proportion (e.g., a greater allowance would be made in the case of a proprietor of a hotel or school, or alternatively an agreed sum may, in such cases, be added back in respect of the proprietor's board residence, and that of his wife and family (if any) unless employed in the business (otherwise than as a partner), the whole of the rent then being allowed as a deduction). A similar apportionment of such expenses as rates, light, heat, repairs, etc., will often be necessary. Any portion of the premises used solely for business purposes will be subject to capital gains tax on the disposal (see Chapter 29, § 13).

Example

James Brown, a retail greengrocer, lives on his own shop premises. His Profit and Loss Account for the year ended 31st December 1984 was as follows:

PROFIT AND LOSS ACCOUNT FOR THE YEAR ENDED 31ST DECEMBER 1984

	£		£
Wages and salaries	10,400	Gross profit	14,900
Rates.	750	Dividends	150
Lighting and heating	300		
Repairs to premises	300		
Bank interest	100		
Sundry trade expenses	450		
Net profit	2,750		
	£15,050		£15,050

The items of rates and light and heat represent his total expenditure in those directions. A charge of £100 per week for proprietor's salary is included in the charge for wages and salaries. One third of premises expenditure is private.

The assessment on James Brown for the year 1985–86 will be computed as follows:

	£	£
Net profit as per Profit and Loss Account for the year ended 31st December 1984.		2,750
Add: Repairs to premises (one-third).	100	
Lighting and heating (one-third)	100	
Rates (one-third)	250	
Proprietor's salary	5,200	
		5,650
		8,400
Deduct:		
Taxed dividends		150
Case I, Schedule D, Assessment, 1985–86 . . .		£8,250

Where an employee resides on business premises, the employer is entitled to deduct from his profits for Schedule D purposes the rent of the whole building, including the part used as a residence.

Profits from illegal transactions
When the Income Tax Acts charge tax on profits, no distinction is drawn between those from legal and illegal sources, and even if a trade or business is illegal, the profits can be assessed. Thus profits from street betting, though the latter is illegal, have been held to be assessable. (*Southern* v. *A.B.* (1933))

Profits from betting
Where a person attends race meetings and bets systematically, he is exercising a vocation (i.e., that of betting), and is liable to assessment thereon, the usual deductions in respect of losses and expenses being permissible (*Partridge* v. *Mallandaine*). On the other hand, a person who made his livelihood by betting on horses from his private address at starting prices only, has been held not to

be in receipt of profits or gains assessable to Income Tax, and not to be exercising a vocation. (*Graham* v. *Green* (1925))

No attempt is made to assess football pool winnings, but these are subject to a special levy upon the stake moneys.

§ 5.—ANNUAL PAYMENTS (OTHER THAN INTEREST)

Following the principle of collection of tax at the source, the tax in respect of any annual payments (e.g., annuities, patent royalties, etc.) paid out of profits or gains brought into charge to tax is collected from the person paying such charges, and not from the recipient.

The amount of the charges is not the subject of a separate assessment, but is included in the assessment on the profits or income out of which such payments are made, the amount charged in the accounts being added back in computing profits for Income Tax purposes. The theory is that the payer deducts tax from the annual payments and is thus recouped (see Chapter 1, § 12).

Payments out of profits brought into charge
The following example illustrates the method of dealing with annuities, etc., where the assessment is in excess of the annuity payable during the year of assessment concerned, i.e., where the annual payments are wholly payable out of profits or gains brought into charge.

Example 1

The Profit and Loss Account of Henry Smith, a sole trader, for the year ended 31 December 1984, is as follows:

PROFIT AND LOSS ACCOUNT FOR THE YEAR ENDED 31ST DECEMBER 1984

	£		£
Trade expenses	5,800	Gross profit	22,650
Wages and salaries	6,700		
Annuity	1,000		
Depreciation	550		
Net profit	8,600		
	£22,650		£22,650

For 1985–86 Smith will pay annuities of £1,200.
It is required to show Smith's assessment for 1985–86.

HENRY SMITH: INCOME TAX COMPUTATION, 1985–86

	£	£
Net profit as per Profit and Loss Account for the year ended 31st December 1984		8,600
Add: Depreciation	550	
Annuity	1,000	
		1,550
Assessment, 1985–86		£10,150

Notes. (1) In adjusting profits the amount of the charges paid in the accounting period (£1,000) is added back. The charges payable in 1985–86 are not the subject of a separate assessment since they are wholly payable out of profits or gains brought into charge, i.e., they do not exceed the 1985–86 assessment (£10,150).

(2) For 1985–86 Smith has a statutory income from his business of £10,150. The annual payments made in 1985–86 (£1,200) are however deductible in computing his "Net Total Income" (see Chapter 2, § 2).

Payments from insufficient profits

Where there are no assessable profits, or where the assessable profits are less than the annual payments (e.g., annuities, patent royalties, etc.), made in the year of assessment concerned (i.e., where the annual payments are *not* wholly made out of profits or gains brought into charge to tax), an assessment will be made on the amount by which the annual payments exceed the assessable profits and it is the duty of the taxpayer to render an account of such payments to the Inspector for this purpose.

Example 2

The Profit and Loss Account of F. Forward for the year ended 31st March 1985 is as follows:

PROFIT AND LOSS ACCOUNT FOR THE YEAR ENDED 31ST MARCH 1985

	£		£
Trade expenses............	52,000	Gross profit	137,500
Wages and salaries	68,000		
Annuity...................	10,000		
Depreciation..............	6,500		
Net profit	1,000		
	£137,500		£137,500

For 1985–86 F. Forward will pay an annuity of £20,000. It is required to show the assessments for 1985–86.

F. FORWARD: INCOME TAX COMPUTATION, 1985–86

	£	£
Net profit as per Profit and Loss Account for the year ended 31st March 1985........		1,000
Add: Depreciation........................	6,500	
Annuity.............................	10,000	
		16,500
Adjusted profit........................		£17,500
Schedule D Case I Assessment, 1985–86...........................		17,500
Annual payments to be covered.........		2,500
Assessment under s. 53, I.C.T.A. 1970		£20,000

Note. It will be observed that a taxpayer must, in one way or another, pay to the Inland Revenue in respect of any year of assessment *at least* the amount of tax deducted from any annual charges in that year.

A s. 53 assessment is only made where the annual payments of a year of assessment exceed the sum of the assessments otherwise raised and the gross amount of income which has suffered tax by deduction.

Example 3

The profits of J. Wood for the year ended 31st January 1985, as adjusted for income tax purposes, are £3,000. He receives dividends in 1985–86 amounting to £9,000.

In the year 1985–86 he pays annuities of £4,500 and patent royalties amounting to £2,000.

The Schedule D assessment for 1985–86 will be on the profits of the preceding year, i.e., £3,000; and this together with Dividends £9,000 (gross) = £12,000, which covers the Annuities (£4,500) and Royalties (£2,000), so there will be no s. 53 assessment.

A s. 53 assessment will also be made where an annual payment is charged to capital, even though there may be sufficient profits to cover the payment. Conversely, income credited to capital is regarded by the Inland Revenue as not available to cover annual payments charged to income.

§ 6.—VALUATION OF STOCK-IN-TRADE AND WORK IN PROGRESS

As previously explained, the Schedule D, Case I or II profit is based in the first instance on normal accounting principles. In preparing the accounts, it is normal to value stock at the "lower of cost, net realisable value or replacement price" and it is permissible to value certain items, or certain groups, on any of these bases, i.e., not to take a global evaluation.

As regards work in progress, the accountancy profession regards as acceptable any one of the following methods of valuation:

(1) Prime cost;
(2) Marginal cost, i.e., prime cost plus variable overheads; or
(3) Prime cost plus all overheads.

The prime cost of an item is the sum of the wages, materials and expenses directly expended thereon, while overheads are costs which cannot be directly allocated to any particular article but which must be apportioned over production.

The stock value used in the accounts will normally be acceptable for tax purposes, although not in all cases. In particular, some adjustment may be required where there has been a change in the method of valuation. Set out below is the Inland Revenue practice concerning changes in the basis of valuation, together with a note from the Inland Revenue concerning the application of Statement of Standard Accounting Practice no. 9 in relation to stock valuation.

INLAND REVENUE PRACTICE WITH REGARD TO A CHANGE IN THE BASIS OF STOCK VALUATION (published in the *Accountant*, 17th November 1962)

"Change in basis of stock valuation

"1. The Revenue accepts any method of computing the value of work in progress and finished stock which is recognised by the accountancy profession, so long as it does not violate the existing statutes as interpreted by the courts. Such a basis is referred to in this note as a 'valid basis'. The expression 'non-valid basis' is used to denote a basis which does not accord with the standard of acceptability referred to in the first sentence of this paragraph, and includes a valuation which, although in form made on a recognised basis, gives insufficient regard to the facts. Having regard to the principle of consistency, there would need to be good reason for any change in an existing valid basis.

"*Change from one valid basis to another valid basis*
"2. Where a change from one valid basis to another valid basis is accepted, certain consequences normally follow. The opening stock of the basis year of change is valued on the same basis as the closing stock. Whether the change is to a higher or lower level, the Revenue normally does not seek to revise the valuations of earlier years. It neither seeks to raise additional assessments, nor does it admit relief under the 'error or mistake' provisions.
"3. It is not possible to define with precision what amounts to a change of basis. It is a convenience, both to the taxpayer and to the Revenue, not to regard every change in the method of valuation as a change of basis. In particular, the Revenue encourages the view that changes which involve no more than a greater degree of accuracy, or a refinement, should not be treated as a change of basis, whether the change results in a higher or a lower valuation. In such cases the new valuation is applied at the end of the year without amendment of the opening valuation.
"4. What constitutes a good reason for change in the existing basis is a question to be answered by reference to the facts of each case. Possible examples of such justified changes are that of a company absorbed by a group and adapting its basis to the group's principles, or a concern adjusting its basis to conform to some alteration in the nature of its trade.

"*Change from a non-valid basis to a valid basis*
"5. When a change in the basis of valuation is first made from a non-valid basis to a valid one, the new basis is applied to both the opening and closing values of the year of change. In addition, a review is made of past liabilities, but in cases where there is no question of past irregularities (that is, fraud, wilful default or neglect) the Revenue would not in any event seek to recover tax for past years or an amount greater than that involved in the uplift of the opening valuation of the year of change."

EXTRACT FROM STATEMENT OF STANDARD ACCOUNTING PRACTICE NO. 9 (SSAP 9) (APPENDIX 3)

"*This appendix is for general guidance and does not form part of the Statement of Standard Accounting Practice.*
"The accountancy bodies have received the following statement from the Board of Inland Revenue in response to their request for clarification of the Revenue's practice on the publication of SSAP 9, *Stocks and Work in Progress.*

"*Changes in basis of valuation*
"1. After the publication of N22, the Revenue explained their practice with regard to changes in basis of valuation in a statement published in the *Accountant* on 17th November 1962. The practice set out in that statement applies to changes made as a result of the adoption of SSAP 9 in the following way. References to stock in trade cover manufacturing work in progress but not professional work in progress or work under long-term contracts.
"2. First, the basis set out in SSAP 9 will be regarded as a valid basis, and will be accepted as a good reason for a change from a previously valid basis. Therefore on such a change the opening stock of the year of change is to be valued on the same basis as the closing stock of that year. Whether the change is to a higher

or a lower level, the valuations of previous years will not be revised. Further assessments for past years will not therefore be raised nor will relief under the 'error or mistake' provisions be admitted on this account.

"3. Where the existing basis of stock valuation is valid under recommendation N22 and is such that the adoption of the new standard could be argued to be merely a refinement and not a change of basis, the Revenue will be prepared to accept a valuation of the opening stock in the year of change by reference to the new standard, *i.e.* the argument that there has only been a refinement, so that the opening valuation should be the same as the closing valuation of the preceding year, will not be used.

"4. Where stock has been brought into accounts in the past on a basis which was not a valid basis under recommendation N22 the Revenue must reserve the right to review past liabilities. However, where there is no question of past irregularities (i.e. fraud, wilful default, or neglect), the Revenue would not in any event seek to recover tax for past years on an amount greater than that involved in the uplift of the closed valuation of the year preceding the year of change to a valid basis within the old code.

"5. These comments are made on the basis of existing law and practice. The Revenue reserve the right to reconsider their attitude in the event of any change in the law, and in any case, at the expiry of 3 years.

"*Discounted selling price*

"6. Where stock is valued at current selling prices less the normal gross profit margin in the circumstances described in paragraph 4 of Part I of the Statement, the valuation will be acceptable only if the further test, set out in paragraph 14 of Appendix I to the Statement is clearly satisfied. It it considered that the selling price to be used for the purpose of discounting should normally be the original price fixed for the article determined by operating the normal mark-up on the original price.

"*Replacement cost*

"7. Where the value of the raw material content forms a high proportion of the total value of stock in process of production and the price of the raw materials is liable to considerable fluctuation, it is common practice to make rapid changes in selling prices to accord with the changes in the price of the raw material. In cases of this kind the replacement cost basis may be extended to cover stock in process of production and finished stock as well as to the stocks of raw material.

"*Long-term contracts*

"8. When a loss on a contract as a whole is foreseen, a proportion of the overall loss, calculated either by reference to time normally up to the due completion date under the terms of the contract, or to expenditure incurred, may normally be taken into account year by year during the remainder of the contract period so long as all contracts, profitable or otherwise, are dealt with similarly. Further, when the work on a long term contract has been substantially completed, so that it is possible to assess the financial outcome of the contract with reasonable certainty, the Inland Revenue do not normally object to account being taken, at that point, of the foreseeable further expenditure representing obligations arising out of the contract up to the time of final delivery and also of a reasonable provision to allow for expenditure under any guarantee or warranties included in the contract. Beyond these limits it is not permissible for tax purposes to take account of expenditure which has not then been incurred. It follows that a provision for an expected future loss made in accordance with paragraph 9 of Part I of the Statement would be disallowed for tax purposes to the extent that it is in excess of the amount determined above.

"9. Where there is a change in the basis for treatment of long-term contracts, the opening figure in the year of change must, for taxation purposes, be the same as the closing figure for the preceding year. The Inland Revenue will not accept a claim for a tax-free uplift based on the grounds that the opening and closing figures in the year of change must be on the same basis. Alternatively, the Inland Revenue would accept the continuance of the existing basis for long-term contracts current at the beginning of the year of change, with the new basis being applied only to contracts entered into in or after the year of change."

TRADING STOCK CONSUMED BY THE TAXPAYER

Where a trader takes goods from his trading stock for the enjoyment of himself and his household, the Revenue insist upon the inclusion of the retail market value of the goods consumed in the computation of profits for tax purposes (*Sharkey* v. *Wernher* (1956)). In a wholesale business, the wholesale price is employed.

Where, however, services are rendered by the business to its proprietor or his household, these should be valued at cost, without addition for profit.

In the same way, where a trader incurs expenditure upon the construction of fixed assets, the appropriate sum to capitalise is the cost of the work done.

Example

Before adjustment for the undermentioned items, the accounts of John Benbow for the year ended 30th June 1984, show a profit of £10,800.

It is ascertained that:

(i) Benbow, who is a grocer, has withdrawn from his trading stock goods which cost him £1,000 and which he would normally sell for £1,120 for the use of himself and his family.

(ii) An assistant has employed his spare time: (*a*) in constructing shop fittings estimated to be worth £2,450, (*b*) in repainting the shop front (value of work done estimated to be £500) and (*c*) in decorating a bedroom (value of work done estimated to be £120). It is estimated that the cost of the assistant's services was: (*a*) £1,100, (*b*) £250 and (*c*) £60. The materials involved have already been treated correctly in the accounts.

Ignore Capital Allowances.

JOHN BENBOW INCOME TAX COMPUTATION, 1985–86.

	£
Profit for the Year ended 30th June 1984	10,800
Add: Market value of goods consumed	1,120
Cost of assistant's time:	
Capital work—construction of shop fittings	1,100
Decorating bedroom	60
Assessment, 1985–86	£13,080

§ 7.—CASH BASIS

Certain professionals, such as surgeons and counsel, keep their accounts on a cash basis, on the grounds that they cannot sue for their fees. That is to say, whilst expenditure is charged on the normal accruals basis, income is only credited when received.

POST-CESSATION RECEIPTS

(*a*) *Position prior to 1968*
Any sums collected after the cessation of the business were, prior to the Finance Act 1968 (now incorporated in the Income and Corporation Taxes Act 1970), regarded as being covered by the assessments made upon it during its continuance, and were not therefore assessable unless they fell within the special provisions of ss. 143, 145, 146, 147, 148, 149 and 151, I.C.T.A. 1970. The previous practice was to insist upon the preparation of Income and Expenditure Accounts upon the normal accruals basis for at least the first three years. If a change to the cash basis was then made, cash receipts from debtors outstanding at the date of the changeover were then brought into account as cash received.

(*b*) *Current position*
Sections 144, 146, 150 and 151, I.C.T.A. 1970 provide that where, after 19th March 1968, a trade, profession, etc., which has been previously assessed on the "cash basis", is permanently discontinued, or is so treated for tax purposes, or changes its basis so that receipts may drop out of assessment, all sums received on or after the discontinuance or change, which arise from the carrying on of the trade, etc., in any period prior to the discontinuance will be assessable under Case VI, Schedule D to the extent that they are not otherwise assessable to tax, or fall within the provisions of ss. 143, I.C.T.A. 1970 (post-cessation receipts). There are provisions for the deduction of expenses, losses and unused capital allowances in arriving at the amount assessable.

In the case of an individual who was born before 6th April 1917, and was carrying on the trade, etc., at 18th March 1968, any net amount chargeable upon him under Case VI, Schedule D is reduced by 5% for each year, or part year, by which his age on 5th April 1968 exceeded 51 years, up to a maximum of 75% if he was then 65 or over. An individual born on 1st January 1916 would be taxable on 90% of the net amount, while an individual born in 1900 would be taxable on 25% of the net amount.

The Case VI, Schedule D assessment is treated as earned income if the profits for earlier years qualified as such.

Where a sum is received in any year of assessment beginning within six years of the discontinuance, etc., an election may be made within two years after that year of assessment for the sum to be treated as received on the date of discontinuance, or on the last day before the change of basis.

§ 8.—COMPREHENSIVE EXAMPLE

Frank Penrose has been in business for eight years, making up accounts to 30th September annually. His Profit and Loss Account for the year ended 30th September 1984, is as follows:

	£	£
Sales		390,000
Less: Cost of sales—		
Purchases	290,000	
Add: Stock at 1st October 1983	40,000	
	330,000	
Less: Stock at 30th September 1984	60,000	
		270,000
Gross profit		120,000

	£	£
Wages..................................	76,000	
Rates and ground rent	6,500	
Insurance................................	4,400	
Repairs and renewals	14,600	
General expenses.........................	23,000	
Depreciation.............................	12,000	
		136,500
Net loss		£16,500

You are given the following additional information:

(1) Wages includes £215 in respect of Penrose's personal class 2 N.I. contributions, and £2,080 paid to his wife who acts as bookkeeper-typist.

(2) Insurance includes loss of profits insurance £450.

(3) The charge for repairs and renewals includes £6,500 expended on the reconstruction of a warehouse. It is estimated that repairs to the original building would have cost £2,500. Also included in the charge is the cost of replacing two office desks, £200. Capital allowances are not claimed in respect of office furniture.

(4) The general expenses consist of:

Legal expenses:	£
Settling a dispute with a customer	315
Preparing service agreements	50
Protection of trading rights............................	200
Costs of successfully refuting allegations of breaches of the law in relation to the business.......................	350
Costs of successfully appealing against an Income Tax assessment..	200
Registration of a trade mark	100
Payment for the cancellation of a contract to build a new factory..	2,500
Cost of raising a loan.................................	500
Advertising...	3,000
Loss of cash by embezzlement by a cashier...............	2,100
Interest charged on hire purchase agreements.............	750
Other items (allowable)	12,935
	£23,000

(5) The class 4 N.I. contributions for 1985–86 amount to £276. (N.B. this would be calculated on the current profits less capital allowances and stock relief at 6.3%.)

Compute Penrose's assessment for 1985–86:

Ignore capital allowances and stock relief.

F. PENROSE INCOME TAX COMPUTATION, 1985–86

	£	£
Net Loss as per Profit and Loss Account for the year ended 30th September 1984		16,500
Deduct: Social Security—own	215	
Reconstruction of warehouse	6,500	
Legal expenses: Income Tax appeal	200	
Cancellation of contract to build new factory..............................	2,500	
Depreciation............................	12,000	
50% of N.I. contributions	138	
		21,553
Adjusted profit....................................		£5,053

Notes.

(1) The N.I. contributions of the proprietor of a business are merely a form of drawings.

(2) Where an asset is reconstructed in lieu of repairs, no deduction can be claimed for the notional cost of the repairs obviated by this course of action.

(3) The cost of replacing the two office desks is allowed as a renewal.

(4) It is assumed that the interest charged on hire purchase agreements relates solely to the period under review.

(5) Costs of raising loan finance are allowable.

(6) For 1985–86 onwards, 50% of the class 4 N.I. contributions are deductible.

5. Capital Allowances—Sole Traders and Partnerships

§ 1.—INTRODUCTION

EFFECT OF FINANCE ACTS 1984 AND 1985

In an attempt to promote efficient investment the Chancellor, in his 1984 Budget speech, outlined a radical change in the structure of providing tax relief for businesses.

The change outlined was to phase out in three annual stages initial and first-year reliefs for investments in capital equipment and buildings and to replace these with a lower rate of Corporation Tax (see Chapter 14). Writing-down allowance is, however, to remain, and the Finance Act 1985 introduces a quicker form of granting allowances for short-life assets and retains the 100% allowance for Scientific Research expenditure (see below).

The alterations made to allowances for capital expenditure enacted in the Finance Act 1984 refer only to machinery and plant, industrial buildings and assured tenancies, but the Finance Act 1985 enacts the changes for discontinuing other forms of initial allowance, namely on:

    (i) agricultural buildings
    (ii) hotels
    (iii) dredging

with effect from 1st April 1986. In addition expenditure on patents and know-how after 31st March 1986 will be written off by means of a 25% writing-down allowance.

Date expenditure incurred

The Finance Act 1985 also clarifies the definition on which the date expenditure for capital allowances is incurred. This now falls in line with generally accepted accounting treatment (see below for specific details).

Granting of relief

The Finance Act 1985 alters the date on which relief is given for writing-down allowances for *machinery and plant* by providing that relief is available on the date expenditure is incurred rather than the date on which the asset is brought into use. This has effect for periods of account ending after 31st March 1985. The system of allowances is also re-coded so as to differentiate between assets used wholly and exclusively for the purposes of the trade and others. The distinction for motor cars still applies and assets used partly for the trade are then segregated into a notional trade pool (see below).

All these provisions *apply equally to sole traders and partnerships.* Whilst allowances will continue to be available in some degree in the period up to 31st March 1986, after this date their relevance is very greatly reduced, and the detailed rules that follow should be read with this thought in mind.

GENERAL RULES

The Capital Allowances Act 1968 and F.A. 1971 (in respect of expenditure incurred on machinery and plant after 26th October 1970), as amended by subsequent Finance Acts, contain the provisions for capital allowances (i.e. deductions on account of "depreciation") in connection with:

    (1) Machinery and plant. (§ 5)
    (2) Industrial buildings and structures. (§ 6)

(3) Agricultural land and buildings. (§ 7)
(4) Mines, oil wells, etc. (§ 8)
(5) Capital expenditure on scientific research. (§ 10)
(6) Dredging. (§ 12)

The provisions relating to capital allowances in respect of patents are contained in the Income and Corporation Taxes Act 1970. Provision for capital allowances in respect of know-how is contained in ss. 386 and 387, I.C.T.A., 1970, and for cemeteries and crematoria, s. 141, I.C.T.A. 1970.

Although usually thought of in connection with Cases I and II of Schedule D and Corporation Tax, allowances also apply in other circumstances, e.g., an employee may in certain circumstances claim capital allowances against his Schedule E assessment.

ALLOWABLE EXPENDITURE

Capital allowances are given in respect of capital expenditure. Such expenditure is excluded in arriving at the amount of profits for the purposes of Schedule D, Cases I and II. Once it is established that capital expenditure has been incurred, it is necessary to identify the nature of the expenditure (see the list at the start of this chapter) and follow the rules for the type of expenditure concerned. If the expenditure does not fit into any of the categories for which capital allowances are given, no relief will be due.

EFFECT OF GRANTS

(a) *regional development grants*

These grants, paid under Part I of the Industry Act 1972, are payable in respect of expenditure incurred after 22nd March 1972 for certain buildings, new plant, machinery and mining works in development areas, special development areas and intermediate areas, and derelict land clearance areas, as defined. The cash grant, depending on the area, does *not* reduce the amount on which capital allowances are claimable (unlike other subsidies and grants). For example, if a trader received a regional development grant of 20% in respect of plant costing £100,000, he is entitled to claim a First Year Allowance (see below) on the whole £100,000, as well as receiving the grant.

(b) *other grants/subsidies (s. 84, C.A.A. 1968)*

Non-regional development grants towards the cost of capital assets have the effect of reducing the asset cost for Capital Allowance purposes. Grants under the Industry Act 1972 for *non* capital assets which are *not* regional development grants are treated as trading receipts (s. 42, F.A. 1980) (see § 4 below for further details).

FIXTURES (s. 59, F.A. 1985)

This legislation reverses the decision in *Stokes* v. *Costain Property Investment Ltd* (1984) where it was held that as lessee the taxpayer company was not entitled to capital allowances on fixtures which become part of the building since they belonged to the landlord (N.B. No relief was due to the landlord as no trade was carried on).

Thus for expenditure incurred after 11th July 1984 on building fixtures where a lease applies, an allowance is given to the lessee incurring the expenditure even though in law the asset belongs to the landlord.

Where there is any dispute in law as to whether a fixture is part of a building, the dispute for allowance purposes is determined by the Special Commissioners.

§ 2.—MANNER OF GRANTING RELIEF

Relief for capital allowances can be given in two ways:
(1) in taxing a trade,
(2) by discharge or repayment of tax.

The manner of relief which is appropriate in a particular case will depend upon the circumstances in which the allowances fall to be due.

ALLOWANCES GIVEN IN TAXING A TRADE (s. 70, C.A.A. 1968)
In general, capital allowances due to a trader in respect of assets used in his trade are given "in taxing a trade".

Allowances are given as a deduction from the assessment on trading profits (not as a deduction in arriving at the trading profits). If there are excess allowances, they may be used to create or augment a loss and relief claimed accordingly (see Chapter 7, Losses). Any unused allowances may be carried forward, without time limit, and deducted from future assessments on the profits of the same trade.

ALLOWANCES GIVEN BY DISCHARGE OR REPAYMENT OF TAX (s. 71, C.A.A. 1968)
Allowances given "by discharge or repayment of tax", are usually expressed to be available primarily against a specified source of income. The principal allowances given by discharge or repayment are:
(1) Agricultural buildings allowance
(2) Industrial buildings allowance where the building is leased.

Example

In 1984–85 Foodbotham builds a factory, for £100,000 available for industrial buildings allowance, which he then lets to Watchbender.

Foodbotham will be entitled to industrial buildings allowances (see § 6), which will be given by discharge or repayment of tax and will be available primarily against his income from letting the factory.

The basic rule for these allowances is that they are to be deducted from the income of the "primary" class for the year concerned, any excess being deductible from income of the same class in future years, without time limit.

SET-OFF AGAINST OTHER INCOME
If the allowances due exceed the "primary" source of income for the year of assessment concerned, the taxpayer may elect that the excess is deducted from his total income in the year the expenditure is incurred *and* the following year. Any excess still unutilised is then carried forward against future income from the "primary" source. An election must be made within two years of the end of the year of assessment in which the allowance would be relieved.

Example (first year relief)

Taking the facts from the previous example, the industrial buildings allowance due to Foodbotham for 1984–85 is £54,000 (see § 6 below). His rental income for the year is £4,500 and he has other income of £12,600. If Foodbotham makes an election to set excess capital allowances against his total income, his position will be as follows:

	£	£
Rental income		4,500
Less Capital allowances		4,500
		—
Other income		12,600
Total income		12,600
Excess capital allowances		12,600
Taxable income		Nil

Industrial buildings allowance	£	£
Amount due..............................		54,000
Used: Primary source....................	4,500	
Total income	12,600	17,100
Carried forward against rental income........		£36,900

Where an unused allowance due for one year is treated as forming part of the allowances due in the next year of assessment, and therefore eligible for set off against total income, set-off is made from allowances of the earlier year first.

Example (second year relief)

Continuing from the previous example, assume that in 1985–86 Foodbotham is entitled to a further industrial buildings allowance of £4,000. His rental income is £6,500 and his other income totals £14,200. If he elects to set all available excess capital allowances against his total income, his position for 1985–86 will be as follows:

	£	£
Rental income.............................		6,500
Less Capital allowances		6,500
		—
Other income.............................		14,200
Total income		14,200
Excess capital allowances...................		14,200
Taxable income...........................		Nil
Industrial buildings allowance		
Brought forward		36,900
Due 1985–86		4,000
		40,900
Used: Primary source....................	6,500	
Total income......................	14,200	20,700
Carried forward against rental income........		£20,200
Made up of: 1984–85 (balance)		16,200
1985–86		4,000
		£20,200

Since the 1984–85 allowances are used first, the allowance due for 1985–86 is still unused and may be added to a claim against total income for 1986–87. The balance of the 1984–85 allowances may only be carried forward against rental income.

RENEWALS

As an alternative to claiming capital allowances, it is possible to claim the cost of replacements (renewals basis—*Caledonian Railway* v. *Banks* (1880)). Any improvement on the original assets is not allowed to be charged, although it may be claimed as a capital allowance. The renewals basis is very rarely used in practice.

§ 3.—BASIS PERIODS (s. 72, C.A.A. 1968)

General position

Almost all the allowances granted or charges made under the Income and Corporation Taxes Act 1970 (as amended by subsequent Finance Acts), the Capital Allowances Act 1968 and the Finance Act 1971 are dependent, as regards any particular chargeable period, either upon the occurrence of a specific event (e.g., the incurring of capital expenditure on industrial buildings or structures) or upon the fulfilment of a specific condition (e.g., ownership and use of machinery and plant) in what is termed the "basis period" appropriate to that chargeable period.

The basic idea is quite simple: the basis period for a chargeable period is the period, the profits or income of which form the basis of the assessment for that chargeable period. The chargeable period for income tax purposes is the year of assessment. In the case of remuneration assessable under Schedule E the basis period and the chargeable period always coincide.

It is equally simple to ascertain the basis period of a chargeable period of a business assessed under Case I or Case II of Schedule D, where the business is a *continuing one*. Thus, if the accounts of A. Stephens are made up to 30th September, annually, the basis period for 1985–86 will be the year 1st October 1983, to 30th September 1984, and that for 1986–87 will be the year 1st October 1984, to 30th September 1985. Similarly, if the accounts of B. Thomas are made up to 30th June, annually, the year ended 30th June 1984, will form the basis period for 1985–86.

Special rules where basis periods overlap or where an interval arises between basis periods

This simple rule requires amendment, however, where for any reason the profits of some period form the basis of more than one chargeable period or where the profits of some period do not form the basis of any chargeable period. *This will usually be the case in the opening years of a new business, where the normal accounting date is changed, and in the closing years of a business.* The special rules which apply in such cases are:

(1) Where two basis periods would otherwise overlap, the period common to both is treated as falling in the *first* basis period only. (See Example 1).

(2) Where there is an interval between the end of the basis period for one chargeable period and the basis period for the next chargeable period, then, *unless the second-mentioned chargeable period is the year of the permanent discontinuance of the trade*, etc., the interval is treated as forming part of the *second* basis period. (See Example 2).

(3) Where there is an interval between the end of the basis period for the chargeable period preceding that in which the trade etc., is permanently discontinued and the basis period for the chargeable period in which it is permanently discontinued, the interval is treated as forming part of the *first* basis period. (See Example 3).

Example 1—business commencement

Graft commenced business on 6th July 1984, and his first accounts are made up for the year to 5th July 1985. The capital allowance basis periods for the first and second years of assessment (1984–85 and 1985–86) will be:

1984–85: Nine months to 5th April 1985.
1985–86: Three months to 5th July 1985.

For whilst the assessment for 1985–86 will be based on the profits of the twelve months to 5th July 1985, the overlapping period of nine months to 5th April 1985 will be treated as falling in the first basis period only, i.e., 1984–85.

Example 2—business discontinuance (effect of s. 118 I.C.T.A. 1970)

Pearson's business, the accounts of which have been made up annually to 5th July, is permanently discontinued on 5th July 1985. The actual aggregate of the profits of the penultimate and pre-penultimate years of assessment exceeds the assessments for those years on the preceding year basis, so that the assessments for those years will be adjusted to actual profits.

The basis periods for the pre-penultimate, penultimate and closing years (1983–84, 1984–85 and 1985–86) will be as follows:

> 1983–84: Period of two years and nine months from 6th July 1981 to 5th April 1984. The basis period for 1982–83 would be the year ended 5th July 1981. The assessment for 1983–84 is based on the profit of the year 6th April 1983, to 5th April 1984. [If it were not for the provision which makes the period 6th July 1981, to 5th April 1984, part of the basis period for 1983–84, there would be an interval between the basis period for 1982–83 and that for 1983–84, of one year and nine months.]
>
> 1984–85: Year ended 5th April 1985.
>
> 1985–86: Period of three months to 5th July 1985.

Example 3—discontinuance, normal basis

Consider again the facts given in Example 2. Had the aggregate of the actual profits of the pre-penultimate and penultimate years been less than the original assessments for three years, the assessments would not have been adjusted. The assessment for 1984–85 would be based upon profits of the year to 5th July 1983, and that for 1985–86 on those of the three months to 5th July 1985, leaving an interval of one year and nine months the profits of which did not fall to be assessed in any year of assessment. In arriving at the basis periods on the discontinuance, this period of one year and nine months would form part of the earlier basis period, the basis periods being:

> 1984–85: Period of two years and nine months from 6th July 1982 to 5th April 1985.
>
> 1985–86: Period of three months to 5th July 1985.

(The basis period for the year 1983–84 would be the year to 5th July 1982.)

Where, in the case of a new business, the taxpayer exercises the option to be assessed on an actual basis (Chapter 3, § 4) the capital allowance computations for the second and third years are likely to be affected, since there will be a change in the basis periods for these years of assessment.

Note that capital allowance basis periods are used only to allocate additions and disposals to tax years. Capital allowances are then computed for the tax years concerned as though those additions and disposals had taken place in them.

§ 4.—TYPES OF ALLOWANCE

INTRODUCTION

As mentioned earlier, initial and first-year allowances for capital expenditure are to be phased out completely after 31st March 1986, with only writing-down allowance then remaining. The detailed rates in the interim period are shown under the relevant expenditure heading.

INITIAL ALLOWANCE

An initial allowance is based on a percentage of the cost of the asset, given for one year of assessment only, for the year of assessment based on the period in which the capital expenditure was incurred.

The initial allowance is granted on capital expenditure incurred, and is deducted from the cost of the asset for the purposes of calculating allowances other than the first year's writing-down allowance.

This allowance was withdrawn, in respect of expenditure on plant and machinery incurred after 26th October 1970, but is still given for other types of expenditure (e.g. industrial buildings).

FIRST-YEAR ALLOWANCE

A first-year allowance is granted on capital expenditure incurred on new or second-hand plant and machinery on or after 27th October 1970. This allowance replaces the former initial allowance and writing down allowance in the first year. The allowance is deducted from the cost in calculating any writing down allowances in subsequent years.

WRITING-DOWN ALLOWANCE

The writing-down allowance is a percentage allowance which must be considered separately for the two main divisions of (1) industrial buildings and (2) plant and machinery.

For industrial buildings it is an allowance of the same amount each year based on the cost or the "residual value" of the building. It is only granted when the building is owned and in use as an industrial building on the last day of the basis period. It is given for a full year no matter for how short a period it has been so owned or used.

For plant and machinery the reducing balance method is used. The method is to apply a percentage rate (currently 25%) to the cost of the asset in the second year as reduced by any first year allowance received and then to the balance outstanding after deducting previous writing-down allowances, in subsequent years. After 31st March 1986 the allowance will be given in the year of purchase as first year allowance has ceased.

BALANCING ALLOWANCE AND CHARGE

On the disposal of an asset that has received capital allowances its value after deducting those allowances (the written-down value) is compared with proceeds. If the proceeds are less than its value as written down, a further allowance called a balancing allowance is given for the chargeable period based on the basis period in which the disposal occurred. If the proceeds are in excess of the written down value, the allowances granted have been too great and so a balancing charge will arise for the same chargeable period as would a balancing allowance. It should be noted that Capital Gains Tax may be applicable, in addition to balancing charges, where an asset is disposed of for more than its cost price—see Chapter 26.

Except for motor cars costing over £8,000 and other "non-pool" items (see below), no balancing adjustment will arise on the sale of plant and machinery which was originally acquired after 26th October 1970, unless the proceeds exceed the balance of "pool" expenditure. The proceeds are merely deducted from the "pool" value of the plant and machinery (see later) and writing-down allowances are calculated on the balance (refer below for pre 27th October 1970 acquisitions).

These allowances are considered in more detail in the following text.

No balancing adjustments are made in respect of agricultural buildings allowances.

Effect of grants and subsidies (s. 84, C.A.A. 1968)

The cost of any asset on which a capital allowance falls due is reduced to the extent that part or all of the expenditure is met by:

(1) The Crown, or any government or public authority, whether in the U.K. or elsewhere (*unless* the grant is a regional development grant).

(2) Any other person other than the person claiming the allowance.

Example

Freda acquires a new machine for £50,000 on 25th August 1985, and receives from the local authority a grant for £12,000 in respect of the machine.
Freda will be entitled to a first-year allowance as follows:

	£
Cost.	50,000
Less Grant.	12,000
Allowable expenditure for first year allowance.	£38,000

§ 5.—MACHINERY AND PLANT

GENERAL
The Finance Act 1984 has substantially reduced the tax effectiveness of expenditure on machinery and plant by removing in three annual stages the 100% first-year allowance (see below), although the 25% writing-down allowance remains to provide a measure of relief.

DEFINITION
The legislation dealing with allowances available on expenditure incurred is contained in the Finance Act 1971 (for expenditure incurred after 26th October 1970), as amended by subsequent Finance Acts.

There is no definition of machinery and plant in the legislation, and consequently it has been left to the Courts to decide what is, and what is not, plant. It is beyond the scope of this book to consider this question in detail, although the following judgements give a reasonable indication of the areas to be considered:

Lindley L. J. (*Yarmouth* v. *France* (*1887*)). "Plant in its ordinary sense includes whatever apparatus is used by a businessman for carrying on his business—not his stock-in-trade which he buys or makes for sale; but all goods and chattels fixed or moveable, live or dead, which he keeps for permanent employment in his business."

Pearson L. J. (*Jarrold* v. *John Good & Sons Ltd* (*1962*)). "The short question in this case is whether the partitioning is part of the premises in which the business is carried on or part of the plant with which the business is carried on. . . . On the view of the facts, the partitioning undoubtedly can be regarded as 'plant'. . ."

The second judgement seeks to distinguish between expenditure which forms part of the setting from which the trade is carried on (i.e. *not* plant) and apparatus with which the business is carried on (i.e. plant). This "functional" test has been reiterated in subsequent decisions, notably: *C.I.R.* v. *Barclay, Curle & Co. Ltd* (1969); *Cooke* v. *Beach Station Caravans Ltd* (1974); *Dixon* v. *Fitch's Garage Ltd* (1975); *Benson* v. *Yard-Arm Club* (1978); *Cole Brothers Ltd* v. *Phillips* (1982); *C.I.R.* v. *Scottish and Newcastle Breweries Ltd* (1982), as a result of which the *functional test* is now considered the major criterion in determining whether expenditure is or is not machinery or plant.

Whilst a definition of machinery and plant does not exist, the following items are specifically *included*:

(*a*) Motor cars (see below)
(*b*) Ships
(*c*) Expenditure:
(i) On fire safety, following a notice under the Fire Precautions Act, 1971 (s. 17, F.A. 1974; s. 15, F.A. 1975)

(ii) On thermal insulation of industrial buildings (s. 14 F.A. 1975)

(iii) On safety at sports grounds (s. 49, F.A. (No. 2) 1975.

(iv) On altering or replacing authorised quarantine premises to comply with an order made after 1 September 1972, if relief would not otherwise be available (s. 71, F.A. 1980)

(*d*) Alterations to a building which are incidental to the installation of machinery or plant (s. 45, C.A.A. 1968)

SYSTEM OF ALLOWANCES

The F.A. 1971 introduced a new system of dealing with expenditure incurred after 26th October 1970. Consequently, it was necessary to divide expenditure into two separate categories:

Post 26th October 1970
Pre 27th October 1970

These two categories are considered below, although the introduction of s. 39, F.A. 1976 in respect of basis periods ended after 5th April 1976, has meant that expenditure pre 27th October 1970 has now very little application.

POST 26TH OCTOBER 1970 EXPENDITURE

FIRST-YEAR ALLOWANCES

RATES (s. 42, F.A. 1971, as amended by ss. 58, 59 and Schedule 12, F.A. 1984)
The rates of first-year allowance have been, are, and are to be as follows:

22.3.72–13.3.84	100%
14.3.84–31.3.85	75%
1.4.85–31.3.86	50%
After 1st April 1986	Nil

Special provisions apply in the following cases:

(i) for contracts entered into prior to 14th March 1984 (see also 'Date expenditure incurred', below);

(ii) expenditure incurred in development areas;

(iii) contracts in the period 14.3.84 to 31.3.86 where completion takes place after 31.3.85.

The full allowance is only available where the asset is used wholly and exclusively for the purposes of the trade (s. 55, F.A. 1985). In the case of assets provided for non-trade purposes an appropriate proportion of the allowance applies (see below).

It is now (from 31st March 1985) not necessary for the asset to be brought into use at some time for a claim to succeed (see below).

(*i*) *Contract entered into prior to 14th March 1984* (Schedule 12, para. 2, F.A. 1984)

The 100% first-year allowance continues to apply to expenditure incurred after 13th March 1984 and before 1st April 1987 *provided* the sums are paid under a contract entered into prior to 14th March 1984. This also applies to a lessor who acquires the equipment prior to 1st April 1987 under a pre-Budget contract entered into by someone else but which is subsequently novated to the lessor.

Example 1

Oliver enters into a contract for the supply of equipment costing £50,000 on 17th February 1984, paying a deposit of £5000. The equipment is supplied and payment of the balance (£45,000) is made on 7th April 1985.

Since the contract is entered into prior to 14th March 1984 and is executed prior to 1st April 1987, the full 100% allowance is due on the whole £50,000.

The allowance due would be:

£5000	17.2.84
£45,000	7.4.85

(ii) Contracts in development areas (Schedule 12, para. 4, F.A. 1984)
Expenditure in a development area (within the meaning of the Industrial Development Act 1982 or in Northern Ireland or in the Highlands and Islands Development Board) which qualifies for a regional development grant continues to attract 100% allowance *provided* a written offer of assistance for the expenditure was received from the Secretary of State in the period 1.4.1980 to 13.3.1984. There is no time limit as to when the expenditure needs to be incurred.

(iii) Contracts in the period 14th March 1980 to 31st March 1986 with a completion date after 31st March 1985 (Schedule 12, para. 5, F.A. 1984)
It should be noted that these provisions only apply where the sole or main benefit which might have been expected to be gained was the obtaining of a first-year allowance or higher first-year allowance. Accordingly normal commercial contract will not fall within this provision and in practice their application is probably limited.

Introduction
The purpose of this provision is to prevent the obtaining of a higher allowance by bringing forward the date on which expenditure is incurred *if* the date on which the contractual obligations are fulfilled occurs later.

The provisions apply to contracts:
   (a) entered into after 13.3.84 and before 1.4.87; and
   (b) which either specify no date by which the contractual obligations must be performed or specify a date after 31.3.85; and
   (c) which provide that the person incurring the expenditure shall or may become the owner of the machinery or plant.

Effect
Contracts falling within these provisions are then effectively time apportioned in terms of the expenditure incurred over the period between the contract date and the completion date (as in (b) above) to determine the maximum allowable expenditure.

The maximum allowable expenditure is then calculated by taking the fraction of the total contract price of which:

   (a) the numerator
      (i) for the financial year 1984 is the number of complete months in the period beginning on the contract date and ending on 31st March 1985 and
      (ii) for the financial year 1985 is 12 or, if it is less, the number of complete months in the period beginning on the contract date and ending on 31st March 1986;
      and
   (b) the denominator is the number of complete months in the period beginning on the contract date and ending on the completion date or, if it is earlier, 31st March 1987.

N.B. (i) Financial year 1984 is the year ended 31.3.1985.

(ii) Financial year 1985 is the year ended 31.3.1986.

If the actual expenditure incurred is *less* than the maximum allowable expenditure, then this figure will be used. If, as will be usual, the actual expenditure exceeds the maximum allowable expenditure, the excess is carried forward to the following year and deemed to be incurred in that year, for purposes of both the rate of relief and the basis period.

These provisions do not apply to machinery and plant acquired on hire purchase.

ELIGIBILITY (s. 41(1), F.A. 1971 as amended by s. 55, F.A. 1985)

The general rule is that expenditure incurred by a trader in providing plant and machinery for the purpose of his trade qualifies for first-year allowances provided that the items concerned *belong to him* at some time in the chargeable period in which the expenditure was incurred. Expenditure on both new and secondhand plant and machinery is eligible. It is not necessary for the plant and machinery to be in use in the chargeable period and for periods of account ending after 31st March 1985, even if the asset is disposed of prior to usage, an allowance is still granted. The full allowance is, however, only available where the asset is used wholly and exclusively for the purposes of the trade (for non-trade usage see p. 164).

Example 2

Marriott, making his accounts up to 30th June each year, incurs expenditure of £40,000 on 29th March 1985, on a computer. Marriott decides that the computer is not suitable and before using it sells it back to the supplier for £15,000 on 1st June 1985.

His pool of expenditure at 1st July 1984 is £60,000.

His capital allowance computation in respect of the year ended 30th June 1985 is as follows:

		Qualifying expenditure £	Allowances £
Balance b/f from 1985–86		60,000	
Additions:			
Computer	40,000		
F.Y.A. @ 75%	(30,000)		30,000
		10,000	
		70,000	
Less Disposal value (computer)		15,000	
		55,000	
W.D.A. @ 25%		(13,750)	13,750
Qualifying expenditure c/f		£41,250	
Allowances 1986–87			£43,750

The first-year allowance is *not* available in the following cases:

(1) Motor cars (s. 43, F.A. 1971) *unless*

(*a*) of a construction primarily suited for the conveyance of goods;

(*b*) of a type not commonly used as private vehicles and unsuitable for such use;

(*c*) used wholly or mainly for hire to, or for the carriage of, members of the public (e.g. taxis).

To qualify under (*c*) the following further conditions must be satisfied:

- (*a*) (i) the number of consecutive days for which it is on hire to, or used for the carriage of, the same person will normally be less than thirty; and
  - (ii) the total number of days for which it is on hire to, or used for the carriage of, the same person in any period of twelve months will normally be less than ninety; *or*
- (*b*) it is provided for hire to a person who will himself use it wholly or mainly for hire to, or the carriage of, members of the public in the ordinary course of a trade and in a manner complying with the conditions specified in paragraph (*a*) above.

(2) Where the asset is provided for non-trade purposes (a partial claim may, however, apply if some trade usage occurs (see below)).

(3) Expenditure incurred in a period when the trade is permanently discontinued (s. 41(1), F.A. 1971).

(4) Where the acquisition of an asset is from a connected person (Schedule 8, para. 3, F.A. 1971) unless:
- (*a*) the asset has not been used before (s. 68(5), F.A. 1972); *or*
- (*b*) the seller's business is the manufacture or supply of the asset acquired, and the asset has not been used before (s. 68(7), F.A. 1972).

(5) Where it appears with respect to the sale, or with respect to transactions of which the sale is one, that the sole or main benefit of the transaction is the obtaining of an allowance (Schedule 8, para 3, F.A. 1971—subject to (4)(*b*) above).

(6) Where the asset continues to be used in the trade of the seller (subject to (4)(*a*) and (*b*) above).

(7) Certain leased assets (see below).

DISCLAIMER OF ALLOWANCE (s. 41(3), F.A. 1971)

The claim for first-year allowance need not be for the whole amount. A claim can be for any amount.

A first-year allowance not claimed (or only part claimed) cannot be claimed in future years *except* in the case of expenditure on ships, where the allowance is postponed and can be claimed in a later period.

DATE EXPENDITURE INCURRED (s. 56, F.A. 1985)

For expenditure incurred after 17th December 1984, the rules relating to the date expenditure is incurred are clarified.

The general rule is that the date on which expenditure is incurred is the date on which the obligation to pay becomes unconditional (whether or not there is a later date on or before which the whole or any amount of the sum is required to be paid). Thus the date will follow that of normal accountancy treatment in that where there is a legal requirement to make payment that will be the date the expenditure is incurred. This will normally be the date of the invoice, irrespective of actual payment date (but see below).

Anti-avoidance

This general rule is, however, set aside where:

- (i) the obligation to pay is more than four months after the date payment is required to be made, or
- (ii) where the obligation to pay is in advance of the date payment would be made in accordance with normal commercial usage, and a tax advantage is sought.

The date the expenditure will be incurred is the date it is *required to be paid*, even (apparently) if the payment date is earlier.
(N.B. See above for the special cases of contracts spanning 13th March 1984.)

Example 3

	Date obligation to pay is unconditional	Date payment required to be made	Date payment made	Date payment would be made in accordance with normal commercial usage
(1)	31.3.85	31.5.85	1.7.85	N/A
(2)	31.3.85	31.8.85	1.7.85	N/A
(3)	31.3.85	31.7.85	31.5.85	30.6.85

Date incurred
  (1) 31.3.1985 (normal rule)
  (2) 31.7.1985 (date payment required to be paid since more than four months after obligation date)
  (3) 31.7.1985 (date required to be paid since commercial date after obligation date assuming a tax advantage)

These anti-avoidance provisions are modified in the case of assets built under contract where the payment obligation falls within the first month of a new period of account. In these circumstances the expenditure is treated as arising in the earlier period.

HIRE PURCHASE (s. 45, F.A. 1971)
The full cost of the asset is available for first-year allowance (even though some instalments remain outstanding).

Writing-down Allowance

RATE
The rate of writing-down allowance is unaffected by the Finance Act 1984 changes made to capital allowances. It thus remains at 25%, and is not available where a first-year allowance has been claimed. For chargeable periods ending after 13th March 1984 where *no* claim for a first year allowance is made the expenditure not claimed (up to the amount of the cost) is available for writing-down allowance (s. 59, F.A. 1984). This changes the position existing hitherto whereby writing-down allowance was not available in the same year in which first-year allowance was or could have been claimed.

For expenditure in chargeable periods ending after 31st March 1985 a writing-down allowance is available even where the asset is not in use, although no WDA is available if a first-year allowance is claimed.

The F.A. 1985 also allows an effective shorter write-off period where it is anticipated the life of an asset will not exceed five years (see below on short-life assets).

ELIGIBILITY (s. 44(1), F.A. 1971)
Expenditure incurred by a trader in providing plant and machinery for the purposes of his trade qualifies for writing down allowance provided that the machinery or plant belongs to him.

An allowance of 25% is given on the *pool of qualifying expenditure* (see below). This consists of:
  (1) The balance of *qualifying expenditure* from the previous period (i.e. after deducting writing down allowance for that period) *plus*
  (2) The balance of any expenditure in the previous period which qualified for first-year allowance (i.e. after deducting the first-year allowance claimed) *plus*

(3) Expenditure incurred in the period which does not qualify for the first-year allowance *less*

(4) The disposal value to be brought into account in the period. (This will normally be the proceeds of disposal, insurance proceeds, compensation, etc.—see below).

BALANCING ADJUSTMENTS (ss. 44(2) and (3), F.A. 1971)

If the disposal value brought into account exceeds the aggregate of the items of qualifying expenditure, a *balancing charge* equal to the excess is made.

On the discontinuance of a trade, no writing down allowance is available but a *balancing adjustment* is made equal to the difference between the balance of qualifying expenditure and the disposal value brought into account.

SHORT PERIODS (s. 44(2), F.A. 1971)

The writing down allowance is reduced to the extent that the accounts (as opposed to capital allowances) basis period giving rise to a claim is less than one year.

POOLING

All items of expenditure form part of the main pool of expenditure except the following:

(1) Motor cars costing over £8,000 (£5,000 pre 12th June 1979). Each car in this category is treated as forming a "separate trade" distinct from the actual trade or any other trade that may be carried on. Each such car therefore forms a separate pool. (Paras 9–11, Schedule 8, F.A. 1971 as amended by Schedule 11, F.A. 1985)

(2) Motor cars bought after 31st May 1980 and costing less than £8,000. These form part of a separate "Finance Act 1980" pool containing certain expenditure not qualifying for first-year allowances. (s. 69, F.A. 1980)

(3) Certain leased assets ineligible for first-year allowance following Finance Act 1980. These form part of the Finance Act 1980 pool.

(4) Machinery or plant where a subsidy has been received to take account of wear and tear. Each such asset forms a separate pool. (Para 6, Schedule 8, F.A. 1971)

(5) Machinery or plant used only partly for business non-purposes. Each asset forms a separate pool. Only the proportion of the allowance attributable to the business use of the asset is available (see below) (Para 5, Schedule 8, F.A. 1971)

(6) Ships. As noted in connection with first-year allowances, where less than the whole first-year allowance is claimed on a new ship, the remainder of the first year allowance is merely postponed and can be claimed in a later period. The proceeds of disposal of the ship, however, represent disposal value to be brought into account in the main pool (Para 8, Schedule 8, F.A. 1971 and s. 59, F. A. 1984).

Example 4

Falstaff makes up his accounts for the year to 30th June. The written down value of machinery and plant after his 1984–85 computation (all pool expenditure) is £27,000. During the year to 30th June 1984, Falstaff had the following transactions relative to machinery and plant:

	Cost £	Proceeds £
Acquisitions:		
4 Typewriters (31.5.84)	1,000	
2 Lorries (31.8.83)	5,000	
Motor car (11th June 1984)		
(no private use)	7,000	

		£
Disposals:		
2 Filing cabinets........................		75
Lorry..................................		725

The Capital Allowances available for 1985–86 are as follows:

				FA 1980	
			Pool	Pool	Allowances
			£	£	£
WDV brought forward			27,000	—	
Additions (not qualifying for FYA)					
—motor car.........................				7,000	
Disposals—proceeds			(800)		
Expenditure qualifying for WDA..............			26,200	7,000	
WDA 25% × £26,200.......................			6,550		6,550
25% × £7,000......................				1,750	1,750
Additions for FYA					
—typewriters		1,000			
—lorries		5,000			
		6,000			
FYA lorries (100%)	5,000				
typewriters (75%)	750	5,750	250		5,750
Total allowances..........................					£14,050
WDV carried forward			£19,990	£5,250	

SHORT-LIFE ASSETS (s. 57, F.A. 1985)
For expenditure incurred after 31st March 1986 a trader can elect for assets to be *individually* separated from his main pool and for short-life asset treatment to apply.
It should be noted that this provision simply allows for a balancing adjustment to be made specifically to the asset rather than to the entire main pool, and accordingly it is only on sale or disposal that a greater allowance, by virtue of the balancing adjustment, is achieved. Furthermore if the asset is still retained at the end of the fourth period of account after that in which it was purchased, it is transferred into the main pool.

Election
The election for "short-life assets" must:
 (i) be made in writing to the inspector,
 (ii) specify the asset or assets concerned and the date acquired (N.B. Each asset forms its own separate pool)
 (iii) be made within two years of the end of the period of account in which it was acquired
The election does *not* apply to assets that cannot form part of the main pool of expenditure and certain others (see Schedule 12, F.A. 1985) viz:

 (*a*) Ships.
 (*b*) Cars (but not commercial vehicles).
 (*c*) Machinery and plant tax otherwise than in the course of trade.
 (*d*) Cars over £8000.
 (*e*) Non-qualifying leased assets.

(*f*) Plant used partly for trading purposes.

(*g*) Plant attracting transitional relief by virtue of contracts entered into prior to 14th March 1984 or as a result of a regional development grant.

(*h*) Television sets attracting transitional relief.

(*i*) Plant received by way of gift or acquired where previously non-trading use applied, and plant where a wear and tear subsidy is paid.

Example 4

Joe, a sole trader making up accounts to 30th June, purchases two computers on the following dates:

31.5.1986	(1)	£30,000
12.6.1986	(2)	£25,000

Joe elects for short-life asset treatment to apply. The first computer is sold in the year ending 30th June 1989 for £5000, whilst the second is retained after 30th June 1991. Allowances will be as follows:

	Computer (1)	*Computer (2)*	*Allowances*
1987–88 (Year to 30.6.86)			
Additions	30,000	25,000	
W.D.A. @ 25%	7,500	6,250	13,750
W.D.V. c/f	22,500	18,750	
1988–89 (Year to 30.6.87)			
W.D.V. b/f	22,500	18,750	
W.D.A. @ 25%	5,625	4,688	10,313
W.D.V. c/f	16,875	14,062	
1989–90 (Year to 30.6.88)			
W.D.V. b/f	16,875	14,062	
W.D.A. @ 25%	4,219	3,516	7,735
W.D.V. c/f	12,656	10,546	
1990–91 (Year to 30.6.89)			
W.D.V. b/f	12,656	10,546	
Disposal proceeds	5,000		
Balancing allowance	(7,656)		7,656
W.D.A. @ 25%		2,637	2,637
W.D.V. c/f		7,909	10,293
1991–92 (Year to 30.6.90)			
W.D.V. b/f		7,909	
W.D.A. @ 25%		1,977	1,977
W.D.V.—transferred to main pool		5,932	

Disposals to connected persons
Provided both parties to the disposal elect that the asset is transferred at tax written-down value, the acquirer takes the asset in place of the disposer, i.e. he picks up the short-life asset treatment as if he had acquired the asset himself (N.B. The five-year period always commences at the time of the original requisition).

DISCLAIMER OF WRITING-DOWN ALLOWANCE (s. 44(2), F.A. 1971)
There is no obligation upon an individual or partnership to claim the whole of any writing-down allowance which may be due. The taxpayer may claim part of the allowance or no allowance at all.

BALANCING ADJUSTMENTS (s. 44(3), F.A. 1971)
A balancing charge will be made in any period where the disposal value in that period exceeds the qualifying expenditure.

Example 5

Delta, a sole trader making up accounts to 31st December, has a written-down value of "pool expenditure" of £1,500 after 1984–85.

During the year ended 31st December 1984 his only transactions relative to machinery and plant are:

		£
Acquisition of		
	(*a*) printing machine (13.3.84)	7,000
	(*b*) motor car.	1,200
Disposal of		
	old machine (proceeds)	3,450

The capital allowance position of Delta for 1985–86 is as follows:

		Pool £	FA 1980 Pool £	Allowance £
WDV of pool b/f		1,500		
Additions (not qualifying for FYA)				
—motor car			1,200	
		1,500	1,200	
Disposal—proceeds		3,450		
Balancing charge		(1,950)		(1,950)
WDA 25% × £1,200.			300	300
Additions for FYA	£			
Printing machine	7,000			
FYA	7,000		—	7,000
Total allowances.				£5,350
WDV c/f		Nil	£900	

A balancing allowance will be made on the permanent discontinuance of the trade where the disposal value of the machinery and plant to be brought into account is less than the qualifying expenditure. (A balancing charge will arise if disposal value exceeds qualifying expenditure.)

DISPOSAL VALUE (s. 44(5), (6), F.A. 1971)

The disposal value to be brought into account depends upon the event giving rise to the disposal as follows:

(1) If the event is the sale of machinery or plant at market value, the disposal value is the proceeds together with any insurance monies received.

(2) If the event is the sale of machinery or plant at less than market value the disposal value is the market value *unless*:

    (*a*) The expenditure on the acquisition by the buyer determines the allowances available to him (this will be the normal situation) *or*

    (*b*) A charge to tax under Schedule E arises on the buyer.

(3) If the event is the demolition or destruction of the machinery or plant, the disposal value is the residual monies received for what remains of the machinery or plant together with any insurance, and compensation so far as it consists of capital sums received.

(4) If the event is the permanent loss of the machinery or plant in circumstances other than demolition or destruction, the disposal value is the insurance and compensation received, so far as it consists of capital sums.

(5) If the event is the permanent discontinuance of the trade before any event as detailed above has occurred, the disposal value will be the amount subsequently received on the asset's sale, etc., as above.

(6) In the case of any other event, the disposal value equals the market value.

There is a proviso that in no case shall the disposal value exceed the cost of the machinery or plant.

MOTOR CARS (s. 69, F.A. 1980)

As mentioned above, motor cars do not qualify for a first year allowance, and to the extent that they cost over £8,000, are accorded special treatment (see below). Expenditure on or after 1st June 1980 on motor cars costing less than £8,000 is allocated to a separate "Finance Act 1980" pool.

MOTOR CARS COSTING OVER £8,000 (£5,000 pre 12th June 1979) (Paras 9–11, Schedule 8, F.A. 1971)

Vehicles in this category are completely divorced from the main pool of expenditure, and, in fact, constitute a "separate trade". It is therefore necessary to segregate cars under this heading individually, as each car forms its own separate trade.

In the case of a car costing over £8,000, a restriction on the writing-down allowance applies as follows. Writing-down allowance is the *lower* of:

(1) 25% of £8,000, i.e. £2,000. (25% of £5,000, pre 12th June 1979)

(2) 25% of written-down value.

Example 6—writing-down allowances

Elm, making up accounts to 30th September, acquired a motor car for £10,400 on 15th July 1982. For the three years of assessment to 1985–86, the allowances due on the car are as follows:

	Cost £	Allowance £
1983–84 (Year to 30.9.82)	10,400	
Writing-down allowance......................	2,000	2,000
	8,400	

	£	£
1984–85		
Writing-down allowance......................	2,000	2,000
	6,400	
1985–86		
Writing-down allowance......................	1,600	1,600
	£4,800	

Note. The first two years' allowance are restricted to 25% × £8,000 (ie £2,000), whilst the third year is based on 25% of the written-down value.

In the event of the disposal of a motor car costing over £8,000, a balancing adjustment is required.

Example 7—effect of disposal

Birch, making up accounts to 31st December, acquired a motor car for £8,200 on 30th April 1982. Birch sold the car for £5,000 on 19th December 1984.
The allowances are as follows:

	Cost £	*Allowance/(charge)* £
1983–84 (year to 31st December 1982).....	8,200	
Writing-down allowance.............	2,000	2,000
	6,200	
1984–85 (year to 31st December 1983)		
Writing-down allowance.............	1,550	1,550
	4,650	
1985–86 (year to 31st December 1984)		
Sale proceeds (see Note 2).........	5,000	
Balancing charge..................	(350)	(350)

Notes
(1) If the car had been sold for £4,500, a balancing *allowance* of £150 (£4,650 − £4,500) would have been available.
(2) Strictly, since motor cars costing in excess of £8,000 form a separate trade, the disposal constitutes a cessation. This means that the year of disposal is the final year, so that the allowances should be computed thus:

	Cost £	*Allowance* £
1983–84 (year to 31st December 1982).............	8,200	
Writing-down allowance......................	2,000	2,000
	6,200	
1984–85 (year of sale)		
Proceeds	5,000	
Balancing allowance	1,200	1,200

It is, however, the practice of the Inland Revenue, for the sake of simplicity, to treat the allowances as shown in the example, but, of course, the taxpayer is at liberty to choose the method which is most advantageous to him. It will be noted that both calculations overall give exactly the same allowance, so that the only decision relates to the year in which allowances are granted.

HIRE CHARGES (Para 12, Schedule 8, F.A. 1971)
In the case of a hired motor car costing over £8,000, which would not qualify for first-year allowance if purchased, a restriction applies to the rental payments deductible for tax purposes.
   The maximum charge allowed is computed as follows:

$$\frac{£8,000 + \frac{1}{2}(R - 8,000)}{R} \times \text{Hire charge}$$

(where R is the retail cost of the car).

Example 8

   Albert hires a car for £3,500 per annum which has a retail value of £16,000. The allowable deduction is limited to:

$$\frac{£8,000 + \frac{1}{2}(£16,000 - £8,000)}{£16,000} \times £3,500$$

$$= 0.75 \times £3,500$$

$$= £2,625$$

Note. The £875 disallowed rental (£3,500 − £2,625) is irrecoverably lost.

ASSETS USED NOT WHOLLY AND EXCLUSIVELY FOR PURPOSES OTHER THAN THE TRADE
(Para 5, Schedule 8, F.A. 1971, as amended by F.A. 1985)
Allowances, first year and writing down, are granted on such assets on a basis that is just and reasonable having regard to all the relevant circumstances and, in particular, the extent to which the asset is used for non-business purposes.
   The restriction in practice relates preponderantly to motor cars, although it may apply to any asset.
   Assets in this category are *separated from the main pool of expenditure* and are then divided, as to usage, between the "actual trade" (the business usage) and the "notional trade" (the non-business usage). Although allowances are deducted by reference to the total cost, the allowable element is only that which relates to the business usage ("the actual trade").
   On the disposal of an asset within this class, it is necessary to compute a balancing adjustment. Such adjustment is reduced in accordance with the basis on which allowances have been granted.

Example 9

   Oak, making up accounts to 31st July, acquires a motor car for £4,800 on 15th July 1983. It is agreed with the Inspector that Oak's personal usage of the car is 25%. The car is sold by Oak for £2,800 on 17th September 1984.
   The allowances available are as follows:

	Cost	Private usage	Trade usage	Available allowance
	£	£	£	£
1984–85 (year to 31st July 1983)	4,800			
Writing-down allowance..........	1,200	300 ($\frac{1}{4}$)	900 ($\frac{3}{4}$)	900
	3,600			

	£	£	£	£
1985–86 (year to 31st July 1984) Writing-down allowance..........	900	225 $(\frac{1}{4})$	675 $(\frac{3}{4})$	675
	2,700			
1986–87 (year to 31st July 1985) Sale proceeds.................	2,800			
Balancing charge..............	(100)	25 $(\frac{1}{4})$	75 $(\frac{3}{4})$	(75)

Although assets in this category are separated from the pool of expenditure, they do not form a separate trade (as with motor cars costing over £8,000), so that there is no "cessation of trade" when the asset is disposed of.

DEMOLITION COSTS (Para 14, Schedule 8, F.A. 1971)
Where plant is demolished and replaced, the cost of demolition is treated as expenditure on the replacement plant and will thus qualify for first year and/or writing down allowances as appropriate.

If the plant is not replaced, the demolition costs are added to the pool of qualifying expenditure for the period concerned. In this case writing down allowance only will be available.

SUCCESSIONS (Para 13, Schedule 8, F.A. 1971)
Where one person takes over a trade from a predecessor who is connected with him, capital allowances can continue as if there were no discontinuance of the trade. It is necessary for both parties to elect for this treatment and in these circumstances no balancing adjustment will be made on the predecessor, whilst the successor will take over the written down value of the machinery and plant.

Example 10

Lancia transfers his business to Beta Ltd (owned by him) on 31st March 1985 (his year end). At this date the written down value of his machinery and plant is £6,000 (all general pool and used for his trade).

If an election is made by Lancia and Beta Ltd under Schedule 8, Para 13, F.A. 1971, no balancing adjustment on the disposal will befall Lancia, whilst Beta Ltd will acquire the machinery and plant for £6,000. This will then form an addition to Beta Ltd's general pool on which writing down allowances will be available (a first year allowance is not claimable, as the parties are connected and the machinery and plant is second-hand).

Pre 27th October 1970 expenditure

As mentioned earlier, the effects of s. 39, F.A. 1976 mean that expenditure incurred prior to 27th October 1970 has very little future application. For the sake of completeness, however, the few cases to which the provisions do apply are outlined below.

Capital expenditure in this category qualified for initial allowance and writing down allowance.

Initial allowance
The allowance granted was as follows:

Expenditure incurred	*Rate of allowance*
15.4.58–7.4.59	30%
8.4.59–16.1.66	30% (reduced to 10% if investment allowance claimed)
17.1.66–26.10.70	30% (nil, if Investment Income Grant received)

Writing-down allowances

Allowances were granted at 15%, 20% and 25%, depending upon the asset in question. The allowance was computed by reference to the written-down value of the assets, except where the taxpayer had elected for the alternative basis to apply. The alternative basis granted allowances by reference to the useful life of the asset on a straight-line method as follows:

Life of asset	*Annual writing-down allowance*
More than 18 years	$6\frac{1}{4}\%$ p.a.
14–18 years	$8\frac{1}{2}\%$ p.a.
less than 14 years	$11\frac{1}{4}\%$ p.a.

Balancing adjustments

The disposal of an asset under this system necessitated a balancing adjustment (allowance or charge) to be calculated in every case. The allowance or charge is determined by comparing the disposal proceeds with the written-down value of the asset at the date of disposal (a balancing charge never being greater than the allowances granted). It will be noted therefore that under this system individual records of every item of machinery and plant are necessary.

EFFECT OF SECTION 39, F.A. 1976

To eliminate the detailed records that were necessary under the system applying to capital expenditure incurred before 27th October 1970, s. 39, F.A. 1976 was introduced. The section applies to all basis periods ended after 5th April 1976 and treats *all* pre 27th October 1970 expenditure as an addition to the unallowed pool of expenditure in that period.

Example 11

Ash, making up accounts to 31st August, has the following written-down values of machinery and plant following the allowances granted for 1976–77:

		£
Pre *27.10.70 Expenditure*:		
	15% allowance.....................	2,460
	20% allowance.....................	684
	25% allowance.....................	856
Post *26.10.70 Expenditure*:		
	("Pool")...........................	5,000

During the year ended 31st August 1976, Ash acquired the following assets:

	£
Tractor	4,000
Motor car.........................	3,400

The allowances available for 1977–78 are as follows:

		Pool	*Allowances*
		£	£
Expenditure b/f			
Post 26.10.70............................		5,000	
Pre 27.10.70	2,460		
	684		
	856	4,000	
Additions (not qualifying FYA)			
—Motor car..............................		3,400	
		12,400	

		Pool £	Allowances £
Writing-down allowance			
(25% × £12,400)		3,100	3,100
		9,300	
Additions qualifying for FYA			
—Tractor	4,000		
Less FYA	4,000	—	4,000
WD Value c/fwd		£9,300	
Total allowances.			£7,100

The section applies to all expenditure except that on:
(1) Ships
(2) Assets used partly for the trade and partly for other purposes.
(3) Assets where a subsidy has been received for wear and tear.
(4) Cars costing over £2,000.
(5) Leased assets.
(6) Assets where the alternative basis of calculating writing down allowances is operative.
(7) Assets under a hire purchase contract which is uncompleted at the beginning of the basis period to which the section applies.
(8) Assets where the taxpayer elects for the section *not* to operate (an election must be made within two years of the end of the basis period, as mentioned above).

Expenditure on assets in any of the above eight categories will be segregated from the pool of expenditure and allowances calculated thereon accordingly.

Leasing of machinery and plant

(a) General
An individual who is carrying on the trade of leasing is entitled to claim first-year allowance for the equipment leased (subject to anti-avoidance provisions—see below) which are available for set-off against the lease income and then against other income under s. 169, I.C.T.A. 1970.

To qualify for s. 169 relief, however, the individual must be able to demonstrate:
(a) the trade has been carried on for a continuous period of at least six months in or beginning or ending in the year of the claim; *and*
(b) that he devotes substantially the whole of his time to carrying on the trade throughout the year—or if the trade has commenced or ended in the year, for a continuous period of at least six months beginning or ending in that year (s. 70, F.A. 1980).

(b) Exclusion of first-year allowances (s. 64, F.A. 1980)
This section is designed to prevent tax abuses that were considered to be taking place in respect of plant and machinery on lease, particularly assets leased to non-residents.

The section provides that a first year allowance for leased machinery or plant is now only available where it appears that the machinery or plant will be used for a *qualifying purpose* and not any other purpose in the *requisite period*. The section applies (except for transitional cases) to all expenditure incurred after 31st May 1980. The writing-down allowance (25%) is, however, still available (see below for restrictions).

A *"qualifying purpose"* is:
- (*a*) Leasing to a lessee who uses the plant for the purposes of a trade (other than leasing) and, if the lessee had acquired the plant himself, a first year allowance would have been available to him (i.e., the lessee); *or*
- (*b*) The plant is used for short term leasing, either by the person incurring the expenditure or by leasing to a lessee (who is subject to U.K. taxation) who uses it for short-term leasing; *or*
- (*c*) the person incurring the expenditure uses the plant for the purposes of a trade other than leasing.

These requirements are relaxed in the case of ships and aircraft on charter, and transport containers on lease (ss. 64(5), (6) and (7)), *unless* in relation to ships and aircraft the main object or one of the main objects of the chartering was to obtain a first-year allowance (s. 71, F.A. 1982).

Short-term leasing is leasing for periods of normally less than 30 days, where leasing to the same person in any twelve months is normally less than 90 days.

The *"requisite period"* is a period of four years commencing with the date the plant is first brought into use. The period is shortened if the plant is sold by the lessor within the four years.

It will be appreciated from the above limitations that leasing to
- (1) non-residents (not trading in the U.K.),
- (2) exempt traders or
- (3) non-traders

will remove the availability of the first year allowance.

(*c*) *Pooling non-qualifying expenditure* (ss. 65 and 69, F.A. 1980 as amended by Schedule 11, F.A. 1985)
Where the F.Y.A. is denied by s. 64, F.A. 1980, the 25% writing down allowance is available. The assets do, however, form a separate "pool" (technically a separate trade) by reference to which allowances and balancing charges are made. *Included in this pool are all motor cars costing less than £8,000 acquired after 31st May* 1980. See (*f*) below for restriction of 25% allowance.

(*d*) *Recovery of allowances* (s. 66, F.A. 1980)
Where a first-year allowance has been given in respect of leased plant which subsequently during the requisite period is used for a non-qualifying purpose, the "excess relief" (i.e. the difference between the first-year allowance and that available as writing down allowance) is treated as a balancing charge in the period the plant is first used for a non-qualifying purpose.

(*e*) *Transitional provisions* (Schedule 12, F.A. 1980)
The restrictions above apply to expenditure incurred on or after 1st June 1980, *except*:
- (*a*) where the contract to acquire the leased plant or machinery was entered into prior to 27th March 1980 and the plant is brought into use within two years of the contract;
- (*b*) to television sets and similar equipment.

In the case of television sets, the transitional period is from 1st June 1980 to 31st May 1984 (extended to 1986 for Teletext and Viewdata receivers). In these circumstances, the allowance available is:
- (i) 100% for sets delivered on or before 31st May 1982;
- (ii) 75% for sets delivered from 1st June 1982 to 31st May 1983;
- (iii) 50% for sets delivered in the final year (i.e. to 31st May 1984).

(The first four years will be at 100% for Viewdata and Teletext receivers).

In relation to expenditure incurred after 9th March 1982, the reference to television sets includes Teletext adaptors and Viewdata adaptors.

Finally, in the case of machinery or plant acquired in the period 23rd October 1979 to 1st June 1980 which was:
  (i) manufactured or assembled outside the U.K.; *or*
  (ii) manufactured in the U.K. but not less than 25% of the cost is attributable to work done outside the U.K. *and*
  (iii) the plant is leased under a "finance lease" to a non resident (not using the plant for a trade in the U.K.),
the 100% allowance is denied and a 25% allowance is substituted.

(*f*) *Restriction of writing-down allowance for leasing to non-residents* (s. 70, F.A. 1982)
For expenditure incurred after 9th March 1982 on assets leased to non-residents not trading in the U.K., the writing down allowance is reduced from 25% to 10%. The first year allowance is, of course, denied under (*b*) above. The reduction does not apply to short-term leasing (see above). Furthermore, all allowances are withdrawn where lease payments do not follow a normal pattern (s. 70(4), F.A. 1982).
  Transitional provisions apply to lease contracts entered into prior to 10th March 1982 and in certain cases prior to 31st March 1984 (s. 70(10), (11), F.A. 1982).

EXPENDITURE ON PRODUCTION OF FILMS (S. 72, F.A. 1982)
Expenditure incurred on the production or acquisition of a film, tape or disc which would otherwise qualify for capital allowances as machinery or plant (see SP9/79) is to be treated after 10th March 1982 as revenue and not capital expenditure. See SP2/83 for Inland Revenue practice for allowing deductibility of expenditure.
  Transitional provisions apply up to 31st March 1987 to treat the expenditure as capital for contracts entered into before 10th March 1982. Furthermore expenditure on "British films" as certified by the Secretary of State incurred will still qualify for capital allowances, although this proviso will have diminished importance following the Finance Act 1984 amendments to first-year allowances.

§ 6.—INDUSTRIAL BUILDINGS AND STRUCTURES

GENERAL
The provisions contained in the Finance Act 1984 have very substantially reduced the tax relief available for expenditure on industrial buildings, particularly for expenditure incurred after 31.3.86, when the only relief will be the 4% writing-down allowance.

DEFINITION (ss. 7–10, C.A.A. 1968)
Capital allowances are not granted in respect of all premises, but only in respect of those coming within the scope of an "industrial building or structure" as defined by the Capital Allowances Act 1968. To come within the definition, a building or structure must be in use for the purposes of:
  (*a*) a trade carried on in a mill, factory or other similar premises; or
  (*b*) a transport, dock, inland navigation, water, electricity, hydraulic power or tunnel undertaking; or
  (*c*) a bridge undertaking; or
  (*d*) a trade which consists in the manufacture or processing of goods or materials; or
  (*e*) a trade which consists in the storage of (i) raw materials to be used in the manufacture of other goods; (ii) goods or materials which are to be subjected to any process; (iii) goods which have been manufactured but not yet delivered to a purchaser, or (iv) goods imported into the United Kingdom; or

(*f*) a trade which consists in the working of any mine, oil well or other source of mineral deposits, or of a foreign plantation, including any land outside the United Kingdom used for husbandry or forestry; or

(*g*) a trade which consists in ploughing or cultivating land (other than land in the occupation of the person carrying on the trade), or doing any other agricultural operation on such land; or

(*h*) a trade which consists in the catching or taking of fish or shellfish.

Any building (e.g., a sports pavilion) provided by a person carrying on a qualifying trade as mentioned above, for the welfare of workers employed in that trade and used for that purpose ranks as an industrial building or structure. Any building or structure in use as a dwelling house, retail shop, showroom, hotel or office, or partly as such or for some purpose ancillary thereto is *not* an industrial building.

However, buildings for the welfare of persons engaged in a trade within items (*f*) to (*h*) above and which will have no value when the mine, etc., or plantation is no longer worked, are treated as qualifying for I.B.A.

Despite the specific nature of the definition of an industrial building, there have been several cases concerned with its meaning.

Treated as industrial buildings

(i) A drawing office related to the industrial process (*C.I.R.* v. *Lambhill Ironworks* (1950))

(ii) A warehouse in which were stored finished goods manufactured by the taxpayer (even though bought in goods were also stored there)—(*C.I.R.* v. *Saxone, Lilley & Skinner (Holdings) Ltd* (1967))

(iii) A building in which goods were repackaged (*Kilmarnock Equitable Cooperative Society Ltd* v. *C.I.R.* (1966))

Not treated as industrial buildings

(i) Maintenance of plant in premises where the business was plant hire (*Vibroplant Ltd* v. *Holland* (1981))

(ii) A warehouse for imported goods of a trade (not a manufacturer) (*Dale* v. *Johnson Brothers* (1951))

(iii) An employee's house (*C.I.R.* v. *National Coal Board* (1957))

(iv) A crematorium (*Bourne* v. *Norwich Crematorium Ltd* (1967))

(v) A secure area for counting wages (by a security company) (*Buckingham* v. *Securities Properties Ltd* (1979))

By concession (B3—1980) roads within an industrial estate are treated as industrial buildings.

Maintenance/repair businesses

The subjection of goods to a process within the definition of (*d*) above from 10th March 1982 includes repair or maintenance work on any goods or materials, provided that:

(i) the activity does not form part of a retail business, *or*

(ii) the activity does not form part of a trade, which would itself not qualify premises for industrial buildings allowance (e.g. plant hire—see *Vibroplant* v. *Holland* (1981) above).

Accordingly expenditure on buildings for such purposes qualifies after this date for Industrial Buildings Allowance.

Warehousing and storage (I.R. press release 26.3.1982)

In the light of a court decision (understood to be *Crusabridge Investments Ltd* v. *Casings International Ltd* (1979)), Inland Revenue Practice is now in broad terms to grant Industrial Buildings Allowance for buildings used for warehousing and storage by traders and wholesalers where the goods involved are to be used for industrial process. The allowance will not be extended to premises used for storage for retailing purposes.

INITIAL ALLOWANCES (s. 1, C.A.A. 1968)

GENERAL

Where a person incurs expenditure on the construction of a building or structure which is to be an industrial building or structure (as defined above), or incurs *capital* expenditure on any part of an existing building or structure occupied for the purposes of a trade carried on by him*, he is entitled to an initial allowance. This initial allowance will be granted to the person who incurred the expenditure, for the chargeable period in the basis for which the expenditure was incurred.

RATE

The initial allowance for expenditure on qualifying industrial buildings has been, is and will be as follows:

Expenditure incurred†	Rate
13.11.74–10.3.81	50%
11.3.81–13.3.84	75%
14.3.84–31.3.85	50%
1.4.85–31.3.86	25%
After 1.4.86	Nil

Special provisions apply, however, to:
  (i) small workshops;
  (ii) expenditure within enterprise zones;
  (iii) contracts entered into prior to 14th March 1984;
  (iv) expenditure incurred in development areas (but not enterprise zones);
  (v) contracts entered into in the period 14.3.84 to 31.3.86 where completion takes place after 31.3.85.

(*i*) *Small workshops* (s. 75, F.A. 1980 and F.A. 1982)
  (a) *Pre 27.3.83.* Relief is given for expenditure incurred after 26th March 1980 and *before 27th March 1983* on an industrial building whose gross internal floor space is less than 2,500 square feet. Such a building qualifies for a 100% *initial allowance*, which the taxpayer may reduce to such amount as he chooses. Any balance of expenditure after the initial allowance is relieved by way of straight-line writing down allowances at a rate of 25% of cost. If such a building is sold the new owner's writing down allowance is based on the usual 25-year writing-down period.
  A building whose gross internal floor space is greater than 2,500 square feet divided into smaller units qualifies for this relief if each unit is separated from, and under different occupation from, other units. Units are regarded as separate notwithstanding that they are connected by doors required for fire safety purposes, and is also available for common services (e.g. canteens, warehouses) and any ancillary works. See SP6/80.

---

* Such expenditure by a "landlord", in connection with a building or structure occupied for the purposes of a trade carried on by a lessee occupying the building or structure under a lease under which the person who incurred the expenditure has a right to succeed to the property when relinquished by the lessee, is also eligible. Occupation by a licensee in respect of licences granted after 9th March 1982 entitles the landlord to allowances in the same way as occupation by a lessee.
† Expenditure is deemed to be incurred in accordance with s. 56, F.A. 1985 (see above).

(b) *Pre 27.3.85.* The relief is extended for expenditure incurred after 26th March 1983 and before 27th March 1985 if the gross internal floor space of the building is not greater than *1250* square feet. Expenditure incurred on buildings converted in small workshops (1250 square feet) will qualify for allowances notwithstanding the gross internal floor space of the whole building exceeds 1250 square feet provided:

(1) The building has been converted into two or more units.

(2) The units are permanently separated and intended for separate occupation.

(3) The average floor space of the units does not exceed 1250 square feet. It is understood that SP6/80 will apply as above.

This allowance is unaffected by the Finance Act 1984, since it is withdrawn after 27th March 1985.

(ii) *Expenditure within enterprise zones* (s. 74, F.A. 1980)

Allowances of 100% are given in respect of industrial and commercial buildings, located in designated enterprise zones, which covers factories, qualifying hotels, shops and offices, but not dwelling houses, or parts of dwelling houses.

In order to qualify the expenditure must be incurred within ten years after the site has been included in an *enterprise zone.* The taxpayer may elect to take a smaller *initial allowance* and in such cases will qualify for a 25% *writing down allowance,* calculated on a straight line basis.

On sale of the building, a balancing adjustment is made and the new owner's writing down allowance is based on the usual 25-year writing-down period.

This allowance continues to apply to all expenditure incurred and is unaffected by the rate changes above.

(N.B. *This is the only capital allowance of 100% still applying after 31st March 1986 other than scientific research expenditure.*)

(iii) *Contracts entered into prior to 14th March 1984*

Provided expenditure is incurred prior to 1st April 1987, under a contract dated on or before 13th March 1984 the 75% allowance continues to apply. This also applies to expenditure incurred before 14th March 1984 where the trade commences later.

(iv) *Expenditure in development areas*

As with the first-year allowance (see above), expenditure incurred in development areas continues to attract 75% allowance provided an offer for assistance has been received from the Secretary of State in the period 1.4.80 to 13.3.84.

(v) *Contracts after 14.3.84 with later completion dates*

The detailed provisions apply in the same manner as with the first-year allowance for expenditure on plant and machinery (see above). Again, however, it should be noted that this provision only applies where the sole or main benefit was to achieve a higher allowance.

AVAILABILITY

The allowance is granted in respect of capital expenditure incurred on the *construction* of an industrial building or structure or acquisition of a building unused (see above). It follows that expenditure on the purchase of a second-hand building or structure does not qualify for an initial allowance, though capital expenditure on improvements to such a building after it has been acquired second-hand is eligible for such an allowance.

Expenditure on land or any rights therein is not regarded as part of the cost of construction for purposes of capital allowances, though the cost of preparing, cutting, tunnelling and levelling the land is so regarded and treated as a separate building or structure.

Expenditure on alterations to a building to accommodate plant and machinery is eligible for first year allowances and writing down allowances as plant and machinery (s. 45, C.A.A. 1968).

Relief is granted even though the building has not been used as an industrial building or structure at the time the expenditure is incurred (e.g., if payments are made during the course of construction) but will be withdrawn if the building or structure is not an industrial building or structure at the time when it comes to be used.

OFFICE ELEMENT

Where part of a building or structure is, and part is not, an industrial building or structure, the whole building will be treated as an industrial building or structure provided the expenditure on the second part is not more than one-quarter (one-tenth prior to 16th March 1983) of the total capital expenditure incurred on the construction of the whole building or structure.

Although as noted the restriction relates to any non-qualifying element of the building, this is normally that part used as offices.

In the case of a building part of which is non-qualifying and exceeds one quarter of the total cost, only that part of the building which qualifies will be available for allowances.

Example 1

Baker constructs a building prior to 14th March 1984 for use as a bakery incurring expenditure as follows:

	£
Bakery	70,000
Offices	30,000

Initial allowance is 75% × 70,000 = £52,500 (the office element does not qualify).

N.B. It is possible to split the building into qualifying and non-qualifying parts by virtue of s. 87(4), C.A.A. 1968.

CLAIM FOR ALLOWANCE (s. 73(2), F.A. 1981)

For expenditure incurred after 10th March 1981 an individual (or other non-corporate person) may claim that the initial allowance be reduced to an amount specified. Before this date, relief was mandatory.

Example 2

T. Brown, an old-established trader whose accounting year ends on 30th June, incurs, on 27th May 1984, capital expenditure amounting to £10,000 on the construction of a warehouse which falls within the definition of an industrial building or structure for the purposes of the C.A.A. 1968.

An initial allowance of £5,000 (i.e., 50 per cent of £10,000) is available for the year (the year of assessment for the trading year to 30th June in which the expenditure was incurred) although Brown may claim any sum up to this amount.

Where expenditure was incurred by a person about to commence trading, for the purposes of that trade, it will be treated as if it had been incurred on the date on which the trade was set up. Where, however, the expenditure was incurred in a period to which one of the above rates applied, and the trade was set up on a date when another rate applied, the earlier rate applies.

BUILDINGS PURCHASED UNUSED (s. 5, C.A.A. 1968)

Where expenditure has been incurred on the construction of an industrial building and *before the building is used* it is sold, the purchaser will be entitled to initial allowances as if he had incurred the expenditure himself.

The allowable expenditure is, however, limited to the lower of:

    (1) the original cost of construction; or
    (2) the net price paid.

In the case of an acquisition from a developer (i.e. a person carrying on a trade of constructing buildings), the allowable expenditure will be the net price paid. This therefore allows relief for the developer's profit, although it is not entirely clear in this case whether the price is exclusive of the land (which otherwise would not qualify).

WRITING-DOWN ALLOWANCES (s. 2, C.A.A. 1968)

A writing-down allowance is granted for *capital expenditure incurred* on the construction of any industrial building or structure, or expenditure on repairs thereto not deductible from profits for the chargeable period concerned. The allowance is a rate per cent *on the expenditure incurred.* The rates are as follows:

	Rate
Expenditure prior to 6th November 1962	2%
Expenditure after 5th November 1962	4%

A writing-down allowance will only be given where at the end of the basis period the claimant has the "*relevant interest*" in the building and the building is in use as an industrial building. The writing down allowance is given in addition to the initial allowance in the first year, provided the above conditions are satisfied.

RELEVANT INTEREST (s. 11, C.A.A. 1968)

This is the interest in a building or structure (e.g. freehold, leasehold) to which the person who incurred the expenditure was entitled when the expenditure was incurred.

Thus, for example, if X constructed an industrial building at the time he held a 25-year leasehold interest in the land, the allowances will follow the leasehold, so that the sale of the freehold interest would have no effect whatsoever on the industrial buildings allowance. The sale of the leasehold (i.e. the relevant interest) *would* affect future entitlement to allowances (see sections on balancing allowances and charges below).

Example 3

R. Francis and Partners, make up accounts to 31st December, annually. In March 1984, the firm sold its factory premises in Blackpool to Tower Trunks Ltd, and in September 1984, purchased an industrial building in Skegness. The latter building was in use as an industrial building on 31st December 1984.

Since the year to 31st December 1984, forms the firm's basis period for 1985–86, a writing-down allowance will only be granted for that year in respect of industrial buildings "owned" by R. Francis and Partners, and in use as such on 31st December 1984. Thus no writing-down allowance for 1985–86 will be granted to the firm in respect of the Blackpool premises, though a full writing-down allowance will be granted in respect of those in Skegness.

Observe that the writing-down allowance is computed on capital expenditure incurred and not on the "written-down value", i.e., the balance after deducting allowances granted in earlier years. Compare this with the position in regard to machinery and plant.

Example 4—general claim

Humbug, an old-established trader, prepares accounts annually to 30th April. On the 27th April 1984, he incurred capital expenditure amounting to £25,000 on the construction of an industrial building, which was brought into use as such on that date and remains so used.

Humbug will be entitled to capital allowances as follows:

		£	£
1985–86:	(Since the accounting year ended 30th April forms the basis of the 1985–86 assessment).		
	Initial allowance:		
	50 per cent of £25,000	12,500	
	Writing-down allowance:		
	4 per cent of £25,000	1,000	13,500
1986–87:	Writing-down allowance:		
	4 per cent of £25,000		1,000

Example 5—progress payments

Progress, an established manufacturing partnership, had built an industrial building, paying for it (under the terms of the contract, dated 10.1.83) as follows:

	£
10th January 1983	10,000 (on account)
31st December 1983	10,000 (on account)
30th December 1984	25,000 (on account)
30th April 1985	20,000 (balance)

The business occupied the building on 30th April 1984, and it was in use as an industrial building on that date. The accounting year of the business is 31st December.

Capital allowances would be granted as follows:

		£	£
1984–85:	Initial allowance:		
	75% of £10,000 (pre 10.3.82)	7,500	
	75% of £10,000 (post 10.3.82)	7,500	15,000
1985–86:	Initial allowance:		
	75% of £25,000	18,750	
	Writing-down allowance:		
	4% of £45,000	1,800	20,550
1986–87:	Initial allowance:		
	75% of £20,000	15,000	
	Writing-down allowance:		
	4% of £65,000	2,600	17,600

(N.B. The 75% allowance still applies to the expenditure of £25,000 incurred on 30th December 1984 and the £20,000 incurred on 30.4.84, as the original contract was effected prior to 14.3.84.)

REDUCTION OF EXPENDITURE

Any writing-down allowances, taken in conjunction with the initial allowance must not reduce the capital expenditure below "nil". No writing-down allowance is granted after the fiftieth year following the construction of the building or structure where the rate of writing-down allowance applicable is 2 per cent or after the twenty-fifth year where the rate applicable is 4 per cent.

ACQUISITION AND OCCUPATION

There is no restriction of the writing down allowance where the asset is only owned for the latter part of the basis period. Thus if, in the case of a new business, a building is *purchased and occupied* as an industrial building, on the last day of the basis period for the first chargeable period, the full writing-down allowance is due, notwithstanding the fact that the basis period may be less than a full year.

Example 6—new business

B. Hobson commenced to trade on 1st October 1984, making up accounts annually to 30th September.

On 1st December 1984, he paid for, and commenced to occupy a newly constructed industrial building costing £12,000.

The basis periods are (assuming there is no election for the actual basis):

1984–85:	1st October 1984 to 5th April 1985.
1985–86:	6th April 1985, to 30th September 1985.
	(The assessment for 1985–86 is based on the profits of the first twelve months, ie those of the period 1st October 1984, to 30th September 1985. The period 1st October 1984, to 5th April 1985, has already formed the basis period for 1984–85 and does not therefore enter into that for 1985–86).

Capital allowances are therefore computed as follows:

		£	£
1984–85:	Initial allowances:		
	50 per cent of £12,000	6,000	
	Writing-down allowance:		
	4 per cent of £12,000	480	6,480
1985–86:	Writing-down allowance:		
	4 per cent of £12,000		480
1986–87:	Writing-down allowance:		
	4 per cent of £12,000		480

BALANCING ALLOWANCES AND BALANCING CHARGES

Where an industrial building or structure is *sold, demolished,* or *destroyed,* or (without being demolished or destroyed) *ceases altogether to be used,* usually either a balancing allowance will be made to, or a balancing charge will be made upon, the person entitled to the relevant interest before the happening of such event. This balancing allowance or charge will be made for the chargeable period in the basis period for which the sale, etc., took place.

No balancing allowance or balancing charge will however ever be made if the sale, etc., occurs more than twenty-five years after the building or structure was first used (or fifty years in the case of expenditure incurred prior to 6th November 1962).

Furthermore a balancing charge cannot exceed the allowances granted.

Prior to 18th December 1980 no balancing charge or allowance was made if, at the time the building was sold, etc. it was not being used as an industrial building (having previously qualified as one). This anomaly was corrected by s. 74, F.A. 1981 with effect from 18th December 1980.

Example 7

Consul, an old-established trader, makes up accounts to 31st December annually. During the accounting year ended 31st December 1984, he sold two industrial buildings. The first of these was first used in 1945, and the second in 1906.

A balancing adjustment will be made in regard to the first, in the year of assessment 1985–86 (since the year ended 31st December 1984, forms the basis period for that year).

There will be no balancing adjustment in regard to the building purchased in 1906, since that building had been in use more than fifty years.

DISPOSALS AFTER 17TH DECEMBER 1980 (ss. 3 and 4, C.A.A. 1968 as amended by s. 75, F.A. 1981)
In order to block the loopholes that existed in the legislation the calculation of balancing adjustments on disposals which take place after 17th December 1980, was altered.

If the sale, etc., proceeds of the building equal or exceed the capital expenditure, there is a balancing charge equal to the allowances given.

In any other case there is a balancing allowance or charge, as appropriate, equal to the difference between the adjusted net cost and the allowances given.

The following terms are used to arrive at the charge or allowance:

(*a*) *"The relevant period"*
This is normally the period from the date of first use to the date of the disposal (or other event giving rise to the balancing adjustment). If the building had already been used when acquired, "the relevant period" is the period from the date of acquisition to the date of disposal.

(*b*) *"The capital expenditure"*
This is the expenditure on the building on which allowances have been calculated in the hands of the person making the disposal. This will be the initial expenditure on construction or, as appropriate, the residue of expenditure taken over from the previous owner.

(*c*) *"The allowances given"*
This means all industrial buildings allowances, scientific research allowances, mills, factories, etc. allowances given to the taxpayer in respect of the building.

(*d*) *"The adjusted net cost"* is
    (i) where no proceeds are received, the capital expenditure
    (ii) where the proceeds are less than the capital expenditure, the amount by
        which they are less.
In both cases the net cost is reduced by the proportion to which the period of qualifying industrial usage bears to the relevant period (see definition above).

N.B. In cases where proceeds are greater than the capital expenditure, the net cost calculation is otiose, as the balancing charge is simply the allowances given.

Residue of expenditure (s. 4, C.A.A. 1968)
This is simply the difference between the capital expenditure and the allowance given.

Where the building is sold, however, the residue of expenditure (as far as the purchaser is concerned—see below) is increased/decreased by the amount of the balancing charge/balancing allowance resulting from the sale. *The residue of expenditure is restricted, however, to the sale proceeds where this is a lesser sum.*

Example 8

Anton who makes up accounts to 31st March incurred expenditure of £75,000 on the construction of a building. It was first used on 1st July 1980. It was used for industrial purposes from that date to 30th June 1983. It was then used for other purposes until 31st March 1985, when it was sold for £61,000. Allowances given are £46,500.

The calculation of the balancing charge for 1985–86 is as follows:
Since proceeds are less than capital expenditure, the charge is calculated by reference to net cost.

Net cost: £

    Capital expenditure   75,000
    Less Proceeds...........................   61,000

    Net cost £14,000

Reduce by:

    Period of industrial use,
    (1.7.80 to 30.6.83) ....   *36 months*
    Over relevant period
    (1.7.80 to 31.3.85) ....   *57 months*

$\frac{36}{57} \times £14,000$ ....   = £8,842

Balancing charge for 1985–86 is therefore:

    Allowances given   46,500
    Less Net Cost (as reduced)   8,842

    £37,658

The *residue of expenditure* will be the lower of:

    £

(*a*)   Capital expenditure   75,000
    Less Allowances given................   46,500

    Residue prior to sale   28,500
    Add Balancing charge................   37,658

    Residue after sale.....................   £66,158

(*b*)   The sale proceeds £61,000

The residue of expenditure is therefore £61,000

Further effects of non-industrial usage
(*a*) A balancing allowance is reduced to the extent of any reduction in the net cost.

Example 9

Assume the facts are as in Example 9 except that sale proceeds amounted to £1,000.

Net cost: £
    Capital expenditure   75,000
    Less Proceeds....................................   1,000

    £74,000

Reduced as before: $\frac{36}{57} \times £74,000 =$ £46,736

Balancing allowance:	£
Allowances given	46,500
Less Adjusted net cost	46,736
Balancing allowance	236

(b) A balancing charge will arise even though the sale proceeds are less than the residue of expenditure before the sale.

Example 10

Assume the facts are in Example 9 except that the sale proceeds are £10,000. (N.B. The residue of expenditure prior to sale was £28,500.)

Net cost:	£
Capital expenditure	75,000
Less Proceeds....................................	10,000
	65,000

$$\text{Reduced as before: } \frac{36}{57} \times £65,000 = \quad \text{£41,053}$$

Balancing charge:	£
Allowances given	46,500
Less Adjusted net cost	41,053
Balancing charge.................................	£5,447

Note. A balancing allowance of £18,500 would have arisen if the building had been used for qualifying purposes throughout (ie £10,000 − £28,500 = £18,500)

DISPOSALS BEFORE 18TH DECEMBER 1980 (ss. 3 and 4, C.A.A. 1968)
These provisions are outlined in Appendix 3.

SUNDRY POINTS

DEMOLITION (s. 4(11), C.A.A. 1968)
Where an industrial building or structure is demolished, the cost of demolition, less any moneys received for the remains of the property, is to be added to the residue of expenditure immediately before the demolition (and not treated as expenditure on any property by which the demolished property is replaced). It thus has the effect of reducing any balancing charge or increasing any balancing allowance.

MANNER OF GRANTING ALLOWANCES AND CHARGES (s. 6, C.A.A. 1968)
As already stated above, any balancing or other allowance made to a person carrying on a trade will be made in taxing the trade. Where any allowance is made to the lessor or *licenser* (for licences granted after 9th March 1982) of any industrial building or structure, it will be made *by way of discharge or repayment of tax*, and will be available primarily against the following income:
- (a) income taxed under Schedule A, in respect of any industrial building or structure; or
- (b) income which is the subject of a balancing charge in respect of an industrial building or structure under the Capital Allowances Act 1968.

Where a balancing charge is made on the lessor of any industrial building or structure, it will be made by means of an *assessment* on him under Case VI, Schedule D.

PURCHASE OF A SECOND-HAND BUILDING

The writing-down allowances granted to the purchaser of a second-hand building or structure are based on the *residue of expenditure* after sale of the seller, i.e., upon the residue of expenditure before sale plus any balancing charge, or less any balancing allowance *but limited to the sale proceeds*.

The writing-down allowance for any chargeable period is the residue of expenditure after sale reduced in the proportion which the length of the chargeable period bears to the part unexpired at the date of sale of the period of 25 years (or 50 years where the expenditure was incurred before 6th November 1962) *beginning with the date on which the building or structure was first used*. In no case can a writing-down allowance be given after 50* years following the date on which the building or structure was first used.

Example 11—restriction of residue to sale proceeds

, Elsinore purchased the building referred to in Example 9 above. He makes up accounts to 31st March, annually, and has done so for many years.

	£
Residue of expenditure after sale	£61,000

Elsinore will first be entitled to a writing-down allowance in respect of the building in 1985–86 (i.e. the year of assessment in the basis period for which 31st March 1985 fell). On 31st March 1985 there are still $20\frac{1}{4}$ years of the 25-year period from 1st July 1980 to run, so the writing-down allowance is

$$\frac{£61,000}{20\frac{1}{4}} = £3,012.$$

As already stated, the purchaser of a second-hand building or structure is not entitled to any initial allowance.

Example 12—no restriction

Small purchased on 30th June 1984, an industrial building for £100,000. The building was constructed by the previous owners and first used on 1st April 1981 as an industrial building. The original cost was £87,000. The residue of expenditure will, therefore, be £87,000 (residue + balancing charge equal to allowances given).

The proportion of the period of 25 years unexpired at date of sale is $25 - 3\frac{1}{4}$ years $= 21\frac{3}{4}$ years.

The future writing-down allowances will be as follows:

$$\frac{1}{21\frac{3}{4}} \times £87,000 = £4,000.$$

The allowance of £4,000 will be given for 21 chargeable periods, and the allowance for the 22nd chargeable period will be £3,000—assuming that the building is retained by Small for 22 years from date of purchase.

---

* 25 years in cases of expenditure after 5th November 1962.

N.B. It is academic whether or not the previous owners used the building throughout as an industrial building since the balancing charge will simply be the allowances granted as sale proceeds exceed original cost.

LONG LEASES (s. 37, F.A. 1978)

Where expenditure has been incurred on the construction of an industrial building, and a long lease (i.e. one over 50 years) is granted out of the original interest, provided that the lessor and lessee elect, Industrial Buildings Allowance is available to the lessee. This is a departure from the rule whereby only the person holding the relevant interest (see above) can claim the allowance.

The effect of an election is that:

(1) The grant of the lease is treated as the sale of the relevant interest at the time the lease takes effect.

(2) The capital sum paid by the lessee for the grant of the lease is treated as the purchase price of the relevant interest.

(3) The interest out of which the lease is granted ceases to be the relevant interest, and the lease granted becomes the relevant interest.

Example 13

Claude constructs an industrial building on a freehold site in 1984 (after 13th March 1984). The cost of construction amounts to £120,000. Claude grants a 60-year lease to Cedric for a premium of £90,000 one year after first usage of the industrial building. Claude and Cedric elect that s. 37, F.A. 1978 shall apply to the grant of the lease.

Industrial Buildings Allowance will be available to Cedric as follows:

$$\frac{\text{Cost of lease}}{\text{unexpired period at grant of lease}} = \text{Annual writing-down allowance.}$$

$$\text{i.e.} \quad \frac{90{,}000}{25-1} = £3{,}750$$

Claude will be subject to a balancing charge as follows:

	£	£
Cost of building		120,000
Less Initial allowance........	60,000	
W.D.A. (1 yr)	4,800	64,800
		55,200
Sale proceeds (lease)...........		90,000
Balancing charge................		£34,800

Note. The relevant interest is now contained in the 60-year lease, and only the sale of this lease (unless a 50-year plus lease were granted out of it) would allow the Industrial Buildings Allowance to pass. An initial allowance is not available, since the building is not acquired unused.

An election under this section must be made within two years of the lease taking effect. The operative date is in respect of leases taking effect on or after *15th February 1978.* This section will not apply where:

(1) The lessor and lessee are connected with each other (except in the case of a body discharging statutory functions, and the lessee is under the control of that body.)

(2) It appears that the sole or main benefit which may be expected to accrue to the lessor is the obtaining of a balancing allowance.

TIME EXPENDITURE IS INCURRED

This follows exactly the definition for machinery and plant (see above).

HOTELS (s. 38 and Schedule 6, F.A. 1978 as amended by F.A. 1985)

This section allows relief for expenditure incurred after 11th April 1978 on "qualifying hotels". The relief is given by treating the hotel as if it were an industrial building, so that Industrial Buildings Allowance is available.

The provisions relating to I.B.A.s are, however, modified where the expenditure relates to an hotel so that:

(1) An initial allowance of only 20% is available (up to 1.4.86). (The 4% writing-down allowance is unchanged.)

(2) A balancing charge/allowance will arise in the normal situations (sale, demolition etc.), but also in the case where the hotel has ceased to be a qualifying hotel. In these circumstances, a balancing adjustment will occur after a period of two years following the date on which the building ceased to be a qualifying hotel.

(3) Where the hotel falls "temporarily out of the use", the period for which the hotel can remain a qualifying hotel is restricted to two years (for other industrial buildings the period is indefinite).

The definition of a *qualifying hotel* for these purposes is an hotel the accommodation of which is in a building or buildings of a permanent nature and which complies with the following requirements:

(1) It is open for at least four months in the season (April to October); and

(2) During the time it is open in the season:

(*a*) It has at least 10 letting bedrooms;

(*b*) The sleeping accommodation must wholly or mainly consist of letting bedrooms;

(*c*) The services provided for guests normally include breakfast, evening meal, the making of beds, and the cleaning of rooms.

The above requirements are determined by reference to the 12 months *prior* to the end of the basis period. The hotel must also have been used for the purposes of the person's trade.

Example 14

Sawfly, making up accounts for 18 months to 30th June 1983, will have had to comply with the requirements listed above from the period 1st July 1982 to 30th June 1983 for any relief to be available.

Included in the definition "qualifying hotel" are any buildings provided, by the person carrying on the hotel business, for the welfare of the hotel staff (e.g. separate sleeping quarters, or games areas). The accommodation used privately by an individual (whether alone or in partnership) carrying on the hotel business is, however, excluded.

TENANTED BUILDINGS (s. 76, F.A. 1980)

Prior to 27th March 1980, where the first use of an industrial building was by a tenant, the initial allowance was given by reference to the date on which the tenancy commenced, and not the date the expenditure was incurred. Section 76, F.A. 1980 repeals this rule for expenditure incurred after 26th March 1980. In the case of expenditure incurred before 27th March 1980, the initial allowance is due on 27th March 1980 if the building was not let by that date.

DWELLING HOUSES LET ON ASSURED TENANCIES (s. 76 and Schedule 12, F.A. 1982)

Introduction
Capital expenditure incurred after 9th March 1982 and before 1st April 1987 on the construction of a building as a *qualifying dwelling house* by an *approved body*, qualifies for capital allowances on a similar basis to industrial buildings allowance, although it is an entirely new capital allowance. (N.B. Initial allowance is discontinued after 31.3.86.)

Capital expenditure restriction
The capital expenditure on which allowances are granted is restricted to a maximum of £40,000 per qualifying dwelling house. (This is increased to £60,000 if the dwelling house is situated in Greater London). Where the qualifying dwelling house forms part of a block (e.g. flats), the capital expenditure restriction applies to each dwelling in the block with an additional amount being allowed for "common parts" (i.e. those not used for separate occupation but of benefit to all users within the block). The additional amount for the common parts must not exceed 10% of the cost of the houses comprised in any block, and the overall limitation applies to the aggregate of the house and "common parts".

Example 15

Causio, an approved body, incurs capital expenditure in 1984 on the construction of three separate qualifying dwelling houses (A, B, C) as follows:

	£
A	70,000 (in Greater London)
B	30,000 (in Greater London)
C	50,000 (outside Greater London)

Allowances will be granted on the expenditure as follows:

A	60,000 (restricted)
B	30,000 (no restriction)
C	40,000 (restricted)

Example 16

Taxos, an approved body, incurs capital expenditure in 1985 on the construction of a block of four qualifying dwelling houses outside Greater London. The expenditure is as follows:

	£
Houses	140,000
Common area	20,000

Allowances will be granted on the expenditure as follows:

Houses	140,000 (restricted to 4 × £40,000)
Common area	14,000 (restricted to 10% of house cost)

N.B. the maximum expenditure in any event that would be allowed is 4 × £40,000 = £160,000

References to expenditure do not include expenditure on land. Repair expenditure of a capital nature is, however, allowed.

Initial allowance
An initial allowance is granted for both newly constructed qualifying dwelling houses and qualifying dwelling houses acquired unused. The initial allowance

is available even though the building is not used, provided that the allowance will be recovered if the building is not a qualifying dwelling house when first used.

The initial allowance was 75% but has been altered by the Finance Act 1984 in the same manner as for industrial buildings. The rates are therefore:

9.3.82–13.3.84	75%
13.3.84–31.3.85	50%
1.4.85–31.3.86	25%
After 31.3.86	Nil

Similar provisions apply as for industrial buildings (refer above) for:

(a) contracts entered into prior to 14.3.84;
(b) expenditure in development areas;
(c) contracts effected after 14.3.84 with later completion dates.

Writing-down allowance
An allowance of 4% per annum is due provided that the claimant is an approved body and at the end of its accounting period, the building is a qualifying dwelling house.

Definitions

Approved body	is a body falling within s. 56(4) of the Housing Act 1980.
Qualifying dwelling house	is a dwelling house let on a tenancy which is an assured tenancy within s. 56 of the Housing Act 1980 (see over).

A dwelling house will not qualify even let on an assured tenancy:

(*a*) unless the landlord (is a company and either)* is entitled to the relevant interest (see below) or he constructed the building; or
(*b*) if the landlord is a housing association approved by s. 341, I.C.T.A. 1970 or a self-build society within Part I of the Housing Act 1974; or
(*c*) if the landlord and tenant are connected persons; or
(*d*) if the tenant is a director of a company which is the landlord or which is connected with the landlord; or
(*e*) if the landlord is a close company and the tenant is a participator or an associate of a participator (refer to Chapter 19); or
(*f*) if the tenancy is an arrangement between landlords of different houses and qualification arises which would otherwise be denied by virtue of (*c*) to (*e*) above.

Dwelling house	is a house falling within the ambit of the Rent Act 1977.
Relevant interest *Residue of expenditure*	These follow the same lines as Industrial Buildings, but reference should be made to Schedule 12(7), (13), F.A. 1982.

Manner of making allowances
Allowances are given by way of discharge or repayment (see para 2) and are offset primarily against the rental income. Balancing allowances and balancing charges, follow along similar lines to those for industrial buildings but reference should be made to Schedule 12(4), F.A. 1982.

Assured tenancy scheme
The assured tenancy scheme introduced by the Housing Act 1980 allowed bodies approved by the Secretary of State for the Environment to let property at freely

---

* Words inserted by F. (No. 2) A. 1983 for expenditure after 5th May 1983.

negotiated rents outside the provisions of the Rent Acts. This was provided the building commenced on or after 8th August 1980 and the property had not previously been occupied as a residence except on an assured tenancy.

§ 7.—AGRICULTURAL LAND AND BUILDINGS (ss. 68 and 69, C.A.A. 1968)

RATES

	%
Initial allowance	
12.6.78–31.3.86	20
After 31.3.86	Nil
Writing-down allowance	
12.6.78–31.3.86	10
After 31.3.86	4

ELIGIBLE EXPENDITURE

An allowance is granted in respect of capital expenditure incurred by the owner or the tenant of any agricultural land or forestry land on the construction of farm houses, farm or forestry buildings, cottages, fences or other works.

To qualify for the allowance, the expenditure must have been incurred for the purposes of husbandry or forestry on the agricultural or forestry land in question; and it is subject to the following restrictions:

(*a*) where the expenditure is on a *farm house*, the allowance will be granted on only one-third thereof (or such smaller proportion than one-third as may be just, if the accommodation and amenities of the farm house are out of due relation to the nature and extent of the farm; as where, for instance, there is a disproportionate "residential" element in the farm house);

(*b*) where the expenditure is on some asset *other than a farm house* and that asset is to serve partly for the purposes of husbandry or forestry and partly for other purposes, the allowance will be granted on such portion of the expenditure as may be just.

Any Farm Improvement Grant or other grant received from public funds must be deducted in arriving at the amount on which the allowances are calculated.

BASIS PERIOD

For the purposes of income tax, the basis period for a year of assessment means the year to 31st March preceding the year of assessment in question (or the year ended on such other date as may be agreed by the owner or tenant and the Inspector).

WRITING-DOWN ALLOWANCE

Where, *in the basis period for any chargeable period*, the owner or tenant incurs expenditure in the circumstances set out above, he is entitled, for that chargeable period and for each of the succeeding nine chargeable periods, to an allowance equal to *one-tenth of that expenditure*.

INITIAL ALLOWANCE.

Expenditure incurred after 11th June 1978 qualifies for a 20% initial allowance, but this is to be discontinued for expenditure after 31.3.86. The allowance is available in addition to the 10% (4% after 31.3.86) writing-down allowance in the first year.

A claim for initial allowance has the effect of reducing the period of writing down allowance to 8 years overall (30% in the year of claim and 10% for the next 7 years).

Example 1

Frank, a sole-trader farmer, purchases a barn for £12,000 on 15th May 1985.
If Frank claims the full initial allowance in respect of the barn, the allowance will be granted as follows:

$$1985\text{--}86 \ 30\% \times £12,000 = £3,600$$
$$1987\text{--}88 - 1993\text{--}94 \ 10\% \times £12,000 = £1,200$$

Claims (prior to 1.4.86)
In the case of individuals and partnerships, it is necessary for a claim to be made for initial allowance, which may be for *any amount* up to 20%. Should no claim or a reduced claim be made, the period of writing-down allowance is then increased from 8 years (up to a maximum of 10) to accommodate writing-off 100% of the expenditure.

Example 2

A trader claims 4% initial allowance. The balance of expenditure to be written-off after the first year will be 86% (100% − [4% + 10%]). This will be written off over the following 9 years, the first 8 years at 10% and the final year at 6%.

Method of granting allowances
Agricultural buildings allowances are made by way of *discharge or repayment of tax* and will be available primarily against *agricultural income* and *forestry income*. For this purpose, "agricultural income" comprises income chargeable under:
   (*a*) Schedule A, in respect of agricultural land;
   (*b*) Schedule D, in respect of farming or market gardening in the United Kingdom;
while "forestry income" comprises income chargeable under:
   (*a*) Schedule A, in respect of forestry land;
   (*b*) Schedule D (but not Schedule B), in respect of the occupation of woodlands in the United Kingdom.

BALANCING ADJUSTMENTS
Balancing allowances and charges do not arise in relation to expenditure on Agricultural Land and Buildings, but the allowance for the year of change is apportioned between the vendor and purchaser on a time basis. The purchaser will receive the allowances for the unexpired years.

Example 3

Jamie, who is the owner of Tonbridge Farm, has been receiving an agricultural buildings allowance of £1,800 p.a. for the three years up to and including 1984–85. On 5th August 1985, Jamie sells his farm to Mel.
The agricultural buildings allowance for 1985–86 is:

	£
Jamie 4/12ths × £1,800 (6th April 1985–5th August 1985)	600
Mel 8/12ths × £1,800 (6th August 1985–5th April 1986)	1,200

Note. Mel will be entitled to an allowance of £1,800 for 1986–87 and the remaining years until the end of the 10-year period.
(N.B. The 10% allowance continues to apply after 31.3.86 since the original expenditure was incurred before this date.)

§ 8.—MINES, OIL WELLS, ETC.

MAIN ALLOWANCES

Allowances and charges are made under the Capital Allowances Act 1968, to (or on, as the case may be), any person carrying on a trade which consists of the working of a mine, oil well or other source of mineral deposits of a wasting nature who has incurred "qualifying expenditure":

Qualifying expenditure (ss. 51 to 55 and 62, C.A.A. 1968)

Qualifying expenditure is extensively defined but in general can be said to include the cost of searching and testing for mineral deposits and of extracting them. The construction of works which will be of little value (if any) when the source is worked out are also included. Expenditure on buildings for processing raw material (unless it is to be sold as raw material), for the welfare of workers, or for use as offices does *not* qualify. There is however a *de minimis* limit on expenditure on offices within a building of 10% of the overall capital cost (similar in effect to the industrial buildings allowance position).

Abortive expenditure, including applications (See SP4/78) for planning permission is treated as qualifying expenditure if it would have qualified if it had led to production.

Plant and machinery does not qualify unless it is used for exploration.

In general there is no allowance for expenditure on land unless it is outside the United Kingdom. Expenditure on working overseas mineral deposits is eligible.

INITIAL ALLOWANCES

Where a trader incurs expenditure on works of the type and in the circumstances referred to above he will be granted, for the year of assessment in the basis period for which the expenditure is incurred, an initial allowance, as follows:

Expenditure incurred:	*Rate of initial allowance:*
27th October 1970 to date.	40 per cent in general, 100 per cent in a Development Area or in Northern Ireland.

In relation to expenditure incurred after 27th October 1970, a person may claim such initial allowance up to the appropriate percentage as he requires.

WRITING-DOWN ALLOWANCES (s. 57, C.A.A. 1968)

Where before the end of his basis period for any chargeable period, a trader incurs expenditure of the type and in the circumstances referred to above (whether on exploration, developing, etc., *or* on the construction of works), a writing-down allowance will be granted to him, for that chargeable period, in respect of the whole of the said expenditure which he has incurred in the period which begins on 6th April 1946, and ends at the end of the said basis period. This allowance is ascertained by multiplying the residue of the expenditure by the *greater* of the two following fractions:

(a) one which may be conveniently expressed as $\dfrac{A}{A+B}$, where $A =$ the output from the source in question in the basis period for the year of assessment concerned, and $B =$ the total potential future of that source.

(b) one-twentieth.

At the option of the person carrying on the trade, the writing-down allowance for the final chargeable period and also for each of the five previous periods will be recomputed on the basis that A in the above formula = actual output of the basis period *plus* the actual output between the end of the basis period and the cessation. The residue of expenditure is that which remains after deducting allowances (initial and writing down) already granted.

Alternative claims

The above allowances are an alternative to allowance claims for machinery and plant and industrial buildings which will normally be claimed as creating a higher allowance.

BALANCING ALLOWANCES AND BALANCING CHARGES (s. 58, C.A.A. 1968)

Where a person sells, as a going concern, assets subject to allowances under these provisions, this will give rise to a balancing allowance (or a balancing charge, as the case may be). A balancing charge will arise if the sale proceeds exceed the residue of expenditure (i.e. the expenditure on which allowances are available *less* those given).

A balancing allowance will arise if the sale proceeds are less than the residue of expenditure, provided that in no circumstances shall the balancing charge exceed the allowances granted.

In both instances the charge or allowance is reduced if the source on which the expenditure was incurred was worked before 6th April 1946. In such cases the charge/allowance is reduced by A/B, where

A is the total output from the source from the appointed day
B is the total output from the source to the date of sale.

MINERAL DEPLETION ALLOWANCE (s. 60, C.A.A. 1968)

Writing-down allowances are granted also in respect of the acquisition of U.K. mineral deposits, land containing them, or rights over such land. Writing-down allowances are as follows:

First 10 years of working source	$\frac{1}{2}$	royalty value of output in basis year.
Next 10 years.................	$\frac{1}{4}$	royalty value of output in basis year.
Thereafter	$\frac{1}{10}$	royalty value of output in basis year.

Royalty value means the amount of reasonable royalties that would be payable if the source had been acquired under lease, less any royalties actually payable. The total of writing-down allowances, including those deemed to have been granted prior to 1963–64, however, cannot exceed the total capital outlay. Where a source ceases to be worked, a balancing charge or allowance, limited to the part appropriate to years after 1962–63, will be made on the difference between the cost of acquisition (less the residual market value) and the total allowances. Any Investment Incentive Grant received must be deducted in calculating the total capital outlay and the cost of acquisition.

§ 9.—PATENTS

Allowances and charges are made under ss. 378 and 379, I.C.T.A. 1970, to persons who have incurred capital expenditure on the purchase of patent rights.

WRITING-DOWN ALLOWANCES (s. 378, I.C.T.A. 1970)
RATES

Pre 1.4.86—over "life of patent" (see below)
After 31.3.86—25% writing down allowance

Where a trader* incurs capital expenditure on the purchase of patent rights

---

* Similar allowances are made to a *non-trader*, provided that any income receivable by him in respect of the patent rights would be liable in Income Tax (e.g., patent royalties).

which are used for the purposes of his trade, he is entitled to a writing-down allowance in respect of such expenditure. This allowance is given *in equal instalments over seventeen years of assessment*, beginning with the chargeable period in the trader's basis period (as defined in § 3) for which the expenditure was incurred, thus spreading the expenditure over what is, broadly speaking, the legal life of the patent. If the patent rights are purchased for a specified period which is less than seventeen years, the capital expenditure thereon will be allowed in equal annual sums over such shorter period. After 31.3.86 a simple 25% writing-down allowance applies.

BALANCING ALLOWANCES AND BALANCING CHARGES (s. 379, I.C.T.A. 1970)
Balancing adjustments apply where, before the end of the period (seventeen years or such shorter period as may be applicable) during which the writing-down and/or annual allowances were being given, the patent rights have, *inter alia*, come to an end without being subsequently revived, or have been sold. Adjustments also apply where part only of the patent rights is sold.

Example

Modern Appliances prepares its accounts annually to 30th June. On 31st March, 1980, it acquired patents, having ten years to run, at a cost of £1,000. These patents were sold outright by Modern Appliances, on 30th April 1984, for £400.

	£	£
Cost of Patents on 31st March 1980.		1,000
1981–82: Annual allowance—one-tenth of £1,000	100	
1982–83: Do. do.	100	
1983–84: Writing-down allowance do.	100	
1984–85: Do. do.	100	400
Unallowed expenditure.		600
Less: Proceeds of sale.		400
1985–86: Balancing allowance		£200

Example

Assuming the same facts as in the previous example except that the proceeds of sale amounted to £800, there will be a balancing charge of £200:

	£
Cost of patents on 31st March 1980.	1,000
1981–82 to 1984–85: Annual and writing-down allowances	
(as above)	400
Unallowed expenditure	600
Less: Proceeds of sale.	800
1985–86: Balancing charge.	£200

For the purpose of allowance to the payer and charge on the recipient, expenditure on the acquisition of patent rights includes payments for the right to acquire future rights when an invention has been patented.

MANNER OF MAKING ALLOWANCES AND CHARGES (s. 385, I.C.T.A. 1970)
The manner in which effect is given to the various allowances and charges under ss. 378 and 379, I.C.T.A. 1970, is primarily dependent on whether or not the person concerned is carrying on a trade the profits or gains of which are chargeable for the year of assessment for which the allowance or charge is made *and* at any time in his basis period for that chargeable period the patent rights in question were used for the purpose of that trade. If the above conditions apply, then the allowance or charge will be made to or on that person, in taxing the trade, in the manner described in § 2.

In other cases (i.e., where the person concerned is not regarded as a trader):
(*a*) *Allowances* will be made by way of discharge or repayment of tax, and will be available against income from patents (as defined in s. 388 of the Income and Corporation Taxes Act 1970);
(*b*) *Charges* will be made under Case VI of Schedule D.

The manner of assessing capital receipts from the sale of patent rights is dealt with in Chapter 11 § 16.

§ 10.—ALLOWANCES FOR EXPENDITURE ON SCIENTIFIC RESEARCH (ss. 90 to 94, C.A.A. 1968)

RATE (for capital expenditure)
100% in the relevant chargeable period (see below). There are no disclaimer provisions and writing-down allowances do not apply.

(N.B. The 100% allowance still applies, since it was unaffected by the provisions of the Finance Acts 1984 and 1985 relating to the withdrawal of capital allowances.)

DEFINITION
Scientific research means any activities in the fields of natural or applied science for the extension of knowledge.

Scientific research expenditure is divisible into two categories: (1) that of a non-capital nature, and (2) that of a capital nature.

(1) *Non-Capital Expenditure* (s. 90, Capital Allowances Act 1968)
Where a person carrying on a trade:
(*a*) incurs non-capital expenditure on scientific research related to that trade and directly undertaken by him or on his behalf; or
(*b*) pays any sum to an approved scientific research association; or
(*c*) pays any sum to be used for scientific research purposes to an approved university, college, research institute, etc.
the expenditure incurred (or the sum paid, as the case may be) is *allowable as an expense* in computing the profits or gains of that trade for Income Tax purposes.

(2) *Capital Expenditure* (s. 91, Capital Allowances Act 1968)
Where a person:
(*a*) while carrying on a trade, incurs capital expenditure on scientific research related to that trade and directly undertaken by him or on his behalf; or
(*b*) incurs capital expenditure on scientific research directly undertaken by him or on his behalf and thereafter sets up and commences a trade connected with that research,
he will be granted a scientific research allowance of 100 per cent of the expenditure. For expenditure incurred after 31.3.85 land and dwellings are excluded.

For income tax purposes, 100 per cent of the expenditure is allowed in year of assessment for which the year of expenditure is the basis year.

In the case of an overlap between two basis years for income tax purposes or an interval between two basis years, there are provisions (of a substantially similar character to those described in § 2 in the case of the allowances granted under the Capital Allowances legislation) for determining in which basis year any given scientific research expenditure shall be deemed to have been incurred.

Allowances in respect of capital expenditure on scientific research are ordinarily granted in taxing the trade.

SALE OF SCIENTIFIC RESEARCH ASSETS (s. 92, C.A.A. 1968)

(i) Assets acquired prior to 1.4.85

The excess of sale proceeds, together with allowances granted, over the expenditure incurred is treated as a *trading receipt* accruing at the date of sale. The trading receipt is limited to the allowances granted.

Example 1

Quentin incurred expenditure of £70,000 on scientific research assets on 12th August 1980. On 12th December 1984 Quentin sold the assets for £10,000. Quentin makes up accounts to 30th September each year.

A trading receipt included in Quentin's accounts to 30th September 1985 will arise as follows:

	£
Proceeds of sale................................	10,000
Capital allowance...............................	70,000
	80,000
Less Capital expenditure.........................	70,000
Trading receipt	£10,000

Example 2

If in the above example the assets had been sold for £150,000, the trading receipt would be:

	£
Proceeds of sale................................	150,000
Capital allowance...............................	70,000
	220,000
Less Capital expenditure.........................	70,000
	£150,000

The trading receipt would be limited to the capital allowance, £70,000.

Note. The excess of proceeds over cost is subject to capital gains tax.

Where assets cease to be used for scientific research, no balancing adjustment is necessary unless the assets are sold or destroyed. Any proceeds of such destruction are treated in the same manner as sale proceeds above.

Expenditure and sale in same period

In the case of assets sold before the chargeable period in which the allowance would fall due, no allowance is granted unless the sale proceeds are less than the cost, in which case a deduction is allowed in taxing the trade in the period in which the sale occurs. This, effectively, is a balancing allowance.

Example 3

Zaphod, making up accounts to 31st May, incurs expenditure on scientific research assets of £25,000 on 30th June 1983. On 15th December 1983 Zaphod sells these assets for £11,000.

Zaphod has sold the assets before the chargeable period in which the allowance would fall due, i.e. 1985–86 (since the expenditure falls into the basis period to 31st May 1984), but is entitled to an allowance in 1985–86 as follows:

	£
Proceeds	11,000
Capital expenditure	25,000
Allowance	£14,000

(ii) Assets acquired after 31.3.1985.

The above rules are modified to trigger an adjustment when the asset ceases to belong to the trader, and the references to sale proceeds are replaced by references to the disposal value. This in turn depends on the relevant event.

Where the relevant event is the sale, the disposal value is the sale proceeds or open market value if greater. If the relevant event is the destruction, the value is that value immediately before destruction. In any other case the relevant value is the market value (e.g. in the case of a gift).

§ 11.—KNOW-HOW (ss. 386 to 388, I.C.T.A. 1970)

RATE

$$\text{W.D.A}$$

Pre 1.4.86	$\frac{1}{6}$
Post 31.3.86	25%

Relief   Where know-how is acquired for use in a trade after 19th March 1968, a writing-down allowance will be granted of one-sixth of the cost for each year for a period of six years commencing with the chargeable period related to the expenditure.

If the trade is discontinued within the six year period, any balance of expenditure then remaining unallowed will be allowed for the chargeable period related to the discontinuance.

Know-how is defined as industrial information and techniques likely to assist in manufacturing or processing goods or materials or in working (or searching for) mines, oil wells and other mineral deposits, or in agricultural, forestry or fishing operations.

Where a sale of know-how occurs after 19th March 1968, including any consideration for restricted covenants connected therewith, the consideration received is treated as a trading receipt, except where the sale is between bodies under the same control. A non-trading vendor is assessable under Schedule D, Case VI on the net gain.

On the sale of a business, or part of a business, together with know-how, both the vendor and the purchaser are treated as if the consideration for that know-how represents goodwill, unless both parties elect that the consideration is to be treated as representing know-how, in which case the vendor will be taxed as if the consideration were a trading receipt, while the purchaser will be entitled to capital allowances on the sum over the six-year period mentioned above.

§ 12.—DREDGING (s. 67, C.A.A. 1968)

RATES

Initial	
Pre 1.4.86	15%
Post 31.3.86.	Nil
W.D.A. (available in the first year)	4%

Relief Allowances are granted in respect of capital expenditure on dredging incurred for the purposes of a "qualifying trade", for which expenditure, industrial buildings or machinery and plant allowances cannot be claimed.

Provision is made for balancing allowances on the discontinuance of the trade, and for allowances in respect of expenditure incurred prior to 1956–57.

§ 13.—CEMETERIES AND CREMATORIA (s. 141, I.C.T.A. 1970)

Allowances are made in any basis period for: (a) the cost of land (including levelling, draining and otherwise making suitable) sold for interments in that period, and (b) a proportion of residual capital expenditure at the end of the period, based on the number of grave spaces sold in the period to that number plus those still available.

§ 14.—MISCELLANEOUS

(a) POSTPONEMENT OF CAPITAL ALLOWANCES TO RETAIN DOUBLE TAXATION RELIEF (s. 515, I.C.T.A. 1970)
Where a claim for capital allowances would result in a loss of credit for overseas taxes paid, allowances can be postponed to the next chargeable period.

The effect of the postponement is to treat the allowances as arising in the following period, on which first year allowances as appropriate would be available.

The postponement can be in full or part, but only applies to trades assessable under Case I Schedule D, in respect of allowances granted in taxing the trade (see § 2 above), provided that the following conditions are satisfied:
  (1) The law under which the overseas tax is chargeable provides for relief corresponding to capital allowances to be given *but*, on a basis which is less than the corresponding UK allowance in the first year, but greater in subsequent years; *and*
  (2) that the double tax credit relief is actually reduced if allowances are not claimed (if for example other allowances would in any event reduce the credit to nil, the claim will not be competent).
The postponement provisions are extended to trades assessable under Schedule D, Case V for claims made after 5th April 1982 (s. 78, F.A. 1982).

(b) CLAIMS FOR ALLOWANCES OTHERWISE THAN BY ASSESSMENT
Agreement reached with the Inspector of Taxes after 5th April 1982 for capital allowances claims need not be subject to assessment for effect to be given to the claim. This applies equally to stock relief (see Chapter 6).

§ 15.—COMPREHENSIVE EXAMPLES

Example 1

A sole trader commenced business on 6th July 1982, and his first accounts are made up for the year to 5th July 1983.

He incurred expenditure on new machinery and plant as follows:

	£
1982	
July 6	1,000
1983	
March 31	200
June 30...	400
July 31	100

Show the basis periods and relate the expenditure to years of assessment:

    (a) on the assumption that the normal basis is applied in the opening years; and

    (b) on the assumption that an election to apply the actual basis is made.

The normal basis periods for the first and second years of assessment (1982–83 and 1983–84) will be:

1982–83: Nine months to 5th April 1983.

1983–84: Three months to 5th July 1983. (The assessment would be based on the profits of the twelve months to 5th July 1983, but the overlapping period of nine months to 5th April 1983, is treated as falling in the basis period for 1982–83 only.)

Normal basis

The normal basis periods in relation to the expenditure on machinery and plant are computed as follows:

1982–83: The first year of assessment is the actual period from 6th July 1982 to 5th April 1983, and the expenditure of £1,200 (i.e., £1,000 on 6th July 1982, and £200 on 31st March 1983) within this period is considered to be expenditure of the basis period for 1982–83.

1983–84: The second year of assessment is 1983–84, and the basis period is the first twelve months, i.e., 6th July 1982, to 5th July 1983, but of this period the nine months from 6th July 1982, to 5th April 1983, is also the basis period for 1982–83, and there is thus an overlapping period as explained above. In these circumstances, the expenditure of £400, (i.e., on 30th June 1983) during the period of three months from 6th April to 5th July 1983, is considered to be expenditure of the basis period for 1983–84.

1984–85: The third year of assessment is 1984–85 and the normal basis period is the preceding year of the business, i.e., the twelve months to 5th July 1983. This basis period is, however, the same as the basis period for 1983–84, consequently there is again an overlapping period. The expenditure from 6th July 1982, to 5th April 1983, has already been taken into account in the basis period for 1982–83, while the expenditure from 6th April 1983, to 5th July 1983, has already been taken into account in the basis period for 1983–84; thus there is no further expenditure remaining to be regarded as expenditure for the basis period for 1984–85.

1985–86: The fourth year of assessment is 1985–86, and the normal basis period is the preceding year of the business, i.e., the twelve months to 5th July 1984. The expenditure of £100 on 31st July 1983, within the twelve months to 5th July 1984, is considered to be expenditure of the basis period for 1985–86.

Assuming the business elects to claim to have the assessments for the second and third years (i.e., 1983–84 and 1984–85) amended to the actual profits of those years, the basis periods as and from 1983–84 will be amended in the following manner:

1983–84: The basis period will now become the actual period from 6th April 1983, to 5th April 1984, and the expenditure of £500 (i.e., £400 on 30th June 1983, and £100 on 31st July 1983), within this period is considered to be expenditure of the basis period 1983–84. This does not constitute any change as regards the expenditure of £400 on 30th June 1983, but it has accelerated the treatment of the expenditure of £100 on 31st July 1983, by including it in the basis period for 1983–84, in place of the basis period for 1985–86.

1984–85: The basis period will not become the actual period from 6th April 1984, to 5th April 1985, and any expenditure within that period will be considered to be expenditure of the basis period for 1984–85.

1985–86: The basis period will normally be the preceding year of the business, i.e., the twelve months to 5th July 1984, but the period 6th July 1983, to 5th April 1984, already falls in the basis period for 1983–84 (i.e. the periods overlap) and is treated as falling in the first basis period (1982–83), while the period 6th April to 5th July 1984, already falls in the basis period for 1984–85 and is treated as falling in the first basis period (1984–85). Thus there will be no effective basis period for 1985–86.

1986–87: The basis period will normally be the preceding year of the business, i.e. the twelve months to 5th July 1985, but the period 6th July 1984, to 5th April 1985, falls in the basis period for 1984–85 (i.e. the periods overlap) and is treated as falling in the first basis period (1984–85). Thus the basis period for 1986–87 will be the period 6th April to 5th July 1985.

Example 2

Epos, a sole trader manufacturing leather goods, making up accounts to 30th June, has the following transactions relative to capital allowances in the year ended 30th June 1984:

		£
Acquisitions:		
	Fixed plant (pre-14.3.84)	15,000
	Office equipment (post-14.3.84)	2,000
	Motor car.............................	7,500
Disposals:	(at proceeds)	
	Machinery............................	2,500
	Motor car (original cost £5,500 30th	
	May 1978)	4,750

The written-down value of machinery and plant forming Epos's "pool" of expenditure following allowances for 1984–85 was £12,000 and the written down value of the car was £1,793.

In addition to the above transactions, Epos incurred expenditure on 15th May 1984 of £25,000 on a new factory. The factory was in use on 30th June 1984. Included in the cost of £25,000 was £2,750 for thermal insulation. The factory was approximately 8,000 ft^2.

The only other transaction undertaken by Epos related to the sale of his existing factory for £14,000. The factory (always used as such) was constructed in the year ended 30th June 1978, at which date it was brought into use. The cost of construction amounted to £15,000.

The allowances available to Epos for 1985–86 are as follows:

(i) *Capital allowances—machinery and plant*

		Pool £	Motor car (1) £	F.A. 1980 Pool £	Allowances £
Written-down value b/f		12,000	1,793		
Additions not qualifying for F.Y.A.:					
Motor Car				7,500	
Disposals (proceeds)					
Machinery....................		2,500			
Motor car....................			4,750		
			(2,957)		(2,957)
		9,500		7,500	
Additions for F.Y.A.	£				
Fixed plant	15,000				
Office equipment	2,000				
Thermal Insulation					
of industrial building	2,750				
	19,750				
F.Y.A.					
100% × 15,000	15,000				
75% × 4,750	3,562				
	18,562				18,562
Writing-down allowance					
25% × 9,500		2,375			2,375
25% × 7,500				1,875	1,875
Written-down value c/fwd		1,188	£7,125	£6,525	
Total allowances....................					£19,855

(ii) *Industrial Buildings Allowance*

New factory	Value £	Allowances £
Allowable cost (£25,000 − £2,750)	22,250	
Initial allowance		
50% × £22,250............................	(11,125)	11,125
Writing-down allowance		
4% × 22,250...............................	(890)	890
Residue of expenditure	£10,235	
Total allowances...		£12,015

Disposal of old factory		Value £	Allowances £
	£		
Residue of expenditure b/f (£15,000 − £11,100)		3,900	
Capital expenditure	£15,000		

	£	Value £	Allowances £
Allowances given:			
Initial allowance (1979–80): 50%			
× £15,000	7,500		
Writing-down allowance (1979–80 to			
1984–85): 4% × £15,000 × 6	3,600		
	£11,100		

Adjusted net cost:			
Capital expenditure	15,000		
Less Proceeds.	14,000		
	£1,000		

Balancing charge: Allowances given.	11,100		
Less Adjusted net cost	1,000	10,100	£(10,100)
Residue of expenditure for new owner		£14,000	

(iii) *Summary of allowances*	£	£
Machinery and plant:		
First-year allowance.	18,562	
Writing-down allowance	4,250	
Balancing charge.	(2,957)	19,855
Industrial buildings:		
Initial allowance	11,125	
Writing-down allowance	890	
Balancing charge.	(10,100)	1,915
		£21,770

Notes.

(1) The motor car brought forward forms a "separate trade" since it cost more than £5,000 pre 12th June 1979.

(2) Cars costing less than £8,000 and acquired after 31st May 1980 are included in the "Finance Act 1980" pool instead of the main pool.

(3) Thermal insulation of industrial buildings qualifies as expenditure on machinery and plant and hence a first-year allowance is available. This is 75%, since expenditure was incurred after 13.3.84. (Note, of course, that the expenditure on which Industrial Buildings Allowance is available is reduced by this sum).

(4) The disposal of the motor car has not been treated as the cessation of a trade in line with normal Revenue practice.

6.   Stock Relief—Sole Traders and Partnerships

§ 1.—INTRODUCTION

Ending of relief
The Finance Act 1984 abolished stock relief for all periods of account beginning after 12th March 1984. Transitional relief applies for periods straddling this date based on the "all-stocks index" from the start of the period to March 1984.

Historical background
The purpose of stock relief was to give a measure of relief to businesses whose trading stocks and/or work in progress have increased in value as a result of the effects of inflation.

In his Budget statement on 12th November 1974 the Chancellor of the Exchequer announced an interim scheme of relief which had effect for the "1973 accounting period" of companies (but not individuals or partnerships) whose trading stocks at the end of that period were in excess of £25,000.

When this interim scheme was announced, it was hoped that the benefit of the relief could be extended to all businesses in a form which was dependent on the findings of the Sandilands Committee on Inflation Accounting. The report of the Sandilands Committee was still awaited when the Budget was presented on 15th April 1975 and the interim scheme was, in effect, extended for a further year.

The extended relief was made available to individuals and partnerships in respect of the increase in stock values over a two-year base period ending, in most cases, on the last day of the period of account (i.e. the period for which a business draws up its accounts) which ended in 1974–75 (or last such period if more than one). The relief was equal to the amount by which the value of trading stocks at the end of the base period exceeded their value at the start thereof, less 10% of "relevant income" for the periods of account comprised in the two-year base period as computed for the purposes of Schedule D, Case I but *before* taking account of capital allowances or balancing charges or loss relief.

Effect was given to the relief by means of a deduction from the value of trading stock at the end of the last period of account comprised in the base period. The effect of this deduction was to reduce the profits of the trade for that period.

An additional relief equal to 5% of the relief otherwise available for the base period was also given to individuals and partnerships, since they had not been entitled to the interim relief. This additional relief was also deducted from the value of trading stock at the end of the last period of account comprised in the base period, but is not subject to recovery.

In the continued absence of agreement on a viable form of inflation accounting, a third form of stock relief was introduced by s. 37 and Schedule 5, F.A. 1976. Broadly this relief is given for the increase in stock value arising during a period of account less 10% of the relevant income of the business for the period. Relevant income was computed for F.A. 1976 relief *after* taking account of capital allowances or balancing charges but *before* loss relief.

A fourth form of stock relief came into effect, for periods of account ending on or after 14th November, 1980, following a consultative document issued by the Inland Revenue on that date and made law by s. 35 and Schedule 9, F.A. 1981 (see this chapter—§ 3). This relief is calculated by applying the increase, over a period of account in the "all stocks index" to the opening stock (less £2,000). Transitional rules which apply for periods of account beginning before and ending after 14th November 1980 were brought in by s. 35 and Schedule 10, F.A. 1981 (see this chapter—§ 4).

§ 2.—PERIODS OF ACCOUNT ENDING AFTER 12th MARCH 1984

(*a*) *Periods of account commencing after 12th March 1984* (s. 48, F.A. 1984)
No relief is available and no clawback of past relief applies. The provisions relating to offset of losses created by unused relief given for periods ending on or after 14th November 1980 will, however, continue to apply (see below).
(*b*) *Periods of account commencing before 12th March 1984 and ending after that date*
Relief is calculated as for periods ending prior to 12th March 1984 (for which see below) *except* that the period of account is treated as ending on 12th March 1984. Thus relief is calculated on the increase in the all stocks index from the commencement of the period of account to March 1984 *and* no clawback will arise provided cessation etc. takes place after 12th March 1984.

Example

T. Pain makes up accounts to 30th June each year. His stock at 30th June 1983 is £75,000. The indexes are:

June 1983   235.2
March 1984   246.1

The relief available for 30th June 1984 is $£75,000 - £2,000 \times \dfrac{246.1 - 235.2}{235.2} = £3,383$.

New businesses
Relief will be given by reference to the closing stock value discounted by reference to the rise in the all-stocks index between commencement and March 1984.

Unused relief
Losses created by unused relief given for periods ending on or after 14th November 1980 will continue to apply (see below for details).

Successions after 12th March 1984
The election rules for continuance cease to have effect, although the apportionment of relief rules as appropriate continues to operate.

Herd basis election
The time limit for election under Schedule 6, para. (3), F.A. 1970 is extended to two years after the end of the period of account beginning on or after 13th March 1984. The election where otherwise not valid will only apply to the period after 13th March 1984.

§ 3.—PERIODS OF ACCOUNT ENDING AFTER 14th NOVEMBER 1980 BUT BEFORE 13th MARCH 1984

CALCULATION OF RELIEF
As mentioned in § 1, the relief for stock appreciation is calculated simply by multiplying the opening stock (less £2,000) by the "all-stocks index" applying to the period of account in question. (For calculations see below and for transitional arrangements, see § 4.)

Relevant year of assessment (Schedule 9, para. 7, F.A. 1981)

In general, the relevant year of assessment in relation to a period of account is the year for which it is the basis period.

If the period of account forms the basis period for more than one year of assessment, the relevant year of assessment depends on the reason for this. If it is because the provisions for new businesses apply, the relevant year of assessment is the earliest such year. Otherwise (e.g. on a change of accounting date) it is the last such year.

In some circumstances (e.g. when a trade ceases) a period of account may not form the basis period for any year of assessment. In such a case, the relevant year of assessment is that following the year in which the period of account ends.

DEFINITIONS

(1) *Trading stock* (Schedule 9, paras. 28–30, F.A. 1981)

"Trading stock" is property of any description, whether real or personal, such as is sold or is bought to be processed and sold in the ordinary course of the trade, etc. in question, together with materials used in manufacture etc. and work in progress. It does not include:

  (*a*) Securities (i.e. stocks and shares); or
  (*b*) Land, unless held for sale in the course of the trade after being developed by the company carrying on the trade; or
  (*c*) Goods held for letting on hire or hire-purchase.

It will thus be noted that securities (i.e. stocks and shares etc.) are excluded from trading stock for this purpose, as are goods let on hire or hire pur-chase.

Land cannot be included as trading stock unless it is held for sale in the ordinary course of a trade after the construction or substantial reconstruction of buildings on the land concerned. For periods of account beginning after 26th March 1980 a building can be regarded as land in the somewhat unusual case of buildings for which there is no immediately underlying land (e.g. *freehold* flats above the floor). In other words land held as trading stock by a land dealer is not eligible for the relief, but a builder or developer would qualify.

Payments on account reduce the value of trading stock for the purposes of the relief, but it is understood that this reduction is not made for payments received by way of deposits to secure future orders. Furthermore payments on account must be matched against the items of stock concerned and if the amount of the payment on account exceeds the value of an item of stock, that excess is not set against other stock.

Example 1—effect of payments on account of W.I.P.

Gerard is working on three contracts. The value of work in progress on these jobs and the payments on account received in respect thereof are:

	Total £	Job A £	Job B £	Job C £
Value	12,000	4,000	3,000	5,000
Payment on account	10,000	3,000	1,000	6,000
Balance sheet value	£2,000	£1,000	£2,000	£(1,000)
Value for stock relief	£3,000	£1,000	£2,000	£ Nil

If a business is registered for V.A.T. and all its outputs are standard or zero-rated the stock value in the accounts will be "net". However, if the supplies made by the business is wholly or partly exempt supplies to it will nonetheless have borne V.A.T. In such a case any V.A.T. input which relates to trading stock and which cannot be taken into account will be included in the stock value.

If goods are sold subject to reservation of title (i.e. the seller can reclaim the goods if he is not paid), such goods are nonetheless treated as purchases and, if appropriate, stock of the purchaser (provided the seller treats them as sold and not included in his stock).

Work in progress on Government contracts is regarded as remaining the property of the contractor pending final delivery (even though most such clauses contain a clause vesting property therein in the Government Department or Agency concerned).

(2) *Work in progress* (Schedule 9, para. 31, F.A. 1981)

"Work in progress" comprises services performed in the ordinary course of a trade, etc. where performance thereof is partly complete and where it is reasonable to expect that a charge will subsequently be made for those services, together with any article produced or material used in performing those services. This definition of work in progress does not include work wholly completed but not billed.

The purpose of this exclusion is to prevent the giving of relief on work in progress which in reality should be an amount owing by a debtor. However, the Inland Revenue has stated that this definition will not be applied harshly and the relief would only be denied in exceptional cases.

SPECIAL CIRCUMSTANCES

In most cases trading stock for relief purposes is primarily the amount which is brought into account in computing the profits of the trade etc., subject to any necessary adjustment for excess payments on account. There are however a number of special rules for determining the value of trading stock which have to be followed in certain circumstances; these are outlined as follows:

(i) *New businesses* (Schedule 9, para. 19, F.A. 1981)

For new businesses, any actual opening stock for the first period of account is ignored. Instead, a notional figure is calculated by reducing the closing stock in accordance with the movement in the all-stocks index over the period. Relief is then given as if the opening stock were equal to that amount.

Example 2

Patel commenced trading on 1st November 1981 and made up his first accounts to 30th June 1982.
His stocks were:

1.11.81	Nil
14.11.81	Nil
30.6.82	£14,950

Patel's opening stock is ignored and a notional figure is calculated, as follows:

$$\text{Closing stock} \times \frac{\text{Index for month containing day before period began}}{\text{Index for month containing last day of period}}$$

$$= £14,950 \times \frac{211.8 \ (\text{October 1981})}{220.5 \ (\text{June 1982})}$$

$$= £14,360$$

The relief due will therefore be:

Percentage increase in index

$$\frac{206.4 - 195.6}{206.4} \times 100 = \underline{\underline{5.24\%}}$$

Relief due £(14,360 − 2,000) × 3.94% = £487

The relief will be available to Patel in 1981–82 (i.e. the earliest year) since it is a business commencement.

(ii) *Anti-avoidance provisions* (Schedule 9, para. 22, F.A. 1981)
If a person enters into transactions from which it appears that the sole or main object is to obtain:

(*a*) additional relief; or
(*b*) a reduction in clawback; or
(*c*) a reduction in the restriction of carry forward of unused stock relief

then the Revenue have the power to substitute, at the end of the affected period of account, the value of stock which would have been held if the transactions had not been entered into. Where the arrangements were intended to reduce the restriction in carry forward of unused relief any reduction attributable to such arrangements is ignored.

The wording of the paragraph implies that any arrangement would be caught, although the following are mentioned specifically:

(*a*) any acquisition or disposal of trading stock otherwise than in the normal course of trade; or
(*b*) any change in the normal pattern or method of carrying on the trade; or
(*c*) any change in the accounting date of the trade; or
(*d*) any acquisition of trading stock or increase in the value of one person's trading stock which is associated with a decrease in that of a person connected with him (s. 533, I.C.T.A. 1970).

(iii) *Long periods of account* (Schedule 9, para. 23, F.A. 1981)
Where a period of account exceeds eighteen months the Inland Revenue have a right to require that the period of account is divided into notional periods, only the last of which may exceed twelve months. The relief is then calculated for each of such periods and aggregated to obtain the relief for the whole period of account. It will be necessary to use the special rules for valuation of stock at intermediate dates unless stock has actually been taken at the ends of the notional periods of account.

Example 3

George has stock of £150,000 on 31st March 1982 and next prepares accounts to 31st March 1984. It is established that stock at 31st March 1983 is £75,000.

The "all stocks index" is assumed, *for the purposes of this example only* to be:

31st March 1982	216.3
31st March 1983	237.4
31st March 1984	258.2

At first sight the relief (see calculation below) would seem to be:

$$(£150,000 - £2,000) \times \frac{258.2 - 216.3}{216.3} = \qquad \underline{\underline{£28,670}}$$

If the Revenue use their option it is likely that each of the years to 31st March 1983 and 1984, would be the notional periods. The revised relief would be:

	£
Year to 31st March 1983	
$(£150,000 - £2,000) \times \dfrac{(237.4 - 216.3)}{216.3} =$	14,437
Year to 31st March 1984	
$(£75,000 - £2,000) \times \dfrac{(258.2 - 237.4)}{237.4} =$	6,396
Revised relief for the two year period to 31st March, 1984	£20,833

(iv) *Valuation at intermediate dates* (Schedule 9, para. 24, F.A. 1981)
When a stock value is required at some other date than on the commencement of a new business, or at the end of a period of account, and the actual value at the date concerned is not known it is necessary to calculate a notional value. The value taken is such as is "reasonable and just" taking into account all relevant circumstances but in particular:
 (*a*) actual values of stock at the beginning and end of the period of account concerned;
 (*b*) movements in the costs of items comprised in trading stock;
 (*c*) changes in the volume of trade.
If a valuation is needed for an intermediate date during a long period of account these items are taken into account for the long period and not those for each notional period. However, any available information relating to one or more of the notional periods can be used in arriving at a value, since regard must be had to all the relevant circumstances.
 These rules apply (unless actual figures are known) in determining the stock value at 14th November 1980. In that case the period of account is to be treated as divided into two parts.

PAST RELIEF (Schedule 9, paras. 25, 27, F.A. 1981)
Past relief is the aggregate of the "two-year" stock relief (but not the 5% additional relief) and relief under the F.A. 1976 and F.A. 1981 schemes.
 Unrecovered past relief is past relief less any amounts clawed back or written off.
 Any balance of "two-year" stock relief remaining in unrecovered past relief is written off by excluding an appropriate amount from unrecovered past relief brought forward from the period of account ending in 1978–79.
 The actual amount written off was the amount of "two-year" stock relief given, less any amounts recovered subsequently under the claw-back arrangements. In determining whether any relief for these periods has been recovered, claw-backs are set against later years' relief before earlier years' (i.e. on a "last-in-first-out" (LIFO) basis).
 Stock relief under the F.A. 1976 and F.A. 1981 schemes given for later periods of account is to be excluded from unrecovered past relief for any period of account beginning on or after the sixth anniversary of the end of the period of account for which the relief was claimed. In most cases, where accounts have been drawn up annually, the write-off will be made with effect from the day following the sixth anniversary of the period of account concerned. If the sixth anniversary of the period of account in point does not coincide with the end of a period of account (because an intervening period of account was for more or less than twelve months), the write-off is made immediately after the period of account which is current on the sixth anniversary of the relevant period of

account. The same general principles apply as with the write-off of the "two-year" stock relief, including the LIFO principle for identifying the actual amount to be written off.

Example 4

Rick France has had the following stock relief claims and clawbacks.

Period to	Relief (clawback)	Type
30.6.1974	£2,200	F(No.2)A. 1975
30.6.1975	£3,000	F.A. 1976
30.6.1976	£3,500	F.A. 1976
30.6.1977	£6,000	F.A. 1976
30.6.1978	£(7,200)	F.A. 1976
31.1.1979	£4,000	F.A. 1976
31.1.1980	£5,400	F.A. 1976

The allocation of clawback and the write-off dates are shown below:

	30.6 1974 £	30.6 1975 £	30.6 1976 £	30.6 1977 £	30.6 1978 £	30.6 1979 £	31.1 1980 £
Relief	2,200	3,000	3,500	6,000	(7,200)	4,000	5,400
Clawback allocation	—	—	(1,200)	(6,000)	7,200	—	—
Net relief	£2,200	£3,000	£2,300	£—	£—	£4,000	£5,400
Write-off date	1.7.78	1.2.82	1.2.83	N/A	N/A	1.2.86	1.2.86
Note	(a)	(b)					(c)

(a) The last period of account ending in 1978–79 (i.e. year to 5th April 1979) was the year to 30th June 1978. Thus, the two-year stock relief is excluded from the unrecovered past relief brought forward at the start of the next period. At that point it ceases to be vulnerable to any claw-back.

(b) The relief for the year to 30th June 1975 is six years old on 30th June 1981. Had there been no change of year-end, it would therefore have been excluded from unrecovered past relief brought forward on 1st July 1981, and would have ceased to be vulnerable to clawback from that date. Since the year-end changed, there is no period commencing on 1st July 1981, and it is necessary to find the date on which the next period does in fact commence. This is 1st February 1982 and is therefore the write-off date.

(c) The relief for the year to 31st January 1980 is six years old on 31st January 1986. Since the next period of account commences on 1st February 1986 the relief is written off on that date.

The write-off also applies to stock relief for farmers which was "frozen" on the making of a herd basis election.

CALCULATION

(1) *Relief* (Schedule 9, paras. 1, 2, 3, F.A. 1981)
Calculations of stock relief are based on the increase, during a period of account, in the "all-stocks" index prepared and published monthly by the Department of Industry. The percentage increase in the all-stocks index during the period concerned is applied to the opening stock (strictly the closing stock at the end of the preceding period) less a standard £2,000 exclusion.

The relief has to be claimed within two years after the end of the year of assessment in which the period of account ends. However claims can be made for all, none or part only of any stock relief to which the trader is entitled. The unclaimed balance is not available for future periods.

Example 5

Arthur had stock on 1st July 1981 of £47,500. Assuming *(for the purposes of this example only)* that the all-stocks index was 208.2 on 30th June 1981 and 221.6 on 30th June 1982, Arthur can claim stock relief for the year to 30th June 1982 as follows:

Increase in all-stocks index (221.6 − 208.2)	13.4
Percentage increase ($\frac{13.4}{221.6} \times 100$)	6.05%
Stock relief £(47,500 − 2,000) × 6.05%	£2,753

Arthur can, if he wishes, reduce the amount of his claim. Any unclaimed balance cannot be claimed in a future period, so the only beneficial effect of failing to claim relief in full is that the unclaimed amount will not go to increase the unrecovered past relief vulnerable to clawback. Thus, it can be advantageous to make a reduced claim if personal allowances would otherwise be wasted.

(2) *Clawback* (Schedule 9, para. 4, F.A. 1981)
When a person ceases to carry on a trade, stock relief is not available for the period of account during or at the end of which the trade ceases. On cessation any balance of unrecovered past relief will be clawed back. There is also a prohibition on relief and there will be a clawback of unrecovered past relief where the activities of a trade in a period are negligible as compared with their scale in a period beginning within the previous six years.

In determining whether the scale of activities has become negligible the Inland Revenue has issued a practice statement (SP3/81) which sets out a "test of negligible". Under this test activities will be considered negligible if turnover has fallen below $2\frac{1}{2}\%$ of its level during the period of account in which it was at its higher in the preceding six years. (Reduction in turnover as a result of exceptional circumstances e.g. prolonged industrial action will be ignored).

It should be noted that since this test is only a guideline the usual rights of appeal will apply if the taxpayer and inspector are unable to agree.

(3) *Top-slicing* (Schedule 9, para. 6, F.A. 1981)
If a clawback arises and the trader has been carrying on the trade for more than one year, he may claim a top-slicing relief to mitigate his tax liability on the claw-back. In effect, the whole of the clawback is taxed at the rate which would have applied to a fraction of the clawback, this fraction being dependent on the length of time for which the business has been carried on.

The calculation proceeds as follows:
- (*a*) calculate tax on the whole clawback, taking it as the top slice of income for the year.
- (*b*) calculate tax on the "*appropriate fraction*" of the clawback, taking it as the top-slice of income for the year. The appropriate fraction is $\frac{1}{2}$ if the trade has been carried on for between one and two years, and $\frac{1}{3}$ if it has been carried on for two years or more.
- (*c*) multiply the tax on the "*appropriate fraction*" of the clawback by the reciprocal of the "*appropriate fraction*".
- (*d*) the relief is the difference between (*a*) and (*c*).

In making the above calculations, certain other amounts eligible for top-slicing reliefs are excluded from total income. These are:
- (i) Lease premiums.

(ii) Amount treated as premiums on assignment of a lease at undervalue or sale with right to reconveyance.

(iii) Payment on termination of office or employment.

(iv) Gains on non-qualifying life policies.

Deductions from total income are set against other sources of income in priority to the clawback.

Example 6

Ivett ceases trading on 28th February 1984. He has carried on the trade for ten years. There is a clawback of stock relief, on cessation, of £14,000.

Ivett is entitled only to a married person's allowance, and he has the following income for 1983–84 (excluding the clawback):

	£
Schedule D Case I	10,000
Schedule D Case III	400
Schedule E	1,850
	£12,250

Top slicing relief is due as follows:

	£
Income other than clawback	12,250
Less: Personal allowance	2,795
	9,455
Clawback	14,000
	£23,455

Tax on clawback

	£
£5,145 @ 30%	1,543.50
£2,600 @ 40%	1,040.00
£4,600 @ 45%	2,070.00
£4,355 @ 50%	827.50
£14,000	£5,481.00

Tax on appropriate fraction of clawback

Appropriate fraction of clawback is:

$$£14,000 \times \tfrac{1}{3} = £4,667$$

Tax thereon is:

£4,667 @ 30%	£1,400.10

Scaled-up tax

£1,532.30 × 3	=	£4,200.30

Top-slicing relief due

	£
Tax on clawback	5,481.00
Scaled-up tax on appropriate fraction of clawback	4,200.30
Relief due...	£1,280.70

A claim for top-slicing relief must be made within two years after the end of the year of assessment concerned.

Utilisation of relief

(i) *General*
The carry-forward of losses due to unused stock relief given under F.A. 1981 is restricted to six years. Thus it is necessary to distinguish the various components of a carried forward loss, i.e. trading loss, capital allowances and stock relief (see below).

(ii) *Deduction from current profits* (Schedule 9, para. 5, F.A. 1981)
Stock relief is deducted from the amount of assessable profits of the relevant year of assessment. The order in which the various amounts available are deducted from profits is:
  (*a*) current capital allowances
  (*b*) current stock relief
  (*c*) capital allowances from basis period after 14.11.80
  (*d*) F.A. 1981 stock relief brought forward (taking later periods before earlier periods)
  (*e*) other capital allowances brought forward
  (*f*) "old scheme" stock relief brought forward
  (*g*) trading losses brought forward.

(iii) *Set off against general income* (Schedule 9, para. 8, F.A. 1981)
Stock relief may be used to create or augment a loss for set off against general income under I.C.T.A. 1970, s. 168 and s. 169. *However, this is only permissible if a similar claim is made for any available capital allowances.* The reason for this is to give effect to the set-off rules in determining the restriction on carry forward of unused stock relief (see below).
  If such a claim is made the utilisation of the various reliefs is in the following order:
  (*a*) trading loss
  (*b*) capital allowances
  (*c*) stock relief
  A claim for set-off against general income must be made as part of a claim under I.C.T.A. 1970, s. 168. If the relief arises in a partnership, the consent to the claim of all the partners is required.

(iv) *Carry forward of unused relief* (Schedule 9, para. 9, F.A. 1981)
Stock relief not used against current profits or against general income may be carried forward against future profits of the same trade. The order of set off in such a case is shown at (ii) above.

(v) *Restriction of carry forward of unused relief* (Schedule 9, para. 10, F.A. 1981)
Stock relief under F.A. 1981 may not be carried forward to a year of assessment whose basis period begins six years or more after the period of account for which

it was given. The losses are written off irrevocably after this six year period, and if appropriate, claims for capital allowances should not be made (or should be reduced) so that the losses are preserved. Each case will need careful consideration according to its own circumstances.

The order of set-off is as in (ii) above.

SPECIAL SITUATIONS

(1) *Successions* (Schedule 9, para. 20, F.A. 1981)
Special provisions apply on a transfer of stock, at cost or market value, where a trade carried on by a sole trader or partnership is transferred to a company and at the date of the transfer not less than 75% of the ordinary share capital is held by that sole trader or by the partners.

If the predecessor and successor elect (within two years after the end of the period of account in which the transfer takes place), the successor is treated as having carried on the trade since the predecessor began to do so. There is then no clawback on cessation by the predecessor. If the transfer takes place during a period of account, the predecessor receives stock relief based on the movement in the "all stocks index" up to that date applied to opening stock. The successor obtains stock relief based on the movement in the "all stocks index" from the date of transfer to the end of the period, applied to the stock taken over.

If, when the business of a sole trader or partnership is incorporated, any relief remains unused (e.g. because the profits were insufficient), an equivalent amount is excluded from unrecovered past relief taken over by the company.

These rules also apply where only part of a trade is transferred. In such cases unrecovered past relief is apportioned on the basis of the respective values of stock retained or transferred.

(2) *Partnership changes* (Schedule 9, para. 21, F.A. 1981)
A change in the members of a partnership constitutes the cessation of the old partnership and the commencement of the new one, with a consequent clawback of unrecovered past relief.

However, if at least one member of the old partnership continues in the new one, and all "old" and "new" partners so elect, the business may be treated as continuing. Election for this treatment must be made within two years from the end of the successors' period of account commencing on the change. However, the treatment is automatic if an election is made under I.C.T.A. 1970, s. 154(2).

(3) *Farm animals* (Schedule 9, para. 25, F.A. 1981)
Farm animals are treated as trading stock for stock relief unless an election is made under para. 2, Sch. 6, I.C.T.A. 1970, for the "herd basis" to apply. If such an election is made those animals which comprise the "herd" are excluded from stock, with effect from the end of the period of account preceding the one during which the election becomes effective.

Unrecovered past relief at the end of that previous period is apportioned between the "herd" and the remaining stock in proportion to their respective values at that time.

The normal treatment, whereby when a person transfers part of his trade, the unrecovered past relief is apportioned between predecessor and successor by reference to the value of stock transferred and that retained, does not apply to the relief attributable to the "herd", which is instead apportioned on the basis of the respective values of "herd" animals transferred and retained.

(4) *Foreign Trades* (Schedule 9, para. 35, F.A. 1981)
The stock relief provisions apply equally to trades and professions carried on

outside the U.K., and chargeable to Case V of Schedule D unless the remittance basis applies (i.e. the individual is non-UK domiciled or a British subject not ordinarily UK resident).

Stock relief applicable to foreign trades is however reduced to 75% of the normal stock relief claim in the case where income is only 75% chargeable by virtue of s. 23(3), F.A. 1974.

Example 7

Bearos carries on a trade outside the UK which is chargeable under Case V of Schedule D *not* on a remittance basis.

His results for the year to 31 December 1982 are:

	£
Adjusted profits	80,000
Capital allowances	Nil
Stock 31.12.1981	100,000

The percentage increase in the all stocks index for the year to 31.12.1982 is 5.88%.

Bearos is chargeable to tax as follows:

		£
Adjusted profits		80,000
Less 25% relief (s. 23(3), F.A. 1974)		20,000
		60,000
Less stock relief		
5.88% × 100,000	5,880	
less 25% reduction	1,470	4,410
Case V Schedule D assessment		£55,590

7. The Treatment of Losses

§ 1.—INTRODUCTION

The contents of this chapter refer only to losses incurred in trades, professions, employments or vocations, income from which would be assessable under Schedule D, Cases I and II. The treatment of other losses is dealt with in the appropriate chapters of this book, although brief mention (see § 9) is made of relief under s. 37, F.A. 1980.

Each of these reliefs is examined in detail below together with the effect of annual charges including those created or augmented by capital allowances and stock relief.

Losses incurred in carrying on a trading activity are available for relief in a variety of ways:

    (1) Set off against general income.
    (2) Carry back for losses in the first years of trading.
    (3) Carry forward of losses against future trading profits.
    (4) Carry forward where trade transferred to a company.
    (5) Carry back where trade ceases.

§ 2.—SET OFF AGAINST GENERAL INCOME (s. 168, I.C.T.A. 1970)

Section 168 provides that where in:

    (*a*) Any trade, profession, employment or vocation; or
    (*b*) The occupation of woodlands in respect of which application has been made for assessment under Schedule D;

a loss (as adjusted for Income Tax purposes) has been incurred in any year of assessment, a claim may be made for repayment of tax on the amount of the loss to the extent of the tax borne on *any income for the same year*. Where the claim is made before the second instalment of tax has been paid, such second instalment will be amended or cancelled and any further tax still recoverable will be repaid.

Two-year relief
A claim under s. 168 may be made for the year of assessment following that in which the loss was incurred, provided that the trade, profession, vocation, etc., is still carried on in that following year, and in so far as relief in respect of that loss has not already been given.

Thus if a loss occurs for the year ended 5th April 1985, relief under s. 168 may be claimed for *either* 1984–85 or 1985–86; alternatively, the taxpayer may make a claim in 1984–85 and also a claim in 1985–86 in respect of any balance of the loss. No claim could be made for 1985–86, however, unless the business was still carried on in that year.

Priority of claim and carry forward
Where a loss is sustained in the year for which relief under s. 168 is claimed in respect of an earlier loss, the relief for the earlier loss has priority. This provision is of importance, for by utilising the earlier loss first, it enables relief for the second loss to be claimed in the subsequent year of assessment.

Where tax is recovered on a portion only of the loss, the balance may be carried forward (under s. 171, I.C.T.A. 1970) and deducted from subsequent assessments (see § 4 of this chapter).

Year of loss
Except in the case of the first three years of a new business or the last year of a discontinued business, it is not the practice, in arriving at the loss for any year, to "split" accounts, i.e., to apportion the results of two trading periods to the year of assessment concerned, but to treat a loss as applicable to the year of assessment which includes that last day of the period for which the accounts have been made up. The practice of allowing the accounting year to be treated as co-terminous with the year of assessment is not allowed in a year following a claim based on a loss for a year ended 5th April, i.e., on a "split" accounts basis. Nor is it allowed when accounts are made up for irregular periods.

Example 1

D. Drake makes up accounts annually to 5th October. In his accounting year ended 5th October 1985, he suffers an adjusted loss of £1,200. He could split this, treating six-twelfths (i.e., £600) as incurred in 1984–85, and the remainder (£600) as incurred in 1985–86.

Normally, however, the whole loss would be regarded as suffered in 1985–86.

Time limit for claim
The claim for relief under s. 168 must be made within two years after the end of the year of assessment concerned, and thus a claim in respect of the year 1985–86 must be made not later than 5th April 1988.

Restriction of loss offset (ss. 170 and 180, I.C.T.A. 1970)
No relief under s. 168, I.C.T.A. 1970 is given for losses (including capital allowances) unless it is shown that the trade, profession or vocation was being carried on for that year of assessment on a commercial basis and with a view to the realisation of profits in the trade, etc. Section 170 also restricts relief under s. 168(2), I.C.T.A. 1970 which gives relief similar to that under s. 168(1) for the immediately succeeding year of assessment.

For the purposes of s. 170, I.C.T.A. 1970 the fact that a trade was being carried on so as to afford a reasonable expectation of profit is conclusive evidence that it was then being carried on with a view to the realisation of profits.

Section 180, I.C.T.A. 1970 provides that where a loss is incurred in a trade of farming or market gardening, and a loss was incurred in each of the five previous years, then a loss in the sixth year, together with any related capital allowances, is to be disallowed for the purposes of s. 168, I.C.T.A. 1970.

The restriction does not apply where the taxpayer can show that the whole of his activities in the sixth year are of such a nature and carried on in such a way as would have justified a reasonable expectation of future profits if these activities had been carried on by a competent farmer or market gardener who could not have been expected to make a profit until after the period in question.

Section 180, I.C.T.A. 1970 does not apply to a loss incurred in, or any capital allowances the basis year for which is, a year of assessment prior to 1967–68.

Sections 170 and 180, I.C.T.A. 1970 do not, however, prevent relief for any loss from being obtained by carrying forward the loss under s. 171, I.C.T.A. 1970 (See § 4).

Utilisation of loss
If the claimant so requires, the adjustment under s. 168, I.C.T.A. 1970 is made by reference only to the income of the person sustaining the loss, *without extending*

to the income of that person's wife or husband. Relief under s. 168, I.C.T.A. 1970 is given first against the claimant's income of the same class (earned or unearned), and then against his other income. If the claimant does not restrict the claim to his or her own income, the relief is then extended to the income of the claimant's wife or husband (if the wife or husband agrees), being given first against income of the corresponding class (earned or unearned), and next against other income.

Example 2

A. Dormer is a sleeping partner in Black and White, his income for 1985–86 being as follows:

	£
Share of Schedule D Assessment, 1985–86 in Black and White	2,500
Taxed dividends (including tax credit)	30
Salary from Traders Ltd	2,450

His wife received taxed dividends of £300 (including tax credit) in 1985–86.

Black and White incur a loss during the year to 30th September 1985, the share of Dormer in such loss being £4,800.

It is required to show the tax payable by Dormer for 1985–86 after claiming relief in respect of the loss.

STATEMENT OF INCOME TAX PAYABLE 1985–86

	£	£	£
Salary			2,450
Less: Share of loss in partnership		4,800	
Deduct: Amount of loss set-off against income of corresponding class:			
Share of partnership Assessment, 1985–86	2,500		
Taxed dividends	30	2,530	
Balance of loss set-off against earned income			2,270
			180
Wife's taxed dividends			300
			480
Less: Personal allowance			3,455
Taxable income			Nil

Notes (1) As the share of a sleeping partner constitutes unearned income, the loss is set-off first against income of that class.

(2) As Income Tax has been deducted at the basic rate of 30 per cent on the Taxed Dividends of £330 and tax has been deducted under the Pay As You Earn Regulations (see Chapter 8, § 12), from Dormer's salary, the whole of this tax will be repayable.

(3) Dormer may have considered not making a s. 168 claim, but instead carrying the whole of the loss forward under s. 171, as effectively he has lost £2,975 of allowances (£3,455–£480). N.B. *Once a s. 168 claim is made it is not possible to restrict it to income of the corresponding class only. The only choice in this respect is to offset against the spouse's earnings.*

SOLE TRADERS

When a claim under s. 168, I.C.T.A. 1970 is made by a sole trader, the loss is deducted from the total statutory income and the tax payable re-computed. The excess over this of the tax originally borne is then repaid. It should be noted that the loss is deducted primarily from the assessment in respect of the business, etc., in which the loss is incurred.

The following example illustrates the application of the claim in the case of a sole trader.

Example 3

The statutory income of A. Jones, a manufacturer, for 1985–86 is as follows:

	£
Business profits (Year to 30.9.84):	
Schedule D assessment	8,450
Taxed dividends (including tax credit)	200
Wife's taxed dividends (including tax credit)	150

For the year ended 30th September 1985 (the usual date to which the accounts are made up), the result of Jones's trading is a loss (as adjusted for Income Tax purposes) of £5,800. It is required to show the tax recoverable by Jones under s. 168 I.C.T.A. 1970. Jones will have paid or borne tax as follows:

	£
Business profits	8,450
Taxed dividends (self)	200
Taxed dividends (wife)	150
Total statutory income	8,800
Less Personal allowance	3,455
Taxable income	£5,345

TAX PAYABLE

£5,345 at 30%	£1,603.50

On a claim being made under s. 168, I.C.T.A. 1970, Jones's income will be recomputed as follows:

	£	£
Business profits	8,450	
Less Loss	5,800	
		2,650
Taxed dividends (self)		200
Taxed dividends (wife)		150
Total statutory income		3,000
Less Personal allowance		3,455
Taxable income		Nil

Jones will therefore obtain repayment of £1,603.50

PARTNERSHIP LOSSES

In the case of a partnership, no claim under s. 168, I.C.T.A. 1970 can be made by the firm; each partner must claim individually in respect of his share of the loss, his personal income, apart from the firm, being brought into account. It is not necessary, however, for all the partners to claim, and the share of the loss applicable to a partner who does *not* claim under s. 168, I.C.T.A. 1970 will be carried forward under s. 171, I.C.T.A. 1970 (see § 4).

The following example illustrates the application of the claim in the case of a firm.

Example 4

Atkins and Bateman carry on business in partnership, sharing profits three-fifths and two-fifths respectively. The Schedule D assessment on the firm for 1985–86 is £10,000. For the year ended 31st March 1986, a loss (as adjusted for Income Tax purposes) of £8,125 is incurred.

Atkins (aged 50) is married, with one child, aged 9; he has taxed dividends amounting to £1,000 (including tax credit). Bateman is a bachelor with no other income. Both partners having elected to claim under s. 168, it is required to show the tax recoverable by each.

The assessment for 1985–86 will have been divisible:

	£
To Atkins—three-fifths	6,000
To Bateman—two-fifths	4,000
	£10,000

Atkins and Bateman will have paid or borne tax as follows:

	ATKINS £	BATEMAN £
Business profits	6,000	4,000
Taxed dividends	1,000	—
Total statutory income	7,000	4,000
Less Personal allowance	3,455	2,205
Taxable income	£3,545	£1,795

TAX PAYABLE

ATKINS		BATEMAN	
£3,545 at 30%	£1,063.50	£1,795 at 30%	= £538.50

The loss of £8,125 will be divisible:

	£
To Atkins—three fifths	4,875
To Bateman—two-fifths	3,250
	£8,125

On claims being made under s. 168, their incomes for 1985–86 will be recomputed as follows:

	ATKINS £	BATEMAN £
Business profits	6,000	4,000
Taxed dividends	1,000	—
	7,000	4,000
Less: Share of loss	4,875	3,250
Total statutory income	2,125	750
Less: Personal allowance	3,455	2,205
Taxable income	Nil	Nil

	TAX RECOVERABLE	£	£
Tax paid		1,063.50	538.50
Tax recoverable		£1,063.50	£538.50

Note: (i) Following the loss for the year ended 31st March 1986, the assessment for 1986–87 will be "nil".

(ii) Since the s. 168 claim results in a loss of personal allowances, it may be advantageous not to make the claim, but to carry forward the loss under s. 171, I.C.T.A. 1970 (see § 4).

LIMITED PARTNERSHIPS (s. 48, F.A. 1985)
Where the interest of any one partner is limited to the amount of money at risk in the business, any loss made is restricted to the sum at risk.

This provision applies for all periods of account beginning after 19th March 1985. (See Chapter 3 for further details.)

Example 5

Careful is a limited partner in Careful & Reckless. The partners share profits and losses equally. Careful has introduced £12,000 into the business, and during the year ended 31st March 1986 the partnership makes a loss of £40,000.

Careful's loss is restricted to £12,000 on which a s. 168 claim is available, and the balance of the loss of £8,000 (£20,000 − £12,000) is available to carry forward under s. 171.

CAPITAL ALLOWANCES (s. 169, I.C.T.A. 1970)
A claimant for relief under s. 168, I.C.T.A. 1970 *may* require the loss in respect of which the relief is claimed to be increased by any capital allowances *based on the accounting period in which the loss is sustained.*

A claim may be made as above notwithstanding that apart from those allowances a loss would otherwise not arise, i.e., if the allowances based on an accounting period exceed the profits for that accounting period, the balance of capital allowances may be treated as a loss for the purpose of a claim for relief under s. 168, I.C.T.A. 1970.

If any capital allowances are brought forward from earlier years, they cannot be utilised for this purpose, although they may be deducted from any profits of the year in respect of which the claim is made in priority to the capital allowances for that year.

Capital allowances used to augment or create a loss for the purpose of a s. 168 claim must be regarded as having been effectively allowed for all tax purposes and cannot be carried forward. But the amount deemed to have been effectively allowed cannot exceed that of the s. 168, I.C.T.A. 1970 claim, and hence any balance of allowances is available for carry forward.

Where a person has carried on a trade or business in partnership since the end of the year of assessment for which the claim is made, capital allowances can only be utilised as described above for the purposes of a s. 168, I.C.T.A. 1970 claim with the written consent of every partner or the personal representative of a deceased partner. The purpose appears to be to preserve equity between the partners, since they will be jointly liable on any subsequent clawback of capital allowances by way of a balancing charge.

Example 6

A trader prepares accounts to 31st March each year. For the year to 31st March 1985, his adjusted profits were £20,000; capital allowances 1985–86 amounted to £2,000. For the year to 31st March 1986, a loss of £10,000 is sustained; capital allowances 1986–87 amounted to £1,800. The claim under s. 168, I.C.T.A. 1970 for 1985–86 is as follows:

	£	£
Assessment 1985–86	20,000	
Less: Capital allowances 1985–86	2,000	
	———	£18,000
Claim s. 168:		
Loss, Year to 31st March 1986	10,000	
Add: Capital allowances 1986–87	1,800	
	———	£11,800

The capital allowances can also be used to produce a loss.

Example 7—creating a loss

Assume the same facts as in Example 5 except that for the year to 31st March 1986, there was an adjusted profit of £500. The s. 168 claim would be:

	£
1986–87 profit, year to 31st March 1986 ...	500
Less: Capital allowances 1986–87	1,800
	———
Amount of claim (1985–86)	£1,300

Example 8

A long-established trader A. Young has agreed the following figures for taxation purposes.

	£
Adjusted Profit, Year to 30th September 1982	8,000
Adjusted Loss, Year to 30th September 1983	2,000
Adjusted Profit, Year to 30th September 1984	5,000
Capital Allowances brought forward to 1983–84	3,000
Capital Allowances for the year 1983–84	6,000
Capital Allowances for the year 1984–85	5,000
Capital Allowances for the year 1985–86	4,000
Balancing charge 1984–85	1,300
Other annual income (taxed at source) gross	6,000

The position for the years 1983–84 to 1985–86 will be as follows:

	£	£
1983–84 original assessment:		
Profit, year to 30th September 1982		8,000
Less: Capital allowances b/f.	3,000	
Capital allowances 1983–84	6,000	9,000
	———	———
Unused 1983–84 allowance		£1,000

(Alternatively, the £1,000 unused allowances might be relieved under s. 168 for 1982–83.)

	£	£
Section 168 claim: capital allowances available:		
Capital allowances 1984–85		5,000
Deduct: Balancing charge 1984–85	1,300	
Less: Capital allowances b/f.	1,000	300
Available for s. 168 claim		£4,700
Loss, Year to 30th September 1983		2,000
Add: Capital Allowances, 1984–85		4,700
		6,700
Limited to taxed income		6,000
Capital Allowances carried forward		£700
1984–85 Balancing charge		1,300
Less: Capital allowances		1,300
		Nil
Capital allowances, 1984–85 (Balance)		700
Section 168 claim		700
		Nil
1985–86 profit, year to 30th September 1984		5,000
Less: Capital allowances, 1985–86		4,000
Net assessment		£1,000

Example 9—opening year*

P. Nutt commenced business on 1st April 1985, and in his first accounting year to 31st March 1986, suffered a loss of £600. Capital allowances, based on purchases during that year, amounted to £800. He received taxed dividends (including tax credit) of £750. Claims under s. 168 for 1984–85 and under s. 168(2) for 1986–87 are available as follows:

	£
1985–86 Loss, year to 31st March 1986	600
Add: Capital allowances	800
	1,400
Limit of claim against dividends	750
Capital allowances unused	£650
1986–87 Claim against dividends:	
Unused Capital allowances b/f.	£650

---

* Section 30, F.A. 1978 claim may also be made.

Example 10

Suppose in the above example P. Nutt had achieved a profit of £200 and the capital allowances amounted to £1,500. The position would be as follows:

	£
1985–86 Profit, year to 31st March 1986	200
Less: Capital allowances	1,500
Converted loss	1,300
Limit of claim against dividends	750
Capital allowances unused	£550
1986–87 Profit, Year to 31st March 1986	200
Less: Capital allowances b/f.	550
Claim against dividends	£350

Note—Since the claim was for the first year of trading, it would normally be necessary to split the loss according to the accounting period; in the example, however, 31st March would be treated in practice as 5th April, and hence no split is necessary.

EFFECT OF CESSATION ON CAPITAL ALLOWANCES USED IN S. 169 CLAIM

As the capital allowances normally used are those for the year following the year of claim, it may happen that because of a cessation of trading these allowances are not available. If they have already been given, a Case VI assessment will be raised to collect the amount of tax over-allowed.

Example 11

In the year to 30th June 1985, a trader incurs a loss of £20,000. The assessment for 1985–86 is £35,000 less capital allowances £5,000. The capital allowances for 1986–87 are £4,000.

The position for 1985–86 is therefore:

	£	£
Assessment	35,000	
Less: Capital allowances, 1985–86	5,000	
		30,000
Section 168 claim:		
Loss, Year to 30th June 1985	20,000	
Add: Capital allowances, 1986–87	4,000	24,000
		£6,000

STOCK RELIEF (Schedule 9, para. 8, F.A. 1981 ("new relief") and Schedule 5, para. 6, F.A. 1976—"old relief")

Introduction

As mentioned in Chapter 6 this relief ceases to have effect for periods of account beginning after 12th March 1984. The notes below are for completeness.

A claim under s. 168, I.C.T.A. 1970 may be increased by an amount equal to the stock relief entitlement (refer to Chapter 6, § 3 for the bases of calculation), based on the accounting period in which the loss is sustained. The "old" and "new relief" claims follow the same lines *except* a claim for new relief *must* accompany a capital allowance (s. 169, I.C.T.A. 1970) claim—see below.

A claim may be made under this paragraph notwithstanding that apart from the relief no loss would arise. Apart from the order of set off, relief under this paragraph follows along the lines of capital allowances (see above). The claim for stock relief and capital allowances is independent of s. 168, I.C.T.A. 1970, and separate claims can therefore be made as appropriate (see below).

Example—old relief

Smith, who prepares accounts to 30th June each year, has the following results for the year ended 30th June 1980:

Trading Loss	£20,000
Capital allowances	£ 5,000
Stock Relief Claim	£ 7,600

Smith may make a claim for the whole of the £32,600 to be available for relief under s. 168, I.C.T.A. 1970.

It should be noted that Smith would effectively have to make three claims as follows:

Trading Losses	s. 168, I.C.T.A. 1970
Capital Allowances	s. 169, I.C.T.A. 1970
Stock Relief	Schedule 5, para. 6, F.A. 1976.

CLAIMS

(*a*) *New Relief* (See Chapter 6 § 3)
A claim for trading losses alone can be made *but* a claim for stock relief cannot be made unless a claim for capital allowances is also made. Accordingly a stock relief claim *must* accompany a trading loss and capital allowance claim.

(*b*) *Old Relief*
A claim for trading losses alone can be made, or a claim for trading losses, and either or both of capital allowances or stock relief. (N.B. it is not possible to make a claim for capital allowances or stock relief *without* a claim for the trading losses applying.)

ORDER OF SET-OFF

(*a*) *Old Relief*
Where the whole of the loss is not set off under s. 168, I.C.T.A. 1970, the relief granted is attributed firstly to the trading losses, then to the stock relief and finally to the capital allowances.

(*b*) *New Relief*
Where the whole of the loss is not set off under s. 168, I.C.T.A. 1970 the relief granted is attributed firstly to the trading loss then to the capital allowances and finally to the stock relief.

The difference in treatment in relation to both claims and order of set-off for new relief is as a result of the introduction of the six year write-off of stock relief losses (Schedule 9, para. 10, F.A. 1981—Chapter 6 § 3).

WHEN A CLAIM SHOULD BE MADE

Considerable care is necessary before deciding whether a claim should be made under s. 168, I.C.T.A. 1970 (in the case of a loss in a business assessed under

Schedule D) owing to the effect thereof on subsequent assessments where the loss can be carried forward.

If there is a probability that the rate of tax will be reduced during the years following the loss, a claim will usually prove advantageous, since the effect of the claim will be to enable the taxpayer to recover tax on the loss in the years when the rate of tax is highest. On the other hand, if the rate of tax is increased during the succeeding years, more tax will be paid over the whole period than would be the case if no s. 168 claim were made.

It should be borne in mind that if a claim is made repayment of tax will be obtained in the same year in which the loss is incurred (or the following year), and probably the money refunded will be of considerable use to the business, whereas if the loss is carried forward the benefit of a reduction in liability will not be obtained until some years later.

A claim may result in the loss of personal allowances, in that the total statutory income for the year of assessment, *after* deducting the s. 168 loss, may not be sufficient to exhaust the personal allowances for that year. In appropriate circumstances it may be advantageous to restrict the claim to the income of the claimant, without extending it to the income of his or her wife or husband. The question of any liability to higher rates of tax should also be considered.

DETERMINATION OF CLAIMS

Claims under s. 168, I.C.T.A. 1970, are determined by the Inspector of Taxes, subject to the right of appeal to the General Commissioners or Special Commissioners.

§ 3.—RELIEF FOR LOSSES IN EARLY YEARS OF TRADE (s. 30, F.A. 1978)

Where an individual (either solely or in partnership) carrying on a trade sustains a loss in the trade:

- (*a*) in the year of assessment in which the trade is first carried on; or
- (*b*) in any of the next three years of assessment, then relief is available against the claimant's income equal to the amount of the loss, being income for the three years of assessment immediately preceding the year in which the loss has been sustained.

The claim must be made in writing within two years after the year of assessment in which the loss arises.

Relief is granted for earlier years in priority to later years and applies to losses incurred in 1978–79 or subsequently. The relief dovetails into s. 168, I.C.T.A. 1970 (see above) and is therefore graded accordingly, i.e. it:

- (*a*) can include capital allowances and stock relief;
- (*b*) is available primarily against income of the same class; and
- (*c*) can be used to offset income of the claimant's spouse.

A claim under s. 30, F.A. 1978 is independent of other loss relief claims and provided losses are not claimed more than once, claims can be made under different headings. The priority as to the utilisation of the claims rests with the taxpayer although partial claims cannot be made (*Butt* v. *Haxby* (1982)).

Example

Jones began to trade as a market gardener on 1st July 1985, having previously been employed as a sales rep. His results for the period to 5th April 1986 were:

	£
Adjusted Case I loss	23,000
Capital allowances	12,000
Losses available for relief	3,500

Jones's income for the three years to 5th April 1985 was as follows:

		JONES £	WIFE £
1982–83	Earnings	7,000	2,000
	Dividends	2,000	1,000
1983–84	Earnings	11,000	3,500
	Dividends	4,000	1,000
1984–85	Earnings	15,000	5,000
	Dividends	4,500	1,000

A claim under s. 30, F.A. 1978 for the whole of the losses of £35,000 will revise the assessments as follows:

		ORIGINAL		REVISED	
		Self £	*Wife* £	*Self* £	*Wife* £
1982–83	Earnings	7,000	2,000	7,000	2,000
	Dividends	2,000	1,000	2,000	1,000
		9,000	3,000	9,000	3,000
	Less Section 30 claim	—	—	9,000	—
		9,000	3,000	Nil	3,000
		3,000	—		
	Assessment subject to personal allowances	£12,000			£3,000
1983–84	Earnings	11,000	3,500	11,000	3,500
	Dividends	4,000	1,000	4,000	1,000
		15,000	4,500	15,000	4,500
	Less s. 30 claim	—	—	15,000	—
		15,000	4,500	Nil	4,500
		4,500	—		
	Assessment subject to personal allowances	£19,500			£4,500
1984–85	Earnings	15,000	5,000	15,000	5,000
	Dividends	4,500	1,000	4,500	1,000
		19,500	6,000	19,500	6,000
	Less section 30 claim (£35,000–[£9,000 + £15,000])	—	—	11,000	—
		19,500	6,000	8,500	6,000
		6,000		6,000	
	Assessment subject to personal allowances	£25,500		£14,500	

Notes

(1) The claim is not extended to Jones's wife, as this would result in the loss of personal allowances for 1982–83 and 1983–84 and accordingly reduce the claim available for 1984–85.

(2) The tax paid by Jones for 1982–83, 1983–84 and 1984–85 will be repaid as appropriate, together with interest supplement as applicable.

Special Points

Relief will be available under this section unless:

(*a*) relief has been granted under any other provision of the Income Tax Acts (e.g. s. 168);

(*b*) the trade is not carried on commercially and in such a way that profits could not reasonably be expected in the period, or a reasonable time thereafter;

(*c*) the trade has previously been carried on by the spouse of the claimant and the loss is sustained later than the third year of assessment after that in which the trade was first carried on by the other spouse.

§ 4.— CARRYING FORWARD LOSSES (s. 171, I.C.T.A. 1970)

Section 171, I.C.T.A. 1970 provides that where a loss is sustained in any trade, profession or vocation carried on by any person either solely or in partnership, such portion of the loss for which relief has not been obtained under s. 168, I.C.T.A. 1970 (see § 2) or under any other provision of the Income Tax Acts, may be carried forward and deducted from any profits made *in the same trade, profession or vocation* without time limit.

It should be observed that the making of claims under s. 168 is *optional*. Where, therefore, no such claims are made, the *whole* of the loss is carried forward under s. 171, I.C.T.A. 1970 but any claim for relief under this section should be made within six years of the end of the year of assessment.

Any such losses carried forward must be deducted as far as possible from the first subsequent *assessment* for any year following that in which the loss is sustained, any balance of the loss being deducted from the next assessment, and so on. An individual cannot claim to deduct primarily his personal, etc., allowances and to set-off the loss against his taxable income.

A loss for the purposes of this relief is to be computed on the same basis as profits are computed under Cases I and II, Schedule D.

Example

The adjusted results of a business carried on by C. Hill, were as follows:

	£
Year ended 31st March 1980, Profit	500
Year ended 31st March 1981, Loss	2,000
Year ended 31st March 1982, Profit	800
Year ended 31st March 1983, Profit	600
Year ended 31st March 1984, Profit	1,000
Year ended 31st March 1985, Profit	1,200

For 1980–81, the assessment was £500, but a claim was made under s. 168, £500 of the loss of £2,000 for the year ended 31st March 1981, being utilised for this purpose.

The assessments for the years 1981–82 to 1985–86 will be as follows:

	Assessments	
	£	£
1981–82—Profits of preceding year		Nil
1982–83—Profits of preceding year	800	
Less: Balance of loss brought forward	1,500*	
Loss forward	£700	Nil

* Assuming that a claim under s. 168 has been made in respect of the profits to 31st March 1980 (£500).

	£	£
1983–84—Profits of preceding year	600	
Less: Loss brought forward	700	
Loss forward	£100	Nil
1984–85—Profits of preceding year	1,000	
Less: Loss brought forward	100	
		900
1985–86—Profits of preceding year		1,200

Note. The assessment for the year of assessment following the loss will be "nil" in any case, and therefore the *second* year after that in which the loss is sustained is the earliest in which any deduction can be made.

NEW BUSINESS

(a) Restriction of loss carry forward to actual loss
A claim cannot be made to carry forward a *notional loss*, e.g. if a business makes a loss in its first year, it is only the amount of such loss which is available for a carry-forward under s. 171, and not the notional losses which arise as a consequence of the special basis of assessment in the second and third years, *Commissioners of Inland Revenue* v. *Scott Adamson* (1932).

Example

A business was commenced on 1st June 1984. The result for the first ten months ended 31st March 1985, was an adjusted loss of £610, and for the year ended 31st March 1986, an adjusted profit of £1,440.

The assessments upon the business for the first three years were as follows:

	£
1984–85—Assessment	Nil
1985–86—Loss for ten months to 31st March 1985	610
Deduct: Profit for two months to 31st May 1985 ($\frac{2}{12}$ of £1,440)	240
Loss for one year from commencement of business	£370
Assessment	Nil
1986–87—Profit for year ended 31st March 1986	1,440
Assessment (subject to s. 171 claim)	£1,440

As a loss of £610 has been incurred during the accounting period of ten months ended 31st March 1985, and relief has been given on £240 in computing the assessment for 1985–86, only £370 is available for carry-forward under s. 171 in respect of 1986–87. Thus the adjusted assessment for 1986–87 is £1,070 (£1,440 less £370).

Note. Although notional losses of £610 and £370 had been incurred in 1984–85 and 1985–86 respectively, the amount available for relief under s. 171 for 1986–87 is not £980, but only £370, and the total relief granted is the *actual* loss incurred—i.e. £610, of which £240 is allowed in 1985–86 and £370 in 1986–87.

(b) Calculation of assessable profits in second and third years
The above position must be compared with the case where a loss is made in the first period of trading (less than 12 months) and profits are subsequently made. In this case although the loss *cannot* be carried forward (following *Scott Adamson*) it is used in the calculation of the assessable profits. [*Westward Television* v. *Hart* (1968). N.B. this case related to the period when companies were "taxed on the same basis as individuals".]

Example

Nomansland commenced business on 6th July 1983. His first accounts were made up to 31st December 1983, and showed an adjusted loss of £3,000. Accounts for the years ended 31st December 1984 and 1985, showed adjusted profits of £6,000 and £9,000, respectively. The assessments (working in months) will be as follows:

		£	£
1983–84—Actual profits of the year of assessment: 6th July 1983 to 31st December 1983 .... *Loss*		3,000	
1st January 1984 to 5th April 1984: $\frac{3}{12}$ of £6,000 .... *Profit*		1,500	
		———	Nil
1984–85—Profits of the first 12 months' trading: 6th July 1983 to 31st December 1983 .... *Loss*		3,000	
1st January 1984 to 5th July 1984: $\frac{6}{12}$ of £6,000 .... *Profit*		3,000	
		———	Nil
1985–86—Profits of the preceding year			6,000

Note: The taxpayer in effect receives £1,500 over-relief. The loss is effectively allowed for purposes of s. 171, I.C.T.A. 1970 and nothing can be brought forward to 1984–85.

Example

Sandridge commenced business on 6th July 1983. His first accounts were made up to 5th April 1984, and showed an adjusted loss of £9,000. Accounts for the year ended 5th April 1985, showed an adjusted profit of £12,000. The assessments will be as follows:

		£	£
1983–84—Actual profits of the year of assessment			Nil
1984–85—Profits of the first 12 months' trading: 6th July 1983 to 5th April 1984 ... *Loss*		9,000	
6th April 1984 to 5th July 1984: $\frac{3}{12}$ of £12,000 .... *Profit*		3,000	
		———	Nil
Adjusted loss carried forward: £9,000 *less* £3,000 = £6,000			
1985–86—Profits of preceding year		12,000	
Less: Loss brought forward under s. 171		6,000	
		———	6,000

Interaction with other claims

Whereas s. 171, I.C.T.A. 1970, gives relief by reducing the next following assessment(s) on the same business only, a claim under s. 168, I.C.T.A. 1970, can be used against any income for the year of claim and for the subsequent year.

Where a loss brought forward under s. 171 exceeds the Case I, Schedule D assessment of the business, the balance of the loss can be set against any interest or dividends on investments arising in that year of assessment which would be trading receipts but for the fact that they are taxed in some other manner.

Example

Saphire Co. made an adjusted profit of £4,650 in the year ended 30th September 1984, subject to a deduction of £450 in respect of capital allowances. Losses from earlier years amounting to £7,000 are brought forward under s. 171, I.C.T.A. 1970.

The firm received dividends of £1,450 in the year 1985–86 from trade investments. The position as regards 1985–86 will be as follows:

There will be a nil assessment under Case I, Schedule D, computed as follows:

		£
Adjusted profit for the year ended 30th September 1984		4,650
Less:	Capital allowances	450
		4,200
Less:	Losses brought forward under s. 171, I.C.T.A. 1970 ..	7,000
	Losses not relieved	2,800
Less:	Repayment against dividends from trade investments	1,450
	Carried forward under s. 171, I.C.T.A. 1970	£1,350

Saphire Co. would be repaid tax at the basic rate upon £1,450.

FIRMS

In the case of a firm, each partner must claim individually, his share of the loss being deducted from his share of the firm's subsequent assessments. Where a partner retires from the firm, his share of the partnership loss lapses. Thus, where a partner dies or retires, it is advisable to claim under s. 168 in respect of any loss incurred in the year of death or retirement, otherwise the late partner's share of the loss will not be recoverable.* A continuing partner (i.e. a member of both the old and new firms) has the right to have his share of loss carried forward under s. 171, and also to carry forward his share of capital allowances and stock relief which have not been relieved; thus he can set-off his share of any loss before the change against his share of profits after the change, together with his share of any capital allowances which could not be given in the assessments on the firm before the change, owing to insufficient profits.

§ 5.—BUSINESS TRANSFERRED TO A LIMITED COMPANY (s. 172, I.C.T.A. 1970)

The right to carry forward losses attaches to the person owning the business, etc., and not to the business, and normally lapses on a complete change of ownership (see Chapter 3, § 8).

Where, however, a business carried on by an individual or a firm is transferred to a company in consideration solely or mainly of the allotment of shares in the company to the old owner(s), and the total income of the latter for any year

---

* In certain circumstances such a loss may be recovered as a terminal loss (see § 7).

includes any income (whether earned or unearned) derived from the company, that person may treat such income as profits of the business on which he is assessed under Schedule D, for the purpose of carrying forward and setting off any loss sustained in the business prior to the transfer.

The loss once claimed is given in like manner to s. 171 I.C.T.A. 1970 (above) and consequently must be given against the first year in which income arises from the company with only any balance then available for carry forward. In order to claim this relief the individual must have been the beneficial owner of the shares and the company must have continued to carry on the business throughout the year of assessment concerned, or, as regards the year of transfer, from the date of transfer to the following 5th April.

The losses must first be set off against any *earned* income derived from the company (e.g. directors' fees) and then against any unearned income (e.g. dividends). In the latter case, relief will be given by way of repayment, and notice of the claim must be given in writing to the Inspector of Taxes within six years after the end of the year of assessment to which the claim relates.

A partner can claim similar relief in respect of his share of the loss of a firm.

Example 1

J. Webber owned a business which he sold to a private limited company on 1st April 1985, the consideration for the sale being the allotment of shares in the company to Webber and his nominees.

Webber remained the beneficial owner of the shares, and the company continued to carry on the trade, throughout the year 1985–86.

For the trading year ended 31st March 1985, the result of the business was a loss of £30,000, of which £18,000 was used by Webber in a claim under s. 168, I.C.T.A. 1970.

For 1985–86, he received income from the company as follows:

Salary: £10,000.　　Taxed Dividends: £5,000.

It is required to show the claim which may be made for 1985–86.

Webber may claim to carry forward the balance of the loss for 1984–85 (£12,000) and to deduct £10,000 thereof from the salary of £10,000 received by him from the company. He will also obtain repayment of tax in respect of the remaining £2,000 of the loss against the taxed dividends received by him from the company.

Example 2

Box, Cox and Knox, who had been in partnership for a number of years as greengrocers, decided to form a company to be named Apples and Pears Ltd. The company commenced to trade, taking over the partnership business, on 1st July 1983, the consideration for the transfer being 18,000 ordinary shares of £1 each, to be divided equally between the partners. At the date of transfer losses available for carry-forward under s. 171, I.C.T.A. 1970 were as follows:

Box, £600; Cox, £900; and Knox, £1,800.

On 31st December 1983, Box sold his interest in the company to Fox, and on 31st January 1985, Cox sold his interest in the company to Knox, but continued to manage a branch of the company.

Box, Cox and Knox received the following income from the company:

Year ended 5th April	1984	1985	1986
	£	£	£
Salary—Box	200	—	—
Cox	400	960	1,500
Knox	400	600	1,500
Dividends—Box	—	—	—
Cox	—	300	—
Knox	—	300	600

Since Box parted with his shares before 5th April 1984, he can claim no relief for his share of losses, £600.

Cox will receive relief of £400 in 1983–84, against his salary, leaving a nil assessment under Schedule E. Since he has parted with his shares by 5th April 1985, he receives no further relief under s. 172, I.C.T.A. 1970, and the balance of his share of losses, £500, goes unrelieved.

Relief in the case of Knox is given as follows:

	£	£
1983–84—Salary	400	
Less: Loss set off under s. 172	400	
		Nil
1984–85—Salary	600	
Less: Loss set off under s. 172	600	
		Nil
Dividends	300	
Less: Loss set off under s. 172	300	
		Nil
1985–86—Salary	1,500	
Less: Loss set off under s. 172 (balance)	500	
		1,000
Dividends		600

§ 6.—ANNUAL CHARGES ASSESSED UNDER s. 53, I.C.T.A. 1970 (s. 173, I.C.T.A. 1970)

Where a person has been assessed in respect of a payment of an annuity, etc., not made out of profits or gains brought into charge, but made wholly and exclusively for the purposes of a trade, profession or vocation, the amount on which tax has been paid may be treated as a loss in that trade, profession or vocation and carried forward accordingly. This relief will not be granted, however, if the payment has been charged to capital, or is not borne by the person ultimately assessed.

The relief will also be granted in the following cases:

(*a*) on any payment to which the s. 53 applies by virtue of s. 54(3) of the Act (annual interest). (N.B.: the interest, if business interest, will be treated as part of the trading loss (hence effectively relieved under s. 168, I.C.T.A. 1970))

(*b*) on any payment to which the s. 53 applies by virtue of s. 89(1) of the Act (Schedule A, and associated charges: non-residents),

(*c*) on payments of rent referred to in s. 157(4) of the Act (easements in connection with radio relay services),

(*d*) on any capital sum paid in respect of any patent rights assessed under s. 53 by virtue of s. 380 of the Act,

(*e*) on any payment of, or on account of, copyright royalties to which s. 391 of the Act applies, or

(*f*) on any payment to which s. 53 applies by virtue of s. 477 of the Act (manufactured dividends).

§ 7.—TERMINAL LOSSES (s. 174, I.C.T.A. 1970)

Where a trade, profession or vocation is permanently discontinued and a loss (termed a "terminal loss") is sustained in the last *year* for which the business was carried on, such a loss may be carried back and set-off against the assessments on that business for the three years of assessment last preceding that in which the discontinuance occurs, *provided that relief in respect of the loss has not been given under some other provision of the Income Tax Acts.*

Relief is given as far as possible from the assessment for a later rather than for an earlier year.

Where the profits assessed under Cases I and II, Schedule D for any of the three years of assessment preceding that in which the business was permanently discontinued are insufficient to enable the relief under s. 174 to be given, then the relief may be given against any interest or dividends on investments received by the business in that year which would be trading receipts assessable under Case I had it not been for the fact that they were assessed under another Case of Schedule D, or were taxed at the source. This provision affords relief to businesses with investment income.

Calculation of loss

The amount of a terminal loss is to be computed so as to include:

  (*a*) The loss sustained in the trade, etc., in the year of assessment in which it is permanently discontinued, i.e. from the 6th April to the date of the discontinuance;

  (*b*) the relevant capital allowances for that year of assessment;

  (*c*) the loss sustained in the trade, etc., in the part of the preceding year of assessment beginning twelve months before the date of the discontinuance; and

  (*d*) the same fraction of the capital allowances for that preceding year of assessment.

N.B. see p. 229 for reduction of terminal losses for non-trading charges.

"Capital allowances" mean the allowances under the Capital Allowances Act 1968 and F.A. 1971 (as amended by subsequent Finance Acts).

Any amounts which have already been taken into account in reducing the taxpayer's liability must be excluded from the computation of the terminal loss.

Example 1

Finchley, who had traded for many years, showed the following results as adjusted for Income Tax purposes:

		£
Year ended 30th June 1982	....	Profit 5,000
Year ended 30th June 1983	....	Profit 2,500
Year ended 30th June 1984	....	Profit 800
Year ended 30th June 1985	....	Loss 1,200
Six months to date of cessation, 31st December 1985	...	Loss 1,800

The capital allowances, as finally agreed, were:

		£
1983–84	....	300
1984–85	....	240
1985–86.	....	170

It is required to compute the terminal loss and show what relief would be given in respect of the losses in the last two years of the business.

The 1985–86 assessment will be "Nil". The 1984–85 assessment on the profits to 30th June 1983 will be £2,500, less capital allowances of £240, i.e. a net assessment of £2,260.

The terminal loss is computed as follows:

	£	£
(*a*) Loss sustained during 1985–86, i.e. from 6th April to 31st December 1985: Three months to 30th June 1985:		
$\frac{3}{12}$ of £1,200	300	
Six months to 31st December 1985	1,800	
	————	2,100
(*b*) Capital allowances, 1985–86		170

(c) Proportion of losses during 1984–85
period from 1st January to 5th April 1985:
$\frac{3}{12}$ of £1,200 = £300 but this will have
been used in the s. 168 claim for
1984–85 ....   —

(d) Proportionate part of the capital allowances
for 1984–85—$\frac{3}{12}$ of £240—but as these
allowances will have been taken into
account in reducing the 1984–85
assessment, they must be excluded from
the terminal loss. ....   —

Terminal loss £2,270

A claim under s. 168, I.C.T.A. 1970, should be made on a "split" accounts basis in respect of 1984–85. The loss of $\frac{9}{12}$ of £1,200 = £900, will be relieved against the net assessment for 1984–85 of £2,260.

A claim under s. 174, I.C.T.A. 1970, will then be made against the balance of the net assessment for 1984–85 of £2,260 *less* £900 = £1,360; the balance of the terminal loss amounting to £910 (i.e. £2,270 *less* £1,360) may be claimed against the net Case I, Schedule D assessment for 1983–84, of £4,700, there being no balance then remaining to be claimed against the 1982–83 assessment.

Effect of profit in final period

If *in a terminal loss period* a profit arises, this is ignored. It will, however, be necessary to cover this profit to the extent it falls to be taxed. If losses are required to cover any such profit the terminal loss is reduced (see Example 1 above).

Example 2

J. Green, who had traded for many years, showed the same results as Finchley (see Example 1) except that in the year ended 30th June 1985, he made a profit of £1,200 (and not a loss of that amount).

The terminal loss is then computed as follows:

	£	£
(a) Profit or loss sustained during 1985–86, i.e. from 6th April to 31st December 1985:		
Three months to 30th June 1985:		
$\frac{3}{12}$ of £1,200 (= £300 but ignored) .... *Profit*	Nil	
Six months to 31st December 1985 .... *Loss*	1,800	
		1,800
(b) Capital allowances, 1985–86		170
(c) Proportion of losses during 1984–85:		
Not relevant—a profit having been made ..		—
(d) Proportion of capital allowances for 1984–85:		
These will already have been employed in reducing the 1984–85 assessment		—
Terminal loss		£1,970

EFFECT OF ANNUAL CHARGES

(*a*) *Trading*

The profits on which a person has been charged to tax for any year of assessment, and against which the relief under s. 174 is claimed, are to be reduced for the purpose of this relief by any part of those profits applied in payment of any sum from which tax was deducted and not accounted for because the payment was made of profits brought into charge of tax, i.e. annual charges.

The amounts to be excluded are *gross* amounts.

(b) Non-trading

The amount of the terminal loss is to be reduced by the gross amount of any payment made under deduction of tax which would not be capable of being treated as a loss under s. 173, I.C.T.A. 1970. (See § 6).

Thus a payment made under deduction of tax which was not wholly or exclusively laid out or expended for the purposes of the trade or business would fall to be deducted from the amount of the assessment in the basis period for which the payment was made, and also from the amount of the terminal loss.

Example 3

Hendon & Co., ceased trading on 30th September 1985, having made a loss in the year ended 30th June 1985, of £1,200 and a further loss of £280 in the three months to 30th September 1985. The assessments were as follows:

1982–83, £1,100; 1983–84, £800; 1984–85, £450.

The capital allowances were:

1982–83, £40; 1983–84, £30; 1984–85, £25; 1985–86, £20.

Annuities paid wholly and exclusively for the purposes of the trade out of the profits for the relevant years of assessment were:

1982–83, £500; 1983–84, £300; 1984–85, £200.

It is required to show what claims for relief under s. 174, I.C.T.A. 1970, would be made. Assume that the partners had no other sources of income.

The terminal loss is computed as follows:

		£	£
(a)	Loss sustained during 1985–86, i.e. from 6th April 1985 to 30th September 1985:		
	Three months to 30th June 1985 $\frac{3}{12}$ of £1,200	300	
	Three months to 30th September 1985	280	
			580
(b)	Capital Allowances, 1985–86		20
(c)	Proportion of losses during 1984–85, period from 1st October 1984 to 5th April 1985: $\frac{6}{12}$ of £1,200 (N.B. No s. 168 claim.)		600
(d)	Proportionate part of the capital allowances for 1984–85—$\frac{6}{12}$ of £25 but as these allowances will have been taken into account in reducing the 1984–85 assessment, they must be excluded from the terminal loss		—
	Terminal loss		£1,200

Relief under s. 174, I.C.T.A. 1970, would be claimed as follows:

		£
1984–85	Case I, Schedule D Assessment	450
	Less: Capital allowances	25
	Net assessment	425
	Deduct: Annuity	200
	Claim under s. 174, I.C.T.A. 1970	£225

		£
1983–84	Case I, Schedule D Assessment	800
	Less: Capital allowances	30
	Net assessment	770
	Deduct: Annuity	300
	Claim under s. 174, I.C.T.A. 1970	£470
1982–83	Case I, Schedule D Assessment	1,100
	Less: Capital allowances	40
	Net assessment	1,060
	Deduct: Annuity	500
		£560
	Claim under s. 174, I.C.T.A. 1970—Balance of terminal loss	£505

Notes: (1) The amount of £505 is represented by the terminal loss of £1,200 less the adjusted assessments of £470 and £225 for 1983–84 and 1984–85 respectively.

(2) As the annuity was paid wholly and exclusively for the purposes of the trade, it is not necessary to deduct this from the terminal loss. If, instead of this annuity, a gross payment under deduction of tax had been made, say, to a charity under deed of covenant, of £100 per annum, then the amount of the terminal loss would be reduced by £300, the claim for relief in 1982–83 being thus restricted to £205.

PARTNERSHIPS

In the case of the discontinuance of a business carried on in partnership, no relief for a terminal loss can be claimed by a partner who continues to be engaged in the business after the cessation*, but relief may be claimed by the partners who have retired (or the personal representatives of partners who have died) in respect of their shares in the terminal loss, against their shares of the partnership assessments for the three preceding years, as reduced, in appropriate cases, by their shares of the annual charges paid out of the profits of these years.

CLAIMS

A claim for relief under s. 174, I.C.T.A. 1970, may be made at any time within six years after the end of the year of assessment to which the claim relates.

§ 8.—RELIEF FOR INTEREST (s. 175, I.C.T.A. 1970)

Interest claimed against an individual's personal tax liability under s. 75, F.A. 1972, or building society interest, can if a surplus arises be claimed as a loss for ss. 171 and 174, I.C.T.A. 1970 purposes. The interest must, however, be wholly and exclusively incurred for the purposes of the trade, so that the s. 75, F.A. 1972 claim is an optional claim to the normal business deduction.

§ 9.—RELIEF FOR LOSSES ON UNQUOTED TRADING COMPANY SHARES (s. 37, F.A. 1980)

The main provisions of this relief are set out in Chapter 30 (Capital Gains Tax), as although the loss is treated as an income tax loss, it is computed in accordance

---

* The rights of such a continuing partner have already been explained.

with capital gains tax rules. The following points should however be reiterated as applicable to loss relief.

The relief is given first against the individual's earned income, then his other income, then the earned income of the spouse and finally the spouse's other income, subject to an election by the individual to have the spouse's income excluded (as with s. 168, I.C.T.A. relief). Any unutilised relief may be carried forward one year, and is utilised in priority to other s. 37 losses arising in the year.

Claims for relief must be made within two years of the year of assessment in which the loss occurred, or within two years from the second year if carried forward. The relief is given in priority to relief under s. 168, I.C.T.A. or s. 30, F.A. 1978.

8. Schedule E

§ 1.—NATURE OF INCOME ASSESSED UNDER SCHEDULE E (ss. 181–183, I.C.T.A. 1970)

Assessments under Schedule E are made on the income arising from any office or employment and in respect of any annuity, pension or stipend resulting from such employment or payable by the Crown or out of the public revenue of the United Kingdom, except such annuities, etc., as are charged under Schedule C (s. 181, I.C.T.A. 1970). Any pension which is paid voluntarily or is capable of being discontinued, is also assessable under Schedule E (s. 122, I.C.T.A. 1970) except a foreign pension which is assessable under Schedule D, Case V (s. 113, I.C.T.A. 1970).

Broadly speaking, Schedule E embraces all salaries, wages, bonuses, commissions, perquisites, directors' fees and generally all emoluments and remuneration arising from any employment (s. 183, I.C.T.A. 1970).

The tips of taxi drivers, hotel porters, waiters, hairdressers, etc. are also assessable (*Calvert* v. *Wainwright* (1947)), an estimated amount generally being included in the assessment, but the taxpayer has the usual right of appeal. A public benefit to a cricketer has been held to be a gift, and not assessable (since it was a voluntary act) (*Reed* v. *Seymour* (1927)), whereas somewhat similar payments to footballers under service contracts, and presents to successful jockeys, are both assessable (*Corbett* v. *Duff* (1941)).

The following sources of income or gains (which would otherwise fall under Schedule E), are with notable exceptions exempt from Income Tax:
- (1) Wound and disability pensions (s. 365, I.C.T.A. 1970).
     Annuities paid to holders of the Victoria Cross or George Cross and (by s. 26, F.A. 1980) to holders of the M.C., D.F.C., C.G.M., D.S.M., M.M. and D.F.M. (New annuities payable to holders of the Albert and Edward Medals are also exempt.)
- (2) Pensions granted to war widows (s. 9, F.(No. 2)A. 1979).
- (3) War gratuities; payable to members of the armed forces, and defence workers, etc.; and bounties and gratuities payable to persons who have served in the armed forces and who voluntarily undertake a further period of service (s. 366, I.C.T.A. 1970).
- (4) Sickness and disablement benefits from mutual insurance societies for periods of less than one year (Concession A26); but payments by an employer (or under arrangements made by him) to an employee or member of his family in respect of sickness or disability will for 1982–83 onwards be subject to tax (s. 30, F.A. 1981).
- (5) Unemployment benefits, sickness benefits, maternity benefits, and death grants under the National Insurance Acts; but from 1982 payments of social security benefits to the unemployed, other than earnings-related supplement of unemployment benefit, will be subject to tax. Also taxable are supplementary benefits under the Supplementary Benefit (Urgent Cases) Regulation 1981 (s. 27, F.A. 1981, as amended by F.A. 1982). Sickness and maternity benefits from 6th April 1982 are taxable as outlined below.
- (6) Social security benefits, including supplementary pensions and allowances, invalidity benefit, non-contributory invalidity pension, death

grant, child's special allowance and guardian's allowance (except that amount attributable to an increase for a child), attendance allowance and family income supplement (s. 219, I.C.T.A. 1970). Mobility allowance is exempted for payments made after 5th April 1982 (F.A. 1982).

(7) Statutory redundancy payments, and the corresponding amount of any other employer's payment, made under the Redundancy Payments Act, 1965 (s. 412, I.C.T.A. 1970). But such payments are to be taken into account under s. 187, I.C.T.A. 1970, which relates to compensation and termination payments (see § 5).

(8) Wages in lieu of notice but taken into account for s. 187 as above.

(9) Scholarship income and bursaries (s. 375, I.C.T.A. 1970).

(10) Lump sum payments from certain retirement annuity and pension schemes. (See generally ss. 19–26, F.A. 1970 and s. 21, F.A. 1971)

(11) Luncheon vouchers (up to 15p per day). (By concession A3.)

(12) Free coal or cash equivalent given to miners. (By concession A7.)

(13) Compensation for loss of office (see (7) above)—payments up to £25,000.

Extension of Tax liability under s. 219, I.C.T.A. 1970

The following payments are taxable in respect of periods after 5th April 1982:

(*a*) allowances paid under a scheme of the kind described in the Job Release Act 1977

(*b*) maternity pay within the meaning of the Employment Protection (Consolidation) Act 1978 (whether paid during employment or not).

(*c*) payments of statutory sick pay within the meaning of Section 1 of the Social Security and Housing Benefits Act 1982.

§ 2.—BASES OF ASSESSMENT (s. 181, I.C.T.A. 1970)

For 1974–75 and later years tax chargeable under Schedule E is assessed under one of the three cases thereof as explained below.

Case I—Applies where the person holding office or employment is resident and ordinarily resident in the U.K., and taxes the entire emoluments from the employment for the relevant year of assessment. Where, however, the duties of the employment are carried out wholly or partly outside the U.K. *or* the emoluments are foreign emoluments, a deduction may be made from the amount assessable to tax (see below).

Case II—Applies where a person is either not resident, or, if resident, not ordinarily resident, and taxes any emoluments, the duties in respect of which are performed in the U.K., subject to a deduction if the emoluments are foreign emoluments.

Case III—Applies to a person resident (whether or not ordinarily resident) in the U.K. and taxes any emoluments *remitted* to the U.K. in respect of:

(i) Foreign emoluments, the duties in respect of which are carried out wholly abroad;

(ii) Emoluments of a person resident, but not ordinarily resident (otherwise Case I applies) from duties performed wholly outside the U.K.

N.B. Case III only applies to emoluments *not* otherwise taxed under Case I or Case II.

RESIDENCE

No definition in the Taxes Acts exists for the term residence, except that it is stated that if a person is physically present in the U.K. for a period of 6 months (183 days), he will always be a U.K. resident (s. 51, I.C.T.A. 1970).

Residence is a question of fact, and although, if present for 6 months in any year, U.K. residence is automatic, a much shorter time may well suffice to support the assertion of U.K. residence.

Factors establishing residence are:

(1) Whether a place of abode is maintained in the U.K. This will always constitute residence (*Cooper* v. *Cadwalader* (1904)) *unless* a person works full time in a trade, profession or vocation no part of which is performed in the U.K., other than those in the case of an office or employment which are incidental to the performance of the other duties outside the U.K. (s. 50, I.C.T.A. 1970).

(2) Frequency, regularity and duration of visits.

(3) Purpose of such visits.

(4) Past history as to residence.

(5) Ties with the U.K. (family, business etc.).

In the recent case law decision of *Reed* v. *Clarke* (1985) it was held that the taxpayer (a prominent musician) was not resident in the U.K. in the year he was physically not present in the U.K., even though his intention was to return subsequently.

ORDINARY RESIDENCE

As with residence, no definition of ordinary residence exists. The term has, however, been adjudged by the courts to denote residence in a place with some degree of continuity; and that the residence is not casual and uncertain, but occurs in the ordinary course of an individual's life (cf. *Levene* v. *C.I.R.* (1928) and *Lysaght* v. *C.I.R.* (1928)). The Inland Revenue in their explanatory notes (IR 20) take the view that a person visiting the U.K. will be ordinarily resident:

(1) After his visits to the U.K. for 4 consecutive years have averaged 3 months or more a year; or

(2) If there is a place of abode available to him in the U.K. and he has visited the U.K. regularly (however short the period) year by year.

DOMICILE

Although not as important as the residency question, domicile still has a part to play both in income tax (Schedules E and D (IV) and (V)) and in capital gains tax. A person's domicile is a concept of general law, and it is outside the scope of this book to outline more than the basic concepts. The law attributes to any person a domicile of origin which is that of the father unless the child is illegitimate in which case the mother's domicile is taken. The domicile of origin can be changed for a domicile of choice but this requires:

(*a*) Living in a country other than the country of the domicile of origin.

(*b*) Intending permanently to reside in that country.

The domicile of a wife is not now automatically that of her husband, so the factors mentioned above apply equally in determining the wife's domicile. Spouses may therefore have different domiciles, although the point may be difficult to establish where the wife lives with her husband and intends to reside there. (See *C.I.R.* v. *Duchess of Portland* (1981) for domicile of women married prior to 1974.)

Having outlined the terms relevant to the overseas question, it now remains to examine the three cases of Schedule E.

§ 3.—SCHEDULE E, CASE I

A person who is resident *and* ordinarily resident will be fully chargeable on *all* emoluments, unless:

(1) The duties of the office or employment are carried out wholly or partly

outside the U.K. and the person is absent from the U.K. for a *qualifying period* which consists of *at least 365 days*, when a deduction of 100% of the emoluments is allowed (Para. 1, Schedule 7, F.A. 1977).

(2) The emoluments are foreign emoluments (see below).

(N.B. The 30 day relief ceases to apply for 1985–86 onwards—see below for earlier years.)

DEDUCTION OF 100% OF EMOLUMENTS

A qualifying period for the 100% deduction is a period of consecutive days which either:

> (i) consists entirely of days of absence from the U.K., *or*
> (ii) consists partly of days of absence from the U.K. and partly of days of *non*-absence which are included since:
>> (*a*) in any one continuous period they do not exceed 62 days, *and*
>> (*b*) when a period of absence comes to an end the number of non-absence days does not exceed $\frac{1}{6}$ of the total days in the period (this period will include prior periods which are qualifying periods).
>
> (N.B. for the 100% deduction to apply the total qualifying period *must* exceed 365 days).

Example 1

Hermas spends the following periods in and out of the U.K. in respect of the duties of his employment.

	Days out of U.K.	Days in U.K. Per period	Cumulative	Total days
(1)	20			20
(2)		4	(4)	24
(3)	56			80
(4)		20	(24)	106
(5)	75			181
(6)		40	(64)	221
(7)	100			321
(8)		5	(69)	326
(9)	50	(Returns permanently to U.K.)		376

Notes

(*a*) In order to determine whether the entire period constitutes a qualifying period it is necessary to review the periods spent in the U.K. Since not one of these periods exceeds 62 days the only other restriction is the "$\frac{1}{6}$ rule".

The periods ending with days of absence are: (1), (3), (5), (7), (9).

	Total days	Days in U.K.	"$\frac{1}{6}$"
Period (1)	20	—	N/A
(3)	80	4	$\frac{1}{6} \times 80 = 13$
(5)	181	24	$\frac{1}{6} \times 181 = 30$
(7)	321	64	$\frac{1}{6} \times 321 = 53$

greater than

—since the $\frac{1}{6}$ total is broken, the period up to 321 days will *not* constitute a qualifying period so the 100% deduction will not apply.

(*b*) At this point, the period ends and is only restarted with a further day of absence. In the example this is period (9), which itself is not a qualifying period since it is less than 365 days.

It must be noted that a period only ends for the purpose of determining qualification, *after* a period of absence. Accordingly a period in the U.K.

immediately following a period abroad *will not* break the continuity provided it does not exceed:
  (i) 62 days or
  (ii) $\frac{1}{6}$ of the total days *after* the next period of absence

Example 2

	Days of absence from U.K.	Days in U.K.	Total
(1)	2	—	2
(2)		25	27
(3)	160		187

$\frac{1}{6} \times 187 = 31$. Since this is greater than 25, the period is *not* broken.

FOREIGN EMOLUMENTS (paras. 3,4, Schedule 2, F. A. 1974and s. 30, F.A. 1984) A deduction is allowed in computing income assessable under Schedule E Case I and Schedule E Case II where emoluments are foreign emoluments. Foreign emoluments are those of a person *not domiciled in the U.K.* from an office or employment under or with a person not resident in the U.K. (s. 181(1), I.C.T.A. 1970)

Deduction available
The deduction for emoluments assessable as foreign emoluments is to be phased out following the Finance Act 1984.
  The deduction prior to 1984–85 was 50% reducing to 25% where the individual has been resident in the U.K. for 9 of the last 10 years.
  The 25% deduction is abolished for 1984–85, whilst the 50% deduction continues to apply up to and including the year 1986–87 thereafter reducing to 25% for the two years 1987–88 and 1988–89.
  For the 50% deduction to apply to these years, the person claiming must:
  * (i) either have held an employment with a non-resident at any time in the period beginning 6 April 1983 and ending 13 March 1984, or
  (ii) in fulfilment of an obligation incurred before 14 March 1984 have performed duties of the employment in the UK before 1 August 1984, and
  (iii) in both cases have held the employment in the years subsequent to 1984–85.
The above position can be summarised as follows:

	Foreign emoluments with 50% deduction applicable for 1983–84	Foreign emoluments with 25% deduction applicable for 1983–84
1983–84	50	25%
1984–85	50	Nil
1985–86	50	Nil
1986–87	50	Nil
1987–88	25	Nil
1988–89	25	Nil
1989–90	Nil	Nil

(It will be noted that if during the years 1984–85 to 1988–89 an individual becomes U.K. resident in 9 of the last 10 years, the relief ceases to apply.)

A person in receipt of foreign emoluments, the duties of which are performed wholly outside the U.K. is exempted from assessment under Schedule E, Case I (Schedule 2, para. 4, F.A. 1974). The emoluments will however be assessed under Case III if remitted.

Example

Fred (a U.K. resident, ordinarily resident and domiciled) was absent from the U.K. during the period 5th October 1984 to 5th April 1986, working in the Middle East for his London-based company. He then returned permanently to the U.K. Fred had spent 20 days (all in 1985–86) during his period of absence visiting relatives in the U.K.

His earnings for 1984–85 and 1985–86 were:

		£
6th April 1984–4th October 1984 ⎱ 1984–85		4,000
5th October 1984–5th April 1985 ⎰		6,000
6th April 1985–5th April 1986 1985–86		13,000

Fred's assessment to income tax is as follows:

1984–85	£	£
U.K. earnings....................................		4,000
Duties performed outside the U.K...................	6,000	
Less 100% deduction	6,000	—
Assessment		£4,000

1985–86		£
Duties performed outside the U.K..................		13,000
Less 100% deduction		13,000
Assessment		Nil

Note. The 18-month period is a qualifying period, since:
  (i) More than 365 days are spent outside the U.K.
  (ii) No period of consecutive days in the U.K. exceeds 62.
  (iii) The $\frac{1}{6}$ limit is not exceeded

DEDUCTION OF $12\frac{1}{2}\%$ OF EMOLUMENTS (Ineffective for 1985–86 onwards—s. 30, F.A. 1984)
General
The Finance Act 1984 terminates relief for short absences abroad for 1985–86 and subsequent years. For 1984-85 the relief, which previously was 25%, is $12\frac{1}{2}\%$ of emoluments. The reliefs are summarised as follows:

1977/78 to 1983–84	25%
1984–85	$12\frac{1}{2}\%$
1985–86 et seq.	Nil

Qualifying days A day is a qualifying day of absence from the U.K. if:
  (i) It is substantially devoted to the performance outside the U.K. of that employment or of that and other employments; *or*
  (ii) It is one of at least 7 consecutive days on which the person concerned is absent from the U.K. for the purpose of the performance of such duties outside the U.K. and which, taken as a whole, are substantially devoted to the performance of such duties; *or*
  (iii) The person concerned is travelling in or for the purpose of performing such duties outside the U.K.
A day of absence will only be treated as such if the person concerned is absent at the end of the day. (Thus a day of departure will be a qualifying day, whereas a day of arrival in the U.K. will not.)

Emoluments

In ascertaining the emoluments to which the $12\frac{1}{2}\%$ deduction applies, the deduction cannot exceed that proportion of the emoluments as is shown to be reasonable having regard to the nature and time devoted to the duties performed outside and in the U.K. (Schedule 7, para. 4, F.A. 1977). Accordingly, if the circumstances are such that the apportionment of emoluments outside and in the U.K. on an equal basis is unreasonable, a higher (or lower) proportion may be attributed to the non-U.K. duties. In all other cases, the "prescribed proportion" will apply. This is the proportion which:

(*a*) The number of qualifying days (i.e. those outside the U.K.) bear to

(*b*) 365 days (or if a part year, the number of days in the part).

Example

Exodus (U.K. resident, ordinarily resident and domiciled) spent 40 days outside the U.K. working for his employer in 1984–85.

In view of the nature and time devoted to the duties performed outside the U.K., the emoluments have been agreed with the Inspector of Taxes to be apportioned as follows:

	£
U.K. duties	16,000
Non-U.K. duties	4,000
	20,000

Exodus will be assessed in 1984–85 as follows:

	£	£
U.K. duties		16,000
Non-U.K. duties	4,000	
Less $12\frac{1}{2}\%$	500	3,500
		£19,500

N.B. If the prescribed proportion calculation was used, the assessment would be:

	£
Total emoluments	20,000

Prescribed proportion

$$\frac{40}{365} \times 20,000 = \quad \text{............................} \quad 2,192$$

	£	£
U.K. duties (20,000 − 2,192)		17,808
Non-U.K. duties (prescribed proportion)	2,192	
Less $12\frac{1}{2}\%$	274	1,918
		£19,726

FOREIGN EMPLOYMENTS (para. 3, Schedule 7, F.A. 1977 and s. 30, F.A. 1984)
This relief given as a deduction from emoluments, as with the "30 day relief," is to be abolished from 1985/86. Relief for years up to 1985/86 is as follows:

1977–78—1983–84	25%
1984–85	$12\frac{1}{2}\%$
1985–86	Nil

Deduction

The deduction as above applies to emoluments provided:

(1) The duties of an employment are performed wholly outside the U.K.; and

(2) The employment is with a person resident outside the U.K.

In such cases it is not necessary to be absent from the U.K. for 30 days or more. The whole of the emolument will qualify for the $12\frac{1}{2}\%$ deduction.

This deduction is an extension of that described above, since, of course, if the period of absence constitutes a qualifying period, the 100% deduction will apply, while in all other cases $12\frac{1}{2}\%$ deduction (given the two conditions) automatically applies. The question of the $12\frac{1}{2}\%$ deduction thus turns on whether or not the employment is with a U.K. employer. If with a U.K. employer, the "30 day" rules apply; if not, the "foreign employment" rules apply. Furthermore, if the person in receipt of the emoluments is non-U.K. domiciled, relief will be given for foreign emoluments (see above) and not under this head.

Expenses in connection with work done abroad (s. 32, F.A. 1977)

An employee who is resident and ordinarily resident in the U.K., with an office or employment the duties of which are performed wholly outside the U.K. (the emoluments from which are not foreign emoluments) is entitled to a deduction for the following expenses:

(i) travelling from the U.K. to take up the overseas employment and in returning to the U.K. on its termination; and

(ii) the provision of board and lodging, *borne or reimbursed by the employer*, where this is necessary to enable the employee to perform the duties of the overseas work.

In both cases if the expenditure is only partially for the purposes of the employment, only that part will be allowable.

Relief is also available to a person who holds two or more offices or employments, the duties of one or more of which are performed wholly or partly outside the U.K. and where he is required to travel from one place to another to perform those duties. The places must both (or all) be outside the U.K. and the employee must be resident, ordinarily resident in the U.K. and not in receipt of foreign emoluments. The expenditure incurred is treated as a deduction necessarily incurred under the provisions of s. 189, I.C.T.A. 1970 (See § 6).

Furthermore a deduction is allowed for travelling expenditure *borne by the employer* where the employee is absent from the U.K. for a continuous period of 60 days for the purpose of performing the overseas duties in respect of:

(*a*) any journey by the spouse or any child of the employee
(i) in accompanying him at the beginning of the period of absence, or
(ii) to visit him during that period;

(*b*) any journey by the employee at the end of the period to visit his spouse or any child of his;

(*c*) any return journey of (*a*) or (*b*).

The number of journeys in each direction by the same person in any year is restricted to two.

Proposals for 1984–85 et seq.

The Inland Revenue, following the 1984 Budget speech, have issued two consultative documents (March 1984 and January 1985) outlining certain relaxations in the manner in which relief for expenses is allowed. The proposals suggest that from 6th April 1984, s. 32 is amended so that an employee who is resident and ordinarily resident in the U.K. and is required to perform duties outside the

U.K. (either wholly or partly) will be exempt from tax on that part of the travelling costs borne by his employer which relates to the expense of carrying him between the U.K. and the place where he is performing his overseas duties without any limit.

It is not proposed that such exemption should apply to U.K. travel (i.e. from home to the point of departure from the U.K.).

§ 4.—SCHEDULE E CASE II

Schedule E Case II applies to a person non-resident in the U.K., or if resident, not ordinarily resident. Such a person is only chargeable to the extent that duties *are performed in the U.K.* (Thus income from overseas would be wholly exempt under this case.)

If the duties performed constitute foreign emoluments (i.e. for a non-resident employer and the employee is non-U.K. domiciled—see Case I above), then a 50% deduction is allowed in respect of the U.K. duties. This deduction applies up to and including 1986–87 and then reduces to 25% for 1987–88 and 1988–89 *provided* the rules concerning Case I deduction (see above) apply. (N.B. The 25% deduction as with Case I ceases to apply after 1983–84.)

Example

Alonzo, U.K. resident (for 2 years only), but not ordinarily resident or domiciled in the U.K., has the following emoluments in 1984–85:

	£
Duties performed in the U.K.	
(i) For a U.K.-resident employer	5,000
(ii) For a non-resident U.K. employer	6,000
Duties performed outside the U.K.	
(i) For a U.K.-resident employer	2,000
(ii) For a non-U.K.-resident employer	3,000
	£16,000

Alonzo is assessed under Schedule E Case II as follows:

	£
Duties performed in the U.K.	
(i) Wholly chargeable	5,000
(ii) Chargeable as to 50% of foreign emoluments	
= 50% × £6,000	3,000
Duties performed outside the U.K.	
(i) and (ii) both wholly exempt unless remitted to U.K.	
(see Case III)	—
	£8,000

Note. The duties performed outside the U.K. are exempt, as Case II only charges emoluments the duties of which are performed in the U.K.

§ 5.—SCHEDULE E CASE III (REMITTANCE BASIS OF ASSESSMENT)

This Case applies to *overseas income received* (*or remitted*) *to the U.K.* which would otherwise not be chargeable. To be chargeable, the person *must be U.K. resident*, whether or not ordinarily resident.

The Case thus applies to:

(1) Case I exempted emoluments, i.e. those in respect of foreign emoluments for the duties of an office or employment performed wholly outside the U.K., which are *remitted* to the U.K.

(2) The Case II exempted emoluments (i.e. those in respect of duties performed abroad) which are *remitted* to the U.K.

It will be appreciated that income applicable to the 100% deduction under Case I would not fall to be assessed under Case III, as the income is chargeable to Case I even though a deduction of 100% is allowed.

Emoluments received in the U.K. (Constructive remittances—s. 184(4), I.C.T.A. 1970)

Emoluments are treated as received in the U.K. if they are paid, used or enjoyed in or in any manner or form transmitted or brought to the U.K. Furthermore, emoluments arising outside the U.K. are treated as received in the U.K. (and hence assessable) if they are applied outside the U.K. by a person ordinarily resident in the U.K. in or towards satisfaction of:

(1) A debt for money lent to him in the U.K. or for interest on money so lent;

(2) A debt for money lent to him outside the U.K. and invested in or brought to the U.K., or

(3) A debt incurred for satisfying in whole or in part a debt falling within (1) and (2) above.

Where a loan is obtained abroad and is wholly or partly repaid before it is brought into the U.K. it will be treated as remitted at the time it is brought into the U.K. Where overseas income is retained by a lender abroad so as to be available for set-off against the debt it will be treated as having been applied in or towards satisfaction of the debt if the amount of the debt outstanding depends in any way on the amount retained.

Summary of Bases of Assessment under Schedule E 1985–86
(See also chart overleaf)

(1) FOREIGN EMOLUMENTS

	Duties performed wholly in U.K.	Duties performed partly in U.K.	Duties performed wholly abroad
Resident and ordinarily resident	All emoluments less 50% (see text)	All emoluments less 50% (see text)	Remittances (Case III)
Resident but *not* ordinarily resident	All emoluments less 50% (Case II)	(i) Duties performed in U.K.—all emoluments less 50% (Case II) (ii) Duties performed abroad— remittances (Case III)	Remittances (Case III)

(1) FOREIGN EMOLUMENTS—(*continued*)

Not resident	All emoluments less 50%	(i) Duties performed in U.K.—all emoluments less 50% (Case II)	Outside scope of U.K. Tax
		(ii) Duties performed abroad —outside scope of U.K. Tax	

(Note the 50% reduction falls to 25% for 1987–88 and 1988–89 and reduces to nil thereafter.)

(2) OTHER EMOLUMENTS

	Duties performed wholly in U.K.	Duties performed partly in U.K.	Duties performed wholly abroad
Resident and ordinarily resident	All emoluments (Case I)	All emoluments deductions for duties performed abroad based on qualifying days (Case I)	(i) 365 qualifying days absence— all emoluments less 100% (ii) less than 365 qualifying days absence—all emoluments (Case I)
Resident but *not* ordinarily resident	All emoluments (Case II)	(i) Duties performed in U.K.—all emoluments (Case II) (ii) Duties performed abroad —remittances (Case III)	Remittances (Case III)
Not resident	All emoluments (Case II)	(i) Duties performed in U.K.—all emoluments (Case II) (ii) Duties performed abroad—outside scope of U.K. Tax.	Outside scope of U.K. Tax

The position on liability to Schedule E for 1985–86 can be diagrammatically represented (using a flowchart) as follows:

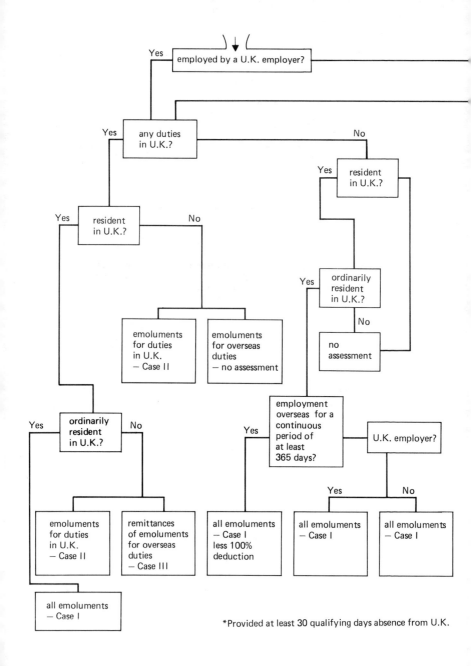

*Provided at least 30 qualifying days absence from U.K.

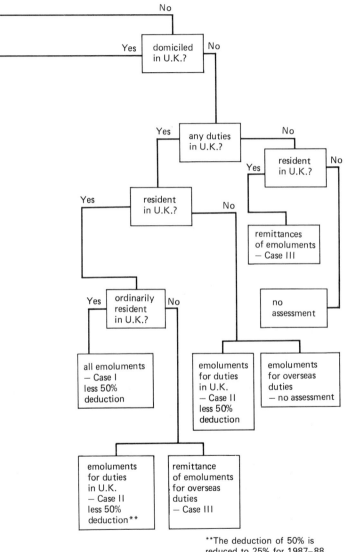

No

Yes — domiciled in U.K.? — No

Yes — any duties in U.K.? — No

resident in U.K.? Yes / No

Yes — resident in U.K.? — No

remittances of emoluments — Case III

no assessment

Yes — ordinarily resident in U.K.? — No

all emoluments — Case I less 50% deduction

emoluments for duties in U.K. — Case II less 50% deduction

emoluments for overseas duties — no assessment

emoluments for duties in U.K. — Case II less 50% deduction**

remittance of emoluments for overseas duties — Case III

**The deduction of 50% is reduced to 25% for 1987–88 and 1988–89.

§ 6.—DEDUCTION OF EXPENSES (ss. 189, 191 and 192, I.C.T.A. 1970)

Any expenses incurred *wholly, exclusively and necessarily* in the performance of the duties of any office or employment of profit, may be deducted from the emoluments of such office for the purpose of an assessment under Schedule E.

A definite distinction is drawn between those expenses incurred *in* the performance of the duties of an employee (e.g. travelling expenses incurred during the actual course of business), and those incurred *in order* to perform one's duties (e.g. travelling expenses incurred in travelling to and from a place of business, or between two separate employments), the former being allowable and the latter disallowable (*Pook* v. *Owen* (1970)—allowable; *Ricketts* v. *Colquhoun* (1925)—not allowable).

Fees paid to an employment agency are not deductible, nor is the cost of travelling to classes in preparation for an examination, even though required by the terms of employment. (*Lupton* v. *Potts* [1969]) The additional cost of travelling by car from home to work is not allowed, even where the car must be employed for business purposes. (*Donnelly* v. *Williamson* [1981])

Clothing is not allowed unless of a special nature (e.g. protective). It was held that the expense of a woman barrister's attire, even though that which would otherwise not be worn, was not deductible (*Mallalieu* v. *Drummond* [1983])

ENTERTAINING (s. 411, I.C.T.A. 1970)

The general rule is that business entertaining expenses are not allowable *unless* the expense is in connection with an overseas customer. Where, however, the director or employee receives an allowance which is for entertaining (this would not cover round sum allowances), or the employer pays the bills for business entertaining or re-imburses the employee, the employee may still claim a deduction for expenses incurred, subject to the ordinary expenses rule, i.e., that the expenses must have been wholly, exclusively and necessarily incurred in the duties of the employment. The proviso is that the expenses are disallowed in computing the employer's tax liability (i.e. disallowed in the Schedule D(i) computation).

Entertaining expenses include the cost of the employee's own meal, etc., and expenditure incidental to the entertaining.

An *overseas customer* must be (*a*) not ordinarily resident in the United Kingdom, (*b*) carrying on a trade or business outside the United Kingdom, and (*c*) a customer or potential customer.

Employees and other authorised agents acting on behalf of overseas principals who satisfy the above conditions are also regarded as overseas customers, provided that they themselves are not ordinarily resident in the United Kingdom.

DIRECTOR'S TRAVELLING EXPENSES

Difficulties have also arisen in connection with the treatment of travelling expenses of directors, and the Board of Inland Revenue has issued notes to assist in clarifying the position:

1. The general principle is that the expense of travelling from home to place of business is not allowable whereas expense necessarily incurred in travelling during the course of business is allowable.
2. Travelling expenses include reasonable hotel expenses where incurred. Where a wife accompanies her husband on a business trip, the expense of which is borne by the employer, the employee is assessable in respect of the travel and subsistence expenses of the wife, but an allowance for the wife's expenses may be given where the wife has some practical qualification directly associated with the husband's trip which she uses regularly during the trip, or where her presence is necessary to act as

hostess at a series of business entertaining occasions for overseas customers which are an essential part of the trip. The wife's expenses may also be allowed where the husband's health is so poor that it would be unreasonable to expect him to travel alone.

In some cases it may be necessary to apportion the cost of the wife's travel and subsistence between business and private.

3. A director who performs his duties at one particular place is not entitled to any deduction for the expense of travelling to that place, and is assessable on the amount of the expense if it is met for him by the company.

4. If a director is required to carry out duties at more than one place, any expense necessarily incurred in travelling between those places is allowable.

5. A director of several associated companies may be regarded as having one place at which he normally acts and is entitled to a deduction for any expense necessarily incurred in travelling from that place to other places of business of the associated companies.

6. A director who gives his services without remuneration to a company not managed with a view to dividends (e.g., a company established for charitable purposes only), is not assessable in respect of any travelling expenses paid to him.

OTHER EXPENSES

(a) Capital allowances
Capital allowances, etc., may be claimed by an individual assessed under Schedule E if the asset is used in earning such income, e.g., a motor car used by a traveller for business purposes.

(b) Clothing/tools
By concession (A1–1980) an employee who has to bear the cost of upkeep of his tools or special clothing is entitled, without enquiry, to a flat rate allowance (as agreed with the trade unions concerned). This does not prevent him from claiming as an alternative the actual expenditure incurred. Clothing expense generally, however, will not be deductible (see *Mallalieu* v. *Drummond* (1983), mentioned above).

(c) Pension contributions
Contributions to approved superannuation funds or statutory superannuation schemes are deductible by the holder of an office or employment from the emoluments of his office.

(d) Subscriptions, etc.
Subject to certain conditions (s. 192, I.C.T.A. 1970) an employee may deduct from the emoluments of any office or employment to be assessed to tax, the following payments, if defrayed out of those emoluments:

(a) Any fee payable in respect of retention of name in the Register of Architects.

(b) Any fee payable in respect of retention of name in the dentist's register or in roll or record kept for a class of ancillary dental workers.

(c) Any fee payable in respect of retention of name in either of the registers of ophthalmic opticians or in the register of dispensing opticians.

(d) The annual fee payable by a registered patent agent.

(e) Any fee payable in respect of retention of name in register of pharmaceutical chemists.

(f) Any fee and contribution to the Compensation Fund or Guarantee Fund payable on issue of a solicitor's practising certificate.

(*g*) The annual fee payable by a registered veterinary surgeon or by a person registered in the Supplementary Veterinary Register.

(*h*) Any annual subscription paid to professional bodies, learned societies, etc. approved for the purposes of s. 192, I.C.T.A. 1970 by the Revenue.

The Revenue may approve any body of persons not of a mainly local character whose activities are carried on otherwise than mainly for profit and are solely or mainly directed to all or any of the following objects:

(i) The advancement or spreading of knowledge (whether generally or among persons belonging to the same or similar positions);

(ii) The maintenance or improvement of standards of conduct and competence among the members of any profession;

(iii) The indemnification or protection of members of any profession against claims in respect of liabilities incurred by them in the exercise of their profession.

Provision is made for the allowance of only part of the subscription where a significant part of the body's activities are directed to objects other than those listed.

Fees, contributions and subscriptions can only be deducted from the emoluments of an office or employment if:

(i) The fee is payable in respect of registration (or retention of a name in a roll or record) or certificate which is a condition or one of alternative conditions of the performance of the duties of the office or employment or, as the case may be, the contribution is payable on the issue of such a certificate;

(ii) the subscription is paid to a body the activities of which are relevant to the office or employment, that is to say, the performance of the duties of the office or employment is directly affected by the knowledge concerned or involves the exercise of the profession concerned.

§ 7.—RETIREMENT BENEFITS (ss. 220 to 224, I.C.T.A. 1970 and ss. 19–26, F.A. 1970)

The above sections contain comprehensive provisions under which directors and other employees of companies are assessed to tax under Schedule E in respect of certain benefits *to be paid to them on*, or in connection with, their retirement from office.*

Premiums paid by employers to insurance societies, etc., and similar payments to a third party with a view to securing retirement benefits to directors or employees will be treated as income of the latter for the year in which the premium, etc., is paid. Provision is made for the *exemption* of certain types of payments including payments under, *inter alia*, any of the following funds or schemes (this applies in the majority of cases):

(i) statutory superannuation schemes;

(ii) approved pension and superannuation schemes (see Chapter 11, § 9);

(iii) schemes in operation before 6th April 1947, where the benefits are by way of annuity or pension, to the extent that the schemes do not relate to directors and/or employees with remuneration exceeding £2,000 per annum; and

(iv) small provident funds and endowment insurance schemes where the premiums paid by the company do not exceed the lower of £100 or 10 per cent of the employee's salary, provided the remuneration of the employee does not exceed £2,000 per annum.

---

* These provisions, which relate to payments made by the *employer* must not be confused with payments made by the *employee* to secure retirement annuities, etc. See also § 9 of this chapter in respect of compensation and termination payments.

Similar provisions apply in the case of amounts set aside by a company with the object of providing for such pensions, etc., instead of being paid to third parties. So long as any such arrangements are in effective operation with any directors or employees, the appropriate sums will be treated as income of the individuals concerned in so far as the benefits proposed will not themselves be assessable to tax under Schedule E. The appropriate sums treated as taxable income of the directors and employees in such circumstances will be assessed as the equivalent amount payable to a third party, e.g., an insurance company, to provide the pension, etc.

Where tax has been charged under the above provisions and the director or employee concerned can show that he has not received, and can no longer claim or expect to receive, any such benefits, the tax deducted may be refunded on relief being claimed within three years of the occurrence of the event which terminated the anticipated benefits.

No tax will be charged in respect of sums laid out in the provision of retirement benefits through unapproved schemes if the duties of the employment are carried out in such circumstances that no tax is chargeable under Schedule E, Cases I and II (see § 4 of this chapter). Similarly, no charge arises if the emoluments are foreign emoluments.

§ 8.—BENEFITS IN KIND (ss. 60–72, F.A. 1976 unless noted)

Income chargeable to Schedule E includes all perquisites and profits whatsoever. (s. 183, I.C.T.A. 1970). However, the decision of *Tennant* v. *Smith* (1892) left some uncertainty concerning the tax position of non-monetary benefits. The legislation contained in the Finance Act 1976, which deals with the taxation of benefits, was in part the statutory solution. Thus benefits derived from employment such as use of a motor car, use of a house or flat or provision of uniform or clothing are subject to taxation. The amount of tax applicable depends upon which of the following groups the employee falls into:

(*a*) Directors or higher-paid employees (see definitions below).

(*b*) All others.

(a) Directors and higher-paid employees (ss. 60–72, F.A. 1976)

GENERAL (ss. 60–63, F.A. 1976)
Tax is chargeable on employees in this category on the *cash equivalent* of the benefit and sums paid by way of expenses.

The cash equivalent is the cost of providing the benefit less so much as is made good by the employee.

All benefits are included under this charging provision, although certain items are excluded and others specifically charged (see below). The cash equivalent for the use of assets other than those specifically charged is as follows:

(i) In the case of land, the annual value;

(ii) In the case of any other asset, 20% of its market value.

DEFINITIONS (ss. 69, 72, F.A. 1976)
The definitions of director and higher paid employees are as follows.

Director means:

(1) A member of the board of directors or similar body, in relation to a company whose affairs are managed by such a board.

(2) The director or other person who manages a company whose affairs are managed by a single director or similar person.

(3) Where the affairs of a company are managed by the members themselves, a member of the company.

It includes any person in accordance with whose directions or instructions the directors of the company (defined as above) are accustomed to act.

Higher-paid employee means every person whose emoluments (inclusive of benefits) exceed £8,500 (£5,000 prior to 1978–79). *Note* expenditure allowable is ignored in calculating the income limit.

Example 1

Taxos receives a salary from Poros Ltd of £7,600 for 1985–86. In addition he is allowed the use of a company car (benefit value say £450) and is reimbursed entertaining expenses of £600. Taxos is treated as a higher paid employee since total income for this purpose is £8,650 (£7,600 + £450 + £600).

A person's employment is not as a director or higher-paid employee merely by reason of it being employment as a director of a company if that person has no *material interest* in the company and either:

    (*a*) His employment is as a full-time working director; or

    (*b*) The company is non-profit-making (meaning that it neither carries on a trade, nor has functions consisting wholly or mainly in the holding of investments or other property), or is established for charitable purposes only.

Material interest is direct or indirect ownership of more than 5% of the ordinary share capital of the company with or without associates.

Full-time working director is a director who is required to devote the whole of a week to the service of the company in a managerial or technical capacity.

BENEFITS EXCEPTED FROM CHARGE (s. 62, F.A. 1976)
The following benefits are specifically exempted:

    (i) Provision in premises occupied by the employer of accommodation, and supplies or services used by the employee solely in performing the duties of his employment (otherwise use of the employer's office would be chargeable!).

    (ii) Where living accommodation is provided (see below for specific charge) alterations of a structural nature to those premises.

    (iii) Provision of any pension, annuity, lump sum gratuity or other like benefit to be given on the employee's death or retirement (the payment can be to the employee, his spouse, children or dependents).

    (iv) Provision of meals in any canteen in which meals are provided for the staff generally.

    (v) Benefits charged otherwise to Schedule E (i.e. to prevent a double charge).

BENEFITS SPECIFICALLY CHARGED
The general taxation charge for benefits as outlined above is the cash equivalent of the benefit.

The following benefits are however charged specifically:

    (i) Motor cars

    (ii) Living accommodation and expenses connected therewith

    (iii) Beneficial loan arrangements

    (iv) Employee shareholdings

    (v) Medical insurance.

(See also vouchers/credit tokens under (**c**) below.)

MOTOR CARS (ss. 64, 65 and Schedule 7, F.A. 1976; s. 48, F.A. 1980; ss. 68 and 69, F.A. 1981)

The benefit assessable on the individual depends upon the element of business use. (Subject to the car being treated as a "pool" car.) The three areas covered are:

(1) Cars not used for business travel, or only insubstantially used. ("Insubstantially" means not more than 2,500 miles of business travel.)

(2) Cars used substantially (i.e. more than 2,500 miles) for business travel.

(3) Cars used preponderantly for business travel. ("Preponderantly" means business travel exceeding 18,000 miles in any one year.)

(1) *Cars insubstantially used.* The benefit assessable is one and a half times the "scale charge" (see below). This also applies to second cars used by the employee.

(2) *Cars substantially used.* The benefit is assessed by reference to a scale of charges depending on the cost and age (and cylinder capacity where appropriate) of the car.

The scales are as follows:

1985–86

TABLE A
CARS WITH ORIGINAL MARKET VALUE UP TO £17,500

Cylinder capacity of car (cm³)	*Age of car at end of year of assessment*	
	Under 4 years £	*4 years or more* £
1,300 or less	410	275
More than 1,300 but not more than 1,800	525	350
More than 1,800	825	550

TABLE B
CARS WITH ORIGINAL MARKET VALUE UP TO £17,500
WITHOUT A CYLINDER CAPACITY

Original market value of car	*Age of car at end of year of assessment*	
	Under 4 years £	*4 years or more* £
Less than £5,500	410	275
£5,500 or more but less than £7,700	525	350
£7,700 or more but less than £17,500	825	550

TABLE C
CARS WITH ORIGINAL MARKET VALUE MORE THAN £17,500

Original market value of car	*Age of car at end of year of assessment*	
	Under 4 years £	*4 years or more* £
More than £17,500 but not more than £26,500	1,200	800
More than £26,500	1,900	1,270

N.B. The Treasury have power to increase the scale levels without the need for separate legislation (s. 64(4), F.A. 1976). This is achieved by statutory instrument.

A deduction is available (up to the amount of the scale benefit) if the employee, as a condition of having the car available for his private use, has to pay his employer a sum of money for that usage.

Example 2

Xerxes uses a Ford Capri 1600 cc car provided by his employer substantially for business travel. The car is two years old at the end of 1985–86.
Xerxes's benefit assessable for 1985–86 from Table A is £525.

(3) *Cars preponderantly used.* The benefit assessed under the above three tables is reduced by one half if travel has been preponderantly business travel (over 18,000 miles p.a.—s. 48, F.A. 1980).

Example 3

Smith, a sales rep, is provided with a Jaguar by his company for the year ended 5th April 1986. Smith's mileage during the year amounted to 35,000 and the cost of the car in 1984 was £18,000.
Smith will be assessed for 1985–86 on the benefit as follows:

	£
Value per Table C.	1,200
Less Reduction due to business travel	600
	£600

CAR FUEL (*1983–84 onwards*)
The scale charge before 1983–1984 was the only charge levied on the employee for the use of the car unless it was shown that a reimbursement of running expenses was made, in which an additional liability (subject to a claim under s. 189, I.C.T.A. 1970) arose. This position was changed for 1983–84 onwards so that the provision of fuel for the car is treated as a taxable benefit.
The cash equivalent of the fuel provided by an employer is also determined by reference to a "scale charge" (s. 64A, F.A. 1976).
The scale charge is set out in s. 64A, F.A. 1976 and as follows for 1984–85:

Table A

Cylinder capacity of car in cm³	*Cash equivalent*
1300 or less	£375
More than 1300 but not more than 1800	£480
More than 1800	£750

Table B

Original market value of car	*Cash equivalent*
Less than £4,950	£375
£4,950 or more but less than £7,000	£480
£7,000 or more	£750

Fuel is provided for a car particularly, but not exhaustively if:
    (*a*) any liability for the supply of fuel is discharged or
    (*b*) a voucher or credit token is used to obtain fuel for the car or
    (*c*) any sum is paid for expenses in providing fuel for the car.
Cars used preponderantly for business usage are granted the same reduction (i.e. 50%) from the fuel scale charge as the car benefit scale charge.
The fuel scale charge is reduced to nil but no other reduction applies where either of the following criteria are met:
    (i) the fuel is *only* made available for business use or

(ii) the employee is required and does make good *the whole of the fuel expense* in connection with the private usage of the car. Partial reimbursement will not revoke the charge.

(This provision is to be contrasted with the reduction in the car benefit scale charge where any contribution made by the employee for the use of the car will reduce the scale charge.)

Pool cars

The scale charge benefit *does not apply* to any car included in a car pool for the use of employees of one or more employers.

A car is a pool car for any year if:

(a) in that year it was made available to and actually used by more than one of those employees and, in the case of each of them, it was made available to him by reason of his employment but was not in that year ordinarily used by any one of them to the exclusion of the others *and*

(b) in the case of each of them any private use of the car made by him in that year was merely incidental to his other use of it in the year *and*

(c) it was in that year not normally kept overnight on or in the vicinity of any residential premises where any of the employees was living, except while being kept overnight on premises occupied by the person making the car available.

A claim for pool car treatment can be made either by any of the employees or by the employer on their behalf.

LIVING ACCOMMODATION PROVIDED (ss. 33 and 33A, F.A. 1977)

The amount assessable is the *annual value* (see below) of the premises or the rent paid by the employer, if greater. Sums paid by the employee for the provision of such accommodation to his employer are deductible in arriving at the assessable benefit.

Annual value

The annual value is the rateable value of the property as set out in s. 531, I.C.T.A. 1970 *unless* the value of the property exceeds £75,000 in which case an additional charge is levied. N.B. this charge only applies for 1984–85 onwards.

Additional charge

The additional charge is the excess cost of the property (including improvements) over £75,000 multiplied by the rate of interest applicable to beneficial loans (see below), currently 12%. Contributions by the employee for the use of the premises will be deducted from the amount assessable.

Example 4

Giles has the use of a company flat during 1985/86, which cost his company £125,000. It is established that the rateable value of flat for s. 531 purposes is £600. Giles contributes £850 for the use of the flat.

Giles' assessment for 1985–86 for the use of the flat is as follows:

	£
Section 531 value	600
Additional charge	
(£125,000 − £75,000) × 12%	6,000
	6,600
Less Contribution	850
Net sum assessable	£5,750

No assessment will arise (either for the rateable value or for the additional charge):

(1) Where it is necessary for the proper performance of the employee's duties that he should reside in the accommodation;

(2) Where the accommodation is provided for the better performance of the duties of his employment *and* his is one of the kinds of employment in the course of which it is customary for employers to provide living accommodation for employees (e.g. police officers);

(3) Where there is a special threat to security, and special arrangements are in force, and the employee resides in the accommodation as part of those arrangements.

Directors cannot avail themselves of (1) and (2) above unless they have:

(*a*) No material interest in the company; *and*

(*b*) They are full-time working directors, or the company is non-profit-making, or is established for charitable purposes.

Accommodation provided for members of the employee's family or household is treated as if it were accommodation provided for the employee.

Example 5

Marina, a full-time working director, is provided with a flat by her company (cost £70,000) during the year 1985–86. Marina has 10% of the ordinary share capital (O.S.C.) of the company and the annual value of the flat has been established at £500. Marina is not required to reside in the flat for security reasons, although it has been agreed with the Inspector of Taxes that the residence is necessary for the proper performance of her duties.

Marina is assessable on this benefit for the year 1985–86 in the sum of £500. This is so, since, as a director with a material interest (more than 5% of the O.S.C.), she cannot avail herself of the exemptions provided where it is necessary to reside in the premises for the proper or better performance of the employee's duties. The cost of the flat is below £75,000 so the additional charge does not apply.

EXPENSES CONNECTED WITH LIVING ACCOMMODATION (s. 63A, F.A. 1976)

Where a director or higher-paid employee is exempted from the charge for living accommodation by one of the three exemptions provided above, and expenditure is paid for by the employer on the provision of:

(1) Heating, lighting or cleaning;

(2) Repairs and maintenance of the premises;

(3) Furniture or other effects in the premises for normal domestic occupation;

the employee will be taxable on the amount which would be added to his emoluments in respect of the expenditure incurred or 10% of his emoluments, whichever is the lesser.

If the accommodation is provided for less than a year, the percentage limit is reduced *pro rata*. Emoluments for these purposes are emoluments of the employment less any capital allowances attributable thereto and payments to approved superannuation, retirement annuity and pension schemes.

Example 6

Theta, a director of Alpha Ltd, who is required to reside in a company house for the better performance of his duties, has the following expenditure paid on his behalf for the premises for the year 1985–86:

	£
Heating and lighting	200
Repairs and maintenance	250
Domestic effects (non assets)	350
	£800

Theta is a full-time working director and has no material interest in the company. His emoluments for the year amount to £5,750.

Theta is assessed on the lower of:

    (a) The expenditure incurred in respect of expenses connected with the accommodation (£800); and

    (b) 10% of emoluments (£575).

The assessment is therefore £575.

Note. Theta is not assessable on the provision of living accommodation and hence the specific legislation relative to expenses provided in respect of the accommodation is applicable.

It is important to note that employees who do not fall within these provisions, i.e.:

    (1) Employees other than directors or higher-paid employees; and

    (2) Directors and higher-paid employees who are not exempted from the charge relative to living accommodation;

will be charged under the normal rules for benefits (in the example of Theta above, this would be £800).

BENEFICIAL LOAN ARRANGEMENTS (s. 66, F.A. 1976)

Where a loan is made to an employee by reason of his employment at a nil rate or rate of interest of less than 12% (15% prior to 6th October 1982), the cash equivalent of the benefit (and hence the amount chargeable to tax) is the difference between the interest paid on the loan by the employee and 12%. An employee benefiting from a loan (i.e. to his spouse) will also be chargeable.

No charge will be made if:

    (i) The cash equivalent is less than £200;

    (ii) In respect of a loan to a relative, no benefit is derived;

    (iii) The interest on the loan would be eligible for relief (e.g. interest on a loan up to £25,000 for the employee's main residence) but where an interest-free loan and another loan exist, both loans are taken into consideration in determining interest eligible for relief;

    (iv) The employee is an individual and the loan is made in the course of his normal domestic, family or personal relationships.

Loans made to such employees and released or written off are taxable in full (unless already charged to tax under Schedule E).

The expression "obtained by reason of employment" is widely drawn (see Sch. 8, F.A. 1976).

EMPLOYEE SHAREHOLDINGS (s. 67, F.A. 1976)

This section applies where an employee or a person connected with him by reason of his employment acquires shares in a company at under market value.

In these circumstances the market value of the shares less any amount paid by the employee is treated as a "notional loan" and the provisions relating to beneficial loans (see above) apply accordingly.

The section is, however, likely to have very little application, since it only applies where the "notional loan" is not otherwise charged as an emolument.

MEDICAL INSURANCE (s. 68, F.A. 1976; s. 72, F.A. 1981)

Medical insurance provided by an employer for an employee (or members of his family) is assessable as a benefit on the cost of providing the insurance.

SCHOLARSHIPS (s. 62A, F.A. 1976)

Scholarships awarded to students by reason of their parents' (or other members of the students' family or household) employment are treated as benefits in kind notwithstanding the provisions of s. 375, I.C.T.A. 1970. This legislation introduced by s. 20 F.A. 1983 reverses the decision in *Wicks* v. *Firth* (1983) where scholarships provided by ICI plc through the medium of a trust for children of the company's employees were not subject to tax on the employee as a benefit.

Taxation as a benefit on scholarships so provided applies to all scholarships awarded after 15th March 1983, *except* those
  (i) Provided under a trust fund or scheme and held by a person receiving full time instruction in an educational establishment *if*
  (ii) in the year payment is made not more than 25% of the total payments made from the fund or scheme do not go to students by virtue of their parents' (or others') employment.

This rule is tightened for 1984/85 onwards so as to include *all* scholarships awarded by reason of directorship or higher-paid employment. Where the scholarship is otherwise provided, i.e. 25% test, the above rules also need to be satisfied. The benefits charge will also not apply to scholarships awarded before 15th March 1983, if the first payment for the scholarship is made before 6th April 1984 and the student is undergoing full-time instruction in the same educational establishment as that when the first payment was made. This provision is relaxed for 1984–85 onwards so that it is not necessary for the instruction to be at the same educational establishment (this only applies, however, to 5th April 1989 or the end of the scholarship, whichever is earlier).

DIRECTORS' P.A.Y.E. (s. 66A, F.A. 1976)
Payments to directors of remuneration by companies without deduction of P.A.Y.E. which is subsequently accounted for is from 6th April 1983 to be treated as a benefit. This provision does not apply to directors without a material interest in the company who are working full-time or to directors of charities or non-profit-making organisations.

EMPLOYEE SUBSIDISED NURSERIES
Following publication by the Equal Opportunities Commission in their manual that employee-subsidised nurseries were *not* a taxable benefit, the Inland Revenue have agreed *not* to tax such benefits for years prior to 1985–86. For 1985–86 onwards such benefits will be fully taxable (I.R. press release 24.4.85).

(b) Other employees

Tax is chargeable on these employees on the *money's worth* of the benefit (i.e. what the employee may sell the benefit for). Thus, for example, the provision of a motor car for an employee (provided some business usage exists) will not be taxable, as the personal usage of the car is not capable of being sold.

Similarly, a suit provided for an employee will only be taxable to the extent of its second-hand value (*Wilkins* v. *Rogerson* (1961)). This will be considerably less than the cost.

Exceptions to this general rule are:
  (1) Provision of cash vouchers, transport vouchers, credit tokens and vouchers capable of being exchanged for goods or services: they are taxed on their *cash equivalent*.
  (2) Provision of living accommodation (see above) but not expenses connected therewith.

(c) Other provisions

Benefits which are not taxable (all employees)
  (1) Luncheon vouchers (if not exceeding 15p per day). (Concession A2–1980).

(2) Provision of a meal in a canteen (provided that the canteen is available to all staff). The "canteen" need not necessarily be on the employer's premises.

(3) Gifts, if of a personal nature, e.g.:
    (i) Marriage gifts;
    (ii) Gifts for passing examinations (*Ball* v. *Johnson* (1971)).

(4) Certain removal expenses (Concession A5).

(5) Miners' free coal (Concession A6–1980).

Vouchers (*other than cash vouchers*) *but including cheque vouchers and transport vouchers* (s. 36, F.(No. 2)A. 1975, amended by s. 44, F.A. 1982)

The provision of a non-cash voucher to an employee including a transport voucher (1982–83 onwards only) is treated as a taxable emolument. The emolument assessable is the cost of providing the voucher, *less* any part of the cost made good by the employee.

The taxable emolument applies to *all* employees, whether or not "higher paid", and the provision of a voucher to the employee's spouse, or his parent or child or any dependant of his is also taxable.

Transport vouchers provided to employees or relatives of employees of passenger transport undertakings (e.g. British Rail, London Transport) are exempted from charge.

A claim under ss. 189, 192 or 194(3) (expenses deductible) can be made for any assessment if it can be shown that the claim would have been competent had the employee incurred the expenditure.

The following are defined by the amending s. 44, F.A. 1982:
    cheque voucher
    employee
    passenger transport undertaking
    relation
    subsidiary
    transport voucher
    voucher.

Credit tokens (s. 36A, F.(No. 2)A. 1975)

As with vouchers the provision to an employee of a credit token *and* any goods etc. received by using the credit token are treated as a taxable emolument. The emolument assessable is the cost of providing the token (e.g. subscription) together with the expense of the goods etc. provided by using the token *less* any amount made good by the employee.

Any expenses which would be deductible as wholly, exclusively and necessarily incurred reduce the assessable emolument.

A credit token is defined as a card, token, document or other thing given to a person who undertakes:
    (*a*) that on the production of it he will supply any money, goods or services on credit, *or*
    (*b*) that where on production of it to a third party, the third party supplies any money, goods or services, he will pay the third party for them.

A credit token is exclusive of non-cash and cash vouchers falling within ss. 36 and 37, F(No. 2)A. 1975.

Cash vouchers (s. 37, F(No. 2)A. 1975)

Any voucher, stamp or similar document capable of being exchanged for a sum of money greater than, equal to or not substantially less than the cost of providing the voucher is treated as pay, if provided to an employee, and subjected to P.A.Y.E.

The taxation of cash vouchers applies to *all* employees and the amount included for P.A.Y.E. purposes is the sum into which the voucher is convertible as mentioned above.

No taxation consequences arise under the section if:

- (*a*) the sum represented by the voucher would have been taxable under Schedule E if received direct or
- (*b*) the voucher is a savings certificate: the accumulated interest thereon is exempt.

Return of benefits

The return of benefits for those who are directors or in higher-paid employment is to be made annually on Form P.11.D (P.9.D for other employees), which is completed by the employer after the end of the financial year in question.

The form P.11.D. requires the following information:

- (1) Entertainment payments made exclusively in respect of entertaining.
    - (*a*) Amount of any round sum allowance.
    - (*b*) Specific allowances for entertaining.
    - (*c*) Sums reimbursed.
    - (*d*) Sums paid to third persons.
        (Show all sums even if disallowable in employer's tax computations where they do not relate to the entertainment of "overseas customers").
- (2) General expense allowance (round sum allowance not exclusively for entertaining).
- (3) Travelling and subsistence.
    - (*a*) Fares, hotels, meals etc. (excluding payments for travel between home and normal place of employment).
    - (*b*) Payments for travel between home and normal place of employment from which tax has not been deducted under P.A.Y.E.
- (4) Cars.
    Details as required for Tables A, B and C plus fuel supplied.
- (5) Living accommodation provided for the director or employee.
    - (*a*) Address and nature of accommodation.
    - (*b*) Gross value for rating of the property.
    - (*c*) Rent, if any, repairs and insurance paid by employer.
    - (*d*) Other expenses borne by employer (rates, etc.).
    - (*e*) Furniture and fittings etc. provided by the employer.
- (6) Subscriptions.
- (7) Private medical, dental, etc., treatment.
- (8) Goods and services supplied free or below market value unless supplied under discount facilities equally available to employees generally.
- (9) Work carried out at the director's or employee's own home or on his property or assets.
- (10) Wages, insurance, keep, etc., of personal or domestic staff.
- (11) Cars, property, furniture, etc., given or transferred to the director or employee.
- (12) Other expenses and benefits.
    - (*a*) Expenses payments.
    - (*b*) Benefits.

By concession (A23–1980) the Inland Revenue do not tax reimbursements by an employer of an employee's travelling expenses of getting himself and his dependants to an employment abroad and returning therefrom to the United Kingdom, provided the emoluments are foreign emoluments.

A notice of nil liability may be granted in respect of particular payments, benefits or facilities if the Inspector is satisfied that on the supply of all relevant information no benefit arises to the particular employees to whom the benefit/payment or facility is made available (s. 70, F.A. 1976).

§ 9.—COMPENSATION FOR LOSS OR REMOVAL FROM OFFICE AND RETIREMENT (EX GRATIA) PAYMENTS (ss. 187 and 188, I.C.T.A. 1970; s. 31, F.A. 1981)

General
Payments which are made to an employee or former employee in connection with the termination of his employment and *which would otherwise escape liability to tax* are wholly or partly liable to tax. Section 187, I.C.T.A. 1970 provides that Income Tax shall be charged under Schedule E in respect of payments to, or on behalf of, or to the personal representatives of, the holder or past holder of any office or employment in consequence of or in connection with the termination of the holding of that office or employment, or any change in functions or emoluments.

Statutory redundancy payments, and the corresponding amount of any other employer's payment, made under the Redundancy Payments Act 1965, are to be taken into account for this purpose, although such payments are otherwise exempt from income tax under Schedule E.

Payments excluded from charge
By virtue of s. 188, I.C.T.A. 1970 the following payments are excluded from charge under s. 187 and hence not chargeable to tax:

(1) Payments made on termination of the office or employment by the death of the holder;
(2) Payments made on account of the injury or disability of the holder of the office or employment;
(3) Sums chargeable to Income Tax in connection with restrictive covenants.
(4) Terminal grants, gratuities, etc., payable to Her Majesty's Forces;
(5) Certain benefits provided for by approved pension schemes and agreements;
(6) Benefits paid to a non-domiciled person employed by a non-resident; and
(7) An amount not exceeding £25,000 (£10,000 prior to 6th April 1981). Where the payment exceeds £25,000 only the excess is chargeable, but is subject to relief (see below). Payments made to the same person in respect of the same office or employment or in respect of different employments with the same employer are aggregated. Earlier payments are then exempted first.
(8) Foreign service—a whole or partial deduction applies to terminal payments in respect of foreign service (see below).

Compensation payments—the charge to tax
The first £25,000 of any payment made by way of damages or compensation for loss, or retirement from office whether under legal obligation or ex-gratia will only be exempted from charge if not otherwise chargeable to tax. Thus for example:

(i) payments made under the employee's service agreement, or
(ii) payments requiring or in anticipation of, the future provision of services

will be chargeable under normal Schedule E rules and hence not exempt.

CALCULATING THE TAX LIABILITY ON PAYMENTS OVER £25,000
Relief for the excess over £25,000 is given for payments up to £75,000. Payments in excess of £75,000 *are fully taxable*. The relief falls in two bands of £25,000, as follows:

(*a*) *£25,000 to £50,000*
The relief is *one half* of the difference between:
  (i) the tax chargeable excluding the lump sum payment, and
  (ii) the tax chargeable including the whole of the taxable lump sum payment, treating the payment as equal to £50,000 (thus the excess over £25,000 up to £50,000).

(*b*) *£50,000 to £75,000*
The relief is *one quarter* of the difference between:
  (i) the tax chargeable including the whole of the taxable lump sum payment treating the payment as equal to £75,000, and
  (ii) the tax chargeable on the basis that the lump sum payment was exactly £50,000 (i.e. the taxable element is £25,000).
The termination payment for the purposes of relief is treated as the "top slice" of the taxpayer's income.

The relief can be calculated simply by ascertaining the tax liability on each of the £25,000 amounts as the top slice of income and then applying the appropriate fraction (i.e. $\frac{1}{2}$ or $\frac{1}{4}$). This method has been used in the example below.

Example 1

Argos receives £120,000 compensation for loss of office from his employer on 7th June 1985. His other income for 1985/86 is as follows:

	£
Salary (same employment)	7,000
Salary (new employment)	8,350

Argos is a married man with no allowances other than mortgage interest paid during 1984–85 of £4,000 (all allowable).
The tax charge on the lump sum is as follows:

	£
Lump sum	120,000
Less exempt....................................	25,000
Taxable..	£95,000

Other income and tax thereon:

	£	£
Salary		15,350
Less Mortgage interest	4,000	
Personal allowance.........................	3,455	7,455
Taxable income.................................		£7,895

Tax thereon	£7,895 @	30%	= £2,368.50

Tax on lump sum:

£				£
8,305	(16,200 − 7,895)	@	30%	2,491.50
3,000		@	40%	1,200.00
5,200		@	45%	2,340.00
7,900		@	50%	3,950.00
7,900		@	55%	4,345.00
62,695		@	60%	37,617.00

£95,000

Total tax liability	£51,943.50

Relief thereon as follows:

(i) *On first taxable £25,000*
Tax is:

£			£	£
8,305	@	30%	2,491.50	
3,000	@	40%	1,200.00	
5,200	@	45%	2,340.00	
7,900	@	50%	3,950.00	
595	@	55%	327.25	
£25,000			10,308.75	

Relief is therefore $\frac{1}{2}$ × £10,308.75 = (5,154.37)

(ii) *On second taxable £25,000*
Tax on this £25,000 is:

7,305	@	55%	= 4,017.75	
17,695	@	60%	= 10,617.00	
£25,000			£14,634.75	

Relief is therefore $\frac{1}{4}$ × £14,634.75 = (3,658.69)

Tax liability on lump sum	
after relief (£51,943.50 − (5,154.37 + 3,658.69))	£43,130.44

Foreign service
Terminal payments in respect of an office or employment which includes foreign service and that foreign service comprises either:
  (a) three-quarters of the whole period of service, or
  (b) the last ten years of service (where the whole period of service exceeds ten years, or
  (c) one-half of the period of service, including ten of the last twenty years where the period of service exceeds twenty years.
are exempt from charge.

Where these conditions are not satisfied a deduction is allowed which is worked out as follows:

$$\frac{\text{length of service}}{\text{whole period of service}}.$$

Foreign service is service the emoluments from which were not charged to tax under Schedule E Case I (Schedule E prior to 1956–57) either by exemption or 100% deduction.

Example 2

Spooner receives £100,000 compensation for loss of office on 26th August 1985. His contract of employment commenced on 26th August 1965 and during his term of office his foreign service amounted to 8 years.

The compensation payment is chargeable to tax as follows:

	£
Lump sum	100,000
Less Exempt.	25,000
	75,000
Less Foreign service deduction:	
8/20 × £75,000 = ...	30,000
	£45,000

Prior to 1984–85 a 50% deduction applied to terminal payments made in respect of employments the emoluments from which were foreign emoluments (see above).

§ 10.—SHARE OPTIONS AND SHARE INCENTIVE SCHEMES

The detailed provisions relating to share option and share incentive schemes are beyond the scope of this book and the following notes are therefore only an outline of the main charging sections and the exemptions afforded by "approved schemes".

SHARE OPTIONS (s. 186, I.C.T.A. 1970)
An option granted by a company to a director or employee to acquire shares is assessable under Schedule E.

Assessments in respect of share options now arise when the option is exercised or assigned or released, and are computed as follows:
  (*a*) Where the option is exercised, the amount assessable will be the difference between the then open-market value and the cost of acquiring and exercising the option.
  (*b*) Where the option is assigned or released, the amount assessable will be the difference between the consideration for the assignment or release, and the cost of acquiring the option.

For the purpose of calculating the capital gains on the subsequent disposal of the shares, the amount assessed under Schedule E is treated as an addition to the cost of acquiring the shares.

If the right is capable of being exercised more than 7 years after it is granted tax may also be charged on the grant of the right (s. 77, F.A. 1972).

Tax so charged will reduce any subsequent charge when the right is exercised.

It is understood that the Inland Revenue tax the liability under Schedule E Case I, and accordingly it may be possible to avoid a charge by becoming non-resident in the year of exercise or utilising the 100% deduction (see above).

Payment by instalments (s 40, F.A. 1982 as amended)
This method of payment ceases to have effect where rights to acquire shares are obtained after 5th April 1984.

For rights obtained before 6th April 1984, and exercised after 5th April 1983, tax is payable in five instalments provided the tax charge exceeds £250 and the option price for the shares is not less than the market value of the shares at the date the option was granted. It is necessary for an election to be made within 30 days after the end of the year in which the charge arises for the instalment basis of payment to apply.

The instalment payment dates are as follows:

First—14 days after application for payment of tax is made under the P.A.Y.E. regulations (i.e. the date the tax would otherwise be payable in full).

Second,—on such dates to secure that the interval between any two consecutive
Third and instalments is the same.
Fourth

Fifth—the 5th April in the fifth year following the end of the year in which the charge arose.

Approved Share Option Schemes (s. 47 and Schedule 10, F.A. 1980)

The charge to Schedule E on the grant or exercise of an option to acquire shares, as outlined above, is exempted if the option is granted under an approved share option scheme. Furthermore any growth in value of the shares (see below) following the exercise is also exempted from charge.

The scheme *must* be linked to an approved savings scheme (S.A.Y.E. scheme) which is to provide the funds for the acquisition of the shares when the option is exercised. Savings must not exceed £100 per month nor impose a minimum on the amount of a person's contribution which exceeds £10 monthly.

Any right which is exercised within three years of being obtained will *not* be exempted from charge to tax.

Persons eligible to participate and conditions as to scheme shares are broadly the same as for "approved profit sharing schemes" (see below) although for the specific details reference must be made to Schedule 10, F.A. 1980.

The appointed day for the commencement of these provisions was 15th November 1980.

Approved Share Option Schemes under s. 38 and Sch. 10, F.A. 1984

This legislation was introduced to provide a form of company incentive to non-shareholding employees or directors outside the somewhat limited application of schemes under s. 47, F.A. 1980.

The legislation provides that share options will not be subjected to an income tax charge (under s. 186, I.C.T.A. 1970 or otherwise) on exercise, but subject only to capital gains tax. (A Schedule E charge will arise, however, on the difference if any between the option price paid and the market value of the option at the date of grant.)

The provisions apply to all schemes which have as their main feature the providing for employees or directors benefits in the nature of rights to acquire shares and whose rules comply with the requirements of Schedule 10, F.A. 1984, the requirements of which relate to:-

(1) Eligible participators
Broadly full-time working directors or employees, who have at the point of participation a material interest in the company (but only if the company is close)

(2) Limitation of rights
Shares capable of being acquired under the scheme must not have a market value in excess of the greater of:—
(a) £100,000 or

(b) four times emoluments (of the current or preceding year whichever is the greatest)

(3) *Type of shares*
These must be ordinary paid-up non-redeemable shares not subject to restrictions which do not apply to other shares of that class.
Shares must be in a quoted company or subsidiary of a quoted company *or* be in a company which is not under the control of another company.

(4) *Exercise of rights*
The scheme must not provide for any person obtaining rights under it to:—
(a) transfer any such rights
(b) exercise any rights within three years of being granted or later than ten years after they are granted—unless by reason of termination of employment.
(c) exercise any rights within three years of any previous exercise of rights.

SHARE INCENTIVE SCHEMES (s. 79, F.A. 1972)
A person who acquires shares (or an interest in shares) as a result of an opportunity offered to him as an employee or director is subject to a Schedule E charge on the growth in value of those shares.
This charge will be in addition to any Schedule E liability that may arise on the acquisition of the shares (e.g. if acquired at less than market value).
The charge to tax will not arise if:
(i) Employees of a company receive as part of their emoluments shares in that company which are determined to an extent in advance by reference to the profits of the company.
(ii) The shares acquired *are not subject to restrictions* (see below) and immediately after the acquisition either:
(*a*) the majority of the available shares of the class acquired, were acquired otherwise than as a result of opportunities offered to employees *or*
(*b*) the majority of the available shares of the class acquired were acquired by employees or directors who control the company.
(N.B. Shares held by an associated company are *not* available shares; thus shares given to an employee in a subsidiary would be caught by these restrictions.)
Restrictions attaching to the shares are:
(i) restrictions not attaching to all shares of the same class;
(ii) restrictions ceasing or liable to cease at some time after the acquisition;
(iii) restrictions depending on the shares being or ceasing to be held by directors or employees of the company (other than restrictions imposed by a company's articles of association). This restriction does not apply to shares falling within (ii)(*b*) above.
The charge to tax under s. 79 is the difference between the market value at the date of acquisition and the market value on the *earliest* happening of the following:
(i) the expiration of 7 years from the date of acquisition of the shares;
(ii) the date the employee ceases to own the shares;
(iii) the date the shares are no longer subject to restrictions.

Example 1

Alpha acquires 500 shares for £1 each on 15 July 1977 as a result of an opportunity offered to him as an employee. The shares are subject to restrictions which do not apply to all shares of that class.

Alpha sells the shares on 24 August 1985 for £10,000.
The market value of the shares was:

15.7.84.	£9,500
24.8.85.	£10,000

The s. 79 charge is:

	£
Market value at acquisition.	500
Market value 15.7.84.	9,500
Schedule E charge.	£9,000

Notes

   (i) The expiration of 7 years occurs before the sale hence this earlier date crystallises the charge.

  (ii) The amount assessable is treated as earned income.

 (iii) The subsequent disposal will produce a charge to capital gains as follows:

	£	£
Sale proceeds		10,000
Less Original cost.	500	
Schedule E charge.	9,000	9,500
Chargeable gain.		£ 500

The acquisition of shares by a director or employee at a discount where an offer for similar shares is made to the public is no longer the subject of a s. 79 change provided certain conditions are satisfied (s. 41, F.A. 1984).

APPROVED PROFIT-SHARING SCHEMES (ss. 53–61 and Schedule 9, F.A. 1978; s. 46, F.A. 1980)

The legislation exempts from charge to Schedule E employees who participate in any profit-sharing schemes, provided certain stringent conditions are satisfied so that the scheme is designated by the Inland Revenue an approved profit-sharing scheme.

An approved scheme is one in which an employee may have appropriated to him shares up to a value (in any tax year) of:

  (i) £1,250 *or*

 (ii) 10% of salary exclusive of benefits, whichever is the greater but with a ceiling of £5,000.

The shares must be held in trust and the employee must agree to the shares being held for a "period of retention" which must not end before the *earliest* of the following dates:

  (1) The second anniversary of the date on which the shares were appropriated. (The minimum period was five years until 5th April 1980.)

  (2) The date of the participant's death.

  (3) The date on which the participant reaches pensionable age (65 for men, 60 for women).

  (4) The date on which the participant ceases to be an employee of the company operating the profit-sharing scheme (but only if through injury, disability or redundancy).

If these conditions are not satisfied, the employee becomes liable to tax under Schedule E for the full value of the shares.

If an employee disposes of his shares after the period of retention, but within 5 years of appropriation, the charge to Schedule E is based on percentage of the value of the shares at the date of appropriation (or of the proceeds of sale, if less), depending on the date of realisation. The percentage is as follows:

	Percentage of value at date of appropriation (*or of sale proceeds, if less*)
Period held	
Before the 4th anniversary of appropriation	100%*
Between the 4th and 5th year of appropriation	75%

Example 2

Smith had appropriated to him 50 shares valued at £9 each in an approved profit-sharing scheme on 1st December 1981. He realised the shares for £1,000 on 31st December 1985. Smith will be charged to Schedule E in 1985–86 on 75% × £450 = £337.50.

Notes
   (1) Smith has held the shares for over 4 years but less than 5 so the 75% charge applies.
   (2) The value of the shares at appropriation is less than the sale proceeds, so the former is used as the basis of the charge.

Example 3

Assume that in Example 2 above the shares had been realised for £300. The charge to Schedule E for 1985–86 would be 75% × £300 = £225.

A participant in an approved profit-sharing scheme is liable to capital gains tax whenever the shares are disposed of. The gain is the difference between the value of the shares at the date of appropriation and the sale proceeds.

Example 4

Given the facts in Example 2 above, Smith will be liable to capital gains tax as follows:
   Gain chargeable = Sale proceeds − Appropriation value
                   = £1,000 − £450 = £550.

Example 5

If the facts were as in Example 3, an allowable loss will arise:

   Allowable loss = Sale proceeds − Appropriation value
                  = £300 − £450 = £(150)

For the complex conditions relating to approval (covering the participants, the shares and the trust) the reader should refer to Inland Revenue booklet I.R. 36 as well as the legislation.

---

*But only 50% where participant ceases to be employed for reasons of injury, retirement, redundancy etc.

§ 11.—SUB-CONTRACTORS IN THE CONSTRUCTION INDUSTRY (ss. 68 to 71 and Schedules 12 and 13, F(No. 2)A 1975; s 47 and Schedule 8, F.A. 1982)

A contractor making payments to a sub-contractor is obliged to deduct income tax at the rate of 30% from the payment unless the sub-contractor holds an exemption certificate. This provision, originally enacted by F.A. 1971, was aimed at preventing the evasion of tax by labour-only sub-contractors ("the lump"). The deduction applies equally to company sub-contractors, but does not apply where a contract of employment exists between the contractor and sub-contractor.

The issuing of exemption certificates was tightened up following the Finance (No. 2) Act 1975 but was subsequently relaxed in the Finance Act 1980.

To obtain a certificate, all applicants must be carrying on a business in the U.K. which:

(1) Includes the carrying out of construction operations (or the supply of labour carrying out construction operations).

(2) Is carried on to a substantial extent by means of a bank account.

(3) Is carried on with proper records.

(4) Is carried on from proper premises with proper equipment, stock and other facilities.

In addition to the above, the applicant if an individual must:

(1) During the 3 years prior to the application have been employed in the U.K. either as the holder of an office or employment, or as a person carrying on a trade, vocation or profession (unless a certificate is held).

(2) Have complied with the Income Tax Acts and the T.M.A. for the 3 years before the application.

(3) Have made the necessary contributions for National Insurance in respect of the 3 years before the application.

If the applicant is a company it must additionally within the 3 years prior to the date of application have complied with all obligations imposed on it under the Income Tax Acts, Corporation Tax Acts or the Taxes Management Act 1970.

On appeal by a person who has been refused a sub-contractor's tax certificate, the Commissioners have the power to review the Board of Inland Revenue's discretion to disregard the appellant's failure to fulfil his tax obligation, provided such failures were *minor and technical* and do not cause doubt as to his likely fulfilment of future obligations.

The term "contractor" is widely drawn for these purposes and includes:

(1) Any person carrying on a business which includes *construction operations*;

(2) Any local authority;

(3) Any development corporation or New Town Commission;

(4) The Commission for the New Towns; and

(5) The Housing Corporation, a housing association, a housing trust, a housing society, and the Northern Ireland Housing Trust and Executive and the Scottish Special Housing Association.

The term also applies to any person carrying on a business if his average annual expenditure on *construction operations* (refer Schedule 13, F(No. 2)A 1975) in the three years ending with the last accounting date has exceeded £250,000. Businesses which have not been carried on for three years are brought in when one third of their total expenditure on construction operations up to their most recent accounting date exceeded £250,000. Moreover, once included in the scheme the *contractor* must continue to operate the legislation until he can satisfy the Board of Inland Revenue that his total expenditure on constructions has been less than £250,000 in three successive years.

This condition will be satisfied if:

(*a*) He has been employed or self-employed in the U.K. for a three-year period in the six years prior to the date of his application;

(*b*) He has not been so employed or self-employed during the rest of that six-year period; and

(*c*) He spent the whole or part of the remainder of the period outside the United Kingdom and has satisfactory evidence of this.

In determining whether the *three years' employment test* under (*a*) is satisfied, periods of unemployment totalling six months are ignored.

School and college leavers and others offering a guarantee (s. 47 and Schedule 8, F.A. 1982)

The above provisions gave the Inland Revenue the power to introduce by regulation (via statutory instrument) an extension of certificate holders exempted from the tax deduction imposed under the construction industry scheme.

The regulations were issued on 1st December 1982 (S.I. No. 1391 (1982)) and extend the issue of special tax deduction certificates to those leaving full-time education and others who can offer a guarantee.

The regulations provide for:

—a weekly limit of £150 on the total payments (net of materials which may be paid without deduction of tax to a sub-contractor holding a 714S certificate);

—special vouchers to be given by sub-contractors holding 714S certificates as receipts for payments made without deduction of tax;

—any payments over the £150 limit to be made under deduction of tax;

—the form of the 714S certificate;

—the form of the special voucher to be used by the 714S certificate holder;

—the form, content and amount of the guarantee for applicants for a 714S certificate other than those applying for reason of full-time education.

Certain other amendments to the general scheme are also made by the above provisions. In particular the Inland Revenue has power to make regulations specifying certain circumstances in which payments are to be made under deduction of tax.

§ 12.—PAY AS YOU EARN

The statutory provisions relating to the deduction of income tax from salaries, wages etc., assessable under Schedule E, have been incorporated in ss. 204 to 207, I.C.T.A. 1970; while the regulations relating to "Pay As You Earn" have been consolidated in the Income Tax (Employments) Regulations (e.g. I.T. (Employments) No. 13 Regulations 1982 introduced *inter alia* provision to bring within the tax procedures social security benefits paid to the unemployed, to those temporarily laid off and those involved in trade disputes.

The "Pay As You Earn" provisions apply to all emoluments assessable to Income Tax under Schedule E, except those assessable under Case III, of Schedule E. It should be observed that "Pay As You Earn" is merely a method of collection of tax under Schedule E. The territorial scope of P.A.Y.E. was considered in *Clarke* v. *Oceanic Contractors Inc* (1983) where it was held that a non-resident company making payments to individuals in the North Sea (brought within the U.K. by s. 38 F.A. 1973) were assessable to Schedule E via the P.A.Y.E. system because of their trading presence in the U.K.

(a) The operation of "Pay As You Earn"

The essential feature of the scheme is that, week by week (or at whatever intervals the employee's emoluments are payable to him), the employer shall deduct tax in accordance with the figures set out in a series of "Tax Tables." These tables, which have the general appearance of ready reckoner tables, are divided into weekly parts for employees paid at weekly intervals, one for each week in the Income Tax year. Thus, the table for Week 1 will apply to any pay day falling within the period 6th April to 12th April (both dates inclusive); the table for Week 2 will apply to any pay day falling within the period 13th April to 19th April (inclusive); and so on right through the Income Tax year. Similarly Monthly Tax Tables (for the "Income Tax months," see below) are provided for employees paid monthly or at longer intervals.

Those from 6th April 1983 will not include qualifying mortgage interest payments on loans up to £25,000 (£30,000 for 1984–85) but relief for which is given at source (see Chapter 11, §2). The Tax Tables, which have been prepared by the Commissioners of Inland Revenue, contain a list of figures known as '*Codes*'. These codes determine the total net allowances and reliefs (with the exceptions which are referred to later—see below) to which the taxpayer is entitled for the year of assessment.

As regards each person who is assessable under Schedule E, the Income Tax authorities will work out his Code Number for the year of assessment concerned, in accordance with the details of the allowances claimed by the employee on his last Income Tax Return, and by reference to his circumstances as known to the Income Tax authorities at the time of fixing the Code Number. In arriving at this Code Number, the authorities may also, in appropriate cases, take into consideration the following additional factors (using the allowances for 1985–86):

(1) Untaxed income against which a portion of the allowances will be set. For instance, if a married man receives untaxed interest of £40, his personal allowance of £3,455 will, in all probability, be partially set against his Schedule D, Case III, income, leaving him with net allowances amounting to £3,415. His Code Number would therefore be 341H. This principle is not adopted where there is considerable untaxed income, or where the employee objects, since it spreads the collection of Schedule D tax over the whole year and the employee is in fact paying tax some months before liability arises.

(2) Any tax overpaid for any previous year, which has not been repaid.

(3) Any tax remaining unpaid for any previous year, which is not otherwise recovered. Small amounts of net tax will be cancelled.

(4) Tax deducted from annual charges (annuities, etc.).

Alternatively, separate notices of assessment may be sent out in respect of untaxed income other than the main source of income under Schedule E, but it is more probable that, for the purpose of simplification, such "other income" will be set off against the allowances to which the employee is entitled, for the purpose of arriving at the employee's Code Number.

If all the reliefs due to an employee have been set off against other income, the Inspector may determine that tax shall be deducted at the basic rate (Code O), while where the emoluments will be included in a Schedule D assessment (e.g. a practising accountant acting as secretary to a company), or if the Inspector is satisfied that the emoluments will not be chargeable to tax, then he may determine that no tax shall be deducted (Code N.T.). Where tax will be payable on some of the emoluments at the higher rates for 1985–86 Code OT will operate and the tax tables will provide for the correct deductions to be made. (See Chapter 2 for the personal tax structure for 1985–86.)

The following code numbers provide for tax at a specified rate:

D1 Tax at the higher rate of 40 per cent.
D2 Tax at the higher rate of 45 per cent.
D3 Tax at the higher rate of 50 per cent.
D4 Tax at the higher rate of 55 per cent.
D5 Tax at the higher rate of 60 per cent.

When the employee's Code Number has been worked out, it is entered on a "*tax deduction card*", which is issued to the employer by the Inspector. The purpose of this card and the form which it takes are explained later on, but before the Tax Deduction Card is issued to the employer the Inspector sends a *"notice of coding"* to the employee*, an example of which is given below:

Notice of coding, 1985–86

Allowances: £

Expenses, superannuation, etc.	—
Personal allowance.....................................	3,445
Wife's earned income allowance	—
Housekeeper	—
Dependent relatives	100
Building society interest payable (loan over £30,000)	4,000
	7,555

deduct: Allowances to be set against other income, as follows:

Untaxed interest......................................	378
Allowances to be Set against Pay......................	£7,177

Your code number is 718 H

N.B. Building society interest paid for loans under £30,000 is now given by way of deduction from source and not in the code notice (see Chapters 11 and 12 for full details).

"H" and "L" denote the higher and lower personal allowances respectively. This facilitates recoding by the Inland Revenue, when necessary, but where the employee objects to this, the letter "L" is used.

If the employee does not agree the details on the Notice of Coding, he may give notice of objection, stating the grounds thereof, to the Inspector within 30 days of the date the Notice of Coding was issued, who may then agree an amended Notice with the employee. Failing agreement with the Inspector, the employee may appeal to the General Commissioners for the district in which he resides or for the district in which the coding was determined (or to the Special Commissioners, if he resides in Northern Ireland or is a non-resident), and their decision is final.

THE TAX DEDUCTION CARD
This card (Form No. P.9), which is issued to the employer by the Inspector *after* the Notice of Coding has been sent to the employee (as explained above), and which has the employee's Code Number specified thereon, constitutes an authorisation to the employer to deduct tax from any payment of emoluments to the employee during the year of assessment to which that card relates (or, as the case may be, to repay tax to the employee) by reference to that employee's Code Number.†

---

* Where, however, an employee's Code Number for the year of assessment is the same as his Code Number for the previous year of assessment, he need not be notified.

† The Inspector may issue a Tax Deduction Card to the employer, notwithstanding the fact that the employee has objected or appealed against the Code Number which is specified thereon, and the employer must deduct (or repay) tax by reference to that Code Number. If the Code Number is amended, particulars thereof will be sent by the Inspector to the employer, who will henceforward deduct (or repay) tax by reference to the amended Code Number.

The Tax Deduction Card is ruled horizontally to cover 53 weeks (the extra week is to allow for the fact that there will sometimes be 53 weekly pay days falling within the Income Tax year), and there are vertical columns headed as follows:

(1) (a)–(c) National Insurance Contributions.
— Week No.
(2) Gross pay in the week.
(3) Total gross pay to date.
(4) Total free pay to date as shown by Table A (see below).
(5) Total taxable pay to date.
(6) Total tax due to date as shown by Table B (see below).
(7) Tax deducted or refunded in the week.
(8) Tax refunded in the week.

National Insurance Contributions payable, are collected under the P.A.Y.E. system. An extra column has been provided on the extreme left of the tax deduction card in which the employee's National Insurance contribution is entered.

In the case of employees paid at monthly or longer intervals, a month (referred to as an "Income Tax month") covers the period from the 6th of one month to the 5th of the following month (both dates inclusive). Month 1 is that which covers the period from 6th April to 5th May (both dates inclusive); Month 2 covers the period from 6th May to 5th June; and so on throughout the Income Tax year.

The Inland Revenue authorities are, however, prepared to allow an employer to use his own card or form, so long as it shows, in a readily comprehensible manner, the same information as the official card, and they have had an opportunity of commenting on the proposed card or form before it is printed.

The appropriate particulars must be filled in by the employer in the columns specified above on the occasion of each payment of emoluments to the employee. If, however, the necessary figures of emoluments and tax deducted are incorporated by the employer in his pay records, he need show only the totals for the Income Tax year on the Tax Deduction Card (or the totals up to the last week of employment, if the employee has left during the year); but he must also undertake to keep his pay records intact for at least three years after the end of the Income Tax year.

DEDUCTION AND REPAYMENT OF TAX

Before describing the method of computing the amount of tax to be deducted (or repaid, as the case may be) from each payment of emoluments to the employee, it is desirable to explain the principle on which the Tax Tables, which are designed to give the necessary figures, have been constructed.

The Tax Tables, which have been prepared by the Commissioners of Inland Revenue, are divided into two parts:

(a) *Free Pay Table* (referred to as "Table A"), which indicates the amount of non-taxable (or free) pay to date according to the Code Number of the employee; and

(b) *Taxable Pay Table* (referred to as "Table B"), which indicates the total amount of tax due to date on any figure of taxable pay, i.e. total pay less free pay.

In brief, the Tax Tables are so constructed that, as far as possible:

(a) the total tax payable in respect of any emoluments for any year of assessment is deducted from the emoluments paid during that year; and

(b) the tax deductible (or repayable) on the occasion of any payment of emoluments is such that it makes the total net tax deducted from the beginning of the year of assessment up to the occasion of that payment a proportionate part of the total tax payable for the year of assessment, in the ratio that the part of the year which ends with the date of the payment bears to the whole year.

Thus, the Free Pay Tables apportion the personal allowances, etc., to which an individual is entitled according to his Code Number over the Income Tax year so that an equal proportion is allocated to each weekly (or monthly) pay day in order to determine the non-taxable pay to date. Similarly, the Taxable Pay Tables are constructed so that the cumulative tax to date can be determined on the basis of the cumulative taxable pay to date.

The procedure which the employer is required to follow in completing the Tax Deduction Card when making any payment of emoluments to an employee will now be described. The procedure set out below is that which is applicable to employees who are paid weekly; in the case of payments at intervals other than weekly (e.g. monthly) a similar procedure is adopted by reference to the Monthly Tax Tables.

(1) At each pay day complete columns 2 and 3 of the employee's Tax Deduction Card by entering the gross amount of the pay (including overtime, bonus, commission, etc.) before any deductions in column 2 and extend the total gross pay to date to column 3; the date of the pay day may be entered for record purposes in the column provided but this is not essential.

(2) Refer to Table A (Free Pay Table) for the week in which the pay day falls and in the column headed "Code" find the Code Number entered on the employee's Tax Deduction Card; in the next column of Table A immediately to the right of this Code Number appears a figure of free pay to date which should be entered in column 4 of the Tax Deduction Card.

(3) Subtract the figure of free pay to date (column 4) from the total gross pay to date (column 3) and enter the difference (if any) in column 5 as total taxable pay to date. If the amount in column 4 is more than the amount in column 3, no entry is made in column 5.

(4) Refer to Table B (Taxable Pay Table) and find the amount of tax which applies to the figure of total taxable pay to date (column 5) and enter the amount of total tax due to date in column 6. Subtract the amount entered in column 6 for the previous pay day from the amount entered in the same column for the current pay day and the difference represents the amount of tax to be deducted from the current pay. This amount is entered in column 7. If the amount entered in column 6 for the current pay day is less than the amount entered for the previous pay day the difference represents the amount of tax to be refunded to the employee. This amount is entered in column 7, followed by the letter "R".

(5) Refer to the National Insurance tables to find the amount of contribution which applies to the gross amount of pay for that week and enter it in column 1(a) and the employee's share in column 1(b) or (c).

After the end of the Income Tax year, the employer must give a certificate on a form—No. P.60—supplied by the Inland Revenue authorities to each employee who is in his employment on that date, and from whose pay tax has been deducted. The certificate will show the gross amount of wages paid to the employee during the year and the total tax (less refunds) deducted. (In the case of an employee taken on during the year, the certificate will also include, in a separate section, details of the pay and tax in the previous employment; this information will be obtained from the previous employer, see below.)

BECOMING UNEMPLOYED

Where a person becomes unemployed after having had tax deducted under "Pay As You Earn," he will only be entitled to a repayment of tax provided he is not claiming unemployment benefit. If benefit is claimed the D.H.S.S. will keep a record of the taxable benefit and at the end of the period of benefit claim make any appropriate repayment of tax.

DEATH

Where a person dies after having had tax deducted under "Pay As You Earn," any repayments of tax which become due will be made by the Inland Revenue authorities to his nearest relative or other personal representative.

PAY

The following are emoluments for the purposes of the "Pay As You Earn" provisions: salaries, wages, overtime, bonuses, commission, pensions, holiday pay and any other emoluments liable to Income Tax. The employer will make a return at the end of the year of any income from which tax cannot be deducted, e.g. that in the form of shares. Benefits in kind, such as: accommodation occupied rent free in the performance of the duties of the employment; refunds of, or payments on account of, expenses actually incurred by the employee in the performance of the duties of the employment; and reasonable lodging allowances; are not normally income, and should not be treated as pay for "Pay As You Earn" purposes.

Awards under a suggestion scheme, provided they are of reasonable amount (normally not exceeding £10), are not regarded as taxable and should therefore be treated as emoluments.

MEAL VOUCHERS

By concession (A2–1980) meal vouchers are not taxed provided that certain conditions are complied with. The conditions are that (*a*) vouchers must be non-transferable and used for meals only; (*b*) where any restriction is placed on their issue to employees they must be available to lower paid staff; and (*c*) the value of vouchers issued to an employee must not exceed 15p for each full working day. Any excess over this amount is taxable.

BONUSES, ETC. IN RESPECT OF EARLIER YEARS

Tax is deducted (or repaid) in accordance with the "Pay As You Earn" provisions from *any* payments of emoluments notwithstanding that such emoluments may have been earned, wholly or partly, in a previous Income Tax year, and tax will be deducted from such a payment in accordance with the provisions relating to the year in which the emoluments are paid. The Inland Revenue authorities will, however, for assessment purposes, correctly relate the payment to the year of assessment in which it was earned, and will make such amendments as are necessary to arrive at the correct liability for the different years of assessment.

CHANGE OF CODING

For any of the reasons set out below, an employee's Code Number may be wrong, and hence, until the correct Code Number is ascertained, the wrong amount of tax—it may be either too little or too much—will be deducted from his emoluments:

(i) He may have omitted to send in his Income Tax Return, with the result that the Inland Revenue authorities will probably not have granted him all the allowances to which he is entitled.

(ii) He may have filled in his Income Tax Return incorrectly. [He has rights of objection and appeal, as explained above, but pending the settlement thereof, the Inspector may issue a Tax Deduction Card to the employer, bearing the Code Number which is the subject of the objection or appeal, and the employer must deduct (or repay) tax by reference to that Code Number.]

(iii) He may become entitled to further allowances (e.g. he may get married or he may reach the age of 65), or, conversely, he may no longer be entitled to certain allowances. He should notify the Inspector of these changes, and if he does not agree the details on the amended Notice of Coding, he has the same rights of objection and appeal as he had in respect of the original Notice of Coding.

Until he is notified by the Inspector of any change in an employee's Code Number, the employer must continue to deduct tax by reference to the old Code Number. At the first pay day after the employer has received notification of the amended Code Number from the Inspector, the calculation of total free pay is made by reference to the amended Code Number, in order to ascertain the amount of tax which is repayable (or the additional tax which is payable, as the case may be).

CHANGE OF EMPLOYMENT

By means of the following provisions, the continuity of the "Pay As You Earn" scheme is ensured in cases where an employee changes from one employer to another*:

(1) If the employer ceases to employ an employee in respect of whom a Tax Deduction Card has been issued to him, he must forthwith send a certificate (No. P.45) to the Inspector, containing the following particulars:

(*a*) the name of the employee;
(*b*) any number used to identify the employee;
(*c*) the date on which the employment ceased;
(*d*) the employee's Code Number;
(*e*) the number of the week† in the Income Tax year in which the last payment of emoluments was made to the employee, and the cumulative emoluments at the date of that payment;
(*f*) the cumulative tax on the emoluments referred to in (*e*) above.

(2) The employer must also make, on the prescribed form, two copies of the certificate referred to in (1) above, and hand them both over to the employee on the day on which the employment ceases. [These copies are, in point of fact, exact ones, as the "prescribed form" is furnished with a carbon backing to the top two of its three parts.]

(3) Immediately he commences his next employment the employee must deliver the two copies of the above-mentioned certificate to his new employer, who must:

(*a*) insert on one copy of the certificate any number used to identify the employee, and the date on which the employment commenced, and forthwith send that copy to the Inspector from whom he usually receives Tax Deduction Cards;
(*b*) prepare a Tax Deduction Card in accordance with the particulars given in the copies of the certificate (i.e., he must transfer to the Tax Deduction Card the details shown on the certificate regarding Code Number, total pay to date, etc., and complete the Tax Deduction Card by entering details of total free pay to date and total tax due to date as shown by the appropriate Tax Tables); and
(*c*) on paying any emoluments to that employee, deduct or repay tax by reference to that employee's Code Number in the manner described above, and keep the Tax Deduction Card in respect of that employee, as if the total pay and total tax due to date

---

* The retirement of an employee on a pension is *not* treated as a cessation of employment for "Pay As You Earn" purposes if the emoluments are paid by the same person both before and after the retirement.

† Or the number of the "Income Tax month" in the case of employees paid monthly.

represented emoluments paid and tax deducted by the new employer.

If, however, a repayment of tax amounting to more than £20 is due from the new employer to the employee on the first pay day in the new employment, the new employer must forthwith notify the Inspector, and he must not make the repayment until he is authorised to do so by the Inspector. If the repayment does not exceed £20, it may be made without obtaining the Inspector's authority.

(4) If the employee objects to the details of his cumulative emoluments from his old employment being disclosed to his new employer, he may deliver the two copies of the certificate (see (2) above) to the Inspector before he commences his new employment. The Inspector will then issue a Tax Deduction Card (which will *not* contain any details of the cumulative earnings and cumulative tax in the old employment) to the new employer in respect of that employee, and will instruct the new employer to deduct tax, by reference to the employee's appropriate code, in accordance with the Tax Tables for Week 1.

(5) When the new employer gives the employee a certificate after the end of the Income Tax year (as explained above) he must include therein the emoluments paid to the employee by the previous employer (or employers) and the tax deducted from such emoluments.

If the employee is entitled to any late payment of wages after he has left his old employment, his previous employer must deduct tax therefrom by reference to the Tax Tables for Week 1, the reason for this being that the previous employer is no longer aware of the employee's cumulative earnings and cumulative tax deductions.

EMERGENCY CODE (CODE 'E') PROCEDURE

If an employee, upon changing his employment, immediately follows the procedure explained above, there should be little or no disturbance of the normal routine of computing his correct liability to tax from week to week. If, however, he is dilatory in handing the two copies of his certificate to his new employer, then the latter will have no knowledge of the total pay and tax deducted in respect of the old employment, nor of the employee's Code Number. In such circumstances, the new employer must deduct tax under what is known as the Emergency Code procedure. That is, he will make out a Tax Deduction Card bearing Code 'E' in respect of the new employee and will record thereon, as regards each payment, the date thereof, the gross amount of the emoluments, and the amount of tax (if any) deducted therefrom; but tax is deducted as if the payment had been made on the preceding 6th April, i.e. in Week 1 (in other words, the new employer must treat each payment of emoluments as a single payment on its own, and must not take into account the emoluments and tax deductions of previous weeks during which that employee has been employed by him). The actual amount of tax deductible in respect of graduated scales of weekly and monthly remuneration is set out in the Emergency Code Table. Furthermore, tax will be deducted on the basis of the new employee being a single man without dependants. The result may be that the employee will temporarily suffer an over-deduction of tax.

The Regulations provide that if an employer makes any payment of emoluments to an employee in respect of whom he has not received a Tax Deduction Card from the Inspector (other than, *inter alia*, an employee who has delivered to him, on commencing employment, the two copies of the certificate from his previous employer—see above) and that payment is equivalent to emoluments at a rate exceeding £42 per week (or £183 per month), the employer shall, on making the first such payment, forthwith notify the Inspector of the name and address of the employee, the date on which his employment commenced, and such other particulars as may be necessary to secure the issue of the appropriate Tax

Deduction Card. The Inland Revenue authorities will then have the task of tracing the previous employment, which may, in some cases, occasion a certain amount of delay. When this has been done, a notice will be issued to the new employer by the Inspector, showing the correct Code Number, and the total earnings and total tax under the old employment. Henceforward, tax deductions will be made in the normal way in accordance with the weekly (or monthly) Tax Tables, and any over-deduction of tax which may have occurred during the weeks (or months) when the Emergency Code was in use will be automatically corrected on the first pay day on which the new Code Number is operative, in the manner described above.

The Emergency Code procedure will also be followed in cases where a new employee is taken on who has not previously been in employment. In such cases the Inland Revenue authorities, on receiving the employer's notification (Form No. P.46) that he has made a payment of emoluments to that employee (see previous paragraph), will take such steps as are necessary (e.g. by obtaining from the employee an Income Tax Return, if he has not previously made one) to obtain details of the reliefs and allowances to which the new employee is entitled. When they have received this information, the Inland Revenue authorities will advise the employer of the correct Code Number.

EMOLUMENTS PAID AT OTHER THAN WEEKLY INTERVALS

Where an employee's emoluments are paid *monthly*, tax will be deducted therefrom in accordance with the Monthly Tax Tables which are compiled on similar principles to the Weekly Tax Tables described in the foregoing pages. The computation of the cumulative emoluments and the cumulative tax deductions will be made on similar lines to those which have been described in the case of employees who are paid weekly.

Where an employee who is paid monthly or quarterly receives a payment in respect of overtime or other extra earnings at an earlier date in the month than the date on which the main emoluments are paid, a strict comparison of the cumulative emoluments and the cumulative tax deductions up to the time of paying the overtime, etc., earnings might show that a repayment of tax was due to the employee. The Regulations provide, however, that in such circumstances a repayment shall *not* be made to the employee on the lines set out above, but that the Regulations shall have effect as if the overtime, etc., payment was made on the same date in that Income Tax month as the date on which the main emoluments are paid.

Where emoluments are paid at regular intervals other than regular intervals of a week or a month, any such payment is to be deemed, for the purpose of the Regulations, to have been made on the date on which it would have been made if a payment had been made on the last day of the preceding year. Thus, if an employee is paid at regular intervals of three weeks, his first emoluments in 1985–86 will be deemed to have been paid to him on 26th April 1985 (i.e. 3 weeks after 5th April 1985); his second on 17th May 1985; and so on. Tax will be deducted from these emoluments (or repaid, as the case may be) in the manner already described, by reference to the Tax Tables for the week in which such payment is deemed to fall.

Although the method already described for the operation of "Pay As You Earn" will apply to the majority of cases the Regulations also provide for a number of modifications of the main method (e.g. the Simplified Tax Tables). A description of such alternative methods of deduction of tax is considered to be beyond the scope of this book.

MISCELLANEOUS MATTERS

Tax-free Emoluments

Where an employer makes a payment to an employee in respect of his Income

Tax, the amount of the emoluments which the employer pays to the employee is deemed, for "Pay As You Earn" purposes, to be such a sum as will include the amount assessable on the employee in respect of the payment made by the employer in respect of the employee's Income Tax.

Married Women
Where a married woman is in employment, she will, in all probability, receive a separate Notice of Coding. The additional Personal Allowance, up to the maximum of £2,205 (see Chapter 2, § 3) will be taken into account in arriving at her Code Number.

Annuities, etc., from which tax is deducted
If not covered by income taxed at the source, an amount is deducted from allowances in order to make up the difference.

Building Society Interest Payable
This is added to allowances, unless relief given under MIRAS (see Chapter 11).

(b) Collection of tax from employers

Within 14 days of the end of each Income Tax month (as defined for "Pay As You Earn" purposes) the employer must pay to the Collector all amounts of tax which he was liable to deduct from emoluments paid by him during that Income Tax month, *less* any amounts which he was liable to repay on making payments of emoluments during the same month plus the amount due in respect of Class I National Insurance. The employer must also contribute an amount in addition to the contributions deducted from the employees' emoluments.

If, as regards any Income Tax month, the amount which the employer is liable to pay to the Collector exceeds the amount which he actually deducted from emoluments paid by him during that month, the Commissioners of Inland Revenue, on being satisfied that the employer took reasonable care to comply with the "Pay As You Earn" Regulations and that the under-deduction was due to an error made in good faith, may direct that the excess shall be recovered from the employee and not from the employer.

If the total of the amounts which the employer was liable to repay on making payments of emoluments during any Income Tax month exceeds the total of the amounts which he was liable to deduct during that month, he shall be entitled either:

    (*a*) to deduct the excess from any subsequent payment which he is liable to make to the Collector; or

    (*b*) to recover the excess from the Commissioners of Inland Revenue.

Proceedings for the recovery of any amount which an employer is liable, under these Regulations, to pay to the Collector in respect of any Income Tax month may be brought as if the said amount had been charged on the employer under Schedule E.

(c) Return by employer (Form P35)

Not later than 14 days after the end of the year of assessment, the employer must return the Tax Deduction Cards to the Collector, completed so as to show, in respect of each employee, the total National Insurance deducted, the total emoluments and the total net tax deducted therefrom, details of superannuation fund contributions, payments for expenses, holiday pay (where tax was not deducted therefrom when it was paid out to the employee) and pay from which tax could not be deducted (e.g. income in the form of shares in the company). If, however, an employer with a large number of employees wishes to retain the

Tax Deduction Cards (whether these are official cards or cards specially printed by the employer) he may do so, provided that he undertakes to supply the Collector at the end of the year with a separate document for each employee showing:

(*a*) The whole of the particulars required at the top of the official Tax Deduction Card (including the employee's National Insurance number), corrected as at the end of the year as regards amendment of the Code Number, changes in works number, etc.;

(*b*) The particulars of "gross total pay" and "total tax due" which would have been entered on the Tax Deduction Card on the last pay day at the end of the year (or the last week or month of the employee's employment);

(*c*) In the case of an employee leaving during the year, particulars of any pay issued after he left and of any tax deducted from that pay;

(*d*) The information asked for at the bottom of the Tax Deduction Card, i.e. particulars of certain superannuation contributions and, in the case of an employee taken on during the year, particulars of the pay and tax in the previous and present employments respectively; and

(*e*) Particulars of deductions in respect of National Insurance contributions.

Where the Tax Deduction Cards are retained by the employer and not returned to the Collector, the employer must undertake to keep the whole of the Tax Deduction Cards intact for so long after the end of the year as the Inland Revenue authorities may require.

The following particulars must also be entered on the reverse side of all Monthly Tax Deduction Cards before they are returned by the Collector.

(1) Except for cards of directors or of employees whose remuneration plus expenses exceeds £8,500 per annum (in whose case a form P11D must be completed—see § 5 of this chapter), payments made to employees for expenses, distinguishing between (i) amounts included in total gross pay for the year, and (ii) amounts not included in gross pay for the year if more than £25 in the year but excluding any payments towards any expenses that were actually incurred by the employee in connection with his employment.

(2) In all cases, fees, bonuses, etc., paid after the end of the year distinguishing between (i) any payment included in total gross pay for the year which relates to a previous year, and (ii) any payment relating to the year which will be made after the end of the year.

(3) In all cases payments from which tax could not be deducted.

Officers of the Inland Revenue Department are empowered by law to make inspections of employers' records from time to time in order to satisfy themselves that the correct amounts of tax are being deducted and paid over to the Collector.

(d) Assessment

The Notice of Assessment (which is issued by the Inspector) is issued after the end of the year of assessment*, and it shows both (i) the amount of tax which was due in respect of that year (i.e. after adjusting in respect of, *inter alia*, any emoluments which were paid in one Income Tax year but earned in a different Income Tax year—see above), and (ii) the amount of tax which was deducted from emoluments, which the employee will be able to compare with the certificate which was given to him by his employer after the end of the Income Tax year.

---

* Section 204, I.C.T.A. 1970 authorises the deduction or repayment of tax by the person making a payment of emoluments, notwithstanding that when the payment is made no assessment has been made in respect of the emoluments.

In the majority of cases the two amounts will be almost identical, but there may be some cases where either too much or too little has been deducted during the year of assessment.

If too much tax has been deducted from the employee's emoluments during the year of assessment, the Inspector may (and must, if the employee so requires) repay the difference to the employee instead of taking it into account in arriving at the employee's Code Number for a subsequent year. If too little tax has been deducted, the Inspector may require the employee to pay the difference to the Collector instead of taking it into account in arriving at the employee's Code Number for a subsequent year, but a small underpayment will be cancelled.

In arriving at the amount of any such over- or under-deduction, the actual net tax which was deducted from the employee's emoluments during the year of assessment is adjusted in respect of:

(a) any tax which the employer was liable to deduct from the employee's emoluments but failed to deduct, having regard to whether the Commissioners of Inland Revenue have or have not directed that that tax shall be recovered from the employee; and

(b) any tax overpaid or remaining unpaid for any previous year, small underpayments being cancelled.

The employee may object against a Notice of Assessment, by giving notice to the Inspector within 30 days of the date of the Notice of Assessment. If the employee is not satisfied with the amendment which is made by the Inspector, he may appeal to either the General or Special Commissioners, with a further right of appeal to the High Court on a point of law.

No formal assessment is necessary where the tax deducted from the income assessable is the same as that that would be deducted at the year end when all the relevant circumstances are known (s. 205, I.C.T.A. 1970)

Section 206, I.C.T.A. 1970 and s. 35, T.M.A. 1970 provide for an assessment to be made in respect of any emoluments, expense allowances, benefits in kind, etc., paid in respect of a year earlier than the year of receipt, at any time up to six years after the year of receipt. The period of six years is reduced to three years in the case of deceased persons.

Readers who require a more detailed knowledge of the "Pay As You Earn" provisions are referred to the "Employer's Guide" (P.7) and other explanatory literature issued by the Board of Inland Revenue.

§ 13.—RETURNS

A Return must be made by every employer, *when required to do so*, showing:
1. The names and addresses of all persons employed by him; and
2. The remuneration paid to such persons for the year concerned, including any bonuses or other fluctuating emoluments.

The employer also has to include on a supplementary form details of casual or part-time employees paid more than £25 per annum.

Where the employer is a limited company or other body, the Return must be made by the secretary or officer performing the duties of secretary.

The above Return must include (i) the amount of all payments made to such employed persons in respect of expenses or on their behalf except where the payment for expenses represents merely a recoupment by the employer to the employee, and (ii) any payments made to employees for services rendered in connection with the trade or business, whether the services were rendered in the course of their employment or not.

Furthermore, the Inspector of Taxes can demand a Return from any person carrying on a trade or business, of all payments (in excess of £15 per person in the year concerned) made to persons who are not employees for services rendered to the trade or business, including services in connection with the formation, acquisition, development or disposal of the trade or business and payments made for copyrights; the Return must include details of the names and addresses of such persons and the amounts paid to them. Similar Returns must also be made, when required by the Inspector of Taxes, by any body of persons carrying on any activity, even though this does not amount to the carrying on of a trade, e.g. a professional society.

These provisions enable the Revenue authorities to raise assessments under Schedule E on the amount of the payments, leaving the recipient to claim in respect of any expenses which have been incurred by him wholly, exclusively and necessarily in the performance of the duties of his employment.

Employers may be required to give details of payments for expenses and provision of benefits in kind to directors and employees (see § 6 of this chapter).

The regulations dealing with the question of the deduction of tax at the source from employees' remuneration contain provisions regarding the rendering of certain returns by employers. Further details of these returns are given in § 11 of this chapter.

Where the duties of an employment are carried out in the United Kingdom for a non-resident employer for a period in excess of thirty days but for the benefit of a person resident or trading in the United Kingdom the person so benefiting is required to report this on a return of employees. He is not required to provide details of payment made in respect of the employment.

§ 14.—DIRECTORS' REMUNERATION: ACCOUNTS/EARNINGS BASIS OF ASSESSMENT

Although the strict legal basis of assessment is the remuneration voted in the accounts, apportioned between the appropriate tax years, in practice the Revenue will accept that for administrative simplicity the accounts year is co-terminous with the end of the tax year in which it falls (i.e. the Accounts year to 31st December 1985 would be the tax year 1985–86). The earnings basis will always be adopted in the opening and closing years.

§ 15.—DIRECTORS' FEES "FREE OF TAX"

Where directors' fees are paid "free of tax" (i.e. the tax thereon is paid by the company), the fee payable by the employer is deemed, for the purpose of computing the tax deductible from the fee for "Pay As You Earn" purposes, to be such a sum as will include the amount assessable on the director in respect of the payment of tax by the employer on his behalf. In other words, the payment of tax by the company is regarded as being an additional fee, and the company will be allowed to charge as an expense against profits the Schedule E tax so paid.

Similar remarks apply to the payment of employees' salaries "free of tax."

In the case of "free of tax" fees, salaries, pensions, etc., payable under a pre-war contract or enactment (which has not been varied or amended on or after 3rd September 1939), the amount payable to or for the benefit of the recipient in respect of his Income Tax *shall not exceed the amount which would have been payable if the 1938–39 rates of tax still applied* (i.e. if the standard rate of tax were 27p and the various pre-war reliefs and allowances were still in force), (s. 423, I.C.T.A. 1970).

§ 16.—WEEKLY WAGE-EARNERS

Weekly wage-earners, employed by way of manual labour, are assessed on their actual earnings for the year of assessment, as in the case of other employees who are assessable under Schedule E (see § 2 of this chapter).

By concession (A1–1980), manual workers are allowed to deduct from their wages the cost of any tools, and also of clothes where the nature of the employment causes abnormal wear and tear. A scale of deductions for each particular trade is usually agreed by the respective trade union with the Board of Inland Revenue. Effect is given to the estimated expenses for the year of assessment in arriving at the tax to be deducted from the weekly payments of wages during that year (see § 11 of this chapter).

9. Schedule D, Cases III to VI

SCHEDULE D: CASE III

§ 1.—NATURE OF INCOME ASSESSED UNDER CASE III (s. 109, I.C.T.A. 1970)

With effect from 6th April 1985 bank deposit interest paid (and other interest paid by "deposit-takers") to individuals will be subject to tax deduction at source—on the same lines as building societies—and hence will cease to be Case III interest (see below). This will to a great extent reduce the applicability of assessments under (D) (iii).

The position for 1984–85 and earlier years is as follows:
   (1) Any interest, whether yearly or otherwise, or any annuity or other annual payment, but not including any amount chargeable under Schedule A;
   (2) Income from securities bearing interest payable out of the public revenue (e.g. $3\frac{1}{2}\%$ War Loan), except that charged to Schedule C;
   (3) All discounts.

Other items assessable are:
   (a) Savings bank interest. See § 2, however, regarding interest on Ordinary Deposits in the National Savings Bank and Trustee Savings Banks, and Chapter 4, § 8, regarding interest credited to the Profit and Loss account of a trader;
   (b) Small maintenance payments (see § 3 of this chapter);
   (c) Rents assessable under ss. 156 and 157 I.C.T.A. 1970 (i.e. rents payable in connection with mines, quarries and electric line wayleaves);
   (d) Sums received under sickness and disablement policies after the expiration of a period of twelve months.

(Assessments after 1984–85 will continue to apply to:
   (a) non-interest items
   (b) interest not subject to deduction at source—see below)

The ascertainment of the amount of income assessable under Case III is facilitated by the rights of the Inland Revenue to obtain Returns from persons paying untaxed interest exceeding £15 per annum (see Chapter 1, § 14). In practice, this request is not usually made for amounts less than £150.

§ 2.—INTEREST PAID ON DEPOSITS WITH BANKS ETC. (s.26 and s.27 and Schedule 8, F.A. 1984)

Introduction
As mentioned above, with effect from 6.4.85 banks and other deposit-takers will be required to deduct tax from interest payments to depositors who are *individuals* (with certain exceptions). Interest will then be taxed currently and not in accordance with the rules of Schedule D Case III. The deposit will be termed a composite rate deposit.

The deduction rules do not apply to the National Savings facilities. Thus National Savings Ordinary Account, the Investment Account, the Income Bond and the Deposit Bond will continue to be paid gross.

Composite rate deposits
The deduction of tax will follow the same basis as that applicable to building societies (i.e. use of a composite rate—currently understood to be $25\frac{10}{4}\%$). This rate will be determined in the year preceding the year in question and whilst it will always be less than the basic rate of tax the depositor will be treated as if basic rate had been paid. As with building society interest however, no tax can be repaid in the event of a nil tax liability.

Example 1

In 1985–86 Delta receives bank deposit interest of £70. Delta will be treated as having received interest of £70 and having paid tax thereon of £30, irrespective of the tax paid by the bank. He will thus only pay further tax if a liability to higher rate tax applies.

Banks, etc. affected
The requirement to deduct tax on all post-6.4.85 deposits applies to all "deposit-takers" on "relevant deposits".

Deposit-takers
These are defined as:
- (a) the Bank of England;
- (b) any recognised bank, licensed institution or municipal bank (within the meaning of the Banking Act 1979):
- (c) the Post Office;
- (d) any trustee savings bank within the meaning of the Trustee Savings Bank Act 1981;
- (e) any bank formed under the Savings Bank (Scotland) Act 1819 and
- (f) any person or class of person who receives deposits in the course of his business or activities and who is for the time being prescribed by order made *by the Treasury* by statutory instrument for these purposes.

Relevant deposits
These are all deposits made by individuals and groups of individuals (e.g. partnerships consisting of individuals)—companies are therefore excluded.
This will also apply to personal representatives who receive interest in that capacity.

Excluded deposits
A deposit is not a relevant deposit and consequently interest deduction does not apply if:
- (a) a qualifying certificate of deposit has been issued in respect of it or it is a qualifying time deposit;
- (b) it is a debt on a debenture ("debenture" having the meaning given in s. 744 of the Companies Act 1985) issued by the deposit-taker;
- (c) it is a loan made by a deposit-taker in the ordinary course of his business or activities;
- (d) it is a debt on a security which is quoted on a recognised stock exchange (within the meaning of s. 535 of the Taxes Act);
- (e) in the case of a deposit-taker resident in the United Kingdom for the purposes of income or corporation tax, it is held at a branch of the deposit-taker situated outside the United Kingdom;
- (f) in the case of a deposit-taker who is not so resident, it is held otherwise than at a branch of the deposit-taker situated in the United Kingdom; or
- (g) the person to whom any interest in respect of the deposit is payable has certified in writing to the deposit-taker liable to pay that interest that—

  (i) at the time when the declaration is made, the person who is beneficially entitled to the interest is not, or, as the case may be, all of the persons who are so entitled are not, ordinarily resident in the United Kingdom; or

(ii) in a case of a personal representative, the deceased was, immediately before his death, not ordinarily resident in the United Kingdom.

Also excluded are:

(a) deposits held on general undesignated client accounts where the holder is beneficially entitled to the interest but required by law to make payments to the clients concerned—such deposits include those of solicitors and estate agents.

(b) deposits forming part of a premiums trust fund of a Lloyds underwriting syndicate required to meet claims and liabilities.

Effect on Schedule D Case III and transitional rules
Bank deposit interest prior to the introduction of the tax deduction provisions was assessed according to the rules of Schedule D Case III—see below.

For the year 1985–86, however, this basis of assessment will cease and the income will be assessed currently as with building society interest.

Transitional provisions
The effect of the change of basis of assessment means that the cessation provisions apply (*but* see below) with the following amendments:

(i) the source is treated as ceasing immediately before it becomes a composite rate deposit;

(ii) where the source becomes a composite rate deposit with effect from 6.4.85 (which will be the majority of cases) the penultimate year of assessment (i.e. 1983–84) will *not* be revised.

Example 2

James has had a deposit account with a bank for a number of years. From 6.4.85 the bank is required to deduct tax from interest paid.
Interest is as follows:

	£
Year to 5.4.82	300
5.4.83	320
5.4.84	400
5.4.85	450
5.4.86 (taxed at source)	300

Assessments will be:

	£
1982–83 (y/e 5.4.82)	300
1983–84 (y/e 5.4.83)	320
1984–85 (y/e 5.4.85)	450
1985–86—taxed at source	

Notes

(i) 1984–85 is taxed on an actual basis since this is the year of deemed cessation;

(ii) 1983–84 remains on a preceding year basis since the bank is subject to tax deduction rules as from 6.4.85.

§ 3.—BASIS OF ASSESSMENT

The basis of assessment for bank interest prior to 1984-85 and other Case (III) income is as follows:

1. FOR THE YEAR OF ASSESSMENT IN WHICH THE INCOME FIRST ARISES
The actual amount of such income, i.e. the actual income from the date the income first arises to the following 5th April.

2. FOR THE SECOND YEAR OF ASSESSMENT
   (a) If the income first arose on 6th April in the preceding year (that is, if it was a full year's income)—the income of the preceding year; but the taxpayer may make a claim for reduction of the assessment to the actual income of the second year. The claim must be made within six years after the end of the year of assessment.
   (b) If the income first arose on some date other than 6th April in the preceding year—(that is, if it was *not* a full year's income)—the actual income of the second year.

3. FOR THE THIRD YEAR OF ASSESSMENT
The income of the second year, except that if the income arising in the first year was not a full year's income, the taxpayer may make a claim for reduction of the assessment to the actual income of the third year. The claim must be made within six years after the end of the year of assessment.

4. FOR SUBSEQUENT YEARS
For subsequent years the income of the preceding year, subject to any adjustment which may be necessary if the source of the income ceases (see below).

Income is not apportioned for the purpose of assessment under Case III, Schedule D, e.g. interest received gross on $3\frac{1}{2}$ per cent War Loan in respect of the six months ended 1st June 1985, is regarded as income arising in 1985–86 (i.e. the year in which it was received), and it is immaterial for Income Tax purposes that the greater part of it (four months' interest) accrued in the year 1984–85.

The examples that follow apply up to the years 1983–84 for bank deposits and following that year for non-composite-rate bank deposits (see above).

Example 1

On 10th July 1980, A. Brown opened a deposit account with his bank, and received interest as follows:

	£
1980–81	30
1981–82	85
1982–83	60
1983–84	70

There was no change in the capital sum on deposit.
The assessments under Case III for 1980–81 to 1983–84 will be as follows:

1980–81 (part year)	£30—actual income.
1981–82 (full year)	£85 actual income (since the first year (1980–81) was *not* a full year).
1982–83 (full year)	£85—income of preceding year, but, as the first year's income was not a full year, Brown may claim before 6th April, 1989, to have this reduced to £60, the actual income for 1982–83.
1983–84 (full year)	£60—income of preceding year.

Example 2

On 1st June 1979, D. Evans opened an account with his bank under an arrangement by which interest is credited on the excess of any balance over £100. He received interest as follows:

	£
1979–80.	Nil
1980–81.	20
1981–82.	70
1982–83.	60
1983–84.	80

Interest first accrues on the account from 1st August 1980.

The assessments under Case III for 1979–80 to 1983–84 will be as follows:

1979–80.	Nil
1980–81 (part year)	£20—actual income of year in which income first arises.
1981–82 (full year)	£70—actual income (since the first year's income (1980–81) was *not* a full year).
1982–83.	£70—income of preceding year but, as the first year's income was not a full year, Evans may claim before 6th April 1989, to have this reduced to £60, the actual income for 1982–83.
1983–84 (full year)	£60—income of preceding year.

All income falling under Case III may be aggregated and assessed in one sum; but where there is any change in the source of any particular item (e.g. where a new source is acquired or a source is parted with), the liability on that item must be computed separately, despite the aggregation for purposes of assessment (see Example 8 below).

CESSATION OF SOURCE

The following provisions normally have effect:

Where the source of any income falling under Case III ceases, the assessment for the year of assessment in which the cessation takes place is to be based on the actual income from the preceding 6th April to the date of cessation. If the actual income for the year *preceding* the year in which the source ceases is *greater* than the assessment for that year, an *additional assessment* will be made so that the total assessment for that year shall be on the actual income.

There is *no* provision for a *reduction* of the assessment for the year preceding the discontinuance in a case where the actual income is less than the assessment. On the other hand, the assessment for the year in which the source of income ceases *must* be amended to the actual income, whether this is greater or less than the normal assessment.

Example 3—revision of penultimate year to actual*

B. Chart received bank interest on a deposit account, which he closed on 30th June 1983, as follows:

	£
1981–82.	100
1982–83.	120
1983–84.	75

There were no changes in the capital sum on deposit.

---

*Refer to §2 for bank deposits ceasing as a result of the introduction of the composite rate from 6.4.85.

The assessments under Case III for 1982–83 and 1983–84 would be as follows:

The original assessment for 1982–83 of £100 would be increased to the actual income of £120.

The original assessment for 1983–84 would be reduced from £120 to the actual income of £75.

Example 4—no revision of penultimate year*

R. Adams received bank interest on a deposit account, which he closed on 30th September 1983, as follows:

30th June 1981, £60; 31st December 1981, £90;
30th June 1982, £40; 31st December 1982, £70;
30th June 1983, £50; 30th September 1983, £30;

There was no change in the capital sum on deposit.

The assessments under Case III for 1982–83 and 1983–84 would be as follows:

1982–83, £150 (income of preceding year)—there is *no* provision for reduction of this assessment to the actual income of £110.

1983–84, £80 (actual income)—replaces income of preceding year of £110.

Example 5

D. Dawson had the following transactions in $3\frac{1}{2}$ per cent War Loan:

£5,000 purchased in January 1982.
£3,000 purchased in April 1983.
£2,000 sold in April 1984.
£4,000 sold in October 1985.

Interest on $3\frac{1}{2}$% War Loan is payable on 1st June and 1st December.

All purchases and sales were made *cum div*.

The Case III assessments for 1982–83 to 1984–85 will be as follows:

1982–83—£175. Actual income of the year of assessment (i.e. $3\frac{1}{2}$ per cent on £5,000 for twelve months).

1983–84—£280. Income based on previous year is £175 but additional purchase of £3,000 stock in April 1983, must be treated as a separate source of income, and accordingly the assessment in respect of this stock will be based on the actual income received—i.e. £105. The total assessment for 1983–84 is therefore £280 (i.e. $3\frac{1}{2}$ per cent on £5,000 for twelve months plus $3\frac{1}{2}$ per cent on £3,000 for twelve months).

1984–85—£210. Income based on previous year is £280 but £2,000 stock sold in April 1984, must be treated as a separate source of income, and the assessment thereon will be based on the actual income received in the year. No income was received, and the total assessment will be reduced to £210 (i.e. $3\frac{1}{2}$ per cent on £6,000 for twelve months).

1985–86—£140. Income based on previous year is £210 but £4,000 stock sold in October 1985, must be treated as a separate source, and as only one payment of interest is received on this stock in 1985–86 (i.e. in June 1984), the assessment thereon will be £70, the actual income received in 1985–86, and the total assessment will be reduced to £140 (i.e. $3\frac{1}{2}$ per cent on £2,000 for twelve months plus $3\frac{1}{2}$ per cent on £4,000 for six months).

Note. (1) Although Dawson actually owned £5,000 War Loan during part of the year 1981–82 the income thereon did not *first arise* until 1st June 1982, and therefore 1982–83 is the first year of assessment.

Additions to and withdrawals from deposit account (see example 8 below)
Where the rate of interest on a security is *constant* (e.g. $3\frac{1}{2}$ per cent War Loan),
the assessment for any year must always equal the interest actually arising during
that year. In the case of interest on a deposit account, the assessment will normally
be on the preceding year basis (subject to the modifications for the early and
closing years). Additions to and withdrawals from the account, following the
decision in *Hart* v. *Sangster* (1957), are in strictness treated as addition or
cessation of a source of income. However, in view of the complicated calculations
involved in attaching interest to each separate transaction affecting the deposit
account, in practice, unless the sums involved are significant, the ruling will not
be followed.

Cessation of income
Relief from assessment under Case III applies where a source of income continues
to be held after the income therefrom has ceased. Apart from these provisions,
when the preceding year basis is applicable an assessment would normally be
made if income arose in the preceding year although no income arose in the year
of assessment or subsequently. Thus, s. 121, I.C.T.A. 1970, provides, therefore,
that the year in which *income* last arises is to be treated as the year of cessation,
at the option of the taxpayer, instead of the year when the *source* ceases to be
held. Two options are available to the taxpayer:

(1) *Cessation of source and income*
The normal cessation provisions apply (see above) but where no income arose in
the last two years of the source of income, the assessments are to be similarly
adjusted for the last year of assessment when the income arose and for the
preceding year. A claim to apply these alternative cessation provisions must be
made (*a*) within two years after the end of the year of assessment in which the
source ceases to be held, or (*b*) not later than eight years after the end of the year
of assessment, in which *income* last arose from that source.

(2) *Continuance of source but cessation of income*
The cessation provisions will not normally apply (see above) in these circumstances, but where the source of income has not ceased but has been held for a
period of six consecutive years of assessment without any income arising, then
provided income arose for the year immediately preceding those six years, a claim
may be made for the cessation provisions to be applied as at the end of those six
years.
    A claim to apply these alternative provisions must be made within eight years
from the end of the year of assessment in which income last arose. The normal
cessation provisions are then applied for the last year of assessment when the
income arose and for the year before that.

CHANGES IN SOURCE
The following example illustrates the method of dealing with changes in the source
of items of income which form the subject of a Case III assessment. For the
purposes of the actual assessment, all income falling under Case III may be
aggregated and assessed in one sum.

Example 6

A portion of X. Young's capital is invested in $3\frac{1}{2}$ per cent War Loan and a part is on deposit
account at a bank. The actual income from these sources for the years 1980–81 to 1983–84
is as follows:

	1980–81	1981–82	1982–83	1983–84
	£	£	£	£
War Loan	70	70	70	35
Bank deposit account	35	47	15	Nil

The War Loan was purchased in 1948 and sold in September 1983, while the bank deposit account was opened in 1947 and closed in October 1982.

It is required to show the assessments for 1981–82 to 1984–85.

1981–82. The original assessments will be as follows:

	£	
War Loan..............	70	(income of preceding year)
Deposit account	35	(income of preceding year)
	£105	

As, however, the deposit account was closed in 1982–83, the assessment in respect thereof for 1981–82 will be increased to the actual income of 1981–82, £47, involving an additional assessment of £12, and making the total Case III assessment for 1981–82, £117.

1982–83. The original assessments will be as follows:

	£	
War Loan..............	70	(income of preceding year)
Deposit account	47	(income of preceding year)
	£117	

As the deposit account was closed in 1982–83, the assessment for that year is reduced to £15. Thus the amended Case III assessment for 1982–83 is £85, i.e. £70 plus £15.

1983–84. The original assessments will be as follows:

	£	
War Loan..............	70	(income of preceding year)
Deposit account	Nil	
	£70	

As, however, the War Loan was sold in September 1983, only one payment of interest was received, and in view of the cessation of income the assessment for 1982–83 will be amended to the actual income of that year, £35. As the source of income in the case of the bank deposit account ceased in 1982–83, there will be no assessment thereon for 1983–84. Thus the amended Case III assessment for 1983–84 is £35.

1984–85. As the War Loan was sold in 1983–84 the source of income ceased in that year, and there will be no assessment thereon for 1984–85.

Sale of securities cum div.
Where a security, carrying interest which is payable without deduction of tax, is sold *cum dividend* between two interest dates, the portion of the purchase price representing the accrued interest to the date of sale is not assessable to Income Tax under Schedule D, Case III on the seller, but the full interest is assessed on the purchaser (*Schaffer* v. *Caltermole* (1980)), following the decision of *Wigmore* v. *Summerson* (*Thomas*) & *Sons Ltd* (1925)). The accrued interest will, however, form part of the consideration on the sale for the purposes of Capital Gains Tax.

Systematic disposal of securities *cum dividend* may, however, create an income tax charge in relation to the accrued interest under the provisions of s. 30, I.C.T.A. 1970.

EXEMPTION OF FIRST £70 OF N.S.B. INTEREST (s. 414, I.C.T.A. 1970; s. 59, F.A. 1980)

The first £70 of interest on *ordinary* National Savings Bank accounts, while still to be included in a taxpayer's return of income, is exempt from Income Tax in the case of an individual. This exemption applies equally to *both* husband and wife. The exemption does *not* apply to National Savings Bank investment accounts or ordinary or special investment deposits with Trustee Savings Banks. Before 21st November 1979, interest paid or credited on ordinary deposits with a Trustee Savings Bank was also exempt up to £70.

It should be noted that the composite rate deposit scheme does not apply to National Savings investments.

Example 7

B. Chart received interest upon an ordinary deposit with a National Savings Bank account opened many years ago as follows:

   1984–85—£100

B. Chart's assessment is:

   1985–86 £30 (£100 − £70)

Example 8

H. Hyde and his wife have received the following interest on banking accounts for the year ended 31st December 1984:

	Mr. H.	Mrs. H.
	£	£
National Savings Bank ordinary account.............	50	30
Investment Account of the National Savings Bank.......	—	25

In each case the deposit was made in 1956.

The assessment under Case III, Schedule D, for 1985–86 will be £25 made up as follows:

	£	£
Mr Hyde:..		
National Savings Bank Ordinary Account	50	
Less Exempt....................................	50	—
	—	
Mrs Hyde:	£	£
National Savings Bank Ordinary Account	30	
Less Exempt....................................	30	—
	—	
National Savings Bank Investment Account............		25
		—
		£25

§ 4.—PAYMENTS UNDER MAINTENANCE ORDERS (s. 65, I.C.T.A. 1970, as amended by F.A. 1982)

"Small maintenance payments" (as defined below), which would otherwise be paid net of tax under ss. 52 and 53 (see Chapter 1, § 12) are paid gross and are assessed on the recipient under Case III, Schedule D. Income Tax is, however, to be computed in all cases on *the payments falling due in the year of assessment*, as far as they are paid in that or in any other year.

(*a*) *Orders made prior to 31st July 1982*

(i) *Payments prior to 6th April 1983*

"Small maintenance payments" means payments under an order made by a Court in the United Kingdom:

   (*a*) to or for the benefit of one party to a marriage for their maintenance, by the other party to the marriage, and required to be made weekly at a rate not exceeding £33 per week, or monthly at a rate not exceeding £143 per month; or

(b) to any person for the benefit of, or for the maintenance or education of, a person under 21 years of age (not being a payment referred to in (a) above); and required to be made weekly at a rate not exceeding £18 per week, or monthly at a rate not exceeding £78 per month.

(ii) *Payments after 6th April 1983*

F.A. 1982 alters slightly the definition of small maintenance payments.

For payments made after 6th April 1983 the term means annual payments, which would otherwise fall within ss. 52 or 53, I.C.T.A. 1970, under an order made by a Court in the U.K.:

(a) by one of the parties to a marriage to or for the benefit of the other party to that marriage for that other party's maintenance at a weekly rate not exceeding £33, or a monthly rate not exceeding £143; or

(b) to any person under 21 years of age for his own benefit, maintenance or education at a weekly rate not exceeding £33, or a monthly rate not exceeding £143 (not being a payment within (a) above); or

(c) to any person for the benefit, maintenance or education of a person under 21 years of age at a weekly rate not exceeding £18, or a monthly rate not exceeding £78 (not being a payment within (a) or (b) above).

(b) *Orders made, varied or revived after 30th July 1982 (i.e. passing of F.A. 1982)*

Payments made under these orders will follow the revised small maintenance definition (see (ii) above) regardless of whether the first payment is made before or after 6th April 1983.

The above limits are altered periodically by statutory instrument.

The payer of any small maintenance payment is entitled, in computing his total income for Income Tax purposes for any year of assessment, to deduct therefrom any such small maintenance payments as have been made by him in respect of that year.

SCHEDULE D: CASES IV AND V

§ 5.—NATURE OF INCOME ASSESSED UNDER CASE IV (s. 109, I.C.T.A. 1970)

Income arising from securities in any place outside the United Kingdom is assessed under Case IV. "Securities" for this purpose implies that there is some fund against which the holder can proceed and that there are two owners of the fund, i.e. the holder of the securities who has the first right to proceed against the fund and the residual owner. Thus the type of security to which Case IV applies is debentures in a foreign company, a mortgage on foreign property, or foreign government, etc., stocks (except such income as falls under Schedule C, see Chapter 10, § 20). Conversely, stocks and shares in companies are not securities for the purpose of Case IV, the incoming arising from any such stocks or shares or shares in companies abroad being assessable under Case V.

Only persons resident in the United Kingdom are liable to tax under Case IV, Schedule D.

§ 6.—BASIS OF ASSESSMENT UNDER CASE IV (ss. 122 to 124, I.C.T.A. 1970)

Arising basis

The basis of assessment for Case IV is exactly the same as for income assessable under Case III, i.e. the actual income arising in the preceding year, whether such income is remitted to the United Kingdom or not.

The basis of assessment in the opening and closing years is as stated previously for Case III (see § 2 of this chapter).

If the Commissioners of Inland Revenue are satisfied that any person liable to tax under Case IV, Schedule D, is not domiciled in the United Kingdom or that that person is a British subject and is not ordinarily resident in the United Kingdom, then the basis of assessment under Case IV is to be the actual amounts remitted to the United Kingdom within the preceding year.

§ 7.—NATURE OF INCOME ASSESSED UNDER CASE V (s. 109, I.C.T.A. 1970)

Income assessable under Case V falls into two classes:
  (1) Income arising from possessions (other than securities assessable under Case IV) out of the United Kingdom, which arises:
    (*a*) from the carrying on by a person, either solely or in partnership, of any trade, profession or vocation; or
    (*b*) from any pension or annuity.
  (2) Income arising from other possessions out of the United Kingdom, i.e. where the income is in the nature of unearned income.
Only persons resident in the United Kingdom are liable to tax under Schedule D, Case V (see Chapter 1, § 7).

§ 8.—BASES OF ASSESSMENT UNDER CASE V (ss. 122 to 124, I.C.T.A. 1970; ss. 22 and 23, F.A. 1974)

The different bases of assessment are as set out below:

(1) FOREIGN TRADES (sub-heading (1)(a) above) (s. 23. F.A. 1974 as amended by F.A. 1984)
  (*a*) In the case of persons resident, domiciled and ordinarily resident in the United Kingdom, the profit (for the preceding year) is chargeable to tax whether or not remitted to the United Kingdom. A deduction of 25% was allowed from chargeable profits assessable up to and including 1983–84. The Finance Act 1984 abolishes this deduction with effect from 1985–86 and reduces it to $12\frac{1}{2}\%$ for 1984–85. Similar provisions apply to losses, capital allowances and stock relief (see below).
  The deduction can thus be summarised as follows:

Years to 1983–84.....................	25%
1984–85	$12\frac{1}{2}\%$
1985–86 (et seq.)	Nil

  The remittance basis will still apply in the case of a person not domiciled in the United Kingdom or, being a British subject, not ordinarily resident in the United Kingdom.
  Where a deduction applies to the assessable profit the 75 per cent assessment basis applies; relief is restricted to the same percentage of any losses, capital allowances, stock relief, etc. This will therefore cease to have effect for 1985–86 and is restricted to $12\frac{1}{2}\%$ for 1984–85. Relief for losses incurred in foreign trades is, broadly speaking, only allowable against the following other foreign earned income:
  (1) Foreign trading income, assessable under s. 23, F.A. 1974;
  (2) Foreign pensions or annuities, assessable under s. 22, F.A. 1974;
  (3) Foreign emoluments, assessable under Schedule E.

(2) FOREIGN PENSIONS OR ANNUITIES

(sub-heading (1)(b) above), s. 22, F.A. 1974. In the case of persons resident and domiciled in the United Kingdom, 90 per cent of the pension arising in the preceding year is chargeable to tax whether or not remitted to the United Kingdom (prior to 1974–75 the remittance basis applied). The remittance basis will still apply in the case of pensions received by persons not domiciled in the United Kingdom or, being a British subject, not ordinarily resident in the United Kingdom.

(3) INCOME FROM OTHER FOREIGN POSSESSIONS

(sub-heading (2) above). The actual income of the preceding year, whether remitted to the United Kingdom or not; thus the basis of assessment is the same as for Cases III and IV.

Remittance basis

If, as in the case of Case IV, the Revenue are satisfied that any person liable to tax under Case V, under (2) above is not domiciled in the United Kingdom or that the person is a British subject and is not ordinarily resident in the United Kingdom, then the basis of assessment under Case V, whatever the source of income, is the actual amount remitted to the United Kingdom within the preceding year. Income arising from securities outside the United Kingdom, forming part of the investments of a foreign life assurance fund of an assurance company is treated on a similar basis.

Example

Romeo, who is domiciled, resident and ordinarily resident in the United Kingdom, has the following sources of income for 1985–86.

(i) Securities of a foreign government, the interest upon which is payable through a London paying agent.

(ii) Mortgage debentures of a foreign company, the interest upon which is paid, and retained at Romeo's direction, by a bank in Rome.

(iii) Profits of his hairdressing business in Madrid, some of which are retained in Spain, whilst the remainder are remitted to the United Kingdom.

(iv) Dividends from shares in a foreign company, retained at Romeo's direction by a bank in Iceland.

Ignoring double taxation reliefs, state how United Kingdom Income Tax will be charged. United Kingdom Income Tax will be charged as follows:

(i) Tax will be deducted by the United Kingdom paying agent, who will suffer tax under Schedule C thereon.

(ii) Interest upon mortgage debentures of a foreign company, payable abroad, is charged under Case IV, Schedule D, as income from foreign securities. The assessment is (normally) the actual income arising in the previous year. This is not affected by the fact that Romeo has chosen to retain the interest abroad and not to remit it to the United Kingdom, since Romeo is resident and domiciled in the U.K.

(iii) Profits of a hairdressing business in Madrid are charged under Case V, Schedule D, the assessment being on the whole of the profit for the preceding year. Again, this is not affected by Romeo only partially remitting the profits (see (ii) above).

(iv) As (ii), except that the charge will be under Case V, Schedule D, and not Case IV.

New and discontinued sources of income

The rules relating to new and discontinued sources of income and the consequent adjustments to assessments in the opening and closing years, and the provisions with regard to cessation of source or income, are as stated previously for Case III (see § 2 of this chapter).

Thus it may be stated that the provisions relating to Case III in effect apply to Cases IV and V with the possible difference that Case IV and/or Case V income *may* be measured according to the amounts remitted to the United Kingdom, whereas in Case III the measurement is according to the amount "arising" during the appropriate basis year.

Where income, having been assessable under Case IV or Case V, becomes chargeable by deduction at source, the source is treated as discontinued. Where income, having been charged at source, becomes chargeable under Case IV or Case V, the source is regarded as a new source for Case IV and Case V purposes.

Where a business previously assessed under Case V, as a foreign possession, becomes liable under Case I because of a change in the place of control, it is not assessed as a new business but as a continuing one. Losses sustained prior to the change are not, however, eligible for carry forward under s. 171, I.C.T.A. 1970.

§ 9.—CONSTRUCTIVE REMITTANCES (s. 122, I.C.T.A. 1970)

Any income arising outside the United Kingdom which would be charged to tax under Cases IV or V, if *remitted* to the United Kingdom, shall be treated as remitted (and so assessable) if it is applied outside the United Kingdom by a person ordinarily resident in the United Kingdom in or towards satisfaction of:

(1) A debt for money lent to him in the United Kingdom or for interest on money so lent;

(2) A debt for money lent to him outside the United Kingdom and invested in or brought to the United Kingdom; or

(3) A debt incurred for satisfying in whole or in part a debt falling within (1) or (2) above.

Where a loan is obtained abroad and is wholly or partly repaid before it is brought into the United Kingdom it will be treated as remitted at the time it is brought into the United Kingdom. Where overseas income is retained by a lender abroad so as to be available for set-off against the debt it will be treated as having been applied in or towards satisfaction of the debt if the amount of the debt outstanding depends in any way on the amount retained.

Example

Carl (non-United Kingdom domicile), whilst resident and ordinarily resident in the United Kingdom is a partner in the firm of Carl, Marks and Co., which carries on business in Rome.

No remittances are made to the United Kingdom during 1984–85 out of the partnership profits, but Marks, who lives in Switzerland, lent Carl £5,000, £1,000 of which was remitted to the United Kingdom in May 1984, after the loan had been repaid out of partnership income.

Carl will be assessed under Case V, Schedule D, in 1985–86 on £1,000, since a remittance of that amount will be deemed to have been made on the date the loan was received in the United Kingdom and is assessed on the usual preceding year basis.

§ 10.—RESIDENCE AND DOMICILE (refer to Chapter 8 for narrative of terms)

"Residence" is of major importance in determining liability to U.K. taxation since *prima facie* people can only be subject to U.K. tax if they have a U.K. source of income or they are U.K. resident. A resident person will be subject to U.K. tax on U.K. source income and will also be subject to tax on non-U.K. source income unless non-domiciled. The following items outline the principal areas of taxation where residence and domicile are in point.

(1) Under the provisions relating to Cases I and II, Schedule D, the profits of a trade, profession, vocation, etc., are assessable wherever the trade,

etc., is carried on if it is controlled by a person resident in the United Kingdom.

(2) Non-residents are only liable in so far as they derive income from any property, trade, profession, vocation, or employment in the United Kingdom.

(3) Under the provisions relating to Cases IV and V, Schedule D, a British subject who is resident but not ordinarily resident in the United Kingdom, is assessed on the "remittance" basis.

(4) A foreign subject who is resident in the United Kingdom is liable to tax in the United Kingdom, under the provisions relating to Cases IV and V, Schedule D, on amounts remitted to the United Kingdom.

(5) A person who is ordinarily resident in the United Kingdom is assessable to United Kingdom tax on the whole of his income wherever it arises (subject to the provisions relating to Cases IV and V which are determined by the "remittance" basis where he is not domiciled in the United Kingdom).

(6) A person who is resident but not domiciled in the U.K. is, in respect of overseas income, assessed under Schedule D (Case IV or V) and certain Schedule E income (see Chapter 8) on a remittance basis.

The above issues are all dealt with more fully under the appropriate chapter subject heading.

§ 11.—CASE I OR CASE V?

In practice problems sometimes arise in connection with businesses which are situated abroad, to determine whether the assessment on such businesses shall be according to the provisions relating to Case I or those of Case V. The effect of determining this problem one way or the other may be considerable—it is in fact the problem of whether the whole of the profits of the business shall be assessed to United Kingdom tax or whether only such part as is attributable to, for example, a shareholding (i.e. a dividend) shall be assessable.

In the solution of this problem the question of control of the business is paramount and this is, in turn, connected with the question of residence.

In the case of a natural person (i.e. an individual) the residence of the natural person is determinable by reference to the facts not the least of which is physical presence.

Although not directly relevant to this chapter, it is worthwhile comparing the individual residency position with that of a company. In this case it is then essential to ascertain the place from which the real control of the day to day affairs of the business emanates in order to determine the residence of the corporation for taxation purposes.

The following are matters to which regard must be paid in determining the place of control of a business carried on by a company:

1. The domicile of a limited company is the country in which it was incorporated.

2. The situation of the registered office is to be taken into account but is by no means conclusive.

3. The place where the directors hold their meetings is important.

4. The location of the physical assets in relation to the type of business may be a guide to the place where central management abides.

5. The place where general meetings are held.

6. The place where the accounts are kept and the offices situated.

The above are merely some of the factors which must be considered but it cannot be too strongly emphasised that the answer to the essential question, "Where does the central management and control abide?" must always be dependent on the facts of each case. One point, however, is perfectly clear and that is that control of a company for tax purposes does not automatically follow merely because a majority of the shares is held; it is the directors who control the company and this they do until they are removed by the shareholders.

If, then, a business is controlled in the United Kingdom, the total profits of that business, wherever earned, will fall to be assessed under Case I, Schedule D; if the business is not controlled in the United Kingdom it is a foreign possession and the provisions relating to Case V, Schedule D, will apply.

In the case of an individual or partnership the business will also be "carried on abroad" if it can be shown to be managed and controlled from abroad. This will of course be considerably difficult to demonstrate where U.K. residency of the individual or majority of the partners exist.

§ 12.—UNREMITTABLE OVERSEAS INCOME (ss. 418 and 419, I.C.T.A. 1970)

Where a person satisfies the Commissioners of Inland Revenue that he is unable to transfer the amount of any overseas income to the United Kingdom or to realise the overseas income outside the territory in which it has arisen, owing to some restriction imposed in that territory and despite any reasonable action on his part, then such income will not be assessed when it first arises.

On the Commissioners becoming satisfied that it is reasonably possible to transfer the income, additional assessments will then be made for the original year or years so as to bring in the amounts previously unassessed, and such additional assessments may be made at any time within six years of the date at which remittance was considered to be reasonably possible. The value of any previously unremittable overseas income which has become remittable shall be ascertained by reference to the generally recognised market value in the United Kingdom or, if there is no such value, in accordance with the official rate of exchange of the territory concerned. It is necessary for a person to give written notice for these provisions to be applied and such notice must be given before the relevant assessments have become final and conclusive. Any appeals against the assessments may be made to the General or Special Commissioners.

A person who receives remittances from sources assessable under Cases IV or V, Schedule D or Case III, Schedule E (see Chapter 8, § 1) is allowed to spread them back provided he can show that the remittance was delayed because of the law of the territory where the income arose or the action of its Government or because it was impossible to obtain foreign currency in that territory, and that the inability was not due to any want of reasonable endeavour on his part. Thus, so much of the receipt as represents income which arose before the basis year as fulfils the foregoing conditions is to be included not in that basis year, but in the basis year for the year in which it arose. Similar provisions apply in respect of pensions or increases of pensions granted retrospectively.

A claim must be made within six years of the end of the year of assessment in which the income is received in the United Kingdom.

§ 13—NON-RESIDENTS' EXEMPTION FROM TAX ON CERTAIN SECURITIES (ss. 99 and 100, I.C.T.A. 1970)

BRITISH GOVERNMENT SECURITIES

The Treasury has power to issue securities with a condition that the interest thereon shall not be liable to tax, so long as the securities are in the beneficial ownership of persons who are not ordinarily resident in the United Kingdom and if issued with this condition, are non-taxable.

SECURITIES OF FOREIGN STATES
Dividends payable in the U.K. on securities issued by an overseas state or territory to a non-U.K. resident are not chargeable to tax.

SCHEDULE D: CASE VI

§ 14.—NATURE OF INCOME ASSESSED UNDER CASE VI (ss. 109 and 125, I.C.T.A. 1970)

Assessments under Case VI are made on any annual profits or gains not falling under Cases I to V or charged under any other Schedule. The assessment is on a current year basis unless the Inspector of Taxes directs that it should be based on an average of the profits or gains arising in any year. In practice this direction is very rarely exercised, and where it is exercised appeal can be made to the General or Special Commissioners (s. 125, I.C.T.A. 1970).

Tax is charged under Case VI for example on:
(1) Profits accruing from the letting of *furnished* houses, unless an election has been made for assessment of the profit in respect of the house under Schedule A, in which case only the profit in respect to the letting of the furniture is assessed under Case VI as unearned income—see below for furnished holiday lettings;
(2) Sub-underwriting commissions;
(3) Certain "balancing charges" (see Chapter 5, § 6);
(4) Capital profits or sums received for the sale of patent rights (see Chapter 11, § 15).

Furnished lettings—computation of profits
In computing the profits from letting furnished houses, all expenses incurred should be deducted; such expenses will include any rent payable, repairs, rates, insurance of contents, wear and tear of furniture (normally 10% of gross rent—see example), cost of all services provided, etc.

Example

J. Preston now lives with his son, following the death of his wife. Preferring not to sell his own home, he has let it furnished from 1st April 1985, at a rent of £200 per calendar month, Preston bearing the rates of £450 per annum.

The Inland Revenue will generally accept that depreciation of furnishings can be taken as 10%* of the gross rent. Expenses of letting were £220, and the cost of insuring the contents was £130. No election has been made to have the rent attributable to the house assessed under Schedule A.

Show Preston's Case VI computation for 1985–86.

Computation: 1985–86

		£
Rent.		2,400
Deduct:	£	
Rates paid by owner	450	
Insurance (contents)	130	
Wear and tear of furniture 10% of rent	240	
Letting expenses	220	1,040
Assessment under Schedule D, Case VI		£1,360

---

* Inland Revenue Statement of Practice A19.

The nature of the profits and the basis on which they have been computed must be stated to the Commissioners. In no case is an average of a period greater than one year to be taken.

Special provisions for furnished holiday lettings (s. 50 and Schedule 11, F.A. 1984)
The income from commercially let furnished holiday accommodation is treated as a trade (Schedule 11, para. 1) although taxed under Schedule D case (vi). The provisions relating to trading income are therefore specifically identified thus:

    (i) payment of tax can be made in two instalments (s. 4, T.A. 1970 and s. 30, F.A. 1978)
   (ii) relief for losses applies (ss. 168 to 175 and 177, 178, T.A. 1970 and s. 30, F.A. 1978)
  (iii) retirement annuity relief applies (ss. 226, T.A. 1970)
  (iv) the earned income definition applies (s. 530, T.A. 1970)
   (v) relief for capital allowances is granted
  (vi) roll-over relief for C.G.T. applies (ss. 115 to 120, C.G.T.A. 1979)
 (vii) relief for transfer of business applies (s. 124, C.G.T.A. 1979)
(viii) relief for transfer of business assets applies (ss. 126, C.G.T.A. 1979)
  (ix) relief for loans to traders applies (ss. 136, C.G.T.A. 1979)
   (x) relief for pre-training expenses applies (s. 39, F.A. 1980)

In addition expenses are treated as deductible as if the activity were a trade; hence the rules applicable to Schedule D case (i) apply.

Accommodation is treated as commercially let and furnished (and hence the reliefs apply) if:

    (i) it is let on a commercial basis with the view to the realisation of profits and
   (ii) it is furnished and the tenant is entitled to the use of furniture.

In addition, to qualify as holiday accommodation:

   (a) it must be available for commercial letting to the public generally as holiday accommodation for periods which in total are not less than 140 days;
   (b) the periods for which it is so available must amount to not less than 70 days;
   (c) the periods for which it is so let during the season must amount to at least 90 days; and
   (d) for a period comprising at least seven months (not necessarily continuous), it must not normally be in the same occupation for a continuous period exceeding 31 days.

The holiday accommodation provisions must apply by reference to the year of assessment in question or in the case of commencement or cessation to the twelve months beginning with commencement or to the twelve months ending with cessation.

These rules apply for 1982–83 onwards.

(N.B. C.G.T. retirement and roll-over relief also apply—see details in Chapter 30.)

§ 15.—CASE VI RELIEF IN RESPECT OF LOSSES (s. 176, I.C.T.A. 1970)

Where a loss is sustained by a person in any transaction of such a nature that, if any profits had arisen therefrom, he would have been assessed in respect thereof under Case VI, the amount of the loss may be deducted from *any* assessment made on him under Case VI for the same year. Such portion of the loss for which relief has not been obtained in this manner may be carried forward and deducted from *any* profits assessable *under Case VI* for subsequent years of assessment.

Example

T. Thrush has the following income for 1985–86:

	£
Salary...	6,000
Profit on sub-underwriting commission...................	64
Loss on furnished letting.............................	(78)

The 1985–86 assessable income is:

		£
Salary.....................................		6,000
Case VI—Underwriting commission......................	64	
—Furnished lettings (loss)......................	(78)	Nil
	(14)	
Total assessable (Schedule E).........................		£6,000

N.B. the £14 Schedule D Case VI loss will be carried forward to set against future Case VI assessments.

10. Schedules A, B and C

SCHEDULE A

§ 1.—INCOME ASSESSABLE (s. 67, I.C.T.A. 1970)

The charge to tax under Schedule A is imposed upon the annual profits or gains arising in respect of rents or receipts from land and buildings as follows:

(*a*) rents under leases of land in the United Kingdom;

(*b*) rent-charges, ground annuals, feu duties and any other annual payments relating to land;

(*c*) other receipts arising from, or by virtue of, ownership of an estate, or interest in, or right over, land or any incorporeal hereditament or incorporeal heritable subject in the United Kingdom, except for:

    (i) certain mineral rents and royalties, charged to tax under s. 156 or s. 157, I.C.T.A. 1970, mines and quarries, etc. or profits or gains chargeable under s. 112, I.C.T.A. 1970

    (ii) annual interest (i.e. mortgage interest, debenture and loan interest);

    (iii) rent payable under a lease where the tenant is entitled to the use of furniture and if within the terms of the lease, entitled to services.

In the case of (iii) furnished lettings and lettings with services are assessable under Case VI of Schedule D. The landlord is, however, entitled to elect to be assessed under Schedule A for any year in respect of the income attributable to the use of the property providing written notice is given to the Inspector within two years after the year of assessment. The income attributable to the use of the furniture will, however, continue to be assessed under Case VI. Cases (i) and (ii) are taxed under Schedule D Case III.

§ 2.—MISCELLANEOUS RECEIPTS

Many receipts can be received in respect of land other than rent receivable under a lease. Thus, easements, wayleaves, sporting rights, etc., are assessable under Schedule A.

Where a person who occupies and uses land assessed under Schedule B achieves profit or gain in a year of assessment from payments or any easement over or right to use the land, an assessment under Schedule A will be raised on him for the amount by which the profit or gain exceeds the Schedule B assessment.

§ 3.—METHOD OF ASSESSMENT (s. 69(1), I.C.T.A. 1970)

Profits or gains chargeable to Schedule A may be assessed in one or more assessments if they arise from more than one source. Thus the amount of rent to be assessed may be assessed wholly in the district in which the taxpayer resides or in a district in which any of the premises are situated, or separate assessments may be made by each district in which the property is situated. A taxpayer may receive, therefore, notices of assessment from various income tax districts for property he owns, and lets.

§ 4.—BASIS OF ASSESSMENT (s. 69(2), I.C.T.A. 1970)

ACTUAL BASIS

The assessment under Schedule A is made upon the profits to which the person becomes entitled during the year of assessment (i.e. "actual" basis). Accordingly, as tax is payable on the assessment on 1st January within the year of assessment, provision is made for the sum assessed to be based on the sources of income and the amounts brought into account in the immediately preceding assessment year. The amount so estimated is adjusted in respect of sources of income disposed of, if the person concerned makes a written declaration to the Inspector before 1st January, informing him of the sources which have ceased and stating the rents to which he will become entitled in the year. If the Inspector is satisfied that a decreased amount of rent will be received because of the cessation of a source the amount to be assessed will be decreased proportionately. After the end of the year of assessment when the actual profits are determined an adjustment by way of an additional assessment or repayment of tax or set-off, will be made.

Example 1

Alpha received income from letting property during the year to 5th April 1985 of £1,360. His allowable deductions amounted to £960. For the year 1985–86 he will receive an assessment under Schedule A of £400 which will be adjusted to the actual profit achieved during the year to 5th April 1986 when this can be determined.

Example 2

Using the facts of Example 1, if Alpha had sold a house on 30th June 1985, that had an annual rental in 1985–86 of £120 and for which allowable deductions for that year had been £72, and Alpha had given notice of this to the Inspector, the Schedule A assessment raised for 1985–86 until such time as the actual profit could be ascertained, would be £364 arrived at as follows:

	£	£
Amount assessed for 1984–85		400
Deduct: Rent of property sold	120	
Less: Deductions 1984–85	72	
	£48	
Three-quarters thereof:		36
1985–86 Assessment		£364

Non-residents (s. 89, I.C.T.A. 1970)

Where rent is paid directly to a person whose usual place of abode is outside the U.K., basic rate income tax *must* be deducted from the payment and accounted for to the Inland Revenue.

(N.B. Section 78, T.M.A. 1970 will apply where rent is collected by a letting agent in the U.K. so that in these circumstances the onus of accounting for the tax lies with the agent—see Chapter 1.)

§ 5.—DEFAULTING PERSONS—COLLECTION FROM LESSEES AND AGENTS (s. 70, I.C.T.A. 1970)

If the person liable to pay tax on the profits arising defaults, provision is made for the tax to be collected from any lessee of the land (called a derivative lessee). The Commissioners may give a derivative lessee notice in writing requiring him to pay to them sums on a date or dates specified to satisfy the tax not collected.

The amount of such tax to be demanded from the derivative lessee must not exceed the amount of rent payable by him for such land, for that period to the person in default or to another derivative lessee.

The tax paid can be deducted from future rent payable. If the tax is deducted from rent payable to another derivative lessee it may be that he is unable to recover the whole of the tax from rent which he in turn must pay to a superior landlord during the following twelve months. In such a circumstance he may recover the tax which he has suffered and cannot pass on from the Inland Revenue.

If rents are collected by an agent for a defaulting person the Commissioners may require the agent to pay over to the Collector of Taxes all rents collected for the defaulting person, including moneys then in hand, until such time as the unpaid tax has been satisfied.

§ 6.—RELIEF FOR RENT NOT RECEIVED (s. 87, I.C.T.A. 1970)

The amount of rent to be brought into account is that due in the year. In order to avoid taxing rent that should have been received but was not in fact received provision is made for relief in certain circumstances. If the landlard has not received the amount he was entitled to by reason of the default of a person and he has taken all reasonable steps, including the process of law, to obtain payment, or, if the amount receivable was waived, without consideration, to avoid hardship, he may claim relief for the sum not received and the adjustment will be made by repayment of tax or otherwise. If the sum is subsequently received, without time limit, the landlord must notify the Inland Revenue within six months. An adjustment will then be made and an additional tax payment will be required.

Example 1

Beta had been assessed on rents receivable less outgoings for 1985–86 in the sum of £1,200. During the year arrears of rent had accumulated on one property, amounting to £6 and Beta had been advised that this would not be recovered except by legal processes which would cost Beta more than £6. Arrears of £20 rent had also accumulated during the year on a house occupied by a widow old age pensioner who had been ill and Beta told her that he would forego the arrears to avoid her hardship.

In June 1986, Beta advised his Inspector of Taxes of these facts. The assessment of £1,200 would be amended to £1,174 and if Beta had paid the tax due on £1,200 he would receive a repayment of tax on £26.

If the widow subsequently came into money and decided to pay Beta the arrears of rent, Beta would receive an assessment for £20 even though the payment may be made more than six years after 5th April 1986.

DISPOSAL OF PROPERTY (s. 86, I.C.T.A. 1970)

If property subject to a lease is sold and rent was payable in advance, the rent is apportioned between vendor and purchaser for purposes of assessment. The years of assessment in which the receipt will fall will be the year of assessment in which the rent is due in the case of the vendor, and the year of assessment in which the day following completion falls in the case of the purchaser.

Similarly, payments to be made by the purchaser for outgoings on the property accruing over the date of sale and allowed in the completion statement are apportioned to the vendor, and are treated as having been paid immediately before the completion date. Care must be taken here not to allow apportioned expenditure falling due to the purchaser, for he is not entitled to deduct expenses incurred for a period prior to his becoming landlord (see § 7 of this chapter).

§ 7.—ALLOWABLE DEDUCTIONS (s. 72, I.C.T.A. 1970)

Subject to further provisions allowable deductions are stated to be payments made by the recipient (subject to certain stated exceptions):

Types of expenditure
    (*a*) in respect of any maintenance, repairs, insurance or management;
    (*b*) in respect of any services provided by him otherwise than by way of maintenance or repairs being services which he was obliged to provide but in respect of which he received no separate consideration;
    (*c*) in respect of rates or other charges on the occupier which the person chargeable was obliged to defray;
    (*d*) in respect of any rent, rent charge, ground annual, feu duty or other periodical payment reserved in respect of or changed on or issuing out of land.

Specific requirements
  The further provisions relating to such deductions are that:
    (1) the payment must have become due in the year of assessment concerned or at an earlier time falling within the currency of the lease (see below);
    (2) the payment in respect of maintenance and repairs must be incurred by reason of dilapidations attributable to a period falling within the currency of the lease;
    (3) any other payment must be incurred in respect of a period falling within the currency of the lease;
    (4) the payment must be in respect of premises comprised in the lease.
Where the person chargeable became the landlord after the lease began references to the currency of the lease shall not include any time before he became the landlord.
It will be observed that (2) above excludes payments which are made during the currency of the lease on dilapidations which arose before the commencement of the lease.

Interest
The question of deductibility for interest paid from rental income is dealt with in Chapter 11.

Example 1

Apple acquired a long lease on factory premises on 1st June 1985. The premises were in need of extensive repairs which Apple carried out before subletting the premises to Titus Ltd under a lease commencing on 30th September 1985. Under the terms of the lease to Titus Ltd, Apple was responsible for repairs, for the payment of rates and for providing a resident caretaker.

The premises were let at a rental of £7,500 to 5th April 1986, payable in advance.
Expenses incurred by Apple during the year 1985–86 were as follows:

	£
Repairs—arising before 1st June 1985	12,000
arising after 1st June 1985.	1,600
Ground Rent (full year)	2,400
Rates—from 30th September 1985.	600
Insurance—from 1st June 1985, for a full year	150
Caretaker's Wages, etc., from 1st June 1985.	680
Management Expenses	800
	£18,230

The assessment under Schedule A for 1985–86 will be as follows:

	£	£
Rent Receivable:		7,500
Less: Deductions:		
Repairs	1,600	
Ground Rent—10 months	2,000	
Rates................................	600	
Insurance—10 months................	125	
Caretaker's Expenses..................	680	
Management Expenses	800	5,805
Assessment		£1,695

Notes:
(1) The Ground Rent and Insurance would normally be restricted to the length of the qualifying period falling within the tax year, i.e. 10 months from 1st June 1985 to 5th April 1986.
(2) Provided a taxpayer is consistent in application, expenses may be deducted on a payments or expenditure basis.
(3) The repairs of £12,000 are disallowed because they arose in respect of dilapidations which took place before G.H. Ltd acquired the long lease, on 1st June 1985.
(4) The period from 1st June 1985 to 30th September 1985, is a "previous qualifying period"—see below.

Example 2

John owned premises which he leased to Larry. Extensive repairs to the premises were required and as John could not afford to pay for them he sold the property to Paul subject to the lease to Larry. Paul duly carried out and paid for the repairs.

Although the repairs arose during the currency of the lease to Larry (and Paul receives rent under the lease from Larry) he cannot deduct from that rent the cost of the repairs as these arose during a period prior to the date he became the landlord.

Extension of "expenditure period"

If the above provisions were not modified they would be very stringent because a person negotiating a further lease of premises would not be allowed to charge the cost of making good dilapidations arising before the lease commenced nor would a person acquiring property be allowed to charge the cost of making good dilapidations that arose during his ownership but prior to the commencement of a lease of the property. Furthermore, each lease would have to be considered separately. The provisions are modified in these respects so that the period of the lease is extended to accommodate expenditure incurred prior to the lease commencement. First. it is necessary to consider the definition of certain expressions (ss. 71 and 72, I.C.T.A. 1970):

(i) **A previous qualifying period** is a period,
(*a*) during which the person chargeable was the landlord in relation to a previous lease of the premises, *being a lease at a full rent*; or
(*b*) which was a void period beginning either with the termination of such a lease as (*a*) above, or beginning with the acquisition by the person chargeable of the interest in the premises giving him the right to possession of them.

However, a period will not be a previous qualifying period if it

precedes a period which is not in itself a previous qualifying period and which ended before the beginning of the lease.
  (ii) **A void period** is defined as a period during which the person chargeable was not in occupation of the premises or any part thereof, but was entitled to possession thereof.
 (iii) **A lease at full rent** is defined as a lease under which the rent reserved under the lease (including an appropriate sum in respect of any premium under the lease) is sufficient, taking one year with another, to defray the cost to the lessor of fulfilling his obligations under the lease and of meeting any expenses of maintenance, repairs, insurance and management of the leased premises which fall to be borne by him.
 (iv) **A tenant's repairing lease** is defined as a lease where the lessee is under an obligation to maintain and repair the whole, or substantially the whole of the premises comprised in the lease. This categorisation of leases at full rent between tenant's repairing leases and others is important when considering utilisation of losses arising from leases of different premises (see above).

Bearing these definitions in mind it is provided that where premises are let under a lease at a full rent, the afore-mentioned deductions from rent receivable by the lessor may include payments that became due in, or are in respect of, a previous qualifying period.

Where the circumstances are such that a qualifying period is only applicable to part of the premises an apportionment of rents and payments is made.

Example 3

Ray owns premises which he had let to Tim at £2,400 per year under a lease at full rent. The lease terminated on 30th June 1985. During the period 6th April 1985, to 30th June 1985. Ray had received the rents due on 1st May and 1st June 1985, and had incurred expenditure attributable to that period of £700. The premises remained vacant until 1st September 1985, during which period Ray incurred further expenditure of £200 including the cost of repairs. On 1st September 1985, he negotiated a new lease for £1,500 per year with Vance being a lease at full rent. For the period from 1st September 1985, to 5th April 1986, he incurred expenditure of £300. All rents were payable on the first day of each month, in advance.

As the void period began immediately following the termination of a lease for full rent under which Ray was the landlord, it is a qualifying period and the expenses of that period are allowable and may be set off against the rent of the subsequent letting. Had the previous lease to Tim not been a lease at full rent, the following void period would not be a qualifying period and neither the expenses of the period of that lease so far as they exceeded the rent received for that period, nor the expenses of the void period, would be allowed as a deduction against rent received from Vance.

The Schedule A assessment for 1985–86 will be £200 computed as follows:

	£	£	
Rent receivable—6.4.85 to 30.6.86		400	($\frac{2}{12}$ × £2,400)
—1.9.85 to 5.4.86		1,000	($\frac{8}{12}$ × £1,500)
		1,400	
Deduct: Expenses:			
6.4.85 to 30.6.85	700		
1.7.85 to 31.8.85	200		
1.9.85 to 5.4.86	300	1,200	
		£200	

Example 4

Kraken owns premises which he let to Gorgon under a lease for full rent at £2,400 per year payable monthly in advance. The lease terminated on 30th June 1985. For the period from 6th April to 30th June 1985, Kraken had received rent of £400 and had incurred expenditure of £250. Between 1st July and 31st July, repairs that had arisen during the tenancy of Gorgon were carried out at a cost of £1,750.

Having no immediate tenant Kraken occupied the premises himself from 1st August to 30th September 1985. During that period he negotiated a further lease at full rent with Medusa whereby he received a rent of £2,880 per year payable monthly in advance the lease commencing on 1st November 1985.

Expenditure attributable to the various periods was from 1st to 31st July, £60 in addition to the cost of repairs of £1,750; from 1st August to 30th September, £150; from 1st October to 31st October, £80 and from 1st November 1985 to 5th April 1986, £310.

(1) The period 6th April 1985, to 30th June 1985, is during the currency of the lease and the surplus assessable is NIL. The deduction in respect of the repairs of £1,750 arising during the currency of this lease is restricted to £150 (£400 less £250), and the balance of £1,600 is not allowable as explained below. For the purpose of considering the remaining periods it is a qualifying period but there is an interval of time between the termination of this lease and the commencement of the lease to Medusa which is not itself a qualifying period.

(2) The period 1st July 1985, to 31st July 1985, is a void period commencing with the termination of a lease for full rent. It would be a qualifying period but for the following period 1st August 1985, to 30th September 1985, being a non-qualifying period. This latter period causes an interval of time to elapse between qualifying periods, and, accordingly, no deduction of the £60 expenses for this period is allowable against the proceeds of the lease to Medusa. Furthermore, the balance of the £1,750 (i.e. £1,600) spent during this period in repairs arising during the currency of the lease to Gorgon is not deductible, as the period 6th April 1985, to 30th June 1985, is now not a qualifying period.

(3) The period 1st August 1985, to 30th September 1985, is the period Kraken himself occupied the premises and so it is not a qualifying period. Expenses of £150 for this period are not deductible from the subsequent letting.

The period 1st October 1985, to 31st October 1985, is not a qualifying period because although it is a void period it has not begun on the termination of a lease at full rent nor on the acquisition of the premises by Medusa. The expenses of £80 are again not deductible from the subsequent letting.

The period 1st November 1985, to 5th April 1986, is during the currency of a lease at full rent and the surplus arising is £1,130 [($\frac{6}{12}$ × £2,880)—£310].

Kraken will be assessed under Schedule A for the year 1985–86 in the sum of £1,130, i.e. £1,130 for the period 1st November 1985, to 5th April 1986, plus *NIL* for the period 6th April 1985, to 30th June 1985.

It will be observed how costly the two months occupation of the premises by Kraken has turned out to be. The intervention of this non-qualifying period has caused an assessment of £1,130 to be raised for a year in which Kraken suffered expenses of £760 in excess of income.

Had Kraken *not occupied the premises* but allowed them to remain empty until 1st November 1985, the whole of the period 1st July 1985, to 31st October 1985, would have been a void period commencing with the termination of a lease at full rent and ending with the commencement of such a lease and the total expenses of £2,600 would have been deductible. Thus, a loss of £760 would have been carried forward to 1986–87 in place of the assessment of £1,130 that has arisen for the year 1985–86.

Example 5

Duck purchased some premises on 1st May 1985, but did not occupy them. He negotiated a lease for full rent of the premises commencing 1st October 1985.

During the period 1st May 1985, to 30th September 1985, he incurred £300 on repairs which were necessary when the premises were purchased, £60 on repairs which arose during the period and a further £80 on expenses for the period. The period from 1st May 1985 to 30th September 1985, is a qualifying period because it is a void period commencing with the acquisition of the interest in the premises by Duck and ending with the commencement of a lease for full rent and during which Duck did not assume occupation.

Accordingly, the repairs of £60 and the expenses of £80 can be deducted from the rent received under the lease commencing on 1st October 1985. The repairs of £300 are not deductible because they arose prior to the acquisition by Duck of his interest in the premises.

SET-OFF AGAINST OTHER LEASES

Leases at full rent
In the case of a lease at a full rent (*not being a tenant's repairing lease*) a chargeable person may deduct from rent any payment in respect of other premises,

    (*a*) providing that it was a payment that could have been properly deducted from the rent of those premises had the rent been sufficient, or

    (*b*) providing, in the case of other premises which were leased at a full rent, but the lease had come to an end and was followed by a void period, the payment was one which could have been deducted if the lease had continued to the end of the year of assessment.

A deficiency in respect of a property leased at full rent, and not on a tenant's repairing lease, can be carried forward, or set off against rents from other properties leased at full rent, except properties on tenant's repairing leases.

Tenant's repairing leases
A deficiency in respect of a property on a tenant's repairing lease at full rent can be carried forward against profits of the same property, or set off against rents from other properties leased at full rent, but not against rents from property on tenant's repairing leases.

If a lease which was a lease for full rent becomes a tenant's repairing lease or a tenant's repairing lease becomes a lease at full rent the above provisions will apply from the date of change as if a new lease had commenced on that date.

In circumstances where a person retains part of some premises but receives rent for the remainder of the premises and parts of the premises are used in common (i.e. entrance hall, stairs, etc.) any allowable payments in respect of the parts used in common are eligible for deduction from the rent received.

Example 6

Taylos owned and leased premises in Watford and other premises in Manchester, both being leases at a full rent. During the year ended 5th April 1986, the premises in Watford became empty as a result of the termination of the lease on 1st June 1985. A further lease was entered into on 1st January 1986, which provided for repairs to the premises to be the responsibility of the tenant.

The rents and summarised expenses are as follows:

		£ Rent	£ Expenses
Watford Premises:	Period 6.4.85–1.6.85	600	450
	Period 2.6.85–31.12.85	Nil	300
	Period 1.1.86–5.4.86	400	440
Manchester Premises:	Year to 5.4.86	2,000	1,200

The assessment on Taylos under Schedule A for 1985–86 will be £610, as follows:

		£	£
Manchester Premises:	Rent..........................	2,000	
	Less: Expenses	1,200	800
Watford Premises:	Rent 6.4.85–1.6.85	600	
	Less: Expenses to 31.12.85	750	(150)
			650
	Rent 1.1.86–5.4.86	400	
	Less: Expenses	440	(40)
			£610

Notes:

(1) The period 2.6.85 to 31.12.85 is a void period, being a period following the termination of a lease at full rent, and thus deductions during this period may be added to those for a period of the lease.

(2) A deficiency arising on a lease at full rent may be set-off against a surplus arising on other premises leased at full rent. The lease from 1st January 1986, is a tenant's repairing lease and the deficiency is deductible from a surplus arising on a lease at full rent.

(3) Had the Manchester premises been leased on a tenant's repairing lease the deficiency of £150 could not have been deducted, nor could the £40 deficiency. (In the case of the £150, because deficiencies on leases at full rent cannot be offset against surpluses on tenant's repairing leases; and, in the case of the £40, because tenant's repairing leases cannot be offset against other tenant's repairing leases.)

Leases not at full rent

Where a lease is not at full rent, losses arising can only be offset against income from the *same property* under the *same lease.*

Synopsis of loss offsets

	Loss Offset	
Type of Lease	*Current Year*	*Carry Forward*
1. Lease at full rent	Against any lease at full rent	Against any lease at full rent
2. Tenant's repairing lease	Against any lease at full rent	Against: (*a*) Any lease at full rent (*b*) Same property (any lease)
3. Lease *not* at full rent	NONE	Only against same lease of same property

§ 8.—LAND MANAGED AS ONE ESTATE (s. 73, I.C.T.A. 1970)

Whether or not land is managed as "one estate" is a matter of fact in each case. The only reference in the Taxing Acts to such an estate is that "an estate means land in one ownership managed as one estate". Thus, the principles used and established as to what comprised land managed as one estate for the purposes of maintenance relief will apply equally for the purpose of these provisions.

If, at the end of the year 1962–63, the land then comprised therein was managed as one estate and the owner for the time being so elects, the following provisions will apply:

    (1) if during any part of a year of assessment any part of the estate is not the subject of a lease, the landlord will be deemed to have received for that period a rent equal to the proportion of the annual value that the period bears to a year, except where such part of the estate is occupied by the owner wholly and exclusively in connection with the management of the estate or for the purposes of a trade;

    (2) if during any period during a year a part of the estate is let for an amount less than an amount receivable under a lease for full rent, that property shall be brought into account as if a rent equal to the annual value had been received under the lease;

    (3) payments made in respect of premises comprised in the estate cannot be deducted from rents of properties not comprised in the estate.

The annual value for this purpose is the rent the property might currently be expected to command, on the assumption that the tenant pays the rates and the landlord pays the cost of repairs and insurance etc. (s. 531, I.C.T.A. 1970).

The election must be made in writing to the Inspector, and

    (*a*) must be made within twelve months after the end of the first year of assessment for which the person making it became entitled to make it, or such further time as the Commissioners may allow;

    (*b*) except in the case of the first election that can be made under this paragraph, shall not have effect unless the like election has had effect as respects the immediately preceding ownership;

    (*c*) shall apply throughout the ownership of the person so making it.

The election can only be given in respect of property dealt with as one estate at the end of the year 1962–63. However, if the estate owner had an interest in a trust before the end of the year 1962–63 which might result in him becoming the owner of trust properties and those properties were managed in conjunction with his own properties as one estate at any time before the end of 1962–63 they may be included in his election even though they are acquired when his interest falls in after 1962–63.

Example 1

Goose owned houses Nos 1 to 10 inclusive First Avenue which were dealt with as one estate at the end of 1962–63.

Goose himself occupied No. 1. His aunt occupied No. 2 at a nominal rental. No. 3 was used entirely for estate management.

At the end of 1962–63 he also owned Nos 6 and 7 Second Avenue but these had not been dealt with as one estate with Nos 1 to 10 First Avenue.

Goose may allow each house to be dealt with separately for purposes of Schedule A for 1964–65 and subsequent years or he may make the required election to have Nos 1 to 10 dealt with as one estate when they will be dealt with collectively. He cannot include Nos 6 and 7 Second Avenue in the estate.

He may include in the estate either No. 1 or No. 2, or both houses or he may exclude them. If he includes them expenditure on them will be allowed providing he brings into account the full annual value as computed under s. 531, I.C.T.A. 1970, as rent received. Expenditure on No. 3 can be included without the necessity of bringing in its annual value.

In July 1973, Goose acquired Nos 26 to 35 inclusive First Avenue which were dealt with as one estate at the end of 1962–63 and for which the previous owner had given notice of election. If Goose wishes to do so, he can make an election in respect of these houses which will be dealt with as one estate, but as one estate on their own; they will not be combined with Nos 1–10. If he does not make this election each house will be dealt with separately.

In December 1974, Goose bought Nos 36 to 45 and Nos 50 to 60 First Avenue. Nos 36 to 45 were not dealt with as one estate at the end of 1962–63 and so Goose cannot make an election for these houses which will be dealt with separately. Nos 50 to 60 had been dealt with as one estate at the end of 1962–63 but the previous owner had not made the required election and thus Goose cannot make an election in respect of them.

In June 1975, houses numbered 11 to 25 First Avenue came into Goose's ownership as remainderman of his father's estate. These had been dealt with as one estate with houses 1–10 First Avenue before his father had died in 1945. Under his will Goose had inherited Nos 1–10 and Nos 11 to 25 had formed part of his father's estate and had been left in trust for the life of Goose's mother with remainder over to Goose. Goose may make an election in respect of these properties so that they can be dealt with as one estate with Nos 1 to 10, because Nos 1 to 25 had been dealt with as one estate before the end of 1962–63 (i.e. in 1945) and before the end of that year Goose had an interest in the trust containing houses 11 to 25 which could result in him becoming the owner of them. Houses Nos 1 to 25 can, therefore, be dealt with as one estate.

Example 2

Zeus Ltd owned three shops which they leased at the following rentals, payable monthly in advance.

	£
Shop A....................................	4,000 per year
Shop B....................................	5,000 per year
Shop C....................................	3,000 per year

As they owned and managed these three shops as one estate at the end of the year 1962–63 they gave the required election for them to be managed as one estate for subsequent years.

The lease on Shop A expired on 31st July 1985, and the shop remained empty until a new lease was negotiated to commence on 1st January 1986, at a rental of £4,500 per annum payable monthly in advance. The annual value of Shop A determined according to s. 531, I.C.T.A. 1970 is £5,280.

The allowable expenses of all the shops can be taken as £4,800 per year.

The assessments under Schedule A for the years 1984–85 and 1985–86 raised on Zeus Ltd. will be as follows:

		£
1984–85	Rents received..........................	12,000
	Less: Expenses	4,800
	Schedule A assessment..............	£7,200

1985–86—Rents receivable:...............	£	£
Shops B and C..............		8,000
Shop A—6.4.85–31.7.85	1,000	
1.1.86–5.4.86	1,500	
Annual Value, Shop A:		
1.8.85–31.12.85...............		
($\frac{5}{12}$ × £5,280)	2,200	4,700
		12,700
Less: Expenses		4,800
Schedule A assessment. .		£7,900

In the period 1.8.85 to 31.12.85, Shop A is not leased, and therefore, for this period, the annual value must be used.

Example 3

If, in Example 2, Shop A had been occupied by an associate at a beneficial rental of £2,500 per year and the annual value determined according to s. 531 was £4,000, then the rental of £2,500 would be ignored and £4,000 would be brought into account.

Example 4

If, in Example 2, Shop A had been occupied by Zeus throughout the two years for the purpose of managing the estate, the assessments would have been in the sum of £3,200 for each of the years 1984–85 and 1985–86, computed as follows:

	£
Rent received—Shops B and C	8,000
Less: Expenses—Shops A, B and C	4,800
Schedule A assessment	£3,200

No annual value of Shop A is brought into account.

Example 5

Hermes owned premises in Bristol which were dealt with as one estate. During the year 1985–86 he had received rent from these properties of £1,000. In addition two of the premises had been empty during the year and the proportion of their annual value to be brought into account is £400. The allowable expenses on these properties were £1,500 during the year 1985–86.

Hermes also owned other premises in Bath which were not included as one estate with the Bristol properties. Rents received during 1985–86 from the Bath properties amounted to £2,000 and the outgoings amounted to £1,100.

An assessment of £900 will be raised on Hermes for 1985–86 as follows:

	£	£
Bristol Properties:		
Rents received	1,000	
Annual Value brought in	400	1,400
Less: Expenses		1,500
Deficiency		£100
		£
Bath Properties:		
Rents received		2,000
Less: Expenses		1,100
Schedule A assessment		£900

The deficiency on properties managed as one estate cannot be set off against the surplus on other properties but it may be carried forward and set off against a future surplus on the Bristol properties.

§ 9.—DEDUCTIONS FROM OTHER RECEIPTS (s. 74, I.C.T.A. 1970)

The following deductions can be made from such sums as wayleaves, easements, sporting rights, etc., assessed under Schedule A:

(*a*) so much of any payment made in respect of maintenance, repairs, insurance or management of premises to which the said sum relates and which constitutes an expense of the transaction;

(*b*) so much of any rent-charge, ground annual, feu duty or other periodical payment which constitutes an expense of that transaction;

(*c*) so much of any other payment which constitutes an expense of that transaction not being an expense of a capital nature;

(*d*) where, in or before the year, a person entered into any like transaction, any expenses as above not previously deducted, and any amounts not deducted in the current year.

Difficulty may be experienced on two points. First, only the expense of the transaction is deductible so that part of any expense may be disallowed on the grounds that it was not an expense of the transaction. Second, expenses from like transactions incurred either during the assessment year or in an earlier year (after 5th April 1964) can be deducted. No guidance is given as to what constitutes a like transaction. The grant of fishing rights and the grant of shooting rights would seem to be like transactions both being the granting of sporting rights but whether or not the Inland Revenue require a more close association than this (i.e. two grants of fishing rights) is an open point.

SPORTING RIGHTS (s. 75, I.C.T.A. 1970)

If a person in possession of land is in the practice of granting sporting rights for payment but for some reason he does not grant such rights, expense which he has incurred in that year which would have been eligible for deduction from the payment had it been received can be claimed as a deduction from the rent received from any other leases provided they are leases for full rent. There is no provision for carrying forward such expense to the following year.

The expenses incurred in respect of sporting rights are to be reduced where:

(1) the person in possession of the land exercises sporting rights himself, or

(2) he invites someone else to exercise them, or

(3) the person in possession is a "close company" (see Chapter 13), and the rights are exercised by a director or participator, unless the exercise of such rights leads to a charge to tax under Schedule E as a benefit.

The amount by which the expense is to be reduced is an amount which might reasonably be expected to have been paid for the exercise of the rights, by the person exercising them had he given full consideration therefor.

Sporting rights are defined as rights of fowling, shooting or fishing, or of taking or killing game, deer or rabbits.

Example 1—easement

Jason owned land through which ran a river. Neighbouring land was bought for use as a dairy farm and the owner came to an agreement to pay Jason £180 per year payable yearly in advance for the right to water his cattle at the river. It was agreed that Jason would repair a fence bordering marshland and build further fences to provide a way to the river and a watering compound. Jason decided to hard core part of this way. He also bought cinders for drainage of a gateway through which the cattle would pass but this had been necessary each year. The agreement was signed and the rights commenced on 5th April 1984.

The expenses incurred by Jason were as follows:

		£
1984–85—Repairs to fence		40
	Erecting new fence	70
	Hard core	45
	Cinders for gateway	5
	Share of cost of agreement	8
1985–86—Repairs to fences		12
	Cinders for gateway	4
	Repairs to hard core	6

The assessments raised on Jason under Schedule A will be as follows:

		£	£
1984–85—Rent receivable			180
	Less: Repairs to fence	40	
	Cinders for gateway	5	45
	Schedule A assessment		**£135**

(*Note:* Other expenses are capital)

		£	£
1985–86—Rent receivable			180
	Less: Repairs to fences	12	
	Cinders for gateway	4	
	Repairs to hard core	6	22
	Schedule A assessment		**£158**

Example 2—sporting rights

Titan owned a farm and adjacent land. The farm was let on a lease at full rent for £1,300 per year. The lease terminated on 31st March 1985, and Titan sold the farm to the farmer. The adjacent land was stocked with game and Titan granted shooting rights in 1983–84 for £1,200. In 1984–85 no shooting rights were granted. In 1985–86 he allowed a party of friends to shoot for part of the year. It was agreed that had his friends paid a fair price for these rights they would have paid £600.

The deductible expenses of the farm were £460 in 1983–84 and £415 in 1984–85. The expenses of preservation of game on the adjacent land and the gamekeeper's wages amounted to £850 each year.

Titan will be assessed under Schedule A as follows:

	£	£
1983–84—Rent of farm	1,300	
Less: Expenses	460	840
Shooting rights	1,200	
Less: Expenses	850	350
Schedule A assessment		**£1,190**

	£	£
1984–85—Rent of farm	1,300	
Less: Expenses	415	886
Shooting rights	Nil	
Less: Expenses	850	850
Schedule A assessment		**£35**

	£
1985–86—Shooting rights—agreed value	600
Less: Expenses	850
Loss	**£250**

There is no provision to carry forward such a loss. The loss could be set against Schedule A profits, but as there are no such profits, the loss is irrecoverable.

§ 10.—EXPENDITURE ON SEA WALLS (s. 76, I.C.T.A. 1970)

Where in any year of assessment after 1963–64 the owner or tenant of any premises incurs expenditure in the making or repairing of any sea wall or other embankment necessary for the preservation or protection of the premises against the encroachment or overflowing of the sea or any tidal river, he shall be treated as making in that year of assessment and in each succeeding 20 years of assessment (21 years in all), a payment equal to one twenty-first part of the expenditure incurred.

If the ownership of the premises is transferred during the 21-year period, the relief is apportioned between the transferor and the transferee on a day to day basis for the year in which the transfer was made. For subsequent years relief is to be given wholly to the transferee.

If there is a change in the lessee (he being entitled to the relief) and a payment is made by the incoming lessee to the outgoing lessee for the expenditure, the relief will be transferred to the incoming lessee in the same manner as on a change of ownership. If no such payment is made the relief will be transferred to the landlord.

Any such expenditure which has also been claimed under provisions relating to relief for expenditure on plant and machinery or on agricultural land, or any other capital allowances must be excluded.

Example 1

On 10th April 1985, Wally leased premises by the sea, to Pear for 20 years at an annual rental of £5,000. Allowable expenses amounted to £2,000 per annum. In November 1985, it proved necessary to build a sea wall to prevent erosion and this work cost £31,500.

The Schedule A assessment on Wally for 1985–86 will be £1,500 as follows:

	£	£
Rent received..............................		5,000
Less: Expenses	2,000	
Allowance for sea wall, $\frac{1}{21} \times$ £31,500	1,500	3,500
Assessment		£1,500

Example 2

On 30th June 1986, Wally sold the premises to Bear who allowed Pear to continue the tenancy under the same terms as before. Bear's expenses were £1,650.

The Schedule A assessment for 1986–87 will be as follows:

Wally:	£	£
Rent received..............................		1,250
Less: Expenses (say)	500	
Allowance for sea wall:		
Proportion: $\frac{1}{4} \times$ £1,500	375	875
Assessment		£375

Bear:	£	£
Rent received..............................		3,750
Less: Expenses	1,650	
Allowance for sea wall:		
Proportion: $\frac{3}{4} \times$ £1,500	1,125	2,775
Assessment		£975

Example 3

Assume that, in Example 2, Wally was not the owner of the premises but that he held them on a lease from Colin, the terms of which made him responsible for the building of the sea wall; Pear is the sub-tenant on the same terms as in Example 2, and Wally assigns his lease to Bear instead of selling the property to him.

If Bear pays Wally a sum of money in consideration for the building of the sea wall, then Bear will be entitled to the allowance for the sea wall and the position will be the same as in Example 2. If, however, Bear did not pay anything in consideration of the sea wall, the right to the allowance that would otherwise be available to him, passes to Colin (i.e. the landlord).

§ 11.—SUPPLEMENTAL PROVISIONS AS TO DEDUCTIONS (s. 77, I.C.T.A. 1970)

A deductible sum is to be deducted for the year of assessment in which it is paid. If it cannot be so deducted by reason of an insufficiency of income it is to be deducted from the earliest year of assessment for which it can be deducted.

Any payment must be reduced to the extent that it is balanced by the receipt of insurance moneys, or money recovered by any other person.

No deduction is allowed for any payment which is made under deduction of tax.

No amount is to be deducted more than once and will not be deductible if it has been allowed elsewhere as a deduction in computing the income of a person under any Schedule.

PREMIUMS ON SHORT LEASES

§ 12.—LEASES CONCERNED

The premiums covered by these provisions are those paid under leases of not more than 50 years duration. If it were not for these provisions a landlord could receive rent in some other form and so avoid tax thereon. Accordingly, the provisions are designed to bring into charge any receipt of money or value received which is in the nature of rent or a payment in commutation of rent.

Transactions in connection with leases can also give rise to liability to Capital Gains Tax (see Chapter 29). In such circumstances, the amount chargeable under Schedule A is excluded from liability under Capital Gains Tax.

§ 13.—PERSONS CHARGEABLE

Because the term landlord is used throughout these provisions they are not restricted to owners of land but extend to any lessor of land. It is also provided that sums received by other persons which, had they been landlords, would have been charged as rent received, will be assessed to tax under Case VI of Schedule D.

§ 14.—CHARGEABLE AMOUNT (s. 80, I.C.T.A. 1970)

When a landlord is to be paid a premium under the terms of such a lease, he will be treated as if he were entitled, at the time the lease was granted, to a rent equal to the premium reduced by one-fiftieth for each complete year except the first comprised in the lease. The amount so brought in is in addition to any actual rent received. The term of the lease is to be treated as ending on the earliest date that it could be terminated on notice being given by the landlord or lessee. If there are any circumstances which suggest it is likely that the lease will in fact terminate before its expiration the period of the lease will be reduced to a term ending on that expected termination. If circumstances are such that the duration of the lease falls to be determined on a date after the lease has terminated, the duration of the lease will be extended to that date (s. 84, I.C.T.A. 1970).

Example 1

On 1st October 1985, Edwin granted a lease of premises to George for a term of 16 years on payment of a premium of £15,000.

Edwin will be assessed under Schedule A for 1985–86 on £10,500, deemed to be additional rent received, as follows:

	£
Premium received..............................	15,000
Less: $\dfrac{16-1}{50} \times £15,000$	4,500
Chargeable amount......................	£10,500

WORK CARRIED OUT BY LESSEE

If the terms under which any lease is granted are such that the tenant is required to carry out any improvements on the premises, the lessor shall be deemed to have received a premium, in addition to any other premium required, equal to the amount by which the landlord's interest immediately after the commencement of the lease (including the tenant's obligation) exceeds the landlord's interest at the same time without the tenant's obligation to carry out the improvements. However, if the work is such that it could be deducted in computing the Schedule A assessment on the landlord, if carried out by the landlord, it will be disregarded. It will be appreciated that no liability under this provision can arise to any person other than the landlord.

Example 2

Assume that in Example 1 George was also required to make certain structural alterations to the premises under the terms of the lease, which will cost him £3,000.

The assessment on Edwin for 1985–86 under Schedule A will include £12,600, as follows:

	£
Premium £15,000 + £3,000.......................	18,000
Less: $\dfrac{16-1}{50} \times £18,000$	5,400
Chargeable amount......................	£12,600

SURRENDER OF LEASE

Where, under the terms of the lease, a sum becomes payable by the tenant in lieu of the whole or part of the rent for any period, or as consideration for the surrender of a lease, the lease shall be deemed to have required the payment of a premium to the landlord, in addition to any other premium, of an amount equal to that sum. In computing the amount to be taxed the duration of the lease is to be treated as the period in relation to which the sum is payable and it will be deemed to have arisen when the sum becomes payable by the tenant.

Example 3

Assume that in Example 1, George wished to surrender his lease on 30th September 1992, and it was agreed that he could do this on payment of £1,500 to Edwin. George duly paid £1,500 on 30th September 1992, and surrendered the lease.

There are nine complete years of the lease still to run at the date of surrender and thus this is the number of years to be taken into account.

An amount of £1,260 will be included as additional rent received in the Schedule A assessment made on Edwin for 1992–93, as follows:

	£
Amount paid for surrender	1,500
Less: $\dfrac{9-1}{50} \times £1,500$	240
Chargeable amount	£1,260

VARIATION OR WAIVER

Where a sum becomes payable by the tenant, otherwise than by way of rent, as consideration for the variation or waiver of any of the terms of a lease, the lease shall be deemed to have required the payment of a premium to the landlord, in addition to any other premium, of an amount equal to the sum payable. In computing the amount to be taxed the duration shall be taken as the period commencing with the date the variation or waiver takes effect and ending with the date such variation or waiver ceases to have effect. The rent will be treated as having become due on the date of the contract providing the variation or waiver is entered into. If such a payment is made to any person other than the landlord it can only be assessed to tax under Case VI if that person is connected with the landlord.

This provision is applicable even if the lease was taken out prior to 6th April 1963 (the effective date lease premium provisions commenced) providing the contract for variation or waiver was entered into on or after 4th April 1963.

Example 4

Assume in Example 1, that on 30th September 1990, in consideration of a waiver of terms of the lease, not affecting the period thereof, George paid Edwin a further sum of £5,000. Eleven complete years of the lease remain.

A further amount of £4,000 will be included in the Schedule A assessment made on Edwin for the year 1990–91, as follows:

	£
Additional payment treated as a premium	5,000
Less: $\dfrac{11-1}{50} \times £5,000$	1,000
Chargeable amount	£4,000

PREMIUM PAID BY INSTALMENTS

Where premiums are payable by instalments, the amount chargeable to tax may, if the person satisfied the Board that he would otherwise suffer undue hardship, be paid at his option by such instalments as the Board may allow, over a period not exceeding eight years.

OTHER POINTS

The provisions which require the Schedule A assessment for any year to be based on particulars of the previous year are not to apply to premiums (other than those paid by instalments) brought into account because they fall into charge for one year only.

Relief for sums due but not received is given in the same manner and under the same conditions as relief is given for rent due but not received.

§ 15.—SALES WITH A RIGHT TO RECONVEYANCE (s. 82, I.C.T.A. 1970)

A further form of dealing is to sell an estate or an interest therein on terms that it will be or may be reconveyed at a future date to the vendor or someone connected with him. If there is such a dealing an assessment may be made under Case VI of Schedule D on the vendor. *No assessment will be made if the lease is granted and begins to run within one month of the sale.*

Providing the earliest date at which the property could be reconveyed is less than two years after the sale, the amount of the charge is the amount by which the sum received on the sale exceeds the price at which the property is to be reconveyed.

If the earliest date for reconveyance is after two years from the date of sale, the amount charged is the excess of the amount received on the sale over the price payable on reconveyance by one-fiftieth for each complete year (except the first year) in the period which commences with the date of sale and ends with the earliest date on which the reconveyance can be made.

For these purposes connected persons has the same meaning as connected persons for Capital Gains Tax purposes.

Example 1

Kite sold land for £25,000 on 1st August 1985, reserving an option to repurchase the land at any time after 30th September 1986, at £22,000.

The earliest date of repurchase is within two years of the date of sale and accordingly Kite will be assessed under Case VI for 1985–86 as follows:

	£
Sale price	25,000
Repurchasing price	22,000
Chargeable amount	£3,000

Example 2

If, in Example 1, the option to repurchase was at any time after 30th September 1991 (i.e. six complete years) at £19,000 the Case VI assessment, year 1985–86 would be:

	£
Sale price	25,000
Repurchasing price	19,000
	6,000
Less: $\dfrac{6-1}{50} \times £6,000$	600
Chargeable amount	£5,400

If the terms of sale are such that the date of reconveyance is not fixed and the price at which the property is reconveyed varies with the date, the price of the reconveyance is to be taken as the lowest possible under terms of sale, thus, giving rise to the greatest liability. In such a case the vendor, within 6 years after the date of the reconveyance, may substitute the actual date of the conveyance for the date previously taken and claim repayment of tax accordingly.

Example 3

If the option to repurchase in Example 1 was as follows: at any time after 30th September 1987, but before 30th September 1989 at £21,000; at any time after 30th September 1989, but before 30th September 1991, at £19,500; at any time after 30th September 1992, at £18,000; the Case VI assessment for 1985–86 would be as follows:

	£
Sale price..	25,000
Lowest repurchase price...........................	18,000
Less: $\dfrac{7-1}{50} \times$ £7,000	840
Chargeable amount.......................	£6,160

If, in fact, Kite exercised the option at 31st December 1989, the Case VI assessment for 1985–86 would be adjusted as follows:

	£
Sale price..	25,000
Repurchase price	19,500
	5,500
Less: $\dfrac{5-1}{50} \times$ £5,500	440
Adjusted chargeable amount..............	£5,060

This would lead to a repayment of income tax on, or a set-off of, £1,100 (£6,160 − £5,060).

Sundry points
The period to be taken into account is the complete number of years from the date of sale to the date of repurchase, less one year.

In each of the above examples top-slicing relief could be claimed by the individual under Schedule 3, I.C.T.A. 1970 (see § 21 of this chapter).

There is no relief for a loss which may arise under these provisions (s. 176 (4), I.C.T.A. 1970).

The provisions relating to relief for rents due but not received apply equally to the above provisions.

It should be kept in mind that a transaction such as the sale of land with a right to reconveyance can become assessable under the provisions relating to Capital Gains Tax. In such circumstances amounts chargeable under Case VI will be excluded in computing liability under Capital Gains Tax.

§ 16.—DEDUCTIONS FROM PREMIUMS (s. 83, I.C.T.A. 1970)

As the provisions relating to the taxing of premiums apply to all landlords, relief must be afforded to a lessor who pays a premium for the lease to his superior landlord.

Accordingly, relief is afforded where tax becomes chargeable on a premium or it would have become chargeable but for other exemptions from tax, and a further liability accrues subsequently in respect of a premium for the same lease or interest.

The amount chargeable on the subsequent letting is called the later chargeable amount and the amount chargeable on the earlier letting is called the amount chargeable on the superior interest.

The relief available is the "appropriate fraction" of the amount chargeable on the superior interest. The appropriate fraction is A/B, where:

   A is the period in respect of which the later chargeable amount arose; and

   B is the period in respect of which the amount chargeable on the superior interest arose.

For this purpose the period in respect of which an amount arose is either the duration of the lease, or the period taken to be the duration of the lease. These definitions are applied in the following example.

Example 1

Lake grants a lease to Knoll for 21 years in consideration for a premium of £12,000 and Knoll sublets the premises to Park under a lease for 16 years at a premium of £10,000. The amount chargeable on Lake is the amount chargeable on the superior interest; the amount chargeable on Knoll is the later chargeable amount. The appropriate fraction is 16/21.

The relief is granted by deducting from the amount chargeable on the subsequent letting the appropriate fraction of the amount chargeable on the prior acquisition.

Example 2

Taking the facts as stated in Example 1, the amount chargeable on Knoll is £1,514 computed as follows:

		£
Lake: Premium		12,000
Less: $\dfrac{21-1}{50} \times £12,000$		4,800
Chargeable amount...........................		£7,200
Knoll: Premium		10,000
Less: $\dfrac{16-1}{50} \times £10,000$		3,000
Chargeable amount subject to relief............		7,000
Relief:		
$\dfrac{16}{21} \times £7,200$..		5,486
Amount assessable		£1,514

Example 3

Suppose that on the termination of the first sub-lease, Knoll granted a further lease to Field for a period of four years at a premium of £3,200. Knoll will be assessed on a further £1,637 arrived at as follows:

	£
Premium	3,200
Less: $\dfrac{4-1}{50}$ × £3,200	192
Chargeable amount subject to relief.	3,008
Relief:	
$\dfrac{4}{21}$ × £7,200.	1,371
Amount assessable	£1,637

It will be observed, that taking into account the one year that the premises were not sublet, the relief afforded to Knoll amounts to the sum chargeable on Lake (i.e. 16/21 + 4/21 + 1/21 × £7,200 = £7,200).

The above relief is available to Knoll even if Lake has claimed relief under Schedule 3, I.C.T.A. 1970 (see § 21 of this chapter).

No relief is given for any deficiency that may arise by reason of the above computation.

Example 4

Suppose that the premium paid by Park to Knoll in Example 1 was not £10,000 but was only £7,000, the position would be as follows:

	£
Lake: Amount chargeable as before.	7,200

	£
Knoll: Premium	7,000
Less: $\dfrac{16-1}{50}$ × £7,000	2,100
Chargeable amount subject to relief.	4,900
Relief:	
$\dfrac{16}{21}$ × £7,200.	5,486
Amount assessable	Nil

No relief is afforded in respect of the excess £586.

Where for any reason, such as a change in the period taken for the duration of the lease, a recalculation becomes necessary, additional assessments or repayments will be made accordingly.

If only part of the premises are sublet, the appropriate fraction is to be justly apportioned. Such apportionment may thus be made on area floor space, cubic capacity, or value, or any other method that is just in the circumstances.

Example 5

Suppose in Example 4, Knoll had sublet only half the premises to Park.

	£
Lake: Chargeable amount as previously	7,200

Knoll: Chargeable amount subject to relief . . . .

£ 4,900

Relief:

$$\frac{16}{21} \times £7,200. \ldots \ldots \ldots \ldots \ldots \ldots \text{£5,486}$$

One-half thereof   2,743

Amount assessable £2,157

§ 17.—RELIEF FOR PREMIUMS RECEIVED ("TOP SLICING RELIEF")
(s. 85 and Schedule 3, I.C.T.A. 1970)

Because the inclusion of a chargeable amount, in respect of a premium received, falls for assessment wholly in one year, the rate of income tax payable by an *individual* on that chargeable amount may exceed the rate that would have been payable on the chargeable amount had it been spread evenly over the period taken in arriving at that amount.

Accordingly Schedule 3, I.C.T.A. 1970, offers relief in a rather complicated manner so that the charge to tax represents as nearly as possible, the tax that would have been charged had the chargeable amount been spread evenly over the relevant period.

Relief is afforded for any increase in the rate of tax brought about by the inclusion of premiums. This is because the inclusion of such an amount in one year may considerably increase the rate of income tax paid.

For the purposes of this relief, certain terms are defined.

Chargeable sum means an amount chargeable as a premium or as a sale with a right to reconveyance (see above) and the amount charged on the assignment of a lease at undervalue, whether assessed under Schedule A or Case VI of Schedule D.

Relevant period is the period of the lease taken into account when arriving at the chargeable amount.

Yearly equivalent is the chargeable sum divided by the number of years and fractions of years in the relevant period (i.e. the period of the lease).

CALCULATION OF THE RELIEF

The relief necessitates two calculations.

First, it is necessary to calculate the rate of tax payable on the chargeable amount if no relief were given. For this purpose the chargeable amount is taken as the highest part of the person's income and any deductions from income must be taken, so far as possible, from other income.

Secondly, a computation must be made in the same manner replacing the chargeable amount by the yearly equivalent. The rate of tax applicable to the yearly equivalent is then determined by treating it as the highest part of the income.

The tax payable on the chargeable amount at the rate determined under the first calculation is reduced to the tax payable on the chargeable amount at the rate determined by the second calculation.

DEDUCTIONS

Deductions which attach themselves specifically to the chargeable amount such as an industrial buildings allowance on the leased premises are deductible from the chargeable amount and the yearly equivalent, so far as they are not covered by rent assessable under Schedule A. After making such a deduction the amount to be brought into account to determine the rate of tax applicable to the yearly equivalent is the balance of the yearly equivalent that remains. If the effect of the deduction is to reduce the yearly equivalent to nil, the rate of tax applicable is that which is applied to the highest part of the remainder of the income. If the rate of tax applicable is chargeable at two or more rates those rates are to be applied to the chargeable amount in corresponding proportions.

MORE THAN ONE CHARGEABLE AMOUNT

Where an individual's total income includes more than one chargeable amount, the order and manner in which the amounts are to be taken for the purpose of calculating the tax payable by reference to the yearly equivalent is as follows:

  (1) Amounts in respect of longer relevant periods are to be taken before amounts for shorter relevant periods.
  (2) If amounts arise in respect of two or more relevant periods of equal length, they are to be added together and taken as one amount received for that relevant period.
  (3) For the purposes of total income the yearly equivalents which have not been dealt with (because they apply to a shorter relevant period) and yearly equivalents that are reduced to nil by deductions, are to be ignored.
  (4) If a reduction has been made in calculating the rate of tax applicable to one yearly equivalent, it cannot be deducted again in computing the rate of tax applicable to another yearly equivalent.

For the purpose of total income the above amounts are to be treated as the highest part of the total income of an individual notwithstanding any provision in the Income Tax Acts directing other income to be treated as the highest part of his total income, but any amount which is to be included in total income for payments received on retirement or on removal from an office or employment, under s. 187, I.C.T.A. 1970, is to be excluded from total income when computing the relief, and amounts included by virtue of s. 399, I.C.T.A. 1970 (gains arising in connection with life policies etc.) and only included up to the amount of the "appropriate fraction".

Example 1

During the year 1985–86 Carn granted two leases of land as follows:

  (1) To Egie, for a term of 20 years at a premium of £40,000.
  (2) To Hall, for a term of 10 years at a premium of £25,000.

The rents applicable to the leased lands are:

Lease 1—£2,350. Lease 2—£1,000.

He has no earned income but has investment income of £10,000 gross for the year 1985–86. He owns his own house upon which he paid building society interest of £330 in 1985–86. He also paid bank interest of £235 in that year. (Loan fixed pre-March 26th 1974.)

He is a married man.

His tax position for 1985–86 will be as follows.

Ignoring relief afforded by Schedule 3, I.C.T.A. 1970.

	£	£	£
Income Tax:			
Investment income		10,000	
Less: Building society interest.......	330		
Bank interest................	Nil	330	9,670
Lease (1)			
Annual rent		2,350	
Premium.........................	40,000		
Less: $\dfrac{20-1}{50} \times £40,000$	15,200	24,800	27,150

	£	£	£
Lease (2)			
Annual rent		1,000	
Premium........................	25,000		
Less: $\dfrac{10-1}{50} \times £25,000$	4,500	20,500	21,500
			58,320
Deduct:			
Personal allowance.........			3,455
			£54,865

Income tax payable:	£
On £16,200 @ 30%	4,860.00
3,000 @ 40%	1,200.00
5,200 @ 45%	2,340.00
7,900 @ 50%	3,950.00
7,900 @ 55%	4,345.00
14,665 @ 60%	8,799.00
£54,865	£25,494.00

As the chargeable amounts of £24,800 and £20,500 form the highest part of the income, they suffer tax as follows:

		£
On £14,655	@ 60%	8,799.00
7,900	@ 55%	4,345.00
7,900	@ 50%	3,950.00
5,200	@ 45%	2,340.00
3,000	@ 40%	1,200.00
6,635	@ 30%	1,990.50
£45,300		£22,624.50

Claiming relief under Schedule 3, the yearly equivalents of the chargeable amounts are:

$$\text{Lease (1)} \quad \frac{\text{Chargeable amount}}{\text{Period of lease}} = \frac{24,800}{20} = £1,240$$

$$\text{Lease (2)} \quad \frac{\text{Chargeable amount}}{\text{Period of lease}} = \frac{20,500}{10} = £2,050$$

Substituting the yearly equivalents for the chargeable amounts, the liabilities become:

Lease 1

	£	£	£
Income tax:			
Investment income		10,000	
Less: Building society interest...........	330		
Bank interest....................	—	330	9,670
Annual rents of lands			3,350
Lease (1) (being for the longer period)			
Yearly equivalent....................			1,240
			14,260
Deduct: Personal allowance............			3,455
			£10,805

Income tax payable: £
  On £10,805 @ 30%   3,241.50

The rate of income tax applicable to the yearly equivalent of £1,240 is therefore:

               £
   1,240 @ 30%   372.00

The income tax chargeable on the full amount of £24,800 is therefore:

$$£372.00 \times 20 = £7,440$$

(20 years is the period of the lease.)

Lease 2   £
  Income *less* deductions and allowances as above (including
  Lease (1)).. 10,805
  Lease (2) yearly equivalent.................................... 2,050

                  £12,855

The rate of tax payable on the yearly equivalent of £2,050 is therefore:

  2,050 @ 30%   £615

The income tax chargeable on the full amount of £20,500 is therefore:

$$£615 \times 10 = £6,150$$

(10 years is the period of the lease.)

Relief available under Schedule 3, I.C.T.A. 1970:

	£	£
Amount applicable to chargeable amounts in normal computation...........................		22,624.50
Amount by reference to yearly equivalents		
Lease (1)	7,440	
Lease (2)	6,150	13,590.00
Amount of relief		£9,034.50

For 1985–86, Carn's liability to tax will therefore be the original computation of £25,494.00 *less* relief of £9,034.50 = £16,459.50.

§ 18.—RIGHT TO REQUIRE INFORMATION (s. 19, T.M.A. 1970)

For the purpose of obtaining particulars of profits or gains chargeable to tax under Schedule A, the Inspector may by notice in writing require information from:

  (*a*) any lessee, occupier, or former lessee or occupier of land (including any person having, or having had, the use of land) as may be prescribed by the Commissioners of Inland Revenue as to the terms applying to the lease, occupation, or use of the land, and where any of these terms are established by any written instrument, to produce the instrument to the Inspector;

(*b*) any lessee or former lessee of land on any consideration given for the grant or assignment to him of the tenancy.

(*c*) any person who as agent manages land or is in receipt of rent.

Failure to furnish the particulars required will lead to penalties being imposed in accordance with ss. 93, 95 and 98 of T.M.A. 1970.

SCHEDULE B

§ 19.—NATURE OF INCOME ASSESSED UNDER SCHEDULE B (ss. 91 and 92, I.C.T.A. 1970)

The charge of Schedule B tax is confined to the occupation of woodlands in the United Kingdom managed on a commercial basis and with a view to the realisation of profits. The Schedule B assessment is an amount equal to one-third of the annual value of the land, the annual value being arrived at in accordance with the provisions of s. 531, I.C.T.A. 1970, on the assumption that the lands, instead of being woodlands, were let and occupied in their natural, unimproved state.

A right to elect for assessment under Schedule D is available under s. 111, I.C.T.A. 1970 and once made stands until the occupier changes, when the assessment will revert back to Schedule B. An election may be made within two years from the end of the year of assessment (or accounting period, for Corporation Tax), and must extend to all woodlands so occupied on the same estate, with the exception, if claimed, of woodlands planted or replanted within the previous ten years.

If an amount is received for an easement in respect of such land assessed under Schedule B, the Schedule A assessment on such an easement will be limited to the amount by which it exceeds the Schedule B assessment or the relative proportion of the Schedule B assessment.

Tax under Schedule B is payable in full in one sum on 1st January in the year of assessment.

Occupier (s. 51, F.A. 1984)

An occupier for the purposes of occupation *does not include* a person who in connection with any trade carried on by him has the use of woodlands for the purpose of:

(a) felling, processing or removing timber; or

(b) clearing the lands or part of them for replanting.

This applies for usage after 13th March 1984 and reverses the decision in *Russel* v. *Hird* (1983), which held that such a person was in occupation.

SCHEDULE C

§ 20.—NATURE OF INCOME ASSESSED UNDER SCHEDULE C (s. 93, I.C.T.A. 1970)

Assessments under Schedule C are made on interest, dividends, etc., payable in the United Kingdom *out of any public revenue* in the United Kingdom or elsewhere, where payment is entrusted to an agent resident in the United Kingdom.

Schedule C is concerned almost exclusively with the interest, etc., on Government Stocks (whether of the United Kingdom, the Commonwealth or a foreign state) where payment is entrusted to any agent (e.g. a banking company) resident in the United Kingdom, i.e. where the agent deducts tax and remits the net interest to the individual stockholders. Where payment is not entrusted to an agent resident in the United Kingdom, i.e. where the foreign or Commonwealth Government remits the gross interest direct to the stockholders in this country, the income is assessed direct on the recipient under Case IV of Schedule D, so that an individual recipient is never assessed directly under Schedule C.

So far as the recipient of interest is concerned, he receives his interest net after deduction of tax at the basic rate in force at the date of payment. No regard is had in fixing the rate to the period over which the interest accrued.

§ 21.—THE BASIS OF ASSESSMENT (s. 94 and Schedule 5, I.C.T.A. 1970)

The assessment is based on the actual amount of interest etc., arising in the year of assessment, *and is made on the bank or other agent to whom payment is entrusted*. The agent deducts tax at the basic rate in force at the time of payment, and must pay over the tax so deducted to the account of the Commissioners of Inland Revenue at the Bank of England.

The recipient of the interest can claim repayment of the tax deducted if he is not liable to Income Tax or if he has suffered tax in excess of his true liability.

§ 22.—INTEREST ON GOVERNMENT SECURITIES

Where interest is received gross, it is not assessed under Schedule C but is assessed direct on the recipient under Case III of Schedule D. An individual is never assessed direct under Schedule C.

§ 23.—RATE OF TAX DEDUCTED

The rate at which tax is deducted from interest, etc., falling under Schedule C is the basic rate in force *at the date of payment*, irrespective of the fact that the rate may have changed during the period in which the interest accrued.

Example 1

Interest on $3\frac{1}{2}$ per cent War Loan is payable half-yearly on 1st June and 1st December. For the year 1978–79 the basic rate of tax was 33 per cent and for 1979–80, 30 per cent.

If application had been made to the Bank of England for the interest to be paid "net", tax would be deducted at 30 per cent from the payment of interest made on 1st June 1979, irrespective of the fact that for four-sixths of the period in respect of which the interest was paid the basic rate of tax was 33 per cent.

Where the rate of tax is increased *during* the year of assessment and tax has not been deducted from the first payment of interest at the full effective rate of tax for the year, an increased deduction of tax is made from the second payment of interest during the year, so that the full rate of tax will have been deducted from the total interest payable during the year of assessment.

Example 2

The basic rate of tax for 1985–86 is 30 per cent, and assuming that the rate for 1986–87 is 33 per cent. Then in the case of interest on 4 per cent Funding Loan payable 1st May and 1st November, if tax was deducted at 30 per cent from the interest paid on 1st May 1986, tax would be deducted at 36 (33 plus 3) from the interest paid on 1st November 1986; thus the total interest for 1986–87 will be subject to the basic rate of 33 per cent.

Converse provisions apply where the rate of tax is decreased during the year, a reduced deduction of tax being made from the second payment of interest.

Where the rate of tax is increased, and the agent entrusted with the payment of any interest has not deducted tax at the rate ultimately in force for the year in question (in the manner described above), the additional tax may be recovered from the recipients of the interest by a direct assessment under Case VI of Schedule D. Where the rate of tax is reduced and tax is deducted at a higher rate than that ultimately in force for the year in question without subsequent adjustment (see above), repayment of the excess tax deducted may be recovered on application by the recipient of the interest either by:

(*a*) Adjustment against some subsequent assessment upon the recipient; or

(*b*) Inclusion in the next refund of tax made to the recipient; or

(*c*) Immediate repayment of the excess tax.

11. Miscellaneous Items and Claims

§ 1.—INTEREST PAYABLE

(*a*) *Witholding tax* (s. 54, I.C.T.A. 1970)
Individuals normally pay interest in full without deduction of tax. In the following cases, however, interest must still be subject to deduction of tax at the basic rate:—
> (1) Interest paid to a person who normally resides abroad.
> (2) Interest paid by companies and local authorities (including partnerships with a company member).

(The witholding requirement in these cases does not apply in respect of interest payable to a UK bank or interest paid by such a bank in the ordinary course of its business.) Refer to § 2 for witholding tax on qualifying interest paid after April 1983.

(*b*) *Interest qualifying for income tax relief* (s. 75 and Schedule 9, F.A. 1972, s. 19 and Schedule 1, F.A. 1974)
Generally, relief is only given for 1973–74 and subsequent years on loans effected *after* 26th March 1974 if they are for qualifying purposes, which are:
> (1) Purchase, improvement or development of land (including buildings, caravans (as defined) and house-boats), in the United Kingdom:
>> (*a*) On loans not exceeding £30,000 for the principal private residence of a person, or such a residence of a dependent relative or former or separated spouse (within the £30,000 limit). In the case of a dependent relative or former spouse, the accommodation must be provided rent-free. Bridging loan interest is available for the above properties for a period of 12 months, or such longer period as the Board will allow in appropriate circumstances.
>> (*b*) On loans to acquire property (i.e. land, buildings, caravans or houseboats) which are let in any period of 52 weeks when interest is payable and falling wholly or partly in a year of assessment at a commercial rent for more than 26 weeks; or, when not so let, is either:
>>> (i) available for letting; or
>>> (ii) used as (*a*) above; or
>>> (iii) prevented from being let by reason of repair or reconstruction.
>> (*Note:* the £30,000 limit does not apply in this case but interest is only available for offset against the rental income.)
>> (*c*) Where the property is, at the time the interest is paid, used by the borrower as a residence (or so used within 12 months of the loan, if interest is paid within 12 months of the loan) or it is intended at that time that the property be used in due course as the borrower's only or main residence and he is living in job-related accommodation. (Job-related accommodation is that which meets the criteria for exclusion of a Schedule E charge as set out under Section 33, Finance Act 1977—see Chapter 2.) Relief under this provision is limited to loans up to £30,000. With effect from 6th April 1983 this relief is extended to individuals engaged in a trade, profession or vocation who are required to live in job-related accommodation (e.g. publicans).

(2) Purchase of plant for business purposes by employees or partners. (Schedule 9, para. 10, F.A. 1972)

(3) Acquiring ordinary shares in or lending finance to a *Close Company*

    (i) Where the individual owns over 5% of the ordinary share capital (i.e. has a "material interest") at the date the interest is paid. (It is not necessary for the individual to be employed by the company.) The relief is denied if the company exists wholly or mainly for the purpose of holding investments or other property and the borrower resides in property belonging to the company, unless the borrower has worked for the greater part of his time in the actual management or conduct of the business of the company or of an associated company (Schedule 1, paras. 9 and 10, F.A. 1974).

    (ii) Where at the time the interest is paid the individual has worked for the greater part of his time in the management or conduct of the business the "5% rule" is relaxed and any share ownership, given the other conditions, qualifies interest for relief. In both cases the close company must be a trading company or a company satisfying the conditions of subparas (2)·(*b*) and (*c*) of para. 3A, Schedule 16, F.A. 1972.

(4) Acquiring shares or lending finance to an "employee-controlled" company where:

    1. The individual or spouse is a full-time employee of the company and

    2. The company is 50% owned by full-time employees (or their spouses). Ownership of more than 10% of the company by an individual or spouse means the excess is treated as a non-employee-controlled holding. Where, however, both are full-time employed, share holdings are not combined for the purpose of the restriction (in view of this restriction this relief will have little application) (Schedule 1, paras. 10C and 10D, F.A. 1974).

It will be appreciated that relief under the paragraphs will only be necessitated where the company is not close, when relief would be available under (3) above.

(5) Purchase of an interest in a partnership (Schedule 1, paras. 11 and 12, F.A. 1974)

(6) Acquiring shares, or lending money to a co-operative (Schedule 1, para, 10(A) (B), F.A. 1974).

(7) Payment of estate duty or Capital Transfer Tax on personalty (eligible for one year only) (Schedule 1, para. 17, F.A. 1974).

(8) Purchase of a life annuity where the annuitant is 65 or over and at least 90 per cent of the loan is used for this purpose (Schedule 1, para. 24, F.A. 1974). The maximum loan is £30,000

There is no relief on bank overdraft interest incurred on or after 26th March 1974. (Relief continued for 1974–75 only on the interest on a pre-26th March 1974 overdraft, but limited to interest on the debit balance at 26th March 1974.)

Loans Prior to 26.3.1974
Relief continued on loans effected before 26th March 1974, (if non-qualifying), with the first £35 disallowance, *up to 5th April 1982*. This also applied to a bank overdraft converted to a loan before 6th April 1975 (limited to the interest on the debit balance at 26th March 1974).
The above restrictions do not apply to normal business interest.

Obtaining Relief

In the case of a business, bank interest paid is allowed as a deduction in computing the profits for Income Tax purposes. Where, however, such interest is paid "out of profits or gains brought into charge," by a person not carrying on a business (e.g., an employee whose salary, out of which the bank interest is paid, is taxed under Schedule E), the payer thereof may, by making a claim within six years after the end of the year of assessment, recover tax on the amount of the interest. In other words, he is placed in the same position as if the interest had been allowed as a charge against his income in the first place.

A certificate of the interest paid should be obtained from the bank to support the claim. In the case of bank interest, it is common in practice to take the interest paid for the year ended 31st December *within* the year of assessment in question, although where interest is charged quarterly it is usual to take the interest for the year ended 31st March.

Repayment of tax on the whole amount of the interest paid will be made if the taxpayer's taxable income includes sufficient income on which tax has been borne.

Example

T. Bishop's income for 1985–86 consists of a fixed salary, payable monthly, of £10,000 per annum and fixed investment income (taxed at source) of £200 per annum. During the year ended 31st March 1986, he pays mortgage interest (without deduction of tax) amounting to £300 and personal bank loan interest of £70. The loan was advanced in 1973. He is a bachelor aged 63 but he maintains a dependent relative who has an income of £200 per annum.

The assessment raised on Bishop for 1985–86 (disregarding the adjustment for interest paid) is computed as follows:

	£	£
Salary		10,000
Investment income (gross)		200
Total income		10,200
Less: Personal allowance	2,205	
Dependent relative	100	2,305
Taxable income		£7,895
Tax thereon at 30%		2,368.50
Deduct Tax borne at source, £200 at 30%		60.00
Net tax payable		£2,308.50

When a claim is made in respect of interest paid, the liability to tax will be recomputed as follows:

	£	£
Income (as above)		10,200
Less: Interest paid (£300)		300
Total income		9,900
Less: Personal allowance	2,205	
Dependent relative	100	2,305
Taxable income		£7,595

	£
Tax thereon at 30%..........................	£2,278.50
Deduct Tax borne at source (as above)	60.00
Net tax payable.............................	£2,218.50

T. Bishop is therefore entitled to a repayment of £90.00 (*i.e.* £2,308.50 *less* £2,218.50), on making a claim within six years of 5th April, 1986. Alternatively, however, the estimated interest payable may be taken into consideration in computing the amount of tax which is deductible from T. Bishop's salary under "Pay As You Earn" (see Chapter 8, § 12).

The bank loan interest is disallowed, as not relating to "protected interest" (an allowance of £45 (£80–£35) would have been available up to 5th April 1982).

Business interest
Excess interest, if paid for business purposes, can be carried forward under s. 171, I.C.T.A. 1970 or used under s. 174, I.C.T.A. 1970 (s. 175, I.C.T.A. 1970—see Chapter 7 § 8.)

§ 2.—INTEREST QUALIFYING FOR INCOME TAX RELIEF PAID TO BUILDING SOCIETIES AND OTHERS

PAYMENTS AFTER APRIL 1983 (ss. 26—29 and Schedule 7, F.A. 1982)

Mortgage interest deduction at source (the MIRAS scheme)
The Finance Act 1982 changes fundamentally the method by which tax relief is granted on qualifying interest payments (i.e. primarily mortagage payments).

From 1st April 1983 qualifying interest (see para. 1) paid by a qualifying borrower to a qualifying lender will be paid under deduction of income tax at the basic rate. The lender thus only pays "net" interest and accordingly receives tax relief at source. The applicable date is 6th April 1983 for borrowers other than building societies (e.g. banks).

The deduction of tax at source is only mandatory where loans are not above £30,000 (£25,000 for 1982–83). These provisions will be mandatory for all loans taken out after 5th April 1987 and accordingly the relief will need to be apportioned where the loan exceeds £30,000.

Qualifying borrower (Schedule 7, para. 13, F.A. 1982)
This is any individual making qualifying interest payments other than an individual or his spouse receiving a special exemption or immunity from Schedule E tax.

Qualifying lender (Schedule 7, para. 14, F.A. 1982)
These are essentially building societies, local authorities and recognised banks. The complete list is set out in para. 14.

Effect of MIRAS payments
To account for the fact that basic rate tax has been "deducted at source" the borrower is treated as having received income equivalent to the deduction to which he is entitled (s. 26(4)).

For basic rate taxpayers the effect, therefore, is to ignore the interest paid in calculated taxable income, although no charge to tax is made when income is insufficient to cover the gross interest paid. For higher rate taxpayers, since a higher rate deduction is available, the effect is to increase the basic rate tax back by the amount of the allowable interest.

Example

Alpha, Beta, Gamma and Delta are single men each paying gross mortgage interest of £2,000 (under MIRAS) during 1985/86. They have the following income.

	£
Alpha	1,800
Beta..........	3,000
Gamma........	10,000
Delta	25,000

The tax position for 1985/86 is as follows:

	Alpha £	Beta £	Gamma £	Delta £
Income	1,800	3,000	10,000	25,000
Gross mortgage interest	1,800	2,000	2,000	2,000
Total income	Nil	1,000	8,000	23,000
Charge to tax re mortgage interest	1,800	2,000	2,000	2,000
	1,800	3,000	10,000	25,000
Less: Personal allowance	2,205	2,205	2,205	2,205
Taxable income.............	Nil	795	7,795	22,795

Tax thereon				
Alpha	—			
Beta £795 @ 30%		238.50		
Gamma £7,795 @ 30%			2,338.50	
Delta £18,200 @ 30%				5,460.00
£3,000 @ 40%				1,200.00
£1,595 @ 45%				717.75
Less:				
Mortgage interest relief at source (£2,000 @ 30%) ...	(600.00)	(600.00)	(600.00)	(600.00)
Effective tax paid	£(600.00)	£(361.50)	£1,738.50	£6,777.75

(N.B. (i) Alpha can only cover £1,800 of mortgage interest and hence his charge to tax is restricted accordingly.

(ii) Delta is a higher rate taxpayer and hence his basic rate band is increased by the mortgage interest £2,000.)

It is interesting to note that an individual (option mortgage aside) is better off under MIRAS than previously where mortgage payments create an excess of personal allowances (in practice this will be unusual except possibly in those cases where fluctuating Schedule D earnings arise).

Other points
    (*a*) For deduction of tax to apply it is necessary for the borrower to notify the lender that he is a qualifying borrower.
    (*b*) Loans exceeding the £30,000 limit are available for tax deduction at source but restricted to the interest on £30,000 (it is understood in practice that very few lenders are prepared to operate the MIRAS scheme for loans over £30,000. N.B. it is not mandatory above this level).

(*c*)   The Inland Revenue have issued regulations (the Income Tax (Interest Relief) Regulations 1982) (1.10.82) which set out the procedures in relation to operating the deduction of tax at source scheme.

(*d*)   Section 28, F.A. 1982 allows deduction of tax from interest payments in respect of combined payments (i.e. those containing capital and interest).

(*e*)   Relief applies up to £30,000 in the case of an individual moving house in respect of bridging finance.

(*f*)   MIRAS is not an allowable deduction under Schedule D(i), (ii) or (vi).

As a result of the changes the option mortgage scheme ceases to have effect. The mortgage option scheme applied in certain special cases, within the Housing Subsidies Act 1967, and allowed tax to be deducted at source. (Refer to s. 27(2), (3), (4) F.A. 1982 for transitional arrangements.)

PAYMENTS BEFORE APRIL 1983

Where interest is paid to a Building Society in full under the special arrangement sanctioned by the Inland Revenue authorities for Building Societies (i.e. paid gross see § 11, § 12), the borrower may claim an allowance equal to the amount of the interest (unless the interest is paid under the Option Mortgage Scheme introduced by the Housing Subsidies Act 1967) (s. 343, I.C.T.A. 1970). Repayment of tax may be claimed on the interest against the tax paid on any income. Interest paid to banks is paid gross as s. 54, I.C.T.A. 1970 (see § 1) does not apply.

The interest taken into account for the purpose of the claim is that payable during the Income Tax year concerned. The computation would be the same as in the previous example in § 1 above.

§ 3.—NON-RESIDENTS (s. 27, I.C.T.A. 1970)

An individual who is not resident in the United Kingdom is *not* entitled to the usual allowances and reliefs unless he or she is:

1.   A British subject *or* a citizen of the Republic of Ireland; *or*
2.   A person who is or has been employed in the service of the Crown, or who is employed in the service of any missionary society, or in the service of any native State under the protection of Her Majesty; *or*
3.   Resident in the Isle of Man or the Channel Islands; *or*
4.   One who has previously resided within the United Kingdom and is resident abroad for the sake of his or her health or the health of a member of his or her family resident with him or her; *or*
5.   A widow whose late husband was in the service of the Crown.
6.   Individual residents of certain countries with which the U.K. has Double Taxation Agreements, in which relief is specified.

The amount of tax payable by a non-resident must not, however, be reduced below an amount which bears the same proportion to the amount which would be payable if tax were chargeable on the whole of his income from all sources (including income not subject to United Kingdom Income Tax), as the amount of the income subject to United Kingdom Income Tax bears to the total income from all sources.

This relief is *not* affected by the provisions in the Finance Act 1984 concerning foreign earnings (see Chapter 8).

This relief is subject to the provisions of any double taxation agreement between the UK and the country of residence of the individual concerned.

Example

Angus is a British subject resident abroad in a country which has no double taxation agreement with the U.K. He is married, but without children. His total income for 1985–86 is:

	£
Unearned income liable to U.K. tax......................	6,750
Earned income not liable to U.K. tax	3,950
	£10,700

	£
Unearned income liable to U.K. tax......................	6,750
Less: Personal allowance	3,455
Taxable income...................................	£3,295

TAX PAYABLE

	£
Tax thereon at 30%.................................	988.50

The amount of tax payable by Angus will however be based on total income (world income), as this gives the greater liability:

Total income from all sources

	£	£
Earned	3,950	
Unearned	6,750	
		10,700
Less: Personal allowance		3,455
Taxable income........................		£7,245

	£
Tax thereon at 30%.................................	2,173.50

$$\text{Proportion applicable to U.K. income} = \frac{6,750}{10,700} \times £2,173.50 = £1,371.13$$

N.B. This is less than the £2,025 which would be payable if no relief were given for the personal allowances (i.e. £6,750 @ 30% = £2,025).

Effect of certain government securities

Where the income of a non-resident includes interest derived from $3\frac{1}{2}$ per cent War Loan or from certain other British Government securities (see Chapter 10 § 22), which are exempt from United Kingdom Income Tax when in the beneficial ownership of a non-resident, the amount of such interest must be included in the total income for the purpose of the computation of liability to tax, but is excluded from income subject to U.K. income tax in ascertaining his proportionate liability to Income Tax as a non-resident or British subject resident abroad.

Example

J. Player is a British subject resident abroad in a country which has no double taxation agreement with the U.K. He is married with no children. His total income for 1985–86 is £3,800 as follows:

	£
Dividends from British companies (including tax credit)	300
Untaxed interest from $3\frac{1}{2}$ per cent War Loan.	150
Untaxed interest abroad	3,200
Dividends abroad (gross)	150
	£3,800

It is required to show the claim which may be made by J. Player in respect of the United Kingdom Income Tax deducted at source from his dividends.

	£
Player has borne United Kingdom Income Tax on £300 at 30%	90.00

If the whole of Player's income were liable to United Kingdom Income Tax, his liability would be as follows:

	£
Total Income	3,800
Less: Personal allowance	3,455
Taxable income	£345

TAX PAYABLE

	£
On £345 at 30%	103.50

The proportion borne by the income subject to United Kingdom Income Tax to the total income is

$$\frac{300}{3,800}$$

Player is therefore liable for

$$\frac{300}{3,800} \times £103.50 \dots \dots \dots \dots \dots \dots \dots \dots \quad 8.17$$

Thus he may claim repayment of . . . .   £81.83 (£90.00 − £8.17)

Note 1. The liability in respect of the U.K. income is covered by personal allowances and hence the greater liability by reference to world income will prevail.

Note 2. As interest on $3\frac{1}{2}$% War Loan is exempt from Income Tax in the hands of non-residents, it has been excluded from income subject to U.K. income tax in computing Player's proportionate liability to tax as a British subject resident abroad.

INCOME ELIGIBLE FOR DOUBLE TAX RELIEF

Where the income of a non-resident entitled to claim under the provisions of s. 27, I.C.T.A. 1970, includes United Kingdom dividends, interest, royalties, etc., in respect of which relief (other than credit) is available under a Double Taxation Agreement so as to limit the rate of United Kingdom tax chargeable (but not so as to confer exemption), the income is treated as follows for the purpose of ascertaining the proportionate liability;

(*a*) The tax chargeable in respect of the income is to be excluded.

(*b*) The income is to be excluded from income liable to United Kingdom tax.

(*c*) The income is to be included in total income from all sources.

(*d*) The double taxation relief in respect of the income is to be excluded in calculating the tax chargeable on total income from all sources.

The above provisions do not apply so as to increase the tax payable by a person to more than would have been payable if the double taxation relief had not been available.

Example

A. Ross, a non-resident British subject, is resident in a country which has a Double Taxation Agreement with the U.K. under which the rate of U.K. income tax on dividends and interest is limited to 15 per cent. He is single and has the following unearned income for the year 1985–86:

	Gross £
U.K. rents (not subject to double taxation relief)	2,000
U.K. dividends and interest (U.K. tax deducted at 15 per cent, i.e. subject to double tax relief)	1,000
Foreign income (unearned)	7,000
Total income	£10,000

U.K. tax of £600 has been paid by direct assessment on the U.K. rents.

	£
Total Income as above	10,000
Less: Personal allowance	2,205
Taxable income.	£7,795

	£
Tax thereon at 30%.	2,338.50

The proportion borne by the income liable to U.K. income tax (and not subject to double taxation relief) to total income is:

$$\frac{2,000}{2,000 + 1,000 + 7,000} = \frac{2,000}{10,000}$$

The liability is therefore:

	£
$\frac{2,000}{10,000} \times £2,338.50$	£467.70

Notes

(1) Again the world income calculation of liability prevails, as the U.K. taxable income (£2,000) is covered by the personal allowance.

(2) If double taxation relief had not been available, the U.K. income tax payable would have been as follows:

$$\frac{2,000 + 1,000}{2,000 + 1,000 + 7,000} = \frac{3,000}{10,000} \times £2,338.50 = £701.55$$

Unless a non-resident comes within the classes of person specified above, he will be liable at the basic rate of tax on his income from the United Kingdom, without any deductions for allowances and reliefs, but no liability will arise in respect of interest from $3\frac{1}{2}$ per cent War Loan, etc.

§ 4.—TRUST INCOME IN RESPECT OF MINORS (see Chapter 12 for trust taxation)

Income Tax is payable in full on the income of a trust at the basic rate plus additional rate (15%) where the trust is discretionary or accumulating and the portion accruing to each beneficiary comes to the hands of the recipient taxed at the source. Consequently any allowances or reliefs to which the beneficiary may be entitled must be claimed by way of repayment of tax.

The 15% additional rate continues to apply to discretionary or accumulating trusts notwithstanding the abolition of investment income surcharge for 1984–85 onwards.

The claims which may be made by trustees (or a trust corporation) on behalf of an infant beneficiary under a will or settlement, depend upon whether the trust is (1) non-discretionary and non-accumulating (i.e. the interest is absolute) or (2) discretionary or accumulating. In both these cases, where the settlement is made upon a child by the parent, the income will not be that of the child but that of the parent (i.e. the settlor). This does not apply to a married child or a child aged over 18.

(1) NON-DISCRETIONARY, NON-ACCUMULATING TRUSTS

The trustees may claim repayment of tax year by year in respect of allowances, etc., applicable to the gross income from the trust due to the infant, irrespective of the amount expended on maintenance. On coming of age the infant may claim (if the trustees have failed to do so) in respect of previous years. In each case the usual time limit of six years applies, e.g., a claim in respect of 1985–86 must be made before 6th April 1992.

Example 1—absolute interest

The share of B. Dixon (an infant) in the income of a trust for 1985–86 is £2,400 (including tax credit). The interest of the infant in the trust is absolute.

The claim that can be made by Dixon's trustees in respect of 1985–86 is as follows:

	£
Trust income	2,400
Less: Personal allowance	2,205
Taxable income	£195

	£
Tax thereon at 30%	58.50
Tax deducted at source, £2,400 at 30%	720.00
Amount repayable	£661.50

(2) DISCRETIONARY OR ACCUMULATING TRUSTS (ss. 16 and 17, F.A. 1973)

Where income is applied in maintaining or educating the child, or is paid to the child, repayment of tax may be claimed in respect of the income so applied or paid.

The "gross" amount corresponding to the net amount actually expended in cash is taken to represent the income of the infant from the trust for the year concerned.

N.B. the income paid will be deemed to be that of the parent if the trust settlement was created by the parent and the child is under 18 and unmarried (s. 437, I.C.T.A. 1970).

Example 2—contingent interest

The share of F. Cater (an infant) in the income of a discretionary trust for 1985–86 is £1,000 (gross), of which the trustees have, in accordance with the provisons of the will, expended in cash £188 in maintenance and education.

Calculate the income tax repayment due to Cater assuming that he has no other income. The trustees may claim on the basis of Cater's income for 1985–86 being:

$$£188 \times \frac{100\%}{55\%} = £341.82 \text{ (gross).}$$

		£
Tax has been suffered on £342 at 45% (30% + 15%) ...		153.90
Cater's liability is:	£	
Total income	342	
Less: Personal allowance	2,205	
Taxable income	Nil	
Tax repayable		£153.90

In the case of accumulation trusts which are contingent on the individual reaching a specified age or marrying, personal allowances can be claimed up to 1968–69 on income accumulated up to the happening of the contingency (s. 228, Income Tax Act 1952).

§ 5.—SUBSCRIPTIONS TO CHARITIES

It is a common practice for subscribers to charities to sign an agreement (i.e. a deed of covenant) to pay their annual subscriptions for a period of more than three years, i.e., at *least, four annual payments* or until previous death of the subscriber. Payment is made in this manner since the subscriber is treated as making an annual payment (from which income tax is deducted) and the charity then reclaims the tax as itself being exempted from taxation.

Example 1

Generous makes a deed of covenant with a registered charity to make a payment which after deduction of tax equals £70.

In the year 1985–86 Generous will, on making the payment, complete form R.185E as follows:

	£
Gross payment	100
Tax witheld	30
Net payment	70

The charity can then reclaim the £30.

Relief for higher rate tax
Income tax relief at rates above basic rate will be allowed as far as payments do not exceed £10,000 in any one year (£5,000 for 1983–84 and 1984–85).

Example 2

K. King whose sole income is his salary of £2,500 per annum, has covenanted to pay such a sum as will leave a net sum of £56 per annum after deduction of Income Tax to a charity for a period of four years, or his life, whichever is the shorter. Show the tax payable by King in 1985–86:

(a) If he is single;
(b) If he is married.

To find the gross equivalent of the net sum when the basic rate is 30% it is necessary to work as follows:

$$\text{Gross equivalent} = \text{net sum} \times \frac{£1}{£1 - \text{basic rate}} = £56 \times \frac{100}{70} = £80$$

K. KING—STATEMENT OF INCOME TAX PAYABLE 1985–86

(a) Assuming he is single:

	£
Salary	2,500
Less: Personal allowance	2,205
Taxable income	£295

TAX PAYABLE

On £295 at 30%	£88.50

King will deduct £24 (i.e., £80 at 30%) when paying the charity, and it thus costs him £56 net to make the payment.

(b) Assuming he is married:

	£
Salary	2,500
Less: Personal allowance	3,455
Taxable income	Nil

King will pay the charity £56 (i.e., £80 less £24). In addition he must account to the Revenue for the tax deducted. That is to say, instead of suffering no tax he must pay £24 (see above). The cost to him is thus £80 (£56 plus £24).

Example 3

John Green covenants to pay a charity an annual subscription of £400 covenanting for four years from 1st May 1985 and is liable to pay some tax at 50%. The position for 1985–86 will be as follows:

	£	£
Gross covenant		400
Less Tax deducted and recovered by charity @ 30%	120	
Tax allowed in higher rates assessment, £400 @ 20%	80	200
Net cost to John Green		£200

In practice the deed is often arranged so that the payment is net of tax, and on receipt of the payment together with R. 185E the charity is able to make a repayment claim.

§ 6.—EXEMPTIONS OF CHARITIES FROM INCOME TAX (s. 360, I.C.T.A. 1970)

Institutions such as university colleges, public schools and religious and scientific institutions established in the United Kingdom for charitable purposes are exempted from tax on, *inter alia:*
(1) Rents and profits of lands, tenements, etc., under Schedule A;
(2) Interest, annuities, dividends or shares of annuities, under Schedules C and D;
(3) Annual payments under Schedule D;
(4) Profits from a trade carried on by the charity, where *either*: (i) the trade is exercised in the course of carrying out a primary object of the charity, or (ii) the work in connection with the trade is mainly carried on by the beneficiaries of the charity;
(5) Gains otherwise assessable to Capital Gains Tax. In each case the rents, interest, profits, etc., must be applied for charitable purposes only.

Claims for exemption or repayment under this section must be made within six years after the end of the year of assessment to which they relate.

§ 7.—CLERGYMEN AND MINISTERS OF RELIGION (s. 194, I.C.T.A. 1970)

When computing the Schedule E liability of a clergyman or minister of religion, expenses in connection with a property occupied by him from which to perform his duties that are made good to him will be disregarded except so far as they are attributable to any part of the premises which are let and for which he collects rent. Furthermore, the value to him of any expenses in connection with the provision of living accommodation for him in the premises is also disregarded (unless he is in director's or higher-paid employment).

Expenditure incurred by the clergyman or minister on rent, maintenance, repairs, insurance or management of the premises used mainly or substantially in the performance of his duties entitles the minister or clergyman to a deduction not exceeding *one quarter* of the expenditure incurred.

§ 8.—MUTUAL AND CO-OPERATIVE SOCIETIES (s. 345 and 346, I.C.T.A. 1970)

All societies registered under the Industrial and Provident Societies Acts, 1893 to 1928, such as a co-operative society, are assessed on the profits of their trading with members and non-members alike. Any discounts, rebates, dividends or bonuses granted to members or non-members on their transactions with the society (e.g., the Co-op "divi") are not deemed to be part of the recipient's income for Income Tax purposes.

A registered society must pay dividends, interest or bonuses on its share capital, mortgages, loans, deposits, etc., without deduction of tax, and the recipients will be assessed under Case III, Schedule D.

§ 9.—SUPERANNUATION FUNDS (ss. 19–26, F.A. 1970, previously s. 208, I.C.T.A. 1970, which was repealed from 6th April 1980)

It is beyond the scope of this book to consider these provisions in any detail or to comment on non-approved schemes, and the following notes are therefore a brief outline of the provisions relating to approved schemes.

Exemption from Income Tax is allowed in respect of income from investments (including dealings in financial futures) or deposits of an approved super-annuation fund, and the ordinary annual contributions of employer and employ-ees are allowed as expenses, for the year in which paid, in computing assessments under Cases I or II, Schedule D, or Corporation Tax, and Schedule E, respectively. An approved fund is also exempt from Capital Gains Tax. No allowance is made in respect of any contribution by an employee which is not an ordinary annual contribution. Such a contribution made by an employer will be allowed as an expense, though the Commissioners may direct that it shall be spread over a period of years.

It will satisfy the Commissioners that the fund is approved if:

- (*a*) the fund is *bona fide* established under irrevocable trusts in connection with some trade or undertaking carried on in the United Kingdom by a person residing therein;
- (*b*) the fund has for its sole purpose the provision of annuities for employees either on retirement at a specified age or on an earlier incapacity, or for widows, children or dependants on the death of the employee;
- (*c*) the employer is a contributor to the fund; and
- (*d*) the fund is recognised by both the employer and employees.

The Commissioners may, if they think fit, and subject to such conditions as they may think proper to impose, approve a fund, or any part of a fund, where the above conditions (*a*) to (*d*) are not wholly satisfied. Thus, they may approve when:

- (i) The rules of the fund provide for the return of contributions in certain contingencies; or
- (ii) The main, but not the sole, purpose of the fund is the provision of annuities; or
- (iii) The trade or undertaking is carried on only partly in the United Kingdom and by a person not residing therein.

The Regulations made by the Commissioners provide, *inter alia*, that application for the approval of any fund or any part of a fund for any year of assessment shall be made in writing before the end of that year by the trustees of the fund to the Inspector of Taxes for the district in which the office of the fund is situated or the fund is administered. Application must be supported by a copy of the instrument establishing the fund, two copies of the rules and the most recent accounts of the fund, and any other information which the Commissioners may reasonably require. The Commissioners have power to withdraw their approval in regard to any fund or part of a fund if the circumstances so warrant.

The Inland Revenue office dealing with the approval of pension schemes is the Superannuation Funds Office (S.F.O.), to which details of schemes should be submitted. The S.F.O. has produced a set of practice notes (IR20) which provide an extremely helpful guideline to occupational pension schemes, to which reference should be made.

REPAYMENT OF SUPERANNUATION CONTRIBUTIONS.

Where any contributions (including interest thereon, if any) are repaid to an EMPLOYEE during his lifetime, or where a lump sum is paid in commutation of or in lieu of an annuity, Income Tax on such repayment or payment shall (except in the case of employees whose employment was carried on abroad, or widows, children or dependants of such employees) be paid by the trustees of the fund at ten per cent. of the actual sum repaid. (Refer to S.F.O. Memoranda 54 and 64 dealing with cases where repayment of contributions is not allowed.)

Where contributions (including interest thereon, if any) are repaid to the EMPLOYER, the trustees shall deduct Income Tax therefrom at the basic rate in force for the year in which the repayment is made.

Dividends and other income from investments of a superannuation fund established under an irrevocable trust in connection with a trade carried on wholly or partly abroad and which has for its sole purpose the provision of superannuation benefits in respect of persons employed in the trade wholly outside the United Kingdom, will be exempt from income tax.

A "controlling director" (a director who controls over 5 per cent of the ordinary share capital of a company) is eligible for benefit under an approved pension scheme.

§ 10.—PURCHASED LIFE ANNUITIES (ss. 230 and 231, I.C.T.A. 1970)

This section provides that the capital element of a purchased life annuity (other than a retirement annuity), whenever purchased, is not treated as an income annuity or annual payment. The capital element is normally that part of a payment bearing the same ratio to the total payment as the value of the purchase price bears to the actuarial valuation of the payments. The capital element is constant throughout the period of payment being based on mortality tables at the commencing date of the annuity, and excludes any element of discounting.

Example

C. Carter in 1972 purchased for £2,000 a life annuity of £230. Assuming the capital element based on mortality tables at the commencing date and excluding any element of discounting is agreed at £200, compute the amount receivable by C. Carter in 1985–86. In 1985–86 C. Carter will receive a net amount of £221.00 computed as follows:

	£	£
Capital element of annuity		200.00
Balance of annuity.........................	30.00	
Less: Tax at 30%.........................	9.00	21.00
Net amount receivable.......................		£221.00

Note. The net amount receivable in future years will be affected only by a change in the rates of income tax to be deducted from the income element of £30 per annum.

§ 11.—BUILDING SOCIETY AND BANK ARRANGEMENTS (s. 343, I.C.T.A. 1970 AND s. 26, F.A. 1984)

Special arrangements exist with regard to the taxation of building societies, since, as a large proportion of their investors and borrowers are exempt from tax, deduction of tax from interest on deposits, mortgages, etc., would involve a large number of repayment claims from individual investors or borrowers.

With effect from 1984–85 the Treasury will by statutory instrument determine a rate which will be for the following year:
  (a) the reduced rate for building societies;
  (b) the composite rate for banks, etc. (see Chapter 9).

The main provisions affecting investors and borrowers are set out below. It is important to note that the provisions affect interest from banks, etc. for 1985–86 onwards.

Investors
  (1) Interest paid by the Society or Bank to its investors free of Income Tax. Although a recipient is required to include the amount received in his Income Tax Return, no Income Tax assessment is raised on him at the basic rate of tax nor is he entitled to any repayment of tax thereon. (Companies are, however, entitled to repayment.) Such interest is, however, assessable to higher rates of tax and the Investment Income Surcharge as though they were a net amount corresponding to a gross amount from which notional tax at the basic rate has been deducted. For

the purposes of life assurance relief and age allowance interest received, including the notional tax (i.e., the "gross") from building societies is included in ascertaining the total income from all sources. Furthermore, such interest is to be regarded as taxed income available to set-off against annual charges of the investor in the case of ss. 52 and 53, I.C.T.A. 1970 (payments out of profits or gains brought into charge to income tax). Only the net amount received can be taken into account for determining whether any sum is due to the Revenue. Interest must also be included as income of a dependent relative in computing the amount, if any, of the allowance for a dependent relative. Where a repayment of tax accrues to an individual, the notional tax on the interest received can be offset in the most favourable manner (see example below).

Example 1

A. Brown, who is aged 68 and single, has the following income for 1985–86:

	£
Taxed Dividends (including tax credit)	1,200
Building Society Interest.	140

It is required to show the amount of Income Tax recoverable by Brown for 1985–86. The claim that can be made by Brown in respect of 1985–86 is as follows:

	£	£
Taxed dividends		1,200
Building society interest.	140	
Add Notional tax.	60	200
		1,400
Less: Age allowance		2,690
		Nil

Tax repayable (*dividends only*): £1,200 at 30% = £360

Example 2

C. Charles, a single man, has an income in 1985–86 of £2,200 as follows:

	£
Dividends (including tax credit)	1,800
Building society interest.	400

His tax position will be as follows:

	£	£
Dividends		1,800
Building society interest.	400	
Add Notional tax.	171	571
		2,371
Less Personal allowance.		2,205
Taxable income.		£166

Tax payable:	£	£
On £166 at 30%...........................		49.80
Less Notional tax on building society interest		
(restricted to £166 at 30%).............	49.80	
Tax credits on dividends	540.00	589.80
Tax repayable		£540.00

(N.B. The building society interest is offset in priority to the dividends; hence only partial restriction on the repayment applies.)

Borrowers

Mortgage interest paid by the borrower to the Society or Bank before 1st April 1983 is paid without deduction of tax and is allowed as a deduction from his income for income tax purposes. For payments after 1st April 1983 and relief generally, see § 2.

§ 12.—VALUATION OF TRADING STOCK ON A DISCONTINUANCE OF TRADE (s. 137, I.C.T.A. 1970)

In order to ascertain the true profit that a trader makes from carrying on his business it is necessary to make adjustments for the stock on hand at the commencement and close of the period under review.

Where a trade is discontinued, the trading stock must be valued as follows for Income Tax purposes, no matter what method was used in the past:

(*a*) In the case of any trading stock:
(i) which is sold or transferred for valuable consideration to a person who carries on or intends to carry on a trade in the United Kingdom; *and*
(ii) the cost of which may be deducted by the purchaser as an expense in computing the profits or gains of that trade for Income Tax purposes; the stock is to be valued at the amount realised on sale or the value of the consideration given for the transfer.
(*b*) Any other trading stock (e.g., stock acquired by the purchaser as a fixed asset) is to be valued at the amount which it would have realised if it had been sold in the open market at the discontinuance of the trade.

For this purpose, "trading stock" is defined as property of any description which is either:
(i) property such as is sold in the ordinary course of the trade or would be so sold it were mature or if its manufacture, preparation or construction were complete; *or*
(ii) materials such as are used in the manufacture, preparation or construction of any property referred to in (i).

If any question arises under (*a*) above, it is to be determined for the purposes of both the trades concerned in the following manner:
(*a*) Where the same body of General Commissioners have jurisdiction with respect to *both* trades, the question is to be determined by them, *unless* all parties agree that it shall be determined by the Special Commissioners.
(*b*) In any other case the question is to be determined by the Special Commissioners.

These provisions apply in the case of a complete change of ownership and in the case of a partial change in a partnership except where notice is given for the continuance principles to be applied (see Chapter 3, § 8). They do *not*, however, apply where the trade of a single individual is discontinued by reason of his death.

Work in progress
Similar provisions apply to the valuation of work in progress at the discontinuance of a profession or vocation (s. 138, I.C.T.A. 1970).

§ 13.—DEBTS WRITTEN OFF (s. 136, I.C.T.A. 1970)

Where a trading deduction has been allowed, for a debt incurred in connection with the trade, then if the whole or part of the debt is subsequently released, the amount released is treated as a trading receipt in the period in which the release takes place.

Example

Absent acquires trading stock from Palmos Ltd for £10,000 during his year ended 31st March 1980. The £10,000 remains unpaid and Palmos Ltd decides to write-off and release Absent from his obligation to pay the outstanding sum on 15th March 1985. The debt release on 15th March 1985 will constitute a trading receipt during Absent's year ended 31st March 1985 and will be taxable accordingly.

§ 14.—SALE OF COPYRIGHTS AND COPYRIGHT ROYALTIES (ss. 389 and 390, I.C.T.A. 1970)

(1) SALE OF COPYRIGHTS FOR LUMP SUM
From the very nature of their profession, such persons as authors and playwrights are sometimes engaged for several years on a particular work, and if they are remunerated therefor by means of a lump sum payment for the copyright, their earnings may be of uneven incidence as between one year and another. Thus their earnings may be high in the year in which the lump sum payment is received, and low in the year (or years) in which the work was in progress. Such unevenness of earnings might penalise the author, playwright, etc. (particularly if he became liable to higher rates of tax in the year in which his earnings were high), as compared with what his liability to tax would have been if his earnings had been more evenly distributed over several years.
   Section 389, I.C.T.A. 1970, endeavours to alleviate the above hardship, and provides that where:
   (*a*) the author (this includes a joint author) of a literary, dramatic, musical or artistic work assigns the copyright therein wholly or partially, or grants an interest in the copyright by licence; and
   (*b*) the consideration for the assignment or grant consists wholly or partially of a lump sum payment (this expression includes an advance on account of royalties which is not returnable) the whole amount of which would, but for this section, be included in computing the amount of his profits or gains for a single year of assessment; and
   (*c*) the author was engaged on the making of the work for a period of more than 12 months,
the author may claim, not later than six years after the end of the year of assessment referred to in (*b*) above, to have the payment spread in the following manner for Income Tax purposes:
   (i) *If he was engaged on the making of the work for more than 12 months but not more than 24 months*—as if only one-half of the payment had been received on the actual date of receipt, and as if the other half had been received one year previously.
   (ii) *If he was engaged on the making of the work for more than 24 months*—as if only one-third of the payment had been received on the actual date

of receipt, and as if one-third had been received one year previously and the remaining one-third two years previously.

Assignment

Further relief is given by s. 390, I.C.T.A. 1970, where the copyright or interest is assigned more than ten years after the initial publication. The relief to be granted depends upon whether the copyright is assigned or granted for a period greater or less than six years.

Where the copyright is assigned or granted for a period of, or exceeding, six years, the amount will be treated as receivable in six equal instalments, at yearly intervals, commencing on the date of receipt. If the copyright is assigned or granted for a period of less than six years, the amount is treated as receivable in equal instalments over the number of whole years involved, but no relief is available if the copyright is assigned or granted for a period of less than two years.

A claim cannot be made under s. 390 if a prior claim in respect of the same payment has been made under s. 389.

Where the author permanently discontinues his profession, or dies, s. 390 provides that any subsequent instalments are treated as having been receivable together with the last instalment due before the discontinuance or death, unless the author (or his personal representatives) elects for the assessments to be recomputed as if the assignment had been for a lesser period ending with the day before the discontinuance or death. Such election must be made within two years of the discontinuance or death.

(2) COPYRIGHT ROYALTIES

The principle of spreading liability to taxation applies equally to any payment of or on account of royalties or sums payable periodically which become receivable within two years of the date when the work was first published, performed or exhibited, provided the author, etc., has spent more than one year on the production of the work. (The provisions are the same as for lump sum payments except that of course the relief available under s. 390 will not apply—since no assignment).

If the work took less than two years, one-half of the copyright royalties will be treated for taxation purposes as received on the day of actual receipt and the other half as having been received one year earlier. Where the work took more than two years, one-third of the copyright royalties will be treated as received on the day of actual receipt, one-third one year earlier and one-third two years earlier.

A claim in respect of such a periodical payment may be made at any time within eight years of the end of the year of assessment in which the work was first published, etc.

§ 15.—CAPITAL RECEIPTS FROM SALE OF PATENTS (ss. 380 and 381, I.C.T.A. 1970)

Where a person resident in the United Kingdom sells all or part of any patent rights and the net proceeds of the sale consist wholly or partly of a capital sum, he will be charged to tax thereon under Case VI of Schedule D, in *six equal sums*, for the year of assessment in which the sum is received by him and each of the five succeeding years of assessment.

The recipient of the capital sum may (by notice in writing to the Inspector not later than two years after the end of the year of assessment in which he received the said sum) alternatively elect that the whole sum shall be charged to tax for the year of assessment in which it was received.

Where the recipient of the capital sum had acquired the patent rights by purchase and the price paid by him consisted wholly or partly of a capital sum, he will be assessed on the capital sum received *less* the amount of the purchase price which was paid by him.*

Example

Modern Appliances prepares its accounts annually to 30th June. On 31st March 1980 it acquired patents, having ten years to run, at a cost of £1,000. The patents were sold outright by Modern Appliances on 30th April 1984, for £1,200.

The allowances and charges under the I.C.T.A. 1970 will be computed as follows:

	£
Cost of patents on 31st March 1980......................	1,000
1981–82 to 1984–85: writing-down allowances at £100 per annum	400
Unallowed expenditure...................	600
Less: Proceeds of sale................	1,200
Chargeable to tax as follows	(600)

	£	
1985–86: Balancing charge..................	400	
Capital profit......................	200	
		£600

Notes.—(1) The balancing charge is restricted to the amount of the writing-down allowances (£400) already granted in respect of these patents. (Refer to Chapter 5 for calculation of allowances)

(2) The capital profit of £200 will be assessable in equal sums over the six years 1984–85 (year of receipt) to 1989–90 inclusive.

Where the person in receipt of the capital sum for which a charge under s. 380 I.C.T.A. is applicable dies:

(*a*) no sums shall be chargeable for any period subsequent to the date of death, and

(*b*) the sums that would have been chargeable in periods following the date of death are charged in that year.

To prevent hardship by the application of this provision, the personal representatives may by notice (within 30 days of the issue of the assessment under this section) require that the tax assessed shall not be greater than that that would be payable had the capital sums been spread over the period to the date of death.

§ 16.—PATENT INCOME (ss. 383 and 384, I.C.T.A. 1970)

Income from patent rights is regarded as earned income in cases where the recipient actually devised (whether alone or jointly with any other person) the invention in respect of which the patent was granted.

Where a patentee receives royalties in respect of the user of a patent, over a period of six complete years or more, he may require that the Income Tax payable thereon shall be reduced to the amount which would have been payable by him if that royalty were spread equally over the six years up to and including the year

---

* But where, between the date of the purchase and the date of the sale, he has sold *part* of the patent rights and the proceeds of that sale consisted wholly or partly of a capital sum, such proceeds must be deducted from the above-mentioned purchase price in computing the amount on which he is chargeable under Case VI of Schedule D.

of receipt. Where the period of the user is less than six complete years, the spread, instead of being made over six years, is made over the number of complete years in the period of the user.

Example

R. Roberts receives £7,200 on 5th July 1985, in respect of the user of his patent by S. Snow for a period of eight years ending on that date.

If he so wishes, Roberts may claim that the royalty be spread equally over the six years ended on 5th July 1985, and not deemed all to have been received on that date.

§ 17.—SPECIAL ASSOCIATIONS, BODIES, SOCIETIES ETC.

For the tax treatment of these bodies, refer to Chapter 23.

§ 18.—UNDERWRITERS (s. 39 and Sch. 16, F.A. 1973)

Profits from underwriting transactions
Underwriting profits based on underwriting accounts of a Lloyds syndicate (a collection of individual "names"—see below) are assessed to tax as trading profits under Schedule D, Case 1, and are drawn up each calendar year.

Income is only treated as earned income in the case of *working* "names". (A *"name"* is an underwriting member on the list of participants in a syndicate at Lloyds.) To qualify as a working name a member must spend at least 75% of his time in the Room at Lloyds or within the office of an underwriting agent. Non working names make up the majority of members.

Non-underwriting profits of syndicate
Other income related to investment of the funds and investment of the "deposit" required by the name is unearned and liable to investment income surcharge. Gains realised by the sale of investments are subject to capital gains on the individual in the normal manner, except 30% capital gains tax is deducted by the syndicate managers.

Basis of assessment and payment of tax
The assessment for a tax year is based on the profits from the underwriting account ending in that year (e.g. profits for calendar year 1985 would be assessed for tax in 1985–86). No opening and closing rules apply.

The nature of the business means that profits cannot be determined for some while and the account is in practice closed at the end of the third year. Tax is only due one year and a day after closing the account year for earned income, and 23 months after for investment income (1st January and 1st December 1988 respectively for the account year 1985).

Losses
General trading loss provisions under s. 168 or 171, I.C.T.A. 1970 or s. 30, F.A. 1978 apply. However, s. 168 relief is available against income in the same or *preceding* year of assessment (instead of the same or following year).

Order of set-off is as follows;

	Non-working name *(income treated as unearned)*		*Working name* *(income treated as earned)*
Self:	(*a*) Investment income (*b*) Earned income	Self:	(*a*) Earned income (*b*) Unearned income
Spouse:	(*a*) Investment income (*b*) Earned income	Spouse:	(*a*) Earned income (*b*) Unearned income

Offset against the spouse's income is optional.

Special Reserve Fund, transfers and withdrawals (Schedule 10, I.C.T.A. 1970)
Amounts paid into a Special Reserve Fund as a safeguard against possible future
liabilities are treated as an annual charge on which 30% basic rate tax has been
deducted. Relief is therefore available from higher rate tax and investment income
surcharge. The maximum transfer (after basic rate grossing-up) is £7,000 or 50%
of the member's underwriting profits. Withdrawals from the fund grossed up
accordingly consitute additions to income for higher rate and I.I.S. purposes.

§19.—DEEP-DISCOUNT SECURITIES (s. 36, F.A. 1984)

Securities issued after 13th March 1984 at a "deep discount" are liable to income
tax on redemption or sale.
A deep discount is a discount which:
  (a) represents more than 15% of the amount payable on redemption of the
      security, or
  (b) is 15% or less but exceeds half $Y\%$ of the amount payable (where Y is
      the number of complete years between the date of issue of the security
      and the redemption date).
      (The effect of this provision is that the discount cannot be greater than
      $\frac{1}{2}\%$ per annum.)

Example 1

Freebody issues stock on 10th April 1984 at a discount of 10% redeemable:
  (i) on 10th April 1990
  (ii) on 10th April 2005
(i) The stock redeemable on 10th April 1990 will be deep discount, since $Y = 6\%$ and
$\frac{1}{2}Y = 3\%$ (the discount being 10% is therefore greater).
(ii) The stock redeemable on 10th April 2005 will not be deep discount since 21
years $\times \frac{1}{2}\% = 10\frac{1}{2}\%$, which exceeds the discount given.

Securities for these purposes are any security other than:
  (i)   shares
  (ii) securities issued where the amount payable is determined by reference
        to the movement in the R.P.I.
  (iii) securities which fall within the meaning of 'distribution' for the purpose
        of s. 233 2(C), I.C.T.A. 1970.
Income tax is assessed on such deep-discount securities under Schedule D, Case
III or Case IV (where the source is offshore) by reference to the accrued income
attributable to the period between acquisition and disposal. *The assessment
notwithstanding the normal Schedule D, Case III or IV rules is on an actual basis.*
The accrued income is the sum of the 'income elements' for each 'income period'
in the period of ownership.

Income element
This is calculated by reference to the following formula:
$$\frac{A \times B}{100} - C$$
where A is the adjusted issue price (i.e. the issue price plus any income elements
        for previous periods—this would only apply where acquisition occurred
        after issue).
      B is the yield to maturity (redemption).
      C is the amount of interest, if any, attributable to the income period.
(The yield to maturity is the percentage rate at which the issue price would need
to grow on a compound basis over the years to equal the redemption price.)

Income period

The income period is:

    (i) where the security carries interest, any period to which a payment of interest falls, and

    (ii) in any other case, any year ending immediately before the anniversary of the issue of the security or such lesser period where the redemption date falls within a year of the last anniversary.

The income element for any period (the short period) falling within an incme period is then simply calculated pro rata to the length of the short period.

Any excess receivable over the accrued income is subject to Capital Gains Tax.

Example 2

Rupert acquires securities on 15th June 1984 issued by Bear Ltd. at a 10% discount. The total purchase price is £9,000. The securities are redeemable on 15th June 1986 and pay no interest. The yield to maturity is 4.5% (say). Calculate the tax liability of Rupert assuming that he sells the securities for £9,500 on 15th June 1985.

The income element is, since we are dealing with one period exactly:

$$\frac{90 \times 4.5}{100} \dots\dots\dots\dots\dots\dots\dots\dots\dots\dots\dots\dots\dots\dots = 4.05$$

The total income is therefore £405 (since £10,000 of securities are held).
Rupert will therefore be taxed:

	£
1985–86 D(III)............................	405

and to Capital Gains Tax (as appropriate)
based on:

		£
Cost..		9,000
Proceeds	9,500	
Less assessed to D(III)	405	9,095
Gain		95

Anti avoidance (s. 46 and Schedule 11 F.A. 1985)

Provisions have been included in the Finance Act 1985 to counter the device of a company acquiring securities and issuing its own deep discount stock in place of the securities acquired, so as to enable the holder of the deep discount stock to defer his tax liability. With effect from 19th March 1985 stock issued in such a manner will be taxed on an annual basis.

§ 20.—OFFSHORE "ROLL-UP" FUNDS (ss. 90–95, F.A. 1984)

Gains attributable to funds invested offshore are subject to income tax (under Schedule D, Case VI) with effect from 1st January 1984 where the fund is a non-qualifying fund (as defined).

Prior to this date "income" is taxed as a capital gain.

The income element is only taxed on receipt of the funds from the fund.

Example

Egbert invested £6,000 in an offshore roll-up fund on 1st January 1983. On 1st July 1985 Egbert realises his investment for £9,000. The value of his part of the fund on 1st January 1984 was £7,800.

Egbert will be taxed in 1985–86 as follows:

	£
Schedule D, Case VI (£9,000 – £7,800)	1,200
To CGT (£7,800 – £6,000)	1,800

§ 21.—BOND WASHING

Securities transferred after 27th February 1986 cum div will be subject to income tax on the income element which was previously treated as part of the capital gain.

The interest element is treated as accruing on a day-to-day basis and taxed accordingly.

§ 22.—DEDUCTION OF TAX WHERE RATE CHANGES

Where tax has been legally deducted from interest, etc., at a rate different from that ultimately in force for the year of assessment concerned, the method of effecting the necessary adjustments will depend on whether or not the interest is paid out of profits or gains brought into charge to tax.

The following is a brief summary of the position:

	INTEREST, ETC., PAID OUT OF PROFITS OR GAINS BROUGHT INTO CHARGE.	INTEREST, ETC., NOT PAID OUT OF PROFITS OR GAINS BROUGHT INTO CHARGE.
(a) *Where rate is increased.*	Increased deduction from next payment; if no subsequent payment, the amount not deducted may be recovered from the recipient.	Increased deduction from next payment; if no subsequent payment, paying agent must supply Commissioners of Inland Revenue with lists of recipients' names and amounts paid to them, and recipients then assessed under Case VI, Schedule D in respect of the under-deduction.
(b) *Where rate is reduced.*	Decreased deduction from next payment; if no subsequent payment, the excess deduction should be made good by the payer.	Recipients may claim repayment of excess tax deducted.

Example

The rate of tax for 1978–79 was 33 per cent, whereas the rate for 1979–80 is 30 per cent. On 30th April 1979 Excelsior Ltd paid a half-year's Debenture Interest and deducted Income Tax at 33 per cent. When paying the following half-year's interest on 31st October 1979, Excelsior Ltd should deduct tax at 27 per cent (i.e., the correct deduction of 30 per cent. less 3 per cent. to compensate for the previous over-deduction).

§ 23.—METHOD OF MAKING CLAIMS

In making a claim for repayment of tax, the appropriate form should be obtained from the Inspector of Taxes, and duly completed. In many cases a statement of the total statutory income from all sources for the year in respect of which the claim is made is required.

Vouchers proving the payment of tax on the various forms of income must be submitted with the claim. The following is a brief summary of the vouchers required.

INCOME	VOUCHERS REQUIRED
From Trade or Profession, Letting of Property, Occupation of Woodlands Bank or other interest received "gross".	The Collector's receipts for tax paid under Schedules A, B or D.
Dividends, Interest, etc., received after deduction of tax.	The dividend counterfoil or a certificate from the person deducting the tax.
Dividends received by means of "coupons."	A certificate from the Bank through which the coupons were cashed, or from the agents paying the coupons.

The claim should be sent to the Inspector for the district in which the taxpayer carries on business or, in the event of there being no business, for the district in which he resides.

When the tax is payable by instalments and the first instalment has been paid but the second instalment is still outstanding, a claim will first have the effect of reducing or cancelling the amount of tax payable on the second instalment before a repayment is made of tax already paid on the first instalment.

Where annual charges are payable during the year of assessment, tax at the basic rate on the full amount thereof must be retained in charge.

A taxpayer can make interim claims for repayment of tax throughout the year instead of waiting until the end of the year, e.g., when he is not liable to tax by virtue of the amount of his net total income and tax is deducted at the basic rate from dividends, he can reclaim such tax periodically throughout the year.

There is a special procedure in respect of the repayment of tax which has been over-deducted under Schedule E.

12. Estates and Settlements

TAXATION OF THE ESTATE

Introduction
This chapter deals with the somewhat complicated legislation concerning the tax treatment of:
    (i) The estate of a person following death and
    (ii) Settlements made by an individual either during lifetime or on death.
These items are separately dealt with below.

THE TREATMENT OF THE ESTATE FOLLOWING DEATH

§ 1.—POINTS TO BE CONSIDERED ON A PERSON'S DEATH

INCOME TO DATE OF DEATH
When preparing the return of the deceased's income to the date of death, the personal representatives would be well advised to obtain from the deceased's Inspector of Taxes a copy of the last return submitted by him. This will ensure, so far as possible, that no items are omitted, but it also ensures that assets revealed by the Income Tax Return are shown in the Inland Revenue Affidavit for capital transfer tax purposes.

The rules of apportionment do not apply to income tax as they do to capital transfer tax. Thus, whilst for capital transfer tax purposes dividends received after death are apportioned on a time basis, the part prior to death being regarded as capital of the estate and that after death as income of any life-tenant, no such apportionment is made for income tax purposes. Thus, if A. Arnold died on 5th June 1985, his sole source of income being a government security paying interest quarterly on 5th January, 5th April, 5th July and 5th October, he would have no income for tax purposes for 1985–86, and hence no repayment claim could be made to take advantage of any personal allowances of the deceased.

The position in the year of death may be summarised as follows:
    (i) *Schedule A:* The amount to be included is the amount of rents due less payments made in the period 6th April to the date of death.
    (ii) *Schedule B:* The Annual Value of any property is apportioned on a day-to-day basis, that from the 6th April preceding death to the date of death being income of the deceased. Thus, if woodlands of Annual Value £60 were occupied by a person who died on 5th November 1985, the 1985–86 Schedule B assessment upon him to the date of death would be seven-twelfths of £60, i.e., £35.
    (iii) *Schedule D, Cases I and II:* The cessation provisions will apply, the assessment for the final year being on an actual basis, and those for the penultimate and pre-penultimate years being subject to adjustment to actual at the option of the Inland Revenue.

    Where, however, the widow of the deceased succeeds to the business, the Inland Revenue will, by concession (A7–1980) continue the normal preceding year basis throughout. The assessment for the year of death will then require to be apportioned between deceased and his widow on a time basis. It is however open to the widow to claim the statutory basis.

This concession also applies if a deceased wife's business passes to her husband.

Concession A8–1980 allows brought forward capital allowances to be set against the profits of the final year of trading in priority to current allowances. The current allowances are then available for a loss relief claim under ss. 168 and 169 I.C.T.A. 1970 whereas they would otherwise have been carried forward and therefore wasted.

(iv) *Schedule D, Case III:* The cessation provisions will apply, the assessment for the final year being on an actual basis, and that for the penultimate year being subject to adjustment to actual at the option of the Inland Revenue.

As regards bank interest, National Savings Bank Interest, etc., only the interest which has been credited to the account to the last due date for applying for interest should be included in the return, and not the interest accrued to the date of death. Frequently, however, interest up to the date of death is credited to the account and the item is thus "apportioned" for tax purposes.

(v) *Schedule D, Cases IV and V:* As Case III.

(vi) *Schedule D, Case VI:* The most common type of income met with under this Case is profits from furnished lettings, and the assessments in respect of these sources of income are based on rents arising less payments made in the period from 6th April to the date of death.

Underwriting commissions are treated in the same way as Schedule E income (see below).

(vii) *Schedule E:* The amount to be included is the amount of income earned for the period to the date of death, whether or not this was paid to the deceased during his lifetime.

(viii) *Capital Gains Tax.* The amount to be included is the net gains of the deceased in respect of disposals of chargeable assets in the period 6th April to date of death.

(ix) *Dividends.* The amount of dividends received before the death is included as income of the deceased. Dividends received after death are income of the estate, even if they accrued before the death.

(x) *Interest, etc. taxed at source.* The position is similar to that applying for dividends.

(xi) *Charges on income.* The amount of such charges as mortgage interest, bank interest and annuities to the last due of payment should be regarded as applicable to the deceased.

(xii) *Allowances.* Personal allowances are not apportionable and therefore the full annual reliefs are given in respect of the period to the date of death. In the case of a married man, the full higher personal allowance will be given for this period and the widow will be entitled to a single personal allowance in respect of the period from the date of her husband's death to the following 5th April, and widow's bereavement allowance.

The position is different when the wife dies; in the year of his wife's death the widower is entitled to the higher personal allowance for the complete year and in the return of his income for that year he should include his wife's income up to the date of her death. He cannot claim housekeeper allowance for the period from the wife's death. (*Rossi v. Blunden* (1933).)

A surviving wife could, however, claim housekeeper allowance in addition to the other personal allowances for the period from the date of her husband's death, if she was otherwise so entitled.

(xiii) *Receivable annuities.* If the deceased is in receipt of an annuity which ceases on his death, and is expressed to accrue from day to day, the accrued proportion due from the last due date of payment is not his income for taxation purposes as it did not come to him during his lifetime. (*Bryan* v. *Cassin* (1942).)

(xiv) *Life tenancy*. If the deceased was the life tenant of an estate, the accrued income from the last payment up to the date of death is income of the estate (as for receivable annuities) (*Wood* v. *Owen* (1940)).

DUTIES OF PERSONAL REPRESENTATIVES

When a person dies his property passes not to the intended beneficiaries or legatees under his will as on intestacy. Instead it rests (albeit temporarily) in the hands of his personal representatives. Any liabilities or obligations upon the deceased which do not cease on his death also pass to the personal representatives. Personal representatives is a term which includes executors appointed under a will as well as administrators appointed (on the intestacy of the deceased) under letters of administration granted by the Court.

The duty of the personal representatives is, broadly, to collect in all the deceased's property, pay off his debts and to distribute the residue amongst the beneficiaries and legatees.

Personal representatives are liable to account for any *income tax liability* of the deceased person. They must make returns to the date of death, are assessable to tax on his behalf for the period prior to death, and liable to pay any income tax assessed upon the deceased out of the assets of the estate.

However, if they should neglect or refuse to make a payment of income tax, the Revenue can proceed against them for the collection and recovery of the unpaid tax, just as they can against any other defaulting taxpayer.

The usual time limits apply, except that any assessments must be made not later than the end of the third year of assessment after that in which the death occurred. Thus, if the death occurred on 24th December 1985 (that is, in the year 1985–86) any assessments on the deceased's income must be made before 6th April 1989.

Assessments made because of fraud, wilful default or neglect by the deceased can be made upon the personal representatives. However, such assessments can only be made in respect of years of assessment ending within six years before his death. Such assessments must also be made before the end of the third year of assessment after that in which the death occurred.

HUSBAND'S RIGHT TO DISCLAIM TAX LIABILITY ON DECEASED WIFE'S INCOME
(s. 41 I.C.T.A. 1970)

A husband has the right to disclaim responsibility for unpaid tax relating to his wife's income. By doing this he is making the liability a charge against his wife's estate and thereby relief is obtained for capital transfer tax. The liability on the wife's income is calculated as if an election for separate assessment had been in force (unless it already is). The disclaimer which has to be made in writing, must be notified to the Inspectors within two months of the granting of probate or within such longer period as her executors or administrators allow.

If the husband himself has also died, his personal representatives can make the disclaimer.

There is no equivalent provision for a wife (or her personal representatives) to disclaim tax liabilities on her husband's income because such a liability would automatically fall upon his estate.

WIFE'S INCOME

In the case of a deceased person who was a married man, the liability to account for his income tax liability to the date of death covers that of both the husband and of his wife living with him prior to his death, so that tax on the wife's income for the period to the date of death must also be paid by the personal representatives.

§ 2.—INCOME OF THE ADMINISTRATION PERIOD (ss. 426 to 433, I.C.T.A. 1970)

In order to review the position it is necessary to introduce a number of technical terms connected with the administration of the estate of a deceased person.

Whether a deceased person left a will stating how he wished his property (in the widest sense) to be disposed of, or died intestate (without making a will) it is possible to distinguish between two basic types of gift:

(*a*) *legacies* (termed "devises" if they involve land) which are gifts of some article, property, or sum of money; and

(*b*) *residuary gifts*, i.e. those of the whole or part of the balance of the estate after paying the debts, expenses of administration and legacies (or devises).

Upon the death of a person intestate the disposition of his estate is governed by statutory provisions. These provide for a statutory legacy to the widow (or widower) of the deceased (if any), and for the residue to be paid to, or held on behalf of, his nearest relatives, e.g. his widow and children.

Having determined the taxation liabilities of the deceased to the date of his death, the next consideration is the taxation position relating to the period during which the personal representatives are administering the estate to the point where they can say the amount of residue has been ascertained.

During the administration period (i.e. until all the assets of the deceased's estate have been gathered in, and all debts and death duties paid and the net residue of the estate determined) any income arising is deemed to be that of the beneficiaries for higher rate tax and investment income surcharge. Income tax at basic rate is assessed upon the personal representatives, and payments to the beneficiaries are made net of income tax at basic rate.

Personal representatives

Personal representatives as such are *not liable* to the higher rates of tax on income received by them but they must account to the Inland Revenue for all Income Tax at the basic rate payable in respect of income received by them.

The exemption from Income Tax of the first £70 of National Savings Bank interest is not extended to personal representatives. Accordingly, they should state clearly on the form (R. 185 E) issued to beneficiaries the amount of such interest comprised in the beneficiaries' income. The reason for this is that the beneficiary may already be in receipt of such interest in excess of £70 on his own account, but if not, he can claim repayment of income tax on production of the form R. 185 E.

Personal representatives as such cannot claim personal allowances and reliefs but they may claim other reliefs such as losses, expenditure on agricultural properties, void relief, etc.

It is important to understand the distinction between personal representatives (which includes executors and administrators) on the one hand and trustees on the other in order to appreciate the methods by which different classes of beneficiaries are assessed on the income received by them from an estate.

The income of the estate which comes to the personal representatives in that capacity is the income of the executors. Income which comes to trustees is income of the beneficiaries who have a vested interest the moment it is received by the trustees (*Cobbett* v. *C.I.R.* (1942)).

The difference between absolute, vested, contingent and limited interests can be said to be as follows:

Distinctions between interests in the estate

(i) An *absolute* interest in the residue of an estate is an interest that is complete and unconditional. In other words, the beneficiary has the right, on completion of the administration of the estate, to payment of the capital of the residue of that estate (either directly, or indirectly via the trustees).

(ii) A *limited* interest is an interest in the residue of an estate (in the period in which a beneficiary has an interest which is not an absolute interest) where the beneficiary has the right, on completion of the administration of the estate, to payment of the income from the residue (either directly or indirectly, via a trustee).

(iii) A vested interest is a present fixed right of future enjoyment or other future interest which does not depend upon an uncertain period or event.

(iv) A contingent interest is an interest to take effect either on a dubious and uncertain person or upon a dubious and uncertain event. A contingent interest becomes a vested interest when the contingency has happened.

So far it has been assumed that the deceased disposed on his whole interest in his estate (i.e., his possessions) immediately, either as legacies (or devises) or residuary gifts. But this is not always the case, for many people create by their wills what are termed trusts, i.e., arrangements whereby property is handed over to the care of one or more persons, known as trustees, to be applied for the benefit of some person (or persons) called the *cestui que trust* (or *cestuis que trustent* if more than one).

Frequently a person is to have the enjoyment of the income from the property during his lifetime; he is then said to have a life interest in the property. Where the Will directs that the property held in trust (i.e., the trust fund) shall on the cessation of the limited interest (e.g., the life interest) go on to some other person, that person is said to have a remainder and referred to as the remainderman. The will may also make provision for the payment of an annuity for the duration of the life of the donee, or for some shorter period. Such a donee is termed an annuitant.

Once the fund has been ascertained from which a life-tenant is to receive income, with remainder over to a stated person or persons, both the life-tenant and the remainderman have *vested* interests. *Vested* and *absolute interests* it should be noted are not synonymous for under no circumstances could the life tenant be said to have an absolute interest. The life-tenant's interest is not complete as the right is only to the income of the fund.

Executor or trustee

It is now necessary to determine when a person is an executor and when a trustee and at what point his capacity changes from that of executor to that of trustee. Generally speaking, during the period of administration until ascertainment of residue his position is that of an executor, but on ascertainment of residue his capacity changes to that of trustee. At the point where the executor gives his assent to a legacy he becomes a trustee to the legatee. However, if the legacy is a pecuniary legacy, the amount of the legacy must have been appropriated to a separate fund capable of identification.

A specific legacy, i.e., one of a specific asset such as "my £5,000 holding of $3\frac{1}{2}$ per cent War Loan" or "my cow Sally" carries with it the net income earned by its subject-matter from the date of the testator's death. In the case of a *specific legacy* the legatee has a vested interest in that property from the death of the deceased which becomes absolute upon the assent of the Executor. Accordingly all the income arising from the property comprised in the legacy will be the income of the beneficiary from the date of death.

In the case of other legacies a vested interest in the property cannot arise until such time as the property comprised in the legacy is identified by appropriation to a specific fund. The income from the property prior to the appropriation is *not* the income of the legatee.

Whether or not the income is received in the capacity of executor or trustee also determines whether expenses are allowable deductions. If these are incurred as Executor they are deductible, if incurred as Trustee they are not deductible.

As income which it is the duty of the trustees to pay over to the beneficiary is income of the beneficiary at its inception, income to which the beneficiary is entitled is his income whether he receives it or not and he cannot avoid it falling into his total income merely by refusing to accept it. Similarly sums which the beneficiary is entitled to have applied for his benefit are to be included in his total income.

Specific legatees

Usually some time will elapse between the death of the deceased and the personal representatives giving their assent to a specific legacy. However the income is nevertheless related back to the date of death. If the deceased, in his will, expressly excludes the Apportionment Act 1870, the whole of the income arising from the specific legacy due and payable after death is income of the legatee. If the Apportionment Act 1870 is not excluded then the proportion accrued due up to the date of death will not pass to the legatee and accordingly it will not be included as his income for assessment.

The calculations required to determine the income accrued to the date of death are more laborious than complex. A detailed discussion thereof is, however, outside the scope of this book.

Pecuniary legatees

A pecuniary legacy, simply stated, is a legacy of a certain sum in cash and by its nature no income is normally produced by such a legacy. However, the deceased may have stipulated that the legacy is to be paid at some future time. If a fund is to be set aside to meet the legacy, the legacy will carry the income of this fund which will be accumulated up to the time when it is handed over to the legatee as accumulated income, which is now liable to higher rate tax and investment income surcharge.

If no such fund is set aside then the income from the sum ultimately payable falls into residue and will form income of the residuary beneficiaries.

Whether or not a fund is to be set aside to meet the pecuniary legacy will depend on the terms of the will and the taxation position of the accumulated income depends upon the status of the beneficiary. If the beneficiary has a vested interest in the legacy and only the payment is deferred then the income is the beneficiary's for taxation purposes, but if the interest is contingent it is not the beneficiary's income for tax purposes.

Example 1

A gift of £1,000 to my son, John, to be paid to him on attaining 18 years of age is clearly a gift now to be paid over later and John has a vested interest, and will be taxable on any income arising from the fund set aside to meet the gift, year by year.

Example 2

A gift of £1,000 to be paid to my son if he should attain the age of 18 years, is a gift contingent upon his attaining 18 years and the income from any fund set aside to meet the gift is therefore accumulated and paid to John, if and when he attains 18 years of age. He is not liable to tax on that income year by year.

Annuities

FROM RESIDUARY ESTATE

Where a simple annuity is given by will the personal representative paying the annuity is empowered to deduct Income Tax at the basic rate, so that the annuitant actually receives a net sum after the deduction of tax. Thus, if the basic rate of tax is 30 per cent. and the will provides for payment of an annuity of £100 per annum, the annuitant will receive £70 (i.e., £100 less £100 at 30 per cent) together with an Income Tax Certificate showing: Gross Income £100; Tax £30; net £70; and will include £100 as part of his total income for tax purposes.

"TAX FREE" ANNUITIES

Where a will provides for payment "of such a sum as after deduction of income tax at the basic rate will amount to £x", this will represent the net sum to be received by the beneficiary, and the income tax certificate will read, if the payment specified is one of "such a sum as after deduction of income tax at the basic rate will amount to £70": gross income £100; tax £30; net £70; the net income being grossed up at the basic rate in order to find the gross. Any refund of tax which the annuitant receives from the Inland Revenue because of the annuity will belong to him, just as would any refund from that referred to in the preceding paragraph.

The position becomes rather more complicated where the words used in the bequest indicate that the payment is to be free of the annuitant's *individual* liability to income tax, for the annuitant is then liable to refund to the trustees such portion of his personal reliefs, in terms of tax, as the amount of the annuity bears to his total income for tax purposes (*Re Pettit, le Fevre* v. *Pettit* (1922)).

The following words have been held to bring an annuity within this rule: "to be paid free of all duties and free of Income Tax at the current rate for the time being deductible at source"; "free from Income Tax at the current rate for the time being deductible at source"; and "such a sum in every year as after deduction of Income Tax for the time being payable in respect thereof will leave a clear sum of £x".

Example

A single person has the following income for 1985–86:

	£
Tax-free Annuity under brother's will.	1,750
Dividends (including tax credit)	4,000
Untaxed Interest	2,000

The Income Tax refund would be calculated as follows:

	Income £	Tax credit £
Tax-free annuity grossed up at 30%	2,500	750.00
Dividends	4,000	1,200.00
Untaxed interest	1,000	—
	7,500	1,950.00
Less: Personal allowance	2,205	
Taxable income	5,295	
Less On taxable income, £5,295 at 30%		1,588.50
Repayment		£361.50

The refund to the trustees of the brother's estate would be calculated as follows:

Cash value of allowances: £2,205 at 30% = £661.50

$$\frac{2,500}{7,500} \times £661.50 = £220.50$$

Out of his repayment amounting to £361.50 the annuitant would pay £220.50 to the Trustees and retain the balance himself.

The refund to the Trustees is treated as trust income of the year in which it is received. For this purpose it is grossed up at the basic rate of tax. In the above case, the trust income for 1986–87 would be increased by: gross £314, tax £94, net £220 (assuming a basic rate of 30% for 1986–87).

Where an annuity is directed to be paid out of capital (e.g., upon there being a deficiency of income) the trustees must deduct tax at the basic rate of income tax (under s. 53, I.C.T.A. 1970), and the gross amount of the annuity will form part of the annuitant's income for the year in the normal way. The trustees must then hand over to the Inland Revenue tax on the annuity under s. 53.

PRE-WAR "TAX-FREE" ANNUITIES (s. 422, I.C.T.A. 1970)
To alleviate the burden upon trust funds from which "tax-free" annuities are paid under deeds made before 3rd September 1939, a special relief applies. The effect is:

(i) The annuitant receives only the appropriate fraction of the stated sum, the fraction being $\dfrac{100-30}{72.5}$ when basic rate is 30%;

(ii) The gross amount of the annuity is found by applying the 1938–39 rates of tax to the full stated amount of the annuity;

(iii) The refund to the trustees is calculated at the 1938–39 tax rates and reliefs, and $\dfrac{100-30}{72.5}$ of the sum obtained is paid to the trustees.

ANNUITIES PURCHASES FOR A CAPITAL SUM (s. 230, I.C.T.A. 1970)
If the will provides for an annuity to be purchased, the capital sum provided is used to purchase the annuity. The annuity is paid to the beneficiary, who is liable to tax thereon.

Section 230 I.C.T.A. 1970 provides that any annuity within its scope is to be regarded as partly income and partly capital, and the capital element is not subject to tax. Certain types of annuity are excluded. These are:

(i) an annuity which, apart from s. 230 would have to be regarded as containing a capital element;

(ii) an annuity which has been granted as a result of the annuitant making payments which have ranked as life insurance premiums or pension contributions;

(iii) an annuity purchased in pursuance of any direction in a will or settlement;

(iv) an annuity which is in fact a pension.

Residuary legatee having a limited interest (ss. 426 and 431, I.C.T.A. 1970)

In the period from the date of death to the completion of the administration of the estate ("the administration period") the tax position of a beneficiary having a limited interest in the residue of the estate is as described below. Any sums received by persons with a *limited interest* in the residue of the estate (e.g., by a life tenant), between the date of death and the completion of the administration of the estate are treated as income of the year of assessment in which they are paid. Any sum paid after the interest ceased (e.g. after the death of the life tenant) is treated as income of the last year in which the interest subsisted. As the income will have suffered tax at the basic rate, it must be grossed up.

On the completion of the administration, the total amount received during the administration period is deemed to have accrued from day to day over that period, and to have been paid to the beneficiary as it accrued due and treated as the income of the beneficiary for the year of assessment in which it is deemed to have been paid. When the actual figures are known, adjustments may be made to assessments at any time before the end of the third year following the year of assessment in which the administration was completed.

Example 1

P. Pidgeon died on 5th October 1982, and the residue of his estate was ascertained and the administration of his estate completed on 5th January 1985. S. Snipe, who is life tenant of the residue, received the following amounts during the administration period:

	£
31st December 1983	94
1st May 1984	94
31st December 1984	94
1st May 1985	245
31st December 1985	490
5th January 1986	1,684
	£2,700

Provisonal assessments would be:

    1983–84   £94 grossed up at 30% = £134.
    1984–85   £188 grossed up at 30% = £268.

These would be adjusted on the coming to the end of the administration to the following (working in months for purposes of demonstration):

Year	Period	Months	Proportion of £2,700	£	Grossed up at	£ (nearest)
1983–84	5th October 1983 to 5th April 1984.	6	6/27	600	30%	867
1984–85	6th April 1984 to 5th April 1985.	12	12/27	1,200	30%	1,714
1985–86	6th April 1985 to 5th January 1986.	9	9/27	900	30%	1,286
		27		£2,700		

Foreign source

Income from a foreign estate is deemed paid gross and charged to income tax under Case IV, Schedule D in the hands of the beneficiary: if any of the income has borne U.K. income tax the assessment is reduced to that extent.

Example 2

Partridge is a beneficiary of a foreign estate. The total income of the estate is £1,800, of which £600 has borne U.K. Income Tax.

The Case IV, Schedule D assessment on Partridge is thus:

	£
Gross income of estate	1,800
Less: subject to U.K. Income Tax	600
Case IV, Schedule D	1,200

Partridge is also deemed to receive a net payment of £420 (£600 − 30%). In his tax return this payment will be grossed up.

Residuary legatee having an absolute interest (ss. 427 and 431, I.C.T.A. 1970)

In the administration period the position of a beneficiary having an absolute interest in the residue of an estate is as described below.

Where a person is entitled to an absolute interest in the residue (i.e., to the whole or part of both income and capital) it is necessary to ascertain the income from residue for each year of assessment during which the administration continues. The residuary legatee's share (the whole if he is sole residuary legatee) is income in his hands for tax purposes.

Residuary income for this purpose is found by deducting from the aggregate gross income of the estate for the year of assessment:

    (i) Any annual interest, or other annual payments, forming a charge on residue (e.g., an annuity charged on residue);

    (ii) Expenses incurred in the management of the income which are a proper charge on income (or would be but for a contrary provision in the will);

    (iii) Any income of the estate to which a specific legatee or devisee is entitled.

If the deductions allowable are greater than the gross income of the estate during any particular year the excess may be deducted from the income of the preceding or any subsequent year. Expenses particularly include testamentary and administration expenses and debts *properly payable out of residue* together with interest on those debts. It is important to note that if such expenses are not charged primarily and exclusively against residue they are not allowable.

Since the amount due to the residuary legatee cannot be exactly determined until the residue is ascertained, provision is made for payments on account to be grossed up, and regarded as income of the year in which paid, and for adjustment on the completion of the administration in the same manner as was described in the case of a limited interest. Note however that the beneficiary is deemed to receive the income of each year on an actual basis and not, as for a limited interest, on a day-to-day accruals basis over their whole period.

Once the residue has been ascertained, the rules explained above cease to operate. The trustees of the estate must account for tax on the income, deducting tax from payments made to beneficiaries. It is the practice of the Inland Revenue to treat as the beneficiary's income the actual amount payable to him, grossed at the basic rate, or his proportionate share of the statutory income of the trust, whichever is the lower.

By concession (A13–1980) deficiencies (i.e. where expenses exceed income of a particular year) are allowed as a deduction in computing the income. Income from a foreign estate is dealt with in the same manner as for a limited interest.

A further concession (A14–1980) allows a beneficiary who is not resident and not ordinarily resident to make various claims (listed below) as though the income had arisen to him directly. The claims (which must be made within three years after the tax year in which the administration is completed, and six years after the tax year in which the income arose, whichever is the later) are:

Section 27, I.C.T.A. 1970	Personal relief for non-residents
Section 99, I.C.T.A. 1970	Exemption for non-residents from tax on income for certain U.K. government securities
Sections 100 and 159, I.C.T.A. 1970	Exemption for non-residents from tax on income tax from overseas securities
Double taxation agreements	

Relief from excess liability for capital transfer tax paid on accrued income (s. 430, I.C.T.A. 1970)

The whole of the income received and due and payable after death, is income of an absolute residuary beneficiary whether or not part accrued due prior to the death. However, this income was an asset of the deceased's estate, and thus a beneficiary paying higher rates of income tax and investment income surcharge (*excesss liability*) would find that his total liabilities on such income exceeded the amount of the income as follows:

	£	£
Accrued income		100.00
Income tax thereon at 60%	60.00	
Capital Transfer Tax thereon (say) 50%	50.00	
		110.00
Cost of receiving this interest		£10.00

In order to avoid such a position arising, relief is given from *excess liability* on such income to *absolute beneficiaries*.

To give effect to the relief the following steps are necessary:

(*a*) Reduce the accrued income by any liabilities attaching specifically to such income and deducted from the deceased's estate for capital transfer tax purposes.

(*b*) Determine the average rate of capital transfer tax to be applied.

The procedure to give effect to the relief is as follows:

(i) Ascertain the gross amount of accrued income less the charges attributable thereto.

(ii) Deduct income tax at the basic rate in force during the year of assessment *during which the deceased died.*

(iii) Apply the agreed rate of capital transfer tax and determine the amount of capital transfer tax applicable to this accrued income.

(iv) Gross up the amount of capital transfer tax so ascertained at the basic rate of income tax in force during the year in which the deceased died.

(v) Deduct the resultant figure from the gross income of the residuary estate attributable to the absolute beneficiary.

The deduction can be expressed by the following formula, grossed up at the basic rate:

$$\frac{\text{Accrued income less Income Tax at basic rate and liabilities attached thereto}}{\text{Total value of the estate}} \times \frac{\text{Total capital transfer tax payable}}{}$$

The deduction from income for capital transfer tax is a relief for *excess liability* only. The figure for basic rate purposes is that arrived at immediately before deducting the relief.

Tax deduction certificates

It is the duty of executors and trustees to supply the estate beneficiaries with certificates of deduction of Income Tax (Form R.185E) in order to enable the beneficiaries to show the correct amount of trust income in their returns and to make any claims for which relief can be obtained by them. In order to issue correct tax certificates, all items of income and expenditure must have been dealt with properly from the tax angle, and it is therefore not amiss to suggest that personal representatives (or trustees) should review their accounts with this in mind before issuing Tax Deduction Certificates. Having done this, they should issue the appropriate certificates as soon as they can, so that the beneficiaries' Income Tax affairs can be dealt with, i.e., so that any beneficiary who is entitled to a reclaim does not have to wait an excessive time through the laxity of the personal representatives or trustees.

It should be realised that the income of the beneficiary is derived from the underlying sources of trust income, so that if the trust income consisted, for instance, solely of building society interest, no repayment could be claimed in respect of tax "deducted by the trust"; the beneficiary would be regarded as having received £x (the sum actually paid over) of building society interest, exempt from Income Tax but to be grossed-up for higher rate tax and investment income surcharge purposes.

Where, however, only part of the trust income is from a building society (or similar source, e.g. National Savings Bank Ordinary Account interest exempt from tax), trust expenses may be treated as having been met from either taxed or exempt funds as may be to the benefit of the taxpayers concerned. Any excess of the building society interest over the expenses set against it should be disclosed separately on Form R.185 E since it may be of value to beneficiaries in covering annual charges.

The preceding paragraph applies only to persons having a share of estate income, and not to annuitants, who are unaffected by the underlying income of the trust but suffer deduction of tax under ss. 52 and 53, I.C.T.A. 1970.

Comprehensive example—trust income forming basis of R.185E

The following is a cash account of trust income rendered to the sole life tenant for the year to 5th April 1986.

Receipts			Payments	
	£	£		£
Dividends		245	Income Tax on War Loan	
Building Society			Interest	72
Interest		40	House—Repairs.	20
War Loan Interest. . . .		240	Mortgage Interest	
Rent of House.	100		(to an individual)	80
Less: Schedule A,			Annuity to Albert Jones	
tax paid	24	76	(given by the Will).	196
		—		
			Executors' Fees and Expenses	79
Add: Tax refund			Payment to Life Tenant.	140
re mortgage			Balance, c/d.	38
interest paid				
gross.		24		
		—		—
		£625		£625
		══		══
Balance, b/d.		38		

Show in summary form the return of trust income and outgoings which will be rendered to the Income Tax authorities on form R.59 and the figures for the tax certificate to be given to the life tenant.

RETURN OF TRUST INCOME

	Gross	Income Tax
	£	£
Dividends	350	105
War loan interest	240	72
House—Schedule A, assessment	80	
Schedule A tax.		24
	—	—
	670	201

Charges on income:	£	£	£
Annuity to Albert Jones...................	280		
Mortgage interest	80		
	——	360	108
		£310	£ 93

Summary:			
Income less charges.....................			310
Less: Income Tax		93	
Expenses and fees of executors.....	79		
Less: Building society interest	40		
	——	39	
		——	132
Income of life tenant			£178

Figures for tax certificate (R. 185E):

	(nearest) £
Gross amount of beneficiary's income (£178 grossed-up at 30%) ..	254
Income tax suffered thereon.....................................	76
Net payment actually made to the beneficiary	140

Death of life tenant

It is unusual for a will to extend the exclusion of the Apportionment Act 1870, beyond the testator's death to the death of the life tenant. Thus, in many cases an apportionment of the income accrued due to the date of death of the deceased will be necessary. The income of the estate immediately preceding and following the life tenant's death will fall into three categories:

(*a*) Income due and payable prior to the life tenant's death is income of the life tenant.

(*b*) Income accrued due at date of death but due and payable after the date of death passes to the life tenant's free estate.

(*c*) Income accrued from the date of death to the date of due payment passes to the remaindermen of the settled estate who in many cases will not be the same persons as the beneficiaries of the deceased life tenant's free estate.

The Inland Revenue are not bound by the Apportionment Act 1870, but these assessments must follow the income. On the death of a life tenant the income of the various interested persons for taxation purposes is the division as shown above, namely:

(i) *Life tenant.*

The life tenant's income tax return will include the income due and payable prior to the date of death less any eligible expenses due and paid prior to that date.

(ii) *Personal representatives of the life tenant's free estate.*

These personal representatives will be issued with a form R.185E showing the gross amount of accrued income to date of death less the accrued proportion of eligible expenses.

(iii) *Remaindermen of the settled estate.*

The remaindermen will be issued with a form R.185E showing their share of the income accrued from the date of death, together with income wholly attributable to a period after death received during the period covered by the form. When the administration is complete and their share of the residue is handed over to the remaindermen the final form R.185 and form R.59 are completed.

Although the personal representatives receiving the accrued income under (ii) receive it as capital of the estate it is nevertheless deemed to be income of the absolute beneficiaries (*Stewart* v. *CIR* [1952]) and of the life tenants if the Apportionment Act 1870 is excluded, who will be liable to *excess liability* or who may use it for purposes of repayment claims.

The remaindermen of the settled estate have a *vested interest* in the residue from the death of the testator and an *absolute interest* therein on the death of the life-tenant. The only expenses which can be deducted therefore are those that are laid down as allowable deductions in the case of *absolute interests*.

SETTLEMENTS MADE DURING LIFETIME OR ON DEATH
General

Although settlements are often regarded simply as trusts, for income tax purposes the definition includes any disposition, trust, covenant, agreement, arrangement or transfer of assets (s. 444, I.C.T.A. 1970). Where a trust is formed by the settlement the tax liability in respect of the income from the trust falls on the trustees (see below) unless the trust is ineffective by virtue of the anti-avoidance provisions. In other cases the income from the settlement will be that of the recipient unless once again the anti-avoidance provisions apply.

§ 3.—TAX ON TRUST INCOME

INTRODUCTION

Trustees are taxed on trust income, in a representative capacity, at basic rate of income tax and at the 15% *additional rate on income of discretionary and accumulation trusts* (see below). For other trusts the tax liability of the trustees is limited to tax at basic rate.

Income payments to the beneficiaries of the trust are then deemed made after deduction of tax: at basic rate and at the 15% additional rate in the case of discretionary and accumulation trusts and at basic rate only in other cases. Assessments to higher rate of income tax and to the investment income surcharge are made directly upon beneficiaries.

Some settlements are ineffective for income tax because of anti-avoidance legislation. The anti-avoidance rules are dealt with later in this chapter.

INCOME TAX LIABILITY OF TRUSTEES (ss. 68(1) and 114(1), I.C.T.A. 1970, ss. 13 and 76, T.M.A. 1970)

Income is assessed on trustees as the persons receiving it, and the normal rules of assessment, collection, etc. apply.

Assessments are raised upon the trustees to cover tax on income not taxed at source (e.g. rent, deposit interest), but there is no assessment upon trustees if the income is mandated direct to the beneficiary.

Overseas income due to a non-resident beneficiary is not subject to U.K. tax if it is mandated direct to the beneficiary (if ascertainable): *Williams* v. *Singer* (1920); *Kelly* v. *Rogers* (1935).

Personal allowances are not available to trustees (in that capacity) but non personal reliefs (e.g. trading losses, capital allowances, rent deficiencies, interest) can be claimed. However there is no general allowance for a deficiency of income in one year to be set against a surplus in another.

Trustees are not assessable to higher rate tax nor, in general, to investment income surcharge. This is irrespective of quantity of income, and applies even if whole income of a trust is due to one beneficiary. There is, however, a 15%

additional rate tax on accumulation and discretionary settlements. Whilst there is no general relief for management expenses for basic rate tax liability (*Aikin* v. *Macdonald's Trustees* [1894]) there is *de facto* relief to a beneficiary, because he receives trust income after deduction of tax *and* expenses.

Example

			Beneficiaries	
			A	B
			£	£
Trust income	1,000			
Basic rate tax	300	700		
		—		
Expenses		70		
		—		
		630	315	315
		—	—	—
Gross up at 10/7.	900		450	450
			═══	═══
Expenses	70			
	—			
Gross up at 10/7.	100			
	———			
	1,000			
	═══			

These details will be shown on forms R.59 and R.185E. It will be noted that the net income of the beneficiary does not, because of the deduction of expenses, gross up to the total income of the trust.

If income is mandated direct to an entitled beneficiary he obtains no relief for expenses (e.g. bank charges).

Income payments to beneficiaries represent income from which tax at basic rate (or in the case of accumulation and discretionary trusts, at basic rate and 15% additional rate) and expenses have been deducted. A beneficiary may be entitled to a repayment of tax if he is not taxable in full at basic rate, or in other cases tax at higher rates and investment income surcharge (excess liability) will be due.

Unpaid higher rate tax liabilities of a beneficiary are recoverable from the trustees of discretionary trust but are not otherwise due from trustees (s. 36 I.C.T.A. 1970, *CIR* v. *Pakenham & Others* (1928)).

Accumulation and discretionary trusts (ss. 16 to 18, F.A. 1973)

Income accumulated as payable at the discretion of trustees (or any other person) is subject to tax at the additional rate of 15% as well as at the basic rate of income tax, in the hands of the trustees. The additional rate continues to apply to these trusts notwithstanding the abolition of Investment Income Surcharge for 1984–85 and after.

Allowance is given for trustees' expenses provided these are properly chargeable to income under general law (despite prohibition in trust instrument) or if they are authorised to be paid from income under the trust instrument (despite a requirement to charge them to capital under general law).

However, there is no additional rate tax on income due to a beneficiary under a fixed entitlement before it is distributed (even if payment to other beneficiaries is discretionary).

Income treated as income of a settlor under anti-avoidance rules (described in this chapter) is also excluded from the charge since it will be included in the beneficiaries' gross income and subject to *excess liability* there.

The additional rate tax is due on the gross income of a trust (unless excepted category) after deduction of proper expenses. The following points should also be noted:

(a) Building society interest is grossed up.

(b) Apportioned income of a close company (including A.C.T.) is included as income.

(c) Income from a deceased's estate is deemed paid to discretionary trustees net of basic rate tax.

(d) Scrip dividends are grossed up (if taxable under s. 34, F(No. 2)A 1975).

The following returns are required:

Form 31 (return of income, etc.); and

Form 32 (calculation of additional rate liability).

Example 1

The following figures relate to the N. Tale (1969) Trust. The trust is discretionary.

	£	£
Bank interest		500
U.K. dividends	840	
Tax credit	360	
	—	1,200
Building society interest	490	
Gross up by 3/7	210	
	—	700
Apportionment of close company income	560	
A.C.T. thereon	240	
	—	800
Income from personal representatives	350	
Gross up by 3/7	150	
	—	500
		3,700

		£	£
Less: Gross interest paid		400	
Allocation to specific purpose		200	
Expenses chargeable —to income	280		
Gross up by 3/7	120		
	—	400	
Income treated as income of settlor		NIL	
Income of annuitant	420		
Gross up by 3/7	180		
	—	600	
		—	1,600
Chargeable at additional rate			£2,100
Tax thereon at 15%			£315

Discretionary payments of income to beneficiaries are *deemed* to have suffered tax at basic and additional rate but ss. 52 and 53 I.C.T.A. 1970 do not apply.

Example 2

Payment to beneficiary			550
Gross up:			
Income tax at	30%		
Additional rate tax at	15%		
	45% =		450
Deemed income			£1,000

This treatment does not apply if income is accumulated and the payments made out of capital. Any amounts treated as income of settlor under anti-avoidance rules are not (since the charge is a notional one) treated as income of subject to this special tax charge.

Income becomes capital when the trustees so resolve (or where, for example, a transfer is made from an income bank account, or when the trustees pass an appropriate minute, or sign trust accounts which record the relevant transfer).

Trustees must account for the tax which is *deemed* to be deducted at basic and additional rates from payments to beneficiaries but can set against this.

(*a*) Tax charged at basic and additional rates (under s. 16, F.A. 1973) on trustees' income. Any interest received from a building society must be evidenced by a certificate from the society.

(*b*) Tax charged at additional rate on apportionment of close company income.

(*c*) Tax at basic rate on apportioned close company income where dividend subsequently paid.

(*d*) Tax equivalent to 2/3 of *net* income available for distribution (i.e. not transferred to capital account) on 5 April 1973. This arbitrary figure approximates to the average rate of tax suffered on undistributed income at 7/9, 8/3, etc. still in hand on that date.

Example 3

The following figures relate to the R. Teast Trust:

		£	£
At 5th April 1973	Net income available for distribution.		
	(£2,500 gross at 38.75%)		£1,531
1973–74	Gross income	1,500	
	Less: Basic rate 450		
	Additional rate 225		
		675	
			£825
	Payment to beneficiary	1,700	
	Gross up at 45%	1,391	
		3,091	

	£	£
Tax due		1,391
Less: Set off		
Tax on net income available at 5.4.1973–2/3 × £1,531................	1,021	
Tax on 1973/74 income...................	675	
		1,696
Carry forward to 1974–75		£305

1974–75

	£	£	£
Gross income		1,500	
Less: Basic rate	495		
Additional rate	225		
		720	
			£780
Payment to beneficiary		1,400	
Gross up at 45%		1,145	
Gross		2,545	
Tax due			1,145
Less: Set off			
Brought forward from 1973–74.............		305	
Tax on 1974–75 income...................		720	
			1,025
Liability..................................			£120

Example 4

The following figures relate to the D. Risory Trust

1985–86

	£	£
Gross income	1,000	
Less: Basic rate	300	
Additional rate	150	
	450	
		£550
Payment to beneficiary	nil	
Tax due		nil
Less: Set off		
Tax on 1985–86 income		450
Carry forward to 1986–87		£450

1986–87

	£	£
Gross income	1,000	
Less: Basic rate (say)................	400	
Additional rate	150	
	550	
		£450

	£	£
Payment to beneficiary	1,000	
Gross up at (say) 55%	1,222	
Gross	2,222	
Tax due		1,222
Less: Set off		
Brought forward from 1985–86	450	
Tax on 1986–87 income (say)	550	
		1,000
Liability		£222

The additional rate charge on the income of accumulation and discretionary trusts does not, in general, apply to personal representatives acting in that capacity.

If an accumulation or discretionary trust receives overseas income, double tax relief is available, primarily to the trustees but is passed on to the beneficiaries, provided that the trustees certify that a distribution is made out of income from an overseas source and which has suffered foreign tax.

Treatment of taxation in the books of a trust estate

The Institute of Chartered Accountants recommends that the taxed income of a trust should be shown gross in the accounts and that any annuity payments made to beneficiaries should be charged in the accounts at gross amounts. When this recommendation is followed, an Income Tax Account must be opened in the books of the trust, which will be debited with all tax deductions at the source from taxed income or charged under direct assessments, and credited with tax deducted from payments made to beneficiaries or recovered under repayment claims made by the trustees on behalf of beneficiaries; any balance will be charged to Income Account.

Capital Gains Tax payable on the disposal of the trust assets should be dealt with in a separate Taxation Account, and will normally be charged to Capital Account.

§ 4.—DEEDS OF COVENANT

Provided the settlement is irrevocable, capable of exceeding six years (three years for charities) and not made to an unmarried minor, a deed of covenant covering a settlement can be an extremely effective tax planning device. N.B. apart from deeds made to charities, covenanted donations are only effective for basic rate tax.

Consider the following example:

Example 1—utilisation of covenants

Miss Lomax, who lives with her parents, has a salary of £3,000 per annum. Her parents have a pension of £2,500 per annum. They are not yet 65. Their tax positions for 1985–86 will be as follows:

MISS LOMAX—STATEMENT OF INCOME TAX PAYABLE 1985–86

	£
Salary	3,000
Less: Personal allowance	2,205
Taxable income	795
Tax payable	
On £795 at 30%	£238.50

MR AND MRS LOMAX—STATEMENT OF INCOME TAX PAYABLE 1985-86

	£
Pension	2,500
Less: Personal allowance	3,455
Taxable income	Nil

Total tax payable by the members of the family is thus £238.50. Let us assume that Miss Lomax contributes £350 per annum towards the support of her parents, in addition to her share of household expenses. If she does this in the normal way, the Income Tax payable will be as shown above. If, however, she executes a deed of covenant to pay a net sum of £350 per annum net the position will be as follows:

MISS LOMAX—STATEMENT OF INCOME TAX PAYABLE 1985–86

	£
Salary	3,000
Less: Personal allowance	2,205
	795

Tax payable on salary
On £795 at 30% £238.50

MR AND MRS LOMAX—STATEMENT OF INCOME TAX PAYABLE 1984–85

	£
Pension	2,500
Deed of covenant (£350 × $\frac{10}{7}$)	500
	3,000
Less: Personal allowance	3,455
Taxable income	Nil

Since £150 was deducted on payment of the covenanted sum (i.e. £500 at 30%), a repayment of £150 will be due to Mr and Mrs Lomax, since their total income, inclusive of the covenant (£3,000), is less than their personal allowance.

The net tax payable by the members of the family is thus £88.50 (£238.50 − £150.00) showing a saving of £150 on the making of a deed of covenant.

Student deeds of covenant
These can be used in a similar advantageous manner to supplement as appropriate any student grant. It is normal for the covenant to terminate at the earlier of seven years or when the student ends full-time education. It is interesting to note that the Inland Revenue have published a guide to student covenanted payments including a specimen deed form.

§ 5.—SETTLEMENTS—ANTI-AVOIDANCE PROVISIONS
General

INTRODUCTION
A settlement (broadly) separates control over property or income (placing it in the hands of trustees) from the beneficial interest therein. Before the introduction

of the provisions now in ss. 434 to 459, I.C.T.A. 1970 a settlor could set aside income in a trust so that it was not taxable in his hands. The purpose of the anti-avoidance provisions is to render ineffective for income tax purposes any settlement in which the settlor benefits. However, although the provisions are widely drawn they recognise that not all settlements have tax avoidance motives. The provisions attack specific types of avoidance rather than attempt a blanket disallowance. Furthermore the provisions do not effect general validity of trusts at law or for other tax purposes (e.g. capital transfer tax).

The anti-avoidance provisions fall under the three main headings:

Short-term settlements (ss. 434 to 436, I.C.T.A. 1970)

Settlements on children (ss. 437 to 444, I.C.T.A. 1970)

Settlements where the settlor may benefit (ss. 445 to 456, I.C.T.A. 1970)

In addition, certain settlements are ineffective for excess liability only (ss. 457 to 459).

Short-term settlements (ss. 434 to 436 I.C.T.A. 1970; s. 48 F.A. 1977; s. 55, F.A. 1980)

If there is a disposition (i.e. any trust, covenant, agreement or arrangement) whereby income is payable to or for the benefit of any person for a period which cannot exceed six years the income is treated as though it remained that of the disponer (if living). However, this will not apply if the disposition was made for valuable and sufficient consideration and is not wholly included in the income of the person making the payment (reversing the decision in *C.I.R.* v. *Plummer* [1979]).

This anti-avoidance provision applies only to income capable of being deemed received by a U.K. resident settlor. It does not displace the income of a U.K. beneficiary of a short-term settlement made by a non-resident settlor (*Becker* v. *Wright* [1965]).

As indicated above, this provision renders ineffective any covenant for a period which cannot exceed six years. Put another way, the provision could be said to allow a deduction for payments under a covenant for a period which can exceed six years. However, the conditions are applied narrowly. It is not sufficient that a deed is made for seven years (i.e. more than six). If the last payment is due less than six years after the deed the covenant is ineffective (*C.I.R.* v. *Hostel of St Luke Trustees* [1930]). However, the test is whether payments could have been (under the terms of the deed) for a period in excess of a six years and not whether payments were, in fact, made for a period exceeding six years (*C.I.R.* v. *Black* [1940]). Because of this, covenants for the life of an individual are effective as they are capable of exceeding six years. The payment under a covenant must be for a constant amount, although it has been held that a covenant for a constant fraction of yearly income is effective (*Gardner Mountain* v. *D'Ambrumenil* [1940]).

The Inland Revenue make the following stipulation (in Statement of Practice A1) before they will accept a deed as being valid:

(i) There must be evidence of payment and of deduction of tax.

(ii) They will require declaration of non-reciprocity (i.e. there must be no stipulation or understanding as to a counterbalancing benefit of the covenantor).

(iii) The attestation clause must include the word "sealed".

Example

H. Hart makes a covenant to pay annually on 31st December the sum of £100 to B. Hart (his brother). The covenant is for a period of seven years commencing from 6th April 1985.

Provided the covenant is signed by 31st December 1985, the covenant will be valid for *income tax* purposes, since payments could cover a period exceeding 6 years. This would not be the case were the deed of covenant signed on 1st January 1986 or later.

Charitable covenants
For charitable covenants *payments* made after 5th April 1980 qualify if the period can exceed *three* years, irrespective of the date of covenant. The maximum annual payment on which relief is granted is £10,000 (£5,000 for 1984–85 and 1983–84).

Ineffective settlements
If the payment is made under a deed which is held to be ineffective, so that the settlor becomes chargeable to income tax, he is entitled to recover the tax so paid from the trustee or other person to whom the income was paid. For this purpose the settlor can obtain a certificate from the Inspector showing the amount of income on which he has become chargeable and the amount of the tax. This recovery of tax is on the basis that the income "recharged" upon the settlor is the highest part of his income. Basic rate tax would have been withheld at the time of payment, and it is thus the higher rate tax charge and investment income surcharge which are subject to recovery from the recipient. If the settlor receives an additional tax repayment, following the treatment of a repayment as his income, he is required to account to the recipient for an amount appropriate to the payment. If there is more than one recipient these adjustments are apportioned between them.

Where there is more than one settlor each is dealt with separately.

Settlements on children (ss. 437 to 444, I.C.T.A. 1970)

INTRODUCTION
Settlements by parents on their infant children are, in general, ineffective. This has the effect that income paid out of a settlement, during the settlor's life, to the benefit of an unmarried minor child is aggregated with the income of the settlor (i.e. of the parent concerned).

For this purpose, "child" includes not only a natural child but also a stepchild, an adopted child, a child of divorced parents or an illegitimate child.

A "settlement" includes any disposition, trust, covenant, agreement, or transfer of assets. For example, it has been held to include a gift of shares or an N.S.B. deposit (*Hood Barrs* v. *C.I.R.* [1946]); (*Thomas* v. *Marshall* [1953]).

There is a danger that divorce and separation settlements may create a trust (*Yates* v. *Starkey* [1957]), but court orders under the Matrimonial Causes Act 1973 should not.

A "settlor" is the person by whom a settlement was made, or who has provided the funds, or who has made the reciprocal arrangements so that another person actually makes the statement, in effect, on his behalf.

"Income" includes any income chargeable to income tax by deduction or otherwise (or would be so chargeable if received in the United Kingdom by a person who is resident and ordinarily resident). This definition does not apply to income which is deemed, by this anti-avoidance rule, to be that of the settlor.

It is important to distinguish between revocable and irrevocable settlements. A settlement is, broadly, revocable, in the following circumstances:
  (i) if income or assets which would otherwise be paid or applied to or for the benefit of the settlor's child (or during his or her life) are instead paid to or applied to the benefit of the settlor or, during the life of the settlor, to or for the benefit of the settlor's wife or husband; or
  (ii) if a penalty is payable by the settlors if he fails to comply with the provisions of the settlement.

However, a settlement will be treated as *irrevocable* if the only reason for *not* treating it as such was one or other of the following:
  (*a*) where the settlement provided for the reversion of the income as assets

to the settlors (or husband or wife) only on the child's bankruptcy or upon the child's executing an assignment of or change in the income or assets; or

(*b*) where, despite the fact that the settlement can be brought to an end by any person's act or default no benefit can, during the lifetime of the settlor's child, accrue to the settlor (or husband or wife); or

(*c*) the trust is a protective trust (within s. 33, Trustee Act 1925) and the income is held for the benefit of the settlor's child. However, this does not prevent the settlement from being *revocable* if the trust period is for less than the life of the child, or if the settlement specifies some event which would, if he or she were entitled absolutely to the income of the trust period, deprive the child of the right to receive some or all of the income.

GENERAL RULE

Income paid out of a settlement to or for the benefit of the settlor's unmarried minor child is aggregated with that of the settlor for the year of assessment in which the payment is made.

This general rule does not, however, apply for any year in which the settlor is a non-resident, nor if the amount of income paid to or for the child's benefit does not exceed £5.

If a settlement is deemed ineffective, appropriate adjustments are made as between the settlor and the trustees or any other person to whom payment has been made (see § 15).

Example 1

I. Ingle covenanted in January 1981 to pay the sum of £500 per annum to his son Isaac until Isaac attained his 25th birthday, payment being made annually on 31st December. Isaac was eighteen on 25th December 1985.

Payments made prior to that on 31st December 1985, would be disregarded for tax purposes. That is to say, they would not be regarded as increasing the income of Isaac, or as diminishing that of his father. That made on 31st December 1985, and all later payments would effectively reduce the father's income for income tax purposes and would be treated as part of that of his son Isaac.

Example 2

If, in the preceding example, Isaac had married on 20th December 1983, the payments would have been effective for taxation purposes from that date; and the payment on 31st December 1983, would have effectively reduced his father's income for income tax (basic rate only) purposes and increased his own.

Example 3

J. James deposited £500 in a National Savings Bank ordinary account in the name of his new-born son Joseph in the hope that the interest would be exempt for tax purposes in the hands of his son; J. James himself having over £2,000 invested in a National Savings Bank ordinary account. No tax saving would arise since the interest on the National Savings Bank deposit made by the father would, for tax purposes, still be his and not his son's, and would not qualify for the exemption of £70, which would have been fully used against the interest on the father's account.

Remoter ancestors

The above restrictions apply in relation to parent and infant, unmarried child. A settlement by a grandfather on his minor grandson or made otherwise than by parent to unmarried infant child would not therefore be caught by these restrictions, unless reciprocal arrangements had been made.

Interest paid by trustees is deemed to be paid to the settlor's unmarried minor child if appropriate. The amount so deemed is:

$$\text{interest paid} \times \frac{\text{actual payment to child}}{\text{income of settlement} \atop \text{less expenses}}$$

This deeming provision does not apply to interest paid for a qualifying purpose (e.g. under s. 75, F.A. 1972), nor to interest paid to the settlor as to the wife or husband if they are living together.

In the above calculation the income of the settlement includes income chargeable to income tax by deduction, or by assessment insofar as it would be chargeable if received in the United Kingdom by a person domiciled, resident and ordinarily resident therein. Apportionments of income from a close company (inclusive of A.C.T.) are also included. If the settlor is not domiciled in the United Kingdom, or if he is not resident, or not ordinarily resident in the United Kingdom, the deemed income of the settlement is limited to the income which would be chargeable upon him had he received it.

Also, for the purposes of this calculation, expenses do not include sums (other than interest) distributed to beneficiaries and treated as their income (or which would be so treated if they were domiciled, resident and ordinarily resident in the United Kingdom).

It should however be noted that, whilst this provision may deem interest to be paid to the child (and therefore aggregated with the settlor's income) it does not affect the tax liability of the person receiving the interest.

ACCUMULATION SETTLEMENTS

Income of a settlement which is accumulated is not treated as that of the parent settlor unless paid out for maintenance or otherwise. Such settlements can therefore still provide a tax benefit where the settlor's tax rate exceeds 45% (i.e. the tax payable on the accumulated funds).

OTHER POINTS

The Revenue can require the provision of relevant information from any party to a settlement.

Whilst income can be aggregated with that of the settlor there is no relief if a loss (e.g. if a trade is carried on) is sustained.

If there is more than one settlor to a settlement each is treated as though he were the only settlor. There are rules for allocating the income and property originating from particular settlors.

Revocable settlements, etc.

RELEASE OF OBLIGATION (s. 445, I.C.T.A. 1970; s. 55, F.A. 1980)

If an *income* settlement contains a power whereby all or part thereof can be revoked *by any person* so that the obligation on settlor (or spouse) to make annual payments ceases, the income of the revocable part of the settlement is treated as being the settlor's.

If the settlement cannot be revoked for at least six years (three years if in favour of a charity) this treatment does not apply until the revocation can be exercised.

For this purpose a power of revocation includes the power to reduce annual payments made by the settlor or spouse.

REVERSION OF PROPERTY (s. 446, I.C.T.A. 1970)

If a *capital* settlement contains a power whereby all or part thereof can be revoked *by any person* so that the settlor (or spouse) could become entitled to some, or all, of the income or capital of the settlement the income or the revocable part thereof is treated as the income of the settlor.

If the settlement cannot be revoked for at least six years this treatment does not apply until the revocation can be exercised.

For this purpose a power of revocation includes the power to diminish the property comprised in the settlement or to reduce payments made thereunder to persons other than the settlor or spouse.

RETENTION OF INTEREST (s. 447, I.C.T.A. 1970)

Where a settlor retains an interest in all or part of the income or property of a settlement (so that income or capital may be *in any circumstances* paid to the benefit of settlor or spouse) the income of that part is treated as the income of the settlor, insofar as it remains undistributed.

If the settlor's retained interest is not in the whole of the income arising to or the whole of the property comprised in the settlement, only a proportionate part of the income is treated as that of the settlor.

Income which has already been treated as the income of the settlor because the settlement is a revocable settlement (see above) is deducted from (or eliminates) any amounts chargeable under this provision.

A settlor is deemed to have an interest in income arising to, or in property comprised in, a settlement if such income or property could be paid or applied to the benefit of the settlor (or husband or wife). However, this does not apply if the settlor's interest arises only in the following circumstances:

(*a*) bankruptcy of or deed of arrangement by beneficiary; or

(*b*) in a marriage settlement, death of both parties, or of children of the marriage; or

(*c*) in a contingent trust, death of beneficiary below the vesting age.

Furthermore, it also does not apply whilst some person is alive and under 25 and during whose life the settlor cannot benefit (except in the above circumstances). However it could apply for an unmarried settlor, if a benefit could arise to a possible future wife, or if there is specific intention to provide a benefit to a future wife.

DISCRETION TO BENEFIT SETTLOR (s. 448, I.C.T.A. 1970)

If all or part of the income of a settlement or of the property comprised in a settlement, is capable, by a discretionary power, of being paid or applied to the benefit of the settlor, the whole of such income is treated as the income of the settlor. This does not apply to income which is already treated as that of the settlor under some other provision.

If the discretion cannot be exercised for at least six years from the time the income first arose to, or property was comprised in, the settlement this treatment does not apply until discretion can be exercised.

Furthermore such treatment does not apply if the settlor's interest arises only on the bankruptcy or death of other beneficiaries.

SUPPLEMENTARY PROVISIONS (ss. 449, 454 to 456, I.C.T.A. 1970)

The following points should be noted:

(i) Any tax charged under any of the provisions described above is assessable under Case IV Schedule D;

(ii) The settlor is taxed as though he actually received the income and entitled to normal relief;

(iii) If a settlement is ineffective, adjustments are made between the settlor and the trustees or any other person who receives the income. A settlor may require a certificate from the Revenue of tax levied on trust income;

(iv) If a settlor receives a repayment of tax an appropriate part thereof must be paid over to the trustees or to any other person who receives the income.

(v) Income which is deemed to be that of a settlor (because the settlement is ineffective) is treated as the highest part of his income.

Income arising under a settlement includes income chargeable to income tax by deduction or otherwise or would be so chargeable if received in the United Kingdom by a person domiciled, resident and ordinarily resident therein. This includes apportioned income of a close company plus A.C.T. However if a settlor is not domiciled, or not resident, or not ordinarily resident in the United Kingdom the amount of income which can be deemed to be his is limited to the income which would be chargeable to tax upon him if he did receive it. "Settlements" include any dispositions, trusts, covenants, agreements or arrangements and "settlor" includes a person by whom the settlement was made, or who has provided the funds, or who has made reciprocal arrangements.

Disallowance of deduction (s. 450, I.C.T.A. 1970)

No deduction is available for annual payments to a trust made by a settlor (or spouse) to the extent that the income of the trust is undistributed (and therefore not otherwise taxable). However the prohibition on deduction does not apply to undistributed income which is taxable upon the settlor of a revocable settlement. The prohibition also applies to annual payments made to a company which is connected with the settlement (i.e. it is a close company, or would be if resident in the United Kingdom, and its participators include the trustees of or a beneficiary under the settlement).

Capital payments, loans, etc.

POSITION AFTER 5TH APRIL 1981 (ss. 451, as amended, and 451A, I.C.T.A. 1970; ss. 43 to 44, F.A. 1981; s. 63, F.A. 1982)

Definitions
A capital sum is any payment by way of a loan, any repayment of a loan, or any other sum paid otherwise than as income and not for full consideration. However, this does not include a payment arising on the bankruptcy, death, etc. of the beneficiary. Payments to the husband or wife of a settlor are included, as are payments to the settlor (or spouse) jointly with some other person.

The definition is extended to cover payments to third parties at the settlor's discretion, or because he has assigned to them his right to receive such payments. It also covers any sums which are otherwise paid or applied by trustees for the benefit of the settlor. These extensions of the definition apply even though such payments would not otherwise be treated as capital sums payable to the settlor.

General rule
Capital sums paid by trustees to the settlor (or spouse), whether paid directly or indirectly, are deemed made out of the income available up to the end of the year concerned (and deemed to be the settlor's income for that year).

Prior to 6th April 1981 the amount of such payments treated as the settlor's income was related to the accumulated undistributed income of the settlement for each year until the capital payment was fully covered. The position is now clarified, so that once income has covered part of a capital payment it cannot be taken into account again. Furthermore, the income can cover a capital payment only in the year in which the capital payment is made or in the next *eleven* years.

Any capital payments made before 6th April 1981, but which have not under the old rules been matched with income, are treated as a payment made on 6th April 1981.

EFFECT

Capital sums which are deemed to be income of the settlor (or spouse) are net income and must be grossed up for tax at basic rate and 15% additional rate. This is achieved by an assessment under Case VI, Schedule D, subject to normal personal deductions and reliefs.

These provisions are widely drawn and are apt to apply to innocent transactions in which there was no intention to avoid tax.

(i) A settlor's wife lent money to trustees for the purchase of investments. Following the sale of the investments, the loan was repaid. The money repaid was taxed on the settlor at the gross equivalent of the loan repaid. *C.I.R.* v. *De Vigier* (1964).

(ii) Shares in a company were settled in trust for children. The settlement received income from the company. The company cleared the settlor's bank overdraft. This payment was taxed on the settlor at its gross equivalent. *Bates* v. *C.I.R.* (1966).

(iii) Trustees advanced monies to the settlor out of accumulated income, satisfied by a transfer to them of securities. The transfer was a "capital sum". *McClone* v. *C.I.R.* (1967).

However, some payments, somewhat anomalously, escape liability.

(*a*) Shares in a company were sold by a settlor to a settlement. The settlor's current account was credited with his remuneration and debited with payments made by the company to him, or on his behalf. Such payments were not "capital sums". *Potts Executors* v. *C.I.R.* (1950).

(*b*) A guarantee of trustees' overdraft and the deposit with the bank of an equivalent amount used to purchase shares was not a "capital sum" (but was a revocable settlement under s. 447, I.C.T.A. 1970). *C.I.R.* v. *Wachtel* (1970).

Example

In 1980–81 the trustees of the Forlorn Settlement made a capital payment to the settlor of £10,000.

The settlement had the following undistributed income (after tax) as follows:

	£
1979–80............................	1,800
1980–81............................	2,200
1981–82............................	2,400
1982–83............................	2,300
1983–84............................	2,500

	£	£
Capital payment....................................		10,000
Less: Income 1979–80..........................	1,800	
1980–81..........................	2,200	4,000
Balance unmatched at 6th April 1981..............		6,000
Less: Income 1981–82..........................	2,400	
1982–83..........................	2,300	
(part) 1983–84..........................	1,300	6,000
		Nil

Income available in the settlement up to the end of a tax year is the aggregate of income which has not been distributed *less*:

(i) income which has already covered a capital payment;

(ii) previous capital sums paid to the settlor;

(iii) income taxed as a revocable settlement;

(iv) charges disallowed;

(v) annual payments. Treated as the settlor's income under settlements which are ineffective for *excess liability* purposes.

(vi) income from an accumulation settlement for children taxed as income of the settlor;

(vii) amounts deemed to be income of the settlement by apportionment of the income of a close company. This also includes amounts which would have been apportioned had the company been incorporated and resident in the United Kingdom;

(viii) tax at basic rate and 15% additional rate on the accumulated un-distributed income less items (iii) to (vii) (i.e. on items (i) and (ii)).

LOANS

If the capital sum paid to a settlor is by way of a loan, there is no tax charge on the settlor for any year of assessment later than that in which the loan is repaid. If there have been previous loans and repayments, a new loan is only treated as the settlor's income if it exceeds the cumulative total of earlier loans which have been treated as his income.

Where the capital sum is a repayment to a settlor of a loan made to the settlement by him there can be no tax charge upon the settlor for any year of assessment after one in which he makes a further loan equal to or greater than the amount repaid.

COMPANY PAYMENTS

Certain payments made by companies are within the scope of this provision. Thus a capital sum (as above) paid to a settlor in a year of assessment by a company connected with a settlement can be treated as the settlor's income if there has been an *associated payment* (see below) made directly or indirectly to the company by the trustees of the settlement.

A company is connected with a settlement if it is a close company (or would be if it were U.K. resident) whose participators include the trustees or a beneficiary of the settlement.

In relation to a particular capital sum paid to a settlor, an associated payment means another capital sum paid to the company by the trustees of a settlement at any time within the five years before or five years after the date on which the capital sum concerned was paid to the settlor. This also applies, within the same time limits, to any other sum paid or asset transferred to the company by the trustees which is not paid, or transferred for full consideration in money or money's worth. This treatment is extended to include any capital sum paid by, or any associated payments made to, companies which are associated with each other (as defined by s. 302 I.C.T.A. 1970).

The general definition of a capital sum also applies to company payments, and the tests for payments to a settlor by a company or to a company by trustees are the same as those applied to payments to settlors by trustees.

If a capital sum is caught by these provisions it is treated as having been paid as income to the settlor, to the extent that it falls within the total of associated payments made up to the end of the year of assessment in which the capital sum is paid. Any sum which is not treated as paid to the settlor in such year of assessment but which falls within the total of associated payments up to the end of the next year (less any amounts already taken into account in the first year) is treated as being to the settlor in such next year. This process can be repeated for subsequent years as often as may be necessary.

Special rules apply to payments made to a settlor by way of the making or repayment of a loan. Such payments are not treated as being income of the settlor if the whole of the loan is repaid within twelve months of the date on which it was originally made. There is a further condition that the total period for which loans remain outstanding within any period of five years does not exceed twelve months. This is applied on a cumulative basis to all loans made or repaid by all (if more than one) companies connected with the settlement.

Settlements ineffective for higher-rate tax and additional rate purposes

Certain settlements of income (i.e. covenants) are ineffective for higher rates of income tax and for the 15% additional rate. The way in which this is achieved is described below.

A settlement on or after 7th April 1965 of income from property of which the settlor has not divested himself absolutely, is not deductible in computing the settlor's income for higher rate tax and investment income surcharge purposes.
Exceptions
The following annual payments are, however, deductible:

(1) under partnership agreements to, or for the benefit of, a former partner, or the widow or dependants of a deceased former partner, provided the payments are made under a liability incurred for full consideration.

(2) By an individual for full consideration in connection with the acquisition of the whole or part of a business. The payments must be made to, or for the benefit of, the individual from whom the business was purchased, or to, or for the benefit of, a former partner where the business was acquired from a partnership. Payments are also admissible if made to, or for the benefit of, an individual from whom a business, or part of it, was acquired by a partnership or a preceding partnership. References to an individual include his widow or dependents, if he is deceased.

(3) Under a settlement made by one party to a marriage to the other in consequence of divorce, nullity or separation. The separation may be under a Court order or by agreement or in such circumstances that the separation is likely to be permanent.

(4) To a charity for a period of more than 3 years (1981–82 onwards) and not exceeding £10,000.

These provisions do not apply to income of which a settlor has divested himself absolutely. In other words, no benefit can in any way accrue to the settlor or to his spouse.

Income which is already treated as that of the settlor (or spouse) under some other provision cannot again be treated as his income under this provision.

If a covenanted payment is caught by these provisions it is nonetheless still treated as a deduction in computing the settlor's income from all sources. However, an equal amount is then added to his income. This can have the effect of converting earned income into investment income (*Ang* v. *Parrish* [1980]).

A settlement made on or after 10th April 1946, but before 7th April 1965, is not deductible unless the income is payable to an individual for his own use.

Effect of restrictions

It is important to realise that the restrictions discussed above apply only for Income Tax. The settlements are not otherwise affected by the Income Tax Acts. It is therefore provided that where the income of a settlement is treated as that of the settlor, he must pass on to the trustees or beneficiaries any additional reliefs he may obtain as a result, and can claim from them any additional Income Tax paid.

13.   Double Taxation

§ 1.—INTRODUCTORY

Double taxation arises because countries generally tax the income of their own residents from whatever source it arises, and also the income of non-residents in so far as it accrues within the country concerned. The principle of double taxation is comparatively simple; it is only in considering reliefs which are given to offset the hardship caused by this double taxation that difficulty is experienced.

There are three methods by which relief for double taxation is given:

(1) *Treaty relief*—under the terms of a double taxation agreement negotiated with another country a credit may be given against United Kingdom tax arising on foreign income for any foreign tax which has been paid on the same income. In some cases the double tax agreement may provide for income to be exempt from tax in one country or the other or for the tax rate to be reduced (e.g. with holding tax on interest). Where there is an agreement the relief is claimed under s. 497, I.C.T.A. 1970 and the detailed rules for calculation of the relief are found in ss. 500–512, I.C.T.A. 1970. However, reference must be made to the agreement itself in order to ascertain the precise effect.

(2) *Unilateral relief*—where no double tax agreement has been negotiated the United Kingdom may unilaterally allow a credit against United Kingdom tax due on overseas income for any foreign tax paid on the same income. If there is no agreement, or if there is an agreement but it does not provide any relief in respect of the particular class of income concerned, then unilateral relief may be claimed under s. 498, I.C.T.A. 1970. In such cases the rules set out in ss. 500–512, I.C.T.A. 1970 are also followed.

(3) *By deduction* (s. 516, I.C.T.A. 1970). If no claim for relief under ss. 497 or 498, I.C.T.A. 1970 is available or if the taxpayer elects not to take a credit (following s. 511, I.C.T.A. 1970), he may deduct the foreign tax from the foreign income assessable in the United Kingdom. The effect of this is that United Kingdom tax is charged on the amount of the overseas income *after* deducting the foreign tax thereon. An election not to take a credit applies to the whole of the tax on the source of income in question. It is not possible to take part of the tax as credit and part by deduction.

It is important to appreciate the difference in effect which is achieved by giving relief for credit rather than deduction. This can best be illustrated by means of a simple example showing the net income remaining after both United Kingdom and foreign taxes.

Example

O. B. Joyful (a United Kingdom resident) receives overseas income of £1,000 (foreign tax thereon is 25%). He pays U.K. income tax at 30% (it is assumed that his personal allowances have been set against income from other sources).

	Credit				Deduction
	£	£	£	£	£
Overseas income.........			1,000		1,000
Less: Foreign tax		250	250	250	250
Net income before U.K. tax			750		750
U.K. income tax @ 30% on £1,000...............	300			at 30% on £750 225	225
Less: Credit for foreign tax	250				
		50	50		—
Overall tax liability		£300			£475
Net income after U.K. and foreign tax			£700		£525

§ 2.—RECIPROCAL EXEMPTIONS—DOUBLE TAX TREATIES

As indicated above, in the double tax agreements which have been negotiated certain classes of income have been exempted from taxation in one of the countries involved. Thus it is recognised that it is more appropriate to subject to taxation some categories of income (or capital gains) in the country in which the income originates rather than that in which the recipient resides.

In practice it is necessary to consult the particular agreement concerned, but the following forms of income are commonly exempt from *United Kingdom taxation:*

(1) Profits of a foreign resident from operating ships or aircraft.*

(2) Industrial or commercial profits derived by a foreign resident, in so far as they are not attributable to a permanent establishment in the United Kingdom.

(3) Royalties (including rentals in respect of films) and other amounts paid for the use of copyrights, patents, trade marks, etc., derived from a United Kingdom source, received by a foreign resident, except in so far as he is carrying on a business in the United Kingdom.

(4) Interest or dividends derived from a United Kingdom source by a foreign resident. (In some Double Taxation Agreements, exemption from United Kingdom taxation is not given, but provision is made for withholding tax to be deducted from interest or dividends at a lower rate than the United Kingdom basic rate of income tax). Withholding tax no longer applies in the United Kingdom in respect of dividends following the introduction of the Imputation System of Corporation Tax in the United Kingdom with effect from 6th April 1973. Many treaties are being renegotiated so that the relevant tax credit (see Chapter 15) is paid to the non-U.K. resident shareholder less tax at a reduced rate (often 15 per cent) on the deemed "gross" (i.e., cash dividend plus tax credit.)

(5) A salary or pension paid by a foreign government as official remuneration.

(6) A pension or a purchased annuity derived from a United Kingdom source by a foreign resident.

---

* The term "foreign resident" is used in this chapter to indicate a resident in the state which is the other party to the agreement.

(7) Fees, etc., for services rendered by a foreign resident employed by a foreign resident, provided the former is not in the United Kingdom for a period exceeding 183 days in the aggregate in the tax year concerned.

(8) The remuneration of a foreign professor or teacher who visits the United Kingdom for the purpose of teaching at an educational establishment for a period not exceeding two years.

(9) Payments received from home by a foreign student or business apprentice receiving full-time education or training in the United Kingdom.

(10) Capital Gains arising in the U.K. to a foreign resident.

Reciprocal relief is given to persons resident in the other country to that mentioned above, in respect of foreign taxation in that country.

(N.B. s. 54, F.A. 1985 introduces legislation (to be ratified) to prevent certain companies operating in a "unitary tax state" reclaiming a tax credit.)

§ 3.—TAX CREDITS

A tax credit is an amount allowed as a deduction from the United Kingdom tax payable on income which has already been taxed in another country. The general rules relating to tax credits are set out in Sections 500–512, I.C.T.A. 1970 but, in the case of relief under the terms of a double taxation agreement, reference should also be made to any particular rules contained in the agreement with the country concerned.

A tax credit is under U.K. law only allowed to a person who is resident in the United Kingdom for the period of assessment. The position has however been relaxed by concession (November 1975) in relation to *U.K. branches of overseas banks*. In these cases the foreign tax paid is offsetable as if the branch were a U.K. resident.

The foreign tax which is eligible for relief is generally the tax chargeable on the income concerned for the period in question and not, if different, the amount of foreign tax actually paid in the period.

Tax sparing
In certain countries relief is given from tax which would otherwise be payable on the profit of new businesses or businesses carried on in certain areas. The purpose of this arrangement is to encourage the development of new industries in the countries concerned. This is sometimes known as a pioneer relief or tax sparing. Some recent treaties allow the United Kingdom taxpayer to treat as foreign tax paid the amount of tax which he would otherwise have paid were it not for the exemption. He therefore becomes entitled to a tax credit for foreign tax even though none has in fact been paid. Tax sparing applies *only* to U.K. residents. (The 1975 concession applicable to U.K. branches of overseas banks *does not* apply to tax sparing).

Foreign income chargeable to U.K. tax
Where foreign income is chargeable to United Kingdom tax on the arising basis the amount brought into charge is the gross income from the source concerned and no deduction is made, in determining the amount of income to be assessed, for the foreign tax. If income from the source concerned is taxed on the remittance basis (i.e. on sums actually received in the United Kingdom), the amount to be assessed is the amount received in the United Kingdom grossed up by the amount of foreign tax payable. If the income concerned is a dividend, credit relief may also be available for the underlying tax on the profits out of which the dividend was paid. In such a case the income must be grossed up for the underlying tax also.

Underlying tax
Most of the recent double-taxation agreements preclude relief for underlying tax where the taxpayer receiving the dividend is an individual. *Relief for underlying tax claimed unilaterally is only ever given to companies.*

Utilisation of credits
To the extent that a foreign tax credit is not utilised (e.g. as a result of surplus personal allowances or the overseas tax rate exceeding the U.K. tax rate—see § 5 below), the surplus credit is lost, as carry forward or back is not possible. See Chapter 5 § 15 for postponement of capital allowances to preserve a tax credit.

Limitation of tax credit for certain loan interest (s. 65, F.A. 1982)
To prevent abuses of the double taxation relief system that were considered to be taking place by banks engaged in overseas lending, a tax credit restriction of 15% of the gross interest applies to interest arising after 1st April 1982. For loans in existence on 1st April 1982, the restriction only applies to interest arising after 1st April 1983.

The foreign tax to be credited against the U.K. lender's corporation tax liability is the *lessor* of:
   (i) 15% of the gross interest, or
   (ii) The actual tax withheld or spared (see above).
Any excess of actual tax (not tax spared) will then be allowed as a deduction (see para. 1).

A further amendment is that tax spared is to be included in the amount of interest on which corporation tax is charged. This was previously *not* included and was available for full credit relief. The 15% limitation applies to the gross interest exclusive of the tax spared.

§ 4.—RELATIONSHIP OF U.K. INCOME AND FOREIGN INCOME

Difficulty may be encountered in relating the income assessable under the rules applicable under United Kingdom income tax law with the amount of income computed under the foreign regime. Similarly there may be disparity between the United Kingdom income tax charge and the foreign tax for which credit is sought. There are four main problem areas.

First, in many cases the income will be charged to United kingdom tax on the preceding-year basis, while the foreign country may charge tax on a current-year basis. Most treaties now deal with this problem by providing that the credit for foreign tax paid on foreign income is given against United Kingdom tax chargeable (on whatever basis) on the same income.

Second, difficulty will be encountered in the opening and closing years of a business. In a case where the profit of one period of account forms the basis of assessment for more than one year for United Kingdom income tax purposes (e.g. for the years of assessment following the commencement of a business) but for a single year for foreign tax purposes, the foreign tax paid in respect of the profit assessable for that period can be used as a credit against United Kingdom income tax for more than one year of assessment.

Example 1

O. Dear is resident in the United Kingdom and on 1st January 1983 commenced a new trade in Cantonia. In the year to 31st December 1983 her profits from Cantonia were £10,000 and Cantonian tax thereon was £3,000 (on a current year basis).

	Basis	Profits	Tax credit
		£	£
1983–84	Actual to 5th April 1984		
	3/12 × £10,000	2,500	
	3/12 × £3,000		750
1984–85	First twelve months	10,000	3,000
1985–86	Preceding year	10,000	3,000
			£6,750

Third, a particular difficulty arises on cessation, where, for United Kingdom tax purposes, there may be a period of account which does not form the basis of any United Kingdom assessment, while foreign tax is payable in respect of the profits of that period. In such a case the foreign tax paid for those periods is taken back and added to the actual foreign tax paid for the period of account on commencement of the business. The aggregate of these amounts is then compared with the tax credit allowed on commencement and if the amount allowed exceeds the aggregate of the actual credits, an assessment is made to income tax under Schedule D Case VI so that the excess relief is recovered. However, if the foreign tax paid exceeds the credit given in the opening years, there is no provision for an additional credit.

Example 2

Following the facts of Example 1, O. Dear ceases to trade and the profits of the year to 31st December 1988 do not form the basis of any assessment to United Kingdom income tax. The profits for the year are £8,000 and Cantonian tax thereon is £2,400.

	£	£
Tax credit given in opening year		6,750
Actual Cantonian tax:		
Year to 31st December 1983	3,000	
Year to 31st December 1988	2,400	5,400
Recovery under Schedule D, Case VI...............		£1,350

(i.e. an assessment of such amount as gives a tax liability at basic rate of income tax of £1,350).

In some double taxation agreements it is provided that United Kingdom tax is to be computed by reference to the profit charged to tax in the foreign country.

Fourth, there may be occasions when for United Kingdom income tax purposes a loss is sustained, while for foreign tax purposes there is a profit upon which foreign tax is paid. There is no provision giving relief in such a case. Similarly there may be occasions when there is a loss for foreign tax purposes and a profit for United Kingdom income tax purposes. There is no credit available for foreign tax in such a situation, even though tax may be paid in respect of other periods in excess of the maximum amount which can be allowed as a credit. It is however possible to claim the non available credit as a deduction and hence increase the loss.

§ 5.—COMPUTATION OF TAX CREDITS

The calculation of the maximum tax credit which may be allowed in respect of income which has suffered overseas tax is to be made by reference to an individual taxpayer's marginal (or top) rate of tax. The actual credit will be limited to the amount of the foreign tax suffered, if less.

For the purpose of calculating the maximum credit available, income from overseas is computed before deducting any foreign tax, and in the case of dividends underlying (or indirect) tax may (in appropriate cases but not for individuals) be taken into account.

Example

B. Hunt, a married man, has the following income for the year 1985–86:

	£
Salary	18,000
United Kingdom dividends	2,500
Foreign dividend (declared gross)	3,000

The foreign dividend is paid out of profits which have borne foreign tax at the rate of 40 per cent, and the declared dividend is subject to foreign withholding tax at the rate of 15 per cent. The relevant double taxation agreement provides for tax credit relief in respect of the indirect foreign tax. (This would not be available under unilateral relief since Hunt is not a company.)

The calculation of the maximum tax credit is as follows:

	£	£	Excluding foreign income £	Including foreign income £
Salary			18,000	18,000
United Kingdom dividends			2,500	2,500
Foreign dividend:				
Net.		2,550		
Withholding tax.	450	450		
Indirect tax.	2,000	2,000	—	5,000
Total foreign tax.	£2,450			
			20,500	25,500
Less: Personal allowance.			3,455	3,455
Taxable income.			£17,045	£22,045

INCOME TAX PAYABLE

	£	£		£	£
On	16,200 @ 30%	4,860.00	On	16,200 @ 30%	4,860.00
	845 @ 40%	338.00		3,000 @ 40%	1,200.00
				2,845 @ 45%	1,280.25
	£17,045	5,198.00		£22,045	7,340.25

The income tax attributable to the foreign dividend is therefore £2,142.25 (£7,340.25 − £5,198.00) and the tax credit cannot exceed this amount. The credit to be allowed will therefore be £2,142.25 notwithstanding the actual foreign taxes suffered is £2,450.

If there is more than one source of foreign income, each is dealt with separately but in the order which is most advantageous to the taxpayer, which will normally mean that the income that has borne the highest foreign rate of tax is treated as the top slice of income.

DIVIDENDS THROUGH PAYING AGENTS

Section 159, I.C.T.A. 1970 authorises agents in this country to deduct tax when paying dividends from a foreign company. Usually the Commissioners of Inland Revenue make arrangements with the agent whereby he deducts tax at a lower rate than the basic rate, in effect giving shareholders a provisional measure of relief from double taxation.

The arrangements made differ considerably; typically they might be:
    (i) deduction of tax at the basic rate less the equivalent of the withholding tax (e.g., if the withholding tax is 10%, 20%); or
    (ii) deduction of tax at half the basic rate (i.e., 15%).

The provisional credit will be adjusted if necessary, depending on the claimant's marginal rate.

14. Corporation Tax—General Principles

§ 1.—INTRODUCTION

Prior to F.A. 1965, the income of companies was charged to income tax and where appropriate profits tax, irrespective of whether or not that income was distributed to the company's shareholders. If the company made a distribution (e.g. a dividend), there was no further liability to income tax upon the company when it paid the dividend and the income tax paid by the company upon its income was deemed to satisfy the income tax liability (but not surtax) of the shareholders on the dividends.

Under the corporation tax system introduced by the Finance Act 1965, the tax liabilities of companies and their shareholders are separated. Companies became liable to corporation tax on their profits (i.e. both income and chargeable gains). If a company paid a dividend, it was required to deduct therefrom and pay over to the Inland Revenue income tax at the standard rate in force.

This new system was itself "reformed" by the Finance Act 1972. Under the reformed system the separate corporation tax on a company's profits has been retained but there is now a link between the taxation of a company and its shareholders. The new system is generally known as the "imputation" system. As before, the company's profits remain chargeable to corporation tax. However, if the company makes a qualifying distribution (e.g. a dividend) in an accounting period, the company makes a payment (proportionate to the amount of the distribution) known as "advance corporation tax" (A.C.T.). This payment is taken into account when the company subsequently pays the corporation tax on its profit for that accounting period.

Where the shareholder receiving the distribution is an individual, he is treated as receiving a dividend equal to the amount of the distribution together with the A.C.T. payable in respect thereof. However he is entitled to a tax credit which can be set against his income tax liability upon the distribution and in appropriate cases a repayment may be made or a further liability may be due. The treatment of distributions received by another United Kingdom company is dealt with elsewhere in this work (Chapter 15, § 4).

Companies are required to deduct income tax from annual charges and to pay such tax over to the Inland Revenue.

§ 2.—SCOPE OF CORPORATION TAX (ss. 238–240, 243, 246, I.C.T.A. 1970)

Corporation tax is chargeable on the profits (both income and chargeable gains) of "companies". For this purpose a company is defined by s. 526(5), I.C.T.A. 1970 as including any body corporate or unincorporated association. Thus corporation tax is charged not only on the profits of limited or unlimited companies incorporated under the Companies Acts but also on such bodies as, for example, golf clubs, trade unions or political associations. Partnerships are, however, specifically excluded in the definition as are local authorities and local authority associations. Holiday clubs and thrift funds are also treated as outside the scope of corporation tax (Concession C4—1980) and there are special rules for loan and money societies (Concession C3—1980).

A company which is resident in the United Kingdom is chargeable to corporation tax (and not income tax as capital gains tax) on its income and chargeable gains wherever these may arise, i.e. whether in the United Kingdom or overseas.

Non-resident companies are chargeable only if they carry on a trade in the United Kingdom through a branch or agency, and then only in respect of the trading income, income from property and chargeable gains attributable to the branch or agency wherever arising. A non-resident company will be liable to income tax in respect of any other income arising in the United Kingdom which is not chargeable to Corporation Tax (subject to exemption under Double Tax Treaty).

The United Kingdom is extended, for tax purposes, to include the territorial sea of the United Kingdom and also the designated areas of the United Kingdom sector of the Continental Shelf and covers particularly North Sea oilfield transactions under which profits of overseas companies operating therein will be treated as United Kingdom profits (s. 38 and Schedule 15, F.A. 1973).

The residence of a company is not, in general, dependent on the country of registration or incorporation of the company nor upon the country in which the shareholders reside. It is resident where the central management and control of the conduct and policy of its business in fact exercised (see *De Beers Consolidated Mines Ltd* v. *Howe* (1906); see however the Inland Revenue consultative document *Company Residence*, issued on 26th January 1981 which indicates probable changes in the question of company residence although the proposals have been "shelved" *pro-tem.*). However, these general rules may be overriden by the terms of a Double Tax Treaty (see Chapter 20). For example, under the U.S.-U.K. treaty a company incorporated in the U.S.A is resident there.

Dividends or other distributions received from United Kingdom resident companies are not included in profits for corporation tax purposes.

Annual payments received under deduction of tax (e.g. debenture interest, royalties) are included in profits. The income tax deducted from such payments is set against corporation tax due for the period in which the annual payment concerned is received. If the corporation tax due is insufficient for such set-off the excess income tax is repaid, but not before the normal due date for payment of Corporation Tax (if there had been any).

§ 3.—BASIS OF ASSESSMENT (ss. 243, 244, 247, I.C.T.A. 1970, ss. 18, 20 F.A. 1984)

Assessments to Corporation Tax are for accounting periods and not for years of assessment, and are on the profits arising in each accounting period, i.e. on an actual basis.

FINANCIAL YEAR

The financial year for Corporation Tax purposes runs to 31st March, and when a Company's accounting period covers more than one financial year the total assessable profits must be apportioned on a time basis.

A financial year is to be identified by the year in which it *begins*, i.e. the "financial year 1984" means the year beginning 1st April 1984 and ending 31st March 1985.

Example

A company's accounts are prepared for the year to 31st December 1985. The accounting period is divided as follows:

(a) Period 1st January 1985, to 31st March 1985.
(b) Period 1st April 1985 to 31st December 1985.

The profits for period (a) will be charged at the rate of corporation tax relevant to the year ended 31st March 1985 (financial year 1984), and the profits for period (b) charged at the rate relevant to the year ended 31st March 1986 (financial year 1985).

The rates for corporation tax for the various financial years are as follows:

Financial years		
	1964–66	40%
	1967	42.5%
	1968	45%
	1969	42.5%
	1970–72	40%

Introduction of imputation system on 1st April 1973

	1973–82	52%
	1983	50%
	1984	45%
	1985	40%
	1986	35%

There is a special "small companies" rate of corporation tax applied to the *income* of companies with small *profits* (see § 14).
The "small companies" rates of corporation tax for the various financial years are as follows:

Financial years		
	1973–78	42%
	1979–81	40%
	1982	38%
	1983 onwards	30%

There is provision for marginal relief where a company's profits exceed a stipulated lower limit, but do not exceed a stipulated higher limit. (See § 14.)
Since 1st April 1973 capital gains realised by companies are charged at the full rate of corporation tax after a reduction:

Financial years		
	1973–82	11/26
	1983	2/5
	1984	1/3
	1985	1/4
	1986	1/7

In effect chargeable gains realised by companies suffer tax at 30%:

1973–82	$15/26 \times 52\%$	30%
1983	$3/5 \times 50\%$	30%
1984	$2/3 \times 45\%$	30%
1985	$3/4 \times 40\%$	30%
1986	$6/7 \times 35\%$	30%

If an assessment is made before the Finance Act fixing the rate of corporation tax for the relevant financial year has been passed, such assessment will be made according to the rate of corporation tax fixed either in the previous Finance Act or in the appropriate budget resolution. The House of Commons must pass a resolution fixing the rate of corporation tax not later than 5th May following the end of the financial year concerned. There are provisions for adjustments, whether by way of further assessment or repayment, if the rate finally fixed differs from the rate used provisionally.

Special provisions apply to the undermentioned bodies:

   (*a*) Approved investment trusts and authorised unit trusts (ss. 354 to 359, I.C.T.A. 1970)

   (*b*) Savings Banks

   (*c*) Industrial and Provident Societies

   (*d*) Co-operative Housing Associations

   (*e*) Self-Build Housing Societies   (ss. 339 to 347, I.C.T.A. 1970)

   (*f*) Building Societies

   (*g*) Co-operative Trading Associations

   (*h*) Mutual companies

   (*i*) Company partnerships (ss. 155, I.C.T.A. 1970)

   (*j*) Statutory bodies (ss. 348–353, I.C.T.A. 1970)

Special exemptions apply to the undermentioned bodies: (ss. 360 to 364, I.C.T.A. 1970)

   (*a*) Registered charities

   (*b*) Agricultural Societies

   (*c*) Scientific Research Associations

   (*d*) British Museum

   (*e*) Funds for reducing the National Debt

(See also Chapter 23).

§ 4.—ACCOUNTING PERIODS (s. 247, I.C.T.A. 1970)

Corporation tax for any financial year is charged on a company's profits arising in that year, but assessments to corporation tax are made by reference to its accounting periods.

If a company's accounting period does not coincide with a financial year it is necessary to apportion the profits of the accounting period between the financial years concerned. The appropriate rate of corporation tax is then applied to each part of the profits. Where an apportionment to different periods is necessary, it is calculated on a time basis.

Corporation tax is assessed on the basis of the profits of an accounting period, but for this purpose an accounting period *cannot exceed twelve months*. Thus, whilst the accounting period for corporation tax purposes is usually the period for which a company makes up its accounts, the following situations override this normal rule and will always mark the end of an accounting period or the commencement of another (or the first).

An accounting period *ends* in the following circumstances:

   (*a*) The expiration of twelve months from the beginning of the accounting period.

   (*b*) An accounting date of the company.

   (*c*) The company beginning or ceasing to carry on any trade (or if more than one, all of them).

   (*d*) The company ceasing to be resident in the United Kingdom.

   (*e*) The company ceasing to be within the charge of tax.

An accounting period *begins* when the previous accounting period ends or the company comes within the charge to corporation tax, for example:

   (*a*) when it commences to carry on business;

   (*b*) when it becomes resident in the United Kingdom;

   (*c*) when it acquires its first source of income;

Where a company's period of account exceeds twelve months, it is divided into *two* accounting periods, the first ending after the first twelve months, the second ending at the end of the period of account.

Example

A company makes accounts up to 30th September 1983. The next accounts are made up for the eighteen months to 31st March 1985, and thereafter annually. The accounting periods of the company for corporation tax purposes will be:

Period 12 months ended 30th September 1983
Period 12 months ended 30th September 1984 (first 12 months)
Period 6 months ended 31st March 1985 (remainder of 18 months)
Period 12 months ended 31st March 1986

There are a number of special circumstances which can affect a company's accounting period.

(a) Where a company carries on more than one trade and makes up accounts for each of these trades to different dates, i.e. it does not produce general accounts for the whole of the company's activities, the company's accounting period will end on the accounting date of such one of its trades as determined by the Commissioners of Inland Revenue.

(b) If a chargeable gain accrues to or an allowable capital loss is suffered by a company at a time which is otherwise within an accounting period one will be treated as beginning at that time so that the gain or loss will accrue in that period.

(c) Where a company is wound up, an accounting period ends and a new one begins with the commencement of the winding-up. Thereafter an accounting period runs for twelve months until the final period which ends on the completion of the winding-up. A winding-up commences on the passing by the company of a resolution for the winding-up of the company, or on the presentation, to the court, of a petition to that effect.

(d) If the beginning or end of an accounting period of a company is uncertain, the Inspector of Taxes may make an assessment for any period, not exceeding twelve months, that appears to him to be appropriate in the circumstances. The company has a right of appeal if it is able to show the true accounting period, in which case the Inspector may revise the assessment accordingly. See *Pearce* v. *Woodhall-Duckham Ltd* (1978).

In practice accounting periods of 52 weeks (e.g. to the last Saturday in the month) will be treated as equivalent to a regular twelve-month period, provided that agreement thereto is obtained from the Inspector of Taxes.

§ 5.—PAYMENT OF CORPORATION TAX

DUE DATE (ss. 243 and 244, I.C.T.A. 1970)

Corporation tax is normally payable within nine months from the end of the accounting period (or within 30 days from the date of issue of the assessment, if later).

Where a company was trading before 1st April 1965, the corporation tax assessed on the company for any accounting period must be paid within the same time interval from the end of the accounting period as there was between the end of the basis period of the trade for the year 1965–66 and 1st January 1966 *provided* the company continues to be within the charge to corporation tax in respect of the trade. This rule will not apply unless the interval is longer than nine months. As with the normal case the payment date will be extended to 30 days after the date of issue of an assessment (if that is later).

Example 1

Smith and Co. Ltd. is an old established trading company which makes up its accounts to the 30th June annually. There has been no change of accounting date since 1965–66.

The same time interval applies as between the old income tax basis period for 1965–66 and 1st January 1966, provided the time interval was more than nine months. The time interval is eighteen months. Therefore the due date for the accounting period to 30th June 1985 is the later of 30 days after the date of the assessment, or 1st January 1987.

Example 2

Assume that Smith and Co. Ltd (above) changed its accounting date and made the next accounts to 31st December 1985.

The time interval was calculated as eighteen months after the end of its accounting period. Therefore, the due date is the later of 30 days after the date of the assessment, or 1st July 1987.

Example 3

Jones Ltd commenced business on the 1st October 1984 and makes up its first year's accounts to 30th September 1985.

As this company commenced trading after 31st March 1965, the due date for payment will be the later of 30 days after the date of assessment, or nine months from the end of the accounting period (i.e. 1st July 1986).

TAX UNDER APPEAL (s. 55, T.M.A. 1970, s. 68, F.A. 1982)
Tax charged by an assessment is treated as due and payable on the date indicated above unless an appeal is lodged within 30 days of the issue of the assessment (s. 31, T.M.A. 1970). If the tax charged by the assessment is excessive an application can be made (to the Inspector) for the Commissioners to determine that part of the tax may be postponed. This application must state the amount by which the company is considered to be overcharged to tax and the reason for that belief and must be made within the 30-day period.

This period is extended (with no time limit) for assessments issued after 27th July 1982 if there is a change in the circumstances of the case as a result of which the company has grounds for believing that it has been overcharged to tax.

It is important to note that the application for postponement of tax is separate from any appeal against the assessment itself made under s. 31, T.M.A. 1970, but it can only be made if that appeal is lodged.

Any tax which is not postponed becomes due and payable 30 days after the company's tax liability has been agreed, or after determination by the Commissioners, unless the normal due date is later.

If, after a determination has been made, it appears that the amount of tax held over is excessive, or as the case may be, insufficient, either the Inspector or the company can apply for the determination to be varied.

Both the initial determination of the amount of tax to be held over and any subsequent variation thereof can be made by agreement between the Inspector and the appellant. The matter will normally be decided by the Commissioners only when the parties are unable to reach agreement.

The rules dealing with payment of tax pending the determination of an appeal apply for all assessments with the exception of assessments to recover A.C.T., or Income Tax not accounted for under the CT61 collection procedures.

INTEREST ON OVERDUE TAX (ss. 86 to 92, T.M.A. 1970, s. 69, F.A. 1982)
Interest on overdue tax is charged from a *"reckonable date"* until actual payment. The rate of interest is:

Before 1st July 1974	6%
1st July 1974 to 31st December 1979	9%
1st January 1980 to 30th November 1982	12%
1st December 1982 to 30th April 1985	8%
After 30th April 1985	11%

In determining the reckonable date, it is necessary to split the tax payable as follows:

(1) Tax not under appeal.
(2) Tax under appeal:
   (*a*) Tax determined as payable (i.e. not postponed) following appeal;
   (*b*) Balance of tax payable, if any, being the difference between the ultimate liability and the tax paid following determination, e.g. Latepay Ltd receives an assessment to corporation tax in the sum of £15,000. Latepay Ltd appeals against the assessment, and the tax is determined at £8,000. When the accounts have finally been agreed, revised assessment is £10,000. The balance of tax payable is then £2,000.

The reckonable date is then:

(1) *Tax not under appeal.* The later of:
   (*a*) Normal due date.
   (*b*) 30 days after the issue of the assessment.
(2) *Tax under appeal.*
   (*a*) *Determined as payable.* The later of
      (*a*) Normal due date.
      (*b*) 30 days after the issue of the assessment.
      (*c*) 30 days after the Commissioners' determination (or agreement with H.M. Inspector of Taxes).
   (*b*) *Balance of Tax.* The *later* of:
      (*a*) the due date as if there had been no appeal *and*
      (*b*) the *earlier* of:
         (i) The date on which the tax finally becomes due and payable (normally following the revised assessment); and
         (ii) six months after the normal due date.

In the case of assessment issued after 27th July 1982 where an assessment has been appealed and the final revised assessment is greater than the original assessment, *for interest purposes* the final revised assessment is treated as issued at the date of the original assessment.

This only applies where an appeal has been lodged. In other cases interest on the excess tax charged by the final revised assessment will run from the later of:

   (*a*) the normal due date
   (*b*) 30 days from the issue of the revised assessment.

The reckonable date (which need not be an ordinary business day) can never be earlier than the normal due date. Therefore if no appeal is made on an assessment issued before the normal due date, or if, although an appeal is made, there is no application for postponement of tax, the reckonable date will be the normal due date.

If an appeal is made but the claim for postponement of tax is refused, or if already granted is withdrawn more than 30 days before the normal due date, then the reckonable date will be the normal due date.

Interest, *except* in the case of the balance of tax due under appeal, commences on the date on which tax becomes payable (see payment of tax above).

The exception means that in cases where the final agreed assessment in respect of tax under appeal is some time after the dates shown by the above table, interest will commence to run *even* though the tax is not due for payment. It is therefore essential to review the amount of tax outstanding as a result of an appeal, at the dates shown in the table to ensure that the final tax liability will not be greater than that already paid.

Although there is no lower limit on interest charged the Board has power to waive interest of less than £30 (prior to 1st August 1980 the limit was £10) on an assessment. Interest paid on overdue tax is not an allowable deduction.

These provisions do not apply to the CT 61 collection procedures for Advance

Corporation Tax or Income Tax deducted from annual payments by companies. Interest on such payment runs from fourteen days after the end of the CT 61 return period, without the need for an assessment (which is normally made only where the return procedure has not been complied with). The same rate of interest and *de minimis* limit applies.

It should be noted that if an assessment is raised to recover tax lost (albeit temporarily) due to fraud, wilful default or neglect interest is charged from the date which would have been the normal due date if the proper procedures had been followed.

Payments of interest on unpaid tax are not deductible in computing profits for corporation tax.

If an assessment, upon which interest has been paid, is subsequently reduced because of a relief due to and claimed by the company such interest is waived as repaid.

Where the reason that tax remains unpaid is that is related to overseas profits which cannot be remitted because of foreign exchange control restrictions no interest will be charged for the period during which such restrictions apply. Upon their removal interest will run from three months after the profits become remittable.

REPAYMENT SUPPLEMENT (s. 48, F.A. (No. 2) 1975)
A "repayment supplement" is paid to companies which receive delayed refunds of:

(*a*) Corporation tax.
(*b*) A.C.T.
(*c*) Income tax deducted from charges.
(*d*) Tax credits on franked investment income.

The supplement is *not* subject to taxation.

"Repayment supplement" is paid where a repayment exceeds £100 and the repayment is made more than twelve months after the material date. Interest runs at the appropriate rate for each complete tax month (to the 5th of the month) contained in the period beginning with the relevant date, and ending at the end of the tax month in which the order for the repayment is issued.

The rate of repayment supplement (which is related back to the relevant date) is:

before 6th April 1974	6%
7th April to 5th January 1980	9%
6th January 1980 to 5th December 1982	12%
6th December 1982 to 5th May 1985	8%
After 6th May 1985	11%

To ascertain the relevant date, it is first necessary to establish the *material date*. The material date is the normal due date of payment of tax (i.e. 9 months after the end of the accounting period) or possibly later if the company was trading before the financial year 1965.

The relevant date is then:

(1) *In respect of tax paid more than a year after the material date*, the relevant date is the anniversary of the material date that occurs next after the date of payment.
(2) *In any other case* (i.e. tax paid within a year of the material date), the first anniversary of the material date.

Example

Material date 1st January 1983.
Date of payment of tax:
    (i) 12.1.84 (Tax paid more than a year after the material date)

(ii) 12.8.85 (Tax paid more than a year after the material date)
(iii) 30.6.83 (Tax paid within a year of the material date)
(iv) 31.12.83 (Tax paid within a year of the material date)

The relevant date is

    (i) 1.1.85   (i.e. the anniversary of the material date that occurs next following the payment)
    (ii) 1.1.86   (i.e. the anniversary of the material date that occurs next following the payment)
    (iii) 1.1.84   (the first anniversary of the material date)
    (iv) 1.1.84   (the first anniversary of the material date)

Repayments arising as a result of A.C.T. carried back to a previous accounting period (see Chapter 15, § 3), or loans to participators repaid (see Chapter 19, § 8), are to be treated as corporation tax which has been paid for the accounting period in which they arose.

If corporation tax is paid on several different dates, then the repayment will be matched to the later, rather than the earlier, payments.

CERTIFICATES OF TAX DEPOSIT

Certificates of Tax Deposit, available to companies, are evidence of deposits made by the taxpayer for payment of tax. It is not necessary for the deposit to be specifically set against a tax liability, although deposits *cannot* be made against P.A.Y.E. or be deducted from payments to subcontractors. Interest is payable gross on the deposit but is subject to tax. Interest is payable up to a maximum period of 6 years from the date of deposit to the date of payment of the tax.

Withdrawals for cash may be made at any time, although interest is then reduced.

TAX ON COMPANY IN LIQUIDATION (ss. 245, 247(7), I.C.T.A. 1970)

Special arrangements have been made to enable the liquidation of a company to be completed, notwithstanding that the rate of corporation tax for the final and penultimate financial year is not, at that time, known.

Accordingly the last known rates and fractions, etc. for corporation tax is used. Thus where a rate has been fixed for the final year by a Finance Act, or proposed in a budget resolution, that rate is used. In other cases the rate fixed or proposed for the penultimate year is used.

In order to facilitate the completion of the winding up the liquidator will agree with the inspector the date upon which he expects the winding up to be completed. That date will cause the end of an accounting period, and assessment can be raised on that basis. If that date turns out to be wrong there is still an accounting period ending at the date originally anticipated, but a new accounting period runs for the period up to the actual completion of the winding up. All other accounting periods during the liquidator's administration run to the anniversary of his appointment.

§ 6.—CHARGES ON NON-RESIDENTS (ss. 78 to 85, T.M.A. 1970)

If a non-resident company has a branch or agency in the U.K., the branch or agent will be assessed on the profits thereof notwithstanding that the branch or agency has not actually received the profits. The profits from the branch or agency itself are of course assessed and charged on the branch or agency.

In cases where the profits of a branch or agency are not otherwise determinable, the inspector can estimate the profits on the basis of a percentage of turnover. A decision on this point by the Inspector can be subject to appeal to the General or Special Commissioners.

Where a non-resident has manufactured goods outside the U.K. but sells them in the U.K. through a branch or agency, he has the right to elect that he is taxed on the basis of the profits that a merchant buying and selling (but not manufacturing) the goods could reasonably expect.

These rules do not apply where the agent in the U.K. is carrying on a brokerage or general commission business on normal commercial terms and is not otherwise connected with the non-resident (i.e. the non-resident is 'trading with' the U.K. rather than 'trading in' the U.K.).

By concession (B13—1980) interest (e.g. bank interest) is not assessed on the non-resident unless connected with a branch or agency that the non-resident has in the U.K.

These provisions do not apply to rents paid by a tenant direct to a non-resident and from which tax, at basic rate is deducted on payment (s. 89, T.A. 1970).

Any chargeable gains realised by a branch or agency are dealt with in the same manner as other profits.

§ 7.—COMPUTATION OF PROFITS (ss. 129, 238, 239, 250, 251, 265, I.C.T.A. 1970)

Taxable profits
Corporation Tax is chargeable in respect of the "profits" (i.e. income and chargeable gains) of a company and these profits are computed under the same Schedules and Cases as apply for purposes of income tax and the rules applicable to chargeable gains.

The income from various sources and any chargeable gains which arise in an accounting period are then aggregated to arrive at the total profits for that accounting period.

Profits are chargeable under the following Schedules and Cases:

Schedule		*Income arising*
A		Income from property—rents and premiums.
B		Occupation of woodlands.
D	Case I (or II)	Profits (losses) of a trade (or profession).
	III	Untaxed interest arising in the United Kingdom.
	IV	Untaxed interest arising from foreign securities.
	V	Untaxed income arising from foreign possessions.
	VI	Miscellaneous income (losses) i.e. income (losses) not falling under any other Schedule or Case.
Chargeable gains		Capital gains (less allowable losses), reduced by the appropriate fraction (see §12).
Unfranked Investment Income		⎰Income from which United Kingdom income tax is deducted—interest, royalties, annuities—but not distributions from a company resident in the United Kingdom. (These distributions are called "franked investment income".) Payments received from another company without deduction of income tax as the result of an election in force. Building society interest—at the grossed-up amount.

The income of companies, although *computed* by reference to the rules of income tax, is charged to corporation tax on the *actual* profits arising in accounting periods, applying the law which is operative for the income tax year of assessment in which the accounting period concerned *ends*. Reference should be made to the relevant chapters of this work for the rules of compution of various sources of income. Except for unremittable income and gains (e.g. due to foreign exchange control), the full amount arising is brought into account even though it has not been received in the United Kingdom.

Profits chargeable to corporation tax
From the total of profits assessable to corporation tax, "charges on income" are deducted to arrive at the profits chargeable to Corporation Tax.

Example

The computation of profits chargeable to corporation tax for Hanway Ltd for its accounting period ended 31st March 1986 is as follows:

	£	£
Schedule A.		800
Case I, Schedule D.		26,000
Case III, Schedule D.		1,200
Case V, Schedule D.		1,000
Chargeable gains	10,000	
Less 1/4	2,500	7,500
		36,500
Charge on income (loan interest)		3,000
Profits chargeable to corporation tax		£33,500

It must be remembered that the deduction for "charges" relates only to "charges" actually paid in the accounting period and must not include any deduction for charges accrued.

§ 8.—TRADING PROFITS

Trading profits are normally derived from accounts which have been prepared on commercial and accounting principles. Whilst the trading profit so derived will form the basis of the taxable trading profit, the tax legislation imposes different criteria in arriving at the taxable profit so that a number of adjustments are required. The main adjustments fall into one of the following categories.

(*a*) Increase a profit per accounts, or reduce a loss, by the amount of any expenditure charged in the accounts which is not an allowable deduction for tax purposes.

(*b*) Reduce a profit per accounts, or increase a loss, by the amount of any income or profits credited in the accounts, not assessable to corporation tax.

(*c*) Increase a profit per accounts, or reduce a loss, by the amount of any income credited other than to profits, assessable to corporation tax.

(*d*) Reduce a profit per accounts, or increase a loss, by the amount of any expenditure charged other than against profits, but an allowable deduction for tax purposes.

It is very important to remember that the computation of profits assessable to corporation tax is done in accordance with the provisions of I.C.T.A. 1970. It is therefore essential to distinguish between Case I, Schedule D profits (trading profits) of a company and other profits. This is no way affects the principles and mechanics of arriving at profits assessable to corporation tax. What must be done however, is to segregate the adjusted profits or losses on each Schedule or Case, and it is the sum of all these items which is assessable to corporation tax. In practice this is not really complicated, as the bulk of a company's income will be Case I or trading income, but it should be remembered that income under any other Case or Schedule should be shown as income received under that Case or Schedule.

The deductions allowable or not allowable from trading profits may be found in Chapter 4, to which the following may be added:

(i) *Deductions allowable*

    (*a*) Directors' fees, unless not laid out wholly and exclusively for the purposes of the trade, e.g. if to infant children (*Copeman* v. *Flood* [1940]).

    (*b*) Pre-trading expenses, if incurred after 31st March 1980 (see below).

    (*c*) Incidental costs of obtaining loan finance after 31st March 1980.

    (*d*) Salaries of employees seconded to charities.

(ii) *Deductions not allowable*

    (*a*) Loans made to directors which prove irrecoverable.

    (*b*) Defalcations by a director.

    (*c*) Dividends and other distributions paid or payable.

    (*d*) Pre-trading expenses, if incurred before 1st April 1980 (see above).

    (*e*) Costs of raising share capital.

    (*f*) Legal expenses in respect of a proposed increase in capital.

    (*g*) Loss of capital invested in a subsidiary company.

    (*h*) Payments of Corporation Tax.

    (*i*) Interest on arrears of Corporation Tax.

The treatment of capital allowances and stock relief in the computation of trading profits of companies is dealt with in Chapters 16 and 17.

§ 9.—FRANKED INVESTMENT INCOME (s. 239, I.C.T.A. 1970 and s. 88, F.A. 1972)

If a company resident in the United Kingdom receives dividends and other distributions from another company in the United Kingdom, it will not be liable to corporation tax thereon, as such dividends will have been paid out of profits which have already been subjected to corporation tax. Furthermore the dividends will have given rise to *advance corporation tax* (A.C.T.). Such A.C.T. will not generally be repayable, but may be set off against A.C.T. payable on dividends paid. The dividends thus received are referred to as "Franked Investment Income" which is defined as the dividend *including* the attached A.C.T.

A parent company and its subsidiaries may jointly elect that dividends paid by the subsidiary to its parent should be paid without accounting for A.C.T. Such dividends are not regarded as franked investment income in the hands of the parent company but will be treated as group income. Group income is also not subjected to any further corporation tax charge. (See Chapter 22, § 3.)

§ 10.—UNFRANKED INVESTMENT INCOME (s. 240, I.C.T.A. 1970)

This includes interest on loans, debentures, most government securities, building society deposits ("grossed-up"); and other charges, such as royalties and annuities, from which income tax has been deducted before receipt, and which were treated as charges on the profits of the company making the payment and which have, therefore, not borne corporation tax.

Unfranked investment income is charged to corporation tax and the income tax already suffered is utilised as follows:

  (i) to offset tax deducted from charges paid;

  (ii) to offset corporation tax payable;

  (iii) to obtain repayment, but such repayment will not be made prior to the normal due date for payment of corporation tax for the accounting period concerned.

Unfranked investment income also includes any receipt by one company from another company in the same group, which is a charge on income of the paying company but which has been paid gross under a group election.

§ 11.—BUILDING SOCIETY INTEREST (s. 343, I.C.T.A. 1970)

Building society interest is grossed-up at the basic rate of income tax for the year of assessment in which it is paid or credited, and the gross sum treated as income of the company for the accounting period in which it was paid or credited. The notional income tax is available for relief in the same way as income tax deducted from income received under deduction of income tax.

Example

A company received building society interest of £1,470 in the year to 31st March 1986. The amount included in profits for corporation tax is:

$$£1,470 \times \frac{100}{70} = £2,100$$

		£
Corporation tax thereon at (say) 40%	=	840
Less: Credit for income tax (£2,100 − £1,470)		630
Net corporation tax payable	=	£210

§ 12.—CHARGEABLE GAINS (s. 265, I.C.T.A. 1970, s. 93, F.A. 1972)

A company's chargeable gains are not charged separately to capital gains tax but are included (subject to the allowance of capital losses, including those brought forward from earlier periods) in the total profits on which corporation tax is chargeable.

Chargeable gains are in effect charged to corporation tax at a lower rate of 30%, equivalent to the rate of capital gains tax for individuals. This is achieved by excluding a fraction of the gain, the balance being charged at the full corporation tax rate. The amount excluded is an appropriate fraction of the net chargeable gains (i.e. chargeable gains less allowable losses, including those brought forward).

The appropriate fractions for the various financial years are as follows:

	Reduction	*Balance*	
1973–1982	11/26	$15/26 \times 52\%$	30%
1983	2/5	$3/5 \times 50\%$	30%
1984	1/3	$2/3 \times 45\%$	30%
1985	1/4	$3/4 \times 40\%$	30%
1986	1/7	$6/7 \times 35\%$	30%

Example

Babel Ltd has net capital gains of £100,000 in the accounting period ended 31st March 1986. The liability to corporation tax, at 40%, is as follows:

	£
Capital gain...	100,000
Less: abated (1/4)...................................	25,000
	£75,000

Corporation tax at 40% = £30,000

(N.B. chargeable gains are always charged at the full rate of corporation tax.)

§ 13.—CHARGES ON INCOME (ss. 248, 249 and 251, I.C.T.A. 1970)

Charges on income include:
- (a) Yearly interest*—e.g. interest on loans, debentures and mortgages.
- (b) Annuities.
- (c) Annual payments e.g., payments under four-year covenants to charities.
- (d) Patent royalties.
- (e) Mineral rents and royalties.

Payments treated as charges on income are not allowed as deductions in computing profits from any particular source (e.g. trading profits). Such payments are instead deducted from the company's total profits for the period for which they are *paid*. *This deduction is made after all other deductions* (e.g. loss reliefs) *except group relief* (see Chapter 22, § 7).

Interest paid to banks
Yearly interest incurred wholly and exclusively for the purposes of a trade, payable in the U.K. to a U.K. bank, is deductible in computing trading profits. In this case the company has no option to determine which treatment is applied (*Wilcock v. Frigate Investment Ltd* [1982]). Short interest paid to a U.K. bank (or a member of the Stock Exchange, or a discount house) not wholly and exclusively income for the purposes of the trade is treated as a charge.

To summarise, interest, either short or yearly, paid to banks which is *not* wholly and exclusively incurred for the purpose of the trade will be treated as a charge, as will *any* yearly interest paid to any other person.

Interest payments to banks etc. are treated as being paid when the company's account is debited therewith.

Conditions concerning the allowability of charges on income
Payments *must be:*
- (i) out of profits brought into charge to corporation tax;
- (ii) for valuable and sufficient consideration (except in the case of covenanted donations to charities);
- (iii) actually paid in the accounting period (or debited in the payer's books, in the case of interest to banks, etc.).

Payments *must not be:*
- (iv) charged to capital (except for interest paid in any accounting period ending after 31st March 1981);
- (v) not ultimately borne by the company;
- (vi) dividends or other distributions (see s. 233, I.C.T.A. 1970)

In the case of payments to *non-residents* the above conditions must all be met, and in addition one of the following must be met:
- (a) the payments must be subject to income tax at basic rate; or
- (b) the payments must be made out of income taxed under Schedule D, Cases IV or V: or
- (c) the payment is annual interest by a United Kingdom resident trading company (or its 75% subsidiary) which meets the following further conditions:
  - (1) the contract does or could require the interest to be paid outside the United Kingdom, and
  - (2) the interest is in fact paid outside the United Kingdom, and

---

* Yearly interest is always treated as a change on income unless paid to a bank, etc. (see below).

(3) *either*   the liability to pay the interest was incurred wholly or mainly for an overseas trade;

      or   the interest is payable in foreign currency wholly or mainly for the purposes of a trade carried on anywhere (except in the case of interest paid to partnerships or companies within common control).

With the exception of covenanted donations to charity, payments by a non-resident company must be incurred wholly and exclusively for the purpose of a trade carried on in the United Kingdom through a United Kingdom branch or agency and paid to a United Kingdom resident.

(N.B. The requirement under (*a*) is deemed to be met if under the terms of a double tax treaty the tax deductible is reduced to nil or below the basic rate.)

Further condition

For interest to be deductible as a charge, one of the following conditions must also be fulfilled:

  (i) the company must exist wholly or mainly for the carrying on of a trade; or

 (ii) the interest must be laid out wholly and exclusively for the purposes of the company's trade; or

(iii) the company is an investment company (see Chapter 23, § 1) or an authorised unit trust; or

(iv) the interest relates to a loan for the purchase or improvement of land for occupation by the company and, in general, the conditions for relief on interest paid for such a purpose. Land is regarded as occupied by a company and satisfying the conditions if it is not used as a residence (in which case the £30,000 limit does not apply). Alternatively the land can be used as an individual's only or main residence, or as job-related accommodation, in which case the £30,000 loan limit is applied separately to the loan.

An anti-avoidance provision prevents the deduction of interest paid under any scheme whose main purpose is the obtaining of the relief (s. 38, F.A. 1976). A similar provision prohibits any deduction for annual payments undertaken for non-taxable consideration (s. 48, F.A. 1977).

§ 14.—SMALL COMPANIES RATE (s. 95, F.A. 1972)

A reduced rate of corporation tax, known as the "small companies rate" applies where a company's *profits* (as defined for the purpose of the small companies rate) do not exceed a maximum amount which is fixed for each financial year. It should be noted that whilst a company's entitlement to the small companies rate of corporation tax is determined by reference to the company's "profit" the lower rate is applied only to the company's income.

A company's "profits" (P) for this purpose are computed as for corporation tax but with the addition of "franked investment income" (i.e. dividends received from other U.K. companies, including the attached tax credit). Dividends received from another company within a group (see Chapter 22) are excluded, even if advance corporation tax is paid, dividends without any A.C.T. being accounted for to the Inland Revenue.

"Income" (I) for the purpose of the small companies rate is the amount of profits as computed for corporation tax, less the amount included therein in respect of chargeable gains (s. 85(6), F.A. 1972).

The small companies rate of corporation tax has been as follows:

Financial years 1973 to 1978	42%
Financial years 1979 to 1981	40%
Financial year 1982	38%
Financial year 1983 onwards	30%

The maximum level of profits for the purpose of determining an entitlement to the small companies rate has been as follows:

Financial years 1973 and 1974 .... £25,000
Financial year 1975 .... £30,000
     1976 .... £40,000
     1977 .... £50,000
     1978 .... £60,000
     1979 .... £70,000
     1980 .... £80,000
     1981 .... £90,000
     1982 onwards £100,000

If a company's profits exceed this lower maximum amount but do not exceed a higher maximum amount, the full rate of corporation tax is charged but subject to a tapering relief. The higher maximum amount has been as follows:

Financial years 1973 and 1974 .... £40,000
     1975 .... £50,000
     1976 .... £65,000
     1977 .... £85,000
     1978 .... £100,000
     1979 .... £130,000
     1980 .... £200,000
     1981 .... £225,000
     1982 onwards £500,000

The tapering relief is calculated by the following formula:

$$(M - P) \times \frac{I}{P} \times \text{a fraction fixed by Parliament}$$

where M = higher maximum amount
    P = profit for purposes of small companies rate
    I = income for purposes of small companies rate
The fraction fixed by Parliament has been as follows:

Financial years 1973 and 1974 .... 1/6
     1975 .... 3/20
     1976 .... 4/25
     1977 .... 1/7
     1978 .... 3/20
     1979 .... 7/50
     1980 .... 2/25
     1981 .... 2/25
     1982 .... 7/200
     1983 .... 1/20
     1984 .... 3/80
     1985 .... 1/40
     1986 .... 1/80

Example 1

For the year ending 31 March 1986 Malibu Castings Ltd has trading profits of £80,000, untaxed interest of £10,000 and paid charges on income of £5,000.

	£
Case I, Schedule D..................................	80,000
Case III, Schedule D.................................	10,000
	90,000
Less: Charges on income............................	5,000
Profits chargeable to corporation tax....................	£85,000

The "Profits" are below the lower maximum amount of £100,000 (for the financial year 1985) and the "small companies rate" applies.

Corporation Tax on £85,000 at 30%.....................	£25,500

Example 2

Suppose in Example 1 that the company's franked investment income was £150,000 and trading profits were £380,000. The "Profits" would then be £535,000 (i.e. profits chargeable to corporation tax £385,000 + F.I.I. £150,000), which is above the higher maximum amount, so that the full 50% rate of corporation tax is payable.

Example 3

Surfrider Ltd has trading profits of £25,000 for the accounting period to 31st March 1986 and a capital gain of £20,000.

	£	£
Case I, Schedule D.......................		25,000
Chargeable gain	20,000	
Less: 1/4	5,000	15,000
Profits chargeable to corporation tax.........		£40,000

The "small companies rate" applies as the profits are below £100,000. The corporation tax payable will be:

Financial year 1985				£
Income:	£25,000 at 30%	=		7,500
Chargeable gain:	£15,000 at 40%	=		6,000
	£40,000			£13,500

Example 4

For the year ending 31st March 1986 Beachway Ltd has trading profits of £102,000, untaxed interest of £2,400, net rents of £3,000 and a capital gain of £7,667. The company made annual payments of £5,000. The company also received dividends from U.K. companies of £1,400.

	£	£
Case I, Schedule D........................		102,000
Case III, Schedule D.......................		2,400
Schedule A..............................		3,000
Chargeable gain:	8,000	
Less: 1/4	2,000	6,000
		113,400
Less: Charges on income		5,000
Profits chargeable to corporation tax.........		£108,400

"Income" = £108,400 − £6,000 = £102,400
"Profits" = £108,400 + £2,000* = £110,400

Corporation tax will be subject to the marginal "small companies rate" relief, as total "profits" (which include chargeable gains and F.I.I.) exceed £100,000 but are less than £500,000.

The corporation tax payable will be:

Financial year 1985			£
Income:	£102,400 at 40%	=	40,960
Chargeable gains:	£6,000 at 40%	=	2,400
	£108,400		43,360

Less: Marginal relief

$$(M) \text{ £}500,000 - (P) \text{ £}110,400 \times \frac{(I) \text{ £}102,400}{(P) \text{ £}110,400} \times \frac{1}{40} = \qquad 9,034$$

Corporation tax payable	£34,326

The lower and upper maximum amounts are reduced proportionately if an accounting period is of less than 12 months.

Example 5

Shortchange Limited had the following results for the 9 months to 31 December 1985:

	£	£
Case I, Schedule D.............................		96,000
Case III, Schedule D............................		2,000
Chargeable gain................................	6,000	
Less: 1/4......................................	1,500	
		4,500
		102,500
Less: Charges on income........................		10,000
Profits chargeable to corporation tax..............		£92,500
F.I.I..		£53,000
Profits chargeable to corporation tax..............		£92,500
Less: Chargeable gains.........................		4,500
"Income".......................................		£88,000
"Profits"		
Profits chargeable to corporation tax..............		92,500
Add: F.I.I.		53,000
Profits		£145,500
(M) £500,000 × 9/12		£375,000
(min.) £100,000 × 9/12		£75,000

---

* Profits are inclusive of franked investment income. The dividend of £1,400 must therefore include the attached tax credit of £600 to represent F.I.I.

The corporation tax will be subject to the marginal "small companies rate" relief as its total "profits" (which include chargeable gains and F.I.I.) exceed £75,000 but are less than £375,000.

The corporation tax payable will be:

				£
Financial year 1985				
Income:	£88,000 at 40%	=		35,200
Chargeable gains:	£4,500 at 40%	=		1,800
	£92,500			£37,000

Less: Marginal relief

$$(M)\ 375,000 - (P)\ \pounds145,500 \times \frac{(I)\ \pounds88,000}{(P)\ \pounds145,500} \times \frac{1}{40} = \qquad 3,470$$

Corporation tax payable   £33,530

Effect of charges

For the purposes of calculating "income" for small companies relief deductions that can be taken from more than one type of income—in this case, charges are deducted from income *other than* capital gains first (s. 85(6), F.A. 1972).

Associated companies

Where a company is "associated" with one or more other companies the upper and lower profit limits are split equally between them.

For the financial year 1982 onwards the revised limits are:

Number of associated companies	2	3	4
Lower maximum amount.........	£50,000	33,333	25,000
Upper maximum amount.........	£250,000	166,667	125,000

If the profits of an associated company are below the revised limit applicable to it the "unused" amount *cannot* be transferred to another associated company.

Companies are "associated" if they are under the "control" of the same person or persons. Control is defined as

    (a) having or being able to acquire over 50% of control

      or

    (b) being able to acquire over 50% of the companies' income

      or

    (c) being entitled to more than 50% of the companies' net assets in a winding up.

However, companies which are not carrying on a trade or business (i.e. dormant companies) are ignored as are companies controlled by relatives (other than spouse or minor children) provided there is trading interdependence (Concession C11-1980).

Accounting period spanning two financial years

If a company's accounting period falls into two financial years and there is a change in the lower and upper maximum amounts different limits will apply to the parts of the accounting period which fall into each financial year. Those parts of the accounting period which fall in each financial year are treated as separate accounting periods and the profits and income of the company for that accounting period are apportioned between them on a time basis.

The lower and upper maximum amounts are reduced on a time basis in proportion to the amount of each financial year falling within the company's accounting period and applied to the profits of each notional accounting period.

The appropriate fraction for each financial year is applied in the formula for the calculation of marginal relief if appropriate.

Example 6

For the year to 30th September 1982 Fruitbat Ltd had trading profits of £120,000, untaxed interest of £20,000, chargeable gains of £6,760 (realised on 30th June 1982) and paid charges on income of £2,000 on 31st December 1981 and £4,000 on 30th June 1982. It also received dividends from U.K. companies of £2,100 on 31st January 1982 and £6,300 on 31st August 1982.

		Total	F.Y. *1981* (6/12)	F.Y. *1982* (6/12)
		£	£	£
Case I, Schedule D.............................		120,000		
Case III, Schedule D.............................		20,000		
Chargeable gain	6,760			
Less: 11/26	2,860	3,900		
Total profits....................................		143,900		
Less: charges on income		6,000		
Profits chargeable to corporation tax..............		137,900		
"Income" = profits chargeable to C.T..............		137,900		
Less: Chargeable gains		3,900		
		£134,000	£67,000	£67,000
"Profits" = profits chargeable to C.T.		137,900		
F.I.I. (£8,400 × 100/70).................		12,000		
		149,900	£74,950	£74,950
Higher maximum amount			£112,500	£250,000
Lower maximum amount........................			£45,000	£50,000
Profits chargeable to C.T........................		137,900		
Corporation tax at 52%		71,708		

Less: Marginal relief
  (i) *to 31.3.1982* ....
$$((M) \text{£}100,000 - (P) \text{£}74,950) \times \frac{(I) \text{£}67,000}{(P) \text{£}74,950} \times \frac{2}{25} \qquad 2,685$$

  (ii) *to 30.9.1982*
$$((M) \text{£}250,000 - (P) \text{£}74,950) \times \frac{(I) \text{£}67,000}{(P) \text{£}74,950} \times \frac{7}{200} \qquad 5,477$$

Corporation tax payable £63,546

Example 7

Snap Ltd, Crackle Ltd and Pop Ltd are associated companies. For the year to 31st March 1986 they had the following results

	Snap Ltd £	Crackle Ltd £	Pop Ltd £
Schedule A	4,000		1,000
Case I, Schedule D	50,000	26,000	54,000
Case III, Schedule D	3,000		2,000
Capital gain	31,200		10,400
Dividends from U.K. companies	5,600	420	4,200
Charges on income	(5,000)		(40,000)

Computations

		Snap Ltd £	Crackle Ltd £	Pop Ltd £
Schedule A		4,000		1,000
Case I, Schedule D		50,000	26,000	54,000
Case III, Schedule D		3,000		2,000
Chargeable gain	24,000 / 8,000			
Less: 1/4	6,000 / 2,000			
		18,000		6,000
Total profits		75,000	26,000	63,000
Less: Charges on income		5,000		4,000
Profits chargeable to corporation tax		£70,000	£26,000	£59,000
"Income" = Profits chargeable to C.T.		70,000	26,000	59,000
Less: Chargeable gains		18,000		6,000
		£52,000	£26,000	£53,000
"Profits" = Profits chargeable to C.T.		70,000	26,000	59,000
F.I.I. (£5,600 × 100/70)		8,000	(£420 × 100/70) 600	(£4,200 × 100/70) 6,000
		£78,000	£26,600	£65,000
Higher maximum amount (£500,000 ÷ 3)		£166,667	£166,667	£166,667
Lower maximum amount (£100,000 ÷ 3)		£33,333	£33,333	£33,333

§ 15.—WHERE ACCOUNTING PERIODS DO NOT COINCIDE WITH PERIODS OF ACCOUNT

If a company's period of account has to be split into two or more accounting periods, the profits must be allocated between the various accounting periods. The following rules are applied:

(i) Trading income (Cases I, II or V (trades only), Schedule D) is computed for the whole period of account, before deducting capital allowances or adding balancing charges. This amount is then apportioned to the various accounting periods on a time basis. Capital allowances and balancing charges are calculated for each accounting period and the above amounts are adjusted accordingly.

(ii) For all other Cases and Schedules the actual income for the accounting period must be ascertained.

(iii) Chargeable gains are assessable in the accounting period in which they arise.

(iv) Charges on income are deducted from the *total* profits of the accounting period in which they are paid.

A composite set if covering several years may be apportioned between the various accounting periods on the basis of the facts (see *Marshall Hus & Partners Ltd* v. *Bolton* [1981]).

§ 16.—ADMINISTRATION

CARE AND MANAGEMENT (s. 1, T.M.A. 1970)
The administration of corporation tax is in the hands of the Board of Inland Revenue. The chief officials concerned with the administration of Corporation Tax are the same as for Income Tax (see Chapter 1, § 5).

RETURNS OF PROFITS (ss. 10 to 12, T.M.A. 1970)
Every company that is chargeable to corporation tax for an accounting period and which has not made a return of its profits (including chargeable gains see Chapter 14) within one year following the end of the accounting period concerned is required to notify the Inspector of Taxes that it is so chargeable. Failure to do so will render the company liable to a penalty of £100.

Normally the Inspector issues a return form on which the company is required to make a return of its profits giving the following details:

(*a*) each source of income and the amount of income therefore

(*b*) disposals giving rise to chargeable gains as allowable cases

(*c*) charges on income deducted against profits

(*d*) taxed income

(*e*) management expenses, capital allowances and balancing charges.

(*f*) A.C.T. paid (and, if appropriate, surplus A.C.T. carried forward).

In practice Inspectors of Taxes often accept computations in lieu of the formal return form.

OTHER RETURNS
Companies can be called upon to make returns relating to the income of, as chargeable assets disposed of by, other persons. These are listed in Chapter 1 and Chapter 26, § 13.

POWER TO OBTAIN DOCUMENTS (ss. 20, 20A–20D, 22–24, T.M.A. 1970)
The Inland Revenue's power to obtain documents (see Chapter 1, § 15) in relation to income tax also applies to documents required for the purpose of corporation tax.

ASSESSMENTS (ss. 29, 30, 34, 36, 39, 41, T.M.A. 1970)

Notices of assessment are sent out showing the amount of the assessment and the amount of tax payable. A notice to pay is attached and, if no appeal is made against the assessment the tax due should be paid to the collectors by the appropriate date.

Assessment (under Case VI, Schedule D) can also be raised to recover tax which has been repaid erroneously.

The normal time limit for making an assessment is six years after the end of the accounting period concerned, however, this time limit is extended if there has been *neglect, fraud or wilful default.*

An assessment is normally based on the information supplied by returns or computations supplied by the company to be assessed. If, however, the Inspector is dissatisfied with the return or computations (or if none has been submitted) he may make an assessment to tax to the best of his judgement. Notices of all assessments to tax must be served on the company assessed. The notice must state the date on which it is issued and the time within which an appeal against the assessment may be made.

If an Inspector (or the Board) discovers that any profits that ought to have been assessed have not been assessed, that an assessment is insufficient, or that excessive relief has been given, an assessment (or further assessment) can be made to bring into assessment the amount which, in their opinion should be charged.

The term "discover" has been the subject of considerable legal argument but, arising out of the dicta in the House of Lords in *R* v. *Kensington Commissioners ex parte Aramayo* (1916) a "discovery" arises whenever it newly appears that the taxpayer has been undercharged. From this it will be seen that the word "discover" has a very wide meaning.

RIGHT OF APPEAL

The general rules pertaining to appeals also apply to appeals against corporation tax assessments (see Chapter 1, § 18). The General Commissioners who will hear appeals against corporation tax assessments are those for the place where the company carries on its trade or business, or where it has its head office or principal place of business, or where it resides. The special rules relating to appeals in respect of tax on chargeable gains also apply (see Chapter 26, § 13).

ERROR OR MISTAKE (s. 33, T.M.A. 1970)

Where tax has been paid on an assessment, and it is subsequently found that the assessment was excessive owing to some error or mistake in any return or statement made for the purpose of such assessment, e.g. omission to claim capital allowances in respect of machinery or plant an application for relief may be made to the Revenue within six years after the end of the accounting period during which the assessment was made. No relief will be granted in the case of any error as to the basis on which the liability ought to have been computed, where the return was in fact made on the basis, or in accordance with the general practice, obtaining at the time of making the return.

CLAIMS (ss. 42 and 43, Schedule 2, T.M.A. 1970)

Certain reliefs can only be given if the taxpayer concerned makes a claim. Most claims are made to an Inspector of Taxes, but certain claims have to be made direct to "the Board". If a taxpayer is dissatisfied with an Inspector's decision on a claim, an appeal must be lodged within, in most cases, 30 days following receipt of written notice of the decision.

In most cases appeals against a decision by an Inspector on a claim are made to the General Commissioners, although the taxpayer can elect to have the appeal heard by the Special Commissioners.

Where there is already an outstanding appeal against an assessment concerning the same source of income as that to which the claim relates, the appeal is to the same body of Commissioners as the one which will hear the appeal against the assessment.

Appeals against a decision by an Inspector on "top-slicing" relief for lease presuming taxable under Schedule A (Schedule 3, I.C.T.A. 1970) can only be made to the General Commissioners.

In the undernoted cases, appeals against decisions or claims by an Inspector must be made to the Special Commissioners only:

(*a*) Management expenses of owners of mineral rights (s. 158, I.C.T.A. 1970);
(*b*) Various claims by insurance companies (ss. 310, 311 and 315, I.C.T.A. 1970);
(*c*) Various claims by friendly societies and trade unions in respect of pension and life assurance business (ss. 331, 332 and 338, I.C.T.A. 1970);
(*d*) Claims for tax exemption by Savings Banks (other than TSBs) (s. 339, I.C.T.A. 1970);
(*e*) Spreading of patent royalties (s. 384, I.C.T.A. 1970);
(*f*) Copyright payments (ss. 389 and 391, I.C.T.A. 1970);
(*g*) Spreading of payments to painters, sculptors, etc. (s. 392, I.C.T.A. 1970);
(*h*) Double taxation relief (ss. 497 and 498, I.C.T.A. 1970).

Appeals against a decision on a claim by "the Board" can only be made to the Special Commissioners.

The general time-limit for claims is six years from the end of the year of assessment concerned, but certain claims specify a shorter period.

TIME LIMITS (ss. 34, 36, 37, 39, 41, T.M.A. 1970)

The general rule is that an assessment to tax may not be made after the expiry of six years from the end of the chargeable period to which the assessment relates. However, in the case of fraud or wilful default an assessment may be raised at any time. Such an assessment may only be made with the leave of the General or Special Commissioners which is given on their being satisfied by an Inspector or other Officer of the Board that there are reasonable grounds for believing that tax has been lost by the Crown owing to the fraud or default of the taxpayer.

Section 37, T.M.A. 1970, extends the time limit for making assessments to recover any tax loss attributable to a person's neglect. Neglect is defined as negligence or a failure to give any notice, make any return, or produce or furnish any document or other information required by the Taxes Acts. An additional assessment under this section may be raised in respect of any of the six years of assessment preceding any 'normal accounting period' for which an assessment has been made within the normal six-year time limit on the person concerned for tax lost, wholly or partly on account of their own neglect. Such assessment must be made before one year from the time when the end of the tax lost in the normal accounting period has been finally determined. Such additional assessment may only be made with the leave of the General or Special Commissioners.

There is also provision for an additional assessment to be raised with the leave of the General or Special Commissioners for any accounting period even though more than six years has expired since the end of that accounting period. But only provided that the Commissioners have reasonable grounds for believing that tax for an accounting period ending not earlier than six years before the end of the year for which an assessment is now to be raised was (or may have been) lost to the Crown owing to the neglect of the person concerned.

DOUBLE ASSESSMENT (s. 32, T.M.A. 1970)

Where, by error, an assessment has been made more than once on the same profits, relief may be claimed and the excess tax paid reclaimed. The claim must be made within six years after the end of the accounting period concerned. The normal rights of appeal are available.

COLLECTION AND RECOVERY (ss. 60 to 70, T.M.A. 1970)

The Collector of Taxes will, when tax becomes due and payable, issue a demand to the last known address of the company concerned. On payment the collector must issue a receipt if requested to do so.

If tax due and payable is not paid, the Collector can distrain on the taxpayer's goods and chattels, and if, after holding them five days, the tax is still unpaid, they can sell them by public auction. Any surplus remaining after payment of tax and related costs is returned to the taxpayer. In order to carry out the distraint, after the Collector has obtained a warrant signed by the General Commissioners, he can break into the taxpayer's premises, with the assistance of the police if necessary.

Unpaid tax liabilities for one year only rank as a preferential debt in receivership or liquidation. Any other unpaid tax liabilities rank as non-preferential debts along with those of unsecured creditors.

Similar rules apply in Scotland, with necessary modifications. Recovery proceedings can be started in the Magistrate's Court, in the County Court, dependent upon the amount involved or in the High Court.

Interest on overdue tax ranks along with the assessment to which it relates. In practice this is not enforced in the case of insolvent companies.

PENALTIES, ETC.

Failure to inform of liability to charge (s. 10, T.M.A. 1970)

Every company which is chargeable to corporation tax and which has not delivered a statement of profits for that accounting period shall, not later than one year after the end give thereof notice that he is so chargeable. Such notice must ordinarily be given to the Inspector of Taxes. The penalty for failure to give such a notice is not to exceed £100. This is a maximum penalty, and the Commissioners of Inland Revenue have power to mitigate it.

Failure to deliver statements, etc. (s. 94, T.M.A. 1970)

Where a company has been required by a notice (under s. 11, T.M.A. 1970) to deliver any return, statement, declaration, list or other document, to furnish any particulars, to produce any document or to make anything available for inspection, and fails to do so it will normally be liable to a penalty not exceeding £50. If failure continues after it has been declared by the Court or Commissioners before whom proceedings were commenced, the company is liable to a further penalty not exceeding £10 for each day during which failure continues. The penalty mentioned in this paragraph is not chargeable if the failure is remedied before proceedings for recovery of the penalty are commenced. If the failure continues after two years from the date the notice is served the penalty can be increased to £50 plus the amount of tax due on the relevant profits.

In both these instances the penalty is restricted to £5 if for each offence the taxpayer shows that there were no profits to be included in the tax return for the year concerned.

Fraudulent or negligent returns (ss. 96, 97, 98, 99, T.M.A. 1970)

Where a company negligently delivers an incorrect return or statement or makes any incorrect return, statement or declaration in connection with any claim for any allowance, deduction or relief; or submits incorrect accounts; it is liable to a penalty not exceeding £50 plus the amount of the difference between the correct tax chargeable and that chargeable on the basis of the returns, etc., actually made.

In the case of fraud, the penalty for doing these things is £50 plus twice the amount of the difference computed as above.

For negligence in relation to other returns, statements, certificates, etc., the penalty is a fine not exceeding £250. In the case of fraud, the penalty is a fine not exceeding £500. Any person who assists in, or induces, the making or delivery of any return, accounts, statement or declaration which he knows to be incorrect is liable to a penalty not exceeding £500.

Furthermore, if having made a return which is subsequently discovered to have been incorrect, a company fails to notify the Inspector of the error, it is guilty of negligence.

Refusal to deduct tax (s. 106, T.M.A. 1970)
If a company refuses to allow deduction of income tax, a penalty of £50 will be incurred. Any agreement to pay interest, rent or other annual payments gross is void.

Procedure for recovery (ss. 100, 101, T.M.A. 1970)
An Inspector of Taxes may, without an order of the Commissioners of Inland Revenue, commence before the General Commissioners proceedings for the recovery of the penalties, for the lesser type of failure to deliver a return, statement, but the penalty recoverable is then limited to £50.

In all other cases, no proceedings can be commenced for the recovery of a penalty except by order of the Commissioners of Inland Revenue. Proceedings may be commenced either before the General or Special Commissioners, or in the High Court. Once an assessment is final it can be taken as conclusive evidence of the existence of the profits included therein.

Time limit for recovery (s. 103, T.M.A. 1970)
Where an assessment has been made within the normal six-year time limit for the purpose of making good to the Crown a loss of tax wholly or partly attributable to fraud, wilful default or neglect, provision is made for the making of assessments for earlier years not withstanding that they would normally be out of time. The sole purpose of any such assessment must be the making good to the Crown of a loss attributable to neglect. Normally, assessments can be made only in respect of the six years immediately preceding the earliest assessment which is still in date and which relates to a loss attributable to fraud, etc., though the Inspector may apply for leave to make assessments in certain cases to the General or Special Commissioners.

If the Inland Revenue prove the existence of fraud, they will not need to rely on the above provision, for ss. 34 and 36, T.M.A. 1970, gives them power to amend or make assessments for the purpose of making good to the Crown losses attributable to fraud or wilful default at any time.

Interest on tax recovered (ss. 88, 89, T.M.A. 1970)
Where an assessment is made for the purpose of making good to the Crown a loss of tax wholly or partly attributable to the fraud, wilful default or neglect of any person, the additional tax charged by the assessment carries interest (see s. 5) from the date of which the tax ought to have been paid until payment. The Commissioners of Inland Revenue have power to mitigate any interest so due, at their discretion.

Criminal proceedings (ss. 104, 105, T.M.A. 1970)
It is also open to the Revenue to instigate criminal proceedings for fraud and perjury in addition to the penalties described above. However they may, at their discretion, agree to a pecuniary settlement instead of instigating criminal proceedings.

Mitigation of penalties (s. 102, T.M.A. 1970)
The Board have a discretion to reduce these penalties in appropriate cases (e.g. if the taxpayer co-operates in the enquiry).

MISCELLANEOUS

Responsibility (s. 108, T.M.A. 1970)
All cuts required to be done to or by a company are done to or by its "proper officer". This will normally be the company's secretary but when a company is in the course of being wound up its "proper officer" is the liquidator.

Tax on loans to participators (s. 109, T.M.A. 1970)
Tax at a rate equivalent to A.C.T. on loans to participants is treated as though it were corporation tax and in general, the normal collection and recovery provisions apply.

VALUATION (ss. 110, 111, T.M.A. 1970)
The Revenue have power to inspect premises for valuation purposes and to enter premises to inspect assets for such purposes.

DOCUMENTS (ss. 112 to 115, T.M.A. 1970)
The Revenue have authority to prescribe the form of various returns and other documents. If an assessment or a return is lost or destroyed, the Revenue may issue or make new ones, but not so as to require the taxpayer to pay the tax due more than once. Minor errors in assessments do not render them invalid.

Tax returns, assessments etc. can be sent to taxpayers through the post to their last known address, place of business or place of employment. If a taxpayer submits Form 64-8 to the Inspector, copies of assessments can be sent to the taxpayer's accountant or other agent.

15. Corporation Tax—Distributions and Annual Payments

§ 1.—PAYMENT OF TAX ON "QUALIFYING DISTRIBUTIONS" (s. 232, I.C.T.A. 1970; ss. 84, 86, 87, F.A. 1972; s. 34, F.A. (No. 2) 1975)

A "qualifying distribution" is any distribution (see § 2) other than a bonus issue of redeemable share capital or securities, of the company itself or of another company from whom such bonus items have been received.

When a "qualifying distribution" is made by a company the company must make a payment to the Revenue of *advance corporation tax* (A.C.T.). This distribution together with the appropriate A.C.T. is called a "franked payment". The recipient's total income comprises the distribution plus a tax credit equal to the A.C.T. at the rate in force for the financial year in which the distribution is made.

The rates of A.C.T. for various financial years have been as follows:

Financial year	Ratio of A.C.T. to distribution	Year of assessment	Basic rate of tax
1973	3:7	1973–74	30%
1974	33:67	1974–75	33%
1975	35:65	1975–76	35%
1976	35:65	1976–77	35%
1977	34:66	1977–78	34%
1978	33:67	1978–79	33%
1979 onwards	3:7	1979–80 onwards	30%

Example 1

Turncoat Ltd paid a dividend of £700 on June 1985. This gives rise to a liability to account to the Revenue for A.C.T. at $3/7 \times £700 = 300$.

The method of payment of the tax is that the company makes a remittance of corporation tax to the Revenue and in so doing the individual tax payer has his basic rate of tax satisfied. However, it must be stressed that A.C.T. is not a withholding tax on the dividend but is precisely as stated, i.e. an advance or interim settlement of part of the company's corporation tax liability on its profits of the accounting period in which the distribution is made.

Any individual resident in the United Kingdom who receives a qualifying distribution from a UK resident company is entitled to regard the amount he has received as *net*, together with a tax credit equal to the A.C.T. paid by the company on the distribution, which he may set against his income tax liability on the dividend. This may also apply to some non-residents under the terms of a double-tax treaty.

The rate of A.C.T. has been fixed for each year as noted above and this has the effect of establishing the tax credit *for each year* at an amount which is the equivalent of the basic rate of income tax for each of these years applied against the company's distribution when "grossed-up" at that rate. Consequently, whenever an individual is entitled to a tax credit in respect of any distribution received, that distribution together with the relevant tax credit is regarded as his income for income tax purposes and the tax credit is set against his tax liability, and only the balance is payable or repayable as the case may be.

Example 2

Following example 1, the shareholder concerned is deemed to receive income of £1,000 (i.e. £700 dividend *plus* £300 tax credit).

If the recipient of a qualifying distribution made by a United Kingdom resident company is another such company that other company is entitled to a tax credit. The manner in which the tax credit is treated once in the hands of the recipient company is dealt with elsewhere. However, if the recipient company is exempt from corporation tax, or if the distribution itself is expressly exempt, a repayment of the amount of the tax credit will be made.

Distributions made by a United Kingdom resident company are chargeable to income tax under Schedule F, and this liability is met by the company making the distribution paying A.C.T. This A.C.T. is imputed by way of a tax credit as though it were a payment (at source) of income tax.

In two circumstances the recipient of a distribution is not entitled to a tax credit, viz:

(i) where the distribution is not a qualifying distribution;
(ii) where the recipient is resident in a country (not in the UK) with which the UK has no double tax treaty which provides for repayment of the tax credit.
   The receipt of such a distribution has the following consequences.
   (*a*) there is no assessment to income tax at basic rate upon the recipient;
   (*b*) income tax is payable only at higher rates less basic rate;
   (*c*) the distribution cannot cover annual payments;
   (*d*) the *actual* amount of the distribution is included in the recipient's total income;
   (*e*) it is thought that such distributions would be treated as the top-slice of an individual's income.

§ 2.—MEANING OF "DISTRIBUTION" (ss. 233–237, I.C.T.A. 1970, Schedule 22, F.A. 1972)

For the purposes of corporation tax a dividend is a "distribution" but there are several other matters which are also treated as being distributions:

(1) A capital dividend.
(2) Any other distribution out of the assets of a company except insofar as it represents a repayment of share capital or is in return for "new consideration".
(3) Redeemable shares or securities issued in respect of shares or, after 5th April 1972, securities in a company otherwise than wholly for new consideration. The value of redeemable share capital includes any premium payable on redemption, winding up, etc. The value of any security is the principal amount thereby secured together with any premium payable on maturity, winding up. etc.
(4) Interest or other distribution out of the assets of a company in respect of securities (except to the extent of any principal secured thereby), if the securities fall into any of the following classifications:
   (i) Securities issued after 6th April 1965 as redeemable securities (as in (3) above).
   (ii) Securities convertible, either directly or indirectly, into shares, or securities issued after 5th April 1982 and carrying the right to receive shares or securities, but not in either event being securities quoted on the Stock Exchange.

(iii) Securities under which the consideration given by the company for the use of the principal amount thereby secured is dependent upon the results of the company's business, or where the consideration given represents more than a reasonable commercial return. (It is only the amount in excess of such a reasonable commercial return that is treated as a distribution).

(iv) Securities issued by the company but held by a non-resident company where:

    (*a*) The issuing company is a 75% subsidiary of the other company;

    (*b*) Both are 75% subsidiaries of a third company, not resident in the United Kingdom;

    (*c*) Both the issuing company and the non-resident company are 75% subsidiaries of a resident company, *unless 90% or more of the share capital of the issuing company is held by a UK resident company. A 75% subsidiary is classified according to issued ordinary share capital.* There is no such qualification in respect of "90% or more of the share capital";

(v) Securities which are connected with shares in a company such that a holding is, in effect, part share and part loan.

(5) A transfer of assets or liabilities by a company to its members, or *vice versa*, giving rise to a benefit to the member (by reference to the market value of the assets concerned) in excess of any new consideration given.

If the company is a 51% subsidiary of the member receiving the benefit, or both are 51% subsidiaries of a third company, and in all cases the companies are resident in the United Kingdom, such an excess is not treated as a distribution.

A transfer of assets (other than cash) or liabilities between companies is not treated as a distribution provided both companies are resident in the United Kingdom, and neither is a 51% subsidiary of a non-resident company; and where neither at the time of the transfer nor as a result of it, are they under common control.

(6) If share capital is issued otherwise than for *"new consideration"*, and a repayment of share capital either accompanies or precedes such issue, an amount in respect thereof may be treated as a distribution, being the lower of:

(i) The amount paid up on the new shares; or

(ii) The amount repaid on the old shares less any amount thereof previously treated as a distribution.

In order to give protection to genuine preference share issues, no amount is treated as a distribution where the repaid capital:

(i) Existed on 6th April, 1965 as issued and fully paid preference shares; or

(ii) If issued after 6th April, 1965, was issued as fully paid preference shares wholly for new consideration not derived from ordinary shares.

Provided the company is not controlled by five or fewer persons, the above provisions do not apply to a bonus issue of share capital (other than redeemable shares), and made more than ten years after a repayment of share capital.

Limitation of distribution definition in respect of certain "interest" payments (s. 60, F.A. 1982)

Payments falling within (i), (ii), (iii) or (v) above and for loans, etc, made after 8th March 1982 are *not* to be treated as distributions except to the extent that the interest represents more than a reasonable commercial return.

This limitation was introduced to prevent lenders, primarily banks, from artificially creating distributions from what were in effect payments of loan interest. The mechanics were simply to make a small amount of the "interest" dependent upon the results of the companys' business, so that the interest became a distribution.

The arrangement arose primarily since in the early years of the borrower's business trading losses were likely to arise so that the relevance of a tax deduction for the interest payment was not of prime importance. As the payment would *not* be taxable in the hands of the recipient (as a distribution), a lower effective borrowing rate, ignoring the tax deductability, could therefore be achieved. ACT had, of course, to be accounted for by the borrower.

Transitional arrangements exist to treat this type of loan interest as a distribution if:

  (i)   the loan does not exceed £100,000, and
  (ii) the borrower is obligated to repay both the loan and interest within five years, and
  (iii) the loan was entered into before 9th March 1982 or prior to 1st July 1982 provided negotiations were in progress prior to 9th March 1982.

The limitation does not apply to companies exempted from U.K. tax on distributions under any section other than s. 239, I.C.T.A. 1970 (i.e. U.K. resident companies). Thus seemingly non-residents exempted under s. 246(2), I.C.T.A. 1970 would not caught by the limitation.

Certain of the terms above require further explanation:

(a) *New consideration*

This term means consideration not provided directly or indirectly out of the assets of a company, and in particular does not include profits retained by capitalising a dividend. A distribution is treated as made, or *consideration provided*, out of a company's assets if the cost thereof falls upon the company. However, consideration derived from the value of any share capital or security of a company (as from voting, or other rights therein) is not treated as "*new consideration*" unless it consists of:

  (i)   Money or value received from the company as a "qualifying distribution" (i.e. any distribution other than a bonus issue of redeemable share capital or securities, of the company itself or of another company from whom such bonus items have been received).
  (ii) Money received from the company as a payment which for those purposes constitutes a repayment of that share capital or of the principal secured by that security; or
  (iii) The giving up of the right to that share capital or security on its cancellation, extinguishment or acquisition by the company.

In cases (ii) and (iii), an amount is not treated as new consideration to the extent that it exceeds any new consideration received by the company for the issue of the share capital or security in question, or if the share capital constituted a qualifying distribution on issue, to the extent that such amount exceeds the nominal value of that share capital.

(b) *Repayment of share capital*

If share capital is issued as paid up capital otherwise than for new consideration, and the amount paid up was not at the time of issue treated as a *qualifying distribution*, then subsequent distributions will not in general be treated as repayment of share capital. However, if those subsequent distributions and other relevant distributions previously made exceed the aggregate of the amounts paid up (and not treated as qualifying distributions), such excess is treated as a repayment of share capital.

All shares of the same class, and all shares issued in respect of other shares, or converted or exchanged for other shares are treated as representing the same share capital. If share capital is issued at a premium which represents *new consideration*, that premium is treated as part of the share capital in determining whether any distribution represents a repayment of share capital. Of course, any premium which is applied to pay up share capital must be ignored. Premiums paid on redemption of share capital are not treated as repayments of capital.

In order to deter the issuing of stock dividends (as an optional alternative to cash dividends) which would otherwise not be income in the hands of the shareholders, such dividends are deemed to be income on which basic rate tax has been satisfied. However higher rates and investment income surcharge would be due. Dividends of this kind are now rare.

§ 3.—TREATMENT OF A.C.T. PAID (ss. 85, 103, F.A. 1972, s. 52, F.A. 1984, s. 54, Sch. 13, F.A. 1985)

The A.C.T. which a company has paid in respect of distributions in an accounting period is available for set-off against its liability to corporation tax for that same accounting period. This set-off refers to A.C.T. on dividends paid *in* the accounting period and not in respect of it.

Limitation of set-off
There is a limit to the amount of A.C.T. which may be set-off in this way. The limit pre-supposes that the entire income chargeable to corporation tax is a franked payment, i.e. distribution plus A.C.T. at 3/7 thereon, If follows that, at the 1985–86 basic tax rate of 30% the relevant A.C.T. is 30% of the chargeable *income*; (i.e. taxable profits exclusive of capital gains). This is the *maximum set-off* against the basic corporation tax liability—the net result is known colloquially as "mainstream" corporation tax.

Surplus A.C.T.
It may happen that a dividend is paid in an accounting period but there is no corporation tax liability, or the A.C.T. paid exceeds the 30% set-off limit. In such a case the "*surplus A.C.T.*", may, on a claim within two years, be treated as A.C.T. paid for accounting periods *beginning in the two years prior* to the year of surplus (dealing with a later period before an earlier one). This set-off is still subject to the limit applying in those earlier years and could still leave a surplus. This surplus is carried forward and is dealt with as A.C.T. paid in respect of later accounting periods.

For the purpose of the set-off calculations income is taken as the amount of the profits on which corporation tax falls finally, less chargeable gains.

For accounting periods ending after 31st March 1984 surplus A.C.T. may be carried back for set-off against corporation tax paid for accounting periods beginning within the six years prior to the accounting period concerned. This carry-back is restricted to A.C.T. arising in respect of dividends actually paid in the accounting period concerned. Surplus A.C.T. brought forward from an accounting period ending prior to 1st April 1984 is not eligible for the six year carry-back.

Accounting period straddling two financial years
There are problems when a company's accounting period falls within two financial years in which the rate of A.C.T. is not the same. The maximum set-off against the corporation tax is determined by apportioning the income of the company between two notional accounting periods for the periods up to 31st March and from 1st April, calculating the maximum A.C.T. set off for each part as if it were a separate accounting period and aggregating the result.

Example 1

This example illustrates how the set-off of A.C.T. reduces a company's mainstream corporation tax bill, in a simple case in which the company distributes only a small proportion of its taxable income.

In the year to 31st March 1986 Parameter Ltd has income of £550,000 and pays dividends of £63,000 in that year.

			£	£
A.C.T.	= £63,000 at 3/7	=		27,000
Corporation tax liability	= £550,000 at 40%	=	220,000	
Less: A.C.T.		=	27,000	
Mainstream corporation tax payable at the due date			———	193,000
Total corporation tax paid		=		£220,000

Example 2

This example illustrates a case where the A.C.T. paid in an accounting period is more than can be set against the corporation tax for that period, and shows how "surplus" A.C.T. may be carried back and set against the corporation tax of a previous accounting period.

In the following year to 31st March 1987, the same company (from Example 1) has income of £78,000 but the dividend paid remains unchanged at £63,000 (it is assumed that the rates of A.C.T. remain unchanged).

			£	£
A.C.T.	= £63,000 at 3/7	=		27,000
Corporation tax liability	= £78,000 at 30%	=	23,400	
Less: A.C.T. £78,000 × 30%		=	23,400	
Mainstream corporation tax payable at the due date	=		———	—
Total corporation tax paid		=		£27,000

The company is entitled to further relief in respect of £3,600 A.C.T. not available to reduce its mainstream charge for that accounting period. At its option it can carry this forward to a subsequent accounting period, or obtain immediate repayment by set-off so as to reduce the mainstream corporation tax for the previous accounting period. In the latter case, the computation for account period to 31.3.86 would be recalculated as follows:

			£	£
Corporation tax liability	= £550,000 at 40%	=	220,000	
Less: A.C.T.				
A.P. to 31.3.86		£27,000		
A.P. to 31.3.87		£ 3,600	30,600	
		———	———	
Revised mainstream corporation tax payable		=		189,400
(Compare corporation tax originally payable				
at due date)		=		(193,000)
				———
Repayment				£3,600

Example 3

This example illustrates a case in which a company's taxable income is reduced by a loss carried back from a later year, and shows how "surplus A.C.T." may arise: a surplus which may be carried back to a previous accounting period, or carried forward to set against the corporation tax due on a later accounting period's profits.

If the company in Example 1 paid a dividend of £336,000 for the year to 31st March 1986 but incurred a loss of £124,000 in the year to 31st March 1987 and paid no dividend, the position would be:

Revised computation for A.P. to 31.3.86

Profits for A.P. to 31.3.86	£550,000	
Less: Loss in A.P. to 31.3.87	124,000	
	£426,000	

Corporation tax liability		
Income: £426,000 at 40%		170,400
Less: marginal relief		
$(M)\ 500,000 - (P)\ 426,000 \times \dfrac{(I)\ 426,000}{(P)\ 426,000} \times \dfrac{1}{40}$	=	1,850
		168,550
Less: maximum A.C.T. for A.P. to 31.3.86 (£426,000 × 30%)		127,800
Revised mainstream corporation tax payable		40,750
Compare corporation tax originally payable at due date =		
£550,000 at 40% = £220,000 − (336,000 × 3/7) £144,000	=	76,000
Repayment		£35,250

A.C.T. available to be carried forward or back:
(£336,000 × 3/7 = £144,000 − £127,800 = £16,200)
The repayment for A.P. to 31.3.86 is reconciled as follows

Loss carried back =	£124,000 at 40% = £49,600	
Add: marginal relief	1,850	51,450
Less: A.C.T. in excess of limit =		16,200
Repayment as above		£35,250

Example 4

This example illustrates a case in which a company's total profits include a capital gain, and shows that the set off of A.C.T. applies only in respect of corporation tax on income.
In the year to 31st March 1986 a company has a trading profit of £520,000 and realised a capital gain of £126,000. It pays a dividend of £385,000 in that year.

			£	£
A.C.T.	£385,000 at 3/7	=		165,000
Corporation tax liability				
Income:	£520,000 at 40%	=	208,000	
Gains:	£126,000			
Less: 1/4	£ 31,500			
	£ 94,500 at 40%	=	37,800	
			245,800	
Less: maximum A.C.T. (£520,000 × 30%)		=	156,000	
Mainstream corporation tax payable at the due date		=		89,800
Total corporation tax paid		=		£254,800

Example 5

This example illustrates a case in which a company's accounting period falls into two financial years, and there is a change in the rate of A.C.T.

In the year to 31st December 1979 a company has income of £50,000. Because of the change of rate of A.C.T. there are (for A.C.T. set-off purposes) two separate accounting periods:

(a) 1st January 1979 to 31st March 1979; and
(b) 1st April 1979 to 31st December 1979.

	A.C.T. and set-off rate	Income £	Notional Distribution £	Maximum A.C.T. set-off £	
(a)	33/67 (33%)	12,500 (3/12)	8,375	4,125	(i.e. effectively 33% of £8,375)
(b)	3/7 (30%)	3,750 (9/12)	26,250	11,250	(i.e. effectively 30% of £37,500)
			£15,375		

Change in ownership of company (s. 101, F.A. 1972)

Special provisions apply regarding the restriction of A.C.T. carry-forward. Where, within a period of three years, there has been both a change in the ownership of a company and a major change in the nature or conduct of its business; or where there has been a change in the ownership of a company after a decline in the volume of business carried on to small or negligible proportions. These provisions virtually identical to those which restrict the right to carry-forward unrelieved trading losses.

§ 4.—FRANKED INVESTMENT INCOME (ss. 88, 89, F.A. 1972)

If a company, resident in the U.K., is the recipient of a qualifying distribution, the distribution together with the tax credit thereon is referred to as Franked Investment Income (F.I.I.) This definition of F.I.I. applies for all purposes of the Taxes Acts. F.I.I. is not chargeable to corporation tax in the hands of a U.K. resident company.

If, in an accounting period, a company receives F.I.I. it may set such F.I.I. against any *franked payments*, and A.C.T. is only due if these franked payments exceed the F.I.I. It should be noted that for the purpose of the set-off and accounting for the A.C.T. the distribution received and that paid must always be inclusive of the tax credit.

Example 1

Green Ltd's accounting period ends on 31st March 1986. The company receives F.I.I. amounting to £1,000 and makes franked payments amounting to £1,500. The excess is £500 and the A.C.T. is calculated as follows:

$$\text{A.C.T.} = \frac{30}{100} \times £500 = £150$$

Example 2

Effect of F.I.I. on A.C.T. liability:

Year to 31st March 1986

Profits assessable to Corporation Tax £90,000

Corporation Tax thereon at 30%. £27,000

Distributions	£35,000		
A.C.T. thereon—3/7		£15,000	
Franked Investment Income	£40,000		
A.C.T. credit—30%		12,000	
A.C.T. to be remitted			3,000
Mainstream Corporation Tax = ...			£24,000

Where there is an excess of F.I.I. over franked payments (known as a "surplus of franked investment income") in any accounting period, that excess may be carried forward to the next accounting period and treated as F.I.I. of that period.

Example 3

Effect of surplus F.I.I.:		£	£
Year to 31st March 1986			
Profits assessable to Corporation Tax			60,000
Corporation tax thereon at 30%			18,000
Distributions	£17,500		
A.C.T. thereon—3/7		7,500	
Franked Investment Income	£30,000		
A.C.T. credit—30%		9,000	
No A.C.T. liability................................			—
Mainstream Corporation Tax = ...			£18,000

Surplus Franked Investment Income carried forward of £5,000 (£30,000 − £25,000) to be treated as F.I.I. of next accounting period.

§ 5.—ANNUAL CHARGES (s. 240, I.C.T.A. 1970)

If a company makes a payment which under I.C.T.A. 1970, ss. 53 or 54, is treated as a charge on income, it must withhold and pay over to the Revenue income tax at the basic rate in force at the time the payment is made.

Where a company receives a payment by way of a charge on income, it is entitled to a repayment of the tax which will already have been deducted by the payer.

To the extent that income tax suffered on charges on income received has not been relieved by set-off against charges on income paid, that income tax may be set-off against the company's corporation tax liability, but any repayment of income tax cannot be made before the due date for payment of corporation tax.

It should be noted that charges on income received are included in a company's total profits and consequently subject to corporation tax.

§ 6.—ACCOUNTING FOR TAX ON DIVIDENDS, OTHER DISTRIBUTIONS AND ANNUAL PAYMENTS

Companies are required to make returns of:
    (i) Qualifying distributions and A.C.T. payable. (Sch. 14, F.A. 1972)
    (ii) Franked Investment Income (F.I.I.) (Sch. 14, F.A. 1972)

(iii) Annual payments and income tax payable. (Sch. 20, F.A. 1972)
(iv) Information concerning non-qualifying distributions. (Sch. 21, F.A. 1972)

Returns of items (i) to (iii) returns have been combined in Form C.T. 61. Item (iv) should be returned on Form C.T. 2.

Returns to the Revenue on Form C.T. 61 are required for return periods ending on

(*a*) 31st March, 30th June, 30th September and 31st December, and
(*b*) for the period ending on the last day of the accounting period if this is not one of the above mentioned dates.

Example

A company with an accounting period ending on 31st May will render forms C.T. 61 for the following return periods:

(i)	1st June to 30th June	1 month
(ii)	1st July to 30th September	3 months
(iii)	1st October to 31st December	3 months
(iv)	1st January to 31st March	3 months
(v)	1st April to 31st May	2 months
		12 months

A return under Schedule 14, F.A. 1972 must be made for each return period in a company's accounting period (as determined for corporation tax purposes) in which the company makes a qualifying distribution.

In addition, where the company has paid A.C.T. for a return period falling within its accounting period and in a later return period in the *same* accounting period it receives F.I.I., a return must be made for that later return period, whether or not the company has made any qualifying distributions in that later period.

Similarly, under Schedule 20, F.A. 1972, a company must make a return of annual payments, etc., made in any return period falling within its accounting period.

Returns are to be sent to the Collector of Taxes within 14 days from the end of a return period. Where, exceptionally, a company makes a qualifying distribution (or annual payment, etc.) on a date which does not fall within any accounting period, a return must be made to the Collector of Taxes within 14 days from the date of that distribution, etc.

Use of Form C.T. 61

Parts A, B and E of this form should be completed for any return period for which the company has to make a return under Schedule 14, F.A. 1972, and Part C for any return period for which it has to make a return under Schedule 20, F.A. 1972. Where the company wishes to set-off income tax deducted from income received in any accounting period against income tax payable or paid in respect of annual payments made in that accounting period, Part D should be completed.

Part F should be completed showing the A.C.T. and income tax payable for the return period. Part G should be completed where a repayment is claimed.

Where, exceptionally, a return has to be made in respect of a qualifying distribution or annual payment, etc., made on a date not falling within any accounting period of the company, Part B should *not* be completed.

Part F should be completed, the declaration on page 4 should be signed and this form together with the appropriate remittance, if any, sent to the Collector by the due date; i.e., within 14 days of the end of the return period to which the return relates. Alternatively, where the return relates to a distribution, etc., which was made on a date which does not fall within any accounting period of the company, Part F must be sent within 14 days of that date. The amount of tax shown in Part F is payable on the date the return is due. Interest is chargeable on overdue tax.

Computation of A.C.T. payable

The amount of A.C.T. payable for any return period falling within an accounting period is calculated by reference to the excess (if any) of the franked payments made by the company in that return period over the F.I.I. received in that return period. The amount of A.C.T. is calculated at the rate of A.C.T. in force for the financial year in which the return period ends on an amount which, when that tax is added to it, is equal to the excess referred to above. Thus if in a return period falling within an accounting period the company pays a dividend of £7,000 and the rate of A.C.T. is 3/7, the company makes a franked payment of £10,000. If during that return period it receives F.I.I. of £4,000, the excess of the franked payments over the franked investment income is £6,000 and A.C.T. of £1,800 is payable; i.e. 3/7 of the amount (£4,200) which when 3/7 (£1,800) is added to it equals £6,000.

Where F.I.I. received in a return period falling within an accounting period is equal to or exceeds the franked payments made in that return period, no A.C.T. is payable.

When, exceptionally, the company makes a franked payment on a date which does not fall within an accounting period, it cannot set-off any F.I.I. in arriving at the A.C.T. payable.

F.I.I. treated as received in a return period

In addition to the F.I.I. actually received in any return period falling within an accounting period, the company is also treated as receiving (in that return period) an amount of F.I.I. equal to the excess of:

   (a) any surplus of F.I.I. received over franked payments made in the previous accounting period; plus

   (b) any F.I.I. received in the accounting period but before the commencement of that return period;

over the total of the franked payments made in that accounting period, but before the commencement of that return period.

The amount referred to at (a) will be reduced if the company has claimed loss relief against the F.I.I. surplus or carried back A.C.T. from a later period.

Franked investment income received after payment of A.C.T.

Where a company has paid A.C.T. in respect of franked payments made in a return period falling in any accounting period, and receives F.I.I. in a later return period falling within the *same* accounting period, *repayment is due* to the company if that F.I.I. exceeds the franked payments made in that later return period. The amount of the prepayment will be the lesser of:

   (a) the A.C.T. paid; and

   (b) the tax credit attaching to the excess of the F.I.I. received in that later return period over the franked payments made then.

Example 1

Payment Ltd makes distributions and receives franked investment income (F.I.I.) as follows during the year ended 31st March 1986. (The unutilised F.I.I. brought forward from 31st March 1985 amounts to £20,000.)

	Dividend paid £	Dividend received £
Qtr. to 30th June 1985	14,000	
Qtr. to 30th September 1985	21,000	5,250
Qtr. to 31st December 1985.....................	14,000	
Qtr. to 31st March 1986		17,500

Payment Ltd will account for these transactions as follows:

Qtr.			£	£	Payable receivable £
1.	30.6.1985				
		Dividend paid	14,000		
		A.C.T. (3/7)....................	6,000	20,000	
		F.I.I. b/fwd 31.3.85..............		20,000	
				Nil	Nil
2.	30.9.85				
		Dividend paid	21,000		
		A.C.T. (3/7)....................	9,000	30,000	
		Dividend received..............	5,250		
		A.C.T. (3/7)....................	2,250	7,500	
				£22,500	
		A.C.T. thereon @ 30%			6,750
3.	31.12.1985				
		Dividend paid	14,000		
		A.C.T. (3/7)....................	6,000		6,000
4.	31.3.1986				
		Dividend received..............	17,500		
		A.C.T. (3/7)....................	7,500		(7,500)
		Total A.C.T. paid..............			£5,250

Notes

1. No A.C.T. is paid in the first quarter as this is covered by A.C.T. brought forward.
2. A.C.T. payable for the second and third quarters will be due 14 days after the respective quarter ends.
3. A.C.T. of £7,500 is repayable in the fourth quarter as A.C.T. in excess of this sum has been paid in the previous quarters *within* the accounting period.

Group income: dividends paid without accounting for A.C.T. (s. 256, I.C.T.A. 1970)
A parent company and its subsidiary (if both are resident in the United Kingdom) can elect jointly that the subsidiary shall pay dividends to the parent without accounting for A.C.T. This election may also be made by two fellow subsidiaries or, subject to certain conditions, when the company paying the dividends is controlled by a consortium of companies. Notwithstanding the election, the company may pay any amount of dividend and account for A.C.T. thereon.
A subsidiary for this purpose is a "51%" subsidiary.

Change in rate of A.C.T.

Where the rate of A.C.T. for any financial year differs from the rate fixed for the previous financial year—

(*a*) the A.C.T. payable in respect of any qualifying distributions made before 6th April, in the financial year for which the rate changes, will be payable at the "old" rate applicable to distributions made in the previous financial year;

(*b*) F.I.I. received after 5th April, in the financial year for which the rate changes, cannot be set-off against franked payments made before that date.

§ 7.—PAYMENTS TO NON-RESIDENTS

Dividends

Under the provisions of certain double tax treaties (e.g. U.K./U.S.) the recipient in certain circumstances is entitled to partial repayment of the A.C.T. applicable to the dividend paid. The repayment is made by the U.K. Revenue (via the Inspector of Foreign Dividends) and has *no* effect on the availability of offset to the U.K. paying company.

Example

A company owning 10% or more of the voting share capital of the U.K. company paying the dividend is entitled to a refund of A.C.T. on a dividend of £70,000 as follows:

	£
Dividend	70,000
A.C.T. at 3/7	30,000
Partial refund: $\frac{1}{2}$ A.C.T.	15,000
Less Withholding tax (5% of dividend plus $\frac{1}{2}$ A.C.T.)	
= 5% × (70,000 + 15,000)	4,250
A.C.T. refund	£10,750

The refund will be made by the Inland Revenue (via the Inspector of Foreign Dividends). Where advance clearance has been obtained, the U.K. company can make the 'A.C.T. refund' direct when paying the dividend.

The refund of A.C.T. has no effect whatsoever on the U.K. company's ability to offset the whole of the A.C.T. paid.

Entitlement to this refund may be withdrawn (from a date to be nominated by statutory instrument) where the recipient company has a presence in a "unitary state". Broadly, a unitary state is one which levies taxes upon a proportion of the worldwide income of such a company rather than on the actual profits earned by the company in that state. The detailed rules are to be found in s. 54 and Sch. 13 of the Finance Act 1985.

The Revenue may make arrangements with a company whereby when paying a dividend on the shares specified in the arrangement the company may also pay an amount representing the excess of the tax credit, to which a qualified non-resident may be entitled under the terms of the double taxation agreement.

Where a company has paid an additional amount on the specific authority of the Inspector of Foreign Dividends, *but not otherwise*, the A.C.T. which the company is liable to pay in respect of the relevant dividend may be reduced by that amount.

In certain circumstances, for example in the case of holding companies receiving only F.I.I., it may be possible, with prior arrangements with the Inspector of Taxes, for early reimbursement to be made, after payment of the dividend but before the next return on form C.T. 61 is due.

Annual payments (including interest)
Annual payments may also be made subject to a reduced rate of tax, withheld under a Double Taxation agreement, *provided* they are the subject of a notice to that effect issued by the Revenue.

§ 8.—PURCHASE BY A COMPANY OF ITS OWN SHARES

INTRODUCTION (s. 53, F.A. 1982)
Changes made by the Companies Act 1981 permit companies to redeem, repay or purchase their own shares. Subject to meeting a number of conditions such transactions will not be treated as distributions so that no liability A.C.T. or income tax arises thereon. Broadly they will be treated as sales of shares by the shareholders concerned and subject to capital gains tax. The new rules apply to payments made after 5th April 1982.

The new rules should assist privately owned companies in the following ways:
- (i) allowing a third-party investor (i.e. not a member of the family) to subscribe for shares which, ultimately, can be repurchased from him;
- (ii) allowing the company to acquire the shares of a family shareholder on his retirement instead of them being acquired by other shareholders who do not wish, or cannot afford to buy them;
- (iii) allowing the company to buy out a dissident shareholder;
- (iv) funding the payment of capital transfer tax on the death of a shareholder.

DEFINITIONS (Schedule 9, Paras 14 to 16, F.A. 1982)
There are a number of definitions of general application:

(a) Associates
The following persons are regarded as being each others' *associates*:
- (i) husband and wife (if living together);
- (ii) a child under eighteen and his or her parents;
- (iii) a person *connected with a company* and the other company. Such a person is also the associate of any other company controlled by such a company;
- (iv) companies under common control;
- (v) trustees holding shares in a company are the associates of:
  —a person who provided property to the trustees (or made a reciprocal arrangement whereby another person provided it to the trustees);
  —the husband or wife or infant child(ren) of such a person;
  —persons who are, or may become beneficially entitled to a *significant* interest in the shares. (For this purpose a person's interest is significant if it is worth more than 5% of the value of all the trust property, excluding any property in which he does not and will not have any beneficial interest).
  This rule does not apply to the trustees of approved pension schemes, nor trusts for the benefit of employees of the company concerned or of other companies within the same 51% group (see Chapter 22, § 3). However, it does apply to trusts which are wholly or mainly for the benefit of directors or their relatives.
- (vi) personal representatives of a deceased's estate holding shares in a company and beneficiaries entitled to a significant interest in the shares (see (v) above):

(vii) a person who is accustomed to act, in relation to the company's affairs, on the direction of another person and that other person.

(*b*) *Connected with a company*
A person is *connected with a company*:
    (i) if he, and his associates, have *control* of the company;
    (ii) if he and his associates own more than 30% of:
        —issued *ordinary share capital*;
        —*loan* capital and issued share capital;
        —voting power;
        (For this purpose loan capital includes any debt incurred for any of the following purposes:
        —for money borrowed, or capital assets acquired by the company;
        —for a right to receive income created in the company's favour;
        —for consideration of a value (at the time the debt was incurred) which is substantially less than the debt (together with any premium thereon)).
        However, loan capital held by a person in the course of a business which includes lending money is ignored in applying the 30% test, subject to the additional condition that such person takes no part in the management or conduct of the company.
    (iii) if, directly or indirectly, he and his associates own rights which would, in a winding up (or otherwise) entitle them to more than 30% of the assets of the company available for distribution to the company's *equity holders* (see Chapter 22, § 7).
For the purposes of the above tests it is not only current ownership of shares, etc. which is considered but also rights to acquire such shares, etc. in the future.

(*c*) *Control*
A person *controls* a company if he is in a position to secure that its affairs are conducted in accordance with his wishes.

(*d*) *Holding company*
A *holding company* is a company whose business (apart from its own *trade*) consists wholly or mainly in the holding of shares or securities of 75% *subsidiaries* (see Chapter 22, § 2).

(*e*) *Quoted company*
A *quoted company* is one whose shares are listed on the official list of a Stock Exchange, or whose shares are dealt in on the Unlisted Securities Market.

(*f*) *Trade (and trading activities)*
Trade does not include dealing in shares, securities, land or future.

(*g*) *Trading company*
A *trading company* is one whose business consists wholly, or mainly, of the carrying on of one or more trades.

(*h*) *Trading group*
A *trading group* is a group of companies the business of whose members, taken together, consist wholly or mainly of the carrying on of a trade or trades. (For this purpose a group is a company and its 75% subsidiaries).

(*i*) *Unquoted company*
An *unquoted company* is a company which is not itself a quoted company nor a 51% subsidiary (see Chapter 22, § 2) of a quoted company.

When considering the ownership of shares, the test is beneficial ownership except where the shares are held on trust (other than bare trusts) or by personal representatives of a deceased person.

References to *payments* made by a company include references to anything else which would otherwise be distributions.

GENERAL CONDITIONS (s. 53(1), F.A. 1982)

If the following general conditions are met, payments made by a company to redeem, repay or purchase its own shares are not treated as distributions, and accordingly the company is not required to account for A.C.T. on the payments, nor are they liable to income tax in the hands of the recipient.

1. The company must be an unquoted company;
2. The company must be a trading company or a member of a trading group;
3. The redemption, repayment or purchase must be made wholly or mainly with the purpose of benefiting a trade carried on by the company or by its 75% subsidiary.
4. The payment must not be part of a scheme whose main purpose or one of whose main purposes is to:
   (i) enable the owner of the shares to participate in the company's profits without receiving a dividend;
   (ii) avoid tax.
5. Certain conditions must be satisfied by the owner of the shares ("the vendor")—see below.

CONDITIONS RE VENDOR (Paras 1 to 4, 8, 9, Schedule 9, F.A. 1982)

The "vendor" must meet the following conditions:

1. If the vendor is an individual, he must be resident and ordinarily resident in the U.K. in the tax year in which the purchase, etc., is made. Where shares are held by a nominee, the nominee must be resident or ordinarily resident. The residence status of a trust is determined according to the capital gains tax rules (see Chapter 26, § 8). The residence status of personal representatives is that of the deceased immediately before his death. A company must be resident of the U.K.
2. The vendor must have owned the shares throughout the 5 years prior to the purchase. Where shares have been transferred between husband and wife or vice-versa, the general rule is that the periods of respective ownership are aggregated. They must, however, have been living together at the time of the transfer, and furthermore, except by reason of the death of the recipient, still be living together at the time of the purchase. For shares acquired by inheritance the period is 3 years and includes ownership by the deceased or his personal representatives. Similarly, on a disposal by personal representatives the 3-year period includes ownership by the deceased. If shares were acquired at different times, acquisitions are identified on a first-in-first-out—F.I.F.O.—basis, whilst disposals are identified on a last-in-first-out—L.I.F.O.—basis. Save in the case of "stock dividends" (See s. 34, F.(No. 2)A. 1975), shares acquired on a take-over or re-organisation in exchange for old shares are deemed to be acquired when the old shares were originally acquired.
3. It is not necessary for all a vendor's shares to be purchased, etc., but his holding must be substantially reduced. This test is primarily on the basis of the nominal value of his shares. This means that he must end up owning not more than 75% of his holding immediately prior to the purchase. There is, however, a second test. This is the basis of his entitlement to participate in the distribution of profits. Such entitlement must be reduced below 75% of its level prior to the purchase.

4. Where appropriate, Rule 3 is applied to the combined holdings of the vendor and his associates.
5. Taking account of the combining holdings of the vendor and his associates, he must not, immediately after the purchase, be connected with the company making the purchase.
6. The purchase must not be part of a scheme by which, ultimately, the vendor and his associates end up with different interests which, had they applied at the time of the purchase, would not have met the conditions. Any transaction within one year after the purchase is deemed to be part of any such arrangements. It is however permissible for an associate to agree to sell some of his shares so that the vendor will satisfy the conditions. Such sale need not of itself satisfy the substantial reduction test. However that test will be applied to the combined holding. The associate must have held his shares for 5 years prior to the purchase and be resident and ordinarily resident in the U.K.

GROUPS (Schedule 9, Paras 5 to 7, F.A. 1982)

General
The 75% tests are modified if the relevant company concerned is a member of a group of companies.

The modification applies if prior to the purchase, etc., the vendor owned shares in one or more members of the group (but not necessarily in the company making the purchase). It also applies if after the purchase, etc., he owns shares in the company making the purchase, and immediately before the purchase he owned shares in one or more group companies. In such cases the test is by reference to the vendor's interest as a shareholder in the group.

The nominal value test is applied as a fraction of the issued share capital of each company, aggregating the result and dividing by the number of companies in the group (whether or not the vendor owns shares therein). Likewise the distributable profits test is by reference to the profits of all companies in which the vendor owns shares and of their 51% subsidiaries. These tests take into account the combined interest of the vendor and his associates in all member companies in the group.

The vendor must not, immediately after the purchase, be connected with the purchasing company or with any company in the same group as the purchasing company.

Definition
In this context the following companies are deemed to be members of a group:
    (*a*) the parent company (not itself being a 51% subsidiary of any other company);
    (*b*) 51% subsidiaries;
    (*c*) companies which have ceased to be 51% subsidiaries but which could again become 51% subsidiaries;
    (*d*) an unquoted and otherwise unconnected company which is carrying on a business, the whole or a significant part of which was taken over from the purchasing company or from another company in the purchasing company's group within three years prior to the purchase;
    (*e*) 51% subsidiaries of a company in (*d*).

ADMINISTRATION (Schedule 9, Paras 11 to 13, F.A. 1982)

Notification
A company which makes a payment which it treats as being outside the distribution rules must notify the revenue thereof within 60 days giving full details.

If any person who is connected with the company becomes aware of an arrangement by which the vendor could re-acquire his shares, such person must notify the Revenue within thirty days of coming to know of both the scheme and the arrangement.

If the inspector has reason to believe that a payment has been made and forms part of such an arrangement, he can ask the company or any person connected with it to provide, within sixty days (or longer by agreement), a declaration stating whether or not such a scheme exists, and such other information as he may require. He may also require from the recipient of such a payment a declaration as to whether or not he received it as beneficial owner, and, if not, details of the person who is the beneficial owner.

Penalties
The usual penalties for failure to make special returns (s. 98, T.M.A. 1970—see Chapter 1, § 24) apply.

CLEARANCE (Schedule 9, Para. 10, F.A. 1982)
A company which proposes to purchase its own shares can apply in advance to the Board for notification from the Revenue that such a purchase will or will not be treated as a distribution. Such an application must be made in writing and contain particulars of the relevant transactions. If any material factors are omitted the notification is void. The Revenue have 30 days in which to call for further information. The company must reply within a further 30 days (or longer *by agreement* with the Revenue) or the application lapses. The Revenue must notify their decision to the company within 30 days of the application or the provision of additional information as the case may be. As to the form of a clearance application, see SP2/82.

PAYMENT OF CAPITAL TRANSFER TAX (s. 53(2), F.A. 1982)
The distribution rules do not apply if, subject to certain conditions, the vendor applies a payment to meet capital transfer tax arising on a death. The conditions are as follows:
1. The company must be unquoted:
2. The company must be a trading company or a member of a trading group;
3. The recipient must apply the whole, or substantially the whole amount received (subject to meeting the capital gains tax thereon) in payment of a capital transfer tax liability arising on death;
4. The capital transfer tax must be paid within two years of the death;
5. The recipient must show that the liability could not have been met, except by means of a payment by the company or another such company, without undue hardship.

PURCHASE FROM A DEALER (s. 54, F.A. 1982)
There are special rules which apply where the vendor is a dealer to whom a profit on the sale of the shares is assessable as trading profit under Case I or II, Schedule D. Accordingly the payment is not treated as income under Schedule F in the dealers' hands, nor is he entitled to any tax credit. The company is not, however, required to provide the usual certificate in respect of the distribution.

These rules apply not only to payments by way of redemption, repayment or purchase of shares, but also to the purchase of rights to aquire shares.

However this does not apply to the redemption of *fixed-rate preference shares* issued to and continuously held by the person from whom they are redeemed. The exclusion also applies to the redemption of other preference shares issued before 6th April 1982 on terms which were settled, or all but settled, before that date.

Fixed-rate preference shares are shares whose only entitlement to participation in dividends is limited to a fixed percentage of the nominal value and not exceeding (together with any premium on redemption) a reasonable commercial return on the capital invested when they were issued. Such shares must have been issued wholly for new consideration and must not carry any rights whereby they could be converted into any other kind of share or could give rise to the acquisition of further shares.

A.C.T. ON DISTRIBUTIONS (s. 55, F.A. 1982)
If the price paid for the purchase of shares is not exempt under the rules described above, it is treated as a distribution upon which A.C.T. is payable in the usual way. Such A.C.T. is available for surrender to a subsidiary company as though it were a normal dividend (See Chapter 22, § 5).

CLOSE COMPANIES (s. 56, F.A. 1982)
Payments made by a company to purchase, etc. its own shares are treated as distributions which should be taken into account in apportionment calculations (See Chapter 19).

16. Corporation Tax—Capital Allowances

Refer to Chapter 5 for detailed provisions.

§ 1.—INTRODUCTORY

In general, capital allowances for corporation tax purposes are computed in the same way as for income tax. However, the treatment is different as regards basis periods and the manner in which relief is given, and in relation to the disclaimer of both first year allowances and writing-down allowance. These differences are set out below, but reference should be made to Chapter 5 for the detailed provisions.

In addition, some small difference arises between the offset of allowances for leased assets not used for the purpose of a trade (s. 48, F.A. 1971).

It should be noted that the detailed provisions contained in the Finance Acts 1984 and 1985 withdrawing allowances are equally applicable to companies.

§ 2.—MANNER OF RELIEF

There are two principle ways in which relief may be given for capital allowances:
- (*a*) in taxing a trade
- (*b*) by discharge or repayment of tax.

(*a*) *In taxing a trade* (s. 73, C.A.A. 1968)
Capital allowances given in taxing a trade are treated as though they were trading expenses in arriving at the adjusted profit or loss of the company for the period concerned. Reference is therefore made in relation to expenditure incurred to the accounting period in which the expenditure takes place. Any balancing charges are treated as though they were trading receipts. If a loss is created, such allowances form an integral part of it and are relieved accordingly (see Chapter 18).

In the case of an investment company, s. 306, I.C.T.A. 1970 provides that capital allowances on machinery and plant may be used to increase the management expenses of the company.

Most allowances (e.g. for plant and machinery) are given in this manner, with only isolated cases as set out below given by discharge or repayment.

(*b*) *By discharge or repayment of tax* (s. 74, C.A.A. 1968)
Such capital allowances are normally given primarily against a specified source of income (e.g. industrial buildings allowances on a let building are given primarily against the rental income).

If the allowances for a period exceed the specified source of income, the excess may be carried forward against future income from that source, without any time limit.

Alternatively, if the company so elects within two years of the end of the accounting period, it may set the excess allowances against the total profits of the accounting period and of the previous period. The carry-back of allowances against total profits is limited to profits of a period equivalent in length to that for which the allowances are given.

Allowances set against total profits are set against later periods in preference to earlier periods, and any amount still unrelieved is carried forward against future income from the specified source.

If there are both current allowances and allowances brought forward from earlier periods, those brought forward are set against the specified source first. Thus, the maximum amount of current allowances is made available for set off against total profits.

Allowances given by discharge or repayment are principally industrial buildings allowance to the *lessor*; and agricultural buildings allowance.

Example 1

Porridge Limited has rental income for the year to 31st March 1985 of £12,000. Its other profits for the period are £7,000 and total profits of the year to 31st March 1984 were £15,000.

The company has capital allowances, to be given by discharge or repayment of tax and available primarily against rental income, of £32,000 for the year. It also has £4,000 of such allowances brought forward from earlier periods.

The set-off of the capital allowances (assuming Porridge Limited makes a claim for set-off against total profits) is as follows:

		Capital allowances	
		b/fwd	current
	£	£	£
		4,000	32,000
Rental income	12,000		
Set-off allowances brought forward	4,000	4,000	—
	8,000	£ —	32,000
Set-off current allowances.	8,000		8,000
	£ —		24,000
Other current profits.	7,000		
Set-off current allowances.	7,000		7,000
	£ —		17,000
Previous year's total profits.	15,000		
Allowances carried back	15,000		15,000
	£ —		
Carried forward against future rental income . .			£2,000

§ 3.—BASIS PERIODS

Almost all the allowances granted or charges made under I.C.T.A. 1970 (as amended by subsequent Finance Acts), the C.A.A. 1968 and the F.A. 1971 are dependent, as regards any particular chargeable period, either upon the occurrence of a specific event (e.g., the incurring of capital expenditure on industrial buildings or structures) or upon the fulfilment of a specific condition (e.g., ownership and use of machinery and plant) in what is termed the "basis period" appropriate to that chargeable period. The basic idea is quite simple: the basis period for a chargeable period is the period, the profits or income of which form the basis of the assessment for that chargeable period. The chargeable period for Corporation Tax purposes is the accounting period.

§ 4.—DISCLAIMER OF ALLOWANCES

A first-year allowance or writing-down allowance can be disclaimed by a company to such amount as the company desires, providing an election is made within two years of the end of the accounting period in which the expenditure is incurred. Note the difference between companies and individuals where a company disclaims and an individual claims.

A first-year allowance once disclaimed (or only part claimed) cannot be claimed in future years *except* in the case of expenditure on ships, where the allowance is postponed and can be claimed in a later period.

17. Corporation Tax—Stock Relief

§ 1.—INTRODUCTION

The purpose of stock relief is to give a measure of relief to businesses whose trading stocks and/or work in progress have increased in value because of the effects of inflation so that whilst, on paper, profits are shown by the accounts of a business such profits remain locked up in stock and are not available for distribution or for use in the business.

In his Budget statement on 12th November 1974 the Chancellor of the Exchequer announced an interim scheme of relief which had effect for the "1973 accounting period" of companies whose trading stocks at the end of that period were in excess of £25,000. The scheme had this restricted application so that a workable scheme could be brought into immediate effect to give quick relief (by repayment of tax already paid, or postponement of tax shortly due) to companies holding substantial trading stocks.

When this interim scheme was announced, it was hoped that the benefit of the relief could be extended to all businesses in a form which was dependent on the findings of the Sandilands Committee on Inflation Accounting. However, the report of the Sandilands Committee was still awaited when the Budget was presented on 15th April 1975 and the interim scheme was, in effect, extended for a further year.

The extended relief was made available in respect of the increase in stock values over a two-year base period ending, in most cases, on the last day of the period of account (i.e. the period for which a company draws up its accounts) which ended in the financial year 1974 (or last such period if more than one). The relief was equal to the amount by which the value of trading stocks at the end of the base period exceeded their value at the start thereof, less 10% of relevant income for the periods of account comprised in the two-year base period as computed for the purposes of Schedule D, Case I but *before* taking account of capital allowances or balancing charges or loss relief.

Effect was given to the relief by means of a deduction from the value of trading stock at the end of the last period of account comprised in the base period. The effect of this deduction was to reduce the profits of the trade for that period.

An additional relief equal to 5% of the relief otherwise available for the base period was also given to companies which were not entitled to the interim relief. This additional relief was also deducted from the value of trading stock at the end of the last period of account comprised in the base period.

In the continued absence of agreement on a viable form of inflation accounting, a third form of stock was introduced by s. 37 and Schedule 5, F.A. 1976. Broadly this relief is given in respect of the increase in stock value during a period of account less 15% of the company's relevant income for the period, relevant income being computed for F.A. 1976 relief *after* taking account of capital allowances or balancing charges but *before* loss relief.

A fourth form of stock relief came into effect, for periods of account ending on or after 14th November 1980, following a consultative document issued by the Inland Revenue on that date and made law by s. 35 and Schedule 9, F.A. 1981. Broadly, this relief is calculated by applying the increase, over a period of account, in the "all stocks index" to the opening stock (less £2,000). Transitional rules which apply for periods of account beginning before and ending after 14th November 1980 were brought in by s. 35 and Schedule 10, F.A. 1981.

Stock relief is withdrawn for periods of account beginning after 12th March 1984, although there are transitional rules (see § 2).

The above rules are set out below for the sake of completeness.

§ 2.—WITHDRAWAL OF STOCK RELIEF (s. 48, F.A. 1984) AFTER 12TH MARCH 1984

Stock relief is not available for periods of account *beginning* after 12th March 1984. Furthermore no clawback of relief previously given will be made for such periods of account.

However, where a period of account begins before 13th March it will be regarded for stock relief purposes as having ended on 12th March. In such cases relief will be limited by reference to the increase in the all-stocks index from the commencement of that period to March 1984.

There will be no clawback of relief where a person ceases to carry on a trade (or the scale of activities of the trade becomes negligible) after 12th March 1984.

The special rules for calculating stock relief are modified for a new business whose first period of account begins before but ends after 13th March 1984. The notional opening stock will be computed by reference to the value of the stock at the end of that period but discounted only by reference to the increase in the all-stocks index up to March 1984.

There will be no clawback of relief arising where a succession takes place after 12th March 1984.

Unused stock relief (carried forward as part of a trading loss) given for periods of account ending after 13th November 1980 will be cancelled to the extent that it remains unused six years after the end of the period to which it relates.

An election for the herd basis may be made for any chargeable period for which profits are computed by reference to the first period of account commencing after 12 March 1984.

§ 3.—PERIODS OF ACCOUNT ENDING AFTER 14TH NOVEMBER 1980 BUT BEFORE 13TH MARCH 1984

CALCULATION OF RELIEF

Relief for appreciation in stock values was is calculated simply by multiplying the opening stock (less £2,000) by the "all stocks index" applying to the period of account in question.

DEFINITIONS

(1) *Trading stock* (Schedule 9, Paras 28–30, F.A. 1981)
"Trading stock" is property of any description, whether real or personal, such as is sold or is bought to be processed and sold in the ordinary course of the trade, etc. in question, together with materials used in manufacture etc. and work in progress. It does not include:
  (*a*) Securities (i.e. stocks and shares); or
  (*b*) Land, unless held for sale in the course of the trade:
      (i) After being developed by the company carrying on the trade; or
      (ii) In the case of a group of companies, held for the purpose of being developed by another company in the group; or
  (*c*) Goods held for letting on hire or hire-purchase.
It will thus be noted that securities (i.e. stocks and shares etc.) are excluded from trading stock for this purpose, as are goods let on hire or hire purchase.

Land cannot be included as trading stock unless it is held for sale in the ordinary course of the trade after the construction or substantial reconstruction of buildings on the land concerned. For periods of account beginning after 26th March 1980 a building can be regarded as land in the somewhat unusual case of building for which there is no immediately underlying land (e.g. *freehold* flats above the ground floor). In other words land held as trading stock by a land dealer is not eligible for the relief, but a builder or developer would qualify.

Payments on account reduce the value of trading stock for the purposes of the relief, but it is understood that this reduction is not made for payments received by way of deposits to secure future orders. Furthermore payments on account must be matched against the items of stock concerned and if the amount of the payment on account exceeds the value of an item of stock, that excess is not set against other stock.

Example 1

Civil Engineers Ltd is working on three contracts. The value of work-in progress on these jobs and the payments on account received in respect thereof are:

	Total £	Job A £	Job B £	Job C £
Value............................	210,000	50,000	70,000	90,000
Payment on account	180,000	30,000	40,000	110,000
Balance sheet value................	£30,000	£20,000	£30,000	£(20,000)
Value for Stock relief	£40,000	£20,000	£20,000	£ Nil

If a business is registered for V.A.T. and all its outputs are standard or zero-rated, the stock value in the accounts will be "net". However, if the supplies made by the business are wholly or partly exempt, supplies to it will nonetheless have borne V.A.T. In such a case any V.A.T. input which relates to trading stock and which cannot be taken into account will be included in the stock value.

If goods are sold subject to reservation of title (i.e. the seller can reclaim the goods if he is not paid) such goods are nonetheless treated as purchases and, if appropriate, stock of the purchaser (provided the seller treats them as sold and not included in his stock).

Work in progress on Government contracts is regarded as remaining the property of the contractor pending final delivery (even though most such clauses contain a clause vesting property therein in the Government Department or Agency concerned).

(2) *Work in progress* (Schedule 9, Para. 31, F.A. 1981)

"Work in progress" comprises services performed in the ordinary course of a trade, etc. where performance thereof is partly complete and where it is reasonable to expect that a charge will subsequently be made for those services, together with any article produced or material used in performing those services. This definition of work in progress does not include work wholly completed but not billed.

The purpose of this exclusion is to prevent the giving of relief on work in progress which in reality should be an amount owing by a debtor. However, the Inland Revenue has stated that this definition will not be applied harshly and the relief would only be denied in exceptional cases.

(3) *Farm animals* (Schedule 9, Para. 25, F.A. 1981)

If farm animals are treated as trading stock, they can be included for stock relief but animals which have been dealt with on the "herd basis" must be excluded.

(4) *Special circumstances* (Schedule 9, Para. 22, F.A. 1981)
In most cases trading stock for stock relief purposes is primarily the amount which is brought into account in computing the profits of the trade etc., subject to any necessary adjustment for excess payments on account. There are however a number of special rules for determining the value of trading stock which have to be followed in certain circumstances.

(i) *New businesses* (Schedule 9, Para. 19, F.A. 1981). For new businesses, any actual opening stock for the first period of account is ignored. Instead, a notional figure is calculated by reducing the closing stock in accordance with the movement in the all-stocks index over the period. Relief is then given as if the opening stock were equal to that amount.

Example 2

Collis Ltd commenced trading on 1st November 1980 and made up its first accounts to 30th June 1981.
Stocks were:

1.11.80.	Nil
30.6.81.	£14,950

Collis Ltd's opening stock is ignored and a notional figure is calculated, as follows:

$$\text{Closing stock} \times \frac{\text{Index for month containing day before period began}}{\text{Index for month containing last day of period}}$$

$$= £14,950 \times \frac{195.6}{206.4} \quad \begin{array}{l}\text{(October 1980)}\\\text{(June 1981)}\end{array}$$

$$= £14,168$$

The relief due will therefore be:

$$\text{Percentage increase in index: } \frac{206.4 - 195.6}{206.4} \times 100 = 5.23\%$$

Relief due: £(14,168 − 2,000) × 5.23% = £637

(N.B. Collis Ltd will not claim transitional provision relief (see § 4), since the 14th November 1980 stock value is nil.)

(ii) *Anti-avoidance* (Schedule 9, Para. 22, F.A. 1981). If a company enters into transactions from which it appears that the sole or main object is to obtain:
    (*a*) additional relief; or
    (*b*) a reduction in clawback; or
    (*c*) a reduction in the restriction of carry forward of unused stock relief
then the Revenue have the power to substitute, at the end of the affected period of account, the value of stock which would have been held if the transactions had not been entered into. Where the arrangements were intended to reduce the restriction in carry forward of unused relief any reduction attributable to such arrangements is ignored.
    The wording of the paragraph implies that any arrangement would be caught, although the following are mentioned specifically:
    (*a*) any acquisition or disposal of trading stock otherwise than in the normal course of trade; or

(*b*) any change in the normal pattern or method of carrying on the trade; or

(*c*) any change in the accounting date of the trade; or

(*d*) any acquisition of trading stock or increase in the value of one person's trading stock which is associated with a decrease in that of a person connected with him (s. 533, I.C.T.A. 1970).

(iii) *Long periods of account* (Schedule 9, Para. 23, F.A. 1981). Where a period of account exceeds eighteen months the Inland Revenue have a right to require that the period of account is divided into notional periods, only the last of which may exceed twelve months. The relief is then calculated for each of such periods and aggregated to obtain the relief for the whole period of account. It will be necessary to use the special rules for valuation of stock at intermediate dates unless stock has actually been taken at the ends of the notional periods of account.

Example 3

Fortell Ltd has stock of £150,000 on 31st March 1981 and next prepares accounts to 31st March 1983. It is established that stock at 31st March 1982 is £75,000.

The "all stocks index" is

31st March, 1981............................	201.7
31st March, 1982............................	218.9
31st March, 1983............................	231.4

At first sight the relief would seem to be

$$(\text{£}150,000 - \text{£}2,000)^* \times \frac{231.4 - 201.7}{201.7} = \qquad \text{£}21,793$$

If the Revenue use their option it is likely that each of the years to 31st March 1982 and 1983, would be the notional periods. The revised relief would then be:

Year to 31st March 1982   £

$$(\text{£}150,000 - \text{£}2,000) \times \frac{(218.9 - 201.7)}{201.7} = \qquad 12,620$$

Year to 31st March 1983

$$(\text{£}75,000 - \text{£}2,000) \times \frac{(231.4 - 218.9)}{218.9} = \qquad 4,169$$

Revised relief for the two year period to 31st March, 1983   £16,789

(iv) *Valuation at intermediate dates* (Schedule 9, Para. 24, F.A. 1981). When a stock value is required at some other date than on the commencement of a new business, or at the end of a period of account, and the actual value at the date concerned is not known it is necessary to calculate a notional value. The value taken is such as is "reasonable and just" taking into account all relevant circumstances but in particular:

(*a*) actual values of stock at the beginning and end of the period of account concerned;

(*b*) movements in the costs of items comprised in trading stock;

(*c*) changes in the volume of trade.

---

* For exclusion of £2,000, see sub-section on "calculation" below.

If a valuation is needed for an intermediate date during a long period of account these items are taken into account for the long period and not those for each notional period. However, any available information relating to one or more of the notional periods can be used in arriving at a value, since regard must be had to all the relevant circumstances.

These rules apply (unless actual figures are known) in determining the stock value at 14th November 1980. In that case the period of account is to be treated as divided into two parts.

(5) *Past relief* (Schedule 9, Paras 25, 27, F.A. 1981)
Past relief is the aggregate of the "two-year" stock relief (but not the additional 5% additional relief) and relief under the F.A. 1976 and F.A. 1981 schemes.

Unrecovered past relief is past relief less any amounts clawed back or written off.

Any balance of "two-year" stock relief remaining in unrecovered past relief was written off by excluding an appropriate amount from unrecovered past relief brought forward from the period of account ending in the financial year 1978.

The actual amount written off was the amount of "two-year" stock relief (including "transitional" relief) given, less any amounts recovered subsequently under the clawback arrangements. In determining whether any relief for these periods has been recovered, clawbacks are set against later years' relief before earlier years' (i.e. on a "last-in-first-out" (L.I.F.O.) basis).

Stock relief under the F.A. 1976 and F.A. 1981 schemes given for later periods of account is to be excluded from unrecovered past relief for any period of account beginning on or after the sixth anniversary of the end of the period of account for which the relief was claimed. In most cases, where accounts have been drawn up annually, the write-off will be made with effect from the day following the sixth anniversary of the period of account concerned. If the sixth anniversary of the period of account in point does not coincide with the end of a period of account (because an intervening period of account was for more or less than twelve months), the write-off is made immediately after the period of account which is current on the sixth anniversary of the relevant period of account. The same general principles apply as with the write-off of the "two-year" stock relief, including the L.I.F.O. principle for identifying the actual amount to be written off.

CALCULATION

(1) *Relief* (Schedule 9, Paras 1, 2, 12, F.A. 1981)
Calculations of stock relief are based on the increase, during a period of account in the "all stocks" index prepared and published monthly by the Department of Industry. The percentage increase in the all stocks index during the period concerned is applied to the opening stock (strictly the closing stock at the end of the preceding period) less a standard £2,000 exclusion.

The relief has to be claimed within two years after the end of the period for which it is due. However, claims can be made for all, none or part only of any stock relief to which the company is entitled. The unclaimed balance is not available for future periods.

Example 4

Klingon Ltd had stock on 1st July 1981 of £47,500. Assuming *(for the purposes of this example only)* that the all-stocks index was 206.4 on 30th June 1981 and 220.5 on 30th June 1982, Klingon Ltd can claim stock relief for the year to 30th June 1982 as follows:

$$\text{Stock relief } £(47,500 - 2,000) \times \frac{220.5 - 206.4}{206.4} \qquad £3,108$$

Klingon Ltd can, if it wishes, reduce the amount of its claim. Any unclaimed balance cannot be claimed in a future period, so the only beneficial effect of failing to claim relief in full is that the unclaimed amount will not go to increase the unrecovered past relief vulnerable to clawback.

(2) *Clawback* (Schedule 9, Para. 13, F.A. 1981)

When a company ceases to carry on a trade stock relief is not available for the period of account during or at the end of which a company ceases to carry on the trade concerned. On cessation any balance of unrecovered past relief will be clawed back. There is also a prohibition on relief and there will be a clawback of unrecovered past relief where the activities of a trade in a period are small as compared with their scale in a period beginning within the previous six years.

(3) *Utilisation of losses*

(i) *General.* The carry forward of losses due to unused stock relief given under F.A. 1981 is restricted to six years. Thus it is necessary to distinguish the various components of a carried forward loss i.e. trading loss, capital allowances, and stock relief (see below).

(ii) *Change of ownership* (Schedule 9, Para. 14, F.A. 1981). I.C.T.A. 1970, s. 483 may prohibit the carry forward of trading losses where there is a change in the ownership of a company and a major change in the nature or conduct of the company's trade. Carry forward of losses may also be prevented if the scale of a company's trading activities becomes small or negligible and before any considerable revival thereof there is a change in the ownership of the company.

To the extent that stock relief is included in losses whose carry forward is prohibited by I.C.T.A. 1970, s. 483, there is an equivalent amount eliminated from unrecovered past relief so that it is no longer liable to be clawed back.

In order to determine the amount of losses to be eliminated, profits are set first against F.A. 1976 relief or the earlier *two-year* stock relief. For this purpose stock relief claimed under those schemes is assumed to have been given before capital allowances.

If there have been clawbacks before the change in ownership of the company, certain assumptions have to be made. Clawbacks of *two-year* stock relief, or F.A. 1976 stock relief are applied to the earliest relief on a first-in-first-out (F.I.F.O.) basis. Furthermore it is also assumed that effect is given to relief from earlier periods before that due for later periods. Where there is a clawback of F.A. 1981 stock relief it is the relief for the latest period which is clawed back before that given for earlier periods.

(iii) *Write-off of Government investment* (Schedule 9, Para. 15, F.A. 1981). The position is similar where a company is prohibited from carrying forward losses because government investment in the company has been written off.

(iv) *Restriction on carry-forward of losses* (Schedule 9, Para. 17, F.A. 1981). Unused F.A. 1981 stock relief can be carried forward for only six years. If it is not utilised within that time the relief becomes, in effect, invalid.

A trading loss computed for corporation tax purposes comprises the following:

(*a*) The trading loss ignoring capital allowances and F.A. 1981 stock relief;
(*b*) Capital allowances for the period less a set off for any trading profit of the period (ignoring capital allowances and F.A. 1981 stock relief);

and

(*c*) F.A. 1981 stock relief for the period, less a set off for any trading profit not absorbed by capital allowances

where any of the following loss reliefs are claimed:

—I.C.T.A. 1970, s. 177(2) (set off against total profits of the same or a preceding accounting period);

—I.C.T.A. 1970, s. 254 (set off against franked investment income);
—I.C.T.A. 1970, s. 258 (group relief)
and the loss available for set off or group relief exceeds the profits or franked investment income of the accounting period concerned, the set off of the loss which is applied is as follows:

1. the trading loss, ignoring capital allowances and F.A. 1981 stock relief;
2. capital allowances for the period, *less* a set-off for any trading profit of the period (ignoring capital allowances and F.A. 1981 stock relief); and
3. F.A. 1981 stock relief for the period, *less* a set-off for any trading profit for the period not absorbed by capital allowances.

Order of loss offset

If trading losses are created or augmented by claims for first year allowances and carried back for set-off against total profits of an earlier accounting period, the loss utilisation is as follows:

1. The amount of the first-year allowances;
2. The amount of the trading loss ignoring capital allowances, and F.A. 1981 stock relief;
3. Capital allowances for the period (less the first-year allowances) less any trading profit of the period (ignoring capital allowances and F.A. 1981 stock relief); and
4. F.A. 1981 stock relief for the period less any trading profit for the period not absorbed by capital allowances.

Example 5

Downer Ltd's results for the year to 31st December 1981 are as follows:

	£
Adjusted loss...	12,000
Capital allowances (F.Y.A.'s £25,000)	28,000
Stock relief...	10,500
Case I loss...	£50,500
Other profits..	£8,200

For the year to 31st December 1980 it had profits chargeable to corporation tax of £16,000. Profits for the year to 31st December 1979 were £14,000 and for the year to 31st December 1978 were £15,000.

Assuming that relief is claimed under I.C.T.A. 1970, s. 177(2) for both accounting periods, the set off is as follows:

	Total Loss £	Trading Loss £	Capital allowances £	Stock relief £
Case I loss available	50,500	12,000	28,000	10,500
Claimed 31.12.1981 (s. 177(2))	8,200	8,200	—	—
	42,300	3,800	28,000	10,500
Claimed 31.12.1980 (s. 177(2))	16,000	3,800	12,200	—
	26,300	—	15,800	10,500
Claimed 31.12.1979 (s. 177(3A))	14,000	—	14,000	—
	12,300	—	1,800	10,500
Claimed 31.12.1978 (s. 177(3A))	11,000	—	1,800	9,200
Carried forward (s. 177(1))	£1,300	£ —	£ —	£1,300

Note

Capital allowances are set off before stock relief in determining the make up of the loss carried forward. However, in determining the amount of loss attributable to first-year allowances available for a three year carry back under I.C.T.A. 1970, s. 177(3A), the first-year allowances are treated as set off last. Thus, the carry-back is the lesser of the first-year allowance claimed and the total losses after the T.A. 1970, s. 177(2) claims.

If trading losses are carried forward under I.C.T.A. 1970, s. 177(1) against future income of the same trade in a later accounting period, the order of set-off against such income is:

1. Capital allowances for previous accounting periods (ending after 13th November, 1980);
2. F.A. 1981 stock relief (for later periods before earlier periods);
3. Trading losses of an earlier accounting period (ending after 13th November 1980). Losses are computed, for this purpose, ignoring capital allowances and F.A. 1981 stock relief. If losses which have been used in an earlier period against franked investment income are re-instated on a surplus of franked payments (see Chapter 40, § 18) they are included as losses of the year in which the surplus arises;
4. Any other losses, capital allowances and relief.

Example 6

Ranger Ltd has the following results:

Year to 30.11.1981	£
Adjusted loss	8,000
Capital allowances	10,000
Stock relief	6,000
Case I loss	£24,000
Trading losses, brought forward	£12,000
Chargeable gain (less 11/26)	£5,000

Assuming that relief is claimed under I.C.T.A. 1970, s. 177(2) in respect of the chargeable gain, its losses carried forward will be:

	£
Post 13.11.1980	
Trading loss (£8,000 − £5,000)	3,000
Capital allowances	10,000
Stock relief	6,000
	19,000
Pre 14.11.1980	12,000
	£31,000

If there are trading profits of £14,000 and £10,000 for the years to 30th November 1982 and 1983 respectively, they will be set-off as follows:

	Total	——Post 13.11.1980—— Capital allowances	Stock relief	Loss	Pre 14.11.80
	£	£	£	£	£
Loss at 30.11.81	31,000	10,000	6,000	3,000	12,000
Set-off year to 30.11.82	14,000	10,000	4,000	—	—
	17,000	—	2,000	3,000	12,000
Set off year to 30.11.83	10,000	—	2,000	3,000	5,000
Carried forward	£7,000	£ —	£ —	£ —	£7,000

Where the period of account is longer than twelve months, relief is apportioned on a time basis between the accounting periods concerned.

Seemingly *two-year* and F.A. 1976 stock relief can be carried forward without restriction.

(4) *Method of relief or clawback* (Schedule 5, Para. 16, F.A. 1981)
Stock relief is given as a trading expense for the period of account concerned. Clawbacks are treated as trading receipts for the period for which the clawback arises.

SPECIAL SITUATIONS

(1) *Cessation of trade* (Schedule 9, Para. 16, F.A. 1981)
No relief is available in the period of account in which a company ceases to trade. Any balance of unrecovered past relief is clawed back (normally in the final accounting period).

(2) *Successions* (Schedule 9, Para. 20, F.A. 1981)
Special provisions apply on a transfer of stock, at cost or market value, in the following circumstances:
(a) A company reconstruction falling within I.C.T.A. 1970, s. 252 (for example, the transfer of a trade between companies with 75% common ownership).
(b) Where a trade carried on by a sole trader or partnership is transferred to a company and at the date of the transfer not less than 75% of the ordinary share capital is held by that sole trader or by the partners.
If the predecessor and successor elect (within two years after the end of the period of account in which the transfer takes place) the successor is treated as having carried on the trade since the predecessor began to do so. There is then no clawback on cessation by the predecessor. If the transfer takes place during a period of account the predecessor receives stock relief based on the movement in the "all stocks index" up to that date applied to opening stock. The successor obtains stock relief based on the movement in the "all stocks index" from date of transfer to the end of the period applied to the stock taken over.

Where the business of a sole trader or partnership is incorporated and any relief remains unused (e.g. because the profits were insufficient), an equivalent amount is excluded from unrecovered past relief taken over by the company.

These rules also apply where only part of a trade is transferred. In such cases unrecovered past relief is apportioned on the basis of the respective values of stock retained or transferred.

(3) *Farm animals* (Schedule 9, Para. 25, F.A. 1981)
Farm animals are treated as trading stock for stock relief unless an election is made under Schedule 6, Para. 2, I.C.T.A. 1970, for the "herd basis" to apply. If such an election is made those animals which comprise the "herd" are excluded from stock, with effect from the end of the period of account preceding the one during which the election becomes effective.

Unrecovered past relief at the end of that previous period is apportioned between the "herd" and the remaining stock in proportion to their respective values at that time.

The normal treatment whereby when a company transfers part of its trade, the unrecovered past relief is apportioned between predecessor and successor by reference to the value of stock transferred and that retained, does not apply to the relief attributable to the "herd", which is instead, apportioned on the basis of the respective values of "herd" animals transferred and retained.

(4) *Foreign trades* (Schedule 9, Para. 35, F.A. 1981)
The stock relief provisions apply equally to trades carried on outside the U.K. and chargeable to Case V Schedule D.

(5) *Houses taken in part exchange* (s. 49, F.A. 1984)
In general, land and buildings only qualify for stock relief if they were bought by a builder for development.

For the period from 15th March 1983 to 12th March 1984 stock relief is extended to houses accepted by builders in part exchange for the sale of new or substantially reconstructed property.

§ 4.—PERIODS OF ACCOUNT BEGINNING BEFORE AND ENDING AFTER 14TH NOVEMBER 1980 (Schedule 10, F.A. 1981)

Companies have the option, for periods of account which begin before but end after 14th November 1980, to claim relief under the F.A. 1976 scheme, but subject to a number of modifications. This modified form of F.A. 1976 relief is available where it gives rise to a greater amount of relief than would be available under the F.A. 1981 scheme. Where the modified F.A. 1976 relief is claimed, it is treated as being relief claimed under the F.A. 1981 scheme.

The calculation is as follows:
1. Take the *lesser* of
   - (*a*) the actual stock value at the end of the period; or
   - (*b*) the stock value at 14th November 1980. (The Revenue have stated that for the purpose of valuing stock at 14th November, any reasonable method of determining the value may be adopted.)
2. Calculate the increase in stock value by comparing the appropriate amount (1(*a*) or 1(*b*)) with the opening stock value.
3. The 15% restriction is applied by reference to the relevant income attributable to the part of the period falling before 14th November 1980 or the end of the period of account, as applicable.
4. Deduct from the relief calculated as above the *lesser* of
   - (*a*) 25% of the F.A. 1981 relief which would otherwise have been available; *or*
   - (*b*) £10,000
5. If part of the stock relief for the preceding period was deferred (see § 2), the company has the further option of claiming relief by reference to the F.A. 1976 scheme without modification, *but restricted* to the amount of relief deferred.

Example

Fisher Ltd's results for the year to 31st December 1980 were as follows:

	£
Stock 31.12.80	68,000
Stock 31.12.79	57,000
Adjusted profit	12,500
Capital allowances	7,000

The all-stocks index was:

December 1980	196.5
December 1979	179.5

It is agreed with the Inspector of Taxes that a reasonable value for stock at 14th November 1980 is £64,000.

Stock relief (new scheme):

$$\text{Relief: } £(57,000 - 2,000) \times \frac{196.5 - 179.5}{179.5} \qquad £5,209$$

Transitional relief:

	£
Closing stock (restricted to 14.11.80 value)	64,000
Opening stock	57,000
	7,000

Relevant income (calculated to 14.11.80, since stock at that date used):

$$£(12,500 - 7,000) \times \frac{10.47}{12} \text{ months} = £4,798.75$$

Restriction: £4,798.75 × 15%	720
	6,280

Further reduction:

A. 25% × New relief (£5,209 × 25%) = £1,302

B. Maximum reduction = £10,000

Lesser of A and B	1,302
Modified old relief	£4,978

The relief due is the greater of the new relief (£5,209) and the modified old relief (£4,978), i.e. £5,209.

If stock relief of £8,500 had been deferred from the previous period, a further calculation would have been necessary, as follows:

	£
Closing stock (N.B. 14.11.80 value is ignored)	68,000
Less Opening stock	57,000
	11,000
Less 15% relevant increase (31.12.79–14.11.80) = 15% × £(12,500 − 7,000)	825
	£10,175

However, the relief will be restricted to £8,500 (i.e. the amount deferred), since this is lower than £10,175. If £12,000 had been deferred, the relief due would have been the maximum of £10,175.

N.B. The deferred option is in addition to the new relief and normal transitional relief, so that if it gives a lesser relief, it will of course *not* be claimed.

§ 5.—PERIODS OF ACCOUNT ENDING BEFORE 14TH NOVEMBER 1980

CALCULATION

(1) *Relief* (Schedule 5, Para. 9, F.A. 1976)

Relief is given on the excess of the value of stock at the end of a period of account over the value of stock at the beginning of that period, subject to a restriction by 15% of relevant income.

For periods of account ending after 31st March 1979 claims can be made for all, none or part only of any stock relief to which a company is entitled. The unclaimed balance is not available in future periods. The relief must be claimed within two years of the end of the period of account concerned.

Example 1

Accounting period to 30th September 1980.

	£	£
Case I, Schedule D...............................	125,000	125,000
(after capital allowances)		
Stock relief claim—full (see below)		(19,250)
Relevant income	£125,000	
Total profits....................................		105,750
Less: Charges on income		5,000
Profits chargeable to corporation tax...............		£100,750
Stock relief:	£	
Closing stock.............................	68,000	
Less: Opening stock.........................	30,000	
Increase in stock value	38,000	
Relevant income (£125,000) × 15%	18,750	
Relief claimed	£19,250	

(2) *Clawback* (Schedule 5, Para. 10, F.A. 1976)

If the closing value of stock is less than the opening value of stock there is a recovery (or clawback) of relief previously given. This is restricted to the lesser of:

(*a*) The reduction in stock value in the period; or

(*b*) The amount of unrecovered past relief (i.e. relief given in earlier periods, less clawbacks) not yet written off.

Clawback is calculated solely by reference to actual stock values and there is no adjustment for 15% of relevant income.

There is also a clawback on cessation of trading (see below).

Example 2

Accounting period to 31st December 1979.

	£	£
Case I, Schedule D.............................	40,000	40,000
(after capital allowances—£20,000)		
Stock relief—clawback...........................		19,000
Relevant income	£40,000	
Total profits....................................		59,000
Less: Charges on income		10,000
	£49,000	

Stock relief:	£
Closing stock..............................	110,000
Less: Opening stock........................	140,000
Reduction in stock value..................... *(a)*	£30,000
Unrecovered past relief .... *(b)*	£19,000

Clawback is lower of (*a*) £30,000 or (*b*) £19,000, i.e. (*b*).

(3) *Deferment of clawback* (Schedule 7, Paras 1–6, F.A. 1980)
Subject to certain conditions it is possible for part of a clawback to be deferred for one year if the fall in stock value giving rise to the clawback was purely temporary. This deferment can be claimed for any period of account ending in or after the financial year 1979. (N.B. This is only relevant for periods of account ending on or before 14th November 1980, when the new system of stock relief was introduced.)

The amount of clawback which is eligible for deferment is the full amount thereof *less* 5% of the opening stock for the period.

Example 3

	1979	*1980*
	£	£
Stock at 31st March............................	25,000	10,000

In the year to 31.3.1980 there would normally be a clawback of £15,000, but if the deferment is claimed the current clawback is reduced to £1,250 calculated as follows:

	£	£
Decrease in stock..........................	15,000	
Normal clawback		15,000
5% of opening stock (5% × £25,000).........	1,250	
Deferred clawback	£13,750	13,750
Immediate clawback........................		£1,250

Where such a deferment is claimed the amount deferred is treated as though it were a clawback for the next accounting period. However, for purposes of calculating unrecovered past relief, relief written off, etc., the deferment is ignored.

If the amount available for deferment (i.e. the decrease in stock value less 5% of opening stock for that period) exceeds £100,000 a further calculation must be made. This is by reference to a ratio (known as the credit ratio) at the start of the period of account ending in the financial year 1979 (the relevant time). That ratio consists of trade creditors less trade debtors at the relevant time, divided by the trading stock at that time. The amount of potential deferment in excess of £100,000 is reduced by the proportion of such excess found by applying the credit ratio to it.

Example 4

	1979 £	1980 £	1981 £
Stock at 31st January	400,000	500,000	335,000
Trade creditors	150,000		
Trade debtors	100,000		

In the year to 31st January 1981 there should be a clawback of £165,000 but if deferment is claimed the clawback is reduced to £30,000, calculated as follows:

	£	£ Deferment	£ Clawback
Decrease in stock	165,000		165,000
Less: 5% opening stock (£500,000)	25,000		
Maximum deferment	140,000		
Amount not subject to further adjustment	100,000	100,000	
	40,000		

Trade creditors − Trade debtors

$$= \frac{150,000 - 100,000}{400,000}$$ Stock

$= 1/8 \times £40,000$	5,000		
Further amount eligible for deferment	£35,000	35,000	
Total deferment		£135,000	135,000
Clawback reduced to			£30,000

Note that the amounts for the fraction are taken as at the start of the period of account ended in the financial year 1979 (and not the year of the stock reduction) and are applied to the excess of the maximum deferment over £100,000. Thus, the further adjustments may not reduce the amount eligible for deferment below £100,000.

No deferment of clawback is possible if:

(i) The trade ceased during the period of account for which the clawback arises; or

(ii) The period for which the clawback arises, or the following period, is longer or shorter than 12 months; or

(iii) The trade is transferred to or from another person in the period of account for which the clawback arises, or in the previous or subsequent period; or

(iv) Clawback (whether deferred or not) arose in the previous period.

Deferment of stock relief clawback must be claimed within two years of the end of the period of account for which the clawback arises.

(4) *Method of relief or clawback* (Schedule 5, Para. 12, F.A. 1976)
Stock relief is given as a trading expense for the period of account concerned. Clawbacks are treated as trading receipts for the period in which the clawback arises.

DEFINITIONS

(1) *Trading stock* (Schedule 5, Para. 29, F.A. 1976 and Schedule 7, Para. 7, F.A. 1980)
"Trading stock" is property of any description, whether real or personal, such as is sold or is bought to be sold or processed in the ordinary course of the trade, etc. in question, together with materials used in manufacture etc. and work in progress. It does not include:

    (*a*) Securities (i.e. stocks and shares); or
    (*b*) Land, unless held for sale in the course of the trade:
        (i) After being developed by the company carrying on the trade; or
        (ii) In the case of a group of companies, held for the purpose of being developed by another company in the group; or
    (*c*) Goods held for letting on hire or hire-purchase.

It will thus be noted that securities (i.e. stocks and shares etc.) are excluded from trading stock for this purpose, as are goods let on hire or hire-purchase.

Land cannot be included as trading stock unless it is held for sale in the ordinary course of the trade after the construction or sustained reconstruction of buildings on the land concerned. For periods of account beginning after 26th March 1980 a building can be regarded as land in the somewhat unusual case of a building for which there is no immediately underlying land (e.g. *freehold* flats above the ground floor). (This reverses the decision in *C.I.R.* v. *Clydebridge Properties Ltd* [1980]). In other words land held as trading stock by a land dealer is not eligible for the relief, but a builder or developer would qualify.

If a business is registered for V.A.T. and all its outputs are standard or zero-rated the stock value in the accounts will be "net". However, if the supplies made by the business are wholly or partly exempt, supplies to it will nonetheless have borne V.A.T. In such a case any V.A.T. input which relates to trading stock and which cannot be taken into account will be included in the stock value.

Payments on account reduce the value of trading stock for the purposes of the relief, but it is understood that this reduction is not made for payments received by way of deposits to secure future orders. Furthermore payments on account must be matched against the items of stock concerned and if the amount of the payment on account exceeds the value of an item of stock, that excess is not set against other stock.

Example 5

Contractors Ltd is working on three contracts. The value of work in progress on these jobs and the payments on account received in respect thereof are:

	Total £	Job A £	Job B £	Job C £
Value..............................	120,000	40,000	30,000	50,000
Payment on account	100,000	30,000	10,000	60,000
Balance sheet value..................	£20,000	£10,000	£20,000	£(10,000)
Value for stock relief claim	£30,000	£10,000	£20,000	£ Nil

If goods are sold subject to reservation of title (i.e. the seller can reclaim the goods if he is not paid) such goods are nonetheless treated as purchases and, if appropriate, stock of the purchaser (provided that the seller treats them as sold and not included in his stock).

Work in progress on Government contracts is regarded as remaining the property of the contractor pending final delivery (even though most such contracts contain a clause vesting property therein in the Government Department or Agency concerned).

(2) *Work in progress* (Schedule 5, Para. 30, F.A. 1976)

"Work in progress" comprises services performed in the ordinary course of a trade, etc. where performance thereof is partly complete and where it is reasonable to expect that a charge will subsequently be made for those services, together with any article produced or material used in performing those services. This definition of work in progress does not include work wholly completed but not billed. The purpose of this exclusion is to prevent the giving of relief on work in progress which in reality should be an amount owing by a debtor. However, the Inland Revenue has stated that this definition will not be applied harshly and the relief would only be denied in exceptional cases.

(3) *Farm animals* (Schedule 5, Para. 25, F.A. 1976)

If farm animals are treated as trading stock, they can be included for stock relief but animals which have been dealt with on the "herd basis" must be excluded.

(4) *Special circumstances*

In most cases trading stock for stock relief purposes is primarily the amount which is brought into account in computing the profits of the trade etc., subject to any necessary adjustment for excess payments on account. There are however a number of special rules for determining the value of trading stock which have to be followed in certain circumstances.

(i) *Opening stock* (Schedule 5, Para. 23, F.A. 1976).

    (*a*) In a case where the trade, etc. was commenced during the period of 12 months up to the beginning of the period of account in question;

    (*b*) where during the period of account concerned there is a major alteration in the conduct of the trade in question resulting in an exceptional increase in the trading stock.

In either of these circumstances trading stock is to be valued, at the beginning of the period concerned, on such basis as is reasonable and just having regard to all the relevant circumstances of the case, but in particular account must be taken of:

    (*a*) The actual opening and closing values of trading stock for the period;

    (*b*) Movements during the period in the costs of items of a kind similar to those comprised in the trading stock; and

    (*c*) Changes during the period in the volume of trade carried on.

Example 6

Camphor Ltd commenced trading as a candle manufacturer on 1st June 1978. It made up accounts to 30th April 1979 and to 30th April thereafter.

The company's stock was:

1st June 1978	£ 4,000
30th April 1979	£16,000
30th April 1980	£24,000

In arriving at the stock relief claim for the 11 months to 30th April 1979, the opening stock (for stock relief purposes only) must be recomputed on a "reasonable and just" basis, taking into account the actual opening and closing stock values, movements in the cost of Camphor Ltd's stock and any change in its volume of business.

Since Camphor Ltd was not carrying on the trade twelve months before the start of the year to 30th April 1980 (i.e. on 1st May 1978) it is possible that the opening stock for stock relief purposes will be similarly recomputed for that year also.

(ii) *Change in basis of valuation* (Schedule 5, Para. 24, F.A. 1976). In any case where the basis of valuation of trading stock at the end of a period differs from that applied at the beginning of the period, the opening stock value must be recalculated on the same basis as the closing stock. It may happen that the new value of trading stock at the beginning of a period is less than the unrecovered past relief of the trade (i.e. the accumulation of relief given in earlier periods less any recovery thereof). If this is the case, the opening stock value is deemed to be equal in amount to the unrecovered past relief even though this is higher than the opening stock value as recalculated because of revision in the basis of valuation of stock applied at the end of the period.

(iii) *Anti-avoidance* (Schedule 5, Para. 22, F.A. 1976). Either the opening or closing value of trading stock for any period of account can be adjusted if it appears that the value thereof has been affected by arrangements by a person carrying on a trade, either alone or with others, such that the sole or main benefit which could be expected to accrue is the obtaining of relief or the reduction of a recovery of relief, and in particular in the following cases:

(*a*) Any acquisition or disposal of trading stock otherwise than in the normal course of the trade in question; or

(*b*) Any change in the normal pattern or method of carrying on the trade; or

(*c*) Any change in the date to which the accounts of the trade are made up; or

(*d*) Any increase in the value of one person's trading stock associated with a decrease in the trading stock of another person connected with him.

In all these cases the stock values concerned are, for stock relief purposes, adjusted to what they would have been had the arrangements not been made.

(5) *Relevant income* (Schedule 5, Para. 31, F.A. 1976)
"Relevant income" is the income of the trade computed on the normal principles of Case I, Schedule D *after* taking account of capital allowances and balancing charges, but before taking account of relief for losses, charges on income, group relief, or any clawback of relief previously given (see below).

(6) *Past relief* (Schedule 5, Para. 26, F.A. 1976)
Past relief is the aggregate of the two-year stock relief (but not the 5% additional relief) and stock relief under the F.A. 1976 scheme. Unrecovered past relief is the accumulated aggregate of past relief less any amounts which have been recovered.

Any balance of "two-year" stock relief remaining in unrecovered past relief was written off by excluding an appropriate amount from unrecovered past relief brought forward from the period of account ending in the financial year 1978.

The actual amount written off was the amount of "two-year" stock relief (including "transitional" relief) given, less any amounts recovered subsequently under the clawback arrangements. In determining whether any relief for these periods has been recovered, clawbacks are set against later years' relief before earlier years' (i.e. on a "last-in-first-out" (L.I.F.O.) basis).

Stock relief under the F.A. 1976 scheme given for later periods of account is to be excluded from unrecovered past relief for any period of account beginning on or after the sixth anniversary of the end of the period of account for which the relief was claimed. In most cases, where accounts have been drawn up annually, the write-off will be made with effect from the day following the sixth anniversary of the period of account concerned. If the sixth anniversary of the period of account in point does not coincide with the end of a period of account (because an intervening period of account was for more or less than twelve months), the write-off is made immediately after the period of account which is current on the sixth anniversary of the relevant period of account. The same general principles apply as with the write-off of the "two-year" stock relief, including the L.I.F.O. principle for identifying the actual amount to be written off.

Example 7

Wolf Ltd has had the following stock relief claims and clawbacks.

Period to	Relief (clawback)	Type
30.6.1973	£2,000)	F.A. 1975)
30.6.1974	£2,200)	F.A. (No. 2) 1975)
30.6.1975	£3,000	F.A. 1976
30.6.1976	£3,500	F.A. 1976
30.6.1977	£6,000	F.A. 1976
30.6.1978	(£7,200)	F.A. 1976
31.1.1979	£4,000	F.A. 1976
31.1.1980	£5,400	F.A. 1976

The allocation of clawback and write-off dates are shown below:

	30.6 1973 £	30.6 1974 £	30.6 1975 £	30.6 1976 £	30.6 1977 £	30.6 1978 £	30.6 1979 £	31.1 1980 £
Relief	2,000	2,200	3,000	3,500	6,000	(7,200)	4,000	5,400
Clawback allocation	—	—	—	(1,200)	(6,000)	7,200	—	—
Net relief	£2,000	£2,200	£3,000	£2,300	£ —	£ —	£4,000	£5,400
Write off date	1.7.78		1.2.82	1.2.83	N/A	N/A	1.2.86	1.2.86
Note	(a)		(b)					(c)

Notes:

(a) The last period of account ending in the financial year 1978 (i.e. year to 31st March 1979) was the year to 30th June 1978. Thus, the two-year stock relief is excluded from the unrecovered past relief brought forward at the start of the next period. At that point it ceases to be vulnerable to any clawback.

(b) The relief for the year to 30th June 1975 is six years old on 30th June 1981. Had there been no change of year end it would therefore have been excluded from unrecovered past relief brought forward on 1st July 1981, and ceased to be vulnerable to clawback from that date.

Since the year end changed, there is no period commencing on 1st July 1981, and it is necessary to find the date on which the next period does in fact commence. This is 1st February 1982 and is therefore the write-off date.

(c) The relief for the year to 31st January 1980 is six years old on 31st January 1986. Since the next period of account commences on 1st February 1986 the relief is written off on that date.

The write-off also applies to stock relief for farmers which was "frozen" on the making of a herd-basis election.

SPECIAL SITUATIONS

(1) *Cessation of trade* (Schedule 5, Para. 10, F.A. 1976)
No relief is available in the period of account in which a company ceases to trade. A final clawback of any unrecovered past relief will be made (normally in the final accounting period).

(2) *Successions* (Schedule 5, Para. 20, F.A. 1976)
Special provisions apply on a transfer of stock, at cost or market value, in the following circumstances:
  (a) A company reconstruction falling within I.C.T.A. 1970, s. 252 (for example, the transfer of a trade between companies with 75% common ownership);
  (b) Where a trade carried on by a sole trader of partnership is transferred to a company and at the date of the transfer not less than 75% of the ordinary shares capital is held by that sole trader or by the partners.
If predecessor and successor elect (within two years after transfer) the successor is treated as having carried on the trade since predecessor began to do so. There is then no clawback on cessation by predecessor.

(3) *Change in the ownership of a company* (Schedule 5, Para. 11, F.A. 1976)
I.C.T.A. 1970, s. 483 applies so as to restrict the carry forward of tax losses in a company where there is both a change in ownership and a major change in the nature or conduct of its trade, and also in certain cases where the scale of the activities has become small or negligible and the ownership of the company changes. To the extent that these losses are attributable to stock relief claims, such amounts are disregarded in computing the unrecovered past relief for clawback purposes. This is sensible, as otherwise there would be effective double taxation.

(4) *Farm animals* (Schedule 5, Para. 25, F.A. 1976)
Farm animals are included in trading stock unless they are the subject of a herd basis election.
    If an election for the herd basis takes effect during a period of account, animals forming part of the herd are not treated as trading stock at any time during the period. The stock at the beginning of the period for which the election for herd basis has effect will thus have to be recomputed omitting the herd which is the subject of the election.
    Any unrecovered relief at the end of the previous period of account is apportioned between the herd and the rest of the stock by reference to their respective values at the point of the election. The unrecovered past relief not relating to the herd is dealt with in the normal way, but the stock relief attributed to the herd is recovered in subsequent periods in the following circumstances:
  (a) In the first period—if the number of animals in the herd at the end of the period is less than the number at the point of election,
  (b) In subsequent periods—if the number of animals at the end of the period is less than the number at the last occasion of clawback.
    The clawback is made in the following proportion:

$$\frac{\text{Reduction in number of animals in period}}{\text{Number of animals at point of election}} \times \text{Unrecovered relief at point of election}$$

If the whole herd is sold and another production herd of the same class acquired (for example, Jersey dairy herd replaced by a Friesan dairy herd), both herds are treated as the same herd for the purposes of computing any clawback of relief.

Example 8

Election for herd basis made on 1st April 1977.
Number of animals in herd:

1.4.1977	300
31.3.1978	450
31.3.1979	480
31.3.1980	270
31.3.1981	465
31.3.1982	225

Value of trading stock at 1st April 1977 is £150,000, of which £50,000 relates to the herd. Total unrecovered past relief is £45,000.

Unrecovered past relief relating to herd:

$$\frac{50,000}{150,000} \times £45,000 = £15,000$$

Clawback, year to 31st March 1980:

$$\frac{300 - 270}{300} \times £15,000 = £1,500$$

Clawback, year to 31st March 1982:

$$\frac{270 - 225}{300} \times £15,000 = £2,250$$

(5) *Foreign trades* (Schedule 5, Para. 27, F.A. 1976)
The stock relief provisions apply equally to trades and professions carried on outside the U.K. and chargeable to Case V of Schedule D.

18.   Corporation Tax—Losses

§ 1.—COMPUTATION OF LOSSES (s. 177(6), I.C.T.A. 1970)

A corporation tax trading loss is computed in the same way as a corporation tax trading profit, by commencing with the trading profit (or loss) and considering which items charged in the accounts are allowable expenses, and those which must be disallowed.

§ 2.—CARRY-FORWARD AGAINST FUTURE INCOME OF SAME TRADE (s. 177(1), (10), I.C.T.A. 1970)

If a company incurs a loss in any accounting period, it may claim under s. 177(1), I.C.T.A. 1970 to set that loss against any trading income from the *same* trade in subsequent accounting periods. The trading income of those subsequent accounting periods is reduced by the amount of the loss brought forward until it is fully relieved. It is essential to show that there is not only continuity of ownership of the trade in the sense that the same company carries on the trade, but also that it is being carried on in future years in the same manner as before. Where losses are carried forward over several years before profitable trading is achieved this must be open to doubt. Refer to § 20 for the effects of a change in company share ownership.

Example 1

Optimist Ltd, making accounts up to the 31st December annually, incurred a loss of £100,000 in the accounting period ended 31st December 1982.

Profits for the next three years were;

31st December 1983	£40,000
31st December 1984	£30,000
31st December 1985	£50,000

The loss may be relieved as follows:

A.P. to 31st December 1983

Case I, Schedule D	£40,000	
Less: Loss relief	£40,000	(Part)
Assessment	Nil	

A.P. to 31st December 1984

Case, I, Schedule D	£30,000	
Less: Loss relief	£30,000	(Part)
Assessment	Nil	

A.P. to 31st December 1985

Case I, Schedule D	£50,000	
Less: Loss relief	£30,000	(Balance)
Assessment	£20,000	

Example 2

Pessimist Ltd made up accounts annually to 31st September 1984. It then changed the accounting date to 31st December.

Adjusted results were as follows

	£	£	
A.P. Twelve months to September 1984			
Case I, Schedule D, Loss	(26,000)		
Period of account 15 months to December 1985			
Case I, Schedule D, Profit.	30,000		
A.P. Twelve months to 30th September 1985			
$\frac{12}{15}$ × £30,000		24,000	
Less: Loss relief	24,000	24,000	(part)
Assessment		£ Nil	
A.P. three months to 31st December 1985			
$\frac{3}{15}$ × £30,000		6,000	
Less: Loss relief	2,000	(2,000)	(Balance)
Assessment		£4,000	

It is necessary to deal with the loss in the above manner because the rates of tax may have varied during the period.

A claim under s. 177(1), I.C.T.A. 1970, to carry losses forward must be made within *six years* of the end of the accounting period in which the loss was incurred. It will normally be sufficient if the claim is incorporated in the computations submitted to the Inspector of Taxes.

§ 3.—TRADING LOSSES SET AGAINST TOTAL PROFITS (s. 177(2), (3), I.C.T.A. 1970)

A loss incurred in a trade may, under s. 177(2), I.C.T.A. 1970, be set against the company's total profits, including chargeable gains of the accounting period in which the loss is incurred. It is understood that the Inland Revenue accept that the wording of s. 177(2) allows loss relief to be obtained against profits of the whole of the accounting period, even though the trade was carried on during part only of that accounting period.

Carry Back
Thereafter losses not utilised in the current accounting period may *if required*, be set against the total profits of preceding accounting periods ending within "a time equal in length to the accounting period in which the loss is incurred."

The amount of the reduction which may be made in the profits of an accounting period falling partly before that time cannot exceed a part of those profits proportionate to the period falling within that time. The loss may thus be set against any profits of the period immediately prior to that in which the loss was suffered, but if part of that previous accounting period falls outside the "equal length" period, the amount of the loss which may be set against the profits is limited to the proportion of the profits falling within the period.

Relief under s. 177(2), I.C.T.A. 1970 is only available for carry-back provided the trade in which the loss arose was also carried on in that period.

A claim under s. 177(2), I.C.T.A. 1970 must be made within *two years* after the end of the accounting period in which the loss was sustained.

Section 177(2), I.C.T.A. 1970 only allows relief for trading losses incurred in trades being carried on in the United Kingdom.

Overseas losses

Losses in trades carried on outside the United Kingdom, assessed under Case V, Schedule D, are excluded from s. 177(2) relief (s. 177(4), although Case V profits can be covered by s. 177(2) losses—see § 6 below).

Example 1

Palindrome Ltd made up accounts annually to 31st December 1984. It then changed the accounting date to 30th June and the next accounts were six months to 30th June 1985.
Adjusted results were as follows:

A.P. Year ended 31st December 1984

	£
Case I Schedule D	100,000
Case III Schedule D	5,000

A.P. Six months ended 30th June 1985

	£
Case I Schedule D Loss	(120,000)
Case III Schedule D	2,500
Chargeable Gains (assessable portion)	5,000

The loss incurred may be applied against profits from other sources for the six months ended 30th June 1985, and a claim may then be made against six months' profits of the preceding accounting period.
The position is therefore:

A.P. Six months to 30th June 1985

	£	£
Case I Schedule D, Loss..................	(120,000)	
Case III Schedule D		2,500
Chargeable Gains (assessable portion)		5,000
		7,500
Less: Loss relief	7,500	(7,500) (part)
Assessment		Nil

A.P. Twelve months to 31st December 1984

	£
Case I Schedule D	100,000
Case II Schedule D.......................	5,000
	105,000
Less: Loss Relief (6/12 of full year's profits) ...	52,500	(52,500) (part)
Amended Assessment		52,500
Balance of loss...........................	£60,000

The balance of £60,000 unutilised loss may then be carried forward under s. 177(1), I.C.T.A. 1970 to be deducted from profits (if any) from the same trade in subsequent accounting periods.

Note. An apportionment is required where a period of account exceeds twelve months and therefore comprises two (or more) accounting periods. The loss is set against the profits of the later accounting period first. (See Chapter 14, § 15.)

§ 4.—EXTENSION OF SET OFF FOR FIRST YEAR ALLOWANCES
(s. 177(3A), I.C.T.A. 1970; s. 60, F.A. 1985)

If a company incurs a loss in a trade in an accounting period for which first year allowances are due, then to the extent that the loss is created or augmented by the first year allowances given (and not disclaimed) that loss can be relieved against the profits of the three years preceding the accounting period in which the loss was sustained. This relief extends the relief due under s. 177(2), I.C.T.A. 1970 and in all other respects follows the same rules. Although it would appear that such relief follows automatically if a claim for set off is made under s. 177(2), I.C.T.A. 1970, none the less the Revenue require separate claims.

For accounting periods ending prior to 13th March 1984 the maximum claim was the amount of the loss which would not have been incurred if the allowances had not been postponed. In certain circumstances, because other reliefs could be affected, the change in the loss could exceed the first year allowances claimed.

Example

For the year to 30th June 1985, Chancer Ltd has an adjusted trading loss of £20,000 of which £16,500 is due to a claim for first year allowances. Chancer Ltd has other profits for the year to 30th June 1985 of £1,000. Profits for earlier periods were:

	£
6 months to 30th June 1984............................	600
Year to 31st December 1983............................	1,000
Year to 31st December 1982............................	8,500
Year to 31st December 1981............................	12,000

The utilisation of the loss is as follows:

	Total £	Not due to F.Y.A. £	Due to F.Y.A. £
Case I Schedule D, loss.....................	(20,000)	(3,500)	(16,500)
Current period—30.6.1985.............	1,000	1,000	—
	(19,000)	(2,500)	(16,500)
Carry back			
6 months to 30.6.1984	600	600	—
	(18,400)	(1,900)	(16,500)
6/12 × year to 31.12.1983..............	500	500	—
	(17,900)	(1,400)	(16,500)
Year to 31.12.1983 (balance)	550	—	500
	(17,400)	(1,400)	(16,000)
Year to 31.12.1982	8,500	—	8,500
	(8,900)	(1,400)	(7,500)
6/12 × year to 31.12.1981..............	6,000	—	6,000
Carry forward from 30.6.1985................	£(2,900)	£(1,400)	£(1,500)

§ 5.—CARRY FORWARD OF EXCESS TRADING CHARGES ON INCOME
(s. 177(8), I.C.T.A. 1970)

Where annual charges are paid in an accounting period and they:
      (*a*) exceed the amount of the profits against which they are deductible; and
      (*b*) include payments made wholly and exclusively for the purposes of a
        trade;
to the extent that the excess comprises trading charges, *the excess* can be used for the purposes of computing a loss to be carried forward, under s. 177(1), I.C.T.A. 1970.

Example 1

Incautious Ltd's trading activities for the accounting period ended 31st December 1985, resulted in a profit of £10,000.
During the year the company paid annual trading charges of £11,000.
The position would be as follows:

A.P. Year ended 31st December 1985:

Profits...	£10,000
Less: Annual charges (part)......................	10,000
Assessment	Nil

The unrelieved balance of annual charge of £1,000 can be carried forward against future accounting periods; or alternatively, if the company ceased business at the end of the above accounting period, would be available for terminal loss relief (see this chapter § 13).

Example 2

Careless Ltd has the following profits for the accounting period ended 30th September 1985:

	£
Case I, Schedule D.............................	20,000
Chargeable gain (assessable portion)	40,000
	60,000
Less: Charges...................................	80,000
Excess charges.........................	£20,000

Charges wholly and exclusively for the purposes of the trade amounted to £15,000. This amount may therefore be carried forward (but not backwards) against profits arising from the same trade. The balance of the excess £5,000 (£20,000 − £15,000) is "lost". (N.B. *Non-trading charges are, by nature of the wording of s. 177(8), set-off in priority to the trading charges.*)

Example 3

Futile Ltd has the following results:

	1983	1984	1985
12 months to 30th June	£	£	£
Case I, Schedule D profit or (loss)	£(10,000)	£2,000	£12,000
Chargeable gains (assessable portion)	2,000	200	—
Charges: For the trade	300	600	800
Other	1,200	400	400

A.P. *12 months to 30th June 1983*	£	
Chargeable gains (assessable portion)	2,000	
Less: Charges.........................	1,500	
Assessment	500	
Loss carried forward	£10,000	

A.P. *12 months to 30th June 1984*	£	
Case I, Schedule D..........................	2,000	
Less: Loss Relief.............................	2,000	(Part)
	Nil	
Chargeable gain (assessable portion)	200	
Less: Charges...............................	1,000	
Excess Charges..............................	£800	
Carry forward—Case I, Schedule D.............	8,000	(Balance)
Charges (restricted to those for the trade)	600	
	£8,600	

(*Note.* No relief available for balance of excess charges of £200)

A.P. *to 30th June 1985*	£
Case I, Schedule D....................................	12,000
Less: Loss Relief......................................	8,600
	3,400
Less: Charges	1,200
Assessment	£2,200

Note. Had the company chosen "set-off against total income" for 1983, no relief would have been obtained for charges of £1,200—it was better to lose charges of £200 in 1984. However, in making decisions of this kind the effect upon cash flow must be considered.

Example 4

12 months to 30th September	1984	1985
	£	£
Case I, Schedule D, Profit (loss)	5,000	(20,000)
Schedule "A"........................	1,000	1,000
Chargeable gain (assessable portion) ..	—	1,500
Charges: For the trade	—	2,000
Other	600	100

A.P. *12 months to 30th September 1984*	
Case I, Schedule D..................	5,000
Schedule "A"........................	1,000
	6,000
Less: Charges.......................	600
Assessment	£5,400

A.P. 12 months to 30th September 1985	£
Schedule "A"........................	1,000
Chargeable gain (assessable portion) ..	1,500
	2,500
Less: Loss Relief....................	2,500 (part)
	£ —

Section 177(2), I.C.T.A. 1970 claim:	£
Assessment (as above)	5,400
Add: Charges............................	600
	6,000
Less: Loss relief	6,000 (Part)
Assessment	Nil

To carry forward against profits from same trade:

		£
Case I, Schedule D, Loss		20,000
Less: Relieved 1984 .... £6,000		
Relieved 1985 .... £2,500		
		8,500
		11,500
Add: Charges (available only for carry forward)		2,000
Carry forward from 30th September 1985		£13,500

Note. There is no relief for the non-trading charges, in 1984 of £600 and 1985 of £100.

§ 6.—FOREIGN TRADES (s. 177(7), I.C.T.A. 1970)

If a loss is incurred in a trade assessable under Case V Schedule D, (a trade controlled outside the United Kingdom), it cannot be relieved against total profits of the same or the preceding accounting period under s. 177 (2), I.C.T.A. 1970. Such losses can be set against future profits of the same trade or used in a terminal loss claim (s. 178, I.C.T.A. 1970) on the cessation of such a trade.

§ 7.—NON-COMMERCIAL TRADES (s. 177(4), (5), I.C.T.A. 1970)

If a trade is not carried on on a commercial basis with a view to profit, any loss sustained can only be carried forward under s. 177(1), I.C.T.A. 1970, or used in a terminal loss claim under s. 178, I.C.T.A. 1970. The loss cannot be relieved against total profits of the same or the preceding accounting period under s. 177(2), I.C.T.A. 1970.

§ 8.—FARMS AND MARKET GARDENS (s. 180, I.C.T.A. 1970)

A loss incurred in carrying on the trade of farming or market gardening cannot be relieved against total profits of the same or preceding accounting period under s. 177(2), I.C.T.A. 1970, if a loss (before capital allowances) was sustained in the trade in each of the accounting periods falling wholly or partly within the preceding five years. Where a loss is so excluded from relief, so are any related capital allowances. This restriction does not apply if it can be shown that the farm or market garden is being operated in such a way that a competent farmer or market gardener would have a reasonable expectation of profit at the start of the period of loss.

§ 9.—OIL EXTRACTION ACTIVITIES (s. 13, Oil Taxation Act 1975, s. 43, F.A. (No. 2) 1975)

Oil extraction activities in the United Kingdom, its territorial sea or the designated licence areas of the North Sea, are treated as being within a "Ring Fence" and constitute a separate trade from all other trades, or from oil extraction activities carried on in other areas of the world. Losses sustained within the "Ring Fence" can only be set against other "Ring Fence" activities following the rules of s. 177(1), (2).

Losses on other activities outside the "Ring Fence" can be set against "Ring Fence" profits in the ordinary way. These restrictions have effect for accounting periods (or parts thereof) falling after 11th July 1974. However, trading losses (from whatever trade) incurred before 1st January 1973 cannot be set against "Ring Fence" profits after that date. A further restriction prevents the set-off of trading losses so incurred before 1st January 1973, to the greater amount of:

(a) trading income of the trade in the period from 1st January 1973 to 1st July 1974; or

(b) £50 million.

§ 10.—LEASING PARTNERSHIPS, ETC. (s. 30, F.A. 1973)

Section 30, F.A. 1973 prevents a company obtaining loss relief arising from first year allowances due in respect of certain lease contracts, and then transferring the lease contract to another company in the same group, which could set its losses arising in subsequent years against the profits arising in the later years of the contract.

See also the provisions, effective from 1st June 1980, in respect of leasing plant, described in Chapter 5 § 6.

§ 11.—COMMODITY PARTNERSHIPS (s. 31, F.A. 1978)

Section 31, F.A. 1978 prevents a company obtaining a loss relief arising from trading in commodity futures in partnership with the main object of creating a loss in order to obtain a tax benefit.

§ 12.—CAPITAL ALLOWANCES GIVEN BY DISCHARGE OR REPAYMENT OF TAX (s. 74, C.A.A. 1968)

Certain capital allowances are expected to be given primarily against a particular source of income (e.g. agricultural buildings allowance is given primarily against agricultural income). Relief is given by deducting the allowance from the "primary" source of income for the same period and any excess is carried forward against future income.

The company may elect that, instead, the allowance be deducted from total profits of the same accounting period and (if required) a preceding period of equivalent length. However such a set off is made only after other relief against the same profits have been exhausted.

§ 13.—TERMINAL LOSSES (s. 178, I.C.T.A. 1970)

Where a company ceases to carry on a trade and suffers a loss in the final 12 months of trading, terminal loss relief may be claimed. This applies to any loss sustained in an accounting period falling wholly or partly within the 12 months prior to cessation. A claim may be made whereby such losses are set against trading income from that trade in the accounting periods falling wholly or partly within three years preceding those twelve months. The relief is applied to later periods first. Terminal loss relief is computed on the basis that all other claims for loss relief have been made.

Where the accounting periods ending within the last 12 months exceed 12 months (i.e. the last period is shorter than 12 months), the losses of the earliest thereof are apportioned on a time basis, and aggregated with those of other accounting periods also falling within that period, to find the amount of the terminal loss.

Example 1

Lastditch Ltd incurred a trading loss of £5,300 in the accounting period of 4 months ended on 30th November 1985, its final period of trading. In the year to 31st July 1985 it made a profit of £5,700.

Lastditch Ltd's terminal loss is:

		£
1.8.85–30.11.85	Case I, Schedule D Loss	(5,300)
Less: Relieved under s. 177(2), I.C.T.A. 1970		
	£5,700 × $\frac{4}{12}$	1,900
Terminal loss		£(3,400)
1.8.84–31.7.85	Case I, Schedule D	5,700
Less: Relieved under s. 177(2), I.C.T.A. 1970		(1,900)
		3,800
Less: Terminal loss claim under s. 178, I.C.T.A. 1970		(3,400)
Profits chargeable to corporation tax		£400

A similar apportionment may be required for the earliest of the accounting periods ending within the three preceding years.

Capital allowances which fall to be made by way of discharge or repayment of tax in respect of the final accounting period may, on a claim, be added to the trading loss for that period for the purposes of terminal loss relief.

Example 2

	Trading income/(loss)	Trading charges
	£	£
A.P. to 31.12.82	4,000	1,600
A.P. to 31.12.83	3,000	1,300
A.P. to 31.12.84	3,000	1,700
A.P. to 31.12.85	− (1,200)	1,000
A.P. to 31.3.86 (3 months)	− (2,800)	100

Section 177(2), I.C.T.A. 1970 claim must first be made for A.P. to 31.12.84, thus reducing the profit to £1,800 (£3,000 − £1,200)

Terminal loss:

	£	£
3 months to 31.3.86	2,800	
Add: Charges	100	
		2,900
12 months to 31.3.85	1,200	
Less: I.C.T.A. 1970, s. 177(2) claim (A.P. to 31.12.84)	1,200	
	—	
Add: Charges	1,000	
	£1,000	
9/12 thereof:		750
Terminal loss		£3,650

Relief:

	Trading income £	Trading charges £	Available for relief £	Relief claimed £
A.P. to 31.12.85				
(3/12)	—	250	—	—
A.P. to 31.12.84	1,800	1,700	100	100
A.P. to 31.12.83	3,000	1,300	1,700	1,700
A.P. to 31.12.82				
(9/12)	3,000	600*	2,400	1,850
				£3,650

§ 14.—LOSSES ARISING UNDER CASE VI, SCHEDULE D (s. 179, I.C.T.A. 1970)

Relief is available where a company sustains a loss in any transaction, and the transaction would have been liable to assessment under Case VI if a profit had arisen. The relief for the loss can only be claimed against the profits of any other transactions which would be assessed under Case VI arising in the same accounting period. An unrelieved balance may be carried forward and so relieved against Case VI profits in subsequent years.

Relief *cannot* be given in this way for losses incurred in the following transactions:

   (*a*) Lease premiums (s. 80, I.C.T.A. 1970)
   (*b*) Assignment of lease granted at undervalue (s. 81, I.C.T.A. 1970)
   (*c*) Sale of land with a right to reconveyance (s. 82, I.C.T.A. 1970)

A claim for relief must be made within *six years* after the end of the accounting period in which the loss is sustained, even if the relief will not be utilised until after the end of the six year period.

---

* Charges of £1,600 less profit £1,000 (3/12 × £4,000), not available for terminal relief.

§ 15.—MANAGEMENT EXPENSES OF INVESTMENT COMPANIES (ss. 304–306, I.C.T.A. 1970)

Management expenses of investment companies are deducted from the total profits of the period in which they are *disbursed*. Any excess is carried forward against total profits of later periods. Excess charges on income, if incurred wholly and exclusively for the purposes of the company's business, are also carried forward as management expenses.

For these purposes relevant capital allowances are treated as an expense of management.

Subject to certain necessary modifications, the management expenses of insurance companies are treated in a similar manner to those of investment companies.

§ 16.—CAPITAL LOSSES (s. 265, I.C.T.A. 1970)

Capital losses are set against chargeable gains (before reduction) of the same accounting period, or carried forward and set against future capital gains. Capital losses cannot be set off against any other type of profit. However, they are carried forward by the company which realised the loss, even if it has ceased to trade or to hold investments.

A capital loss can also be claimed under s. 22, C.G.T.A. 1979 if an asset has become of negligible value.

The following reliefs are also available:
  (i) Relief for loss on a debt on a security (s. 134, C.G.T.A. 1979)
  (ii) Relief for loans made to traders becoming irrecoverable, or guarantees called on such loans (s. 135, C.G.T.A. 1979)
  (iii) Relief as an "income loss" on certain investments in trading companies (s. 36, F.A.1981).

§ 17.—RELIEF FOR INVESTMENT COMPANIES FOR LOSSES ON UNQUOTED SHARES IN TRADING COMPANIES (s. 36, F.A. 1981)

If a company sustains a loss on a disposal after 1st April 1981 on shares acquired *by subscription* in a qualifying trading company, that loss, which would otherwise have been a capital loss, can be treated as an "income loss" and used as such in loss relief claims. There is no restriction on when the subscription takes place.

The company which made the investment must be, and must have been throughout the previous six years, an investment company. A shorter continuous period will qualify, provided the company was not previously a trading company, nor an excluded company. An excluded company is, broadly, a company which deals in shares, securities, land or commodity futures. Furthermore, the investing company must not control, be controlled by, or share common control with the trading company.

If a claim is made within two years after the end of the accounting period in which the loss was incurred, the loss can be set against income arising in that accounting period. If the income is insufficient, the loss can also be used against the income of earlier accounting periods ending within the preceding twelve months. Where a preceding accounting period falls partly within and partly outside the preceding twelve months, the relief is given only against a proportion (on a time basis) of the income of the period concerned.

This relief is given before charges on income, expenses of management or any other reliefs which are deducted from total profits. However, the claim does not displace the relief for an earlier loss.

If the income of these periods is insufficient, the excess is carried forward as a capital loss in the normal way.

§ 18—RELIEF FOR LOSSES AGAINST FRANKED INVESTMENT INCOME (ss. 254 and 255, I.C.T.A. 1970)

Where in an accounting period a company has a surplus of F.I.I. over the franked payments which it has made, it may claim under s. 254, I.C.T.A. 1970 to have the excess regarded as income liable to corporation tax. Such a claim may be made in order that the following losses can be offset:

(i) trading losses against total profits (s. 177(2), I.C.T.A. 1970).
(ii) relief for charges on income (s. 248, I.C.T.A. 1970).
(iii) relief for management expenses (ss. 304, 305, I.C.T.A. 1970).
(iv) capital allowances given by discharge or repayment against total profits, i.e. capital allowances not directly related to a trade (s. 74(3), C.A.A. 1968).
(v) relief for an "income loss" on investment in unquoted shares in trading companies (s. 36, F.A. 1981).

The time limit for these claims is two years after the end of the accounting period in cases (i) and (iv) and (v), and six years after the end of the accounting period in cases (ii) and (iii).

Effects of claim on other profits

Where such a claim is made it can only apply after all profits actually liable to corporation tax have been extinguished by the reliefs claimed. This is an important restriction in relation to a close company as it forces relief for the above items to be given against the assessable portion of chargeable gains, if any, before being given against F.I.I.

Restriction of A.C.T. set-off

Where a claim is made to have surplus F.I.I. of an accounting period treated as income liable to corporation tax, the tax credit attaching to the F.I.I. is repaid to the extent of the relief available. However, two restrictions arise as a result of the repayment:—

(i) the surplus F.I.I. available for carry forward against future A.C.T. liabilities is reduced by the amount on which the tax credit has been repaid;
(ii) the amount of A.C.T. which can be offset against mainstream corporation tax liabilities of the next and following accounting periods, is reduced by the repayment received.

Both these restrictions are necessary to prevent a double advantage being obtained from this kind of claim. If the first restriction was applied on its own it would be possible to obtain relief for the extra A.C.T. paid in a subsequent accounting period by set-off against a mainstream corporation tax liability.

Restoration of losses

The restrictions referred to above make it necessary to provide for the restoration of the corporation tax loss used in the claim, where in a subsequent accounting period the company's franked payments exceed the F.I.I. received. This is done by treating the company as having suffered a loss for corporation tax purposes in the accounting period immediately before the period in which the excess franked payments arise, equal to the lesser of:

(a) the surplus F.I.I. originally treated as income liable to corporation tax: and
(b) the excess of franked payments over F.I.I. for that accounting period.

The effect of a claim of this nature is really to borrow the tax credit attaching to F.I.I. received and consequently give rise to a short term cash flow benefit. This can best be seen by considering a detailed example.

Example

	Corporation Tax Income (Loss)	Taxable prop. of chargeable gains	F.I.I. (gross) (inclusive of tax credit)	Dividends paid to shareholders
	£	£	£	£
A.P. to 31.12.82	− (2,000)	—	1,000	700
A.P. to 31.12.83	− (1,500)	1,000	2,000	700
A.P. to 31.12.84	1,000	—	500	700
A.P. to 31.12.85	6,000	—	—	700

Required: Show the most immediate reliefs that can be claimed in respect of the corporation tax losses.

		£	£	£
(a)	*A.P. to 31.12.82*			
	ACT liability on dividend = 3/7 × £700		300	
	offset by: Tax credit on F.I.I.		300	—

Corporation tax loss of £2,000 c/f

		£	£	£
(b)	*A.P. to 31.12.83*			
	ACT liability on dividend = 3/7 × £700		300	
	offset by: Tax credit on F.I.I.		300	—

Surplus F.I.I. £1,000 (gross)—tax credit
offset by: Corporation tax loss (i.e.
£1,500 less £1,000 = £500)
∴ recover. £150

Surplus F.I.I. £500

Corporation tax loss b/f. and c/f. £2,000

		£	£	£
(c)	*A.P. to 31.12.84*			
	ACT liability on dividend = 3/7 × £700		300	
	offset by: Tax credit on surplus F.I.I. b/fwd.	150		
	Tax credit on F.I.I. received in A.P.	150		
			300	—

Profit for corporation tax purposes 1,000
Less: Loss b/f. 2,000

Corporation tax loss c/f £1,000

(d) *A.P. to 31.12.85*
  ACT liability on dividend = 3/7 × £700 . . . .   £300
                          (i.e. excess
                          franked
                          payments of
                          £1,000)

Profit for corporation tax purposes £6,000
Less: Loss b/f. £1,000
   Loss due to former utilisation of F.I.I.
   and subsequent excess franked
   payments.   500
                     1,500

Profit liable to corporation tax £4,500

	£	£
Corporation tax thereon @ 30%		1,350
Deduct: A.C.T. paid	£300	
Less: Restriction due to s. 254 claim	150	
		150
∴ Mainstream corporation tax due = ...		£1,200

Summary

	£
A.P. to 31.12.83—tax credit recovered.............................	(150)
A.P. to 31.12.85—A.C.T. paid	300
—Mainstream corporation tax paid....................	1,200
	£1,350

Note. If no s. 254 claim had been made the tax payable would have been:

		£	£
(a)	A.P. to 31.12.82: as above		Nil
(b)	A.P. to 31.12.83:		Nil
	surplus F.I.I. of £1,000 instead of £500		
	corporation tax loss of £2,500 instead of £2,000		
(c)	A.P. to 31.12.84:		Nil
	surplus F.I.I. of £500 instead of Nil		
	corporation tax loss of £1,500 instead of £1,000		
(d)	A.P. to 31.12.85:		
	A.C.T. payable (£300 less £150 b/fwd.) .... =		150
	Mainstream corporation tax − £4.500 @ 30% ...... =	1,350	
	Less: A.C.T. paid..... =	150	1,200
	Total tax paid		£1,350

As an alternative to a claim to have F.I.I. treated as income liable to corporation tax for purposes mentioned above, it is possible to make a similar claim in order to obtain relief for trading losses brought forward. This is provided the surplus F.I.I. would have been taken into account as trading income under s. 177(7), I.C.T.A. 1970, i.e. for banks, finance and share dealing companies. This claim would have to be made within six years of the end of the AP to which it related.

It is possible to make a similar claim in order to have surplus F.I.I. taken into account as income liable to corporation tax for the purposes of a terminal loss claim in terms of s. 178, I.C.T.A. 1970. A claim must be made within six years of the company ceasing to carry on the trade.

§ 19.—COMPANY RECONSTRUCTIONS WITHOUT CHANGES IN OWNERSHIP (ss. 252 and 253, I.C.T.A. 1970)

Where one company ceases to carry on a trade and another company carries on the trade in place of the first company, the normal corporation tax cessation and commencement provisions will apply. But s. 252, I.C.T.A. provides continuity of relief by allowing losses incurred by the company ceasing business to be carried forward to the second company, provided that not less than three-quarters of the interest in both companies belongs to the same persons at some time, within two years after the change of trade.

The effect of the provisions above is:

(*a*) The unabsorbed losses of the first company are carried forward to the second company; and

(*b*) The capital allowances computations continue without change, the assets being transferred at their written down value. No balancing charges or allowances will arise.

(*c*) The stock relief computations continue without change, there is no clawback and the balance of unrecovered past relief is transferred to the second company.

The company ceasing to trade cannot, however, claim a terminal loss

If the second company ceases to carry on trade within four years of the changeover date, any terminal loss relief may be set-off against the first company's profits from the same trade. However it is not possible for the successor to make a claim under s. 177(2) or 3A), I.C.T.A. 1970 against the total profits of the predecessor.

A trade carried on by a company is regarded:

(*a*) as belonging to persons owning the ordinary share capital of the company and as belonging to them in proportion to the amount of their holding of that capital;

(*b*) in the case of a company which is a 75% subsidiary company, as belonging to a company which is its parent company, or as belonging to the persons owning the ordinary share capital of that parent company, and as belonging to them in proportion to their holdings of that capital.

§ 20.—CHANGE IN OWNERSHIP (ss. 483 and 484, I.C.T.A. 1970)

Anti-avoidance provisions are contained in s. 483, I.C.T.A. 1970 to prevent abuse of the loss carry forward provisions where the ownership of the company changes. This section provides that if:

(*a*) within any period of three years, there is both a change in the ownership of a company and a *major change* in the nature or conduct of a trade carried on by the company; or

(*b*) at any time after, the scale of activities in a trade carried on by a company has become small or negligible, and before any considerable revival of that trade, there is a change in the ownership of the company;

no relief under s. 177(1), I.C.T.A. 1970 is available. This prevents the set-off of a loss incurred by the company in an accounting period beginning before the change of ownership, against income of an accounting period ending after the change of ownership.

The term "major change" in the nature of the trade is defined as:

(a) a major change in the type of property dealt in, or services or facilities provided in the trade; or

(*b*) a major change in customers, outlets or markets of the trade.

There is a change in the ownership of a company for the purposes of s. 483 if:

(*a*) a single person acquires more than half the ordinary share capital of the company; or

(*b*) two or more persons each acquire a holding of 5% or more of the ordinary shares, and those holdings together amount to more than half the ordinary share capital of the company; or

(*c*) two or more persons acquire a holding of the ordinary shares of a company and the holdings together amount to more than half the ordinary share capital of the company. Where a holding is less than 5%, it is to be disregarded unless it is in addition to an existing holding and together with the existing holding, amounts to more than 5% of the ordinary share capital of the company.

A change in the ownership of a company is disregarded if:

(*a*) immediately before the change, the company is the 75% subsidiary of another company, and

(*b*) (although there is a change in the direct ownership of the company) that other company continues after the change to own the first mentioned company as a 75% subsidiary.

But, if there is a change in the ownership of a company which has a 75% subsidiary, whether owned directly or indirectly, then s. 483 will apply as if there had been a change in the ownership of the subsidiary, unless the change is to be disregarded because of (a) and (b) above.

Where losses brought forward for s. 483 purposes consist of capital allowances or stock appreciation relief, balancing charges and stock relief recovery occurring *after* the change in ownership are reduced by the extent of the respective capital allowances and stock relief "losses" (s. 483(5), I.C.T.A. 1970; Sch. 5, para. 11, F.A. 1976; Sch. 9, para, 14, F.A. 1981 (stock relief)).

19. Corporation Tax—Close Companies

§ 1.—INTRODUCTION

A *"close company"* is a company which is owned or controlled by a small group of persons. However, since it is necessary to group various persons who are in some way related or associated with each other, the number of people involved can on occasions be quite large. The distinctions drawn in company law between a private and public company are not relevant and the term "close company" is specifically defined.

In effect the close company provisions are anti-avoidance provisions directed against groups of persons who would otherwise be able to arrange the affairs of the company to their own advantage by avoiding or deferring payment of tax, or paying tax at a lower rate than would otherwise apply. The principal element of the anti-avoidance provisions is that relating to apportionment of income (refer to § 9 below).

§ 2.—DEFINITION OF A CLOSE COMPANY AND OTHER DEFINITIONS

MEANING OF CLOSE COMPANY (s. 282, I.C.T.A. 1970)

The basic definition of a *close company* is a company which is
- (*a*) under the *control* of five or fewer *participators*; or
- (*b*) under the control of participators who are *directors*.

A company is also close if, were its income to be *apportioned* (see this chapter § 9) amongst its participators, more than 50% of the amount which would be so apportioned, would be apportioned to such participators (*a*) or directors (*b*). Where appropriate, this also includes amounts which have been sub-apportioned through companies which hold shares in the underlying company whose income is being apportioned.

Several other terms which are of general application to close companies are contained in ss. 302 and 303, I.C.T.A. 1970.

PARTICIPATOR (s. 303(1), (2), I.C.T.A. 1970)

A *"participator"* is a person with a share or interest in the capital or income of the company, and includes:
- (i) any person who possesses, or is entitled to acquire, share capital or voting rights in the company;
- (ii) any *"loan creditor"* of the company or any person possessing, or entitled to acquire, rights to receive amounts payable to loan creditors as premium on redemption;
- (iii) any person who possesses, or is entitled to acquire, a right to receive or participate in distributions by the company (excluding additional matters treated as distributions—see § 9 below);
- (iv) any person entitled to secure that income or assets (whether present or future) will be applied directly or indirectly for his benefit.

A person is also treated as being entitled to do something where he is entitled to do it at some future date, or will (at some future date) be entitled to do it.

Any participator in a company controlling another company is also treated as a participator in the latter company.

LOAN CREDITOR (s. 303(7), (8), I.C.T.A. 1970)

A *"loan creditor"* is

(*a*) a person holding redeemable loan capital issued by a company, or

(*b*) a creditor in respect of a debt incurred by a company:

(i) for money borrowed or capital assets acquired by the company, or

(ii) for any right to receive income created in favour of the company, or

(iii) for consideration, the value of which to the company was substantially less than the amount of the debt.

This is extended to include a person who is not the creditor in respect of any such debt, but nevertheless has a beneficial interest therein.

A person carrying on a banking business is not to be treated as a loan creditor in respect of any loan capital or debt issued to the company in the ordinary course of business.

For the purpose of the control test, a recognised money broker will not be treated as a participator of a company carrying on a business as a stock-jobber solely by reason of short term loans or advances arising in the ordinary course of their respective trades (see Concession C10–1980).

DIRECTOR (s. 303(5), (6), I.C.T.A. 1970)

The term *"director"* includes not only persons who are directors within the meaning of the various Companies Acts, but also any person occupying the position of director, by whatever name called, or any person in accordance with whose directions the directors are accustomed to act.

Also included as a "director" is any person who is a manager of the company's business (by whatever name called), who either on his own account, or with associates, owns (or is able to control) more than 20% of the ordinary share capital of the company.

Control, or ownership in this respect may be either direct or indirect, (i.e. via another company) including direct or indirect ownership by associates.

CONTROL (s. 302(2)–(6), I.C.T.A. 1970)

A person has *"control"* of a company if he exercises, or is entitled to acquire, control (either directly or indirectly) over a company. That is, if he possesses or is entitled to acquire:

(i) the greater part of the share capital or voting power of the company; or

(ii) such part of the issued share capital as would entitle him to receive the greater part of the company's income (on the assumption that it were distributed amongst the participators); or

(iii) such rights as would, in the event of a winding up, entitle him to the greater part of the assets available for distribution among members.

If two or more persons satisfy these conditions, they are deemed to have control of the company jointly. All shares held by a nominee of a participator are regarded as being held directly by the principal concerned.

In determining control, a person is also treated as being entitled to acquire anything which he is entitled to acquire at a future date, or will at a future date be entitled to acquire. For the purposes of control, there will also be attributed to a person any rights or powers exercised by any of his associates, and any rights or powers of any company over which a person and his associates have control are also attributed to that person.

ASSOCIATES OF A PARTICIPATOR (s. 303(3), (4), I.C.T.A. 1970)

The following persons are to be treated as *"associates"* of a participator and hence treated as belonging to the proprietor in determining control:

(i) wife (or husband);
(ii) parent or remoter forebear:
(iii) children or remoter issue;   } *"relatives"*
(iv) brother or sister;
(v) business partner;
(vi) trustee(s) of any settlement of which the participator, or any relative (living or dead) is, or was, the settlor;
(vii) joint beneficiaries of a trust or of the estate of a deceased person. However this does not make an individual an associate if he is entitled to benefit under a trust set up for superannuation schemes, etc.; nor does it apply to a trust set up for the benefit of the employees and directors of the company (not wholly or mainly for the benefit of the directors) and the person concerned is neither directly nor indirectly, the holder of more than 5% of the ordinary share capital of the company.

ASSOCIATED COMPANIES (s. 302(1), I.C.T.A. 1970)

Two, or more, companies are *"associated companies"* if at any relevant time (or at any time within one year previously) one has control of the other, or both are under the control of the same person or persons.

The one year rule does not apply when determining associated companies for the purpose of the abatements in the computation of relevant income—see § 9 below.

In determining whether two companies are controlled by the same persons, and are therefore associated for the purpose of the abatement of estate income, it is not normally the practice to seek to attribute to a person the rights or powers of his relatives (other than his wife and minor children) where there is no substantial trading interdependence between the two companies (Concesssion C11–1980).

If, for example, an individual owned all the shares in company A, and his brother owned all the shares in company B, normally it will not be contended that B's powers could be attributed to A so that A could be treated as controlling B's company as well as his own. Similarly, if their father held, say 20% of the shares in each son's company, normally it will not be contended that the powers of the sons should be attributed to him, so that he could be regarded as controlling both companies. The Inland Revenue, however, reserve for consideration all cases where there was a substantial trading interdependence between the two companies.

Cases where companies would be associated if a person had attributed to him the rights and powers of persons who were his associates, will be considered on their facts. There may be some exceptional cases where, without attributing to any person the rights and powers of his associates, two or more companies could be regarded as associated because both are controlled by the same trustee (for example, the trustee company of a clearing bank). This fact alone will not be regarded as a ground for treating such companies as associated; but if there were any connection, past or present, between the companies, the case would need to be considered on its facts. Similarly, it will not be contended that two or more companies are associated merely because they could all be treated as being controlled by the same loan creditor, provided that the loan creditor is an open company, or any other bona fide commercial loan creditor, and there is no other connection between the companies.

ORDINARY SHARE CAPITAL (s. 526(5), I.C.T.A. 1970)

"Ordinary share capital" is all the issued share capital of the company (by whatever name called), other than capital carrying only a fixed rate of dividend, but with no other right to share in profits.

§ 3.—ILLUSTRATIONS OF THE BASIC TEST FOR A CLOSE COMPANY

Example 1

You-Hoo Ltd has the following shareholdings:

	Ordinary shares
Smith—Director	3,000
Brown—Director	600
Jones—Director	750
Green—Director	150
Smith Jnr—works manager (son of Smith)	1,500
Mrs Smith (wife of Smith)	2,000
Jeckyl and Hyde (trustees of settlement made by father of Brown)	6,000
White (cousin of Jones)	3,000
Other shareholders (no relation with above shareholders)	3,000
	20,000

	Shares	Director control	
Smith—Director	3,000	6,500	(1)
Brown—Director	600	6,600	(2)
Jones—Director	750	750	
Green—Director	150	150	
Smith Jnr.—Works Manager	1,500		
Mrs. Smith	2,000		
Jeckyl and Hyde	6,000		
White	3,000		
Others	3,000		
	20,000	14,000	

Notes

(1)
Smith	3,000
Add Associates:	
Wife	2,000
Son	1,500
	6,500

(2)
Brown	600
Add Associate:	
Trustees	6,000
	6,600

The directors and their associates hold more than 50% of the shares and the company is a *close company*. It is not, therefore, necessary to check for control by participators.

Example 2

The share capital of Colours Ltd is owned as follows:

Black—Director	10%
White—Director	10%
Grey—Director	10%
Green	6%
Brown	6%
Pink	9%
Lemon (and six others in equal shares)	49%

None of the above are associates.

(i) The company is *not a close company*, since it is not under the control of five or less participators, or of participators who are directors.

(ii) If Green, Brown and Pink were also directors, the company would be a close company, because it would then be under the control of participators who are directors (51% of the share capital).

(iii) If Green, Brown and Pink were brothers of Black, White and Grey respectively, then the company would be treated as a close company, as these are associates of Black, White and Grey. Consequently, the company would be under the control of less than five participators, because the two brothers in each of the three cases are taken as single participators.

Example 3

Swansong Ltd has the following shareholdings:

	Shares
Amble—Director	2,000
Berk—Director	2,000
Clumsy—Works Manager	2,000
Dubious—Nephew of Amble	2,000
Endora—Sister of Clumsy	2,000
Fearless—Son-in-law of Berk	2,000
Gallant—Trustee of settlement by Berk who has no interest therein	2,000
Harmless—Beneficiary of trust by Berk who has no interest therein	2,000
Idle—Grandson of Berk	2,000
Jolly—Director	2,000
Westwinds Ltd.—A close company	4,000
	24,000

	Shares	Director control	Participator control	
Amble—Director	2,000	2,000		
Berk—Director	2,000	6,000	6,000	(1)
Clumsy—Works Manager	2,000		4,000	(2)
Dubious	2,000			
Endora	2,000			
Fearless	2,000			
Gallant	2,000			
Harmless	2,000			
Idle	2,000			

	Shares	Director control	Participator control
Jolly—Director.....................	2,000	2,000	
Westwinds Ltd.....................	4,000		4,000
	24,000	10,000	14,000

		Not director controlled	Participator controlled

Notes

(1)	Berk........................	2,000
	Add Associates:	
	Gallant......................	2,000
	Idle........................	2,000
		6,000

(2)	Clumsy......................	2,000
	Add Associates:	
	Endora......................	2,000
		4,000

Clumsy is not treated as a director, since a shareholding of 20% (=4,800) is required. The directors and their associates do not control more than 50% of the shares. However, five or fewer participators own more than 50% of the shares, and so the company is a *close company*.

These tests are applied as at the end of the accounting period concerned (see *C.H.W. (Huddersfield) Ltd.* v. *C.I.R.* [1963]).

§ 4.—EXCEPTIONS (ss. 282(3)–(5), 283(1), I.C.T.A. 1970)

The following bodies corporate cannot, by definition, be close companies:
   (i) companies not resident in the United Kingdom;
   (ii) a registered industrial or provident society;
  (iii) a building society;
   (iv) a company controlled by the Crown;
   (v) a company which is controlled by one or more companies which are not close companies;
  (vi) for the five or fewer participators rule only—a company controlled by a non-close company (or companies) and which could only be treated as close by including such company as a participator.

Although a non-resident company cannot be close, in determining whether a U.K. resident company is close it is necessary to include (as a participator or otherwise) any such non-resident company which would, if it was resident, itself be treated as close.

Subject to a number of conditions (see § 5 below) a company is *not* treated as a close company if:
   (i) shares in the company carrying not less than 35% of the voting power have been allotted and are held by the public, and
   (ii) any such shares have within the last twelve months been the subject of any dealings on the stock exchange, and
  (iii) the shares have within those twelve months been quoted in the official list of a stock exchange.

§ 5.—QUOTED COMPANIES (s. 283, I.C.T.A. 1970)

A company in which shares carrying at least 35% of the voting powers are held by the public, and where they have been quoted and dealt with on a recognised stock exchange for the preceding twelve months is not treated as a close company (subject to the conditions noted below) even though the tests described above cannot be met.

The following paragraphs examine in detail the definition of a close company as applied to quoted companies.

(a) Tests for qualification as a non-close company

There are two distinct tests, *both* of which must be passed:

(1) not more than 85% of the voting power is possessed by the company's principal members;

(2) shares carrying 35% or more of the voting power have been allotted/acquired unconditionally and are beneficially held by the public.

Note that if test (1) fails (i.e. the principal members own more than 85% of the voting power) then test (2) cannot be applied.

(b) Shares held by the public

The shares held by the public:

(i) must not carry a fixed rate of dividend (even with a further right to participate in profits);

(iii) must have been dealt in on a recognised stock exchange within the previous year;

(iii) must have been quoted in the official list of a recognised stock exchange.

Shares are treated as *held by the public*, if they are held by:

(i) a non-close company;

(ii) a non-resident company which would be treated as non-close if resident:

(iii) trustees for a superannuation, or similar fund.

However, shares must be treated as *not held by the public*, if they are held by:

(i) a principal member plus his associates;

(ii) any director or associate of a director of the company;

(iii) any associated company of the company;

(iv) a fund mainly for the benefit of past and present employees or directors.

(c) Principal member

(i) "*Principal members*" are persons holding more than 5% of the voting power in the company.

(ii) However, if there are more than five such persons, only the five with the highest percentages are principal members (unless there are no such five because persons possess equal percentages; then the number is six or more so as to include those persons).

Example

(a) 5 shareholders with 10%
10 shareholders with 5%
There are 5 principal shareholders totalling 50%.

(b) 4 shareholders with 10%
10 shareholders with 6%
There are 14 principal shareholders totalling 100%.

(iii) Although it seems that a non-close company is not regarded as a principal member when listing members of "the public", it seems that it is a principal member when testing whether principal members have more than 85% voting power.

(d) Voting power

A principal member's holding consists of all shares carrying voting power possessed by him. To any individual there must also be attributed the voting power of:

    (i) nominees;

    (ii) any companies which he (with or without his associates) controls;

    (iii) *associates:* their voting power is not further defined, but it is considered that it does not cover inchoate power (e.g. of preference shares when a cumulative dividend is in arrears) nor the voting power of non-first-named shareholders where the customary form of Articles of Association applies. It is not stated that where an associate's voting power is attributed to a person, the associate is deemed to have no voting power; indeed there is no procedure for determining who is the person and who the associate.

If the aggregate of all the principal members' voting power (as swollen by multiple attribution of associates' votes) is taken, this figure could often exceed 100%. The wording of the Act is "voting power . . . possessed by all of the company's principal members"; it is hoped that this means principal members' own votes plus any associate of any of them, with each individual *counted once only.*

Since associates' votes can be counted several times, anomalies can arise: thus, if 6 disassociated persons hold 10% each and 5 relatives hold 5% each, the 5 associates are deemed to have 25% each, and are therefore the principal members, and the 10% holders (unless ruled out on other grounds) count as public.

It is evident that this anomaly could combine with that demonstrated in the Example given in (c) above. However, the anomaly only seems to operate on Test (2); since in Test (1) it is the voting power of the public which is counted.

If a non-close company holds 50.1% of the voting power in a company, that company will not be close whatever the other shareholdings. If however, it had 49.9% and four other shareholders each possessed more than 5% then the company would fail Test (1) unless the four others each held $8\frac{1}{2}\%$ or more. It would fail Test (2) in any event.

A non-close company counts as public even if the company is a principal member.

§ 6.—ILLUSTRATION OF THE CLOSE COMPANY TESTS FOR QUOTED COMPANIES

Example 1

Thingamajig PLC, a quoted company, has share capital of 1,000,000 ordinary £1 shares. The shares are held as follows:

	Shares	
Alfred	70,000	
Bernard.	80,000	
Charlie	150,000	
Diamonds Ltd (non-close public company)	320,000	
Ernest	110,000	
Total held by principal members	730,000	(73%)
Other small holdings (all less than 50,000 and including Directors' holdings of 25,000)	270,000	
	1,000,000	

The company is not a close company by Test (1)

Total shares held by principal members............	730,000
Directors' shares................................	25,000
	755,000
Less: shares held by non-close company (Diamonds Ltd.).......................................	320,000
	435,000 (43%)

The company is not a close company by Test (2).

Example 2

Greenham PLC, a quoted company, has share capital of 10,000 ordinary £1 shares. The shares are held as follows:
Green family holdings (%) are:

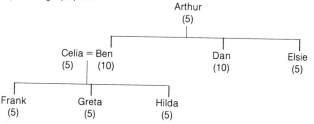

The directors of the company are Ben and Dan (see above), and Yeldham who owns 2%.

Other unrelated shareholdings (all less than 5%) amount to 48%.

Test (1)

The principal shareholders are chosen from:

A, deemed 45%   [A(5%) + B(10%) + D(10%) + E(5%) + F(5%) + G(5%) + H(5%)].
B, deemed 50%   [A + C(5%)].
C, deemed 30%   [C(5%) + B(10%) + F(5%) + G(5%) + H(5%)].
D and E, each deemed 30%   [A(5%) + B(10%) + D(10%) + H(5%)].
F, G, H, each deemed 35%   [A(5%) + B(10%) + C(5%) + F(5%) + G(5%) + H(5%)].

The actual qualifiers are B, A, F, G and H. On the basis suggested above it is thought they possess 50% of the voting power (including associates once only) but with multiple counting, they would be deemed to possess 200%.

It is considered that the company meets Test 1.

Test (2)

Public	48%
Non-public (directors/principal shareholders)	52%
	100%

Note: C, D and E although not principal shareholders [see Test (1)] are associates of Director B.

The company also meets Test (2).

The company is not a close company.

Unlisted securities market
This is *not* considered by the Inland Revenue to represent a recognized stock exchange.

§ 7.—ADDITIONAL MATTERS TREATED AS DISTRIBUTIONS (ss. 284 and 285, I.C.T.A. 1970)

The definition of distributions is modified for close companies and includes benefits paid to participators and interest, above certain limits, paid to directors or their associates.

(a) Benefits (s. 284 I.C.T.A. 1970)
The cost of providing benefits in kind (as defined for Schedule E purposes) for a participator or his associate is treated as a distribution unless the benefits are:
   (i) Benefits assessable on a director or employee under ss. 61–68, F.A. 1976.
   (ii) Living accommodation (as defined by s. 33, F.A. 1977) provided by reason of his employment.
   (iii) Provision for spouse, children or dependants, on death or retirement, of benefits such as a pension, annuity, lump sum, gratuity, etc.
So far as valuation of any benefit is concerned the appropriate Schedule E rules apply.
   The provision of benefits by a close company to a participator is not treated as a distribution where:
   (i) both the company and the participator are resident in U.K.; *and*
   (ii) one is a subsidiary of the other, or both are subsidiaries or a third company which is also resident in U.K.; *and*
   (iii) the benefit arises on, or in connection with, a transfer of assets or liabilities between the company and the participator (or vice versa).
For the above purposes one company is regarded as a subsidiary of the other if it is a "51% subsidiary" (see Chapter 22), except that the definition is modified so a company is not treated as being the owner of:
   (i) share capital (directly owned) of a company, held so that a profit on the sale thereof would be trading receipt; or
   (ii) share capital owned indirectly through a company such as described in (i); or
   (iii) share capital, whether owned directly or indirectly, in a company which is not resident in U.K.
These provisions also apply where benefits are provided under reciprocal and other arrangements between companies, to a person who, although not a participator in the company providing the benefit, is a participator in another company which is a party to the agreements.

(b) Interest paid to directors and their associates (not effective for accounting periods after 26th March 1980)—(s. 285, I.C.T.A. 1970)
Interest paid to directors or their associates in accounting periods ending before 27th March 1980 counted as a distribution when paid by a close company, provided the interest exceeded an overall limit and the director had, either alone or with his associates, a material interest (more than 5%) in the company. Section 45, F.A. 1980 however provided that interest paid to directors or their associates in accounting periods ending after 26th March 1980 is no longer regarded as a distribution.

§ 8.—LOANS TO PARTICIPATORS (ss. 286–287A, I.C.T.A. 1970)

If a close company makes a loan to a participator or to an associate of a participator, the company will be assessed at an amount equivalent to A.C.T. on the amount of the loan. An exception to this rule is where the loan is made in the normal course of a business which includes lending money.

Although a loan to a participator (or to his associate) involves the company in a liability to pay an amount equivalent to A.C.T., the participator receiving it is not treated as having received income of an equivalent amount. *Thus the loan is not a distribution for the purposes of A.C.T.* (and cannot therefore be used to reduce the Corporation Tax liability), nor a reduction of an excess of relevant income over distributions for apportionment (see § 9).

The charge to tax does not arise in the case of a loan made to a director or employee of the company making the loan, or of an associated company, if:

(i) the amount of the loan, together with any other outstanding loans made by the company making the loan (or by any of its associated companies) to the borrower, or to the borrower's spouse, does not exceed £15,000; and

(ii) the borrower works full time for the company making the loan, or any of its associated companies; and

(iii) the borrower does not have a *"material interest"* (see § 7) in the company making the loan, or of any of its associated companies.

If a loan was made before 31st March 1971, it only qualified for exemption if made for the purpose of purchasing a dwelling as the borrower's only or main residence, provided also that it did not exceed £10,000.

If a borrower, previously exempted, acquires a material interest in the company, or in an associated company, at any time when any part of a loan made after 30th March 1971, remains outstanding, then the company is to be treated as loaning him (at that time) an amount equal to the outstanding balance.

A close company is also treated as making a loan equivalent to the debt where:

(*a*) a person incurs a debt to the close company. This does not apply to a debt incurred for the supply of goods or services supplied in the ordinary course of business, unless the credit given exceeds six months, or the credit terms normally given to the company's customers; or

(*b*) a debt due from a person to a third party is assigned to the company.

A close company is regarded as making a loan if a person makes arrangements (otherwise than in the ordinary course of business) whereby a close company makes a loan which would not otherwise be "caught", and some other person makes a payment or transfers property to, releases or satisfies a liability of, a participator (or associate) in the company. This does not apply if the receipt of the payment, etc. is otherwise taxable upon that person.

These provisions apply only to loans made to individuals, except where a company receives the loan or advance in a fiduciary or representative capacity, or where the company is not resident in the U.K.

If the company releases the borrower from the loan, then the grossed up amount becomes his income as at the date of the release, and is liable to tax at the higher rates, and the investment income surcharge on a sum equal to the loan. No repayment of this income tax can be made, and charges on income may not be set against the amount so included in total income.

If the loan were made to a person who has since died, the debt is due from the personal representatives of the deceased, and if the company releases or writes off the loan, the grossed-up equivalent of the amount waived or released is included as part of the estate income. If the loan has already been treated as income of the settlor (e.g. under s. 451, I.C.T.A. 1970), this does not apply unless the amount released (before grossing-up) exceeds the amount so treated.

Where a loan has been made and an amount equivalent to A.C.T. is due an assessment will be raised and tax thereon is due 14 days after the issue of an assessment (unless subject to an appeal). Interest thereon runs from three months after the end of the financial year in which the loan or advance was made, or if later (as will usually be the case) from the date of the assessment.

Where a company has been assessed to an amount equivalent to A.C.T. on any loan, and the loan (or part of it) is repaid, the tax paid by the company (or a proportionate part thereof) is repaid by the Inland Revenue. This would also apply where a loan is distributed *in specie* in a liquidation. Repayment of tax must be claimed within six years from the end of the financial year to which the claim refers.

For the purposes of liability to any assessment of an amount equivalent to A.C.T., the status of the company appears to be determined at the time when the loan is made.

The liability to assessment of an amount equivalent to A.C.T. also covers loans made by a company under the control of a close company to the participators in that controlling company where the loans were made, or debts assigned, after 15th April 1976.

A loan by a company which would not itself be a close company (e.g. a non-resident) but which is controlled by a close company is treated as if made by the close company and accordingly the s. 286 provisions apply.

§ 9.—APPORTIONMENT OF INCOME: INTRODUCTION

The Revenue have power (F.A. 1972, Schedule 16) to apportion undistributed income of a close company amongst its participators. The close companies apportionment rules are, in effect, anti-avoidance provisions. In particular, the provisions are intended to prevent the retention of profits by companies in order to avoid making distributions to shareholders upon which higher rates of income tax and investment income surcharge would be payable. Thus if dividend payments, and other amounts treated as distributions, fall below a certain level, then tax is payable by the shareholders as if they had actually received a dividend.

Without the apportionment of income rules a company could obtain considerable tax advantages for its shareholders by not paying dividends. For example, if an individual participator's income is sufficiently large, the receipt of dividends would give rise to a liability to higher rates of tax and investment income surcharge. There is thus a temptation for companies to retain income, in order to achieve a saving of tax for its participators, particularly where the company is controlled by a small group or family, who would, presumably, not object to leaving money locked up in the company as it is still under their control.

To prevent this form of tax avoidance the Inland Revenue have been given power to apportion or *deem paid* any insufficiency of dividend below a required standard. The participators are then subjected to higher rates of income tax, and investment income surcharge as though they had in fact received the appropriate amount of dividend. Broadly speaking, the amount to be apportioned is the excess of a company's relevant income over its distributions for an accounting period.

Distributions

(*a*) *General*

Distributions for an accounting period are:
      (i) any dividend declared in respect of the period, and paid in that period or within a reasonable time thereafter;
      (ii) all distributions made in the period unless attributable to a previous period.

The additional matters which may be treated as distributions are benefits in kind to participators (if not taxed under Schedule E) and interest paid to directors (or their associates) before 27th March 1980 in excess of certain limits.

Non-qualifying distributions in the form of bonus shares are not treated as distributions for this purpose unless they are made:
      (*a*) to a person other than a close company: or

(*b*) to a close company and the share capital is subsequently distributed to another close company.

(*b*) *Within a group*

Where a group of close companies so wishes, all distributions within the group, for all periods, are included in the distributable profits of the periods for which they are payable (apart from distributions made more than a reasonable time after the end of the period). For this purpose, a group of companies will be regarded as consisting of a parent company which is not itself a subsidiary of another company, and all companies (including companies not resident in the United Kingdom) which are subsidiaries of that parent.

Where a group of close companies wishes to adopt this basis it is required to give an undertaking that the basis will be adhered to irrevocably, as long as the companies remain with the group. To avoid transitional difficulties it is usual for the decision to adopt this basis to be taken with effect from the accounting period in which a group came into being.

Example

In the year ended 31st December 1985, a close parent company received dividends of £50,000 declared by its subsidiaries for the year ended 31st December 1984. The parent declared a dividend of £45,000 for the year ended 31st December 1984 and paid this within a reasonable time after that date. If the group adopted the basis described above, the dividends of £50,000 from the subsidiaries would be included in the distributable profits of the parent, for the purpose of determining its distributable profits, for the year ended 31st December 1984, and not for the year ended 31st December 1985.

ACCOUNTING PERIODS ENDING AFTER 26TH MARCH 1980
For accounting periods ending after 26th March 1980, the consequences of apportionment (see § 10) *for trading companies have been largely negated,* since, after that date, the trading income of such companies is *not* liable to apportionment. The *non-trading income* of such companies may still be apportioned (see § 11).

§ 10.—POWER OF APPORTIONMENT

(*i*) *Power to apportion the excess of a company's relevant income over its distributions* (Para. 1, Sch. 16, F.A. 1972)

The basic premise is that the excess of "*relevant income*" for an accounting period over the distributions made for the period may be apportioned among the participators, with a £1,000 *de minimis* exemption for trading companies. This premise is varied in relation to the activities undertaken by the company (e.g. trading etc.) and the requirements of the companies' business. (See § 11 below.)

Where a company is a trading company, or exists to co-ordinate the activities of a trading group, *no apportionment of trading income* is made.

In the case of an investment company, by concession, no apportionment is made unless the excess of relevant income over distributions exceeds £100.

In the case of an investment company, (by Concession C7–1980) no apportionment is made unless the excess of relevant income over distributions exceeds £250 (or proportionately less for accumulating periods of less than 12 months).

By concession, no apportionment is made where at least 90% of a company is owned by non-residents (see Concession B22-1980).

If a participator is a close company, the apportionment is followed through to be apportioned between the participators of that company.

These provisions continue to have effect, although subject to modification, when a company goes into liquidation.

If income is apportioned to the trustees of a discretionary trust there is a charge upon the trustees for investment income surcharge on the amount so apportioned.

(*ii*) *Power to apportion the whole of the relevant income of a non-trading close company* (Sch. 16, Para 2, F.A. 1972; s. 56, F.A. 1980; s. 47, F.A. 1985)
The Revenue have the power, in the case of a non-trading company, and where the Inspector sees reason for it, to apportion the whole of the company's relevant income, even where there is no excess of relevant income over distributable income. As an example, consider an investment company in which some shares are held by a trust, or other low tax rate person. If dividends are, whether by waiver or otherwise, paid only to such low rate taxpayers there is considerable loss of tax to the Revenue. In such a case there could be an apportionment, even though a dividend sufficient to avoid an apportionment had been paid.

(*iii*) *Power to apportion amounts deducted in respect of certain annual payments* (Sch. 16, Para. 3, F.A. 1972; s. 56, F.A. 1980; s. 49, F.A. 1985)
The Revenue have power to make an apportionment amongst the participators where certain annual payments are made by a close company. These are payments which have been allowed to the company as a deduction for corporation tax purposes, but which would not have been allowed as a deduction for income tax purposes if paid by an individual, or would have been treated as his income in computing his total income. This does not, however, include interest paid wholly and exclusively for the purpose of the company's trade.

Any unused balance of the £10,000 (from 6th April 1985) exemption from higher rate tax on charitable payments under covenant may be set against any amount apportioned to the taxpayer from a covenanted payment to a charity by the close company. Previous limits were:
6th April 1981 to 5th April 1983 £3,000
6th April 1983 to 5th April 1985 £5,000

(*iv*) *Power to apportion interest paid* (Sch. 16, Para. 3A, F.A. 1972)
Interest paid by a close company may, unless exempted (as noted below) be apportioned as if it were income.
This does not apply if the close company is:
    (*a*) a trading company; or
    (*b*) a member of a trading group: or
    (*c*) more than 75% of its income is:
        — estate or trading income; or
        — interest or distributions from a 51% subsidiary which itself is a trading company or a member of a trading group, or 75% of its income is as herein described.
In applying the 75% test, no account is taken of deductions from the company's profits for charges on income, management expenses, or other deductions against total income.
There is no apportionment where the interest paid is for a qualifying purpose, or is paid as a business expense. Neither is there any apportionment for interest paid to a loan creditor. Actual payment of interest to a participator reduces the amount apportionable to that participator.

§ 11.—RELEVANT INCOME

INTRODUCTION (Sch. 16, Para. 8(1), F.A. 1972)
To determine the relevant income of a close company and hence the starting point for apportionment consideration the following general rules are applied in three distinct situations:
    (i) the relevant income of *a trading company*, or *member of a trading group*, is so much of its *distributable income* (other than *trading income*) as can

be distributed without prejudice to the requirements of the company's business;

(ii) the relevant income of *a non-trading company* with some estate or trading income consists of all its *distributable investment income*, plus so much of the *estate, or trading income* as can be distributed without prejudice to the requirements of the company's business so far as concerned with the activities or assets giving rise to the estate or trading income;

(iii) the relevant income of *a non-trading company* with no *estate, or trading, income* consists of all its *distributable investment income*.

DEFINITIONS

(*a*) *Trading company* (Sch. 16, Para. 11, F.A. 1972)

A *trading company* is any company which exists wholly, or mainly to carry on a trade. Also included in the definition of a trading company is any other company whose income does not consist wholly or mainly of *investment income*.

Investment income is income which, were it received by an individual would not be earned income. It also includes any income which has been sub-apportioned through from another company.

(*b*) *Member of a trading group* (Sch. 16, Para. 11, F.A. 1972)

A company is *a member of a trading group* if its only or main purpose is to co-ordinate the administration of two or more trading companies which are either controlled by it or under common control with it.

(*c*) *Non-trading company*

It follows that a *non-trading company* is any company not within the above definitions. Such a company would, therefore, be an investment company or a "pure" holding company (i.e. a parent company which merely holds shares in its subsidiaries but does not co-ordinate their administration.)

(*d*) *Estate income* (Sch. 16, Paras 10(4) and (4A), F.A. 1972)

Estate income is income chargeable to tax under Schedule A, Schedule B, and Schedule D (other than interest) which arises from ownership, occupation or rights over land or buildings, including furnished lettings.

(*e*) *Trading income* (Sch. 16, Paras 10(5) (6), 11 F.A. 1972)

Trading income is income which, if received by an individual, would be treated as earned income.

A special rule applies in respect of close companies carrying on insurance, banking, dealing in securities, and other financial operations. For such companies, income derived from securities (except income from 51% subsidiaries) is treated as estate or trading income (rather than as investment income), provided any profit on the sale of the securities concerned is treated as a trading receipt. Interest on a debt is treated similarly if, should the debt prove to be bad, there would be an allowable deduction when computing the company's trading income.

(*f*) *Investment income* (Sch. 16, Para. 11, F.A. 1972)

Investment income is income which, were it received by an individual would not be earned income. It also includes any income which has been sub-apportioned.

(*g*) *Distributable profits* (Sch. 16, Para. 10(2), F.A. 1972)

In order to compute the amount of *"distributable income"* it is first necessary to calculate the *"distributable profits"* for the period. This is the sum of:

(i) profits on which corporation tax falls finally to be borne, *less* the corporation tax thereon;

(ii) any franked income received, *less* the related tax credit. If any part of the franked income has been offset by losses (under ss. 254 and 255,

I.C.T.A. 1970), charges on income, or management expenses, etc., then this amount must also be excluded.
(iii) group income (i.e. dividends received from subsidiaries) under election to pay without A.C.T. (see Chapter 22).

(*h*) *Distributable income* (Sch. 16, Para. 10(2), F.A. 1972)
Distributable income is distributable profits excluding chargeable gains.
Distributable income is sub-divided into:
(i) estate income (see § 11(d) above)
(ii) trading income (see § 11(e) above)
(iii) distributable investment income (see (i) below)

(*i*) *Distributable investment income* (Sch. 16, Para. 10(3), F.A. 1972)
This is that part of the company's distributable income which is not estate or trading income, *less* the *smaller* of:
(i) 10% of estate or trading income: or
(ii) £3,000 per annum (for accounting periods of less than 12 months this limit is proportionately reduced, and for accounting periods ending before 27th March 1980 the limit was £1,000 only).
For non-trading companies the alternative limit remains at £1,000.

(*j*) *Maximum relevant income: non-trading companies* (Sch. 16, Para. 9(1), F.A. 1972)
There is an arithmetical maximum for relevant income for a company which is neither a trading company, nor a member of a trading group.
It is the distributable investment income after the abatement plus 50% of the estate or trading income. (See Example 3 below)

(*k*) *Maximum relevant income: trading companies* (Sch. 16, Para. 9(2)–(6), F.A. 1972)
The maximum relevant income for trading companies is the distributable investment income after the abatement plus 50% of the estate income. The estate income is itself subject to a prior abatement before applying 50% thereto:
(*a*) if estate income (less corporation tax) is less than the proportion of £25,000 which the estate income bears to the estate and trading income, the amount to be included is *nil*.
(*b*) otherwise there is an abatement of half any excess of that proportion of £75,000 over the estate income.
The figures of £25,000 and £75,000 are proportionately reduced where there are associated companies (even if only associated for part of an accounting period), or where the accounting period is one of less than 12 months. Associated companies may be either trading or investment companies, but completely dormant companies can be ignored.
Except in the calculation of the abatement of investment income trading income is ignored. (See Examples 4 and 5 below.)

ORDER OF SET OFF FOR DEDUCTIONS (Sch. 16, Para. 10(8), (9), F.A. 1972)
Any allowable deductions which can be made from profits of more than one description (i.e. set against total profits) such as charges on income, management expenses, or group relief, are to be applied in the following order:
(1) investment income;
(2) estate income*; } not separated for non-trading companies
(3) trading income*;
(4) chargeable gains

---

* If a non-trading company has estate or trading income which includes development gains, such gains rank after other estate or trading income.

Loss relief claims against franked investment income (under ss. 254 and 255, I.C.T.A. 1970) are set first against franked investment income which is not trading income and secondly (e.g. in the case of banks, insurance companies, etc.) against franked investment income which is trading income.

Example 1

Plumage Ltd, a trading company with one subsidiary, had the following figures for the accounting period of 12 months ended on 31st March 1983.

	Total	Investment income	Estate income	Trading income	Chargeable gains
	£	£	£	£	£
Case I, Schedule D	350,000			350,000	
Schedule A	70,000		70,000		
Case VI, Schedule D	15,000		15,000		
Case III, Schedule D	30,000	30,000			
Chargeable gains					
(*Less:* 11/26)	45,000				45,000
Total profits	510,000	30,000	85,000	350,000	45,000
Less: Charges on income	(130,000)	(1)130,000)	(2)(85,000)	(3)(15,000)	(4) —
Profits on which corporation tax falls finally to be borne	380,000	—	—	335,000	45,000
Corporation tax at 52%	(197,600)	—	—	(174,200)	(23,400)
Profits after corporation tax	182,400	—	—	160,800	21,600
Franked investment Income　60,000					
Less: Tax credit (18,000)	42,000	42,000			
Group income	24,000	24,000			
Distributable profits	248,400	66,000	—	160,800	21,600
Less: Chargeable gain	(21,600)	—	—	—	(21,600)
Distributable income	£226,800	£66,000	—	£160,800	—

Example 2

Following on from example 1, Plumage Ltd has distributable investment income as follows:

	Total	Investment income	Estate income	Trading income
	£	£	£	£
Distributable income	226,800	66,000	—	160,800
Abatements				
(a) Investment income				
Smaller of				
(i) Estate income	—			
Trading income	160,800			
	160,800			
10% = £16,080				

	Total	Investment income	Estate income	Trading income
	£	£	£	£
or				
(ii) £3,000	(3,000)	(3,000)		
(b) Trading income	(160,800)			(160,800)
Distributable investment income		63,000		
Maximum relevant income	£63,000	£63,000	—	—

Chargeable gains—nil.

Example 3

Feathers Investments Ltd, a close company with no associated companies had the following figures for the accounting period of 12 months ended on 31st March 1983.

	Total	Investment income	Estate income	Trading income	Chargeable gains
	£	£	£	£	£
Schedule A	20,000		20,000		
Case VI, Schedule D	10,000		10,000		
Case III, Schedule D	15,000	15,000			
Chargeable gains (less 11/26)	20,000				20,000
Total profits	65,000	15,000	30,000	—	20,000
Less: Charges on income	(5,000)	(1)(5,000)	(2) —	(3) —	(4) —
Profits on which corporation tax falls finally to be borne	60,000	10,000	30,000	—	20,000
Corporation tax					
at 38%	(15,200)	(3,800)	(11,400)		
at 52%	(10,400)				(10,400)
Profits after corporation tax	34,400	6,200	18,600	—	9,600
Franked investment income 21,000					
Less: Tax credit (6,300)	14,700	14,700			
Distributable profits	49,100	20,900	18,600	—	9,600
Less: Chargeable gains	(9,600)				(9,600)
Distributable income	39,500	20,900	18,600	—	—
Less: Abatements					
(a) 50% Estate income	(9,300)		(9,300)		
(b) 50% Trading income	—			—	

	Total £	Investment income £	Estate income £	Trading income £	Chargeable gains £
(c) smaller of					
(i) Estate income	18,600				
Trading income	—				
	18,600				
10% = 1,860					
(ii) or £1,000	(1,000)	(1,000)			
Maximum relevant income	£29,200	£19,900	£9,300		

Example 4

Crest Ltd, trading company with no subsidiaries, had the following figures for the accounting period of 12 months ended on 31st March 1983.

	Total £	Investment income £	Estate income £	Trading income £	Chargeable gains £
Case I, Schedule D	520,000			120,000	
Schedule A	30,000		30,000		
Case III, Schedule D	60,000	60,000			
Chargeable gains (less 11/26)	50,000				50,000
Total profits	660,000	60,000	30,000	120,000	50,000
Less: Charges on income	(30,000)	(1)(30,000)	(2) —	(3) —	(4) —
Profits on which corporation tax finally to be borne	630,000	30,000	30,000	520,000	50,000
Corporation tax at 52%	327,600	15,600	15,600	270,400	26,000
Profits after corporation tax	302,400	14,400	14,400	249,600	24,000
Franked Investment income 27,000					
Less: Tax Credit (8,100)	18,900	18,900	—	—	—
Distributable profits	321,300	33,300	14,400	249,600	24,000
Less: Chargeable gains	24,000	—	—	—	(24,000)
Distributable income	297,300	33,300	14,400	249,600	—

	Total £	Investment income £	Estate income £	Trading income £	Chargeable gains £
Abatements					
(a) Investment income					
Smaller of					
(i) Estate income 14,400					
Trading income					
249,600					
264,000					
10% = 26,400					
or					
(ii) £3,000	(3,000)	(3,000)			
(b) Trading income	(249,600)			(249,600)	
(c) Estate income					
(i) See below*	(300)		(300)		
			14,100		
(ii) 50% of balance	(7,050)		(7,050)		
			7,050		
Maximum relevant					
income	£37,350	£30,300	£7,050	—	

Example 5

Dovecote Ltd, a trading company with no subsidiaries, had the following figures for the accounting period of 12 months ended on 31st March 1983.

	Total £	Investment income £	Estate income £	Trading income £	Chargeable gains £
Case I, Schedule D	114,000			114,000	
Schedule A	16,000		16,000		
Case III, Schedule D	5,000	5,000			
Chargeable gains					
(less 11/26)	20,000				20,000
Total profits	155,000	5,000	16,000	114,000	20,000
Less: Loss relief	(3,000)	(1)(3,000)	(2) —	(3) —	(4) —
Profits on which cor-					
poration tax falls					
finally to be borne	152,000	2,000	16,000	114,000	20,000
Corporation tax at 52%	(10,400)				(10,400)
marginal					
(see below)	(58,952)	(893)	(7,146)	(50,913)	
(i)					
	82,648	1,107	8,854	63,087	9,600

---

* Prior abatement of estate income

$$\frac{£14,400}{£14,400 + 57,600} \times 75,000 = \underline{£15,000}$$

Abatement = $\frac{1}{2}(15,000 - 14,400) = \underline{£300}$

	Total £	Investment income £	Estate income £	Trading income £	Chargeable gains £
Franked investment income 9,000					
Less: Tax credit (2,700)	6,300	6,300	—	—	—
Distributable profits	88,948	7,407	8,854	63,087	9,600
Less: Chargeable gains	(9,600)	—	—	—	(9,600)
Distributable income	79,348	7,407	8,854	63,087	—

Abatements:
(a) Investment income
Smaller of

(i) Estate income	8,854				
Trading income	63,087				
	71,941				
10% = 7,194					
or					
(ii) £3,000	(3,000)	(3,000)			
(b) Trading income	(63,087)			(63,087)	
(c) Estate income					
(i) See below	(188)		(188)		
			8,666		
(ii) 50% of balance	(4,333)		(4,333)		
			4,333		
Maximum relevant income	£8,740	£4,407	£4,333	—	

Notes

(i) Small companies marginal rate applies

"Income" = £152,000 − £20,000 = £132,000

"Profits" = £152,000 + £9,000 = £161,000

Corporation tax at 52% on income   £68,640

Less: Marginal relief

$$(M)£500,000 - (P)£161,000 \times \frac{(I)£132,000}{(P)£161,000} \times \frac{7}{200}$$ 9,728

£58,952

Allocation

Investment income	$\frac{2,000}{132,000} \times 58,952 =$	893
Estate income	$\frac{16,000}{132,000} \times 58,952 =$	7,146
Trading income	$\frac{114,000}{132,000} \times 58,952 =$	50,913
		£58,952

(ii) Prior abatement of estate income

$$\frac{£8,854}{£8,854 + 63,087} \times 75,000 = £9,230$$

Abatement $= \frac{1}{2}(9,230 - 8,854) = £188$

§ 12.—BUSINESS REQUIREMENTS (Sch. 16, Paras 8(2)–(5), 12, 12A, F.A. 1972)

If a company is a trading company or a member of a trading group there is a further restriction upon the amount which it can be called upon to distribute. Such a company need only distribute so much of its distributable income (other than trading income—i.e. its estate income and its investment income) as can be distributed without prejudice to the requirements of its business. Such requirements include not only current requirements but also such other requirements as may be necessary and advisable for the maintenance and development of that business.

For other companies the maximum is:

(i) So much of estate or trading income as could be distributed without prejudice to requirements of the business so far as concerned with the activities or assets giving rise to that income; and

(ii) Its distributable income if any, other than estate or trading income.

A first consideration in determining the level of dividends to be paid is the availability of funds from which to pay them. These funds would comprise cash and liquid resources which can easily be turned into cash. In making a calculation of available funds the *net current assets*, as shown by the company's balance sheet, *may need to be adjusted* in respect of certain items:

CURRENT ASSET ADJUSTMENTS

(i) *Omit* stock and work-in-progress;

(ii) *omit* any asset which is not really liquid and easily realisable, and also any debit balances which would be difficult to call on;

(iii) *include* investments of surplus funds. It might be possible to exclude trade investments if they contribute real value to the company's trade, such as securing a source of raw material supplies;

(iv) *include* loans made, unless they can be treated as trade investments;

(v) *omit* trade debtors if they do not reflect the normal working position of the company (if this policy is followed trade creditors should also be omitted by the same criterion). In any event, it may be possible to omit trade debtors with long-term credit arrangements, or those who present difficulties in obtaining prompt payment, preferably by ensuring there is an adequate allowable provision for bad debts.

CURRENT LIABILITY ADJUSTMENTS

(i) *Omit* trade creditors, subject to the same caveat as indicated in respect of trade debtors;

(ii) *include* taxation liabilities to be met over the next twelve months, and any other reserves made for taxation on a reasonable and consistent basis. Thus the amount set aside from current profits to a deferred tax account should be brought into account. A similar argument can be put forward for the company's liability to meet higher rate tax liabilities on apportionment;

(iii) *include* those dividends provided for in the accounts which remain outstanding at the year end.

Further adjustment of the balance sheet may be necessary if the company's liquidity position has changed since the year end, particularly if the business is subject to seasonal fluctuations, or if there has been any marked change in business conditions.

The company will require a balance of working capital to meet its day to day requirements, and cannot be expected to pay dividends which reduce its available funds below this level. Working capital should therefore be compared with the company's estimated requirements, taken as an appropriate percentage of turnover based on normal credit terms.

A company may be able to claim a retention of profits in order to meet current or future requirements of the business. Such claims must take account of both the past history of the company and its future profit earning capacity. Any claim, however, should itemise specific proposals rather than vague possibilities, and the Inspector is likely to seek an explanation for plans which are not carried out.

REASONS FOR RETENTION OF PROFITS

    (i) *Capital and other longer-term commitments:*
        —replacement of buildings, plant, etc.;
        —purchase of another trade or business;
        —purchase of shares in another company to expand the business;
        —research, development and introduction of new products or methods.

    These commitments should include not only items which are already under obligation, but also those which are in the process of negotiation, under option, or anticipated in the foreseeable future. The Revenue are inclined to argue that future capital commitments should, as far as possible, be met from profits arising between the year end under discussion and the date when payments will fall due, rather than from existing resources.

    (ii) *Contingent liabilities*, such as possible litigation or claims arising from work or services rendered.
    (iii) *Known or anticipated losses* which have arisen since the year end.
    (iv) *Creditors* who have to be paid shortly after the year end.
    (v) *External factors:* hazards caused by U.K. or foreign governments, and from the current economic situation, for example:
        —general state of the industry;
        —anticipated trends of the industry in general, and the company in particular;
        —effect of government credit squeeze on the company's customers;
        —effect of wage claims, price freezes and similar restrictions;
        —difficulty, in view of the above comments, in obtaining new, or continuing, profitable work.

In arriving at the relevant income of a parent company which is a trading company or a member of a trading group, attention is also paid, so far as is reasonable, to the business requirements and resources of companies which are subsidiaries of the parent company, and are trading companies or members of the trading group. This approach may need to be modified in particular cases, for example, where persons other than the parent company have a substantial interest in some, or all, of the subsidiary companies.

To determine the relevant income of a subsidiary company which is a trading company or a member of the trading group, the subsidiary company's requirements would normally be limited to those of its own business. However, in practice the requirements and resources of other companies in the group will be considered if it is appropriate, for example, where the subsidiary company has trading links with the parent company or with another subsidiary in the group.

As noted above, proposed expenditures by subsidiary companies can be taken into account when considering the apportionment position of the parent company, following the Revenue practice. This permits, when computing the relevant income of the parent company of a trading group, the business requirements of its trading subsidiaries to be taken into account. In applying such an approach, one must consider the overall group position on the basis of a consolidated balance sheet for the group. The Revenue practice applies only where the parent company is a "trading company", or is a member of a trading group, whose purpose is to coordinate the administration of two or more trading companies under its control.

Funds may also be set aside for the acquisition of a trade, or of a controlling interest in a trading company or the controlling member of a trading group. This also includes the redemption or repayment of share or loan capital (including any premium thereon) issued in respect of the acquisition, or otherwise meeting obligations arising therefrom. However this does not apply if the trade, asset, shares etc., was owned by an associated company within the preceding year. Likewise it does not apply for acquisition of shares in companies which have been associated within the preceding year. The definition of associated company, control, etc are modified for this purpose and these modifications should be carefully considered in relevant cases.

ITEMS WHICH CANNOT BE TREATED AS BUSINESS EXPENDITURE

It is not possible to justify the retention of funds for the four undernoted purposes, and any amount retained in respect thereof must be regarded as distributable:

  (i) *first business loans (subject to conditions mentioned below)*
      A first business loan is any sum expended, or to be expended, out of the income of the company:
        —in or towards payment for the business, undertaking or property which the company was formed to acquire or which was the first business, undertaking or property of a substantial character in fact acquired by the company; or
        —in redemption or repayment of any share or loan capital or debt issued or incurred in respect of payment therefor; or
        —in meeting any obligations of the company in respect of the acquisition of any such business, undertaking or property; or
        —in redemption or repayment of any share, or loan capital, or debt issued otherwise than for adequate consideration.
 (ii) fictitious or artificial expenditure;
(iii) repayments of loan creditors (except where a company is a trading company or member of a trading group);
 (iv) expenditure by an investment company on land or buildings (except on the improvement of farm or market garden land).

There is some relaxation of the rule whereby close trading companies can not claim the cost of acquiring another trade or company as a reason for not distributing income so as to avoid having their income apportioned. Account can be taken, in certain cases, of the acquisition of a trade, or of a controlling interest in a company which is a trading company or a member of a trading group. The controlling interest (i.e. in excess of *50%* of the ordinary share capital) can be acquired either by a single purchase or over a period. The company can also take account, for apportionment purposes, of a requirement to redeem or repay share or loan capital or debt issued or incurred in respect of such an acquisition, provided the relevant payment does not rank as a distribution for tax purposes.

First business loans etc. of trading companies and members of trading groups can be repaid without apportionment problems and can also be taken into account in determining a company's business requirements if the loans were incurred for the purposes described above and their repayments is not classed as a distribution. Note, however that the first business exclusion rule applies for non-trading companies such as holding or investment companies. Note also that such loans, etc must be incurred for full consideration in bona fide transactions.

These rules do not apply where the acquisition comprises a trade, or an asset to be used in a trade, which at the time of acquisition or at any time within the preceding year was owned by an associated company. Nor can account be taken of any intended acquisition of a trade, or an asset to be used in a trade which, at the end of the accounting period concerned, is owned by an associated company. A similar prohibition applies to the acquisition, or intended acquisition of shares owned by an associated company or by a person who has control of the associated company.

For intended acquisitions the test is applied at the date of acquisition. The time of acquisition of a trade, or of an asset to be used in the trade, or of shares, is either the time at which the contract is made or, in the case of a conditional contract or option, the time when the condition is satisfied and not, if different, the time when the trade, asset or shares is or are conveyed or transferred.

§ 13.—DISTRIBUTIONS (Sch. 16, Paras 10(1), 14, F.A. 1972)

Distributions relating to a particular accounting period are dividends declared in respect of the period. They are set against relevant income for the period in respect of which they are declared, provided they are paid during the period, or within a reasonable time thereafter. However this does not include distributions which have already been taken into account in a previous accounting period.

An excess of relevant income over distributions can be disregarded, to the extent that a company was unable to make distributions because of dividend restraint limitations (e.g. under Counter-Inflation Act 1973) or other legal restraints. However a clause in a company's articles prohibiting distributions would not be effective for this purpose, as it is within the company's power to change the articles.

A distribution is to include anything that would be distribution but for:
(*a*) Schedule 18, Para. 1, F.A. 1980 (demerger provisions)
(*b*) Section 53, F.A. 1982 (purchase by company of its own shares)

§ 14.—MANNER OF APPORTIONMENT (Sch. 16, Paras 4, 15–17, F.A. 1972)

Apportionments, including sub-apportionments through other close companies, are made upon the participators of the company concerned in proportion to their respective interests in the company.

Where appropriate, an apportionment can be made on the basis of the rights of the participators to assets available for distribution amongst participators in the event of a winding-up.

In the case of a non-trading company, a loan creditor may be deemed, for the purpose of apportionment, as having an interest in the company only to the extent that the income to be apportioned is (or has been) available to be applied in redemption of the loan capital or debt concerned.

If the Inspector proposes to make an apportionment he will serve a notice upon the company indicating the amount to be apportioned, and a further notice showing the amount to be apportioned to each participator. Unless an appeal is lodged within 30 days of issue the notice becomes conclusive.

In addition, there is power for the Inspector to raise a further notice of apportionment if the earlier one is shown to be insufficient. Similarly, if a notice is shown to be excessive, because the company's distributable income is smaller than originally anticipated (e.g. if loss relief is claimed), or the distributions made are greater than at first thought, the earlier notice can be amended to reduce the amount apportioned.

§ 15.—CONSEQUENCES OF APPORTIONMENT (Sch. 16, Paras 5–7, F.A. 1972, s. 32, F.A. 1984)

Apportionment is made, as the name suggests, according to the respective interests of the participators in the company.

The effect on an *individual* is that the amount apportioned is treated as if it were a dividend. No A.C.T. is payable as full corporation tax will be paid. There is no entitlement to tax credit, so no repayment can be claimed, and the deemed dividend cannot be used to cover annual payments made under deduction of tax. The deemed dividend plus a *notional tax credit* is regarded as the highest part of the individual's total income, hence higher rate tax and an investment income surcharge are payable.

The effect is similar if an apportionment is made upon the personal representatives of a deceased person.

No assessment for income tax is made upon an individual unless the apportioned amount (including sub-apportionments) is at least £1,000 or 5% of the total amount apportioned, whichever is the less. (For accounting periods ending prior to 6th April 1984 the threshold was £200.)

If an individual's total income includes actual distributions made in respect of an accounting period, and an apportionment is made for the same period, income tax is charged only on the excess of the apportionment over the actual distributions.

If the income apportioned to an individual is distributed subsequently and the distributions in the later period exceed the relevant income for that period, a measure of relief is available to prevent what would otherwise be a duplication of liability. This is achieved by *excluding* from the income of the year concerned the smallest of:

    (i) the amount apportioned;
    (ii) the amount of apportioned income charged to tax;
    (iii) the amount of the subsequent distribution.

Any higher rate tax and investment income surcharge is assessed upon the individual, but if he does not pay the company may be called upon to pay. The Revenue also retains the right to sue the participator if the company in turn does not pay. The company is, in such circumstances liable to pay interest accruing because of non-payment by the participator.

There is no immediate requirement for A.C.T. to be paid in respect of a deemed distribution as the full amount of corporation tax is paid on the profits. However, the notional amount of A.C.T. atributable to the apportioned income is payable if the aggregate of notional A.C.T. plus actual A.C.T. exceeds the maximum available amount allowed by way of set-off for A.C.T. against corporation tax liabilities. This effectively prevents a company accepting an apportionment rather than paying a dividend which would give rise to unrelieved A.C.T.

§ 16.—CLEARANCE (Sch. 16, Para. 18, F.A. 1972)

A trading company, or a member of a trading group, can request the Inspector for a clearance against an apportionment. The request for clearance must:

    (i) be accompanied by a copy of the accounts to which it relates;
    (ii) be accompanied by a copy of the directors' report on these accounts;
    (iii) be accompanied by such further information as is appropriate;
    (iv) be sent to the Inspector of Taxes after the general meeting at which the accounts were approved.

All these conditions must be complied with, otherwise the request may be refused.

The request for a clearance should therefore be submitted with the usual computations. A computation of the potential apportionment should be prepared at the same time, even though a clearance is being requested, so that a comparison of the relevant income with the financial requirements of the company can be made.

The Inspector has the right to call for further information, but he must do so within three months of receipt of the request for clearance. The Inspector must give his decision within three months of receipt of the additional information.

Whenever possible, the accounts on which a clearance is being requested should be submitted shortly after the end of the accounting period concerned. This is to ensure that, should the apportionment clearance be refused, the company will be in a position to make a distribution within "a reasonable period of time".

§ 17.—CESSATION AND LIQUIDATIONS (Sch. 16, Para. 13, F.A. 1972)

If a company commences winding-up or ceases to carry on its trade the whole of its distributable income (other than trading income) is subject to apportionment (i.e. the 50% estate and trading income abatement does not apply although the other abatements are still relevant). Furthermore no account can be taken of the company's business requirements (see below for position of creditors).

These provisions apply not only to the accounting period in which the cessation/liquidation occurs *but also* to any accounting period ending within 12 months of this date.

So great care must be taken in choosing the date for winding-up or cessation. The very best time is immediately after the end of an accounting period so that the total length of time subject to 100% apportionment is just over a year. If the date is just before the end of an accounting period, the period affected is almost two years.

If 100% distribution would prejudice creditors, an appropriate reduction may be made in relevant income. For this purpose, participators and associates are excluded from creditors, except for ordinary trading debts, Schedule E remuneration, commercial rent and copyrights, etc.

It is clearly advisable to clear the apportionment for pre-winding-up accounting periods by paying dividends before going into liquidation, since, *inter alia*, under company law a liquidator cannot pay such a dividend.

It is often difficult to close a liquidation until all apportionments have been agreed and tax thereon paid. This is because of the Revenue's right to collect the unpaid tax from the company. In most cases the Revenue will now agree to the closing of the liquidation if the participators concerned agree to enter into a binding agreement with the Revenue to pay the tax without recourse to the company. In all cases this procedure must be sanctioned by Somerset House.

A problem may arise since, on a reorganisation, in strictness a cessation occurs (i.e. if a trade is transferred from one company which then ceases to trade to another which then starts to trade). It is the Revenue's practice to examine cases where reorganisations are carried out entirely for bona fide commercial reasons, to see whether any relaxation of the 100% apportionment of income on cessation of trade or liquidation can be given. For this purpose, full information about any reorganisation (whether proposed or already carried out) where this problem may arise, should be given to the Inspector of Taxes when the tax liabilities of the company are computed, or when the question of the application of the 100% apportionment to a proposed reorganisation is raised.

§ 18.—RELIEF FOR INCOME TAX PAID ON APPORTIONMENT (s. 74, C.G.T.A. 1979)

Income tax paid following an apportionment of income should be treated as an allowable deduction when computing the capital gains arising on the disposal of shares. If several apportionments occur the income tax thereon should be aggregated. However, where the disposal occurs in a liquidation, the concession (A39–1980) described below will usually be more beneficial.

Where, however, there is an excess of relevant income over distributions for a period after the commencement of a winding-up and an apportionment is made, the resulting liability to higher rate tax (including investment income surcharge) of a participator can be restricted to the excess, if any, over the capital gains tax he has paid and which he shows is attributable to his receipts (as part of the liquidator's distributions in respect of share capital) out of the apportioned income for the period. If this concessionary relief is claimed the statutory relief is foregone.

Both the statutory relief and the concessionary relief assume that tax liabilities on apportionments and on the capital gain arising on a disposal of the shares will fall on the same person. However, there will be cases where income is apportioned through a trust to a beneficiary, who will bear the tax liability upon apportionment. This would also occur in the case of a residuary legatee of an estate under administration. The capital gain, however, falls upon the trustees of the settlement or the administrators of the estate.

The Revenue have now agreed so that where post-liquidation income of a company is apportioned to the beneficiary of a trust, or to a residuary legatee, account can be taken of any capital gains tax paid on that income by the trustees or by the administrators (see Concession D12–1980).

§ 19.—ASSETS OF A CLOSE COMPANY TRANSFERRED AT LESS THAN MARKET VALUE (s. 75, C.G.T.A. 1979)

In the case of a close company transferring an asset to any person:
    (*a*) otherwise than by way of an arms-length transaction; and
    (*b*) for a consideration less than the market value of the asset;
the difference between the consideration passing and the market value of the asset must be apportioned between the issued shares of the company.

Where such an apportionment occurs, and a shareholder disposes of any of his shares, the gain arising must be computed, by excluding from the expenditure relating to the cost of acquisition, the amount apportioned to those shares.

If the person owning the shares is a close company, an amount equal to the amount apportioned amongst the issued shares must be treated in accordance with the rule set out above.

Note: transactions within groups of companies are usually treated as having taken place in circumstances in which neither a loss nor a gain arises.

§ 20.—CAPITAL GAINS OF NON-RESIDENT CLOSE COMPANIES (s. 15, C.G.T.A. 1979)

Chargeable gains realised by certain non-resident companies which, were they resident, in the United Kingdom, would be deemed to be close companies, can be apportioned through to United Kingdom shareholders (See Chapter 20, § 4).

20. Corporation Tax—Foreign Element

§ 1.—ASSESSMENT OF OVERSEAS INCOME AND GAINS (ss. 238 and 243, I.C.T.A. 1970)

INCOME

Overseas income may be assessed under the following cases:

(a) *Case I, Schedule D*

Profits arising from a trade carried on overseas and controlled by a company resident in the United Kingdom.

(b) *Case IV, Schedule D*

Income arising from foreign securities, i.e. interest received on loans made abroad or from sources which are secured on the assets of the company to whom the loan is made, for example interest arising on mortgages or debentures.

(c) *Case V, Schedule D*

Income arising from foreign possessions including, broadly, all foreign sources except those which are foreign securities (e.g. royalties, rents, dividends and, rarely, trading profits from trades carried on overseas and controlled from overseas). Most overseas trades of U.K. resident companies will be assessed under Schedule D, Case I. Profits accruing to a company resident in the U.K., if remitted in the form of dividends, are not regarded as franked investment income and are assessable to corporation tax.

In all cases the amount to be assessed to corporation tax is the *gross figure* of the income arising before any deduction for overseas tax paid.

The amount of overseas tax to be included in the figure assessable varies in the case *of dividends* from foreign companies. In most cases only the withholding tax will be included, but when the British company can claim credit for the "underlying" overseas tax, this must also be included in the gross dividend assessable. The *"underlying tax"* is the overseas equivalent of corporation tax or income tax borne on the profits, out of which the dividend was paid.

Example

Faraway Ltd receives income from two overseas sources:

    (1) Trading profits   £3,500 (net)   (less overseas tax 30%).
    (2) Dividends   £600 (net)   (less overseas tax 20%).

Assessments

Case I

    Trading profits $\left(£3{,}500 \times \dfrac{100}{70} \right) = £5{,}000$ (Gross)

Case V

    Dividends $\left(£600 \times \dfrac{100}{80} \right) = £750$ (Gross)

CHARGEABLE GAINS

A company which is resident in the United Kingdom is assessable on its chargeable gains (as part of its total profits) including those realised overseas.

§ 2.—U.K. BRANCH OR AGENCY OF NON-RESIDENT COMPANY (s. 246, I.C.T.A. 1970)

Where a company is not resident in the United Kingdom, then it is not within the charge to corporation tax, *unless* it carries on a trade in the United Kingdom through a branch or agency. In this case, it is chargeable to corporation tax on the total profits of the branch or agency wherever they may arise.

The chargeable profits of a branch or agency comprise
 (*a*) trading income arising directly or indirectly through or from the branch or agency;
 (*b*) income from property used or held by or for the branch or agency.
Distributions received from United Kingdom resident companies are not included.

Capital gains are included if they relate to:
 (*a*) assets held in the United Kingdom and used for the purposes of the trade at or before the time when the chargeable gain arose; or
 (*b*) assets situated in the United Kingdom and used or held for the purposes of the branch or agency; or
 (*c*) assets acquired for use by, or the purposes of, the branch or agency.

§ 3.—INCORPORATION OF A FOREIGN BRANCH (s. 268A, I.C.T.A. 1970)

If a company which is resident in the United Kingdom but carrying on a business outside the U.K. transfers the trade and assets thereof to a non-resident company, the corporation tax due on the chargeable gains thereby accruing can be postponed. For this postponement to apply the following conditions must be satisfied:
 (*a*) the trade and the whole of the trading assets of the branch business (or the whole of those assets except cash) must be transferred to a company not resident in the United Kingdom; and
 (*b*) the business must be transferred wholly of partly in exchange for shares, or shares and loan stock issued by the transferee company to the transferor company; and
 (*c*) after the transfer the transferor company must own at least 25% of the ordinary share capital of the non-resident company.
 (*d*) there must be a net chargeable gain (or at least *no* allowable loss) accruing to the United Kingdom company.
The relief is given in respect of the net gains on all transferred assets if the United Kingdom company so elects. An effect of such a claim is that relief for allowable losses (which will have been deducted in arriving at the net gains) is also deferred. If only part of the consideration for the transfer is in the form of shares (or loan stock) the amount of the gain which can be deferred is reduced to the proportion thereof which the market value of the shares (or loan stocks) bears to the total consideration.

When the shares (or loan stock) issued by the overseas company are disposed of the deferred gain or a proportionate part thereof is added to the consideration received on the disposal.

A disposal, by the overseas company, within six years of the original transfer, of some or all of the transferred assets triggers a tax charge of such proportion of the deferred gain as the chargeable gains on the assets now disposed of bear to the total of all the chargeable gains on all the relevant assets (before taking account of losses). Intra-group transfers between United Kingdom members of a group of companies or between overseas members of a group of companies do not give rise to liability to pay any part of the deferred tax charge.

In transferring the trade to a non resident company the provisions of s. 482, I.C.T.A. 1970 will be activated, and appropriate action *must* therefore be taken (see Chapter 24, § 8, for s. 482 generally).

Example

Mandrake Ltd has a branch in Ruritania. In 1982 the branch was incorporated and its assets transferred to a new company Mandrake (Ruritania) A.G.

The deemed disposal, at market value, on the transfer to the new company, of the assets of the branch gives rise *prima facie* to the following gains and losses.

	Cost £	Market value £	Gain (*loss*) £
Goodwill	—	50,000	50,000
Land and buildings	100,000	80,000	(20,000)
Plant and machinery	50,000	55,000	5,000
	£150,000	£185,000	£35,000

Net current assets amounted to £15,000.

Mandrake Ltd transferred the assets to Mandrake (Ruritania) A.G. for ordinary shares to the value of £150,000 and £50,000 in cash. At this point Mandrake Ltd owns 100% of Mandrake (Ruritania) A.G. The gain of £35,000 is allocated as follows:

Chargeable now:

$$\frac{£50,000}{£50,000 + £150,000} \times £35,000 = \underline{£8,750} \text{ (before 11/26 reduction)}$$

Postponed liability:

$$\frac{£150,000}{£50,000 + £150,000} \times £35,000 = \underline{£26,250}$$

In 1984 the plant and machinery were sold. This triggers part of the postponed liability as follows:

	£	£
Postponed liability	26,250	
$\dfrac{£5,000}{£50,000 + £5,000} \times £26,250$	2,386	2,386
Chargeable gain (before reduction)		£2,386
Balance of postponed liability	£23,864	

In 1987 Mandrake Ltd sold 49% of the shares in Mandrake (Ruritania) A.G. to a Ruritanian resident for £100,000.

The chargeable gain on the disposal of the shares is increased by a further proportion of the postponed liability.

	£	£
Proceeds		100,000
Less: Cost £150,000 × 49%................		73,500
Gain on disposal of shares		26,500
Add Postponed liability	23,864	
Less: £23,864 × 49%	11,693	11,693
Chargeable gain (before reduction)		£38,193
Balance of postponed liability	£12,171	

§ 4.—NON-RESIDENT "CLOSE" COMPANIES (s. 15, C.G.T.A. 1979; s. 85, F.A. 1981)

A non-resident company which does not carry on a trade in the United Kingdom through a branch or agency is not liable to corporation tax on chargeable gains. However, in the case of a non-resident company which would be close, if U.K.-resident, a gain will be chargeable on a person who holds shares in the company (i.e. a member), if he is resident or ordinarily resident in the United Kingdom.

The proportion of any gain chargeable in this way upon a member is equal to the proportion of the assets of the company to which (at the time of the gain) the member would be entitled on a liquidation of the company; no charge will be made upon a member if his share of the gain is less than 1/20 thereof.

A charge will also be avoided in the following circumstances:
- (*a*) on any amount of the chargeable gain which is distributed:
  - (i) by way of dividend;
  - (ii) as a distribution of capital;
  - (iii) on dissolution of the company within two years from the time the gain accrued, to shareholders, or to creditors of the company; or
- (*b*) where the chargeable gain accrues on the disposal of tangible property, or a lease thereof *used, and used only,* for the purposes of a trade carried on outside the United Kingdom; or
- (*c*) where the chargeable gains are, in fact, assessed to United Kingdom tax; or
- (*d*) where the chargeable gain accrues on the disposal of a debt, owed by a bank, which is not in sterling and which is represented by a sum standing to a person's credit in an account in the bank, and represents money in use for the purposes of a trade carried on by the company wholly outside the United Kingdom.

Any capital gains tax charged by these provisions upon a member, and not reimbursed by the company, is treated as an allowable deduction in computing the chargeable gain arising on the subsequent disposal of the shares in question.

If the company suffers a loss in the disposal of a chargeable asset, it may be set against chargeable gains (subject to the normal rules for set-off) in computing the net chargeable gain to be apportioned to the members. However, losses in excess of gains are not apportioned between the members.

If a member of the non-resident company is also a non-resident close company, the gain is sub-apportioned through that company to the United Kingdom resident or ordinarily resident members thereof.

Where the tax charged upon a member is paid by, or re-imbursed by, the company (or companies) involved this is not treated for the purposes of income tax, capital gains tax or corporation tax, as a payment to the member concerned.

and such payment does not therefore, of itself, give rise to any tax liability on the member, or tax relief to the company making the payment.

Gains realised by a non-resident company after 9th March 1981, can be apportioned to trustees owning shares in the company even though, at the time the gain accrues to the company, the trustees are neither resident, nor ordinarily resident in the United Kingdom.

§ 5.—DELAYED OR "BLOCKED" REMITTANCES

INCOME (s. 418, I.C.T.A. 1970)

Relief in the form of postponement of assessment will apply to a company which is chargeable to corporation tax in respect of overseas income but is prevented from transferring such income to the United Kingdom, by the laws of the overseas country, or by executive action by its government, or because it is not possible to obtain foreign currency in that country. The relief will not be given if the income can be realised outside the country concerned for a consideration in sterling or other currency which is readily convertible into sterling. For postponement to apply the company must also show that it has made all reasonable endeavours to obtain remittance of the income. The postponement applies until any or all of the income becomes remittable, at which point it is brought into charge.

CHARGEABLE GAINS (s. 13, C.G.T.A. 1979)

The same treatment is applied to chargeable gains on assets situated outside the United Kingdom and which cannot (for the reasons outlined above) be remitted to the United Kingdom. The relief cannot be claimed insofar as the company receives a payment in respect of unremittable gains, from the Export Credits Guarantee Department.

§ 6.—DOUBLE TAXATION RELIEF

It will be appreciated that a company resident in the United Kingdom may be taxed on income arising from abroad, and taxed at source at the overseas rate of tax, and may also be subject to assessment on the same figure for purposes of corporation tax. This will give rise to a double assessment to tax on the same amount.

The purpose of double taxation relief is to ensure that the total tax paid by the United Kingdom company does not exceed the greater of the rate of corporation tax or the overseas tax thereon.

TREATY RELIEF

Section 497, I.C.T.A. 1970, enables agreements to be made by the United Kingdom with other countries to provide relief from double taxation where the income concerned has borne, not only U.K. tax, but also local taxes in the foreign country in which the source of the income is located. This relief is achieved either by exemption from tax in one or other country, or by giving credit for the foreign tax paid.

These agreements apply to taxes which are of a similar character to income tax, corporation tax, and capital gains tax. So far as concerns companies as such the agreements cover income derived from foreign sources and chargeable gains arising on the disposal of assets located overseas and chargeable, in either case, to U.K. corporation tax.

Other matters which can be dealt with in such agreements include

(*a*) charging tax on income from sources in the U.K. to persons not resident in the U.K.

(*b*) charging tax on chargeable gains from assets in the U.K. but owned by persons not resident in the U.K.

(*c*) determining the income or gains attributable to a U.K. branch, agency, or establishment of an overseas company.

(*d*) giving a tax credit to non-resident persons on otherwise qualifying distributions.

Where relief is available by way of a credit against U.K. tax for foreign tax paid there are special rules as to the calculation of the credit available and of any limitation thereon (see this chapter § 7–8).

Some overseas countries grant total or partial exemption from tax on certain types of income arising:

(*a*) industrial development;

(*b*) commercial development;

(*c*) scientific development;

(*d*) the provision of education; or

(*e*) from other institutions of a development nature.

Where the double taxation agreement provides for this exemption, then the tax which, but for this exemption, would have been payable is to be taken into account in computing the credit to be allowed against the corporation tax payable on that income.

UNILATERAL RELIEF

Where no agreement is in existence, the tax on income arising in that country will normally be allowed as a credit against tax charged in the country in which the recipient is resident. This is known as unilateral relief and is provided for by s. 498, I.C.T.A. 1970. There are however certain restrictions on the amount of unilateral relief available.

The amount of foreign tax credited cannot exceed the U.K. corporation tax chargeable upon the same income or gain taking each source of income separately. This may cause the credit for foreign tax to be limited if the manner in which the taxable amount of the income or gain is computed in the overseas country is significantly different from that applied in the U.K.

This source by source restriction does not apply where the income is derived from the Isle of Man or the Channel Islands. In such a case the relief is available against the general corporation tax liability.

In the case of overseas dividends, the credit is usually limited to the withholding tax, but in certain circumstances, the underlying tax can also be included in the credit given. This may happen where the recipient owns a material portion of the shares in the foreign company, as opposed to a smaller holding (known as a "portfolio investment").

Relief for underlying tax is available where a dividend is paid by a company resident overseas to a U.K. resident company which controls directly or indirectly not less than 10% of the voting power in the paying company. The relief is also available if the dividend is paid to a subsidiary (i.e. not less than 50% of the voting power) of such a company.

In general the computations for unilateral relief are the same as those described below in respect of treaty relief.

Any claims for relief from double taxation must be made within six years from the end of the accounting period during which the income is received.

§ 7.—LIMITATIONS ON CREDIT (s. 505, I.C.T.A. 1970)

Where relief is claimed, whether under an agreement or by unilateral relief, by way of credit, it is given by allowing the foreign tax on income or on a chargeable gain to be set against the U.K. corporation tax on the same income or gain. If the foreign tax exceeds the U.K. corporation tax against which a credit could be claimed there is no relief for any such excess. In such a case it may be more beneficial to claim foreign tax as a deduction in arriving at the amount of income liable to U.K. corporation tax (refer to ss. 511 and 516, I.C.T.A. 1970).

At its simplest this is comparison of the "net" amount available, after all taxes, in the U.K.

Example 1

Alberto Ltd has received interest of £1,000 from a source in Moravia. Moravian tax of £250 is deducted at source.

Deduction

Interest from Moravia.........................	£1,000
Less: Moravian tax.........................	250
"Cash" in U.K..............................	750
UK tax 30%................................	225
"Net" in U.K.	£525

Assuming that a credit is available under the terms of the U.K.–Moravia double tax treaty, the position would be:

Credit

Interest from Moravia.........................		£1,000
Less: Moravian tax.........................		250
"Cash" in U.K..............................		750
U.K. tax at 30%	300	
Less: Credit for Moravian tax................	250	
Paid to U.K. Revenue........................		50
"Net" in U.K.		£700

The problem is most likely to arise if there is a disparity between U.K. and foreign profits (e.g. due to different systems of capital allowances, stock relief or losses).

Example 2

Weaver Ltd carries on a trade in Bargello. It also has a U.K. trade and pays charges on income.

	Credit £	Total £
U.K. income................................		1,000
Bargello income (tax at 35%)	10,000	10,000
		11,000
Less: Charges on income...................	9,000	9,000
Profits chargeable to corporation tax.........	1,000	2,000
C.T. thereon at 30%........................		600
Foreign tax credit (£1,000 at 35%)		350
Payable.....................................		£250

The Bargello tax paid £3,500 has not been fully relieved. The balance of £3,150 (£3,500–£350) cannot be carried forward or otherwise utilised.

The alternative form of relief is to use the foreign tax to reduce the amount chargeable to U.K. corporation tax.

	Deduction	£	£
U.K. income			1,000
Bargello income		10,000	
Tax at 35%		3,500	
			6,500
			7,500
Less: Charges on income			9,000
Profits chargeable to corporation tax			£ NIL
Charges carried forward			£1,500

Except where the alternative deduction method of relief is being claimed no deduction is given in computing the income liable to U.K. corporation tax for any foreign tax paid.

Example 3

Faraway Ltd is entitled to receive a dividend of £1,000 from a foreign subsidiary. The foreign country concerned imposes a 15% withholding tax. Thus the amount received by Faraway Ltd is only £850. However U.K. corporation tax is charged on the "gross" dividend of £1,000.

If relief is available for underlying tax in the case of a dividend, the "gross" amount of the dividend is further increased (or "re-grossed") to include the underlying tax. The calculations of the credit available are based on this re-grossed amount.

However there is no "re-grossing" of income which has been exempted from tax in the foreign country as part of a scheme to promote industry, commerce, scientific development, education, etc., even though for other purposes such income is deemed to have borne tax.

Example 4

Closeathand Ltd has the following overseas income:

	£	
Trading profits (U.K.)	10,000	
Trading profits (overseas)	1,500	net (local tax £750)
Dividends (overseas)	350	(withholding tax £35 underlying tax £100)

(Note: the company owns more than a 10% shareholding.)

Assessments	£	£
Case I Trading profits (United Kingdom)		10,000
Case I Trading profits (overseas)	1,500	
Add: Local tax	750	2,250
		12,250
Case V Dividends (overseas)	350	
Add: Withholding tax	35	
Underlying tax	100	485
		£12,735

			£
Corporation tax payable at 30%............			3,820
Less: Double taxation relief			
(1) *Trading profits:*	£		
Smaller of £2,250 @ 30%................ =	675		
or overseas tax........................ =	750	675	
(2) *Dividends:*			
Smaller of £500 @ 30% .... =	150		
or overseas tax........................ =	135	135	810
Corporation tax .... =			£3,010

Note: the amount of the credit for foreign tax which is to be allowed against corporation tax may not exceed the corporation tax attributable to that income.

§ 8.—UNDERLYING TAX ON DIVIDENDS (ss. 506–508, I.C.T.A. 1970)

Where, in the case of dividends, the underlying tax is to be taken into account in ascertaining the amount of the credit to be allowed against corporation tax, the amount of tax to be taken into account is the portion of the foreign tax borne on the profits by the company paying the dividend as is properly attributable to the proportion of the relevent profits represented by the dividend.

If under the foreign tax law the divided is increased by any amount which is set against the recipient's tax (i.e. an imputation system) such increase is deducted from the underlying tax.

Considerable difficulties have been encountered, in the calculation of underlying tax, in determining "relevant profits", which had been held in the case of *Bowater Paper Corporation Ltd* v. *Murgatroyd* (1969) to be profits available for distribution and not those actually assessed for foreign tax purposes (e.g. because of a disparity in the treatment of depreciation).

Following representations by the Consultative Committee of the Accountancy Bodies the Revenue have, broadly, agreed to this approach. Where the accounts profits include unrealised gains on currency realignments these are, provisionally, regarded as not available for distribution unless they are in fact used for a dividend or put to a general, and distributable, reserve, or left in the retained earnings account. Realised gains are regarded as available for distribution.

The Revenue regard capital profits as being part of the relevant profits even if they are credited direct to capital reserves.

The underlying rate of tax on a dividend is thus calculated by taking the actual tax liability on the assessed profits, but by applying that tax to the profits available for distribution as shown by the accounts (subject to adjustment for certain amounts taken directly to reserve).

Example

Albion Ltd, a U.K. resident company, received a dividend of £21,250 (after withholding tax of £3,750) from its wholly-owned overseas subsidiary. The profit and loss account of the subsidiary expressed in sterling was as follows:

	£	£
Profit before taxation......................		50,000
Taxation:		
Provision for income tax..................	16,000	
Deferred taxation	8,000	
Overprovision for tax in prior years.........	(1,500)	
		22,500

	£
Profit after taxation	27,500
Proposed dividend	25,000
Retained profit.	£2,500

The actual tax paid by the subsidiary on the above profit was £15,000.
   The profit after tax of £27,500 is the "relevant profit" for double taxation relief purposes (i.e. profit available for distribution).
   The calculations of the underlying rate of overseas tax applicable to the above profit is therefore:

$$\frac{£15,000}{£15,000 + £27,500} \times 100 = 35.29\%$$

The Case V, Schedule D income and double taxation relief arising to the U.K. resident company are as follows:

	£	£	£
Cash received		21,250	
Add: withholding tax		3,750	3,750
		25,000	
Add: underlying tax $25,000 \times \dfrac{100}{64.71} =$	38,634		
Less	25,000	13,634	13,634
Case V, Schedule D		£38,634	
Double taxation relief			£17,384

Determination of profits

The rules to determine the profit figure out of which dividends have been paid are:

(1) if the dividend is paid for a specified period, the profits for that period;
(2) if the dividend is not paid for a specified period but is paid out of specified profits, those profits;
(3) where the above rules do not apply, the profits of the last period (for which accounts have been prepared) which ended before the dividend became payable; and if those profits are insufficient, the profits of the next preceding period, and so on.

Example

Adela Ltd received a dividend in its accounting period to 31st March 1986 from an overseas company in which it holds 40% of the share capital. The amount received in the current accounting period was £11,400 after withholding tax of 5%.
   The net dividend received by Adela Ltd was £11,400; therefore the dividend to Adela Ltd before withholding tax was:

$$£11,400 \times \frac{100}{95} = £12,000 \text{ (withholding tax £600).}$$

The following figures relate to the overseas company:

	A.P. to 31.3.82 £	A.P. to 31.3.83 £	A.P. to 31.3.84 £
Profit per accounts.........................	31,000	18,000	15,000
Provision for tax...........................	10,230	5,940	4,950
	20,770	12,060	10,050
Undistributed profits b/fwd	26,820	47,590	59,650
	47,590	59,650	69,700
Dividend.................................	—	—	30,000
Undistributed profits c/fwd	£47,590	£59,650	£39,700
Adjusted profit per tax computation	£22,000	£17,000	£16,500
Tax thereon at (say) 33%..................	£7,260	£5,610	£5,445

The dividend was not paid out of specified profits, nor out of the profits of a specified period and thus the profits from which the dividend was deemed to be paid are firstly those of the period to 31st March 1985, and then those of the period to 31st March 1984.

	A.P. to 31.3.85 £	A.P. to 31.3.84 £	£
Profit per accounts.........................	18,000	31,000	
Actual tax liability..........................	5,610	7,260	
Effective rate of tax	31.17%	34.57%	
Available for distribution (as above)..........	12,060	20,770	
Therefore dividend deemed derived as to	12,060	17,940	
Proportion of dividend paid to Adela Ltd. $\left(\dfrac{12,000}{30,000}\right) \times \dfrac{£12,060}{(\text{or } £17,940)} =$	4,824	7,176	
Tax at effective rate (as above) (grossed up)..	2,184	3,791	5,975
Profits out of which dividend deemed paid =	£7,008	10,967	
Withholding tax (as above).................			600
Total overseas tax attributable to dividend to Adela Ltd			£6,575

UK corporation tax

		£
Schedule D, Case V "grossed up" dividend as above (£7,008 + £10,967) =		17,975
Corporation tax at 40% (there being other profits)		7,190
Credit for overseas tax		6,575
Net U.K. liability............................		£615

If the arrangements provide for relief for underlying tax for some classes of dividend but not for others, and a dividend is paid for a class which is not within the arrangements credit is nonetheless given provided the dividend is paid to a company which controls, either directly or indirectly, not less than 10% of the total voting power in the company paying the dividend. This also applies where the recipient is a subsidiary (i.e. not less than 50% of the voting power) of such a company.

If an overseas company pays a dividend to a U.K. resident company and the 10% threshold of voting power is exceeded then in computing underlying tax account can also be taken of any U.K. corporation tax or income tax paid by the overseas company on its profits and tax charged by any other country thereon. Furthermore if the overseas company itself receives dividends from a third company also resident outside the U.K. underlying tax relating to that dividend is also taken into account. This also applies to dividends from a fourth company, and from a fifth company, and so on.

Restriction of underlying tax (s. 66, F.A. 1982)
Parallel restrictions to the 15% credit for loan interest (see Chapter 13, § 3) apply to the underlying tax to which a *U.K. bank* or connected company may be entitled. The underlying tax will be restricted if it includes tax on interest which is itself subject to the 15% restriction.

The restriction on underlying tax will apply where the foreign lending is undertaken by a related overseas company and:

(*a*) foreign tax is withheld or spared on the interest that overseas company receives, and

(*b*) its profits are remitted by way of dividend to a U.K. bank or a company connected with a U.K. bank.

§ 9.—A.C.T. AND DOUBLE TAX RELIEF (s. 100, F.A. 1972)

Accounting periods ending before 1st April 1984
A.C.T. is set-off against corporation tax in priority to double taxation relief. This set-off reduces the mainstream corporation tax against which the double taxation relief may be given. Consequently, in certain circumstances, there may be a surplus of double taxation relief. Unlike A.C.T., there is no provision for this surplus to be dealt with, either by repayment or carrying backwards or forwards.

However, a measure of relief is provided in these cases by giving the company concerned a choice when computing the corporation tax assessment as to the order in which it sets its charges or trade losses against its profits (including chargeable gains). In addition, A.C.T. which can only be set against income (not chargeable gains), may be allocated in such a manner as the company chooses. By this method, it would be most advantageous to set charges against chargeable gains (if any) to leave the greatest amount of other income to take against A.C.T. Then the maximum amount of A.C.T. is set against income other than overseas income first, in order to leave the maximum deduction for double taxation relief.

Example 1

This example illustrates how it will usually be advantageous for a company with more than one source of foreign income to opt for (for purposes of credit for foreign tax) its distributions to be made from foreign sources bearing lower rates of foreign tax, before sources bearing higher rates of foreign tax.

In the year to 31st March 1983 a company has income from the following sources:

U.K. trading profits	£15,000
Foreign interest	£5,000 (foreign tax £500)
Foreign branch profits	£30,000 (foreign tax £13,000).

The company distributes £21,000.
ACT due on distribution = £21,000 at 3/7 = £9,000

Liability on U.K. income	£	£
Corporation tax liability £15,000 at 38%.............	5,700	
Less: A.C.T. (restricted)*	4,500	
Mainstream corporation tax payable on due date....	=	£1,200

Liability on foreign interest		
Corporation tax liability £5,000 at 38% = ...	1,900	
Less: A.C.T. (restricted)†	1,500	400
Credit for foreign tax.............................		(400)
Mainstream corporation tax payable on due date....	=	Nil

Liability on foreign branch profits		
Corporation tax liability £30,000 at 38% = ...	11,400	
Less: A.C.T. (balance)	3,000	8,400
Credit for foreign tax.............................		(8,400)
Mainstream corporation tax payable on due date....	=	Nil

Summary	£
Corporation tax payable at time of distribution	9,000
Corporation tax payable on due date:	
(a) U.K. Income.....................................	1,200
(b) Foreign interest.................................	Nil
(c) Foreign branch profits...........................	Nil
	£10,200

Example 2

This example illustrates how a company is able, for purposes of credit for foreign tax, to deem its distributions to be made primarily out of U.K. income in order to maximise its double taxation relief.

In the year to March 31st 1983 a company has income from the following sources:

U.K. trading profits	£200,000
Foreign branch profits	£36,000 (foreign tax £15,000)

The company distributed £147,000 in that year
A.C.T. due on distribution = £147,000 at 3/7 = £63,000

---

* The A.C.T. to be set against the corporation tax on £15,000 is *restricted to* £4,500, the A.C.T. applicable to a distribution of £10,500 or £10,500 + £4,500 = £15,000 gross.
† The A.C.T. to be set against corporation tax on £5,000 is *restricted to* £1,500 (the A.C.T. applicable to a distribution of £3,500 or £3,500 + £1,500 = £5,000 gross).

Liability on U.K. income	£	£
Corporation tax liability £200,000 at 52% =	104,000	
Less: A.C.T. (restricted)*	60,000	
Mainstream corporation tax payable on due date..	=	£44,000

Liability on foreign income		
Corporation tax liability £36,000 at 52% =	18,720	
Less: A.C.T. (balance)	3,000	15,720
Less Credit for foreign tax (no restriction)...........		15,000
Mainstream corporation tax payable on due date..	=	720

Summary	£
Corporation tax payable at time of distribution	63,000
Corporation tax payable on due date:	
(a) U.K. Income......................................	44,000
(b) Foreign income..................................	720
	£107,720

Example 3

Clayville Ltd has the following income and outgoings in the year to 31st March 1983:

U.K. trading profits £10,000.
Overseas royalties £3,000 (after foreign tax £1,500).
Interest paid £2,000.

A distribution of £7,000 was made during the year (A.C.T. payable 3/7 × £7,000 = £3,000).

		Charges	Net	Corp Tax (38%)	A.C.T. Credit	D.T.R.	Net Corp Tax
U.K. profit	£10,000	£2,000	£8,000	£3,040	£2,400	£ —	£640
Sched. D, Case V	4,500	—	4,500	1,710	600	1,110	—
	£14,500	£2,000	£12,500	£4,750	£3,000	£1,100	£640

Notes

(1) The charges are set against the U.K. income so that the maximum credit can be obtained for the foreign tax.
(2) The A.C.T. credit available against the U.K. income is 30% × £8,000, i.e. £2,400. The balance of £600 has to be allowed against the Corporation Tax on overseas royalties.
(3) The Double Taxation Relief is limited to the lesser of the Corporation Tax on the foreign income (£1,710 − £600 A.C.T. = £1,100) or the foreign tax (£1,500).

---

* The A.C.T. to be set against the corporation tax on £200,000 is *restricted to* £60,000 (the A.C.T. applicable to a distribution of £140,000 + £60,000 tax = £200,000 gross).

Accounting periods ending after 31st March 1984 (s. 53, F.A. 1984)

For accounting periods ending after 31st March 1984 the set-off of double tax relief against corporation tax on income which has suffered foreign tax is given in priority to advance corporation tax. Where such double tax relief exceeds the limit of advance corporation tax (presently 30% of taxable income) which could be set off against the corporation tax liability on the foreign income any actual advance corporation tax set-off will be limited to the residual corporation tax liability on the foreign income.

However, surplus A.C.T. can be carried back, or forward, or surrendered, whereas unrelieved double tax relief is irretrievably lost.

Example 4

In the year to 31st March 1986 a company has income from the following sources:

U.K. trading profits	£1,500,000
Foreign interest	£500,000 (foreign tax £50,000)
Foreign branch profits	£300,000 (foreign tax £130,000).

The company distributes £2,100,000.
ACT due on distribution = £2,100,000 × 3/7 = £900,000

	£	£
Liability on U.K. income		
Corporation tax liability £1,500,000 at 40%	600,000	
Less: A.C.T. (restricted)[(i)]	450,000	
Mainstream corporation tax payable on due date		= £150,000
Liability on foreign interest		
Corporation tax liability £500,000 at 40% = ...	200,000	
Credit for foreign tax	50,000	150,000
Less: A.C.T. (restricted)[(ii)]		150,000
Mainstream corporation tax payable on due date		Nil
Liability on foreign branch profits		
Corporation tax liability £300,000 at 40% = ...	120,000	
Credit for foreign tax[(iii)]	120,000	Nil
Mainstream corporation tax payable on due date		Nil
Summary		
A.C.T. payable at time of distribution		900,000
Corporation tax payable on due date:		
(a) U.K. Income		150,000
(b) Foreign interest		Nil
(c) Foreign branch profits		Nil
		£1,050,000
Utilisation of A.C.T.		
Paid on distribution		900,000
Set against corporation tax on:		
(a) U.K. income	450,000	
(b) Foreign interest	150,000	
(c) Foreign branch profits	Nil	600,000
Available for alternative relief		300,000

Notes
  (i) The A.C.T. to be set against the corporation tax on £1,500,000 is *restricted to* £450,000, the A.C.T. applicable to a distribution of £1,050,000 or £1,050,000 + £450,000 = £1,500,000 gross.
  (ii) The A.C.T. to be set against corporation tax on £500,000 is *restricted to* £150,000 (the A.C.T. applicable to a distribution of £350,000 or £350,000 + £150,000 = £500,000 gross).
  (iii) As the foreign tax exceeds the corporation tax due in respect of income from this source the balance of £10,000 is lost.

Example 5

Graveling Ltd has the following income and outgoings in the year to 31st March 1986:

U.K. trading profits £10,000.
Overseas royalties £3,000 (after foreign tax £1,500).
Interest paid £2,000.

A distribution of £7,000 was made during the year (A.C.T. payable 3/7 × £7,000 = £3,000).

		Charges (i)	Net	Corp Tax (30%)	D.T.R. (ii)	A.C.T. Credit (iii)	Net Corp Tax
U.K. profit	£10,000	£2,000	£8,000	£2,400	—	£2,400	—
Sched. D, Case V	4,500	—	4,500	1,350	1,350	—	—
	£14,500	£2,000	£12,500	£3,750	£1,350	£2,400	Nil

Notes
  (i) The charges are set against the U.K. income so that the maximum credit can be obtained for the foreign tax.
  (ii) As the foreign tax paid exceeds the corporation tax due in respect of income from this source, the balance of £150 is lost.
  (iii) The unrelieved balance of A.C.T. is available for alternative relief.

§ 10.—CONTROLLED FOREIGN CORPORATIONS (ss. 82–91, Schedules 16–18, F.A. 1984)

Introduction
Special rules were introduced with effect from 6th April 1984 to prevent tax "leaking" through the use by U.K. residents of companies operating in "low tax" jurisdictions. Such companies are referred to as controlled foreign companies (C.F.C.).
  A country is a "low tax" area if the tax paid by the C.F.C. in its country of residence for that A.P. is less than one-half of the corresponding U.K. tax which would have been payable had it been resident here.

Summary of rules
The rules apply to U.K. resident companies which hold an interest (directly or indirectly) in a C.F.C. where all the following conditions are present:
  (i) the C.F.C. is controlled by U.K. resident persons; and
  (ii) the C.F.C. is resident in a "low tax" area; and
  (iii) the U.K. company, together with connected or associated persons, has at least a 10% interest in the C.F.C.

However, the provisions will not apply where:
- (i) the C.F.C.'s profits for a twelve-month period are less than £20,000; or
- (ii) the C.F.C. remits, by way of dividend, a substantial proportion of its commercial profits to the U.K. and satisfies the "acceptable distribution" test; or
- (iii) the C.F.C. is engaged in activities which fulfil an "exempt activities" test; or
- (iv) the main purpose of the transactions carried out by the C.F.C. is not to achieve a significant underlying reason for the company's existence but to achieve a diversion of profits from the U.K. (the "motive" test).

The Revenue publish a list of countries which are not regarded as "low tax" countries and countries which will be similarly excluded provided the C.F.C. is not subject to certain specified reliefs.

If a C.F.C. does not satisfy any of the three tests, the U.K. company will be liable to tax on its share of the chargeable profits of C.F.C. (if the Revenue so direct).

Imputation of profits of C.F.C.
If the C.F.C. does not satisfy any of the exclusion tests referred to below, its chargeable profits (but not chargeable gains) and its creditable tax may be apportioned to a U.K. resident company.

This only applies if the profits apportioned to that company together with the amounts which are apportioned to connected or associated persons are, in the aggregate, at least 10% of the profits.

The apportioned profits will be separately charged to tax.

Exclusion tests
No charge will arise if the profits of the C.F.C. for any A.P. of twelve months do not exceed £20,000 or, if the A.P. is less than twelve months, a proportionately reduced amount.

A C.F.C. will be treated as having pursued an acceptable distribution policy in respect of an A.P. if:
- (i) a dividend which is not paid out of specified profits is paid for the A.P.; and
- (ii) that dividend is paid during the A.P., or within eighteen months (or at such later time as the Board may allow) of the end of that period; and
- (iii) the proportion of that dividend (or the total dividends if more than one) paid to U.K. residents is at least 50% of the C.F.C.'s available profits for the A.P. attributable to U.K. residents or, in the case of a C.F.C. which is not a trading company, 90% of those profits.

A C.F.C. will be outside the scope of the charge if the following conditions are satisfied:
- (i) The company has a genuine presence in its country of residence.
- (ii) Its business affairs in that country are effectively managed there and the number of persons employed are adequate for the volume of business.
- (iii) The company's main business does not consist of leasing, the holding of or dealing in securities, dealing in goods for delivery to or from the U.K. or to or from connected persons, or the investment of funds which would otherwise be available for investment by person(s) controlling the C.F.C.
- (iv) If the company is engaged in wholesale, distributive or financial business less than 50% of its gross trading receipts are derived from connected persons.
- (v) If the company is a "local holding company" not less than 90% of its gross income is derived from those subsidiaries which must themselves be engaged in exempt activities.
- (vi) If the company is a holding company but not a local holding company, not less than 90% of its gross income is derived from local holding companies or trading companies engaged in exempt activities.

Even if a company fails to satisfy any of the three foregoing exclusions it may still avoid a direction if:
(i) the transactions of the A.P. were carried out for good commercial reasons; and
(ii) the avoidance of tax was not a main purpose of those transactions; and
(iii) where a diversion of profits from the U.K. has taken place it was not one of the main reasons for the C.F.C.'s existence to achieve that diversion.

Territories with a lower level of taxation
The test is whether the local tax payable on the profits of the C.F.C. is less than one-half of the corresponding U.K. tax which would be payable for the A.P. in question.

Special points
(i) The C.F.C. will not be assumed to be a member of a group or consortium. No group or consortium relief may be claimed by the C.F.C. But a U.K. company which has been the subject of a direction may claim group relief against the profits apportioned to it and may also set off A.C.T. against the tax due on these profits. No group income claims may be made in respect of dividends or charges on income paid or received by the C.F.C.
(ii) A C.F.C. may claim relief for trading losses incurred by it in the six years prior to the first A.P. for which a direction is given.
(iii) Capital allowances are available but the acquisition of any asset where the sole or main purpose was to reduce the chargeable profits or corresponding U.K. tax of a C.F.C. will be disregarded. Plant and machinery acquired by a C.F.C. before the first A.P. for which a direction is given will be deemed to have been acquired at the commencement of that A.P. at its market value at that time.
(iv) A C.F.C. may claim relief for unremittable income under s.418, T.A. 1970, if it is prevented from remitting income to the country of its residence by the laws of the territory in which the income arises.
(v) Where a direction is given in respect of the chargeable profits of a C.F.C. for an A.P. a deduction against the tax due may be allowed for the "creditable tax" of the C.F.C. The creditable tax is apportioned in the same proportions as chargeable profits and consists of double taxation relief for any foreign tax attributable to income included in chargeable profits, any U.K. income tax deducted at source from income and any income tax or corporation tax actually charged (e.g. on U.K. branch profits) in respect of the chargeable profits.

§ 11.—CORPORATE FINANCE AND INTERNATIONAL BUSINESS (F.A. 1984)

Interest on quoted Eurobonds (s. 35, F.A. 1984)
The Eurobond market deals in bearer bonds, and interest thereon is always paid gross. U.K. companies issuing Eurobonds have had to do so through an overseas subsidiary to enable interest to be paid gross to investors.
   As from July 1984 interest on a quoted Eurobond will be paid gross if payment is made:
(a) by or through a person not in the U.K.; or
(b) by or through a person in the U.K., if the person owning the bond and entitled to the interest is not resident in the U.K. or the bond is held in a recognised clearing system.
Interest paid without deduction of income tax will be allowed to the paying company as a charge on income.

U.K. companies may make Eurobond issues in London without setting up foreign finance subsidiaries.

Deep-discount securities (s. 36, F.A. 1984; s. 46, Sch. 11, F.A. 1985)

A deep-discount security is a redeemable security issued by a U.K. or overseas company where the difference between the amount payable on redemption (excluding interest) and the issue price is more than $\frac{1}{2}\%$ p.a. over the life of the security or more than 15% overall.

For an investor the discount will be treated as income when the security is sold or redeemed. The charge to corporation tax will be on the income accruing on a compound yield basis over the period of ownership.

To calculate the accrued income it is necessary to establish the annual rate of compound interest at which the issue price has to grow in order to reach the redemption value taking into account any interest payments. The yield to maturity is then used to calculate the accrued income for each income period.

Companies issuing deep-discount securities will be required to show the accrued income for each income period on the certificate relating to the security.

The charge to income tax or corporation tax will apply to disposals of securities on or after 1st April 1984 where the security was issued after 13th March 1984.

The issuing company will obtain relief for the accrued discount as if it were a charge on income paid at the end of each income period. Where the security is held by an associated company or by a company in the same 51% group, relief will be allowed only when the discount is paid on redemption. Relief will be due only on redemption where a close company issues a deep-discount security to a participator, his associate, or a company controlled by him. There is no requirement to deduct income tax from the discount when paid on redemption of the security. Relief to the issuing company will be available for accrued income attributable to income periods ending after 31st March 1984. Relief will be given to the issuer for the incidental costs of issuing deep-discount securities (under s. 38 F.A. 1980).

Securities issued at a discount dependent on the movement of any price index do not qualify.

Action has been taken to counter a form of coupon stripping which would otherwise mitigate the disparity in timing between the tax charge on the investor and the deduction for the issuing company. For example a company might buy interest-bearing securities and itself issue a series of deep-discount bonds with maturities matching each interest payment and the principal sum. In such circumstances the tax charge on the holder of the bond is brought forward so that it applies to the income element of the discount as it accrues during ownership and not only on disposal or redemption.

Acceptance credits (s. 42, F.A. 1984)

Where a trading company raises finance for the purpose of its trade by drawing bills of exchange and having them accepted and discounted by a bank or discount house, it is able to obtain corporation tax relief for the discount suffered at the time of payment of the bills.

From 1st April 1983 relief is available where an investment company raises finance in this way or where a trading company raises finance for capital purposes provided the bank or discount house concerned is bona fide carrying on a business as such in the U.K.

Relief will be given for the discount against the total profits of the period (as reduced by any relief other than group relief) in which the bill is paid. The deduction will be treated as a charge on income. Relief will not be given if the discount is charged to capital or it is not ultimately suffered by the company.

Any incidental costs incurred after 31st March 1983 in obtaining the acceptance of the bill are also deductible in computing trading profits or as a management expense.

Such incidental costs include fees, commissions and any other expenditure wholly and exclusively incurred in connection with the acceptance of the bill.

21. Corporation Tax—Chargeable Gains of Companies

§ 1.—GENERAL

INTRODUCTION (s. 265, I.C.T.A. 1970)

Companies are not liable to Capital Gains Tax but to corporation tax on chargeable gains.

The amount (see below) to be included in the company's total profits in respect of chargeable gains realised by it in an accounting period is that sum left after deducting allowable losses of the same, or earlier, accounting periods.

In general, however, the rules of *computation* of chargeable gains and allowable losses under Capital Gains Tax are applied although certain provisions (e.g. private residence relief; basic exemption) apply only to individuals and not to companies. In most respects, references to income tax are interpreted as applying also to corporation tax, and, unless there is a specific exclusion provisions relating to individuals are also applied to companies. The remaining sections of this chapter are concerned with those provisions which apply only to capital gains of companies.

COMPANIES' CAPITAL GAINS (s. 93, F.A. 1972)

The amount to be included in a company's profits is the net amount of chargeable gains (less allowable losses) reduced by a fraction thereof.

When the full rate of corporation tax is applied to the reduced gains the effective rate is 30% on the full amount of net gains.

The fractions applying for the various financial years are as follows:

1973–1982	11/26
1983	2/5
1984	1/3
1985	1/4
1986	1/7

Example

	1982	1983	1984	1985	1986
Financial year	1982	1983	1984	1985	1986
Fraction	11/26	2/5	1/3	1/4	1/7
Corporation tax rate	52%	50%	45%	40%	35%
	£	£	£	£	£
Net gains	1,000	1,000	1,000	1,000	1,000
Less Reduction	423	400	333	250	143
	577	600	667	750	857
Tax thereon	£300	£300	£300	£300	£300

If an accounting period falls within two financial years, for which different fractions apply, it is necessary to apportion the net chargeable gains on a time basis and apply the appropriate fraction to each part, notwithstanding that the gain will fall in only one financial year.

However if there is a change in the rate of corporation tax, the total profits, including chargeable gains after the appropriate reduction, for the whole accounting period, must be apportioned in addition to the apportionment described above.

Allowable capital losses are set against capital gains, before the reduction of 11/26, of the same accounting period or of later accounting periods. Allowable capital losses are not to be set against any other profits. However, trading losses can be set against chargeable gains (after reduction by 11/26) and included in total profits of the same or an immediately preceding accounting period (see Chapter 18).

Until the financial year 1979, the amount included in total profits of an authorised unit trust (see s. 358, I.C.T.A. 1970), or an approved investment trust (see s. 359, I.C.T.A. 1970), in respect of net chargeable gains was also reduced by a fraction. This fraction varied and was intended to equate with the credits against Capital Gains Tax granted to unit-holders or shareholders in such trusts. In recent years the figures have been as follows:

Financial year	Reduction	C.T. rate	Effective rate
1972	5/8	40%	15%
1973	37/52	52%	15%
1974	71/104	52%	$16\frac{1}{2}\%$
1975–1976	69/104	52%	$17\frac{1}{2}\%$
1977–1979	21/26	52%	10%

Section 81, F.A. 1980 abolished the liability of unit and investment trusts to tax on investment gains. Concurrently the 10% tax credit available to unit-holders or shareholders on gains on sale of unit or investment trust units were also abolished.

§ 2.—RECOVERY FROM SHAREHOLDERS (s. 266, I.C.T.A. 1970)

The Revenue is protected from loss of tax due on of chargeable gains realised by a company where the company makes a capital distribution, other than as a reduction of share capital.

If the corporation tax due in respect of the chargeable gain (as part of total profits) remains unpaid later than six months after the due date, assessments can be raised within two years of the due date (i.e. within a further eighteen months) to recover the tax from the recipient shareholders in proportion to their holdings. A person so charged has a right of recovery against the company. Such assessments can only be made upon shareholders who are "connected" with the company (i.e. controlling the company alone or with others).

A charge made under this provision has no effect upon the liability of a shareholder in respect of chargeable gains realised in respect of his shareholding.

§ 3.—TRANSFER OF ASSETS ON RECONSTRUCTION OR AMALGAMATION (s. 267, I.C.T.A. 1970)

Where assets are transferred from one company to another as part of a scheme of reconstruction or amalgamation, the chargeable gains thereby arising are, in effect, and subject to certain conditions, exempted from corporation tax. This is achieved by deeming that the assets are sold at a price which gives rise to neither a gain nor a loss.

The conditions referred to are:
> (*a*) the scheme must involve the transfer of the whole or part of a company's business to another company;

(*b*) both companies must be resident in U.K.;

(*c*) the transferor company must receive no part of the consideration transfer (except by the other company taking over liabilities of the business);

(*d*) this provision does not apply to those assets which were included in the transferor company's trading stock before the transfer;

(*e*) similarly, the provision does not apply if the assets are acquired as trading stock by the transferee company;

(*f*) the provision does not apply for the transfer of all or part of a company's business to a unit trust for exempt unit-holders.

Where assets were held before 6th April 1965, the transferee company is deemed to have acquired them at the time of original acquisition by the transferor company.

This relief only applies to transactions in course of reconstructions or amalgamations involving the exchange of assets which are carried out for *bona fide* commercial reasons and not part of a scheme having as a main purpose the avoidance of Capital Gains Tax, Corporation Tax or Income Tax.

If as a result of the new restrictions tax falls to be charged, the primary liability is upon the company disposing of its assets. But if such company has been wound up the tax is assessable, in the name of the disposing company, upon the acquiring company. If tax assessed upon a company, as above, remains unpaid six months after the due date then the Revenue may recover the tax from any company which now holds the assets whether as a result of the original transfer or because of a subsequent intra-group transfer. This secondary assessment must be made within two years of the due date.

There is a procedure whereby clearance of a proposed transaction can be sought from the Board.

This provision is also applied in practice (SP 5/85) to a division of a company's undertaking into two or more companies owned by two or more groups from the original shareholders (e.g. on a family split).

§ 4.—INTEREST CHARGED TO CAPITAL (s. 269, I.C.T.A. 1970; s. 38, F.A. 1981)

Prior to 1st April 1981 if a company incurred expenditure on the construction of a building, structure or works which would qualify as allowable expenditure in the computation of chargeable gains on the disposal of building, etc. and that expenditure was met from borrowed money, the interest of which was charged to capital, such interest was an allowable deduction in the computation of chargeable gains. This treatment only applied to interest relating to periods before the disposal. Interest charged to capital in this way could not be deducted from total profits as a charge on income under s. 248, I.C.T.A. 1970.

After 31st March 1981 a company can choose whether to claim interest which has been charged to capital as a charge on income or as an allowable deduction in computing the chargeable gain when the building is disposed of.

§ 5.—GILT-EDGED SECURITIES (s. 270, I.C.T.A. 1970, s. 58, F(No. 2) A 1975)

Gains arising on the disposal of certain Government stocks are exempt unless the disposal occurs less than 12 months after the acquisition thereof. The complex rules for identifying disposals with acquisitions can be summarised as follows:

(i) Acquisitions and disposals of securities on the same day are treated as a single acquisition and a single disposal and matched the one to the other. If the securities so disposed of exceed those so acquired the excess is, in general treated as diminishing a quantity of securities treated as subsequently acquired, taking the earliest acquisitions first.

 (ii) In other cases, each disposal (taking the earliest disposal first) is identified with acquisitions within 12 months preceding the disposal, taking the earliest acquisitions within that period first.

 (iii) If a loss is sustained on the disposal of securities and securities of the same class are re-acquired within one month of disposal (or six months if the re-acquisition is not through a stock exchange), that loss can only be deducted from a chargeable gain on the subsequent disposal of the securities re-acquired.

Although the above rules prevented "bed and breakfast" deals in gilt-edged securities, it was possible to gain benefit by means of a variation of "double-banking". This was achieved by buying new securities before, instead of after the original securities were sold, so they were not identified with each other.

With effect from 2nd July 1986 all disposals of gilt-edged securities and qualifying corporate bonds (whether within 12 months of acquisition or not) are exempt (s. 67, F.A. 1985).

"Bed and breakfast" (all shares)

Companies are prevented, except in respect of small transactions, from establishing allowable capital losses on shares and securities by selling and re-purchasing ("bed and breakfast"), or by purchasing further shares at a lower price and selling part of the new larger holding ("double-banking"). Shares purchased and sold within a "prescribed period" are identified with each other and not with acquisitions and disposals outside the period.

The "prescribed period" is as follows:

 (i) within one month before or one month after a sale through a stock exchange or through ARIEL (Automated Real-Time Investment Exchange Ltd)

 (ii) In other cases—six calendar months before or after disposal.

These provisions apply only for holdings of 2% or more of the issued shares of the company of the class concerned.

There are extensive and complex rules for identifying shares, including not only shares held by the company concerned but also shares held or dealt with by other companies in the same 75% group. These rules do not apply where shares are held as trading stock or to disposals and acquisitions between companies in a 75% group.

§ 6.—LIQUIDATION (ss. 245, 265, I.C.T.A. 1970, s. 19, C.G.T.A. 1979)

The appointment of a liquidator does not give rise to a disposal of a company's assets. The acts of the liquidator are deemed to be those of the company. Transfers between the liquidator and the company, or vice versa, during the course of winding up are ignored. However, distributions during liquidation to shareholders are treated as disposals (or part disposals) by the shareholders.

Disposals of assets during the course of winding-up give rise to chargeable gains or allowable losses in the normal way. Where, however assets are distributed *in specie* (in kind) to the members of the company, the assets are treated as being distributed to and acquired by the member concerned at the market value of the asset at the time of distribution.

In order to prevent delay in the completion of a liquidation, the fraction by which the chargeable gain is reduced before inclusion in a company's total profits and the rate of corporation tax applied thereto, are those applying for the financial year which ended prior to the completion of the winding up. If, before the completion of the winding-up, that fraction or that corporation tax rate become known, then the revised fraction or rate should be used.

22. Corporation Tax—Groups and Consortia

§ 1.—INTRODUCTION

Where two or more companies are members of a group (a definition which has various meanings depending upon the circumstances in which it is being applied) special treatment applies for certain transactions between them. The main areas for which special treatment may apply being:

(a) Payment of dividends without A.C.T. (see § 3);

(b) Payment of charges on income without deduction of income tax (see § 3);

(c) Surrender of A.C.T. (see § 4);

(d) Transfer of chargeable assets on a no gain—no loss basis (see § 5 and 6);

(e) Group relief for trading and other losses (see § 7).

Special treatment also applies under items (a), (b) and (e) to a company owned by a consortium.

§ 2.—DEFINITIONS (ss. 526(5) and 532, I.C.T.A. 1970)

There are a number of definitions of general application although subject, in certain cases, to modification:

(i) *"Ordinary share capital"* means all the issued share capital (by whatever name called) of the company, other than capital the holders whereof have a right to a dividend at a fixed rate, but have no other right to share in the profits of the company.

(ii) *"Preference dividend"* means a dividend payable on a preferred share, or preferred stock, at a fixed rate per cent, or, where a dividend is payable on a preferred share, or preferred stock, partly at a fixed rate per cent and partly at a variable rate, such part of that dividend as is payable at a fixed rate per cent.

(iii) A company is:

(a) a *"51% subsidiary"* of another company if, and so long as, more than 50% of its ordinary share capital is owned *directly or indirectly* by that company;

(b) a *"75% subsidiary"* of another company if, and so long as, not less than 75% of its ordinary share capital is owned *directly or indirectly* by that company;

(c) a *"90% subsidiary"* of another company if, and so long as, not less than 90% of its ordinary share capital *is directly* owned by that other company;

"Owned directly or indirectly" by a company means owned, either

—directly; or

—through another company (or companies); or

—partly directly and partly through another company (or companies).

Note the distinction between 51% and 75% subsidiaries, where ownership can be direct or indirect and 90% subsidiaries, where ownership can only be direct.

Where a company owns less than the whole of another company's ordinary share capital, and in particular where there is a series of companies, it is necessary to consider fractional interests.

Example 1

A Ltd
|
100%
|
B Ltd
|
80%
|
C Ltd
|
80%
|
D Ltd

Relationship	*Interest*
A Ltd—B Ltd	100%
A Ltd—C Ltd	80% (100% × 80%)
A Ltd—D Ltd	64% (100% × 80% × 80%)

Example 2

E Ltd

90%		80%
F Ltd		G Ltd
90%		70%
H Ltd		J Ltd
50%		50%
K Ltd		K Ltd

Relationship	*Interest*	
E Ltd—F Ltd	90%	
E Ltd—G Ltd	80%	
E Ltd—H Ltd	81%	(90% × 90%)
E Ltd—J Ltd	56%	(80% × 70%)
E Ltd—K Ltd	$68\frac{1}{2}$%	(90% × 90% × 50% = $40\frac{1}{2}$%
		+ 80% × 70% × 50% = 28%)

§ 3.—GROUP INCOME (ss. 256 and 257, I.C.T.A. 1970, s. 46, F.A. 1984)

The general definitions in § 2 are modified for this purpose, and some additional definitions apply.

    (*a*) To determine whether a company is a "*51% subsidiary*" of another, ignore:

        (i) share capital which it owns directly or indirectly in a non-resident company; or

        (ii) any share capital which it owns indirectly, and which is owned directly by a company for which a profit on the sale of the shares would be a trading receipt (i.e. a company which buys and sells shares).

(*b*) *"Trading company"* means a company whose business consists wholly or mainly of the carrying on of a trade or trades.

(*c*) *"Trading or holding company"* means a trading company or a company which holds the shares of trading companies which are its 90% subsidiaries.

(*d*) a company is *"owned by a consortium"* if at least 75% of its ordinary share capital is beneficially owned by five or fewer United Kingdom resident companies, of which none beneficially owns less than 5% of that capital; those companies are called the members of the consortium. For payments made after 31st December 1984 the restriction on the number of members (previously five) is lifted. At least 75% of the ordinary share capital must be owned by U.K. resident companies. Since each such company must hold at least 5% there is, in effect, a limit of 20 members.

PAYMENT OF DIVIDENDS WITHOUT A.C.T.

As a general rule, a United Kingdom company which makes a qualifying distribution to another United Kingdom resident company must make a payment of A.C.T. and the recipient company is entitled to a tax credit. However, where both companies are bodies corporate resident in the United Kingdom, and the company paying the dividends is:

(*a*) a *51% subsidiary* of the other, or both are *51% subsidiaries* of a third; or

(*b*) *a trading or holding company owned by a consortium*, the members of which include the company receiving the dividends;

the companies may jointly elect that no liability to A.C.T. is incurred by the paying company, and the recipient company is not entitled to any tax credit. In this situation the dividends are referred to as *"group income"*, not franked investment income of the recipient company.

For this purpose it is the declared amount of the dividend which is paid and not the gross equivalent thereof (i.e. the tax which would otherwise have been paid to the Revenue is not added onto the normal amount of dividend and the aggregate amount paid to the shareholder). The purpose of this procedure is to avoid the need for successive payment to and repayment by the Revenue of A.C.T. relating to dividends paid and received.

Notwithstanding that an election is in force, a company can still pay a dividend together with a payment of A.C.T., if it wishes to do so. This would leave A.C.T. available for set off against the corporation tax liability of the paying company.

The election cannot be made if a profit on the sale of the investment on which the distribution was made would be a trading profit. Neither can it be made if the company receiving the dividend would be entitled because of any exemption from tax, to claim repayment of the tax credit.

Example 1

Kola Ltd has a wholly owned subsidiary Lola Ltd. The results of the companies, for the year ended 31st March 1986, are:

	Kola Ltd	Lola Ltd
	£	£
Trading profit.	340,000	45,000
Interest received	10,000	—
Dividends paid (net).	35,000	17,500
F.I.I. (gross)	—	25,000

(1) If dividends are paid without A.C.T. the position is

	Kola Ltd £		*Lola Ltd* £
Case I, Schedule D..........	340,000	Case I, Schedule D	45,000
Case III, Schedule D........	10,000		
Profits liable to Corpora- tion Tax	£350,000	Profits liable to Corpora- tion Tax................	£45,000

	£			£
Corporation Tax at 40%.....	140,000	Corporation Tax at 30% ... A.C.T. on F.I.I.		13,500
Less: A.C.T. on dividends paid—£35,000 × 3/7	15,000	£25,000 × 30%	7,500	—

Mainstream Corporation
    Tax ....
	£125,000	Mainstream Corporation
		    Tax....................
				£13,500

		Surplus F.I.I.	£7,500	

(ii) If A.C.T. is paid on the dividends the position is

		Kola Ltd £			*Lola Ltd* £
	£			£	
Case I, Schedule D....		340,000	Case I, Schedule D		45,000
Case III, Schedule D...		10,000			
Profits liable to Cor- poration Tax		£350,000	Profits liable to Cor- poration Tax........		£45,000

		£			£
Corporation Tax at 40%...............		140,000			13,500

Less: A.C.T. on
    dividends paid
    —£35,000 × 3/7
	15,000		*Less:* A.C.T. on
			    dividends paid
			    £17,500 × 3/7
				7,500	

Less: A.C.T.
    on F.I.I.
    £25,000
    × 30%....
	7,500	7,500	*Less:* A.C.T.
			    on F.I.I.
			    £25,000
			    × 30% ....
				7,500	—

Mainstream Corpora- tion Tax		£132,500	Mainstream Corpora- tion Tax............		£13,500
			Surplus F.I.I.	Nil	

The benefit in this situation is that Lola Ltd has utilised its F.I.I. and Kola Ltd gains a cash flow advantage in that its A.C.T. liability is reduced to £7,500.

The paying company may pay A.C.T. in respect of "any amount of dividends", which means that A.C.T. can be paid on one dividend but not the next, and/or on a part only of a dividend and not on the remainder.

Dividends paid to shareholders who are not party to a group income election give rise to a liability to account for A.C.T. thereon in the normal way.

Example 2

Slow Ltd has the following share capital

Ordinary shares of £1 each

Rapid Ltd (parent company)	80,000
Others..	20,000
	£100,000

7% Preference shares of £1 each
Rapid Ltd (parent company)   10,000

An interim dividend of 14% is declared on the ordinary shares. A final dividend of 21% is declared on the ordinary shares. An election to pay dividends without A.C.T. is in force between Rapid Ltd and Slow Ltd.

	Dividend paid			A.C.T. paid	
Interim					
£80,000 × 14%	11,200		without A.C.T.	—	
£20,000 × 14%	2,800		with A.C.T.	1,200	(election not avail-able)
	£14,000				
Final					
		£8,400	without A.C.T.	—	
£80,000 at 21%	16,800	£8,400	with A.C.T.	3,600	(notwith-standing election)
£20,000 at 21%	4,200				
	£21,000		with A.C.T.	1,800	(election not avail-able)
Preference					
£10,000 at 7%	£700		without A.C.T.	—	
				£6,600	

PAYMENT OF CHARGES ON INCOME WITHOUT DEDUCTION OF INCOME TAX

Charges on income can be paid by a *51% subsidiary* company to its parent company in full, without deduction of basic rate income tax, if the two companies make a joint election to that effect.

The right of election is also available where both companies are resident in the United Kingdom, and the company paying the charge on income is:

(*a*) the parent of a *51% subsidiary* company; or

(*b*) a fellow *51% subsidiary* of a third company; or

(*c*) a *trading or holding company owned by a consortium*, the members of which include the company receiving the charge on income.

It should be noted that whilst an election to pay charges on income without deduction of basic rate income tax is in force, all charges thereafter must be made gross, even if circumstances arise in which this would be disadvantageous.

PROCEDURE

The joint elections detailed above must be made to the Inspector in writing, setting out all the facts necessary to show that the companies concerned are entitled to make the election.

The election is not effective for dividends paid less than three months after the notice is given and before the Inspector has notified the companies concerned that the election is accepted as valid. In practice, the Revenue may "back date" their approval to validate a payment, or to permit a payment without A.C.T. or deduction of income tax.

An election, once made, continues in force until revoked by notice in writing to the Inspector, by either company, or until the conditions necessary for a valid election cease to apply.

If a company pays a dividend without a corresponding payment of A.C.T., or pays a charge on income without deduction of income tax on the basis of an invalid election, as where no election has been made the Inspector may make such adjustments, assessments or set-offs as necessary to correct the position. If any tax so assessed is not paid by the company within three months of the due date, it can be recovered from the recipient company. The recipient company, in such a case, has a right of recovery of the tax so paid from the paying company.

§ 4.—SURRENDER OF SURPLUS A.C.T. (s. 92, F.A. 1972)

A company can surrender to its 51% subsidiary any A.C.T. paid by it in respect of dividends (but not other distributions) in an accounting period (and not repaid to it i.e.: surplus A.C.T.). The amount of A.C.T. which is available for surrender is limited to A.C.T. paid on dividends of the parent's (i.e. the surrendering company's) current accounting period, and cannot include A.C.T. carried back or forward from other accounting periods. It is a matter of choice for the surrendering company whether it surrenders all, or only part, of the A.C.T. paid by it, and also which of any suitably qualified subsidiaries receive the benefit.

A.C.T. which can be surrendered is referred to as "*surplus A.C.T.*". This can be misleading, as it is possible to surrender *all* A.C.T. paid on dividends.

In order to qualify for the right to surrender A.C.T., both companies must be resident in the United Kingdom, and the subsidiary must have been a 51% subsidiary throughout the parent's accounting period.

Limitation of subsidiaries
A company will only be regarded as a subsidiary if:
    (i) there are no arrangements by which any person could obtain 'control' of the subsidiary company without obtaining control of the parent company;
    (ii) the parent company is beneficially entitled to more than 50% of the profits available for distribution to equity shareholders of the subsidiary company, or would be entitled to more than 50% of any assets of the subsidiary available for distribution to the equity shareholders on a winding-up.
The usual rule for determining a 51% subsidiary is applied, except that the parent company is not treated as the owner of:
    (i) shares held as trading stock;
    (ii) shares owned indirectly through a company which holds them as trading stock;
    (iii) shares owned directly or indirectly in a company which is not resident in the United Kingdom.

Particular points
(1) There is no provision whereby A.C.T. can be surrendered to a company owned by a consortium.

(2) Subject to the restrictions described below, the subsidiary can utilise the surrendered A.C.T. as though it had been paid by the subsidiary itself.

(3) If the parent and subsidiary companies have different accounting periods, the A.C.T. surrendered must be assigned to the appropriate accounting period, or periods, of the subsidiary.

(4) Where a single dividend is paid (or more than one if all were paid on the same day) the subsidiary may apply the benefit of the A.C.T. received on the basis that it had, itself, paid A.C.T. on a distribution on that same day.

(5) Where the surrendered A.C.T. arises from several dividends, the subsidiary must apply the surrendered A.C.T. on the basis that it paid dividends on the actual dates the dividends were paid by the parent. Surplus A.C.T. is apportioned between the dividends and related to the date on which those dividends were paid.

(6) A.C.T. surrendered cannot be set against the corporation tax liability for any accounting period during all, or part, of which it is not a subsidiary of the surrendering company.

(7) A.C.T. surrendered can be used in the current year or can be carried forward, but *it cannot be carried back*. Surrendered A.C.T. must, however, be used in priority to A.C.T. on a subsidiary's own distributions.

An unrelieved balance of A.C.T. in a subsidiary company may thus comprise, in whole or in part, the subsidiary's own A.C.T. which can be carried back to accounting periods beginning in the two preceding years.

(8) A.C.T. which has already been applied, by way of set off, is not available for surrender (and vice versa), so that a double allowance is prevented.

(9) The subsidiary may make a payment to the surrendering company for the amount surrendered. However, such a payment is neither taxable income in the hands of the recipient, nor an allowable deduction to the paying company.

Claims
Claims for this form of relief must be made within six years of the end of the accounting period in which the A.C.T. was paid. The claim is made by the surrendering company, but requires the consent of the recipient subsidiary company which must be notified to the Inspector.

Example 1

Flame Ltd had trading profits of £260,000 in the year ended 31st March 1986, and during that period paid a dividend of £9,000. Its subsidiary, Sword Ltd, had trading profits of £18,000 in the same period. Flame Ltd surrendered £2,000 of its A.C.T. to Sword Ltd. The position was as follows:

Flame Ltd

	£	£
Case I, Schedule D.............................		260,000
Corporation Tax at 40%		104,000
Less: A.C.T. £9,000 × 3/7	3,857	
Deduct A.C.T. surrendered	2,000	1,857
Mainstream Tax................................		£102,143

Sword Ltd

	£	£
Case I, Schedule D.............................		18,000
Corporation Tax at 30%		5,400
Less: A.C.T. surrendered		2,000
Mainstream Tax................................		£3,400

Example 2

The following information relates to Peace Ltd and its subsidiary Quiet Ltd (60%).

	31st March 1985 £	31st March 1986 £
Peace Ltd		
Trading profits..............................	150,000	220,000
Interest	2,000	2,000
Capital gains *less* allowable losses..............	199,333	191,533
Dividends received (net)		
From Quiet Ltd under group election..........	18,090	18,900
From other U.K. companies	13,400	23,100
Dividends paid (net)..........................	127,300	196,000
Interest paid (gross)..........................	22,000	19,500
Quiet Ltd		
Trading profits..............................	44,000	36,000
Capital gains *less* allowable losses..............	—	17,333
Dividends paid (net)		
To Peace Ltd under group election	18,090	18,900
To other shareholders......................	17,500	12,600

In the following calculation the following assumptions are made:
   (i) Peace Ltd only surrenders A.C.T. which it cannot itself use in the current accounting period;
   (ii) Relief is taken as early as possible;
   (iii) Surplus A.C.T. is carried forward by Quiet Ltd;
   (iv) Peace Ltd obtained full relief for A.C.T. in the years to 31st March 1983 and 31st March 1984;
   (v) In the years ended 31st March 1983 and 31st March 1984 the position of Quiet Ltd was:

	31st March 1983 £46,000	31st March 1984 £40,800
Trading profits.......................	£46,000	£40,800
A.C.T. set-off	£7,000	£11,900

	31st March 1985			31st March 1986	
Peace Ltd	£	£		£	£
Case I, Schedule D.........		150,000			220,000
Case III, Schedule D........		2,000			2,000
Capital Gains..............	172,500			147,333	
Less: 1/3...............	57,500	115,000	1/4	36,833	110,500
		267,000			332,500
Charges on income		22,000			19,500
Profits liable to Corpora-tion Tax		£245,000			£313,000
Corporation Tax at 45%....		110,250	at 40%		125,200
Less: A.C.T. set off					
Dividends paid £127,300	54,557		£196,000	84,000	
Dividends rec'd 13,400	5,743		23,100	9,900	
	£113,900	48,814		172,900	74,100

	31st March 1985			31st March 1986	
	£	£		£	£
Maximum set off ([£245,000 − £115,000] × 30%).............	39,000	39,000	([£313,000 − £110,500] × 30%)	60,750	60,750
Surplus A.C.T. surrendered to Quiet Ltd	£9,814			£13,350	
Mainstream Corporation Tax		£71,250			£50,010
Quiet Ltd					
Case I, Schedule D.........		44,000			36,000
Capital gains..............		—		13,333	
Less reduction............		—	1/4	3,333	10,000
Profits liable to corporation tax.................		£44,000			£46,000
Corporation tax at 30%		13,200	(30%)		13,800
Less A.C.T. set off:					
Dividends paid (£17,500)..			(£12,600)		
A.C.T. at 3/7.............	7,500			5,400	
Received from Peace Ltd .	9,814			13,350	
	17,314			18,750	
Maximum set off (£44,000 × 30%).............	13,200	13,200	(£36,000 × 30%)...	10,800	10,800
Surplus A.C.T. carried back	£4,114*				
Surplus A.C.T. carried forward				£7,950	
		Nil			£3,000

Example 3

Hop Ltd has a wholly owned subsidiary Skip Ltd. Hop Ltd draws up its accounts to 31st March, whereas Skip Ltd makes its accounts up to 31st December.

---

* This represents Quiet Ltd's own A.C.T. (that surrendered by Peace Ltd being used in priority). It is therefore available for carry-back.

		£	£	£
31.3.84	£40,800 at 30% =	12,240		
	Less: already set off	11,900	340	340
31.3.83	£46,000 at 30% =	13,800		
	Less: already set off	7,000	6,800	3,774
				£4,114

The companies have the following results:

Skip Ltd	31st December 1984		31st December 1985	
Trading profits	£7,000		£8,000	

Hop Ltd			31st March 1985	
Case I, Schedule D.................................			24,000	
Corporation tax at 30%			9,600	
Less: A.C.T. set off				
Dividends paid (1.12.84)....................	6,700	2,871		
(1.3.85)....................	13,400	5,743		
	£20,100	8,614		
Maximum set off				
(£24,000 × 30%)		7,200	7,200	
Surrendered to Skip Ltd		£1,414		
Mainstream Corporation tax..........................			£2,400	

	31st December 1984		31st December 1985	
Skip Ltd				
Case I, Schedule D.........	£7,000		£8,000	
Corporation tax at 30%				
	2,100		2,400	
Less: A.C.T. set off				
Received from Hop Ltd				
6,700/20,100 × £1,414 ...	471			
13,400/20,100 × £1,414 ...			943	
Mainstream Corporation Tax .	£1,629		£1,457	

Distributions after 6th April 1982
As a result of the introduction of the provisions for a company to acquire its own shares (see Chapter 15, § 8), the reference to dividends for A.C.T. surrender purposes is expanded to include distributions that may arise under the company acquisition of own shares rules.

§ 5.—GROUPS AND CAPITAL GAINS: INTRODUCTION

In general, transactions concerning chargeable assets between companies in a 75% group (as defined for this purpose) do not give rise to an immediate tax liability. Furthermore, there is an extension of the roll-over relief on the replacement of business assets to include re-investment by any company in a group. There are, however, special rules to deal with:
    (i) subsequent sales to persons outside the group;
    (ii) companies which leave the group;
    (iii) appropriations to/from trading stock in one company, and to/from chargeable assets in the other.

DEFINITIONS (s. 272, I.C.T.A. 1970)
The following definitions (or modified definitions) apply for group capital gains purposes.

(*a*) *Company*
The definition of a *"company"* is restricted so that the group capital gains provisions only apply to
- (i) companies as defined by the Companies Act 1985 (or equivalent in Northern Ireland);
- (ii) companies incorporated under any other Act, Royal Charter or letters patent;
- (iii) companies incorporated under the law of a foreign territory;

Only companies which are resident in the United Kingdom can be included in a group for this purpose.

(*b*) *75% Subsidiary*
The general definition of *"75% subsidiary"* applies.

(*c*) *Principal company*
A *"principal company"* is a company which has a 75% subsidiary.

(*d*) *Group*
A *"group"* comprises a principal company and all its 75% subsidiaries, and where a principal company is itself a 75% subsidiary of another company, and therefore a member of a group, then its 75% subsidiaries are also members of that group.

Sub-groups
Note that, where there is a sub-group the main group will include all the 75% subsidiaries in the sub-group, even though the principal company of the main group may have less than a 75% interest, taking account of fractional interest, in the sub-group subsidiaries.

Group changes
Even if there are changes in the composition of a group, it continues to be treated as a group for so long as the same company remains the principal company. If the principal company of a group becomes a 75% subsidiary of another company, and thereby joins another group, all its 75% subsidiaries will also join the new group.

Liquidation
If a company goes into liquidation, the passing of a resolution, or making of an order, for its winding-up (whether it be the principal company or one of the 75% subsidiaries) does not of itself cause the company concerned to leave the group when tracing through the ownership of companies to identify those within a group for capital gains purposes.

Non-residents and dealing companies
A non-resident company breaks a "chain", but dealing companies (where the sale of shares = trading profit) do not.

§ 6.—GROUPS AND CAPITAL GAINS: EFFECT

TRANSFERS OF ASSETS WITHIN A GROUP (s. 273, I.C.T.A. 1970)
Intra-group transfers of assets are treated as if they were made for a consideration which would secure that neither a gain nor a loss was realised. However, on an ultimate disposal to a third party the gain is calculated as the difference between

the disposal price and the price on acquisition by a group member, irrespective of whether the company was the owner on sale. In practice, however, the Revenue claim that the asset must have been *used* by the ultimate company before the disposal occurs.

There are certain occasions when this general rule does not apply, and the disposal gives rise to a chargeable gain.

  (i) A disposal of a debt (of an assessable type) due from a group member by satisfaction of the debt;
 (ii) A disposal of redeemable shares in a company on the occasion of their redemption;
(iii) Capital sums (e.g. compensation) which is, ultimately paid by persons outside the group.

The Revenue regard a transfer of assets by a group company in liquidation as being covered by the general rule. The transfer of an asset, *in specie*, is covered but the shareholder company is treated as having made a disposal (or part disposal) of the shares concerned.

Example

Aardvark Ltd acquired the entire share capital of Bark Ltd. Mark Bark, a shareholder in Bark Ltd, had made a loan of £10,000 to Bark Ltd.

Aardvark Ltd also acquired this loan account (i.e. they took over the right to receive repayment thereof) for a nominal consideration of £1,000.

Later Bark Ltd repaid the loan to Aardvark Ltd.

Aardvark Ltd realised a capital gain of £9,000. This is chargeable, as the transaction is not protected by the group transfer rules.

TRADING STOCK (s. 274, I.C.T.A. 1970)

If a group member acquires an asset as trading stock from another group member where it was held as a fixed asset, the acquiring company is treated as acquiring a fixed asset and immediately appropriating it to trading stock, at market value.

A company which acquires trading stock in these circumstances can elect to defer any capital gain arising by deducting it from the value of the trading stock taken into account in computing the profits of the trade for Case I, Schedule D profit. If the transfer of an asset into the trading stock of another company realises an allowable loss, that loss can, on election, be added to the value of trading stock, thereby converting an allowable capital loss into a trading loss. In effect the assets are being taken into trading stock at their original cost to the transferor company.

Example 1

Cake Ltd acquired a fixed asset for £40,000. The amount is transferred into the trading stock of Bread Ltd, a member of the same group, at which time it is worth £50,000.

The transfer from Cake Ltd to Bread Ltd is deemed to take place at a no gain—no loss price, i.e. £40,000.

When Bread takes the asset into trading stock, it realises a gain of £10,000 (£50,000—£40,000).

Bread Ltd has the option to reduce its stock by deducting therefrom the gain of £10,000. This has the effect of increasing the Case I, Schedule D profits—or decreasing the trading loss—of Bread Ltd.

Example 2

Chip Ltd acquired a fixed asset for £12,000. The asset is transferred into the trading stock of Dale Ltd, a member of the same group, at which time it is worth £8,000.

The transfer from Chip Ltd to Dale Ltd is deemed to take place at a no gain—no loss price, i.e. £12,000.

When Dale Ltd takes the asset into trading stock, it realises an allowable loss of £4,000 (£12,000 − £8,000).

Dale Ltd has the option to increase its stock by addition thereto of the loss of £4,000. (This has the effect of decreasing the Case I, Schedule D profit—or increasing the trading loss—of Dale Ltd.)

Example 3

Frost Ltd acquired an asset as trading stock for £15,000.

The asset is transferred to Flood Ltd, where it will be held as a fixed asset. At this time the asset is worth £25,000.

Frost Ltd credits its trading account with the deemed proceeds of £25,000.

Flood Ltd is now treated as having acquired a fixed asset at an original cost of £25,000 and the asset is transferred to Flood Ltd at a no gain—no loss price of £25,000.

Where a group member disposes of an asset from trading stock to a group member which acquires it as a fixed asset, the company making the disposal is treated as appropriating the asset from trading stock, at market value, immediately before the disposal.

DISPOSAL OUTSIDE THE GROUP (s. 275, I.C.T.A. 1970)
The following additional rules apply on the ultimate disposal outside the group, of assets previously transferred within the group:

   (i) when assets have had capital allowances granted on them, any loss on the sale is restricted for capital gains tax purposes. For an asset used within a group, all the capital allowances which have been granted to members of the group on the particular asset are included, even when the company owning the asset leaves the group.

  (ii) If the asset was originally acquired before 6th April 1965, then all the members of a group are considered to be one person for the purpose of applying the special rules for such assets. This enables a company which disposes of such an asset, which it has acquired by a no gain—no loss intra-group transfer, to obtain the benefit of time apportionment of a gain or loss over the group ownership of the asset, or alternatively it can make an election for valuation as at 6th April 1965.

Example 4

Shake Ltd acquired an asset on 6th April 1960 for £5,000.

On 6th April 1970 the asset was transferred to Rattle Ltd, another member of the group, for £10,000.

On 6th April 1975 it was transferred to Roll Ltd, also a member of the group, for £15,000. Roll Ltd sold the asset on 5th April 1985 for £20,000.

The chargeable gain is computed as follows:

	£
Disposal proceeds	20,000
Less Acquisition cost to Shake Ltd	5,000
Overall gain	15,000
Less Gain accrued before 6th April 1965, 5/25 × £15,000	3,000
Capital gain	12,000
Less 1/3 reduction	4,000
Chargeable gain	£8,000

(N.B. 6th April 1965 valuation is assumed to be disadvantageous).

REPLACEMENT OF BUSINESS ASSETS (ss. 276, I.C.T.A. 1970)

For the purposes of roll-over relief on the replacement of business assets, all the trades carried on by the members of a group are treated as a single trade.

This means that an asset purchased by one company and then transferred to another in the same group which carries on a different trade, would qualify for roll-over relief if sold and replaced, even if the new asset was for another member carrying on a different trade.

The provisions for rolling-over gains where the re-investment is in wasting assets are similarly extended for group members.

REVENUE RIGHTS OF TAX RECOVERY (s. 277, I.C.T.A. 1970)

If a group company has realised a capital gain upon which tax is due and the tax remains unpaid after six months from the due date that tax may be recovered by the Revenue from any member which within two years prior to the disposal date had the necessary financial interest in the asset concerned. This right extends over an eighteen-month period commencing six months after the tax was due to be paid, and ending two years after the tax was due. A company which makes such a payment to the Revenue has a right of recovery from the company realising the chargeable gain.

COMPANY LEAVING A GROUP (ss. 278, 278A and 279, I.C.T.A. 1970)

General rule

A company leaving a group is deemed to have disposed of all its chargeable assets taken over within the group during the preceding six years on a no gain, no loss basis. A company which is in course of winding-up is not treated as leaving the group.

The provisions above do not apply to assets which have been transferred between associated companies which leave the group at the same time. Companies are treated as associated if they, of themselves, would constitute a group.

The chargeable gain realised by the company leaving the group is calculated as if a disposal had been made at market value at the time of the original transfer (*not* the date when the company left the group).

Example

Termite Ltd acquired a building for £100,000 in 1977.

In 1980 the building, now worth £150,000, was transferred to Grub Ltd, another company in the same group. In 1982 Grub Ltd ceased to be in the Termite Ltd group, having been sold to another group. In 1985 Grub Ltd sold the asset for £180,000.

The capital gain position is:

Termite Ltd

1980	No effect.	

Grub Ltd

1980	When Grub Ltd leaves the Termite Ltd group in 1982 it is deemed to have disposed of its asset (acquired from Termite Ltd) in 1980 at the date it acquired it from Termite Ltd, and at the market value of the asset at the time of transfer.	
	Deemed proceeds	£150,000
	Deemed acquisition cost	100,000
	Capital gain	£50,000
1985	Disposal proceeds	£180,000
	Deemed re-acquisition cost	150,000
	Capital gain	£30,000

If any corporation tax due from the company leaving the group on this notional chargeable gain remains unpaid after six months, it can be recovered by the Revenue at any time within the eighteen-month period beginning six months after the tax was due and ending two years after the tax was due to be paid. The Revenue can recover from:

   (i) the principal company of the group at the time the chargeable company left the group; or
  (ii) if different, the principal company when the tax fell due. This provision is extended to include an associated company which owned the asset when the chargeable company left the group, or a company owning the asset when the tax fell due for payment.

Any company making such a payment of corporation tax has a right of recovery against the chargeable company.

Certain mergers

This general rule is relaxed where, *as part of a merger*, a company ("A") ceases to be a member of a group of companies (the "A" group) provided:

   (i) the merger was carried out for *bona fide* commercial reasons; and
  (ii) tax avoidance was not one of the main purposes of the merger.

"*Merger*" means an arrangement whereby:

  (*a*) an acquiring company (or companies), not being part of the "A" group, acquire(s) interest(s) in all or part of the business carried on by company "A"; such acquisition must not be with a view to their disposal; and
  (*b*) one or more companies in the "A" group acquire(s) interest(s) in all or part of the business carried on by the acquiring company, or by a company beneficially owned to the extent of at least 90% (of ordinary share capital) by two or more of the acquiring companies; such acquisition must not be with a view to their disposal.

The following conditions must be met:

   (i) not less than 25% by value (at the date of acquisition) of each of the interests acquired must consist of ordinary share capital, the remainder being share capital (of any description) or debentures or both; and
  (ii) the value of the interest(s) (determined as at the date of acquisition) in the "A" group must be substantially the same as in the other; and
 (iii) the consideration for the interests acquired by the acquiring company in the "A" group must consist of, or be applied in, the acquisition of interest(s) in the other group. For this purpose any consideration which is small by comparison with the total is disregarded.

These special merger rules also apply where any of the companies involved is resident outside the United Kingdom.

Shares in a subsidiary (s. 279, I.C.T.A. 1970)

Where a company leaves a group within six years following an amalgamation or reconstruction, the *chargeable company* upon whom the tax liability described below may fall is the company making the disposal of the shares, and not the company leaving the group. A company is not considered as leaving a group on a winding-up or dissolution.

The chargeable company is treated as though, at the time of the amalgamation or reconstruction, it had sold and immediately re-acquired the shares in the subsidiary at their market value at that time, and thereby realised a gain.

If the chargeable company has ceased to exist before the subsidiary concerned leaves the group, then the assessment is made upon the principal company.

Any corporation tax remaining unpaid by the chargeable company for more than six months after the due date for payment can be recovered by the Revenue at any time within the eighteen-month period beginning six months after the tax was due to be paid, and ending two years after the tax was due. The tax can be recovered from:

   (i) the principal company of the group (as at the due date, or at the time of the amalgamation); or
   (ii) any company taking an interest in the subsidiary as part of the amalgamation or reconstruction in the group.

Any company making such a payment has a right of recovery against the chargeable company.

Example

In 1980 Egg Ltd acquired shares in Chicken Ltd for £100,000.

By 1985 the shares have become worth £300,000 and so in an attempt to sell Chicken Ltd without incurring a capital gain, a new company, X Ltd (not a group member) is formed.

X Ltd acquires the shares of Chicken Ltd from Egg Ltd in exchange for X Ltd shares.

X Ltd is deemed to have acquired the shares at their market value in 1984, i.e. £300,000. When in due course X Ltd sells Chicken Ltd to a third party, the capital gain (if any) arising is calculated by reference to a deemed acquisition cost to X Ltd of £300,000.

Were it not for the provisions of s. 279, I.C.T.A. 1970, Egg Ltd would only realise its gain when it sold its shares in X Ltd. However under the rule, Egg Ltd is deemed to have sold its shares in Chicken Ltd for £300,000 immediately X Ltd acquired the shares, thereby realising a gain of £200,000 (£300,000 − £100,000).

DEPRECIATION TRANSACTIONS WITHIN A GROUP (ss. 280, 281, I.C.T.A. 1970)

Where the share value of a subsidiary is materially reduced by a depreciatory transaction a subsequent loss on the disposal of the subsidiary company's shares may be restricted by the Inspector of Taxes.

A *"depreciatory transaction"* is:

   (i) any disposal of assets at other than market value by one group member to another; or
   (ii) any other transaction to which the company making the ultimate disposal (or its 75% subsidiary) was a party, and where the parties to the transaction were or included two or more companies which, at the time of the transaction, were members of the same group.

A *"group of companies"* for this purpose can include companies which are not resident in the United Kingdom.

"Disposals of assets" include appropriations of goodwill from one group member to another, and *"disposals of shares"* include claims that such shares have become of negligible value.

Any (otherwise) allowable loss on the disposal is reduced on a just and reasonable basis, but depreciatory transactions which occurred when the company making the ultimate disposal was not a group member are ignored.

The provisions do not apply to reduce a gain arising on a subsequent disposal.

A depreciatory transaction which gives rise to an (otherwise) allowable loss may give rise to a chargeable gain in another company. However, if there has been any restriction in the allowable loss, an equivalent reduction in the amount of the chargeable gain is made.

Dividend stripping

This restriction of allowable losses also applies on the disposal of any shares or securities which a "first" company holds in a "second" company, provided the following conditions apply:

   (i) the holding (or aggregate holdings) by a first company amounts to, or is an ingredient in, 10% of all holdings of the same class in the second company;
   (ii) the first company does not own such a holding as a dealing asset;

(iii) a distribution is (or has been) made which materially reduces the value of the holding.

The reference to shares being an ingredient in a holding brings within the scope of these provisions holdings owned by connected persons which, in aggregate, amount to 10% of the total holdings by all persons of shares of the class concerned. The definition of connected persons is, for this purpose, extended to include rights to acquire a holding.

A holding in a company includes any holding of shares or securities which entitle the holder to receive distributions made by the company. Holdings of different classes of shares are treated as separate holdings, as are holdings which differ in the rights or obligations which they confer or impose.

Any distribution which has already been taken into account in computing a chargeable gain, or an allowable loss, realised by the person making the ultimate disposal is ignored.

Example

In 1980 Gull Ltd acquired the entire share capital of Hawk Ltd for £50,000.

Hawk Ltd had acquired a building for £10,000. In 1985 Hawk Ltd transferred the building (then worth £30,000) to Gull Ltd at its book value of £10,000. In 1983 Gull Ltd disposed of its shares in Hawk Ltd for £15,000, at a loss of £35,000.

The transfer of the building at book value is a depreciatory transaction. The apparent loss on the disposal of the shares in Hawk Ltd is restricted by the extent of the depreciation—£20,000 (£30,000 − £10,000). Thus the allowable loss on the disposal of the shares in Hawk Ltd is £15,000 (£35,000 − £20,000).

Note that, if Hawk Ltd had been sold for £60,000, thus realising a *gain* of £10,000, there is no increase in the gain under these rules despite the depreciatory transaction which had taken place.

§ 7.—GROUP RELIEF

GENERAL (s. 258, I.C.T.A. 1970, s. 47, F.A. 1984)

Relief for trading losses and other amounts eligible for relief from corporation tax may be surrendered by the "*surrendering company*", which is a member of a group of companies; and the "*claimant company*", which is a member of the same group, may on a claim to that effect be allowed relief from corporation tax called "*group relief*". The relief can flow either from parent to subsidiary, or vice-versa, or between fellow subsidiaries (note the difference therefore between group relief and A.C.T. surrender). Group relief is also available in the case of companies which are owned by consortia—"*consortium relief*" (see below). Unless expressly stated, the term group relief in this paragraph includes consortium relief.

BASIC REQUIREMENTS

(i) *Group relief*
- (*a*) Two companies are deemed to be members of a *group* of companies if one is the 75% subsidiary of the other, or both are 75% subsidiaries of a third company. (See below for additional qualifications and the effect of arrangements.)
- (*b*) In determining whether one company is a *75% subsidiary* of another, that other is treated as not being the owner of:
  - (i) Share capital which it owns directly as trading stock; or
  - (ii) Share capital which it owns indirectly, and which is owned directly by another company as trading stock; or

(iii) Share capital which it owns directly or indirectly in a non-resident company.

(*c*) A company must be resident in the United Kingdom to be regarded as a member of a group for group relief purposes.

(ii) *Consortium relief*

(*a*) Prior to 27th July 1984 a company was treated as being *owned by a consortium* if all the ordinary share capital was owned directly and beneficially owned between them by five or fewer companies. These companies are called the *members of the consortium.* There must be no shares owned by any individual.

For accounting periods ending after 26th July 1984 the definition of a consortium for group relief requires that at least 75% of the ordinary share capital must be owned by U.K. resident companies. Since each such company must hold at least 5% there is, in effect, a limit of 20 members.

(*b*) Consortium relief is available where the claimant company is a member of the consortium, and the surrendering company is:

    (i) a trading company which is owned by a consortium and which is not a 75% subsidiary of any company; or

    (ii) a trading company which is a 90% subsidiary of a holding company and not a 75% subsidiary of any other company, and the holding company is owned by the consortium; or

    (iii) a holding company which is owned by the consortium and which is not a 75% subsidiary of any company.

(*c*) A *holding company* is a company, the business of which consists wholly or mainly in the holding of shares of companies which are its 90% subsidiaries, and which are trading companies.

(*d*) A *trading company* is a company whose business consists wholly or mainly in the carrying on of a trade or trades.

No claim can be made by a member of the consortium if a profit on the sale, by that member, of shares in the surrendering or holding company would be a trading receipt, nor if the member's share in the consortium in the relevant accounting period of the surrendering or holding company is nil.

Consortium relief differs from group relief in the following respects:

    (i) For accounting periods ending before 11th March 1981 the claimant company must be a member of the owning consortium, i.e. relief is only "one-way" (upwards), thereafter the relief flows in either direction.

    (ii) relief, if given to or claimed by a consortium member, cannot exceed a fraction based on the members' share in the consortium.

The relief is as follows:

    1. Where the claimant company is a member of a consortium, only a fraction of the loss is offsettable.

    2. Where the surrendering company is a member of a consortium, the loss cannot be set against more than a fraction of the total profits of the claimant company.

In both cases the fraction is equal to the members' share in the consortium.

Example 1

Ade Ltd, Bade Ltd, Cade Ltd and Jade Ltd are members of a consortium owning the following percentages in Wade Ltd, a trading company. The results for the year ended 31st March 1986 are also shown.

	% Ownership		Results year ended 31.3.1986
Ade Ltd	15%	Profit	40,000
Bade Ltd	25%	Profit	20,000
Cade Ltd	20%	Profit	15,000
Jade Ltd	40%	Loss	(10,000)
Wade Ltd	—	Loss	(100,000)

Consortium relief can be claimed as follows:

	£	
Ade Ltd..................................	15,000	(15% × £100,000)
Bade Ltd	20,000	(restricted to available profits)
Cade Ltd	15,000	(restricted to available profits)
Jade Ltd.................................	Nil	(restricted to available profits)
	£50,000	

Wade Ltd will therefore have losses to carry forward or back as follows:

	£
Loss for the year	100,000
Less: Consortium relief.....................	50,000
	£50,000

Example 2

Assume in the above example the results were as follows:

		£
Ade Ltd	Loss	(40,000)
Bade Ltd	Loss	(20,000)
Cade Ltd	Loss	(5,000)
Jade Ltd	Loss	(110,000)
Wade Ltd	Profit	80,000

The relief under the consortium provisions is as follows:

Wade Ltd

		£	£
Profit......................................			80,000
Less losses surrendered from:			
Ade Ltd	15% × £80,000	12,000	
Bade Ltd	25% × £80,000		
	but restricted to actual loss.............	20,000	
Cade Ltd	20% × £80,000		
	but restricted to actual loss.............	5,000	
Jade Ltd	40% × £80,000	32,000	69,000
Adjusted taxable profit...........................			£11,000

The other companies will have losses to carry forward or back as follows:

	£
Ade Ltd..............................	28,000 (£40,000 − 12,000)
Bade Ltd	Nil
Cade Ltd	Nil
Jade Ltd.............................	78,000 (£110,000 − 32,000)

"*Payment for group relief* " means a payment made by the claimant company to the surrendering company, under an agreement between them in respect of an amount surrendered by way of group relief. Such a payment may not exceed the amount surrendered.

So far as the Revenue is concerned, the claimant may pay or not pay the surrendering company for the relief. If a payment is made, it will not be taken into account in computing profits and losses, neither will it be regarded as a distribution or a charge, provided it is made:

    (*a*) in pursuance of an agreement between the two companies in respect of group relief surrendered (no specific form of agreement is needed); and
    (*b*) it does not exceed the amount surrendered.

It is generally thought advisable to make some payment where there are minority shareholders, or where creditors' interests might be prejudiced.

There is no time limit for making the payment.

ADDITIONAL REQUIREMENTS FOR GROUP RELIEF ENTITLEMENT (s. 28, Schedule 12, F.A. 1973)

The introduction of first-year allowances created a number of situations where corporation tax losses arise, which cannot be used up in the foreseeable future. This was especially so with shipping and nationalised industries and created the temptation to "sell" the losses to financial institutions.

This was achieved by:

    (*a*) creating an artificial parent for the loss-maker; or
    (*b*) setting up a purpose-built consortium; or
    (*c*) transferring the loss-maker temporarily to a group that could use the losses.

To avoid this position, the 75% subsidiary test (90% re-consortia) was extended, and to qualify for group relief the following additional tests must be satisfied:

    (i) the parent company is beneficially entitled to not less than 75% (or 90%) of the *profits available for distribution to the equity holders* of the subsidiary company; and
    (ii) the parent company would be beneficially entitled to not less than 75% (or 90%) of any *assets* of the subsidiary company *available for distribution on a winding-up*.

The following additional definitions apply for these tests:

    (i) An "*Equity holder*" is a holder of "ordinary shares" or a "loan creditor" in respect of a loan which is not a normal commercial loan, and "profits available for distribution" include only those distributable to such a person in that capacity.
    (ii) "*Ordinary shares*" are all shares other than "*fixed-rate preference shares*", the latter being shares which:
        (*a*) are issued for consideration which is or includes new consideration; and
        (*b*) do not carry any right to conversion into, or for acquisition of further shares or securities; and
        (*c*) carry no rights to dividends other than of a fixed amount or rate, and do not exceed a reasonable commercial return on the new consideration given; and

(*d*) do not carry rights on repayment exceeding the new consideration except to a level given on comparable fixed dividend shares on the Stock Exchange.
(iii) *"Loan creditor"* is as defined for close company purposes (see Chapter 19, § 8), except that bank loans are included.
(iv) *"Normal commercial loan"* means a loan of or including "new consideration" which:
    (*a*) carries no conversion rights or rights to acquire additional securities; and
    (*b*) does not carry interest varying with profits, or value of assets, or at excessive rate; and
    (*c*) does not give any right to an excessive premium on repayment.

If a person has directly or indirectly provided new consideration for any shares in the company, and that person, or any "connected person", uses for his trade any asset belonging to the company and for which there have been claimed:
    (*a*) first-year allowances on plant, or
    (*b*) writing-down allowances on plant, or
    (*c*) initial allowances on mines expenditure, or
    (*d*) scientific research expenditure,
then that person only is treated as being an equity holder in respect of those shares, and as being beneficially entitled to any distribution of profits or assets attributable thereto.

There is an exclusion for new considerations (as defined for distributions—see Chapter 15, § 2) provided by a bank by way of a loan in the ordinary course of its business.

There are detailed and complex rules by which the percentage of profits or assets available for distribution to any other company as equity holder are to be calculated.

Additional regulations also apply in determining a member's share in a consortium. A member's share is the lower of:
    (i) the percentage of the ordinary share capital of the surrendering, or holding, company which is beneficially owned by that member;
    (ii) the percentage of any profits available for distribution to equity holders of the surrendering, or holding, company to which that member is beneficially entitled; or
    (iii) the percentage of any assets of the surrendering, of holding, company available for distribution to equity holders on a winding-up to which that member is beneficially entitled.

Where the percentages have varied during an accounting period, the average percentage is taken.

KINDS OF GROUP RELIEF (s. 259, I.C.T.A. 1970)
    (*a*) *A trading loss* computed as for s. 177(2), I.C.T.A. 1970, is available for set-off against any profits of the same or previous accounting period. Losses caught by:
        (i) Section 177(4), I.C.T.A. 1970—Case V or
        (ii) Section 180, I.C.T.A. 1970—uncommercial or "hobby" farming;
    are excluded, and do not qualify for group relief.
    A trading loss can be wholly surrendered and does not have to be first set against other income.
    (*b*) *Capital allowances* due to the surrendering company, which are to be:
        (i) given by discharge or repayment of tax; and
        (ii) available primarily against a specified class of income.
    Available for:
        Agricultural buildings
        Industrial buildings (let)

Not available for:
>Plant and machinery
>Industrial buildings (used in the trade)
>Patent rights
>Minerals
>Scientific research

(*c*) *Management expenses* of investment companies in excess of profits (ignoring losses or allowances of any other period). Relief under this heading is not available to life assurance companies.

(*d*) *Charges on income* in excess of profits. For this purpose profits are calculated before the deduction of losses or allowances of any other period, or management expenses brought forward.

(*e*) *Limitation of relief for consortium companies*
A member of a consortium is entitled to only a fractional share of the losses, etc., of the consortium company proportionate to its share in that company. (See above.) It should be noted that a claim can only be up to the amount of the claimant's total profits (as reduced by the order of set-off below) any excess will *not* be competent.

RELATION OF GROUP RELIEF TO OTHER RELIEF (s. 260, I.C.T.A. 1970)
The reliefs listed above are available against the *total profits* of the claimant company, i.e. trading profits and investment income and chargeable gains. When applying group relief a certain order of set-off must be observed.

(i) Firstly deduct other reliefs for the period, including relief in respect of charges on income, and assuming the company makes all relevant claims under s. 177(2), I.C.T.A. 1970 (trading losses against profits of same or preceding accounting period) and s. 74(3) C.A.A. 1968 (capital allowances that cannot be fully offset against income of a specified class).

(ii) Ignore relief derived from a "subsequent accounting period" such as:
>(*a*) a trading loss available under s. 177(2) and (3A), I.C.T.A. 1970
>(*b*) capital allowances that cannot be fully offset against income of a specified class under s. 74(3), I.C.T.A. 1970
>(*c*) terminal loss relief under s. 178, I.C.T.A. 1970.

There is some freedom of choice in the application of group relief so that:
>(i) Relief need not be claimed for the full amount available.
>(ii) Relief may be spread over several companies in a group (*Note:* a member of a consortium cannot claim any more than a fraction equal to its share in the consortium company).
>(iii) A claimant company receiving management expenses does not have to be an investment company.

Example 1

Bill Ltd and Ben Ltd are wholly owned subsidiaries of Weed Ltd. The trading results of the three companies for the last accounting period were:

Bill Ltd profit	£5,000
Ben Ltd loss	£20,000
Weed Ltd profit	£10,000

If a group relief claim is made, the position may be as follows:

	Bill Ltd	Ben Ltd	Weed Ltd
	£	£	£
Profits (losses).......................	5,000	(20,000)	10,000
Group relief	(5,000)	15,000	(10,000)
	Nil	(£5,000)	Nil
		(Losses c/f)	

Workings:	£
Losses available for Group Relief: Ben Ltd	20,000
Surrendered to Bill Ltd......................	5,000
	15,000
Surrendered to Weed Ltd	10,000
Unrelieved losses carried forward for relief in future accounting periods	£5,000

Example 2

Fish Ltd has a wholly-owned subsidiary Net Ltd. The results for the four accounting periods ended on 30th June 1985 are set out below.

	30.6.82 £	30.6.83 £	30.6.84 £	30.6.85 £
Fish Ltd				
Trading profit.................	3,000	—	—	14,500
Trading loss..................		(17,000)	(23,000)	
Capital allowances............	(1,000)	(2,700)	(1,500)	(2,100)
Rents received................	2,500	1,300	1,200	1,800
Net Ltd				
Trading profit.................	17,300	18,000	10,900	4,400
Capital allowances............	(8,200)	(4,300)	(3,400)	(2,000)
Bank interest received	2,100	1,100	900	700
Fish Ltd				
Case I, Schedule D (after Capital allowances)	2,000	(19,700)	(24,500)	12,400
Schedule A...................	2,500	1,300	1,200	1,800
Total profits..................	4,500	(18,400)	(23,300)	14,200
Section 177(2), I.C.T.A. 1970	(4,500)	4,500		
	Nil	(13,900)	(23,300)	
Group relief		13,900	8,400	
		Nil	(14,900)	
Section 177(1), I.C.T.A. 1970			14,900	(12,400)
Profits liable to Corporation Tax .	Nil	Nil	Nil	1,800
				(14,900)
Losses to carry forward under s. 177(1), I.C.T.A. 1970				12,400
				£(2,500)
Net Ltd				
Case I, Schedule D (after Capital allowances)	9,100	13,700	7,500	2,400
Case III, Schedule D............	2,100	1,100	900	700
Total profits..................	11,200	14,800	8,400	3,100
Group relief		(13,900)	(8,400)	
Profits liable to Corporation Tax .	£11,200	£900	£ Nil	£3,100

Example 3

Flopsy Ltd and its 100% subsidiaries Mopsy Ltd and Cottontail Ltd have the following profits (losses) for the 12 months ended 31st March 1986:

	Flopsy Ltd	Mopsy Ltd	Cottontail Ltd
Schedule A.........................	(1,000)	—	30,000
Case I.............................	(75,334)	42,000	20,000
Case III............................	37,333	30,000	—
Case VI............................	(6,000)	19,000	—
Capital Gain (loss)			
—before 1/4 reduction.............	—	4,000	(7,800)
Charges on income	(4,000)	(2,000)	—

It is assumed that the losses cannot be carried back to earlier accounting periods under s. 177(2) or (3A), I.C.T.A. 1970.

	Flopsy Ltd	Mopsy Ltd	Cottontail Ltd
Schedule A.........................	—	—	30,000
Case I, Schedule D.................	(75,334)	42,000	20,000
Case III, Schedule D................	37,333	30,000	—
Case VI, Schedule D................	—	19,000	—
Chargeable gain (less 1/4)	—	3,000	—
Charges on income	(4,000)	(2,000)	—
	(42,001)	92,000	50,000
Group relief	75,334	(58,667)	(16,667)
	£33,333	£33,333	£33,333

	Flopsy Ltd	Mopsy Ltd	Cottontail Ltd
Corporation tax at 30%	10,000		10,000
30% on £30,333 ...		9,100	
40% on £3,000		1,200	
	£10,000	£10,300	£10,000

Unrelieved losses
Flopsy Ltd—Schedule A £1,000—c/fwd against future Schedule A income from same property.
   —Case VI £6,000—c/fwd against any future Case VI income.
   Cottontail Ltd—Allowable capital
Loss £7,800—c/fwd against future chargeable gains.

Notes
1. Flopsy Ltd can surrender the whole or a part of its Case I loss without setting it off against its other profits of the same accounting period.
2. Charges on income can be relieved against total profits as reduced by any other relief from tax, other than group relief.
3. Any excess charges can be group relieved or (if incurred "wholly and exclusively" for trade purposes) carried forward.
4. Group relief is allowed as deduction against claimant company's total profits *before* reduction by any relief derived from a subsequent accounting period, but *as reduced* by any other relief from tax (including recharges on income).
5. This allocation of group relief has ensured maximum use of the small companies rate relief.

COMPANIES JOINING OR LEAVING GROUPS (SS. 261, 262, I.C.T.A. 1970, s. 47, F.A. 1984)

Normally to claim relief the surrendering and claimant companies must be members of the same group throughout the whole of:

(i) the surrendering company's accounting period; and
(ii) the claimant company's corresponding accounting period.

Where the surrendering company and claimant company have the same accounting date, no difficulties are experienced in complying with this requirement.

If the accounting dates of the surrendering and claimant companies differ, the group relief must be restricted. The profits and losses of the corresponding accounting period of the claimant and surrendering companies must be computed on a time apportionment basis by applying the following formulae:

(i) for the loss which may be surrendered, apply the fraction $\dfrac{A}{B}$;

(ii) for the profits of the claimant company which the loss may be set against, apply the fraction $\dfrac{A}{C}$;

where: A is the length of the period common to both accounting periods;
        B is the length of the accounting period of the surrendering company;
        C is the length of the corresponding accounting period of the claimant company.

Example 4

Potts Ltd made a trading loss in the 9 months from 1.4.85 to 31.12.85.	£18,000
Panns Ltd made a trading profit in the 12 months from 1.7.84 to 30.6.85.	£20,000

Corresponding accounting period:
1.4.85 to 30.6.85

Potts Ltd could surrender £6,000 (3/9 × £18,000), but Panns Ltd could only claim £5,000 (3/12 × £20,000).

Assuming Panns Ltd makes sufficient profits in its next accounting period, Potts Ltd could surrender the remaining 6/9 of its trading loss to 31.12.85 thus leaving only £1,000 unrelieved.

Example 5

There Ltd (the surrendering company) incurs a loss of £18,000 in the 9 months ended 31st March 1986, while the profits of Here Ltd (the claimant company) are £12,000 and £36,000 for the years ended 30th September 1985 and 30th September 1986 respectively.

Group relief would be available as computed below:

AP to 30th September 1985
Group relief = lower of profit and loss of period common to both companies:

There Ltd $\frac{3}{9}$ × £18,000 (31.3.86).		£6,000	
Here Ltd $\frac{3}{12}$ × £12,000 (30.9.85)	=	£3,000	(i)

AP to 30th September 1986
Group relief = lower of profit and loss of period common to both companies:

There Ltd $\frac{6}{9}$ × £18,000 (31.3.86).	=	£12,000	(ii)
Here Ltd $\frac{6}{12}$ × £36,000 (30.9.86)	=	£18,000	
There Ltd: Loss of A.P. to 31.3.86	=	£18,000	
Relieved by: A.P. of Here Ltd to 30.9.85		(3,000)	(i)
A.P. of Here Ltd to 30.9.86		(12,000)	(ii)
Unrelieved losses	=	£3,000	

The unrelieved losses of There Ltd may be carried forward and relieved against any profits arising in future accounting periods.

COMPANIES JOINING OR LEAVING GROUPS (s. 262, I.C.T.A. 1970, s. 29, F.A. 1973, s. 47, F.A. 1984)
Primarily, group relief is available only where both companies are members of the same group throughout the whole of the surrendering company's accounting period and the claimant company's corresponding accounting period.

However, the date when a company joins or leaves, other than on a normal accounting date, is treated as the finish and start of notional accounting periods (on a time apportionment basis) and the rules for corresponding accounting periods are applied, subject to special rules to prevent double relief.

The rules on joining and leaving groups (suitably modified) also apply for consortia.

The application of group relief where companies leave a group has, following the introduction of s. 29 F.A. 1973 (see below), been largely rendered otiose.

Example

Bambi Ltd became a 75% subsidiary of Dumbo Ltd on 1.3.85, and incurred a trading loss of £60,000 in the twelve-month accounting period from 1.10.84 to 30.9.85.

Dumbo Ltd made profits of £15,000 in the twelve-month accounting period from 1.1.85 to 31.12.85.

7/12 of Bambi Ltd's loss is allocated to period 1.3.85 to 30.9.85.... = £35,000
10/12 of Dumbo Ltd's profit is allocated to period 1.3.85 to 31.12.85 = £8,750

Corresponding accounting period: 1.3.85 to 30.9.85.
Bambi Ltd could surrender £35,000 but Dumbo Ltd could only claim £8,750.

Further restrictions may apply to companies joining or leaving a group or consortium after 13th March 1984 whose accounting period began after 7th November 1983. Although the basic requirement to time-apportion profits and losses of both the claimant and surrendering companies for accounting periods straddling the date upon which a company joins or ceases to belong to a group continues unchanged, where this method would work unreasonably or unjustly such other method of apportionment has to be used as appears just and reasonable (e.g. profits or losses for the periods before and after the change would be ascertained as if separate accounts had been prepared for those periods).

These provisions also apply to consortium relief but subject to the further requirement that the same basis of apportionment shall apply to each member of the consortium.

ARRANGEMENTS (s. 29, F.A. 1973)
It is also provided that two companies which are members of a group which would otherwise be members of a group for group relief purposes will *not* be so regarded if one company has incurred a loss in an accounting period ending on or after 6th March 1973 and arrangements are in existence so that some time after the commencement of that accounting period:
    (i) the first company, or its successor, could leave the group and become a member of another group; or
    (ii) the first company could leave the group and come under the control of another person; or

(iii) a third company, which is not connected to the two companies, would commence to carry on all or part of the trade of the first company (see *Pilkington Bros Ltd* v. *C.I.R.* [1982]).

A similar restriction applies in the case of a company which is owned by a consortium, or which is a 90% subsidiary of a holding company owned by a consortium. The restriction is applicable where, in an accounting period ending on or after 6th March 1973, the trading company has a loss, and arrangements are in existence so that at some time after the commencement of that accounting period:

(i) the trading company could become a 75% subsidiary of a third company; or

(ii) a person, or persons together, owning less than 50% of the ordinary share capital could acquire control of the trading company; or

(iii) any person, other than the holding company to which the trading company is 90% subsidiary, holds or controls or could obtain or control not less than 75% of the voting rights; or

(iv) a third company which is not connected could commence to carry on all or part of the trade of the trading company.

The term "arrangement" is very wide and seemingly could include oral agreements. Even normal commercial agreements will prevent group relief from being claimed. The Revenue have given some guidance as to when they consider "arrangements" to have come into force (see S.P. 5/80). However a single first refusal agreement is not, in general, regarded as an "arrangement" for this purpose (Concession C12—1980).

INTERACTION OF GROUP AND CONSORTIUM RELIEF (s. 39, Sch. 9, F.A. 1985)

For accounting periods beginning on or after 31st July 1985 the general scheme of group and consortium relief is modified. These changes apply where, at the same time, a company is a member of a group of companies and is also either a company owned by a consortium or is one of the joint owners of a consortium company. As a result of these changes it is now possible for the surrendering company's loss to be claimed partly as group relief and partly as consortium relief. Relief can also "flow through" the consortium member to and from other companies in the consortium member's group.

For accounting periods beginning before 1st August 1985, where a company was both a member of a consortium and a member of a group it could surrender a loss, etc., either as consortium relief or as group relief but not partly one and partly the other. For accounting periods beginning on or after 1st August 1985 it is possible for a company to make mixed surrenders of consortium and group relief.

Similarly, for accounting periods beginning before 1st August 1985, where a company owned by a consortium has a loss and a member of the consortium cannot fully use its share of the losses (e.g. because it too has losses) the loss could not be claimed as group relief by other companies in the same group. Likewise no relief could be given for losses suffered by other companies in the consortium member's group against the profits of the consortium owned company. For accounting periods beginning on or after 1st August 1985, consortium relief can be claimed or surrendered via the consortium member between the consortium owned company and members of the consortium member's group.

The modifications made to the scheme of group and consortium relief are intended to make mixed and multiple claims possible whilst preventing insufficient or excessive relief. The new relief is not available where the group/consortium link does not exist throughout the accounting period concerned.

Example

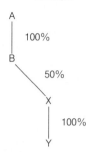

A and B are members of the same group.
B is a member of a consortium which owns X.
X is the consortium owned company, and is a holding company with a trading subsidiary Y.
For accounting periods beginning before 1st August 1985, a loss made by B could be surrendered to A *or* to X, but it could not be shared between them. A loss by X could not be shared between B and Y.

For accounting periods beginning on or after 1st August 1985 mixed claims can be made provided the group/consortium "leg" of the relationship exists throughout the whole of the accounting period. B can claim half of X's loss (provided X has no other profits against which its loss would be set first), or half of the net loss of X and Y combined (where Y has profits). X and Y can claim relief for a loss of B but only to the extent of the proportion of their profits representing B's fractional share in the consortium.

Likewise for accounting periods beginning before 1st August 1985, B could claim relief for the losses, etc., of X and Y, but A cannot. X and Y could claim relief for losses made by B, but not those made by A. For accounting periods beginning on or after 1st August 1985, if A and B are members of the same group throughout an accounting period, the relief can flow through B to and from A.

Claims for losses, etc., of a group/consortium company (Para. 2, Sch. 9, F.A. 1985)
In formulating a claim for consortium relief for a trading loss, or other eligible amount, the loss of a group/consortium company is treated as reduced (or extinguished) by first deducting from it the potential relief attributable to group claims. This is the aggregate amount of group relief that would be claimed if every company within the group which could make a claim in respect of the loss, etc., equal to its total profits.

Where, however, another member of the group has a loss, etc., and group claims are in fact made in respect of the loss, account is taken thereof before computing the aggregate claim referred to above.

Claims for relief by group/consortium company (Para. 3 Sch. 9, F.A. 1985)
Where a consortium claim is made by a group/consortium company in respect of a loss, etc., of a member of the consortium, and because the accounting periods of the companies are not co-terminous, then in formulating the claim the total profits of the group/consortium company against a fraction of which the loss will be set, must be reduced (or extinguished) by first deducting the potential relief available by way of group claims. The potential relief available by way of group claims is the maximum amount of group relief which could be claimed in respect of the losses, etc., of the other members of the group.

Where another member of the group makes claims in respect of the losses of other members of the group, account is taken of the relief which has already been claimed in this way in computing the potential relief available to the group/consortium company.

Trading losses to be set against profits before group relief (Para. 4, Sch. 9, F.A. 1985)

If a company owned by a consortium has sustained a trading loss and in the same accounting period has profits (of whatever description) against which the loss could be set (under s. 177, I.C.T.A. 1970) the amount of the loss which is available to a consortium member is computed on the basis that the company makes a claim to utilise the loss, in the first instance, against such profits.

If the company is a group/consortium company the loss available to a consortium member is calculated before taking account of the potential relief attributable to group claims.

Extension of scope of consortium relief (Paras. 5, 6, Sch. 9, F.A. 1985)

The provisions described below apply where a company is both a member of a consortium and also of a group (a "link company") and the link company could (if it had sufficient profits) make a consortium claim for the loss, etc., of a company owned by the consortium.

A group member which is not itself a member of the consortium can make any consortium claim which could be made by the link company for the same fractional amount to which the link company would be entitled.

However a group member cannot make a consortium claim for a loss, etc., of a company owned by the consortium unless it was a member of the group throughout the whole of the link company's accounting period. In the case of a claim in respect of a corresponding accounting period this test must be met throughout the whole of the periods comprising the corresponding accounting period.

The maximum amount of relief which, in aggregate, can be claimed by group members and the link company, by way of consortium claims, in respect of the loss, etc., of the consortium owned company is the amount which the link company could (if had sufficient profits) otherwise have claimed.

Further provisions apply where there is a link company and another group member which is not itself a member of the consortium has a loss, etc., available for relief.

In such a case, a company which is owned by the consortium can make any consortium claim for the loss, etc., which it could make if the group member were, in fact, a member of the consortium throughout the time in which the link company was a member of the consortium.

The fractional claim available is the same as that which the link company would be able to surrender, except that the accounting period for which the share has to be ascertained is that of the group member which is surrendering the loss.

A company owned by a consortium cannot make a consortium claim for a loss, etc., of a group member unless the group member was within the group throughout the whole of the accounting period concerned.

The maximum amount of relief which, in aggregate, can be claimed by a company owned by a consortium by way of consortium claims relating to losses, etc., of the link company and group members cannot exceed the fractional share of the claimant company's total profits which would be available on a consortium claim for which the link company was the surrendering company on the further basis that the link company and the claimant company have the same accounting period.

Companies joining or leaving the consortium (Paras. 7, 8, Sch. 9, F.A. 1985)

Relief will be prohibited or withdrawn for accounting periods in which companies join or leave the consortium.

CLAIMS (SS. 263 and 264, I.C.T.A. 1970)
There are a number of rules which prevent double relief, whether by obtaining both group relief and some other relief, or by surrendering the same loss, etc., more than once. However, subject to the limitations previously described, group relief can be surrendered and claimed in any desired proportions by suitably qualified companies.

A claim for group relief must have the consent of the surrendering company, be notified to the Inspector, and must be made within two years from the end of the accounting period concerned.

A claim for group relief by a company as a member of a consortium requires the consent of *all* members of the consortium.

GENERAL COMMENTS
(*a*) When considering which company in a group or consortium should claim relief, one should bear in mind the effect (of or on the claim) of:
    (i) double taxation relief;
    (ii) corporation tax rate changes;
    (iii) corporation tax payment date;
    (iv) A.C.T. relief;
    (v) first year allowances (including three-year carry back).
(*b*) The following potential *areas of difficulty* should be noted:
    (i) Failure to ensure that any loss is wholly Case I (i.e. not III, V, VI or Schedule A).
    (ii) Priorities in order of set off.
    (iii) Leaving "uncovered" investment income of a close surrendering company.
    (iv) Payment or non-payment for group relief may have a bearing on share values, and therefore on chargeable gains if shares are disposed of.
    (v) Subsidiaries of a foreign parent can use group relief only if a resident "parent" is interposed between them and the ultimate parent.
    (vi) If a consortium contains a non-resident company, none of its members may claim relief.
    (vii) Companies entering or leaving the group:
      —the sale of a subsidiary without stipulating that consent must be given for the surrender of part losses (if available);
      —as soon as "arrangements are in existence" whereby a subsidiary *could* leave the group, that subsidiary is immediately outside the scope of group relief. An offer for sale would constitute such an arrangement.
    (viii) The distributable income of a close company does not include its chargeable gains, and there will be an overall reduction in a group's distributable income if the surrendering company refrains from setting its losses against chargeable gains but surrenders the maximum loss to the claimant company.
    (ix) In one respect, group relief is more restricted in its application to a consortium than to a group—the whole or any part of an item can be surrendered to a claimant in a group, whereas consortium relief is restricted to the fraction of the member's share in the consortium.

§ 8.—OTHER MATTERS

EFFECT OF LIQUIDATION
When a company goes into liquidation, beneficial ownership of its assets goes into suspense for most purposes. (See *C.I.R.* v. *Olive Mill Spinners Ltd* (1941).

Thus the liquidation of the *parent* company in a group destroys the group relationship (except for capital gains purposes). This has the following effects:

(*a*) prevents group relief from parent and between subsidiaries (unless they are a sub-group).

(*b*) prevents group income payments without A.C.T. and gross annual payments.

(*c*) prevents A.C.T. surrender, because the claimant company cannot be a subsidiary throughout the accounting periods.

However it does not apply where a *subsidiary* goes into liquidation (except in relation to its own sub-group);

It does not apply for the *chargeable gains* provisions for groups of companies, such as:

(*a*) intra-group transfers of chargeable assets at no gain/no loss value.

(*b*) appropriations to and from trading stock/chargeable assets.

(*c*) roll-over and hold-over of chargeable gains on replacement of business assets.

NON-RESIDENT CLOSE COMPANIES (ss. 15 and 16, C.G.T.A. 1979) (See Chapter 15, §4)

Chargeable gains realised by a non-resident close company may be apportioned to United Kingdom resident participators upon whom assessments can be raised for capital gains tax. The gains are calculated on a notional basis assuming that the normal rules which would apply to disposal by United Kingdom residents apply to such a company.

Where appropriate it may be further assumed that the following provisions also apply to such a company:

(i) transfers within a group;

(ii) transfers within a group: trading stock;

(iii) disposal or acquisition outside a group;

(iv) replacement of business assets by members of a group;

(v) company ceasing to be member of a group;

(vi) shares in subsidiary member of a group.

INTER-COMPANY TRADING (s. 485, I.C.T.A. 1970)

Sales and services, etc. between companies under common control (or parent and subsidiary) must be at 'arm's length' prices where one of the companies is non-resident. If not the Revenue have powers to recompute the profits of the companies concerned.

CAPITAL ALLOWANCES

The general scheme of capital allowances on plant and machinery is modified in its application to groups of companies. Where a company acquires an asset from another group member the transfer price is the actual disposal value (proceeds) credited to the seller. The transfer price is debited to the "pool" of unexpired expenditure of the acquiring company. However, the acquiring company is not entitled to any first-year allowance.

The amount of the proceeds from a disposal of plant credited to the "pool" cannot exceed the original cost to the first company of plant acquired by a transaction or series of transactions between connected persons, the proceeds credited to the "pool" are limited to the highest cost of acquisition to any of them.

The effect on claims for losses on company reconstructions in cases where benefits have arisen under the system of capital allowances on plant and machinery through leasing contracts, is that any loss incurred by a company on a leasing contract may be set only against future profits from the same contract if:

(i) the company incurred the expenditure on or after 6th March 1973, on the provision of machinery or plant which is let to another person; and

(ii) the company would otherwise be able to claim relief under s. 177, I.C.T.A. 1970, in respect of losses incurred under the leasing contract; and

(iii) in the accounting period in which a first-year allowance is made to the company, arrangements are in hand for a successor company to take over the company's obligations under the leasing contract.

A company is regarded as a "successor" to another company if the provisions of s. 252, I.C.T.A. 1970 apply to the transfer of the leasing contract, or if the two companies are connected with each other (i.e. under common control).

To determine whether a company would be able to claim relief under s. 177(1), (2), I.C.T.A. 1970 in respect of losses under a leasing contract, the contract must be regarded as a separate trade.

A restriction on the use of company partnerships to obtain group relief and first-year allowances is applied to a company which is a member of a partnership in a trade whereby one member of the partnership receives payment in respect of the profit or loss of the partnership, so that in an accounting period:

(i) the company will only be able to set its share of any trading loss, or charges on income, against its share of the partnership profits; and

(ii) the company's share of the partnership profits will not be available for set-off against non-partnership trading losses; and

(iii) the company's share of the partnership profits will not be available for relieving non-partnership charges on income;

(iv) the company may not set A.C.T. against its corporation tax liability on its share of partnership profits.

Partnership profits assessable under Schedule D, Case VI, are to be treated as chargeable as trading profits, and capital allowances deductible from leasing income are to be treated as trading expenses.

COMPANY RECONSTRUCTION WITHOUT CHANGE OF OWNERSHIP (s. 252, I.C.T.A. 1970)

Where one company ceases to carry on a trade and another company carries on the trade in place of the first company, the normal cessation and commencement provisions will apply for corporation tax purposes. However there is continuity of relief for losses incurred by the company ceasing business if, in the second company, at any time within two years after the change of trade, not less than three-quarters of the interest in both companies belongs to the same persons to whom such an interest belonged at any time within one year before the change. At no time during the above period must the trade be carried on otherwise than by a company, or the relief is lost.

The effects of these provisions are:

(*a*) the unabsorbed losses of the first company are carried forward to the second company; and

(*b*) the capital allowances computations continue without change, the assets being transferred at their pool value, with no balancing adjustments being made.

The company ceasing to trade cannot claim a terminal loss under s. 178, I.C.T.A. 1970. If, however, the second company ceases to carry on trade within four years of the change-over date, any terminal loss relief may be set off against the first company's profits from the same trade.

A trade carried on by a company is regarded:

(*a*) as belonging to persons owning the ordinary share capital of the company, and as belonging to them in proportion to the amount of their holding of that capital; or

(*b*) in the case of a company which is a 75% subsidiary company, as belonging to the company which is its parent company, or as belonging to the persons owning the ordinary share capital of that parent company, and as belonging to them in proportion to their holdings of that capital.

Any ordinary share capital owned by a company may be regarded as owned by any person (or body of persons) who have the power to secure that the company acts in accordance with his (or their) wishes whether by ownership of shares, possession of voting power, or by any power conferred by the articles of association (or other regulatory document).

Ownership referred to above means beneficial ownership, and may be direct or indirect, including fractional holdings.

In determining whether, or to what extent, a trade belongs at different times to the same persons:

—persons who are relatives (husband, wife, ancestor, lineal descendant, brother or sister); and

—persons from time to time entitled to the income under any trust;

are respectively treated as a single person.

23. Corporation Tax—Special Classes of Company

§ 1.—INVESTMENT COMPANIES (ss. 304 to 306, I.C.T.A. 1970)

An investment company is by definition "any company whose business consists wholly or mainly in the making of investments and the principal part of whose income is derived therefrom". For the purpose of this definition, *"income"* includes dividends and other distributions from other UK companies, notwithstanding that they are not taken into account in computing "income" for the purposes of the charge to corporation tax.

An investment company resident in the UK may deduct its expenses of management in computing its profits for corporation tax purposes. These deductible expenses of management must not include any expenses which are deductible in computing income for the purposes of Schedule A. The amount treated as expenses of management must be reduced by the amount of any income derived from sources not charged to tax, other than franked investment income, or group income.

Where in any accounting period the management expenses, together with any charges on income paid in the period (wholly and exclusively for the purpose of the company's business) cannot be wholly allowed by way of a deduction in that period, the balance may be carried forward to the next period and treated as management expenses of that period, thus qualifying for allowance in that period and if need be, in subsequent periods.

As an alternative, an investment company which cannot get full relief for the management expenses of a period by way of a deduction in computing profit for corporation tax, may claim relief for the balance of the expenses against a surplus of F.I.I. Similarly, relief is available for changes on income so far as they are in excess of profits, in the charge to corporation tax.

Capital allowances claimed for capital expenditure on plant and machinery for the purpose of an investment company's business are given against the income of the business for the accounting period. If not fully allowed in this way they are given as an expense of management, and can thus be allowable against capital gains of the period and the profits of future periods, and set against a surplus of franked investment income.

The amount allowable as directors' remuneration under "management expenses" is a question of fact in each case. The onus is left on the company to establish the duties undertaken in the management of the company, and the commercial value of those duties.

Example 1

Bee Investments Ltd is an investment company, and has the following results for the year to 31st March 1986.

	£
Untaxed Interest	6,000
Rents receivable	12,000
Rates and repairs on let properties.	4,000
Rent and Rates on own offices	1,500
Other allowable management expenses	6,000

The position is as follows:

Case III, Schedule D	£	£
Untaxed Interest		6,000
Schedule A		
Rents receivable	12,000	
Less: Rates and repairs......................	4,000	8,000
		14,000
Less: Management expenses—		
Rent and rates on offices................	1,500	
Other expenses.........................	6,000	7,500
Profits chargeable to corporation tax...............		£6,500

Example 2

Hive Investments Ltd is an investment company, and has the following results for the years to 31st March 1985 and 31st March 1986.

	31.3.85	31.3.86
	£	£
Untaxed interest	5,000	15,000
Rents receivable	4,000	3,000
Rates and repairs on let property	800	4,500
Allowable management expenses	10,000	8,600

The position is as follows:

A.P. to 31st March 1985	£	£
Case III, Schedule D		
Untaxed interest		5,000
Schedule A		
Rents receivable	4,000	
Less: Rates and repairs...................	800	3,200
		8,200
Less: Management expenses		10,000
Balance of management expenses		
available for carry forward		£(1,800)

A.P. to 31st March 1986	£	£
Case III, Schedule D		
Untaxed Interest		15,000
Schedule A		
Rents receivable	3,000	
Rates and repairs......................	4,500	
Carry-forward against		
Future rents........................	£(1,500)	
Less: Management expenses		
This period	8,600	
brought forward	1,800	
		10,400
Profits chargeable to corporation tax		£4,600

Example 3

Swarm Ltd is an investment company, and has the following results for the year to 31st March 1985.

	£
Untaxed interest	4,000
Dividends received	49,000
Rents receivable	3,000
Rates and repairs on let property	1,000
Rent and rates on own offices	5,000
Other allowable management expenses	12,000
Dividend paid	28,000

The position is as follows:

A.P. to 31st March 1985	£	£
Case III, Schedule D		
Untaxed interest		4,000
Schedule A		
Rents receivable	3,000	
Less: Rates and repairs	1,000	
	———	2,000
		6,000
Less: Management expenses		
Rent and rates on own offices	5,000	
Other allowable expenses	12,000	
	———	17,000
Balance of management expenses available for relief against Franked Investment Income		£(11,000)
Less: Set off against Franked investment income (s. 254, I.C.T.A. 1970)		10,000
Balance carried forward		£1,000
Dividends received	49,000	
Tax credit 3/7	21,000	
Franked investment income	———	70,000
Less:		
Dividend paid	42,000	
A.C.T. at 3/7	18,000	
Franked payments	———	60,000
Surplus Franked investment income		10,000
Management expenses		(10,000)
Repayment £10,000 at 30%		£3,000

Example 4

Suppose, following example 3, that in the year ended 31st March 1986 the company paid dividends of £54,600 and received dividends of £49,000. The position is as follows:

	£	£
Dividends received	49,000	
Tax Credit 3/7	21,000	
Franked investment income		70,000
Dividends paid.	54,600	
A.C.T. 3/7	23,400	
		78,000
Excess franked payments		£8,000

Management expenses for the A.P. to 31st March 1986 are increased by £8,000, being the lesser of the amount set off in 1984 (£10,000) and the excess franked payment in the current period (£8,000). The company will be required to pay A.C.T. of £2,400 (£8,000 at 30%).

§ 2.—APPROVED INVESTMENT TRUSTS (s. 359, I.C.T.A. 1970, s. 81 F.A. 1980)

Within the general definition of "Investment Companies" are included Investment Trusts, and these qualify for special treatment in the context of tax on Capital Gains. An Investment Trust is defined as a company, approved by the Board of Inland Revenue, which:

(*a*) Is resident in the UK.

(*b*) Is not a close company.

(*c*) Derives income wholly or mainly from shares or securities.

(*d*) Does not have any holding in another company which when acquired represented more than 15% of the value of its investments (treating all holdings in companies which are members of a group as a single holding).

(*e*) Is quoted on a recognised United Kingdom Stock Exchange in respect of a class of its shares or securities.

(*f*) Is prohibited by its memorandum and articles from distributing, as dividend, surpluses arising from the realisation of investments.

(*g*) Does not retain more than 15% of its income from shares and securities in any accounting period.

It is a basic concept that the chargeable gains of an Investment trust are in effect the gains of the many shareholders who have banded together for effective investment purposes.

Prior to 1st April 1980 a double charge to tax on such gains was avoided by taxing the gains made by the company at 10% and by giving credit of up to that amount to the shareholder against capital gains tax on his gains if he disposes of his shares.

In order to achieve an effective rate of 10% on capital gains realised by an investment trust the amount of those gains included in the trusts total profits is after a reduction (for the financial years 1978 and 1979) of 21/26.

Example

	£
Gains realised	10,000
Less: reduction (21/26)	8,077
Chargeable gain included in total profits.	£1,923
Corporation tax (at 52%)	£1,000
Effective rate	10%

After 31st March 1980 investment trusts are exempt from tax on their chargeable gains. However shareholders no longer obtain any credit against gains on disposals of shares in an investment trust.

§ 3.—AUTHORISED UNIT TRUSTS (s. 354, I.C.T.A. 1970, s. 60, F.A. 1980)

An authorised unit trust is a unit trust scheme which has been"authorised" by the Department of Industry under the Prevention of Fraud (Investments) Act 1958. Before 1980–81, the treatment of unit trusts was similar to that of investment trusts. However, s. 60 F.A. 1980 provides that income arising after 31st March, 1980 is chargeable to income tax on the unit holders and not to corporation tax, if the following conditions apply:
- (*a*) Each unit-holder is an individual *or* a trust under which only individuals can benefit; and
- (*b*) The funds of the unit trust are not capable of investment in such a way as to produce income chargeable in the hands of the trustees other than under Schedule C or Schedule D, Case III.

§ 4.—TRUSTEE SAVINGS BANKS (s. 339, I.C.T.A. 1970, s. 59, Sch. 11, F.A. 1980)

Prior to 20th November 1979, Trustee Savings Banks were treated, broadly, as investment companies and were also granted exemption from corporation tax on income from investments insofar as it was applied in meeting interest due to depositors. After that date Trustee Savings Banks are treated in general, in the same way as other banks (i.e. as trading companies).

§ 5.—INDUSTRIAL AND PROVIDENT SOCIETIES (s. 340, I.C.T.A. 1970)

These are defined as any society registered under the Industrial and Provident Societies Act 1965; or under the Industrial and Provident Societies Act (Northern Ireland) 1969.

In general, share and loan interest paid by a registered Industrial and Provident Society is not treated as a distribution. "Share interest" means any interest, dividend, bonus or other sum payable to a shareholder of the society in respect of any mortgage, loan, stock or deposit. It is allowed to the society as a deduction when computing its trading income of the accounting period; or if the society is not carrying on a trade, will be treated as a charge on the income of the society.

Share and loan interest received from a registered Industrial and Provident Society is normally received gross and is subject to corporation tax in the hands of a company receiving it. To enable proper assessments to be made on the recipient, every Society must, within three months of the end of the accounting period, make a return to the Inland Revenue showing:
- (*a*) the name and address of every person to whom the Society has paid, without deduction of tax, sums amounting to more than £15 in that period;
- (*b*) the amount of the sum paid.

§ 6.—BUILDING SOCIETIES (s. 343, I.C.T.A. 1970)

A Building Society is defined as a society incorporated under the Building Society Act, 1962; or the Building Society (Northern Ireland) Act, 1967.

Building Societies, like other companies, are liable to corporation tax on their income; however, s. 343, I.C.T.A. 1970 permits the Inland Revenue to make arrangements with Building Societies so that income tax is not deducted by the Society when paying interest, nor is it directly assessed on the individual concerned, but must be included in the recipient's total income for the year concerned.

A company receiving interest from a Building Society is treated as having received the gross equivalent of the interest received—grossed up at the basic rate of tax in force in the accounting period concerned. The notional income tax arising is available for set-off against the company's corporation tax liability.

Interest on a qualifying certificate of deposit, or on a qualifying time deposit (which in general are dealt in on the money market) is paid gross.

§ 7.—MUTUAL COMPANIES (ss. 345 to 347, I.C.T.A. 1970)

Distributions made by a company carrying on a mutual trade are treated as distributions within Schedule F but only to the extent that they are paid out of profits charged to corporation tax, or out of distributions received from other resident companies. Distributions are not treated in this way if paid out of a surplus on mutual trading which is not within the charge to tax.

Where distributions are made to a company out of a mutual company's F.I.I., the paying company would be able to set-off the income tax deducted against its liability to account for income tax, and the recipient company could treat the distribution as F.I.I.

A similar provision is made in respect of distribution made by a company whose objects do not include the carrying on of a trade, or a business of holding investments, and which has never carried on such a trade or business.

§ 8.—TRADE ASSOCIATIONS

Trade associations, usually set up for the protection or furtherance of the members of a particular trade or profession, are in effect, mutual companies and as such are not liable to corporation tax upon income derived from mutual trading, although they remain liable to tax upon income (and gains) arising under other schedules or cases.

However in most cases the association will have entered into an agreement with the Inland Revenue whereby corporation tax is payable upon any surplus realised by the association. This permits members paying subscriptions, etc to obtain full relief for such payments whereas they would otherwise be restricted to the extent only that the association has applied those payments to purposes which had they been carried out by the members would have been deductible in computing trading profits.

If the association suffers a deficit relief is given as though it was a trading loss, in the usual ways, but subject to the modification that relief under s. 177(2), I.C.T.A. 1970 is available against the total profits of the *six* preceding years.

§ 9.—COMPANY PARTNERSHIPS (s. 155, I.C.T.A. 1970)

A partnership is defined by the Partnership Act 1890 as "the relationship which exists between two or more persons carrying on a business with a view to profit." Thus the situation may arise in which a company is in partnership with an individual(s).

Since the introduction of corporation tax and changes in the basis of assessment of companies and individuals, special provisions were necessary to deal with partnerships. The authority is contained in s. 155, I.C.T.A. 1970, and the main object of the statute is to ascertain the partnership's trading income for an accounting period as if the whole partnership were a company and, from the sum arising, ascertain the share due to the company.

The company's share derived above is then taken out and the company is assessed to corporation tax upon it, while the amount remaining is the share due to the other partner(s) in the partnership and is assessed to income tax on the individuals concerned.

§ 10.—OTHER BODIES

(a) *Local Authorities* (s. 353, I.C.T.A. 1970)
Local authorities (having power to levy a rate) and local authority associations, are exempt from corporation tax.

(b) *Charities* (s. 360, I.C.T.A. 1970)
Charities are, in general, exempt from income tax, corporation tax, capital gains tax and development land tax, provided the income or gains thereof are applicable to, and applied for, charitable purposes.

(c) *Agricultural Societies* (s. 361, I.C.T.A. 1970)
The profits or gains arising from any exhibition or show are exempt, if applied to the purposes of the society.

(d) *Scientific Research Associations* (s. 362, I.C.T.A. 1970)
To the extent that profits, loss or gains of such bodies are applicable to, and applied for, the purposes of scientific research they are exempt from (*inter alia*) corporation tax.

(e) *The British Museum and the Natural History Museum* (s. 363, I.C.T.A. 1970)
The Trustees of these bodies are exempt from tax under Schedules A,D,F, and in respect of chargeable gains.

24. Anti-Avoidance Legislation

§ 1.—INTRODUCTION

In the past high rates of direct taxation and the complexity of tax legislation have led to taxpayers seeking ways of reducing their tax liabilities. Where this is done by fraud or similar means (e.g. by making claims for allowances to which the taxpayer is not entitled; by producing forged documents; by making untrue statements; or by failing to declare a source of income or gain), this is illegal and is known as *tax evasion*.

Tax avoidance, on the other hand, is not illegal. This is the process of arranging a taxpayer's affairs so that he can, lawfully, reduce the amount of tax which he is due to pay (see *C.I.R.* v. *Duke of Westminster* [1935]).

Tax avoidance may amount to no more than the structuring of commercial transactions in such a way that the tax liabilities arising from those transactions are minimised (e.g. making an investment in a way which ensures that there will be an allowable loss if, in the future, the investment is lost) rather than in some other way which achieves the same broad commercial purpose but which gives rise to larger tax liabilities.

At the other end of the scale there are highly artificial schemes which have no real commercial purpose and which have been entered into solely for the tax relief which, by means of narrow interpretation of the statutes and the exploitation of "loop-holes", it is purported will be derived from participation in the scheme. Such schemes are now, in general, ineffective (*W. T. Ramsay* v. *C.I.R.* [1981]).

Indeed, following *Furniss* v. *Dawson* (1984) additional steps inserted into an otherwise commercial transaction for the purpose of reducing the incidence of taxation are also likely to be ineffective.

The purpose of this chapter is to summarise briefly the legislation by which the Revenue can prevent certain specific forms of tax avoidance, in addition to the general power which these decisions give them.

As will be seen from the following sections of this chapter, there are certain areas of recent tax legislation where anti-avoidance provisions have been "built-in" to prevent the mis-use of relieving provisions (e.g. capital allowances, stock relief, foreign earnings, business start-up scheme). There are also a number of tax concepts of general application but which are, in effect, aimed at the prevention of mis-use (e.g. the general rule that transactions between "connected persons" are deemed to be made at market value, whatever the actual transfer price). In other areas, legislation has been introduced to prevent a specific form of mis-use.

§ 2.—LAND

ARTIFICIAL TRANSACTIONS IN LAND (ss. 488 to 490, I.C.T.A. 1970)

The purpose of this provision is to prevent the avoidance of tax by persons concerned with land, or the development of land.

Before the sections can be applied, three conditions must be satisfied:

1. The land concerned must be in the United Kingdom (but the sections can apply to any persons concerned in the land, irrespective of whether they are resident in the U.K. or not).
2. (*a*) A gain of a capital nature is realised from the disposal of land, either by the person acquiring, holding or developing the land, or by any connected person (see s. 533, I.C.T.A. 1970); *or*

(*b*) Where any arrangement or scheme is effected whereby a gain can be realised by an indirect method or series of transactions, by any person who is a party to, or connected with, the arrangement or scheme.

The gain can be made either by such a person for himself or for any other person.

A gain is "of a capital nature" unless it is otherwise already treated as income (e.g. as trading income under Case I of Schedule D, or as a lease premium under Schedule A). This is a very wide definition indeed.

3. (*a*) Land (or any property deriving its value from land) is acquired with the sole or main object of realising a gain on its disposal.

(*b*) Land is held as trading stock (but see below).

(*c*) Land is developed with the sole or main object of realising a gain from its disposal when developed.

Land in this context includes buildings and any estate or interest in land or buildings (e.g. leasehold, freehold reversion).

Property deriving its value from land includes shares in a company, a partnership interest, an interest in settled property where the value thereof is derived directly or indirectly from land, as well as any option, consent or embargo which could affect the disposal of the land.

The meaning of "disposal" is also very wide and includes any arrangement or scheme involving the land, or property deriving its value from land, whereby control of the land is effectively transferred. It can also include any number of transactions if, taken overall, they have the common purpose of disposing of the land.

If these conditions are met, the Revenue can treat the gain as income (either of the person realising the gain, or of the person who transmitted to him the opportunity of realising the gain), assessable under Case VI, Schedule D. The amount of the gain to be treated as income in this way is such amount as is just and reasonable in the circumstances. This will take into account the value of the consideration obtained for disposing of the land and also allows for directly attributable expenses.

For example, account should be taken, in the case of the acquisition of a freehold, and retention on disposal of the reversion, of the way in which profits are computed under Case I, Schedule D. Alternatively, account must be taken of the way in which lease premiums have been treated where the recipient is a dealer in land.

If a gain is computed on the basis of an appropriation of land from fixed assets to trading stock (i.e. the gain arising since the appropriation), this will be a capital gain (under s. 122, C.G.T.A. 1979) on the basis of the market value of the land at the time of appropriation.

Where land has been held for a long time and was originally purchased for occupation or investment, it is only so much of the gain as accrues after there is a change of intention (e.g. a decision to develop) which can be assessed under s. 488, I.C.T.A. 1970.

A gain from the disposal of an individual's private residence is exempted from tax under s. 488, I.C.T.A. 1970 unless it was acquired with the intention of making a gain (when, incidentally, the capital gains exemption would not be available).

When the shares of a company which holds land as trading stock are disposed of, any gain arising thereon is exempt from tax under s. 488, I.C.T.A. 1970 provided firstly that the company subsequently disposes of the land as trading stock in the normal course of its trade, and also that the sale is not part of a wider scheme. The exemption also applies to the disposal of shares in a company which holds 90% of the ordinary share capital of a company which holds land as trading stock.

As previously indicated, s. 488, I.C.T.A. 1970 can apply to a wide range of transactions whereby control of land, or property deriving its value from land, is effectively transferred. It can also apply to transactions, direct or indirect, whereby the value is increased or diminished. Examples of the kinds of transactions to which the Section could apply include:

(a) Any sale or contract, but especially contracts which are above or below full consideration;

(b) Assignment of share capital in a company, or share in a partnership, or an interest in settled property;

(c) Any option, consent or embargo;

(d) Disposal of property etc. in the winding up, dissolution or termination of a company, a partnership or a trust.

However, when seeking to ascertain persons' intentions, the objects and powers of a company, partnership or trust set out in its memorandum, articles of association etc. are not conclusive.

Value derived from property can be traced through any number of companies, partnerships or trusts and attributed to the shareholders, partners or trusts at each stage.

Any expenditure, receipt or consideration or any other amounts can be apportioned as is *just and reasonable* in the circumstances and all necessary valuations made as required for the calculation of the tax charge under s. 488, I.C.T.A. 1970. Whilst tax can be assessed on a person in respect of consideration receivable by some other person, the person assessed has a right of recovery from the recipient of the consideration. Likewise the Revenue have the right to recover tax remaining unpaid (by the person assessed) from the person receiving the consideration.

If the person who is entitled to receive the consideration is not resident in the United Kingdom, the Revenue can direct that it be treated as an annual payment (assessed under Case III, Schedule D), so that income tax must be deducted at source under s. 53, I.C.T.A. 1970 and paid over to the Revenue. However, this does not affect the final liability on the transactions (except to the extent that tax so paid can be offset).

The Revenue have wide powers to obtain information relating to land transactions from persons concerned in transactions. This includes professional advisers, except that a solicitor who has acted only in that capacity need do no more than state that he has acted and give his client's name and address.

Any taxpayer who considers that s. 488, I.C.T.A. 1970 *might* apply to transactions about to be undertaken and to which 3(a) or (c) above apply, can seek a clearance from the Inspector of Taxes that he will not invoke the section.

LAND SOLD AND LEASED BACK—DEDUCTION OF RENT (ss. 491 and 494(10), I.C.T.A. 1970)

Where land is transferred from one person to another by sale, lease etc. and under a lease (widely defined) granted at the same time or later by the transferee to the transferor, or to any associated person, or by some other transaction the transferor or any associated person becomes liable to pay rent (including the income element of a lease premium), the allowance in respect thereof may be restricted.

The restriction applies to deductions claimed in the following circumstances:

1. Schedule A rentals (ss. 71–77 and Schedule 2, I.C.T.A. 1970)
2. Trading profits (Case I, Schedule D)
3. Management expenses (investment and property companies) (ss. 304–305, I.C.T.A. 1970)
4. Schedule E emoluments (s. 189, I.C.T.A. 1970)
5. Occupation of woodlands (s. 111, I.C.T.A. 1970)
6. Case VI, Schedule D

The allowance is restricted to a "commercial rent" for the land concerned. However, if there are later transactions, rent disallowed can be carried forward and, depending on the circumstances, might be eligible for relief on the later event.

In this context "associated persons" are:

1. The transferor in the transaction described above and/or transferor in another similar transaction if they are acting in concert or if the transactions are in any way reciprocal. This also extends to the associates (see below) of such persons;
2. Two or more companies involved in the reconstruction or amalgamation of a company or companies;
3. Associates, namely;
    (*a*) An individual's husband or wife; relatives (brother, sister, ancestor or lineal descendant); husband or wife of a relative;
    (*b*) Trustees of a settlement and the settlor (including persons with whom he has made reciprocal arrangements);
    (*c*) A person or body or bodies of persons (e.g. companies and partnerships) which he controls (see s. 534, I.C.T.A. 1970);
    (*d*) Bodies of persons under common control (see (*c*));
    (*e*) Joint owners of property.

When considering the allowability or otherwise of rent, etc., the following matters should be taken into account:

1. One or more payments for the same period are aggregated.
2. If payments are made for periods which overlap, apportionment is made and the part of the payments relating to the overlap is aggregated; this can include later payments which are related back.
3. The part of a payment which relates to services, use of assets (other than land) and tenants' rates is excluded.
4. Payments for periods later than one year after the date of the payment are related back to the date of the payment.

A "commercial rent" is the normal open market rent which could be expected for a lease of similar terms and duration entered into at the same time, except that rent under the lease taken for comparison will have rent payable at uniform intervals and for a uniform amount (subject to review proportionate to those in the actual lease).

If a payment under the actual lease is not rent, the comparison is made with the rent which could be expected under a tenant's repairing lease of the same duration entered into at the same time as the actual lease. If payments are to be made over a period in excess of 200 years or are perpetual, the comparison is made with a lease for 200 years.

Typical examples of transactions caught by s. 491, I.C.T.A. 1970 are dealings in long leases under which an annual rent charge or other payment arises which is chargeable against profits or income of the payer.

Example

Adam leases land to Bill for payment of a premium and then leases back the land from Bill for a high payment for the first few years. Bill, being a dealer in property, will pay negligible tax on the receipts from Adam (the lease being part of the stock). Accordingly the payment by Bill is restricted to a commercial rent, the excess payment being disallowed for income tax purposes.

LAND SOLD AND LEASED BACK—CAPITAL SUM TAXED AS INCOME (ss. 80 and 82, F.A. 1972)

Where land is sold and leased back to the seller and the lease has no more than 50 years to run and the premises are leased back for less than 15 years, the increased rent is only allowable to the extent that it is a "commercial rent" for the land concerned (s. 491, I.C.T.A. 1970).

Additionally, part of the consideration received for the sale of the original lease is taxed as income under Case I, II or V, Schedule D, depending on the circumstances, and the new rent payable is allowed in full. "Top slicing relief" will be due as in the case of premiums on leases. The taxable part is calculated by the formula:

$$\frac{16 - n}{15}$$

where n = term of new lease.

Example

Sunray Ltd received £100,000 for the assignment of a lease for 40 years. A new lease was granted by the purchaser to Sunray Ltd for a term of 11 years.

The amount taxable as income is:

$$£100,000 \times \frac{16 - 11}{15} = £33,333$$

SALE OF LAND WITH RIGHT TO RECONVEYANCE (s. 32, F.A. 1978)

No relief is available under s. 82, I.C.T.A. 1980 for the premium deemed to have been paid on the sale of land with a right to reconveyance. Thus the avoidance of tax by creating on the one hand a notional premium and a right to reconveyance (usually within a company with substantial accumulated losses), and on the other hand a deduction against rent or trading profits, is prevented.

§ 3.—LEASES OTHER THAN LAND

CAPITAL SUM RECEIVED BY PERSON PAYING RENT UNDER A LEASE (ss. 492 and 494, I.C.T.A. 1970)

Section 492, I.C.T.A. 1970 covers arrangements whereby relief was obtained for payments under leases where the payer was entitled to deduct the payment under any Schedule. The usual method of avoidance was to pay very large capital sums for the first few years of the lease, then nominal sums only for the remainder of the period. The assignment of the rights under the lease in these first few years brought a capital receipt. Now a Case VI assessment will be made on the person receiving such a payment, on the actual basis, to recover the amount previously charged for rent, up to the amount of the capital sum received. Thus if Charles was paid rent of £4,000 which was allowed he received a capital sum of £3,000 in 1983–84, he will be assessed under Case VI, Schedule D for £3,000 in 1983–84.

If more than one capital sum is received (i.e. by persons in succession), the liability on the further capital sum will take into account the payments charged on the previous capital sum. The payments of capital are not of course allowed as a charge against the payer's profits. Capital sums include any sums of money or money's worth.

The deductions referred to above are those claimed in the following circumstances:

1. Trading profits (Case I, Schedule D)
2. Management expenses (investment and property companies) (ss. 304–305, I.C.T.A. 1970)
3. Schedule E assessments (s. 189, I.C.T.A. 1970)
4. Occupation of woodlands (s. 111, I.C.T.A. 1970)
5. Case VI, Schedule D.

This provision applies to any agreement or arrangement whereby payments are made for the use of an asset. It also applies to transactions whereby the payments represent instalments of a purchase price (but normally to hire purchase contracts for plant and machinery).

In general, the amounts taxed under this provision cannot exceed the capital sum actually received. However, if a deduction is obtained in computing profits from a trade or from woodlands, and part of the payments made under the lease by the recipient of the capital sum are not allowed because the period in which the payments would otherwise be allowed is not a period for which the trade (etc.) is taxable, then the taxable amount of the capital sum is computed after taking account of the payments for which no relief is obtained.

As indicated above, leases are widely defined and references to capital sums received from leases are similarly extended to a wide range of transactions:
1. Consideration (in money's worth) received by a lessee for:
    (*a*) Surrendering his rights to the lessor;
    (*b*) Assigning a lease;
    (*c*) Creating a sub-lease, etc.
2. Receiving insurance moneys.
3. Series of transactions.
4. Arrangements whereby the lessee's rights merge with the lessor's.
5. Consideration received by an associate (see § 2).

Where an interest in an asset is disposed of to an associate, the person making the disposal is treated as receiving the greater of:
    (*a*) Market value of the interest;
    (*b*) The value thereof to the transferee; or
    (*c*) Any larger sum actually received.

LEASES OTHER THAN LAND—DEDUCTION OF RENT (s. 493, I.C.T.A. 1970)
Section 492, I.C.T.A. 1970 does not apply to payments which are allowed as deductions in computing trading profits and are made under a lease of an asset previously used for the trade or for another trade by a person who is then, or later, carrying on the first trade and, when previously so used, was owned by the person carrying on the trade in which it was being used. In such a case the deduction is restricted to a commercial rent for the period for which the asset was used.

As for leases of land, there is provision to "store up" otherwise deductible amounts which are restricted by s. 492, I.C.T.A. 1970, and set them against subsequent profits (up to the amount which would then be allowed).

Provisions similar to those applying to leases of land deal with aggregation of several payments in respect of the same period, payments for overlapping periods, carry-forward of non-deducted amounts and relation back of payments in respect of periods more than one year after the date of the payment.

The test of a commercial rent for an asset is applied by comparison of the actual lease with a normal lease giving a rent at a uniform level, payable at regular intervals and being a reasonable return for the market value of the asset for the remainder of its anticipated normal working life.

HIRE PURCHASE (s. 495, I.C.T.A. 1970)
The application of s. 492, I.C.T.A. 1970 is modified for hire purchase contracts. In such a case the overall limit on sums which can be assessed under that Section is restricted, where the capital sum was obtained in respect of the lessee's interest, by deducting therefrom any capital expenditure which for capital allowance purposes remains unallowed at the time of the transfer.

§ 4.—LOANS (s. 496, I.C.T.A. 1970)

Section 496, I.C.T.A. 1970 prevents relief being obtained for interest payments which would otherwise be non-qualifying interest. An example of such a transaction would be the conversion of a non-qualifying interest payment into an annuity, for which relief could be obtained.

Thus if money is lent (or credit given) and the terms of the loan require the payments of an annuity or other annual payment (except interest) chargeable under Case III, Schedule D, the payment is, nonetheless, treated as being a payment of annual interest.

The provision applies whether the transaction is between the lender (or creditor) and the borrower (or debtor) or between either of them and a person connected with the other, or indeed between a person connected with one of them and a person connected with the other. The definition of connected person is that found in s. 533, I.C.T.A. 1970.

If the transaction is one whereby there is a subsequent reacquisition, by the former owner, of securities or other income-producing property, any income arising from the property before the loan is repaid is deemed to be the income of the former owner (by means of a Case VI, Schedule D assessment). This also applies where an option to repurchase is granted.

Where under the terms of a loan a person assigns, surrenders, waives or forgoes income from property (but does not sell or transfer the property), the income arising is nonetheless deemed still to be his (by means of a Case VI, Schedule D assessment). However, if credit is given for the purchase price of any property, and the rights attaching to the property are such that, during the existence of the debt, the purchaser's rights to income which would otherwise have flowed to him are suspended or restricted, he is deemed to have surrendered a right to income of an amount equivalent to the income which is, in effect, forgone by obtaining the credit.

If any income is payable under deduction of income tax, it is the gross amount thereof which is taken into account.

§ 5.—SALE OF INCOME FROM PERSONAL ACTIVITIES (s. 487, I.C.T.A. 1970)

Section 487, I.C.T.A. 1970 prevents the exploitation of an individual's earning capacity by putting some other person (e.g. a company) in a position to enjoy some or all of the profits, gains, income, copyrights, licences or other rights which derive directly or indirectly from an individual's activities, past or present, while the individual concerned (or any other person) receives a capital amount and the main object (or one of them) of the transaction is the avoidance or reduction of liability to income tax.

Any capital sum so received is treated as earned income (although assessed under Case VI, Schedule D), arising when the sum was received.

The Section does not apply to capital sums obtained from the disposal of assets (including goodwill) of a profession or vocation, or a share in a partnership carrying on a profession or vocation, or shares in a company in so far as the value of what is disposed of is attributed to the value of the profession, vocation or business as a going concern. However, these exemptions do not apply to so much of the value derived from an individual's prospective future activities in the occupation (either as partner or as employee) for which he has not (apart from any capital amounts) received full consideration.

The Section is also applied to capital amounts in the form of property or rights deriving their value from an individual's activity (e.g. a stock option which is subsequently exercised), but only where the property or rights are sold or otherwise released, when the amount assessed will be equal to the proceeds of sale or value realised.

Persons who are not resident in the United Kingdom are within this section if the occupation of the individual is wholly or partly carried on in the United Kingdom.

However, when seeking to ascertain a person's intentions, the objects and powers of a company, partnership or trust set out in its memorandum, articles o: association etc. are *not* conclusive.

Any expenditure, receipt or consideration or any other amounts can be apportioned as is *just and reasonable* in the circumstances and all necessary valuations made as required for the calculation of the tax charge under s. 487 I.C.T.A. 1970.

Whilst tax can be assessed on a person in respect of consideration receivable by some other person, the person assessed has a right of recovery from the recipient of the consideration. Likewise the Revenue have the right to recover tax remaining unpaid (by the person assessed) from the person receiving the consideration.

If the person who is entitled to receive consideration is not resident in the United Kingdom, the Revenue can direct that it be treated as an annual payment (assessed under Case III, Schedule D), so that income tax must be deducted therefrom under s. 53, I.C.T.A. 1970 and paid over to the Revenue. However, this does not affect the final liability on the transaction (except to the extent that tax so paid can be offset).

The Revenue have wide powers to obtain information relating to transactions from persons concerned. This includes professional advisers, except that a solicitor who has acted only in that capacity need do no more than state that he has acted and give his client's name and address.

§ 6.—TRANSACTIONS IN SECURITIES

CANCELLATION OF TAX ADVANTAGE (SS. 460–468, I.C.T.A. 1970)
This legislation is to counteract devices where, by "transactions in securities", profits are extracted from a company in the guise of capital but on which income tax would otherwise have been payable (e.g. if paid as dividends).

In order for liability to arise under s. 460, I.C.T.A. 1970, three conditions must be present:

(*a*) As a result of one or more *transactions in securities*,
(*b*) Carried out in one of the *prescribed circumstances* of s. 461, I.C.T.A. 1970,
(*c*) A person is in a position to obtain, or has obtained, a *tax advantage*. Transactions in securities include not only single transactions but also a combination of two or more transactions, or one or more transactions and a liquidation. It also includes the purchase, sale and issue of securities or the alteration of rights attaching to them.
Securities are defined as including shares and stock, and this has been held in *C.I.R.* v. *Parker* (1966) to include also security for payment of a debt, with or without a charge on the property concerned.

TRANSACTIONS IN SECURITIES
Transactions in this context include:

(i) The purchase, sale or exchange of securities;
(ii) Issuing or securing the issue of, or applying or subscribing for new securities;
(iii) The altering, or securing the alteration of rights attached to securities.

In *C.I.R.* v. *Parker* it was held that the redemption of a debenture was a transaction in securities; whilst in *Greenberg* v. *C.I.R.* (1971) it was held that unilateral activity in relation to shares, such as declaring or paying dividends, could also be regarded as transactions in securities.

It was held in *C.I.R.* v. *Joiner* (1975) that transactions carried out in combination with a liquidation are also transactions in securities, but it appears that the liquidation itself is not a transaction in securities. It has however been stated that s. 460, I.C.T.A. will not be invoked in the case of *bona fide* liquidation (i.e. those which are not part of a scheme to obtain a tax advantage).

PRESCRIBED CIRCUMSTANCES
The tax advantage must have been obtained in one of the circumstances prescribed by s. 461, I.C.T.A. 1970 (A to E below).

A. *Abnormal dividend*
Where a taxpayer received an abnormal dividend and is entitled to recover tax in respect of it by reason of:
- (*a*) Exemption from tax;
- (*b*) Setting off losses against profits or income;
- (*c*) Giving of group relief;
- (*d*) Application of franked investment income in calculating A.C.T. liabilities;
- (*e*) Computation of profits or gains from which annual payments are made;
- (*f*) Deduction or set-off of interest.

By way of example, a share dealer buys securities, pays an abnormal dividend and sells the shares, thereby creating a trading loss to set against tax deducted from the dividend (*J. P. Harrison (Watford) Ltd* v. *Griffiths* (1963)).

There are broadly two circumstances in which a dividend is deemed to be abnormal. Firstly, in the case of a fixed-rate dividend, where the amount received exceeds the amount which would be received on the basis that the dividend accrued evenly from day to day over the period of ownership. However, a dividend is not treated as abnormal if during the six months after the purchase of the securities the recipient does not sell, or otherwise dispose of, or acquire an option to sell the securities, or similar securities. The second situation is where a dividend substantially exceeds the normal return on the consideration given for the securities. Account is also taken of the securities' previous history.

B. *Deduction for loss on securities*
Where a taxpayer becomes entitled to a deduction in his profits or gains due to a fall in value of securities which has been produced by a payment of a dividend or other dealings with assets of a company.

As an example, a share dealer buys securities in a company which owns trading stock with a market value in excess of book value. The trading stock is taken out of the company at a low value and sold at a profit. There is then a trading loss on the subsequent sale of the securities.

C. *Other party to A or B*
Whereas provisions to deal with A or B attack the share dealer, C attacks the owner of shares. The shareholder receives, in a non-taxable form, a consideration which is (or represents) the value of assets which are, or could be, available for distribution by way of dividend; or is in respect of future receipts of the company; or is (or represents) the value of trading stock of the company. Meanwhile, another person has received, or will receive, an abnormal amount by way of dividend; or has, or will, become entitled to a deduction for a loss on securities.

An example of such a transaction would be when shareholders in a private company sell their shares to a share dealer, who takes out a large dividend and sells the shares back to the original shareholders. They have thus received a capital consideration in place of the dividend they should have otherwise received.

The reference to future receipts could cover the issue and sale of high-yielding redeemable preference shares. Assets available for distribution mean assets legally, and not necessarily commercially, available for this purpose (*C.I.R.* v. *Brown* (1971)).

Circumstance C can apply even if the recipient of the dividend or claimant of the loss can show a *bona fide* reason for participating in the transaction. Circumstance C could also apply to shareholders in a family company which sells out to a public company which extracts assets by way of dividend, but only if there is foreknowledge by the vendor (*C.I.R.* v. *Garvin* (1979)).

D. *Distribution of profits*

Where a taxpayer receives cash or assets in a tax-free form in connection with a distribution of profits from a company. In this context, *profits* include income, reserves or other assets, and *distribution* means transfer or realisation, including application in discharge of liabilities.

Circumstance D applies only to companies controlled by 5 or fewer people, and other *non-U.K.-quoted* companies. However, Circumstance D is *not* restricted to close companies. Circumstance D does *not* apply to companies controlled by "non-D" companies (see s. 302, I.C.T.A. 1970).

Example

The classic example of a transaction within Circumstance D is the case of *C.I.R.* v. *Cleary* (1967).

Mrs Cleary and Mrs Perrin were two sisters, who each owned 50% in two companies, M Ltd and G Ltd. G Ltd had undistributed profits amounting to about £180,000 and cash of about £120,000. In order to extract cash from the company (the receipt of a dividend would cause a tax liability to arise), Mrs Cleary and Mrs Perrin sold their shares in M Ltd and G Ltd. Each sister received £60,000 in cash from G Ltd for the sale of the shares.

The cash extracted was held to be a net dividend received by the sisters. The extraction of the cash was within the scope of Circumstance D (being a distribution of profits in a tax-free form). It should, of course, not be overlooked that the subsequent distribution by G Ltd of all its reserves as a dividend would give rise to assessable income which would *not* be reduced to allow for the s. 460 assessment.

Other examples of transactions within Circumstance D are the capitalisation of profits followed by a reduction of share capital (as in *C.I.R.* v. *Hague* (1968)), or the use of profits to pay up interest-free debentures (as in *C.I.R.* v. *Parker* (1966)).

Amendments made by Schedule 22, Paras 5 and 6, F.A. 1972 provide that if a company is *not* a D company, an issue of non-redeemable bonus shares more than *ten* years after a repayment of share capital is *not* a distribution. Similarly a repayment of share capital by a company which is *not* a D company more than *ten* years after an issue of non-redeemable bonus shares is not a distribution.

Circumstance D is apt to catch a wide variety of transactions and is concerned with the extraction of assets and reserves in tax-free form (including cases where the recipient is assessed to C.G.T. only).

E. *Non-taxable consideration*

Where two or more D companies are involved, and the taxpayer receives a non-taxable consideration consisting of share capital or securities issued by a D company. This might apply if a D company is put into liquidation and reconstructed as two new D companies, which are subsequently liquidated.

Specifically it can apply where there is a direct or indirect transfer of assets of a D company to another D company, or where, in connection with any transaction in securities involving two or more D companies, the taxpayer receives *non-taxable* consideration which is (or represents) the value of *assets available for distribution*, and which consists of *share* capital or *security* issued by a D company.

If the security received is redeemable share capital, an assessment to nullify the tax advantage can only be made when the capital is repaid in a winding up or a reduction of capital. However, assessment can be made on a former owner of the shares.

If both D and E apply, the deferment in E takes precedence (*Williams* v. *C.I.R.* (1980)).

Several terms are specifically defined for the purposes of Circumstance E:
  (a) *Non-taxable* means that the recipient of the consideration is not taxable thereon as income.

(*b*) *Assets available for distribution* are assets which would have been available for distribution by way of dividend, or trading stock of the company.

(*c*) *Share* includes stock and any other interest of a member in a company.

(*d*) *Security* includes securities not creating a charge on the assets of the company.

A *tax advantage* means a relief from tax or a repayment of tax (e.g. by creating a trading loss qualifying for tax relief), or the avoidance or reduction of an assessment to tax where it is effected by receipts accruing in such a way that the recipient does not pay or bear tax on them, or by a deduction in computing profits or gains. Taxes affected are income tax and corporation tax, but *not* capital gains tax.

Note that the husband and wife (living together) are treated as nominees for each other.

Even if the three conditions mentioned earlier are satisfied, the taxpayer may escape application of s. 460, I.C.T.A. 1970 if he can prove that transactions were carried out for *bona fide* commercial reasons, or in the ordinary course of making or managing investments, and that they were not entered into with the main object of obtaining a tax advantage.

A taxpayer who considers that s. 460, I.C.T.A. 1970 might apply to transactions which he is intending to undertake may apply for a clearance, on the basis that the transaction is a *bona fide* commercial one, that the Revenue will not invoke the Section. Application is made by letter to a special unit at the Revenue Head Office and all relevant background facts should be included. Section 460, I.C.T.A. 1970 is so complex and wide-ranging that the taxpayer should consider applying for a clearance in every case where it is at all likely that it may apply.

The Revenue have power to make adjustments to counteract a tax advantage. This may be by assessment (under Case VI, Schedule D) or by recomputation of profits. Following an adjustment, an allowance may be made for notional A.C.T.

The procedure is as follows:

1. The Revenue notify the taxpayer of their intention to make an assessment.
2. The taxpayer has 30 days in which to make a statutory declaration why he considers no adjustment should be made.
3. If such a declaration is made, the case is referred to a tribunal to determine if there is a *prima facie* case for proceeding. The tribunal is not an appellate body: the taxpayer has no right to appear (*Wiseman* v. *Borneman* (1969)).
4. If the tribunal approves (or if no statutory declaration is made), a notice specifying the required adjustments is issued.
5. The taxpayer can appeal (to the Special Commissioners) against such a notice.
6. A company affected by a notional A.C.T. adjustment can join the appeal. The Revenue also have wide powers to obtain information concerning transactions to which s. 460, I.C.T.A. 1970 might apply.

Not surprisingly, there have been many cases dealing with the interpretation of this complex legislation. These are summarised below.

Against the taxpayer

1. Purchase of shares for cash by a company from shareholder of another company (*C.I.R.* v. *Cleary* (1967); *C.I.R.* v. *Brown* (1971)).
2. Forward dividend strip (*Greenberg* v. *C.I.R.* (1971); *C.I.R.* v. *Tunnicliffe* (1971)).
3. Liquidation and formation of new company (*Marks* v. *C.I.R.* (1973)).
4. Liquidation and sale to a second company (*Addy* v. *C.I.R.* (1975); *C.I.R.* v. *Joiner* (1975)).

5. Shares exchanged to enable dividend to rank as "group income" (*Anysz* v. *C.I.R.* (1978)).
6. Several cases were concerned with transactions involving bonus issues and redemption thereof (or reduction of capital), e.g. *C.I.R.* v. *Parker* (1966); *Hague* v. *C.I.R.* (1968); *C.I.R.* v. *Horrocks* (1968); *Hasloch* v. *C.I.R.* (1971). These cases were before 6th April 1965, and such transactions would not result in distributions under s. 233, I.C.T.A. 1970.

For the taxpayer
1. Redemption of debentures with arrears of interest shortly after purchase by merchant bank. The case was won on the grounds of *bona fide* commercial reasons (*C.I.R.* v. *Kleinwort, Benson* (1968)).
2. Several cases were concerned with transactions involving bonus issues and redemption thereof, e.g. *C.I.R.* v. *Brebner* (1967); *C.I.R.* v. *Goodwin* (1976). These cases were also before 6th April 1965 and would now result in distributions under s. 233, I.C.T.A. 1970.

SALE AND REPURCHASE OF SECURITIES (s. 469, I.C.T.A. 1970)
This section prevents the avoidance of tax on income which would otherwise arise to the owner of securities by the device of agreeing to sell them and subsequently buy them back so that the interest (including dividends) thereon is paid to the "temporary" owner and not to the real owner of the securities. This also applies if the owner of the securities concerned acquires an option, which he subsequently exercises, to buy them back.

In such circumstances any interest paid to the "temporary" owner is deemed to be the income of the true owner (whether or not it would otherwise have been chargeable to tax). If the securities are of a kind the interest on which can be paid without deduction of income tax, the owner is taxable under Case VI, Schedule D, but credit is given for any tax which has in fact been borne. This provision also applies for corporation tax, except that no credit is available.

The repurchase of different, but similar, securities is also caught by this section.

If the "temporary" owner is a dealer in securities, any income which is deemed to remain that of the true owner is ignored in the dealer's accounts. However, if the income is also assessable under the provisions relating to loan transactions, those provisions take precedence.

TRANSFER OF INCOME FROM SECURITIES (s. 470, I.C.T.A. 1970)
Section 470, I.C.T.A. 1970 is concerned with a variation of the above arrangement. It applies where the owner of securities, without selling the securities themselves, sells the right to receive interest therefrom (including dividends and annuities). In such a case the interest is deemed to remain the income of the owner. If the right to interest is sold (or realised) in a way such that the proceeds are taxable under Schedule C, or under s. 159(3), I.C.T.A. 1970 (foreign dividends), the interest deemed to remain the income of the owner is equal to the proceeds.

However, this does not affect the requirement to deduct income tax from interest, etc., notwithstanding that it is deemed to remain the income of the owner. On a subsequent sale, the proceeds are not again treated as the seller's income.

If the interest, etc. is paid gross, an assessment is made on the owner under Case VI, Schedule D, unless he shows that the interest has already been treated as his income and taxed accordingly. Where the income would otherwise have been chargeable on the remittance basis under Cases IV or V, Schedule D, the Case VI, Schedule D assessment is restricted to the amount remitted.

The main purpose of this section is to prevent tax avoidance by selling the right to receive income through agents abroad who are not liable to deduct tax.

PURCHASE AND SALE OF SECURITIES (ss. 471–475, I.C.T.A. 1970)
These sections all deal, in manners appropriate to various classes of recipient, with income received on securities which are purchased by a person (the "first buyer") who, before their subsequent sale, receives interest (including qualifying distributions, dividends, etc.). However, securities held for more than six months are unaffected, as are securities held for more than one month provided the purchase and sale were both at market value and the sale was not made under a contract already in force before the purchase.

The sections are widely drawn and the following points should be noted:
1. A sale under an option is deemed to take place at the option date.
2. A sale of similar securities, or several parcels of securities, is taken into account.
3. Securities held as stock in trade as deemed to be sold and immediately reacquired.

Broadly the sections are concerned with the treatment of the "appropriate amount" of interest, etc. This is the amount of interest, dividend etc. arising since the security went "ex-div" (not of income tax in the case of interest, or the actual amount of a dividend). Section 475, I.C.T.A. 1970 deals with the calculation of the "appropriate amount".

These are three particular situations to which the legislation is applied.

(a) Dealers in securities (s. 472, I.C.T.A. 1970; s. 57, F.A. 1982)
This concerns a "first buyer" who is a share dealer (other than a recognised jobber on the Stock Exchange, a *bona fide* discount house, buying securities in the ordinary course of business), or a "Eurobond" dealer. Where the section applies, then, in the computation of profits or losses of the trade, the price paid for the securities is reduced by the "appropriate amount". This section is currently causing some concern to the banking sector, not covered by the exclusions.

The section does not apply if the transaction has already given rise to a tax charge on the original owner of securities in a sale and repurchase transaction caught by s. 469, I.C.T.A. 1970, nor does it apply to overseas securities.

(b) Persons entitled to exemptions (s. 473, I.C.T.A. 1970)
Where the "first buyer" is otherwise entitled to an exemption from tax which would extend to interest, etc., the exemption is withdrawn for an amount equal to the "appropriate amount". If the "first buyer" is so entitled and he makes an annual payment out of the interest, etc., that payment is treated as made out of profits or gains not brought into charge to income tax, and income tax at the basic rate must be deducted and paid over to the Revenue (under s. 53, I.C.T.A. 1970).

(c) Persons other than share dealers (s. 474, I.C.T.A. 1970)
If the "first buyer" is carrying on a trade, but not a trade of share dealing, and makes a claim for loss relief under s. 168, I.C.T.A. 1970, the "gross" amount of the interest, etc. (or dividend plus related tax credit) is eliminated from the amount eligible for such a claim.

Where the "first buyer" is a company carrying on a trade other than one of share dealing, the gross "appropriate amount" is ignored for all tax purposes, except that the net "appropriate amount" is treated as a capital distribution (see s. 72(5)(b), C.G.T.A. 1979) and accordingly a chargeable gain will arise thereon.

DISTRIBUTION TO REDUCE VALUE OF HOLDING (s. 476, I.C.T.A. 1970)
Where a person whose business consists of dealing in shares or other investments becomes entitled to a dividend on shares and these shares represent 10% or more of any class of the issued ordinary shares of a company resident in the United Kingdom, then, so far as the net dividend is paid out of profits accumulated before the date of the acquisition, it is treated as an untaxed trading receipt, and must be included in the recipient's taxable profits.

A dividend is treated as being paid out of pre-acquisition profits:

   (*a*) If it is declared for a period falling before the date of acquisition. (Overlapping periods are divided for this purpose); or
   (*b*) If the company has no profits in the period from the date of acquisition to the date of payment; or
   (*c*) If, whilst there are such profits, after deducting certain notional dividends, there is no balance available for payment of dividend.

The section contains comprehensive provisions to prevent evasion by several businesses acting in concert, or by acquiring shares over a period.

"MANUFACTURED" DIVIDENDS (s. 477, I.C.T.A. 1970; s. 59, F.A. 1982)

This section applies where securities are sold but the seller agrees to pay the purchaser the amount of a periodical payment due on the securities (e.g. to pay interest, etc. after a "cum-div" sale) and he cannot show that he was entitled to receive the interest as the registered holder of the securities, or to receive it from a person from whom he himself had purchased them. In such a case the seller is treated as making an annual payment out of taxed income. If the previous vendor was non-resident, and the purchase was not made through a broker, the previous vendor must have been a registered holder.

If the seller is non-resident, the liability to deduct tax falls upon the broker acting, unless he can show that the seller falls within the exemptions described above.

The section does not apply to *bona fide* jobbers and dealing brokers buying and selling securities in the ordinary course of their business.

These provisions also apply to marketable bonds issued by building societies and sold after 9th March 1982.

§ 7.—TRANSFERS OF ASSETS ABROAD (ss. 478–481, I.C.T.A. 1970; ss. 45 and 46, F.A. 1981)

These sections are intended to prevent the avoidance of tax *by individuals* who are resident and ordinarily resident in the U.K. by means of transferring assets so that, either alone or as a combined effect of associated operations, income becomes payable to persons resident or domiciled outside the U.K.

If such a transfer is made in such a way that the individual concerned has *power to enjoy* (either immediately or at some time in the future) the income of a person resident or domiciled outside the U.K., then such income is deemed to remain that individual's income.

Where such an individual receives, or is entitled to receive, a capital sum (either before or after the transfer) which is in any way connected with the transfer, then any income which because of the transfer has become the income of a person resident or domiciled outside the U.K. is deemed to remain the individual's income.

In this context a capital sum means, broadly, any loan or repayment of a loan and any other non-income sum (not being a payment for full consideration in money or money's worth). For transactions after 5th April 1981, any sum received by a third person at an individual's discretion, or by his assignment of the right to receive it, is treated as though it were received by the individual himself. However, income will not be deemed to be that of an individual only because he had received a loan, if that loan had been paid off before the beginning of the year.

Although there is no clearance procedure under s. 478, the section does not apply if the individual concerned shows that the transaction was not carried out primarily for the purpose of avoiding tax.

As indicated above, the section applies not only to single transfers, but also to combinations of transactions and associated operations. An associated operation includes any operation of any kind carried out by any person in respect of the asset transferred, or any asset which, directly or indirectly, represents such an asset. It also includes any operation in respect of income arising from the asset, or from any asset which represents accumulations of income arising from such assets.

An individual has *power to enjoy* the income of a person resident or domiciled outside the United Kingdom in the following circumstances:

1. If the income is dealt with in such a way that at some point the individual can receive the benefit therefrom, whether in the form of income or otherwise.
2. If the receipt or accrual of income increases the value of an asset held by or on behalf of the individual.
3. If the individual receives (or could receive) benefit provided out of the income (or out of assets which, as a result of associated operations, represent the income).
4. If the individual could, following the exercise of a power, become entitled to beneficial enjoyment of the income.
5. If the individual can, in any way, control the application of the income.

In determining whether an individual has power to enjoy income, regard is had to the substantial result and effect of a transfer and associated operations and there must be taken into account all benefits, or whatever nature, which accrue to the individual.

In applying the section, the followed definitions are followed.

1. A company incorporated outside the United Kingdom is treated as resident outside the United Kingdom (irrespective of whether, by other rules, it is resident in the U.K. or not).
2. References to an individual also include his or her husband or wife.
3. Assets include property of any kind.
4. A benefit includes any kind of payment.
5. The "gross" amount of apportioned income of close companies can be included (if appropriate) in the income payable to a person resident or domiciled outside the United Kingdom.
6. Assets which represent other assets, income or accumulations of income include shares or other obligations of any company to which such assets, income or accumulations of income have been transferred.

Where the section applies, income tax is assessed under Case VI, Schedule D, but credit is given if any of the income has borne basic rate tax by deduction. In computing an individual's tax liability, the normal deductions and reliefs are allowed as would apply if actual income had been received. Income which has, in fact, previously been distributed is excluded.

If an individual is domiciled outside the United Kingdom, he will not be assessed on income which is deemed to be his if he would not, because of his domicile, be taxed thereon if he in fact received it.

Once an individual has been assessed to tax on deemed income, he will not be charged on it again if he subsequently receives it.

Section 45, F.A. 1981 amends these provisions where there has been a transfer of assets (with or without associated operations) so that income became payable to a person resident or domiciled outside the United Kingdom and an individual who is ordinarily resident in the U.K. but who is not liable to tax under s. 478, I.C.T.A. 1970 (not being the transferor) receives a benefit out of the assets. The new rules apply if the primary purpose of the transfer was the avoidance of tax and the benefit was received, or the income arose, after 9th March 1981, no matter when the transfer or the associated operations took place.

Where the section applies, the value of the benefit is deemed to be the income of the ordinarily resident individual in the year of assessment in which the benefit is received, and is assessed under Case VI, Schedule D. The amount assessed is limited to the cumulative relevant income up to and including that tax year. If the benefit received exceeds the cumulative relevant income, the excess is carried forward against the relevant income of the next year, and so on.

For this purpose *relevant income* is income which arises in the tax year concerned to a person resident or domiciled outside the United Kingdom which can be used, directly or indirectly, to provide the benefit.

However, an individual who is domiciled outside the United Kingdom is not taxable if he receives a benefit outside the United Kingdom, even though there is relevant income, provided the circumstances are such that no tax would arise on any income actually received by him. The provisions of s. 122, I.C.T.A. 1970, by which income applied outside the United Kingdom can, in certain cases, be treated as received therein, are applied as if the benefit received was income arising from foreign possessions.

In the case of an overseas settlement, where a capital payment is made which is deemed by ss. 80 or 81(2), F.A. 1981 to be a chargeable gain in the hands of the beneficiaries, the amount of the gain is left out of account in attributing income to a beneficiary, in order to avoid the income being taxed twice.

No charge is made under s. 46, F.A. 1981 if it is shown that the transactions were not primarily carried out for tax avoidance.

In general, the various definitions in s. 478, I.C.T.A. 1970 also apply to s. 45, F.A. 1981.

Section 46, F.A. 1981 provides that income cannot be taken into account more than once under s. 478, I.C.T.A. 1970 and s. 45, F.A. 1981. If there is a choice as to the persons to whom such income can be attributed, it is apportioned between them on a "just and reasonable basis".

As might be expected, the Revenue have broad powers to obtain information for the purposes of these sections. The persons from whom information can be obtained include not only the taxpayer but also persons acting for him. However, the information which a solicitor can be compelled to provide is strictly limited. This privilege does not apply to accountants. Bankers cannot be compelled to give information about transactions carried out in the ordinary course of a banking business.

§ 8.—MIGRATION OF COMPANIES (s. 482, I.C.T.A. 1970)

Certain transactions are illegal unless carried out with prior Treasury consent:
- (*a*) Transfer of residence outside the United Kingdom by a resident company.
- (*b*) Transfer of the trade or business (or part thereof) of a resident company to a non-resident.
- (*c*) Creation or issue of shares or debentures by a non-resident company controlled by a resident company.
- (*d*) Transfer of shares or debentures of a non-resident company (controlled by a resident company).

A company is deemed to be resident (or not resident) in the U.K. on the basis of a test as to where its central management and control of its trade or business is exercised. Once the residence status of a company has been determined, it is presumed to remain so resident (or not resident) until the contrary is proved.

The holding of investments or property, if that is the principal function of a company, is deemed to be a business.

The mere transfer of assets by a company which does not result in a substantial change in the character or extent of a company's business is not treated as a transfer or part of a trade or business.

The following definitions, apply.
1. "Share", "debenture" and "director" are as defined by s. 455, Companies Act 1948 (ss. 741, 744, Companies Act 1985).

2. "Control" (except in the context of "central management and control") is as defined by s. 534, I.C.T.A. 1970.
3. "Transfer" of shares or debentures includes a transfer of the beneficial interest therein.

Item (3) does not apply to providing the bankers of a company not resident in the United Kingdom with security for payments made by them in the ordinary course of a banking business. This also applies to transactions with insurance companies.

The Treasury consent, if given, to those transactions which are not in the ordinary course of a banking or insurance business may be given specifically to a particular transaction or generally to a class of similar transactions. In the latter case, it may be revoked by the Treasury, and in any event it may be given either absolutely or subject to conditions.

The penalty for non-compliance with this section is a maximum of £10,000 or two years' imprisonment (or both). A company resident in the United Kingdom which infringes the above rule is liable to a fine of £10,000 or three times the tax attributable to the company's profits within the three preceding years. It should be noted that penalties can be imposed on any person who does, or is a party to the doing of, any of the transactions listed above. A director of a company which has infringed these rules is presumed to have knowledge of and be a party to any such acts unless he can prove that they were done without his consent or connivance.

As indicated above, the Treasury can give general consent to a class of transactions and an application for clearance is then not required before carrying out such a transaction. The "general consents" which are currently in force are reproduced below.

GENERAL CONSENTS

1. Transactions falling within paras (a) and (b) of subsection (1) where:
   (*a*) The body corporate resident in the United Kingdom is incorporated after the passing of F.A. 1951 for the purpose of carrying on a new trade or business not previously carried on by any person; *and*
   (*b*) More than 50% of the issued share capital of the body in existence at the time of the transactions in question, or, if there is then in existence share capital of more than one class, more than 50% of the issued share capital of each class, is then, and was when it was issued, in the beneficial ownership of persons not ordinarily resident in the U.K.
2. A transaction falling within para. (c) and subsection (1) consists of the issue, by a body corporate not resident in the U.K. but over which a body corporate resident in the U.K. has control, of shares for full consideration paid in cash to the body issuing the shares, or in (or towards) payment for any business, undertaking or property acquired for full consideration, *unless* either:
   (*a*) The shares are redeemable preference shares; *or*
   (*b*) The shares are issued to, or to trustees for, a body corporate not resident in the U.K. over which the body resident in the U.K. has control, or to, or to trustees for, an individual or individuals who has (or have) control over the U.K.-resident body; *or*
   (*c*) The effect of the transaction is that the U.K.-resident body will no longer have control over the non-resident body.
3. A transaction falling within para. (d) of subsection (1) which consists of the transfer of shares to a body corporate resident in the U.K., unless the effect of the transaction is that the U.K.-resident body which transfers the shares (or causes or permits the shares to be transferred) will no longer have control over the non-resident body.

4. A transaction falling within para. (c) of s. 482(1), I.C.T.A. 1970, where the body corporate not resident in the U.K. was incorporated after 31st December 1951 for the purpose of starting and carrying on a new industrial activity in any Commonwealth territory and is resident in that Commonwealth territory.

"Industrial activity" means any productive, extractive or manufacturing industry, any public utility, fisheries or any form of farming.

5. A transaction falling within para. (b) of s. 482(1), I.C.T.A. 1970, which consists of the outright sale of a business or part of a business to a person not resident in the U.K., provided that:
   (*a*) The sale is for full consideration paid in cash.
   (*b*) The consideration for the sale does not exceed £50,000.
   (*c*) The buyer is not a body corporate over which persons ordinarily resident in the U.K. have control.
   (*d*) The buyer has no interest in the business of the seller, and the seller has no interest in the business of the buyer.
   (*e*) The sale is not associated with any other operation, transaction or arrangement whereby the business (or part of a business) may revert to the seller or to any person who has an interest in the business of the seller.

SPECIFIC CONSENTS

Where specific consent is required, the application should follow a standard format as suggested by the Treasury which is reproduced below.

Information required for all transactions
1. The name of the applicant company.
2. The nature of the business of the company and the place where its main activities are carried on.
3. Whether the applicant is a public or private company.
4. The extent of the overseas holding where U.K. residents hold less than 80% of the share capital of any class.
5. The names of the present and any proposed directors of the company and the addresses of any directors not resident in the U.K.
6. The Tax District in which the company makes its corporation tax returns.
7. Brief details of any previous application which has been made under the section by or on behalf of the applicant company.
8. The nature of the proposed transaction.

For transactions under subsection 1(a) (transfer of residence)
9. The proposed residence of the company.
10. Full details of the means by which it is proposed (*a*) to transfer the residence of the company from the United Kingdom and (*b*) to exercise control and management abroad.

For transactions under subsection 1(b) (transfer of a trade or business or part of a trade or business)
11. The name and address of the transferee. If he is an agent, the name and address of the principal.
12. Whether there is any direct or indirect connection, by means of shareholding or otherwise, between the applicant company and the transferee or his principal.
13. The amount of the consideration for the transfer, how it is to be satisfied, and whether it is regarded as full consideration.

14. If the transfer is to a new company, the reasons why it is necessary for that company to be controlled abroad and full details of the means by which control and management are to be exercised.
15. If part only of the company's trade or business is to be transferred, full particulars of that part. (If separate accounts for that part have been prepared, copies for each of the last five years should be attached; where accounts have not been prepared, an estimate of the turnover and profit in respect of that part for each of these years should be substituted).

For transactions under subsection 1(c) (issue of shares or debentures in a non-resident company)

16. The name of the non-resident company and the nature and extent of the applicant company's control over it (see s. 534, I.C.T.A. 1970, as applied by s. 482(10)).
17. The nature of the business of the non-resident company and the place where its main activities are carried on.
18. The amount and description of the shares or debentures to be issued.
19. The name(s) and address(es) of the person(s) to whom the shares of debentures are to be issued and full details of any direct or indirect connection, by means of shareholding or otherwise, between such persons and either company.
20. Full details of the consideration where the issue is not for cash.
21. If the issue represents capitalisation of profits or reserves,
    (a) How the reserves have been created;
    (b) Whether any repayment of capital, whether directly or by means of associated transactions, is in the contemplation, or, on presently known facts, is possible at a future date.
22. If the issue is other than to the applicant company, the proportion of shares of each class which would be held by the applicant company after the transaction.

For transactions under subsection (1d) (transfer of shares or debentures in a non-resident company)

23. The name of the non-resident company and the nature and extent of the applicant company's control over it (see s. 534, I.C.T.A. 1970, as applied by s. 482(10)).
24. The nature of the business of the non-resident company and the place where its main activities are carried on.
25. The nature and amount of the consideration for the transfer and, where this differs from the current market value, the reasons for the difference.
26. The name(s) and address(es) of the person(s) to whom the shares or debentures are to be transferred and full details of any direct or indirect connection, by means of shareholding or otherwise, between such person(s) and either company.
27. The proportion of the shares of each class in the non-resident company which would be held by the applicant company after the transaction.

For all transactions

28. An estimate of the difference between the amounts of U.K. corporation tax (including A.C.T. and corporation tax on chargeable gains) and income tax, taking into account the close company provisions if applicable which would be payable as a result of the proposed transactions and those payable under existing arrangements.
29. An estimate of the effect of the transaction on the United Kingdom

balance of payments. This estimate should include the provision of the following information:

(*a*) Details of both the current annual value and the expected value after the proposed transaction has taken place of:
    (i) The company's export earnings;
    (ii) All funds remitted to the U.K. to meet tax, head office and other expenses, or out of profits (whether by way of dividends or otherwise).
(*b*) Where application is made under subsection 1(a) or (b), an estimate of the assets and liabilities to be transferred, indicating the extent to which they represent (i) sterling, (ii) other currencies.
(*c*) Where application is made under subsection 1(c) or (d), the amount of any payments or receipts which will be remitted from or to the U.K. as part of the transaction.
30. The reasons in full for the proposed transaction.

(Attention is drawn to the terms of reference of the Advisory Committee, which are as follows: "They will take into account the significance of any new factors or circumstances which are represented to require the proposed change and any compelling reasons for such applications, based on the efficiency and development of the applicant's operations. The Committee will weigh against considerations of this kind the prospective loss of revenue or of foreign exchange to this country which the transaction, if permitted, would entail, and they will inform the Chancellor whether, on a balance of considerations, it would in their opinion be in the national interest that permission should be granted.")

POSSIBLE REPEAL

In January 1981 the Inland Revenue issued a consultative document entitled *Company Residence*. Among other things it put forward the idea of statutorily defining company residence and as a consequence abolishing s. 482, I.C.T.A. 1970. It has been suggested that this section is *ultra vires* E.E.C. regulations. Pending clarification of this it is suggested that clearance be sought in all relevant cases.

§ 9.—SALES AT UNDER-VALUE OR OVER-VALUE (s. 485, I.C.T.A. 1970; s. 17, F.A. 1975)

The Revenue have power to adjust computations for tax purposes when either goods are sold, assets are let (other than furnished lettings) or rights, licences or facilities are given at other than normal market prices, *and* one of the parties to the transaction controls the other, or both are controlled by a third person.

The adjustment comprises substitution of the price which might have been expected to be paid if the parties to the transaction had been independent persons dealing "at arm's length" for the actual price, either:

(*a*) In the seller's computation, if the price paid was under market price, *or*
(*b*) In the buyer's computation, if the price was inflated over market price.
These provisions do not apply in the case of (*a*) above if the buyer is a United Kingdom resident who would normally show the price paid as a charge in his own accounts and computations, or in the case of (*b*) above if the seller is a United Kingdom resident who would normally bring in the price received as a trade receipt in his own accounts and computations.

Any adjustments made by the Revenue under these provisions will not affect the ordinary calculation of capital allowances, etc.

§ 10.—TRANSACTIONS BETWEEN A DEALING COMPANY AND AN ASSOCIATED COMPANY (s. 486, I.C.T.A. 1970)

If a company which carries on a trade of dealing in securities, land or buildings is entitled to a deduction in computing its profits in respect of a depreciation in the value of a right as against an associated company (not itself a dealing company), or if a payment, which is deductible in the computations of the dealing company, is made to the associated company and the depreciation or payment is not otherwise brought into account in computing the profits of the associated company, a Case CI, Schedule D assessment is made upon that company. However, if the associated company is carrying on some other trade or trades, it can elect to include the payment or depreciation as being a receipt of the trade, or of one of them.

A payment which is made to an associated company in respect of abortive expenditure by that company, and for which it does not get any allowance, is, however, excluded.

§ 11.—PERSONS EXEMPT FROM TAX—DIVIDENDS, ETC.

RESTRICTION RE PRE-ACQUISITION DIVIDENDS (s. 22, Schedule 10, F.A. 1973)
Where dividends are received by a person who, because of an exemption, can recover the full tax credit related thereto, but such a person holds more than 10% of any one class of shares, the tax credit related to such part of the dividend as relates to the period before his acquisition of the shares is not repayable. Furthermore, tax will be payable on the gross amount of the dividend in the normal way. The dividend is not available for offset by interest payments (under ss. 52 or 53, I.C.T.A. 1970).

BONUS ISSUES (s. 23, F.A. 1973)
If a bonus issue is treated as a distribution (under ss. 234, 235 or Schedule 22, Para. 3(3), F.A. 1972) and the recipient is entitled to an exemption or a loss relief set-off, the bonus issue and the tax credit related thereto are ignored in any repayment calculation. Furthermore, the bonus issue will be liable to tax, despite the exemption, if it exceeds a normal return on the investment. Such a bonus issue is not available for set-off as franked investment income, nor is it available for ss. 52–53, I.C.T.A. 1970, or to offset interest paid under s. 75, I.C.T.A. 1970.

§ 12.—ANNUAL PAYMENTS FOR NON-TAXABLE CONSIDERATION (s. 48, F.A. 1977)

Action has been taken to counteract tax avoidance schemes incorporating "reverse annuities". Under such schemes a higher-rate taxpayer would sell the top slice of his income for a capital sum, whilst undertaking to pay an annuity over a four- or five-year period. The theory was that the annual annuity payments were deductible in computing the taxpayer's total income for higher-rate tax and surcharge purposes, whilst the capital sum received was exempt from income tax at least.

The section applies to any annuity payment after 29th March 1977, whether made under an annuity contract entered into or before or after that date. The provisions apply to arrangements whereby annual payments (other than interest) chargeable under Schedule D, Case III are made under a liability incurred for a sum which is wholly or partly exempt from tax to the recipient.

These restrictions do not apply to *bona fide* payments made:
    (*a*) To a former partner or his dependents;
    (*b*) Under a maintenance settlement following divorce;
    (*c*) In consideration for the acquisition of a business;
    (*d*) For the surrender of an interest in settled property to a subsequent beneficiary;
    (*e*) In the ordinary course of an annuity business;

(*f*) In connection with a disposal, made before 30th March 1977, of an interest in settled property to a company then carrying on life assurance business in the U.K. or whose business included the acquisition of such interests.

Where the new provisions apply to any arrangement, then any annuity (or other annual payment) paid under such a scheme is made without deduction of income tax and is allowed as a deduction in computing total income.

Similar schemes for companies are also counteracted by these provisions.

§ 13.—DEALINGS IN COMMODITY FUTURES (s. 31, F.A. 1978)

No relief is available for losses sustained in a trade of dealing in commodity futures carried on by a partnership of which one or more of the parties is a company and the arrangements were made for the purpose of obtaining the loss relief. The losses concerned are: s. 168, I.C.T.A. 1970 (set-off against general income of an individual); s. 30, F.A. 1978 (set-off against an individual's general income of earlier years for losses sustained in the early years of a trade); and s. 177(2), I.C.T.A. 1970 (set-off against total profits of a company).

§ 14.—CHANGE OF OWNERSHIP OF A COMPANY

This has been dealt with fully elsewhere, as indicated below:
Losses carried forward (ss. 483–484, I.C.T.A. 1970)—Chapter 17, § 2 and § 3; Chapter 18, § 20.
Advance corporation tax (s. 101, I.C.T.A. 1970)—Chapter 14, § 4.
Stock relief (Schedule 9, Para. 14, F.A. 1981)—Chapter 17, § 3.
Capital gains of companies (ss. 262, 267, 278 to 280, I.C.T.A. 1970)—Chapter 21, § 3.

§ 15.—CAPITAL GAINS

The following anti-avoidance provisions have been dealt with elsewhere:
Paper-for-paper takeover (ss. 87–88, C.G.T.A. 1979)—Chapter 28, § 15.
Value shifting (s. 26, C.G.T.A. 1979)—Chapter 27, § 11.

§ 16.—DEMERGERS (s. 117 and Schedule 18, F.A. 1980)

The demerger provisions apply to transactions which would, but for the rules outlined below, constitute distributions by the company being demerged, unless carried out on the liquidation of the company.

INTRODUCTION

These rules remove a major tax obstacle to the division of a large trading company or group so that two or more of its trades can be managed independently of each other. Such a division occurs when, for example:

1. A conglomerate company A has two trading subsidiaries, and
2. It transfers one of its subsidiaries to a new company which issues its shares to the shareholders of company A, so that
3. Those shareholders then own separately A with its subsidiary and the new company (with its subsidiary).

The provisions apply only to the genuine splitting off of trades, or of trading subsidiaries, from one company to another owned by the same shareholders. They do not apply to, for example, the extraction of cash from any of the companies.

RELIEF FROM A.C.T. AND INCOME TAX

A.C.T. and income tax are not applied to exempt distributions. However, such transactions require the sanction of the Court (under Companies Act 1980, s. 39;

ss. 263, 275, Companies Act 1985) unless there are sufficient profits available for distribution.

The following are exempt distributions:

Type A—a transfer to any or all members of the distributing company of shares of its 75% subsidiary.

Type B—a transfer by the distributing company to the transferee company of a trade.

Type C—a transfer by the distributing company to the transferee company of shares in 75% subsidiaries of the distributing company.

The following points should be noted:
1. Members must be holders of ordinary share capital.
2. Ordinary share capital is as defined by s. 526(5), I.C.T.A. 1970.
3. 75% subsidiaries must be direct subsidiaries of the distributing company.

The following conditions apply to all demergers:
- (*a*) The distributing company, the 75% subsidiaries and the transferee companies must all be resident in the U.K.
- (*b*) The distributing company must be a trading company or a member of a trading group.
- (*c*) The group 75% subsidiary must be a trading company or the holding company of a trading group.
- (*d*) The distribution must be made wholly or mainly for the benefit of trading activities previously carried on by a single company or group, but thereafter by two or more companies or groups.
- (*e*) The distribution must not be part of a scheme or arrangement whose main purpose is:
  - (i) The avoidance of tax (including stamp duty);
  - (ii) The making of a chargeable payment (or an equivalent payment by an unquoted company).
  - (iii) Acquisition by persons who are not members of the distributing company of control thereof, or of any subsidiary or transferee company or fellow group member thereof.
  - (iv) Cessation of a trade, or the sale thereof, after the distribution.

Further conditions apply to *Type A* demergers:
- (*a*) The transfer must:
  - (i) Not be redeemable shares:
  - (ii) Constitute all or a substantial part of its holding in the ordinary share capital of the 75% subsidiary;
  - (iii) Confer all or a substantial part of its voting rights in the subsidiary.
- (*b*) After the distribution, the distributing company must be a trading company or a member of a trading group. This does not apply:
  - (i) On the transfer of two or more 75% subsidiaries resulting in the distributing company being dissolved (there being no net assets remaining);
  - (ii) If the distributing company is a 75% subsidiary of another company.

It should be noted that:
- (i) This prevents the splitting of trade from investment.
- (ii) The demerger provisions *do not* apply to liquidations.
- (iii) The demerger provisions *do* apply to a dissolution under s. 206, Companies Act 1948 (s. 425, Companies Act 1985).

Further conditions apply to *Type B* and *Type C* demergers.
- (*a*) If a trade is transferred, the distributing company must not retain any interest (or only a minor interest) therein.
- (*b*) If shares in a subsidiary are transferred, they must:
  - (i) Constitute the whole or substantially the whole of its holding of the ordinary share capital of the subsidiary;

      (ii) Confer the whole or substantially the whole of its voting rights in the subsidiary.

    There is no condition that the shares should not be redeemable.

(*c*) After the distribution, the only (or main) activity of the transferee company must be the carrying on of the trade or holding the transferred shares.

(*d*) The shares issued by the transferee company must:
      (i) Not be redeemable;
      (ii) Constitute the whole or substantially the whole of its *issued* ordinary share capital;
      (iii) Confer the whole or substantially the whole of its voting rights in the subsidiary.

(*e*) The distributing company must, after the distribution, be a trading company, or a member of a trading group. This does not apply:
      (i) If there are two or more transferee companies, each of which has a trade or shares in a separate 75% subsidiary of the distributing company transferred to it, whereupon the distributing company is dissolved (there being no net assets remaining); *or*
      (ii) If the distributing company is the 75% subsidiary of another company.

The following conditions apply if the distributing company is a 75% subsidiary of another:

(*a*) The group of which it is a member must be a trading group.

(*b*) The requirement for it to be a trading company, or a member of a trading group, *after* the distribution does not apply.

(*c*) The distribution must be followed by one or more *Type A* or *Type C* exempt distributions, so that members of the holding company become members of:
      (i) The transferee company to which the trade was distributed; or
      (ii) The subsidiary whose shares were transferred; or
      (iii) A company (other than the holding company) of which the companies in (i) or (ii) become 75% subsidiaries.

RELIEF FROM TAX ON CAPITAL GAINS

If a distributing company makes a *Type A* exempt distribution, then:

(*a*) The distribution is not a "capital distribution in respect of shares" and no disposal under s. 72, C.G.T.A. 1979 occurs.

(*b*) In applying provisions dealing with the equation of old and new shareholdings on a reorganisation of share capital, the distributing company and the 75% subsidiary whose shares are transferred are treated as being the same company (and the distribution is treated as being a reorganisation of share capital).

(*c*) *Type B* and *Type C* transactions will normally fall within s. 86, C.G.T.A. 1979.

There is no charge to tax on a company ceasing to be a member of a group by reason of an exempt distribution.

RELIEF FROM D.L.T.

There is no charge on a company ceasing to be a member of a group by reason of an exempt distribution.

STAMP DUTY

There is no charge to stamp duty on documents executed solely for the purpose, or on chargeable transactions carried out in an exempt distribution. However, documents must be "nil" stamped.

ANTI-AVOIDANCE

The exemptions do not apply to *chargeable payments*. A chargeable payment is one which is not made for *bona fide* commercial reasons, or forms part of a scheme whose purpose is the avoidance of tax (including stamp duty), being a payment which a company concerned in an exempt distribution makes (directly or indirectly) to its members (or to members of another company) concerned in the distribution; and is made in connection with its shares (or those of another company concerned in the distribution); and is not a distribution, an exempt distribution or made to another company in the same group.

If a company concerned in an exempt distribution is an unquoted company, chargeable payments include payments under a scheme of arrangement made with the unquoted company, and, in the case of a s. 461D, I.C.T.A. 1970 company (extended to include an unquoted company controlled exclusively by a non-D company), chargeable payments include payments under a scheme or arrangement made with such persons.

A company is "concerned in an exempt distribution" if it is the distributing company, a 75% subsidiary whose shares are transferred, or the transferee company. This also concerns any company connected therewith during part, or all, of the period from the exempt distribution to the chargeable payment, and companies connected with such connected companies.

For this purpose a "payment" includes a transfer of money's worth and the assumption of a liability.

Example

The following is an example of transactions caught by the anti-avoidance provisions.

As part of an avoidance scheme there is a *Type A* demerger and the distributing company (or a company connected with it):

    (i) Buys the shares back; or

    (ii) Arranges for the liquidation of the subsidiary; or

    (iii) Otherwise passes out cash in a form not subject to income tax.

The purpose of such a transaction would have been to pass out cash or other assets which would have suffered A.C.T. and income tax if paid as a normal dividend.

The anti-avoidance provisions do not apply:

    1. To an arm's length sale to a third party (e.g. on the Stock Exchange).

    2. On a subsequent (not pre-arranged) takeover by a third party.

If a chargeable payment occurs with five years of an exempt distribution:

    (*a*) It is charged as income under Schedule D, Case VI.

    (*b*) Unless it is a transfer of money's worth, income tax is deductible (s. 53, I.C.T.A. 1970).

    (*c*) It is not deductible as a charge on income, not in computing income.

    (*d*) It cannot be treated as a distribution against relevant income, nor as a subsequent distribution of apportioned income.

    (*e*) It is not treated as a repayment of capital.

If relief from tax on chargeable gains on a company leaving a group by reason of an exempt distribution has been claimed and there is a chargeable payment within five years thereafter, the tax charge is reinstated (time limit for assessment is three years).

If relief from D.L.T. on a company leaving a group by reason of an exempt distribution has been claimed and there is chargeable payment within five years, the tax charge is reinstated (time limit for assessment is three years).

There are clearance procedures so that:

    (*a*) A distributing company can apply to the Revenue for clearance that a distribution will be an exempt distribution.

(*b*) A person making a payment can apply to the Revenue for clearance that it will not be a chargeable payment.

(*c*) A company which becomes (or ceases to be) connected with another company may apply to the Revenue for clearance that payments which it might make thereafter will not be chargeable payments.

25. Value Added Tax

§ 1.—SCOPE OF VAT (ss. 1-2, V.A.T.A. 1983)

VAT is chargeable on the *supply of goods and services* in the United Kingdom and the Isle of Man and the *importation* of goods into the United Kingdom and the Isle of Man is also covered.

No specific goods and services are mentioned in the legislation and thus all goods and services are subject to VAT unless they are specifically mentioned as *exempt*, or are outside the scope of VAT. Certain supplies are zero-rated, which means that they are, technically, subject to VAT but at a rate of NIL.

The tax applies to all goods and services *supplied in the United Kingdom* by a *taxable person* in the course or furtherance of a business carried on by him.

Any person who makes a *taxable supply* whilst he is, or should be, registered for VAT is a *taxable person* and must account to Customs (i.e. the Commissioners of Customs and Excise) for tax charged upon his outputs (i.e. supplies made *by* him) after relief for tax suffered by him on his inputs (i.e. supplies made *to* him), subject to special rules as to accounting and payment on a periodic basis.

The principle of VAT is that a tax will be levied on the value of goods and services at each stage of production and distribution until it reaches the final consumer. The manufacturer will pay VAT on supplies made to him (termed "Input Tax") and charge tax on his sales to the wholesaler (termed "Output Tax"). The manufacturer will deduct the VAT he has paid on supplies made to him from the VAT he has collected from his sales and remit the difference to or claim a refund from the Customs on a periodical accounting basis.

The wholesaler and retailer will repeat the process along the distribution chain until the goods reach the final consumer, the general public.

The final consumer will have to pay VAT on his purchases, but as he is not a taxable trader and cannot therefore pass the VAT on to any other person, he must bear the VAT he has paid.

If, at any stage in this process the VAT paid on supplies exceeds the VAT collected from sales, the excess is refunded to the trader concerned.

Example 1

A person visits a retail shop and purchases an article costing £50.00 on which value added tax of 15% (£7.50) is charged. Total price paid is then £57.50.

The chain of events leading up to the payment of £7.50 VAT may be as under:

		£	VAT transactions
1.	Manufacturer		£
	Amount paid for raw materials	10.00	
	VAT 15%.....................	1.50 =	1.50 paid to supplier
	Total cost	£11.50	
	Sale price to wholesaler.........	25.00	
	VAT 15%.....................	3.75 =	3.75 collected from wholesaler
	Sale price	£28.75 =	£2.25 paid to Customs

(Value added £25.00 less £10.00 = £15.00 @ 15% = £2.25)

2.	Wholesaler	£	£
	Purchase price................	25.00	
	VAT 15%.....................	3.75 =	3.75 paid to manufacturer
	Total cost	£28.75	
	Sale price to retailer	35.00	
	VAT 15%.....................	5.25 =	5.25 collected from retailer
	Sale price	£40.25 =	£1.50 paid to Customs

(Value added £35.00 less £25.00 = £10.00 @ 15% = £1.50)

3.	Retailer		
	Purchase price................	35.00	
	VAT 15%.....................	5.25 =	5.25 paid to wholesaler
	Total cost	£40.25	
	Sale price to final consumer	50.00	
	VAT 15%.....................	7.50 =	7.50 collected from final consumer
	Sale price	£57.50 =	£2.25 paid to Customs

Value added £50.00 less £35.00 = £15.00 @ 15% = £2.25)

4.	Final consumer		
	Purchase price................	50.00	
	VAT 15%.....................	7.50 =	£7.50 paid to retailer
	Total cost	£57.50	

(As the final consumer is not a taxable person, there is no way in which he can reclaim the VAT paid and therefore he must bear the tax).

Example 2

During the quarter ended 31st December 1985 a taxable trader sells goods to the value of £12,000 (VAT charged £1,800). During the same quarter he purchases goods to the value of £8,000 (VAT paid £1,200).

His quarterly VAT account would read:

	£
Output tax due	1,800
Less: Input tax paid........................	1,200
Tax payable to Customs....................	£ 600

The position is the same where a supply of services is involved.

VAT is applied to imports, as if it were a customs duty. This applies not only to goods imported by a taxable person in the course or furtherance of a business, but also to importations by taxable persons otherwise than in the course of their businesses, and also in importations by other (non-taxable) persons.

VAT is under the "care and management" of the Commissioners of Customs and Excise, who are thus made responsible for its administration, collection, etc. The legislation gives them wide powers to make rules and regulations and to exercise their discretion on certain matters. The Treasury has power to issue additional orders, by statutory instrument, which are in effect changes to the VAT legislation.

The Commissioners have issued various notices which set out, in detail, their interpretation as to the application and administration of VAT. In general, these notices do not have statutory authority. However, certain of the VAT regulations have been published in the form of published notices (e.g. Special Schemes for Retailers; Second-hand Schemes; requirements as to the keeping of records) and as such have the force of law. Thus, with these exceptions, VAT tribunals will look to the wording of the legislation rather than to the Commissioners' interpretation of it. Definitions and precedents drawn from experience of income tax, etc, must not be applied. There is a separate body of Customs and Excise cases and precedents which should be consulted. However VAT is not, except in relation to imports, a duty of Customs and Excise and Customs and Excise law must only be applied where the legislation specifically refers to it. Certain regulations made by the Council of Ministers of the European Economic Community ("the Common Market") may also apply.

VAT is charged under either V.A.T.A. 1983 or under Isle of Man Act 1979. Both these Acts, in effect, treat the U.K. and the Isle of Man as one place so that VAT is not charged twice, under both Acts, on the same supplies. Thus a person who is a taxable person under one Act is automatically a taxable person under the other. It also means that the removal of goods and the provision of services between the U.K. and the Isle of Man (or vice versa) are not treated as imports or exports under either jurisdiction. Furthermore re-exports are treated as made from the country from which the original supply was made. Registration for VAT purposes can be made in either the U.K. or in the Isle of Man, but not both.

In the following sections of this chapter, references to the U.K. should be taken as including references to the Isle of Man.

§ 2.—RATE OF TAX (ss. 1, 9, F.A. 1972)

The tax is charged on the value of a supply of goods or services. On the importation of goods the tax is charged on the value of the goods. In either case there are appropriate rules that determine such value.

The standard rate of tax at the commencement of the VAT system on 1st April 1973 was 10% and this continued until 29th July 1974, when it was reduced to 8% for all taxable supplies of goods and services. A higher rate of 25% was introduced on 18th November 1974 on motor spirits (petrol and petrol substitutes) but other road fuels (derv) remained chargeable at the standard rate of 8%.

The 25% higher rate of VAT was extended to include "luxury goods" on the 1st May 1975.

The higher rate of VAT was reduced from 25% to $12\frac{1}{2}$% on 12th April 1976, and was abolished with effect from 18th June 1979.

From 18th June 1979 a single standard positive rate of 15% applies.

The Treasury have powers to vary the standard rate of VAT by means of "regulators". The rate can be increased or decreased by up to one-quarter of its amount. Thus the standard rate of 15% could be varied in this way, by statutory instrument, to any rate in the range of $11\frac{1}{4}$% to $18\frac{3}{4}$%. Such an order, under statutory instrument, automatically lapses after twelve months unless it is continued by a further order or confirmed by a change in the legislation.

The Provisional Collection of Taxes Act 1968 applies to VAT so that temporary effect is given to House of Commons resolutions for changes in the law, and indeed the re-imposition of the tax, pending Royal Assent to a Finance Bill. If a contract for the supply of goods or services has been entered into, but before the goods or services are supplied there is a change in the tax charged on the supply (e.g. on a change in the rate of VAT, or on a change from zero rate to standard rate), then *unless the contract provides otherwise* an appropriate addition or deduction is made to or from the contract price.

§ 3.—TAXABLE PERSONS (ss. 2, 27–32, V.A.T.A. 1983)

The mechanics of VAT are such that, while VAT is charged on the "supply of goods or services" in the U.K., such supplies are made by "taxable persons" who must account to Customs for the tax so charged.

A "taxable person" is someone who makes supplies of goods or services (provided that they are not in the list of "exempt" supplies) and is, or should be, registered for VAT purposes. The requirement to register applies if a person's supplies or his anticipated supplies exceed prescribed limits. There are also provisions dealing with new businesses and allowing for voluntary registration, even though the taxable supplies do not or will not, exceed the prescribed limits.

A supply of goods or services is a "taxable supply" only if it is made "in the course or furtherance of a business" carried on by the taxable person. Thus a person who is not carrying on any business, but who sells, in his private capacity, some article (e.g. furniture) is not making a taxable supply. Likewise an employee whose salary exceeds the registration limit is not, in general, treated as making a taxable supply of his services.

However, it is "persons" who are liable to register for VAT and not the business which they run. Thus a person who carries on several businesses must aggregate the supplies made in each of them in order to determine whether his supplies exceed the prescribed limits for registration. Similarly once a person makes sufficient taxable supplies in the course of a business so that he thereby becomes liable to register in respect thereof, he will have to charge VAT on all his taxable supplies including those made in the course of other businesses which would not, if looked at independently, have given rise to registration (e.g. an accountant who is also letting holiday caravans).

However, a business carried on by a partnership will be registered in the name of the firm, but separate registrations will not be given to separate businesses carried on by the same individuals in partnership even if there are different partnership agreements for each business. This does not apply if the partnerships do not comprise the same individuals. Furthermore where trading is undertaken by separate legal persons (e.g. a company, a partnership, or a club) separate registrations are required even though each of such organisations is represented by the same individual.

Groups of companies (i.e. companies under common control) can apply for group treatment. The effect of this is that supplies to and from members of the group are disregarded. All supplies made to or by group members (other than to and from each other) are treated as made by one "representative" company. That company is responsible for making VAT returns and payments on behalf of all the group members. However, the liability to pay VAT is *joint and several*. (In other words all group members are liable for the full VAT liability arising on all group supplies irrespective of which company actually made the supply.)

A single company carrying on its business through divisions can apply to be registered in respect of each division.

If a receiver is appointed over the assets of a company or if the company goes into liquidation the company continues to be a taxable person. Even though supplies are made or received by the receiver or liquidator such person is acting only as agent for the company.

In strictness any person who makes a supply of goods or services whether as agent or as principal is liable to registration if those supplies exceed the threshold. However, in the case of agents, this would, were it not for special rules which have been introduced to deal with the problem, result in double taxation. The distinction to be made is between disbursements which are monies paid by an agent acting on behalf of his principal and the charges which he, himself, makes for the supply of his services, etc. The form of accounting adopted to deal with this will depend upon the nature of the business and the manner in which it is conducted. In some cases the agent will issue tax invoices, whilst in other cases the supplier will do so direct to the recipient. It is important to distinguish between a true agent and traders (e.g. distributors, employment agents) who act as principal despite their trade title. Accountants, solicitors and other professional men will often act as agents for some supplies and as principals for others.

Clubs, associations and other such organisations are, in general, treated as taxable persons provided the club, etc is a continuing entity separate from persons who from time to time comprise its membership. Similar treatment applies for "project organisations" such as self-build and self-help groups.

Supplies made by the Crown (i.e. by a Government Department) are treated as being taxable supplies made by taxable persons. Supplies between Government Departments are, in general, treated as not amounting to the carrying on of a business. However the Treasury has power to make a direction deeming such supplies to be made in the course of a business and therefore taxable supplies. Most public bodies are entitled to receive refunds of tax charged on supplies to them. Local authorities which make taxable supplies, irrespective of whether such supplies exceed the normal registration limits are liable to register as taxable persons and to charge and account for VAT in the normal way.

§ 4.—BUSINESS (s. 47, V.A.T.A. 1983)

VAT is charged on the supply of goods or services made "in the course or furtherance of a business."

There have been various decisions by VAT Tribunals as to the meaning of business. The following general tests can be applied whether or not there is a business:

(1) *Continuity.* Are the supplies made with any degree of regularity or frequency and as part of a recognisable activity, rather than isolated and irregular transactions?

(2) *Substance.* What is the overall value of the taxable supplies?

(3) *Profit motive.* This is not, of itself, of significance.

(4) *Active control.* Is the supplier actively engaged in the control and management of the assets concerned (including operation through an agent)?

(5) *Domestic activity.* Are the supplies made to members of the public or merely between members of the same organisation?

(6) *Hallmarks of a business.* Are the activities being carried on deliberately and continuously in a way expected of a normal commercial undertaking?

The provision by clubs, associations, or organisations (for a subscription or other consideration) of the facilities or advantages available for its members is deemed to be a business; as is the admission, for a consideration, of persons to any premises.

However, subscriptions to bodies of a political, religious, philanthropic, philosophical or patriotic nature are outside the scope of VAT provided the members obtain no facility or advantage therefrom other than the right to participate in its management or receive reports on its activities.

The term 'business' includes not only trades, but also the carrying on of a profession or vocation. Furthermore, a person who in the course or furtherance of his trade, profession or vocation accepts an office (e.g. a directorship) (which might otherwise be outside the scope of VAT as an ordinary employment), he is, nevertheless, treated as making his supplies, as the holder of that office, in the course or furtherance of his trade, profession or vocation. This is likely to apply to solicitors, accountants, etc who in the course of their professional practice accept appointments as directors, secretaries of companies, etc.

It should be noted that anything which is done in connection with the termination of a business is deemed to be done in the course or furtherance of it, and is therefore a taxable supply. This also applies to the disposal of a business as a going concern, or of its assets and liabilities. However, subject to a number of conditions being met, the transfer of a business as a going concern will usually be taken outside the scope of VAT.

§ 5.—SUPPLIES

GENERAL (ss. 1–3, 47(4)–(6), Sch. 2, Sch. 7., para. 4(6), V.A.T.A. 1983)
VAT is charged upon the supply of goods or services made in the U.K.

For this purpose a supply is defined in very broad terms so as to include all forms of supply *except those made for no consideration*. Various forms of supply are thus included such as sale, purchase, loan, exchange, hire, lease, rental, making up goods from customers' materials, sale on commission, and sale or return. Furthermore anything which is not a supply of goods, but which is done for a consideration, is a supply of services.

Where a person, in the course or furtherance of a trade, profession or vocation, accepts any office (e.g. a professional man who accepts a directorship of a company), services supplied by him as the holder of that office are treated as supplied in the course or furtherance of the trade, profession or vocation. A taxable person accepting an office would be required to charge VAT on the remuneration received therefrom as if it were a supply of services.

The following transactions also represent a supply in the course of business and *prima facie* are subject to VAT:

(*a*) anything done in connection with the termination of a business;

(*b*) the disposal of a business as a going concern, or of its assets or liabilities, whether or not in connection with its reorganisation or winding-up. (But see below.)

In general, anything which is not done for a consideration (e.g. a gift, payment of a dividend) is a non-supply and is outside the scope of VAT. Certain transactions, which might otherwise have been taxable supplies are deemed to be non-supplies.

The Treasury have been given powers to issue, by means of Statutory Instruments, regulations which determine for particular transactions whether they should be treated:

(i) as a supply of goods and not as a supply of services; or

(ii) as a supply of services and not as a supply of goods; or

(iii) as neither a supply of goods nor as a supply of services.

Thus it is provided that the issue of trading stamps is a non-supply unless enclosed with goods for retail sale (See s. 37, V.A.T.A. 1983 and VAT (Treatment of Transactions) (No 1) Order 1973).

Certain transactions concerning motors cars (broadly motor vehicles of private type) are treated as non-supplies

(*a*) disposal of a used car after re-possession thereof under a finance agreement

(*b*) disposal of a used car by an insurer (after a claim)

(*c*) a gift of a car (e.g. as a prize in a competition) provided no input tax has been claimed.

(See VAT (Cars) Order 1980—Art. 7)

Similarly the disposal, after repossession under a finance agreement, marine mortgage or aircraft mortgage (as the case may be), or by an insurer (after a claim) of any of the undernoted goods is a non-supply. The goods concerned are

(i) Works of art, antiques and collectors' pieces

(ii) Motor cycles

(iii) Caravans of less than 2,030 kilogrammes unladen weight, and motor caravans
(iv) Boats and outboard motors
(v) Electronic organs
(vi) Aircraft
(vii) Fire arms
(See VAT (Special Provisions) Order 1981, Arts. 10, 11)

Where an owner of goods assigns his rights thereto to a bank or financial institution, under a hire purchase or conditional sale agreement that is also treated as a non-supply (See VAT (Special Provisions) Order 1981, Art. 12(2)).

Despite the general rule that the disposal of a business as a going concern is a supply in the course or furtherance of a business, nonetheless such transfer is deemed to be a non-supply if the whole of the business (or an identifiable part of it run and accounted for separately) is transferred to a person for use in the same kind of business. If the transferor is a taxable person this treatment applies only if the transferee is already, or will upon the transfer become, a taxable person. A transfer between two persons who are not taxable persons will also be a non-supply thereby avoiding the necessity of registering and charging VAT even though the consideration exceeds the registration threshold (see § 14). However if the transfer is between a taxable person and a non-taxable person (or *vice versa*) this exclusion is not available. (See VAT (Special Provisions) Order 1981, Art. 12(1).)

Further power is given to the Treasury to include as supplies any services (designated in the order) which are not already so treated only because they were done for no consideration. So far no such orders have been made.

Regulations can be introduced to deal with goods which are acquired or produced by a person but not supplied on to any other person (nor incorporated in goods so supplied) but rather are used by that person in his business. They are treated as supplied to him for the business and also as supplied by him in the course or furtherance of the business. A similar power applies to services. This concept is known as self-supply (§ 9).

Special rules distinguish between supplies of goods and supplies of services. Thus where the whole property (i.e. ownership) in goods is supplied, there is a supply of goods. If merely an undivided share of the property in the goods is transferred, or mere possession (as distinct from property) in the goods is transferred, there is a supply of services. However, if possession is transferred under an agreement for sale of the goods, or under an agreement whereby property therein will pass at a specified future date (e.g. a hire purchase contract), there is nonetheless a supply of goods.

The following are specified as being the supply of goods:
  (1) application of a treatment or process to another person's goods (but the exchange of reconditioned articles is a service);
  (2) supply of power, heat, refrigeration or ventilation;
  (3) sale of freehold land and buildings, or the grant, assignment or surrender of a lease for a term certain in excess of 21 years;
  (4) the transfer or disposal of the assets of a business, *except*
      (a) gifts of goods where the cost to the donor is not more than £10 (but not where a series of gifts is made to the same person); and
      (b) gifts to actual or potential customers of industrial samples which are not in a form ordinarily available for sale to the public.

The private use of business assets is a supply of services, but free supplies of services for non-business purposes do not at present give rise to VAT liability although the Treasury has power to issue an order making such supplies taxable.

Goods owned by a taxable person for his business, but which are sold under a power, by another person in or towards satisfaction of a debt owed by the taxable person are, nonetheless treated as supplied by the taxable person.

When a person ceases to be a taxable person any goods then held by him are treated as disposed of by him in the course or furtherance of his business immediately before he ceases to be a taxable person. This does not apply if:

- (*a*) the business is transferred as a going concern to another taxable person; or
- (*b*) the business is carried on temporarily by some person following the death or bankruptcy etc. of the taxable person (pending registration); or
- (*c*) the tax on the deemed supply would not be more than £250. (Prior to 1st June 1980 the limit was £50.)
- (*d*) the taxable person shows that
    - (i) no credit was allowed for input tax on the supply or importation of the goods,
    - (ii) the goods were not acquired as part of the assets originally transferred to him as a going concern
    - (iii) he did not obtain the special relief for stocks held at the start of VAT on which purchase tax, etc. had already been paid.

Where goods acquired primarily for business purposes are used for private purposes, the value of the service is the cost of providing the service, unless a charge is made, when that will be the value of the service.

Certain transactions are treated as a supply of goods and not of services. Thus the exchange of a re-conditioned article for an unserviceable article of a similar kind is a supply of a service and not of goods if it is part of the normal business of the person cercerned. (See VAT (Special Provisions) Order 1981, Art. 13.)

Goods which are lost, destroyed or stolen before being supplied or are dishonestly obtained by a customer are not treated as being supplied. However the trader concerned should ensure that such claims can be justified. Thefts of cash, being after the supply has been made, do not give rise to any adjustment of output tax.

If there is a supply of goods or services under the VAT rules, that supply is classified as being:

- (1) exempt—so that no tax is charged thereon;
- (2) standard-rated—so that tax is charged thereon at 15%; or
- (3) zero-rated—so that tax is charged thereon at 0%.

Compound and multiple supplies

It will often occur that a transaction comprises two or more supplies. Furthermore there may also be one or more considerations therefor. There are several possible situations:

- (1) *Compound supply*—where there are several elements in a transaction, some taxable and some not. In such a case it is necessary to determine the nature of the final compound supply irrespective of the nature of the component parts (e.g. a launderette supplies a licence to use a washing machine, and the supply of water, electricity, etc are integral parts of the overall service). A supply can still be a compound supply even where separate charges are made for different parts of the supply.
- (2) *Multiple supply*—where there is a single transaction under which there are several identifiable supplies of goods or services. Each identifiable supply is treated as a separate supply for VAT purposes and tax levied thereon (or not, as the case may be) on an appropriate proportion of the total consideration. Examples of multiple supplies include:
    —a correspondence course consisting of study notes and model answers (zero rate) and tuition (standard rate)
    —a river cruise consisting of transport (zero rate) and accommodation (standard rate);
- (3) *Two-part tariff*—where there are two or more considerations which relate to a single supply (e.g. an identity card which is linked to a later

supply or transport at a concessionary rate; the purchase of a share in a club which was, necessarily, linked to the payment of an annual subscription, both elements being necessary to secure the right to use the club's facilities).

Mutual supplies
Where each of two parties to a contract are making supplies to the other party, so that there is a set-off or contra between them and only the net difference is paid over, there are nonetheless two supplies for the true gross consideration for the supplies made in each direction and VAT should be charged on each party by reference to the value of the supply made to him. It is incorrect for one party only to charge VAT on the net consideration passing between them.

There are, however, certain exceptions to this rule. Special schemes (see § 18) are operated for acquisitions and disposals of second-hand goods.

§ 6.—TIME OF SUPPLY

GENERAL (ss. 4, 5, V.A.T.A. 1983 Reg. 27 VAT (General) Regulations 1985)
It is necessary to determine the time of supply of goods or services in order to determine the rate of VAT which should be applied (e.g. on a change of rate) and into which period the supply falls for VAT return purposes. Furthermore, if there is a change in the law (e.g. in what is zero-rated or exempt) it may be necessary to determine whether a supply is made before, or after, the change.

For a supply of goods the general rule is that the supply takes place:

(1) if the goods are removed—the time of removal by the customer;
(2) if the goods are not to be removed—the time when they are made available to the customer;
(3) if goods are taken on approval, or on sale or return—when the goods are appropriated by the customer (subject to a limit of 12 months).

However, the date indicated above is pre-empted by the prior issue of a tax invoice or the receipt of cash.

The earliest of these dates is chosen and becomes the "basic tax point".

If the tax invoice is issued within fourteen days of the basic tax point, the tax point is the earlier of the date of issue of the invoice or the payment date. This fourteen-day limit can be extended by agreement in the case of traders who so elect. If the fourteen-day limit is exceeded the tax point is the earliest of the physical time of supply, the date the invoice is issued, or the date upon which payment is received. Special rules apply to determine the tax point in various circumstances.

A supply of services is deemed to take place at the earliest of the time when services are performed, the date when a tax invoice is issued, or the date upon which payment is received. Provided a tax invoice is issued within fourteen days of the date on which the services are performed, both dates are deemed to be the same as the invoice date. As for a supply of goods, the fourteen-day period may be extended in appropriate cases.

Special rules apply to determine the tax point to deal with continuous or periodic supplies and other difficulties. These special rules are contained in VAT (General) Regulations 1980. The time of supply, as determined by the rules described above and below, is referred to as the "tax point".

If a supply is treated as taking place when a tax invoice is issued or when a payment is received that supply comprises only the matters covered by the invoice or payment.

PRIVATE USE OF GOODS (Reg. 17(1))
The private use of goods (as described above) is treated as a service made on the last day of the supplier's VAT accounting period.

PRIVATE USE OF SERVICES (Reg. 17(2))
The private use of services is not, at present, a chargeable supply for VAT. However it is provided that, if it were to become taxable, such supply is deemed made on the last day of the supplier's VAT accounting period.

SERVICES FROM OUTSIDE THE UNITED KINDGOM (Reg. 18)
Services received from abroad and subject to the "reverse charge" procedure (see § 16) are treated as supplied when the supplies are paid for. However, if the consideration is not in money the supply is deemed made on the last day of the supplier's VAT accounting period.

LEASES (Reg. 19)
Where the granting of a lease is treated as a supply of goods (see above) and payments thereunder are made periodically, the supply is deemed to take place when each payment is received, or a tax invoice relating thereto is issued by the supplier, whichever is the earlier.

POWER, HEAT, REFRIGERATION OR VENTILATION (Reg. 20)
Such supplies are treated as made when a payment is received or a tax invoice is issued whichever is the earlier.

"SALE OR RETURN", "ON APPROVAL", ETC. (Reg. 21)
For goods supplied on such terms the supply takes place at the earliest of
  (*a*) appropriation by the buyer;
  (*b*) 12 months after the goods are delivered to the buyer;
  (*c*) on the issue of a tax invoice.
This is subject to the application of the fourteen-day rule. If this applies the tax point is on the earliest of payment or the issue of tax invoice.

RETENTION PAYMENTS (Reg. 22)
If, under the terms of a contract, any part of the consideration is retained pending full and satisfactory completion of the contract, the supply is deemed to take place when a payment is made or a tax invoice is issued, whichever is the earlier.

CONTINUOUS SUPPLIES (Reg. 23)
In general, services supplied over a period of time, and where the consideration is determined or payable periodically, are treated as separate supplies for each part of the period. Each such supply is then treated as made at the earlier of payment or the issue of a tax invoice. This is modified if the supply is made under an agreement for successive payments and the supplier issues a tax invoice which details the required payments over a period of not more than a year. In such a case payment is treated as made as each payment falls due. However if there is a change in the rate of tax (or other relevant change in the law) the invoice can no longer be treated as a tax invoice for payments due after the change.

ROYALTIES (Reg. 24)
Where the consideration for a supply of services is the payment of a royalty, the consideration attributable to such services is not usually ascertainable when the services are performed. Furthermore the use of the benefit of such services by a person other than the supplier will give rise to payments which are determined periodically, which may be in addition to any amount already paid for the supply (e.g. lump sum plus a royalty) and which are not treated as "continuous supplies" (see above). Further supplies are treated as occurring on each occasion on which a payment is made, or when a tax invoice is issued, whichever is the earlier.

BARRISTERS AND ADVOCATES (Reg. 25)
The services of barristers and advocates (in Scotland) are treated as made on the earliest of
> (*a*) when a fee for the services is received;
> (*b*) when a tax invoice is issued;
> (*c*) when the barrister or advocate ceases to practise.

CONSTRUCTION INDUSTRY (Reg. 26)
The supply of services and/or goods in the course of construction, alteration, demolition, repair or maintenance of a building, or civil engineering work under a contract requiring periodic payments is treated as being made on the earlier of receipt of payment (if the consideration for the contract is wholly in money) or on the issue of a tax invoice.

DISCRETION
Notwithstanding the above rules, the Commissioners may, at the request of a taxable person, issue a directive to alter the time of supply to an earlier date than that which would apply under the rules described above. Alternatively they may direct that supplies are treated as made at the beginning or end of a relevant working period.

CHANGE OF RATE OR RE-CLASSIFICATION OF SUPPLY (s. 20, V.A.T.A. 1983, Reg. 28)
When there is a change in the rate of VAT or in the descriptions of supplies within the exempt or zero-rated categories, taxable persons have certain options as to when a supply is treated as having been made.

In those cases where the tax point would normally be governed by the date of payment, the date of issue of the tax invoice, or by a direction of the Commissioners (following a request by the taxable person concerned) and not by the date on which the goods were made available, or on which, under the general rules, the services are deemed to be performed, then the taxable person may elect for the tax point to be fixed by the basic provisions if that gives a different result.

Any provisions which govern the time a supply is made are subject to the overriding right of the taxable person to elect for the use of the basic rules to determine the tax point.

If a tax invoice in respect of a supply to which an election is made is issued before such an election is made, it can be replaced or corrected.

The effect of these arrangements is that traders can account for VAT at the old rate or by reference to the old exemption or zero-rate schedule on supplies actually made before the change but for which the tax point would otherwise be after the change.

The election is not available where the supply concerned is the satisfaction of a debt, or is made under a self-billing scheme.

§ 7.—PLACE OF SUPPLY

GOODS (s. 6, V.A.T.A. 1983)
Since VAT is charged in respect of goods on supplies made in the United Kingdom, it is necessary to determine whether goods are supplied in the United Kingdom or elsewhere. Thus if a supply of goods does not involve their removal to or from the United Kingdom they are treated as supplied there if they are physically in the United Kingdom, otherwise they are treated as supplied outside the United Kingdom. Where a supply of goods involves their removal from the United Kingdom, they are treated as supplied there, whereas goods which are removed to the United Kingdom are deemed to be supplied outside the United Kingdom. Goods which leave and re-enter the United Kingdom en route between places in the United Kingdom are deemed never to have left the United Kingdom.

SERVICES (ss. 6, 8, Sch. 3, V.A.T.A. 1983)

Where a supply is of services it is treated as made in the United Kingdom if the supplier *belongs* there, and outside the United Kingdom in other cases.

Special rules apply to determine in which country the supplier or recipient belongs:

- (*a*) an individual who receives a supply in his private capacity (and not for the purpose of any business carried on by him) is treated as *belonging* in the country in which he has his usual place of residence;
- (*b*) a person (other than a private individual) *belongs* in a country if:
  - (i) he has a business establishment (including a branch or agency) or some other fixed establishment there (and nowhere else); and
  - (ii) he has no such establishment (there or elsewhere) but has his usual place of residence (place of incorporation in the case of a company) there; or
  - (iii) being the supplier of services he has establishments in more than one country, in which case he *belongs* in the country in which is the establishment most directly concerned with the supply; or
  - (iv) being the recipient of services he has establishments in more than one country in which case he *belongs* in the country in which is the establishment which most directly uses the services.

The Treasury has power to make orders varying the rules for determining where a supply of services is made.

Certain services supplied by persons who belong outside the United Kingdom are treated, for the purpose of the reverse charge on imports, as supplied where they are received:

- (1) Transfers and assignments of copyright, patents, licences, trademarks and similar rights.
- (2) Advertising services.
- (3) Services of consultants, engineers, consultancy bureaux, lawyers, accountants and similar services; data processing and provision of information; (*excluding services relating to land*).
- (4) Acceptance of any obligation to refrain from pursuing or exercising, in whole or in part, any business activity as any rights within (1) above.
- (5) Banking, financial and insurance services (including reinsurance services, but not including the provision of safe deposit facilities).
- (6) The supply of staff.
- (7) The services rendered by one person to another in procuring for the other any of the above services.

A special rule applies where any of the above services are supplied by a person who belongs outside the U.K. and they are received by a taxable person who belongs in the U.K. for the purpose of any business carried on by him. Such a person is treated as though he had himself made the supply of services in the U.K. as a taxable supply in the course or furtherance of his business and account for tax thereon. This does not apply where the services fall within the exempt categories. The taxable person is also able to reclaim full value for input tax equivalent to the reverse charge unless he is exempt or partially exempt.

§ 8.—VALUE OF SUPPLIES

GENERAL (s. 10, Para. 11, Sch. 4, V.A.T.A. 1983)

Where the consideration for a supply of goods or services is in money its value is taken as such amount as, with the addition of the tax chargeable, is equal to the consideration. If the supply is not for a consideration, or for a consideration not consisting, or not wholly consisting, of money, the value of the supply is taken as its open market value. Where a consideration is partly for goods and services and partly for some other purpose an apportionment is made. The Commissioners have power to substitute the open market value of a supply where a consideration in money does not represent the true value of the supply and was fixed with a view to securing a reduction of liability to tax. There is also power to prevent a benefit derived when a taxable person sells to individuals who are not taxable persons but who will sell the goods on at an enhanced price. In such a case the taxable person is deemed to supply the goods at the price at which the individuals concerned sell them on.

IMPORTED GOODS (s. 11, Sch. 4, V.A.T.A. 1983)
Where goods are imported their value is (provided there is no other consideration) the basic price payable together with all U.K. taxes, duties (not VAT) and charges arising on importation together with all costs such as commission, packing, transport and insurance to the port of entry. If there is other consideration the goods are valued at open market value (under special E.E.C. rules for valuation for Customs purposes) plus taxes, costs, etc.

DISCOUNTS (Paras 4, 5, Sch. 4, V.A.T.A. 1983)
If goods or services are supplied on terms which allow a discount for prompt payment the consideration is reduced by the discount (even if payment is not made within the required time limit). This rule does not apply where payment can be made by instalments.

This treatment does not apply to turnover discounts.

TOKENS, ETC. (Para. 6, Sch. 4, V.A.T.A. 1983)
Where a right to receive goods or services for an amount stated on a token, stamp or voucher is granted for a consideration, such consideration is disregarded for VAT unless it exceeds the stated amount.

The issue of book or record tokens and similar stamps or vouchers is outside the scope of VAT. This is to avoid the double taxation which would otherwise occur when the voucher is exchanged for goods or services.

Normally, traders who participate in voucher schemes pay a service charge to the organisers. This service charge is subject to VAT.

TRADING STAMPS (VAT (Treatment of Transactions) (No. 1) Order 1973)
The supply of trading stamps in retail outlets is, as with voucher schemes, outside the scope of VAT, but the service charge for supplying the stamps is taxable. However if trading stamps are sold for inclusion in packaged goods which are themselves subject to VAT then the stamps become subject to VAT. The giving of trading stamps to customers by retailers (e.g. in a supermarket) is not a taxable supply.

The supply of trading stamps by the promoter of a trading stamp scheme is dealt with by s. 37, V.A.T.A. 1983 and VAT (Trading Stamps) Regulations 1973.

SELF-SUPPLY OF GOODS (Para. 7(a), Sch. 4, V.A.T.A. 1983)
Goods which are acquired or produced by a taxable person and used by him in his business are deemed supplied at their cost to him.

GIFTS (Para. 7(b), Sch. 4, V.A.T.A. 1983)
Gifts, other than those not exceeding £10 in value and industrial samples, are valued at their cost to the supplier.

TRANSFER OF GOING CONCERNS (Para. 7(c), Sch. 4, V.A.T.A. 1983)
The assets of businesses tranferred as going concerns are deemed transferred at their cost to the transferor.

FREE SUPPLIES OF SERVICES (Para. 8(a), Sch. 4, V.A.T.A. 1983)
If the Treasury issues any orders making such supplies taxable their value will be the cost to the supplier of providing the services.

PRIVATE USE OF GOODS (Para. 8(b), Sch. 4, V.A.T.A. 1983)
Goods which are used by a taxable person otherwise than for business purposes are deemed supplied to him in his private capacity at a value equal to their cost to him in his business capacity.

HOTELS, ETC. (Paras 9, 10, Sch. 4, V.A.T.A. 1983)
Where accommodation at a hotel, boarding house, etc. is on a long-stay basis, a special valuation rule is applied to the part of the stay in excess of four weeks. The consideration for this part of the supply is reduced by the value of facilities other than the right to occupy the accommodation. However, the value of such facilities is not to exceed 20% of the value of the accommodation and facilities.

The value of supplies of food, beverages or accommodation to employees is taken as being the amount paid by the employees, otherwise the value is NIL.

INVOICES IN FOREIGN CURRENCY (Para. 11, Sch. 4, V.A.T.A. 1983)
Invoices expressed in currencies other than sterling must be converted into sterling at the selling rate of exchange at the time of supply.

DISCRETION (Paras 1 to 3, 13, Sch. 4, V.A.T.A. 1983)
If goods or services are supplied or if goods are imported, at a consideration which is below the open-market value thereof and the bargain is not at arm's length, the Commissioners may direct that the supply be treated as made at such open-market value. This does not override the special rule for supplies by hotels, etc. to their employees.

If goods are supplied to non-taxable persons for sale by retail (e.g. at "hostess parties") the Commissioners may direct that the value of such a supply is the open-market value of a retail sale at a specified later date.

§ 9.—SELF-SUPPLIES (s. 3, V.A.T.A. 1983)

A person who has exempt outputs is outside the scope of the value added tax legislation and therefore cannot recover any tax which has been charged to him. He might therefore decide to produce himself items for use in his business in order to minimise the tax charged on his inputs. A partially exempt person may decide to do likewise.

STATIONERY (VAT (Special Provisions) Order 1981, Art. 14)
One possible source of self-supply which could be used to advantage is the supply of stationery. In order to prevent this the Treasury has made an order which provides that the self-supply of stationery and other printed matter of a kind normally produced by commercial printers is to be specially taxable but only if the value of the self-supplies exceeds the normal registration limits.

A person who is normally exempt but for the self-supply must notify the Customs of his liability to be registered if the self-supplies will exceed this limit. He will then become a partially exempt person and will have to keep the usual VAT records and accounts. The records which will have to be kept include:

(a) the quantity and description of the self-supplies;
(b) the date when the goods are used for the purpose of the business;
(c) the value on which tax is to be chargeable; and
(d) the rate and amount of the tax chargeable.

The value which is to be taken is the open market value of the supplies. This is the price that would have been payable for the stationery if it had been purchased from an independent commercial printer. Where such a price is not readily available, the Customs are prepared to accept a valuation based on the cost of production plus an agreed mark up.

Accounting procedure
A partially exempt person making self-supplies of stationery which are taxable can deduct the whole of his input tax on purchases (e.g. paper, ink, plates, machinery), which are used for manufacture of the stationery.

If he has other inputs which cannot be directly related to his taxable outputs, the proportion of deductible input tax must be calculated. For the purpose of this calculation self-supplies should be treated as both an output of, and an input to, the business. The value of the self-supplies should therefore be included with the value of any other taxable outputs and the tax on the self-supplies should be included with the tax on the other inputs to the business.

Example

		£
Value of stationery chargeable at the standard rate (excluding VAT)		40,000
Value of stationery chargeable at the zero-rate		80,000
Value of other taxable outputs (excluding VAT)		880,000
Value of total taxable outputs (excluding VAT)		1,000,000
Value of exempt outputs		250,000
Value of total outputs (excluding VAT)		£1,250,000

$$\text{Percentage of taxable outputs} = \frac{1,000,000}{1,250,000} \times \frac{100}{1} = 80\%$$

		£
Input tax on purchases of materials for manufacture of stationery, say		10,000
Tax on standad rate self-supplies of stationery (£40,000 at 15%)	£6,000	
Other input tax, say	£42,000	48,000

Deductible input tax
£10,000 + [80% of £48,000 = £38,400]   = £48,400

CARS (VAT (Cars) Order 1980, Art. 5)
Another possible source of self-supply concerns private-type motor cars (but not minibuses, caravans, ambulances, prison vans, "London-type" taxis, and other special-purpose vehicles). Input tax on motor cars is, except for purchases for sale by motor dealers, in that capacity, for letting to persons in receipt of mobility allowance, or for conversion, not allowed. This would not apply if a car was assembled or converted by a taxable person from parts, etc on which input tax was allowed. However, where this is done, there is a self-supply at the cost to the trader concerned (excluding input tax already recovered). This could apply where the person making the self-supply is the manufacturer providing cars for his representatives. Another possible application is the case of a garage using a car purchased for stock as a demonstration model.

§ 10.—ZERO-RATING (s. 16, Sch. 5, V.A.T.A. 1983)
This is a term which indicates that the supply of goods and services is a taxable supply but that the tax is charged at a zero or nil rate.

This provision is introduced to enable a trader who supplies goods which are taxed at the zero-rate to reclaim from Customs all the tax he has paid on his purchases or inputs.

Except where otherwise indicated there is also no charge on the importation of zero-rated goods.

The export of goods, the supply of goods as stores on ships or aircraft bound for foreign destinations, and the supply of goods for retail sale to passengers on such ships or aircraft, are also zero-rated.

Schedule 5, V.A.T.A. 1983 contains a list of eighteen groups under which zero-rated goods and services are to be allocated.

GP. 1. FOOD

(1) Although the general rule is that food and drink is zero-rated except where supplied in the course of catering, including "takeaway" supplies of food, certain foods are taxable at the standard rate. These include:
  (i) Ice-cream, ice lollies, etc.
  (ii) Sweets and chocolates.
  (iii) Beverages such as beer, wine, spirits, fruit juices, mineral waters and concentrates, essences, etc for the preparation thereof.
  (iv) Products such as potato crisps, roasted nuts.

(2) In general, feeding stuffs for farm animals are zero-rated but petfoods and bird foods are taxable.

(3) Seeds (including mushroom spawn) used for agricultural purposes are in general zero-rated but seeds and bulbs used for the propagation of ornamental trees, shrubs and flowers will be taxable at the standard rate.

(4) Live animals of a kind generally used as, or yielding or producing, food for human consumption are zero-rated, e.g. cows, poultry, pigs, sheep. But other animals such as horses are taxable at the standard rate.

GP. 2. SEWERAGE AND WATER SERVICES

Water is zero-rated with the exception of distilled, de-ionised, etc water and mineral waters. Collection and treatment of sewerage is zero-rated.

GP. 3. BOOKS AND NEWSPAPERS

The supply of books, booklets, brochures, pamphlets, newspapers, periodicals, children's books and other printed matter (including charts and maps) is zero-rated.

Other printed matter such as plans or drawings for industrial, architectural, engineering and commercial purposes are taxable at standard rate.

GP. 4. TALKING BOOKS FOR THE BLIND

Zero rate applies to the supply of talking books and equipment related thereto for the blind or severely handicapped. These include:

(*a*) Magnetic tape for recording and reproduction of speech.
(*b*) Pre-recorded tapes.
(*c*) Tape recorders.
(*d*) Parts and accessories for use with the above.

} restricted to such use.

Zero-rate also applies to radio sets supplied to charities for free loan to blind persons.

GP. 5. NEWSPAPER ADVERTISEMENTS (to 30th April 1985)
Zero rate applies to the preparation and publication in any newspaper, journal or periodical of any advertisement. From 1st May 1985 such services are taxed at the standard rate.

GP. 6. NEWS SERVICES (to 30th April 1985)
The supply of information to newpapers or to the public is zero-rated. From 1st May 1985 such services are taxed at standard rate.
This provision covers such services to newspapers by news agencies. It does not include the supply of photographs, nor services of advice, such as racing tips, horoscopes, or financial advice.

GP. 7. FUEL AND POWER
All fuel and power is zero-rated. This includes coal, coke, gas, hydro-carbon oils, electricity, heat and air conditioning.
Other fuels which are taxable at standard rate include charcoal, firelighters, peat, wood, greases and paints.

GP. 8. CONSTRUCTION OF BUILDINGS
(1) *New constructions*—zero-rated.
The granting by a person constructing a building of a major interest (e.g. freehold, long leasehold) in the building or its site is zero-rated. A "major interest" is defined as the freehold or a tenancy for a term exceeding 21 years. Zero-rating does not apply to any land sold by the builder other than the site of the building itself. The supply of land in other circumstances is exempt. The supply of materials and services for the construction, alteration or demolition of any building or of any civil engineering work is zero-rated.
A supply of services of repair to, or maintenance of, buildings is taxable at the standard rate.
(i) Interior and exterior decorations.
(ii) Repointing of brickwork.
(iii) Replacing faulty tiles, slates and guttering.
(iv) Cleaning buildings.
(v) Rewiring electric wiring systems.
(vi) Repairs to, or renewal of, plumbing and drainage systems.
(vii) Servicing central heating installations.
(2) *Services (and associated goods) in course of construction, etc.*
The services of architects, surveyors etc. are taxable at the standard rate. Civil engineering works in the grounds of a private residence are taxable at the standard rate.
(3) *Builders' hardware of a kind ordinarily installed by builders as fixtures.* "Luxury" goods installed in private houses are taxable at the standard rate.
With effect from 1st June 1984 all supplies in the construction industry except for the construction of a complete new building (or the substantial reconstruction of a listed building) are standard rated.

GP. 8.A. LISTED BUILDINGS
The granting by a person substantially reconstructing a listed building of a major interest therein.

GP. 9. INTERNATIONAL SERVICES
Various types of services to overseas principals are zero-rated.
For the purposes of this group, a person is an overseas principal or trader if he carries on a business and has his place of business outside the United Kingdom, and is not resident in the United Kingdom.

A taxable person supplying services to overseas traders will need to retain evidence to substantiate the entitlement to zero-rating on those services.

Zero-rating will apply to:

(1) The supply of services relating to land *outside* the United Kingdom. This includes construction, alteration, repair, maintenance, demolition, and civil engineering work, as well as the services of estate agents, auctioneers, surveyors, engineers, etc. However, this does not include any of the items in Sch. 3, V.A.T.A. 1983.

(2). The letting or hire of goods for use outside the United Kingdom throughout the period of hire, provided that the goods are exported by the lessor for the purpose, or at the time of supply are already outside the United Kingdom. This does not apply to the hiring of any means of transport for use in a member state of the E.E.C.

(3) The supply, outside the United Kingdom, of cultural, artistic, sporting, scientific, educational or entertainment services, and services ancillary thereto.

(4) Valuation or carrying out work on goods situated outside the United Kingdom.

(5) Supplying any of the services listed in Sch. 3, V.A.T.A. 1983* to a person in his business capacity (and not in his private capacity) who *belongs* in a member state of the E.E.C. This does not include any services of education, health or training in the United Kingdom (except for a foreign government) nor the provision or organisation of conferences, exhibitions or meetings held in the United Kingdom (unless they constitute advertising) and related services.

(6) Supplying to a person who *belongs* in a country outside the E.E.C.:
   (i) Services listed in Sch. 3, V.A.T.A. 1983* other than insurance and re-insurance (within Group 2, Sch. 6, V.A.T.A. 1983) or dealings with certificates of deposit.
   (ii) Insurance by authorised insurers of marine and transit risks
   (iii) Re-insurance by authorised insurers of marine and transit risks
   (iv) Related services
   The exclusion described at (5) also applies.

(7) Supplying insurance in respect of the carriage of passengers or goods to or from a place outside the E.E.C., and services related to such supply. This does not apply to insurance for boats, aircraft or hovercraft for pleasure purposes.

(8) Supply by the E.C.G.D. or other authorised insurer of credit risk insurance for exports outside the E.E.C.

(9) Financial services in respect of the export, or transhipment, of goods outside the E.E.C.

(10) Carrying out for a person who *belongs* outside the United Kingdom of work on goods for export, or imported temporarily into the United Kingdom for ultimate re-export.

(11) Services in connection with
   (i) Exports
   (ii) (1), (2), (3), (4), (5), (6), or (10) above
   (iii) Supplies made outside the United Kingdom
   This does not include procurement services by a travel agent for a traveller where the services are enjoyed within the U.K.

Services listed in Sch. 3, V.A.T.A. 1983:
(i) Transfers and assignments of copyright, patents, licences, trademarks and similar rights.
(ii) Advertising services.

(iii) Services of consultants, engineers, consultancy bureaux, lawyers, accountants and similar services; data processing and provision of information; (*excluding services relating to land*).

(iv) Acceptance of any obligation to refrain from pursuing or exercising, in whole or in part, any business activity or any rights within (1) above.

(v) Banking, financial and insurance services (including reinsurance services, but not including the provision of safe deposit facilities).

(vi) The supply of staff.

(vii) The services rendered by one person to another in procuring for the other any of the above services.

GP. 10. TRANSPORT

Zero-rating will apply to:

(1) The supply, charter, letting on hire, repair and maintenance of ships exceeding 15 tons designed for commercial use.

(2) The supply, charter, letting on hire, repair and maintenance of aircraft exceeding 8,000 kilos designed for commercial use.

(3) The supply, letting on hire and repair of lifeboats.

(4) The transport of passengers in vehicles, ships or aircraft designed for not less than twelve passengers, or by the Post Office or on scheduled flights.

(5) The transport of passengers or freight between, to or from places outside the United Kingdom.

(6) Any services provided for the handling of ships and aircraft in a port or customs airport.

(7) Pilotage services.

(8) Salvage or towage services.

(9) Any services supplied within and outside the United Kingdom in connection with the surveying of any ship or aircraft.

(10) Arranging for the supply of, or of space in, ships and aircraft, or arrangement for any of the supplies in this group.

(11) Ancillary services, outside the United Kingdom, which are ancillary to the transport of goods or passengers.

(12) Providing to a person in his business capacity (and not in his private capacity) who *belongs* outside the United Kingdom services of handling, storage or transport of imported and exported goods.

Taxable supplies will therefore apply to:

(i) Pleasure boats and yachts, whatever the tonnage.

(ii) Taxis and hire cars.

(iii) Car parking and luggage storage.

But platform tickets and taxi-stand rentals are exempt from taxation.

GP. 11. CARAVANS AND HOUSEBOATS

Caravans are zero-rated if they exceed the limits of size permitted for use as trailers on the public roads. The limits are 7 metres in length and 2.3 metres in breadth and 2,030 kilos in weight. The zero-rating applies therefore to caravans designed primarily as domestic housing.

Smaller caravans capable of being towed on the roads are subject to VAT.

Certain items of expenditure on caravans are taxable, whether or not supplied with zero-rated caravans. These include refrigerators, cookers, curtains and removable furniture.

Houseboats, if immobile and suitable for permanent habitation are also zero-rated.

Zero-rating does not apply to the supply of holiday accommodation in caravans and houseboats.

GP. 12. GOLD

The supply of gold bullion or gold coins, held in the United Kingdom, between Central Banks, or between a Central Bank and an authorised dealer on the London Gold Market is zero-rated. Supplies to persons who are not authorised dealers are taxable at the standard rate.

Gold coins are also taxable on importation into the United Kingdom.

GP. 13. BANK NOTES

The issue of bank notes by the Banks of England, Scotland and Northern Ireland in respect of notes payable to bearer on demand is zero-rated.

GP. 14. DRUGS, MEDICINES, AIDS FOR THE HANDICAPPED

The supply of any goods dispensed by a person registered under the Pharmacy Act 1954, or the Pharmacy and Poisons (Northern Ireland) Act 1925, on prescription of a person registered as a medical practitioner or dentist is zero-rated.

Any drugs and medicines dispensed by a pharmacist without prescription are a taxable supply.

A wide range of medical, surgical and other aids for use by handicapped persons whether supplied directly, or to a charity for that purpose, are also zero-rated.

GP. 15. IMPORTS AND EXPORTS

(1) The zero-rating applies to the supply of imported goods before the delivery of an entry under an agreement requiring the purchaser to make an entry within the meaning of s. 37, Customs and Excise Management Act 1979.

(2) The transfer of goods or services from the U.K. by a person carrying on a business both inside and outside the U.K. Typically this will cover representative offices where only 'supplies' are the provision of information etc. to a foreign head office.

(3) Supplies to or by an overseas authority or trader in connection with a Defence project are also zero-rated.

(4) Supplies of jigs, patterns, templates, dies, punches, etc. to an overseas authority or trader for the manufacture of goods for export.

GP. 16. CHARITIES

The zero-rating applies to new and used goods donated to and sold by a registered charity.

Where, however, goods are sold on commission by a charity, tax at the standard rate will be chargeable to the owner on the amount of that commission. Zero-rating also applies to the supply to an Area Health Board of equipment, including computers and peripheral equipment, for medical research, diagnosis or treatment, and the supply of ambulances.

GP. 17. CLOTHING AND FOOTWEAR

In general most clothing and footwear for young children is zero-rated, but items made of fur (other then mere "trimmings") are usually taxable.

In addition, the zero-rate will apply to footwear and protective helmets used for industrial purposes and to protective helmets for persons riding motorcycles.

Example

Example of a zero-rated trader
Value of goods supplied in the period (output)   £30,000

VAT thereon at Nil%   Nil

Value of goods and services received in the period (inputs)

	£	*Tax paid* £
Goods purchased for resale.....................	20,000 at Nil%	Nil
Telephone	1,000 at 15%	150.00
Stationery...................................	500 at 15%	75.00
Advertising..................................	700 at 15%	105.00
Accounting charges...........................	800 at 15%	120.00
Total tax paid		£450.00

Summary	£
Tax on outputs	Nil
Less: Tax on inputs	450.00
Amount due from Customs and Excise	£450.00

§ 11.—EXEMPT SUPPLIES (s. 17, Sch. 6, V.A.T.A. 1983)

A person who supplies goods or services designated by the Act as "exempt supplies" is not required to charge any output tax on such supplies. If he makes only "exempt supplies" he is not required to register and keep records for VAT purposes. However he is therefore not a taxable trader and cannot reclaim any input tax which he has paid on his purchases. If only some of his supplies are exempt, and others standard or zero-rated, he is "partially-exempt" and a proportion of his inputs, in effect related to the exempt outputs are disallowed (see § 13, below).

The list of goods and services designated as "exempt supplies" is set out in Sch. 6, V.A.T.A. 1983. These consist of the following eleven categories.

GP. 1. LAND

The exemption covers the grant, assignment or surrender of any interest in or right over land, or of any licence to occupy land. If zero-rating also applies, by virtue of Sch. 5 Group 8, the zero-rating takes precedent. Exceptions to this exemption, on which tax is chargeable at standard rate, apply in the undermentioned circumstances:

(a) *The provison of accommodation in hotels, inns, boarding houses, etc.*
Tax is chargeable on the full value of the accommodation, meals and other facilities for the first four weeks of the stay in the hotel etc. For any period exceeding the first four weeks, the value of the supply of the accommodation and facilities is taken to be reduced to the proportion of the value which can be attributed to the facilities other than the right to occupy the accommodation, subject to a minimum taxable value of 20% of the value of the accommodation and facilities. Meals continue to be taxable on the full value arising.

Example 1

A person stays at a hotel for a period of three weeks. The cost of his accommodation is £60 per week and he pays £25 for his meals, a total cost of £85 per week.

		£
The VAT position per week is:	Total cost............	85.00
	Add VAT at 15%......	12.75
	Amount payable	£97.75

Example 2

The above person stays at a hotel for a period of five weeks, cost is £85 per week as above. The value of facilities taken is £10.

The VAT position per week is:

		£
Weeks 1 to 4 inclusive:	Total cost............	85.00
	Add VAT at 15%......	12.75
	Amount payable	£97.75

	£
Week 5: Cost of accommodation.................................	£60.00
Minimum value of facilities taken at 20%	£12.00
Value of facilities supplied..............................	12.00
Cost of meals	25.00
	37.00
VAT at 15%..	5.55
	£42.55

	£
Account rendered by hotel	
Total cost payable	85.00
Add VAT (as computed)	5.55
Amount payable	£90.55

If the actual cost of facilities is more than 20% of accommodation, the actual cost should be shown.

(*b*) *The provision of accommodation in a house, flat, caravan or houseboat used wholly or mainly for the provision of holiday accommodation*
    These are taxable supplies and "house, flat or caravan" includes a chalet, villa or maisonette. Tax is chargeable irrespective of the length of the stay, unlike the situation in (*a*).
(*c*) *The granting of facilities for camping in tents or caravans*
    This is taxable. Camping in this instance refers to temporary stays and does not include long-term occupation of a caravan for residential purposes which would be exempt. Tax is chargeable on the site rental.
(*d*) *The granting of facilities for parking a vehicle*
    This is taxable. This provision covers all car parking arrangements and garaging facilities, other than domestic garaging.

(*e*) *The granting of any right to take game or fish*
This is taxable. This provision applies to the granting of all types of rights to take game or fish, whether by licence, lease or otherwise.

(*f*) *The granting of any right to fell and remove standing timber*
This is taxable. This provision applies where a separate grant to fell timber is made. It does not apply to the sale of land with standing timber.

(*g*) *The granting of facilities for housing or storage of an aircraft, or for mooring, or storage of a ship, boat or vessel*
This is taxable. This only applies to facilities not covered by Group 10 of Schedule 5 (Transport).

(*h*) *The provision to an exhibitor of a site or space at any exhibition or similar event for the display or advertisement of goods or services.*
The supply of "space" for such purposes is taxable at standard rate. If the exhibition is not organised for such a purpose (i.e. where it is organised for the retail sale of goods to persons attending it), the supply of space is exempt unless held in a hotel or similar establishment. Similarly the rent paid by the exhibition organiser is exempt unless the event is held in a hotel, etc.

GP. 2. INSURANCE
The provision of insurance and re-insurance of any description is exempt. Insurance means all the classes of insurance business defined in the Insurance Companies Act.
Insurance broking and insurance agency services are also exempt.

GP. 3. POSTAL SERVICES
The exemption covers the conveyance of postal packets by the Post Office, and the supply of any services in connection with the conveyance of postal packets (excluding telegrams).
The exemption refers to services provided by the Post Office. If, therefore, a taxable person invoices separately to a customer postage and packing, then this charge is taxable.
Services which *are* subject to tax at the standard rate include:

(*a*) The impression by the Inland Revenue and H.M. Stationery Office of postage stamps on customer's own materials.
(*b*) Agency services of sub-postmasters.
(*c*) Printed postage impression services.
(*d*) Sales of stationery.
(*e*) Philatelic services.
(*f*) Post-marking fees.

GP. 4. BETTING, GAMING AND LOTTERIES
The exemption refers to the provision of any facility for the placing of bets or the playing of any games of chance or the granting of a right to take part in a lottery.
"Games of chance" is as defined in the Gaming Act 1968, while "lottery" includes any competition for prizes which is authorised by a licence under the Pools Competitions Act 1971.
Generally the charge for the facilities is the stake money. The measure of exempt output is therefore the money taken in the form of stakes less money paid out as winnings or prizes.
Examples of the *exempt* services are:

(*a*) The gross profits of a bookmaker.
(*b*) The deduction for expenses and profit by a totalisator operator.
(*c*) The deduction for commission and expenses by a pools betting promoter.

(*d*) The charge to play prize bingo, less the value of the prizes won.

(*e*) The house profit from casino games.

(*f*) The takings from gaming machines providing facilities to play a game of chance.

(*g*) The deduction for expenses and profit by the promoter of a lottery.
Examples of services which *are* subject to tax include:

(*a*) Admission charges to any premises where betting or the playing of games of chance take place.

(*b*) Session charges made under s. 14 of the Gaming Act.

(*c*) The subscription to any club and the facilities to which the subscription entitles the member.

(*d*) The supply of gaming or amusement machines.

GP. 5. FINANCE

The issue, transfer or receipt of, or dealings with money, securities, or any note or order for the payment of money is exempt.

The exemption covers banking services in general but does not cover services which are taxable at the standard rate such as:

(*a*) Investment, finance and taxation advice.

(*b*) Portfolio management.

(*c*) Management of trust funds.

(*d*) Executorship and trustee services.

(*e*) Management consultancy.

(*f*) Credit card services.

(*g*) Underwriting of new issues.

(*h*) Miscellaneous services such as debt collection, registrar services, safe custody, stockbroking services, etc.

GP. 6. EDUCATION (INCLUDING RESEARCH)

(1) Education or research by a recognised school or university.

(2) Education or research of a kind provided by a school or university but carried out, otherwise than for profit, by some other body. Training or retraining for a trade, profession or vocation is exempt if carried out otherwise than for profit. Educational and research facilities provided by organisations with a view to profit are not included and will be taxed at standard rate. These will include correspondence, language, management, marketing, computer, business, secretarial, motor, sports and similar schools, as well as commercial research organisations.

(3) Private tuition (other than in recreational or sporting subjects) is exempt if it is in subjects normally taught at a school or university.

(4) The supply of goods and services incidental to such purposes.

(5) Instruction supplemental thereto.

(6) The facilities of youth clubs are exempt.

GP. 7. HEALTH

The supply of medical *services* by persons registered as medical practitioners, dentists, opticians and professional supplementary persons to these (i.e. laboratory technicians, radiographers), nurses, midwives, ancillary dental workers, hearing aid dispensers are exempt whether supplied to National Health Service patients or to private patients.

The supply of *goods* by registered pharmaceutical chemists on the prescription of a registered practitioner is zero-rated, but services are exempt. Supplies by dental technicians are also exempt. Hospital care and medical or surgical treatment and related services are exempt. The provision of a deputy (locum) for a registered medical practitioner is exempt.

GP. 8. BURIALS AND CREMATIONS
The exemption covers the services of undertakers, cemeteries and crematoria.

The exemption is not wide enough to cover all goods and services connected with the above. Supplies of coffins, shrouds, maintenance of graves, flower arrangements and commemorative services are taxed at the standard rate.

GP. 9. TRADE UNIONS AND PROFESSIONAL BODIES
The exemption covers membership, services and related goods supplied by trade unions and non-profit making professional, learned or representational associations.

GP. 10. SPORTS COMPETITIONS
The grant of a right to enter a competition in sport or physical recreation, provided the entry fees are allocated wholly towards the prizes awarded in the competition. This also applies to the grant by a non-profit making body (established for the purposes of sport or physical recreation) of a right to enter a competition in such an activity, unless the consideration consists wholly or partly in a charge which the body normally makes for the use of its facilities or admission to its premises.

GP. 11. WORKS OF ART
The disposal of works of art surrendered, or otherwise dealt with, in settlement of capital gains tax and capital transfer tax liabilities.

§ 12.—CREDIT FOR INPUT TAX AGAINST OUTPUT TAX

GENERAL (s. 14, V.A.T.A. 1983)
A taxable person who makes supplies must account for and pay over to the Commissioners tax due in respect of "prescribed accounting periods". Regulations as to accounting and payment are set out in VAT (General) Regulations 1985.

Returns and payment of tax (Regs. 58, 60)
The normal return is form VAT 100 and the general rule is that such returns must be submitted quarterly (the dates being notified by the Commissioners) and not later than the last day of the month next following the end of the period concerned. Alternatively permission may be given, or an instruction issued for returns to be submitted monthly but within the same time limits. The first return covers the time from the date when liability to be registered first arises up to the normal date for the end of a prescribed accounting period. The Commissioners also have power to order returns to be made for any other period.

If control of the assets of a registered person passes into the hands of a trustee in bankruptcy, a receiver, a liquidator, etc. a return is required up to the day preceding the appointment of such a person.

When a person either ceases to be liable to be registered, or ceases to be a taxable person or has his registration withdrawn by the Commissioners, he must make a final return within one month of such occurrence.

Payment of any tax shown by the return to be due from the taxable person must be paid over within the same time limits.

Sale under a power (Reg. 59)
If goods forming part of the assets of a business carried on by a taxable person are sold under a power exercisable by some other person (e.g. under a mortgage,

or debenture) the supply is deemed made by the taxable person. However the person selling the goods must notify the VAT office of the full details of such sales and pay over the tax due. He must send a copy of this notification to the taxable person concerned. To avoid double taxation this information is then omitted from the normal returns by the seller and the person whose goods are sold.

Set-off (Regs. 61, 62)
VAT returns must record all VAT charged on supplies (estimated if necessary) made by a taxable person and all VAT arising on importations and, after set-off or VAT on supplies made to him the taxable person must make a payment to the Controller of the VAT shown as due by the return. At the end of each prescribed accounting period a taxable person can take credit against the tax which he has charged on his supplies (and is liable to account to the Commissioners therefor) (known as "output tax") for tax which has been charged upon supplies of goods or services, or upon importations, used in his business (known as "input tax"). If goods or services, or importations, are only partly for use in a business and partly for other purposes only the business proportion thereof is allowed as input tax

A claim for input tax is made on the normal VAT return supported by:
- (*a*) a tax invoice provided by the supplier, or, if approved by the Commissioners, an invoice provided by the registered person to himself under a "self-invoicing" scheme;
- (*b*) an invoice from a foreign supplier;
- (*c*) importation documents; or
- (*d*) documents releasing goods from warehouse.

Estimated claims for input tax are allowed provided an exact account and adjustment is made in the next period.

If, at the end of a period, no output tax is due, or if input tax credits exceed output tax, a repayment may be made by the Commissioners. Alternatively it may be held over and credited in a subsequent period. The amount of input tax which can be credited varies as follows:
- (*a*) If all supplies are taxable the whole of the input tax is allowable;
- (*b*) If some, but not all, supplies are taxable supplies only such proportion of the input tax as is attributable thereto is allowable;
- (*c*) If, in the period concerned, or in any previous period, there have been no taxable supplies the allowable proportion of the input tax for the period is determined by the Commissioners.

Persons acting in a representative capacity (Reg. 63)
If a taxable person dies, or becomes incapacitated so that control of his assets passes to a personal representative, trustee in bankruptcy, receiver, liquidators, etc. the requirements as to returns and payment must be complied with by the person having control of the assets. However his liability to pay tax is limited to the assets coming into his hands.

Errors (Reg. 64)
If an error is made in accounting for tax or in a return it must be corrected. The timing and manner of such correction is at the discretion of the Commissioners. Small errors will normally be corrected when the next return is submitted.

Customs have agreed with the Consultative Committee of the Accountancy Bodies that errors of up to £1,000 of VAT underpaid, or over-reclaimed can be dealt with in this way.

ALLOWABLE INPUT TAX (s. 14, V.A.T.A. 1983)
Credit is given for input tax on supplies of goods or services made to a taxable person where such supplies are used or to be used for the purposes of his business.

Thus input tax on supplies made to a person in his private capacity is not allowable. Input tax on supplies made to him in his business capacity will qualify for set off unless they are specifically disallowed (see below) or there is a restriction due to partial exemption (see § 13). Relief may also be available for tax on supplies made for the benefit of a company but prior to its incorporation.

A newly registered person can obtain relief for input tax on goods or services supplied to him, or on importations made before registration. Such a person should notify Customs and Excise that he is an "intending trader" and indicate the date when he anticipates that he will start to trade.

DISALLOWANCE OF INPUT TAX

Goods subject to second-hand schemes (VAT (Special Provisions) Order 1981, Art. 7)
Certain goods, such as works of art, collectors pieces, motor cycles, caravans, boats and outboard motors, electronic organs and aircraft, are frequently dealt with through the second-hand market. To deal with this special arrangements require that tax is only charged on the dealer's margin (if any) between buying and selling prices. Where tax has been paid on this basis no input tax credit is available to the purchaser.

Fittings in buildings (VAT (Special Provisions) Order 1981, Art. 8)
No input credit is available for fittings installed by builders in new houses unless they are materials, builder's hardware, sanitary ware or other articles of a kind normally installed by builders as fixtures.

Entertainment (VAT (Special Provisions) Order 1981, Art. 9)
Input tax related to business entertainment is disallowed unless provided for an overseas customer, and reasonable (in the circumstances) in amount.

Motor cars (VAT (Cars) Order 1980, Art. 4)
No credit is allowed for input tax on the supply (including hire purchase) or importation of a motor car except in the following circumstances
    (i) where the supply is a letting on hire
    (ii) where the car is to be converted into a vehicle which is not a motor car
    (iii) where the car is new and is required by a motor dealer for sale
    (iv) where the car is new and is supplied to a taxable person whose business is supplying cars to disabled persons in receipt of a mobility allowance.

CAPITAL GOODS (s. 36, V.A.T.A. 1983)
The Treasury has power to make regulations to give relief for tax paid on the supply or import, for the purposes of business, of specified descriptions of plant and machinery in cases where all or part of the tax cannot be credited under the normal rules for credit of input tax against output tax. So far, however, no such regulations have been made.

§ 13.—PARTIAL EXEMPTION

GENERAL (s. 15, V.A.T.A. 1983)
A partially exempt person is a person who may have outputs which are taxable, either at the standard rate or zero-rate, and also outputs which are exempt.

A fully taxable person may deduct tax on his inputs from tax collected on his outputs while an exempt person is outside the scope of the tax system and therefore cannot deduct or reclaim any input tax he may have paid.

Therefore a separate scheme is required for the partially exempt person with a mixture of taxable and exempt outputs. Such a person is required to apportion his input tax between taxable and exempt supplies, and can therefore only deduct such part of his input tax that relates to his taxable outputs.

Where, however, in any tax period, a taxable person's exempt outputs are negligible or insignificant in relation to his total outputs, he may reclaim the whole of his input tax for that period as if he was a wholly taxable person, without apportioning it.

A partially exempt person may be able to relate particular types of input directly to particular types of output, e.g. goods bought for resale without any processing. But if an input cannot be related solely either to taxable or exempt inputs, then a calculation will be necessary to ascertain what proportion of the input tax relates to the taxable outputs. The details of the scheme are set out in VAT (General Regulations) Order, 1985.

"LONGER PERIODS" (Reg. 29)

The methods of calculation are normally applied by reference to a taxable person's tax year (for VAT).

METHOD OF CALCULATION (Reg. 30)

There is one "official" method of calculation. Under this method a taxable person may deduct such part of the input as bears the same ratio to the total input tax as the taxable supplies bear to the total supplies.

Other methods may be agreed to or specified by the Commissioners, to cover cases where the above methods would clearly give an unfair result.

Example

	£
Value of outputs chargeable at the standard rate (excluding VAT)	20,000
Value of outputs chargeable at zero-rate	20,000
Value of taxable outputs	40,000
Value of exempt outputs	10,000
Value of total outputs (excluding VAT)	£50,000
Percentage of taxable outputs $= \dfrac{40,000}{50,000} \times \dfrac{100}{1} =$	80%
Total input tax, say	£2,400
Deductible input tax $= £2,400 \times 80\% =$	£1,920

EXCLUSIONS AND LIMITS (Regs. 32, 33, 35)

In these calculations there must be excluded:

(*a*) sale, etc., of land (for a capital sum) habitually occupied for the purposes of the business;

(*b*) supplies (including imports) of goods on which output tax is not charged because input tax was not deductible on acquisition of the goods concerned;

(*c*) transactions in securities (unless that is the business of the person concerned);

(*d*) assignment of a debt;

(*e*) financial dealings and loans (unless that is the business of the person concerned) (except moneylenders, mortgage brokers and pawnbrokers);

(*f*) certain financial dealings and loans within a group treatment;

(*g*) sales, etc., of tied premises;

(*h*) grant of licences to trade within the licenser's own retail premises.

Exempt supplies are treated as taxable if for any prescribed accounting period, or in any longer period the value of the exempt supplies does not exceed certain limits:

(i) £200 per month on average; or
(ii) both £8,000 per month on average and 50% of all supplies; or
(iii) both £16,000 per month on average and 25% of all supplies; or
(iv) 1% of all supplies.

Furthermore if the amount of input tax attributable to exempt supplies is less than 5% of the total input tax (and does not exceed £200 per month) all supplies may, subject to the Commissioners' discretion, be treated as taxable supplies.

DURATION OF USE (Reg. 36)

A partially exempt person has a choice of method to suit his particular trading circumstances and must notify Customs as to the method he decides to adopt. A method once adopted will have to be used for a period of at least two years unless there is a good reason for a change which is approved by Customs. Normally the tax periods for a partially exempt person will be the calendar quarters of the year, i.e. ending 31st March, 30th June, 30th September and 31st December. If, however, a person expects that his input tax will exceed his output tax regularly, he may claim to have a tax period of one month in order that he can obtain earlier repayments.

ADJUSTMENTS (Reg. 34)

Certain further adjustments are made to these calculations for those cases where there has been a provisional allocation of input tax under a method but where not all of his supplies can be treated as taxable supplies. In such a case a taxable person can:

(a) determine the input tax attributable to taxable supplies using one of the methods; and
(b) ascertain whether, overall, there has been an over-deduction or under-deduction of input tax on the basis of a comparison of the amount allowable under one of the methods and the amounts actually deducted, in the same prescribed accounting periods; and
(c) make adjustment for the over-deduction or under-deduction in the next prescribed accounting period following the end of the longer period for which the comparison has been made.

The deduction of input tax claimed on the tax returns will be provisional for each tax period with an adjustment at the end of each tax year to take into account seasonal variations in inputs and outputs. This adjustment is important in order to protect the interests of both the taxable person or the Exchequer, as can be seen by the following illustration:

Example 2

Illustration of quarterly accounting with a year-end adjustment

Quarter no.	Taxable outputs	Exempt outputs	Total outputs	Input tax	Deductible percentage	Deductible input tax
	£	£	£	£	%	£
1	2,000	4,000	6,000	300	$33\frac{1}{3}$	100.00
2	Nil	8,000	8,000	500	Nil	—
3	7,000	1,000	8,000	400	$87\frac{1}{2}$	350.00
4	6,000	2,000	8,000	200	75	150.00
		Total deductible input tax over 4 quarters				£600.00

The year-end adjustment is necessary as, taking the year as a whole, the following position will arise:

Year	15,000	15,000	30,000	1,400	50	£700.00

In this case, the taxable person will be able to claim a further £100 of deductible input tax.

§ 14.—REGISTRATION (s. 2, Sch. 1, V.A.T.A. 1983; VAT (General) Regulations 1985)

REGISTRATION (Paras 1, 3–6, 11, 12; Regs. 4, 5, 37)
Any person who is carrying on a business which has a taxable turnover in excess of the current limit is required to register with Customs. This requirement also includes persons who carry on separate businesses with a combined annual turnover exceeding this limit.

Persons setting up new businesses are required to register on commencement of the business if they have reason to suppose that their turnover will exceed the above limit.

The limits of turnover above which the trader must register have varied periodically. Recent limits have been as follows:

	11.3.81– 9.3.82 £	10.3.82– 15.3.83 £	16.3.83– 13.3.84 £	14.3.84– 19.3.85 £	20.3.85– onwards £
Annual limit	15,000	17,000	18,000	18,700	19,500
Quarterly limit*	5,000	6,000	6,000	6,200	6,500

A person who becomes liable to be registered must notify the Commissioners within ten days after the earliest date on which he knows, or could with reasonable diligence know, that he is so liable. The Commissioners have a discretion to extend this period.

A person who becomes liable to be registered because his turnover for a quarter exceeds the current or the cumulative turnover for four quarters then ending exceeds the current annual limit, must notify the Commissioners within ten days after the end of the quarter concerned. Registration will then take effect from twenty-one days after the end of that quarter, unless an earlier date is agreed upon. Where registration is on the basis of a person's intended supplies upon the making of which he will become liable to be registered, he must notify the Commissioners and request to be registered. The Commissioners will then register him from such date as they agree and subject to any conditions they think fit to impose.

A person whose taxable supplies are zero-rated, or would be zero-rated if he were a taxable person, can apply to be exempt from registration.

A person who makes or intends to make taxable supplies, but who is not or will not be liable to be registered, can apply to register voluntarily.

Exemption from registration and voluntary registration are both at the discretion of the Commissioners and can be withdrawn if the pre-conditions cease to exist.

Where there is a change in the name, constitution or ownership of a business or other event which might require the variation or cancellation of the registration, full particulars thereof must be notified to the Commissioners within twenty-one days of the change. The registration limits can be increased from time to time by statutory instruments.

---

* But only if the taxable supplies in the quarter and the next three quarters are expected to exceed the annual limit.

TRANSFERS OF GOING CONCERNS (s. 33, V.A.T.A. 1983)
Where a business is not closed down but is sold to another person and there is no break in trading, the cancellation of the registration by the vendor and the new registration by the purchaser take place on the same day. This avoids the need for the vendor to pay tax on anything but his "normal" taxable supplies up to the date of the transfer. In particular, he does not have to pay tax on any stocks which he transfers to the purchaser for business purposes. Both parties are responsible for informing the Customs and Excise of the transfer.

DEREGISTRATION (Paras 7–10; Reg. 37)
Existing traders who are at present registered are allowed to deregister if their annual turnover is less than the current "historical" threshold in each of the preceding two years of registration, and is not expected to exceed that amount in the next twelve months, or if the value of taxable supplies will not exceed the current "intended" threshold in the next twelve months.
Recent limits have been as follows:

	1.6.81– 31.5.82	1.6.82– 31.5.83	1.6.83– 31.5.84	1.6.84– 31.5.85	1.6.85– onwards
"Historical" limit	£15,000	£17,000	£18,000	£18,700	£19,500
"Intended" limit	£14,000	£16,000	£17,000	£17,700	£18,500

When a registered person ceases to make taxable supplies or his registration ceases on the historical turnover limits test, he must notify the Commissioners of that fact within ten days thereof. The cancellation has effect from fourteen days after the notification, or as otherwise agreed. If cancellation is on the basis of anticipated turnover the registration ceases from such date as the Commissioners are satisfied that the limits will not be exceeded.
Where a business closes down, the taxable person must inform the Customs and Excise of the fact within ten days, in writing, quoting his VAT registration number. He is then required to make a final return within one month of the date of cancellation and any tax due must be paid for this period.
Input tax on services supplied after de-registration can be claimed back if they were for the purpose of the business carried on before de-registration.
The deregistration limits can be increased from time to time by Statutory Instrument.

GOVERNMENT DEPARTMENTS (s. 27, V.A.T.A. 1983)
VAT applies to taxable supplies by Government departments. Where a supply by a Government department does not amount to carrying on a business, but it appears to the Treasury that similar goods or services might be supplied by taxable persons in the course of or furtherance of any business, then the Treasury may direct that supplies by that department are treated as if made in the course or furtherance of a business carried on by it. The effect is to ensure that there is no unfair advantage to the Government department as compared with other suppliers.
The Treasury can also direct that goods or services obtained by one department from another (e.g. by or from the Crown Estate Commissioners) are treated as *supplied* by that other department. This is also intended to prevent unfair competition as compared with outside suppliers.

LOCAL AUTHORITIES (s. 28, V.A.T.A. 1983)
A local authority which makes taxable supplies is liable to be registered whatever the value of such supplies. Local authorities (and certain other statutory authorities) are entitled to a refund of input tax suffered on supplies to (or imports by) them, insofar as they do not relate to the carrying on of a business by them.

GROUPS OF COMPANIES (s. 29, V.A.T.A. 1983)
Groups of companies (i.e. companies under common control) can apply for group treatment. The effect of this is that supplies to and from members of the group are disregarded. All supplies made to or by group members (other than to and from each other) are treated as made by one "representative" company. That company is responsible for making VAT returns and payments on behalf of all the group members. However the liability to pay VAT is joint and several. In other words all group members are liable for the full VAT liability arising on all group supplies irrespective of which company actually made the supply.

DIVISIONS (s. 31, V.A.T.A. 1983)
A single company carrying on its business through divisions can apply to be registered in respect of each division.

PARTNERSHIPS (s. 30, V.A.T.A. 1983, VAT (General) Regulations 1985, Reg. 9)
Partnerships are required to complete also Form VAT 2 which contains particulars of the full names and addresses of all partners of the business registered on the Form VAT 1. The partnership name will be registered as the taxable person but the individual partners are still jointly and severally liable for the firm's VAT liabilities. It is sufficient for such notice to be given, on behalf of the partnership, by one partner.

Separate registrations will not be given to separate businesses carried on by the same individuals in partnership even if there are different partnership agreements for each business. This does not apply if the partnerships do not comprise the same individuals.

All appropriate notices are addressed to a partnership in the name in which the partnership is registered. For this purpose the partnership is deemed to include all former partners and a notice may be validly served on a partner who has left the partnership until the change is notified to Customs and Excise.

CLUBS (s. 31, V.A.T.A. 1983, VAT (General) Regulations 1985, Reg. 10)
Where registration is made on behalf of a club, association or organisation, whose affairs are managed by its members, or by a committee thereof, the notification must include the full name, address and signature of three members. Although the duty of compliance with VAT regulations falls, in the following order, upon:
(*a*) the officers of the club, etc; or
(*b*) the committee members; or
(*c*) the members
such liability being joint and several, it is a sufficient compliance if any one of them has fulfilled the obligation. With effect from 1st September 1980 no account is taken, in connection with registration requirements, of changes in the membership of a club, etc.

DEATH, BANKRUPTCY (s. 23, F.A. 1983, VAT (General) Regulations 1985, Reg. 11)
If a taxable person dies, or becomes bankrupt or otherwise incapacitated, the Commissioners will treat the person actually carrying on the business as the registered person until some other person is registered. The person carrying on the business must notify the Commissioners within twenty-one days.

§ 15.—AGENTS (s. 32, V.A.T.A. 1983)

The following provisions apply to agents carrying on business in the United Kingdom. They apply to all taxable persons who make disbursements as agents for their clients, for goods or services obtained from third parties.
An agent may be involved with VAT in two ways:
(*a*) in the supply of services to his principal, or

(*b*) as an intermediary in supplies between his principal and a third party.

Most services which are provided by an agent are taxable at the standard rate unless they are specifically zero-rated (i.e. services to overseas principal) or exempt (i.e. insurance business).

Where an agent is a taxable person because the amount of his taxable turnover, e.g. commission, exceeds the current limits for registration, he must account for tax on the supply of his taxable services.

The value on which he will calculate the tax will normally be the amount he charges his principal. The principal, if he is a taxable person, will be able to treat the tax on the agent's commission as input tax.

Where an agent is not a taxable person because the amount of his turnover does not exceed the current limits for registration, he is not required to register and therefore is not a taxable person. He is not required to account for tax on his commission nor must he keep VAT records.

In certain cases, such an agent may be at a commercial disadvantage when he acts as an intermediary between two taxable persons as he is unable to issue tax invoices to the taxable buyers who will not be able to claim deduction or repayment of input tax. In this situation he may wish to apply for voluntary registration in order that he can issue tax invoices in his own name.

The VAT provisions provide for a range of situations which include:

(*a*) where the agent may be either a taxable person or not.

(*b*) the agent may be acting for either the buyer or the seller.

(*c*) the principal, whether buyer or seller, may be either a taxable person or not.

(*d*) the third party may either be a taxable person or not.

(*e*) the principal and the third party may know each other's identity, one may know the other's identity, or neither may know the other's identity.

§ 16.—IMPORTS

GOODS (ss. 1, 19, 24, 25, 35, V.A.T.A. 1983, s. 17, F.A. 1977; VAT (General) Regulations 1985, Regs. 38–51)

VAT may be charged (in addition to customs duties) on goods imported into the United Kingdom, and is charged and paid as though it were a customs duty, and in general, the normal customs procedures are applied.

The charge applies to all imports (unless zero-rated or otherwise relieved) whether by registered or non-registered persons. A registered person can claim VAT paid on importation as input tax in the normal way (subject to any restriction if he is partially exempt).

Most zero-rated goods are not subject to VAT on importation but certain goods which would otherwise be zero-rated are, specifically, excluded from zero-rating and are thus taxable.

There is no VAT when goods are imported but are sold in the United Kingdom prior to "entry" with the purchaser being responsible for making the entry. This is to prevent double taxation (See zero-rate Sch. Gp. 15 item 1).

Special rules apply to determine the value of goods on importation. The value for VAT purposes of goods imported into the United Kingdom is the price paid in money for the goods, together with (if not already included in the price):

(*a*) commission, packing, freight and insurance to the place of importation;

(*b*) customs duties on importation with the E.E.C.;

(*c*) excise duties on importation into the United Kingdom.

Foreign currency conversions are made at the most recent published selling rate of exchange.

If no price in money is payable (or money is not the sole consideration), the value for VAT is as for *ad valorem* duties, together with such duties. A declaration is required for goods exceeding £1,000 in value.

The time of supply of imported goods is determined according to the customs "entry" procedures, or if lodged in a bonded warehouse the time of supply is when they are removed from it.

There are special procedures to deal with special methods of import entry:

(*a*) Transit shed register (at certain airports);
(*b*) Importation through the LACES computer system at London Airports;
(*c*) Postal importations.

Prior to 1st October 1984 (by concession 1st November 1984) where the importation was by a registered taxable person who imported goods in the course of his business, he could take delivery of the goods without paying tax at that time provided he accounted for the tax in his VAT return for the period in which the importation took place. This was known as the "postponed accounting system". Such a person who imported goods and used them for the purposes of his business could, in general, deduct the tax payable thereon as input tax. In effect a registered taxable person held imported goods in his business free of tax. VAT would also have been charged and accounted for if the taxable person made a supply of the goods he had imported.

Example

A taxable person buys goods from United Kingdom sources amounting to £4,000 on which he pays VAT of £600. He also buys goods from overseas sources amounting to £2,000. These were originally deposited in a bonded warehouse but in the accounting period he withdraws these from the warehouse and includes them with the rest of his stock for re-sale. In the tax period he sells goods to the value of £8,000 on which he charges VAT of £1,200. The tax calculation at the end of the tax period would be:

		£
Output tax		
Sales..		1,200
Add tax due on imported goods but not paid at time of import........		300
Total tax due..		1,500
Less Input tax..	300	
Tax on imported goods......................................	600	900
Tax payable to Customs..		£600

From 1st October 1984 onwards, "approved importers" can defer payment of VAT until the 15th of the month following import. Payment is by direct debit.

A private individual, or a taxable person, importing goods for personal use, must pay VAT direct to Customs, unless deferment is allowed.

There is no special rate of VAT for imports so the rate of VAT on imported goods is the same as for goods supplied in the United Kingdom.

SERVICES (s. 7, Sch. 3, V.A.T.A. 1983)
Certain supplies of services are subject to a "reverse charge" to VAT when supplied by a person who belongs outside the U.K. but received by a taxable person who belongs in the U.K. The supplies concerned are:

1. Transfers and assignments of copyright, patents, licences, trademarks and similar rights.
2. Advertising services.
3. Services of consultants, engineers, consultancy bureaux, lawyers, accountants and other similar services; data processing and provision of information (*excluding any services relating to land*).
4. Acceptance of any obligation to refrain from pursuing or exercising, in whole or part, any business activity or any such rights as are referred to in item 1 above.

5. Banking, financial and insurance services (including re-insurance, but not including the provision of safe deposit facilities).
6. The supply of staff
7. The services rendered by one person to another in procuring for the other any of the services mentioned in items 1 to 6 above.

Where such supplies are made to a taxable person in the United Kingdom, they are subject to VAT. If the person making the supply *belongs* in the United Kingdom he will charge VAT in the normal way. If he *belongs* outside the United Kingdom the responsibility to charge VAT rests on the taxable person receiving the supply. This concept is known as a "Reverse Charge". The recipient can also reclaim the VAT as input tax. However, if he is partially exempt he may only be able to recover a proportion.

§ 17.—EXPORTS

GOODS (s. 16, V.A.T.A. 1983)

Goods exported by a taxable person are relieved of VAT by zero-rating, which means that although no VAT is chargeable on the export supply, tax on inputs can be deducted in the normal manner.

Where goods are exported without there being any supply for VAT purposes (e.g. exports on sale or return, transfers to a taxable person's own stocks abroad, or goods sent abroad temporarily for exhibition or processing), no VAT is charged but records should be kept to show the true nature of the transaction.

Supplies of goods in the United Kingdom to overseas traders who do not have a place of business in the United Kingdom are also, subject to certain conditions, zero-rated (broadly proof of export must be obtained). Supplies of goods to an overseas trader who requires them to be delivered to a third person in the United Kingdom for processing, etc. before ultimate export will also, subject to similar conditions, be zero-rated.

Although there are retail export schemes, such schemes are not suitable for some types of purchase (e.g. air travellers). In such cases the "Personal Export Scheme" and the "Over-the-Counter Scheme" cannot be used and alternative procedures must be followed. When the supply is made it is not entered in the supplier's accounts at either standard-rate or zero-rate but is entered in a special record. When evidence of export is obtained the supply is entered as zero-rated. If such evidence is not obtained within one month following the intended date of export, the supply must be recorded at standard rate.

These special provisions do not apply to sales of motor vehicles, nor to goods which should be dealt with under the retail export schemes, including goods sold to Community travellers not exceeding *de minimis* limits.

Most exporters will be registered taxable persons, but an exporter who is not registered (perhaps because he is below the current registration limit) may apply for voluntary registration if he wishes. He may then reclaim the input tax on the goods exported.

The exporter must keep proper records and make returns quarterly.

In cases where exporters find that, as their export outputs are zero-rated, their deductible input tax will regularly exceed their output tax, they will be able to reclaim from Customs.

Where these repayments are material, arrangements can be made with Customs to claim repayments monthly instead of quarterly.

An exporter must ensure that evidence of export is available for production to Customs if required. This evidence will consist of the normal commercial documents, e.g. invoice, consignment note, freight documents, etc., and evidence of the payment received from abroad.

Most shipping and airline companies will be registered taxable persons. Goods supplied to them (i.e. stores and equipment), will bear tax, which will be deductible as usual. Where supplies are made direct to foreign-going craft, these may be zero-rated provided that the supplier can get confirmation of the supply and these are made direct to ship or aircraft concerned. Similar arrangements can be made for supplies intended for sale in ships' shops or on aircraft, provided that these are sold outside the United Kingdom.

Retail export schemes
Retail sales of goods by a registered taxable person to an overseas visitor for export, are zero-rated.

An overseas visitor is described as a person who during the last two years immediately before the purchase has not been in the United Kingdom more than one year.

Two methods of sales are considered:
(i) goods sent direct to the ship or aircraft by which the customer intends to leave the United Kingdom, for export on that ship or aircraft.
(ii) goods sold over the counter to the customer for export on his person or in his hand luggage when he leaves the United Kingdom.

SERVICES
In general the supply of services to a person who belongs overseas are taxable unless they are specifically zero-rated (e.g. under Schedule 5, V.A.T.A. 1983, Gps. 9, 10) or exempt.

§ 18.—SECOND-HAND GOODS (s. 18, V.A.T.A. 1983)

GENERAL
When second-hand goods are sold it will often be the case that the sales are made by private individuals who are not taxable traders selling in the ordinary course of their business. Such sales are thus outside the scope of VAT. Where second-hand goods are sold by a taxable person, VAT must be applied thereto. If the general rules of VAT were applied to a purchase of second-hand goods by a taxable trader from a non-taxable person (e.g. a purchase of a second-hand car by a motor dealer in part exchange for another vehicle), the taxable trader would pay no VAT on the purchase but would have to charge VAT on the sale price. Thus he would have no "input tax" to offset against his "output tax". The problem is dealt with by the issue of regulations which provide that VAT is charged only on the net "value added" by the transaction.

MOTOR CARS (VAT (Cars) Order 1980, Art. 6)
In general, VAT is charged on the margin (i.e. the difference (if any) between the buying and selling price) on sales of used motor cars. Where the used car concerned was imported by the dealer the buying price is taken as the value of the car as assessed for the purpose of charging tax on input together with any VAT (or purchase tax) then charged.

If the car has been self-supplied (See § 9), the buying price is taken as the amount on which VAT was charged together with such tax.

The second-hand scheme does not apply in the following circumstances:
(i) where the supply is a letting on hire
(ii) where the car was produced by the taxable person concerned, provided it was not previously supplied by him in the course of furtherance of his business, nor self-supplied
(iii) if an invoice showing tax on the supply is issued
(iv) if, in the case of a car dealer, he does not keep proper records.

Example

A motor dealer sells to a private individual a car for £2,000 which he took into stock at value of £1,500 in part exchange.

He will pay no VAT on the purchase of £1,500 as this was from a non-taxable person but will only charge VAT on the "value-added", i.e. £500. The VAT on the transaction will be based upon the dealer's margin which is treated as "VAT inclusive". In this case £500 × 3/23 = £65. The dealer does not issue a tax invoice, does not have to declare his margin and does not claim deduction of input tax on the purchase of the car.

OTHER GOODS (VAT (Special Provisions) Order 1981, Arts. 4, 5, VAT (Horses and Ponies) Order 1983)
Broadly similar schemes apply for the following types of second-hand goods:
  (i) works of art, antiques and collectors pieces,
 (ii) used motor cycles,
(iii) used caravans,
 (iv) used boats and outboard motors,
  (v) used electronic organs,
 (vi) used aircraft,
(vii) used firearms,
(viii) horses and ponies.

§ 19.—ACCOUNTING SYSTEM (ss. 14, 40, 48, Sch. 7, paras. 2–8, Sch. 10, para. 17, V.A.T.A. 1983, VAT (General) Regulations 1985, Regs. 12–16, 58–64)

The accounting system is based on "tax invoices". A taxable person must issue a tax invoice which must contain details of the supplies made and the tax chargeable thereon, together with the names and addresses of the persons by whom and for whom the supplies are made. In addition, each invoice must be pre-numbered.
   The recipient of this invoice, if he is a taxable person, must retain this as evidence of his right of set-off of input tax against his output tax.
   A taxable person should therefore adapt his accounting system in such a way that the tax paid by him on his purchases (input tax) can be easily calculated and in addition the tax charged by him (output tax) can be ascertained.
   Special schemes are in operation in respect of retailers who do not normally issue invoices but who nevertheless have to ascertain the amount of their output tax.
   A VAT return is required to be completed at quarterly (or if so authorised, monthly) intervals, a specimen of which is shown below:

Period 1st April 1984 to 30th June 1984

Tax deductible			Tax due		
	£	£		£	£
Input tax			Output tax		
April	3,658		April	4,783	
May	2,794		May	3,516	
June	4,573	11,025	June	5,792	14,091
Over-declarations (if any)		—			
Total tax deductible		11,025			
Payment due to					
Customs		3,066	Under-declaration (if any)		—
		£14,091			£14,091

A return must be made for each accounting period. Documents are not required to be attached to the return but should be filed away by the taxable person as he will be required to produce these from time to time to an inspector from Customs who will visit him for the purposes of checking his VAT returns.

Customs have power to require taxable persons to keep records and documents for a maximum period of six years from the end of the relevant accounting period.

Where accounting is done by means of computers, taxable persons may make arrangements with Customs to enable the appropriate records of print-outs to be preserved.

A return must be made by each due date, even if this is a NIL return, or if the amount payable or repayable is under £1.

Where a taxable person is away from his place of business for a long period of time due to illness or business travel, arrangements must be made for returns to be made at the proper time.

Where failure to make a return takes place, Customs have power to make an estimated assessment of the tax due.

Appeals against this estimated assessment may be made to a tribunal.

VAT repayments may be withheld from a taxable person if he has failed to submit returns or pay VAT due in respect of earlier periods.

If VAT is repaid in error, the Commissioners can raise an assessment to recover the over-repayment.

§ 20.—RETAIL SCHEMES (Sch. 7, para. 2, V.A.T.A. 1983, VAT (Supplies by Retailers) Regulations 1972)

In certain retail establishments tax invoices are not normally given in respect of cash sales. However, the proprietor of these establishments is required to account for the VAT which he charges to his customers.

Gross cash takings are normally the basis on which the retailers may calculate his output tax, but a retailer may opt to include sales to account customers in his gross takings at the time the customer's account is debited and not when the account is paid. This may be of assistance to large retailers who may have difficulty in allocating receipts from account customers or from normal cash customers.

In order to ascertain the amount of this output tax which is included in the retailer's turnover, nine special schemes have been devised to enable the retailer to make this calculation. The retailer may elect to use any one of the nine schemes which best suits his purposes. The schemes apply only to the output tax and there are no special schemes for input tax, which must be calculated in the normal way.

Scheme A

This scheme is intended for retailers whose supplies of goods and services are all subject to VAT at the standard rate.

A record of gross takings must be kept and at the end of each tax period a calculation of the output tax must be made. Where all supplies are subject to tax at the standard rate, the output tax will be 3/23 (15/115) of the takings.

The following is an example of the scheme where all the supplies are taxable at the standard rate.

	£
Daily gross taking for the quarter ended 30th September 1984, say	20,000
Calculate output tax by taking three twentythirds takings	

i.e. $\dfrac{3}{23} \times £20,000 = £2,608.69$

Scheme B
This scheme is intended for retailers whose supplies of goods and services are subject to two rates of tax, zero-rate counting as one rate.

A record of gross takings must be kept and at the end of each tax period a calculation of the output tax must be made. In this scheme, the sales at the lower rate must not exceed 50% of the total sales, e.g.

	£
Daily gross takings for the quarter ended 30th September 1984	20,000
Less Takings at the lower rate (inc. VAT)	1,000
Estimated takings at higher rate	£19,000

Output tax

		£
Higher rate (say 15%) £19,000 × $\dfrac{3}{23}$	=	2,478.26
Lower rate (say 0%) £1,000 × nil	=	Nil
		£2,478.26

The special scheme does not extend to supplies of goods under hire purchase, credit sales or conditional sale agreements, and where receipts from these sources are included in the daily turnover, these must be excluded before the special scheme calculations are made. VAT on this type of sale must be calculated in the normal way and then added to the amount calculated under the special scheme before being remitted, e.g.

	£
VAT calculated under special scheme	2,478.26
Output tax on hire purchase sales, say	200.00
Total output tax for quarter	£2,678.26

Scheme C
In this scheme the sales for the period are calculated by reference to the cost of those sales, to which a "mark-up" fraction is applied to ascertain the assumed amount of the sales to which the appropriate VAT fraction is applied to arrive at the output tax. This scheme is suitable for traders who have supplies of goods at two or more rates of tax—zero rate counting as a separate rate—and whose turnover is less than £75,000 per annum (£50,000 up to 31st March 1983).

The appropriate "mark up" is given for each trade classification. Examples are given below:

Type of business	*Mark up*
Off-licences, confectioners, tobacconists	$16\frac{2}{3}\%$ $(\frac{1}{6})$
Grocers, dairies, butchers, fishmongers and bakers	20% $(\frac{1}{5})$
Greengrocers, fruiterers, radio and electrical goods shops (not TV rental), cycle and pram shops, bookshops and stationers, chemists and photographic shops, music shops (including records)	40% $(\frac{2}{5})$
Jewellers	75% $(\frac{3}{4})$
Other trades	50% $(\frac{1}{2})$

The scheme is applied in the following manner:

	Standard rate 15%	Zero rate
	£	£
Total cost (inc. VAT) of all goods received for retailing in quarter..........................	6,000	4,000
Add Mark up: say $\frac{1}{6}$..........................	1000	—
say $\frac{1}{5}$..........................	—	800
Total assumed sales........................	£7,000	£4,800

Output tax
Standard Rate £7,000 × 3/23 = £913.04

Scheme D
Scheme D may be used to calculate output tax on goods at two or more rates of tax, zero rate counting as a separate rate. It is used extensively by the smaller retailer whose annual taxable turnover is less than £200,000 (£125,000 up to 31st March 1983).

The output tax is calculated by reference to the proportion of the turnover represented by the cost of goods sold at differing rates of tax.

The appropriate VAT fraction is then applied to the estimated sales to arrive at the output tax, e.g.

	£	
Gross takings for period (including VAT).....	12,500	(A)
Cost (inc. VAT) of goods received for resale:		
Standard rate (15%).....................	8,500	(B)
Zero rate (0%)..........................	2,000	(C)
Cost (inc. VAT) of all goods received for resale....................................	£10,500	(D)

Output tax
(a) Standard rate (15%)

$$\text{Formula:}\frac{(B)}{(D)} \times (A) \times \frac{3}{23}$$

$$= \frac{8,500}{10,500} \times 12,500 \times \frac{3}{23} = £1,319.88$$

Scheme E
This scheme may be operated by any size of business to calculate output tax on supplies of goods at two or more rates of tax, again zero-rate counting as a separate rate. In the first period during which the scheme operates, the amount must be ascertained for each positive rate of tax which is payable by customers for goods which have been in stock when the scheme commenced and which have been received in the tax period for retailing. The appropriate VAT fraction is then applied to each separate total and the resultant total will be the output tax for the period. In the second and subsequent tax periods the same calculations as above are carried out but the amounts for the initial stocks are excluded.

Scheme F
This scheme is suitable for retailers of any size of business who supply goods or services at two or more rates of tax and who can distinguish between the rates of tax at the point of sale.

The gross takings for each positive rate of tax during the tax period is computed, and the appropriate VAT fraction is applied, resulting in the output tax for each rate of tax. These are then accumulated for arrival at the total output for the tax period.

Scheme G
Any large or medium-sized business may use this scheme to calculate the output tax at two or more rates of tax, zero-rate counting as a separate rate.

This scheme divides the gross takings for each of the first three tax periods in proportion to the total VAT-inclusive amounts payable to the suppliers for goods at each rate of tax in stock when the scheme first began to be used, together with the goods purchased since for retailing. This gives the assumed takings, including VAT, for goods supplied at each positive rate of tax.

The appropriate VAT fractions are then applied to the takings to arrive at a provisional output tax.

This provisional output tax is then increased by $\frac{1}{8}$ ($1\frac{1}{2}$ in certain circumstances) to allow for the different profit margins and the result is the amount of the output tax for the tax period.

For the fourth and subsequent tax periods, the same procedure is followed but the initial stock is ignored. The disadvantage of this method is the uplift of one-eighth on the provisional amount of the output tax and some traders may feel they are paying more output tax than under one of the other schemes. If this situation arises, they may change to any other scheme provided notice is given to the Customs and Excise. Changes in Schemes are usually made at the end of a twelve-monthly tax period.

Scheme H
This scheme may be used by large or medium-sized businesses to calculate output tax for any number of rates of tax, zero-rate counting as a separate rate of tax.

The gross takings, for each of the first three tax periods of using the scheme, are divided in proportion to the total VAT-inclusive amounts payable by customers for the goods at each rate of tax which were in stock when the scheme was first operated, together with the total of goods received for retailing since that date.

These calculations must take account of the selling price of each different line.

The assumed takings, which included VAT, are then calculated, to which the appropriate VAT fraction is applied to arrive at the amount of the output tax for the period. For the fourth and subsequent periods, the gross takings are divided in proportion to the total VAT-inclusive amounts payable by customers for goods at each rate of tax. Initial stocks are therefore excluded. Output tax is calculated by applying the appropriate VAT fraction for each rate of tax.

Scheme J
This scheme is suitable for large businesses to calculate output tax for any number of rates of tax, again zero-rate counting as a separate rate of tax.

The gross takings for each tax period are divided in proportion to the total VAT-inclusive amounts payable by customers for the goods at each rate of tax in stock at the beginning of the VAT year, together with the amount of goods received for retailing during the tax period. These calculations take into account the selling price of each different line. These calculations give the assumed takings, including VAT, for goods at each rate of tax.

The appropriate VAT fraction is then applied to these assumed takings to arrive at the provisional amount of output tax.

At the end of the trader's VAT year, the total amounts payable by customers for all goods remaining in stock are recorded, and the output tax is calculated for the year by reference to initial and closing stock, receipts of goods and gross takings for the whole year. If the result of that calculation is more than the amount of VAT paid in the year, the difference is payable to the Customs and Excise; if it is less, the excess may be reclaimed from the Customs and Excise.

§ 21.—REFUNDS OF FOREIGN VAT (s. 23, V.A.T.A. 1983; VAT (Repayment to Community Traders) Regulations 1980)

Persons carrying on business in a member state of the E.E.C., other than the United Kingdom, and in certain other countries (if authorised by community directive) who suffer tax on supplies made to them *in the United Kingdom* may obtain repayment of such tax from the United Kingdom authorities.

A similar relief is available for persons carrying on business in the United Kingdom who suffer foreign VAT. The repayment is made by the taxing authority of the country concerned.

§ 22.—DO-IT-YOURSELF BUILDERS (s. 21, V.A.T.A. 1983, VAT (Do-it-yourself Builders) (Relief) Regulations 1975)

Do-it-yourself builders who construct new homes (including a related garage) but who are not in business as builders, may obtain refunds of VAT suffered on goods supplied or imported for incorporation into the building or its site.

The relief is not available for the conversion, reconstruction, alteration or enlargement of existing buildings.

§ 23.—TERMINAL MARKETS (s. 34, V.A.T.A. 1983, VAT (Terminal Markets) Order 1973)

Most supplies between members of the main commodity terminal markets and between members of such markets and their clients are zero-rated provided that the transactions do not result in actual delivery of the commodities.

§ 24.—BAD DEBT RELIEF (s. 22, V.A.T.A. 1983, VAT (Bad Debts Relief) Regulations 1978)

A measure of relief is available to a person who has supplied goods or services for a monetary consideration and has accounted for VAT thereon but who has not been paid for the goods or services because the debtor has become insolvent. Relief is given by way of a refund of the tax chargeable on the outstanding amount.

In this context the debtor must be "formally" insolvent i.e. he is adjudged bankrupt, or, if a company, is in creditors' voluntary, or compulsory winding-up. A receivership does not qualify.

Certain conditions must be met if the relief is to be given:
- (a) the person claiming the relief must prove in the insolvency for the outstanding amount *less* the VAT refund claimed;
- (b) the value of the supply must not have been greater than market value;
- (c) property in the goods must have passed to the debtor.

The regulations set out the relevant claims procedure.

§ 25.—PRIORITY OF VAT IN BANKRUPTCY, WINDING-UP, ETC.
(Sch. 7, para. 12, V.A.T.A. 1983)

If a taxable person should become insolvent (i.e. bankruptcy, liquidation or receivership) Customs have a preferential claim for payment of VAT due in respect of VAT accounting periods falling wholly (or partly—subject to apportionment) within twelve months preceding the relevant date (i.e. appointment of trustee, liquidator or receiver).

§ 26.—ADMINISTRATION

The responsibility for the administration of VAT lies with the commissioners of Customs and Excise.

MAKING REGULATIONS
In this connection they have been given wide powers in relation to the collection and enforcement of the tax. These are summarised below.

(*a*) *Accounting for and payment of tax*
(para. 2 Sch. 7, V.A.T.A. 1983)

(*b*) *Regulations regarding computer produced invoices*
(para. 3 Sch. 7, V.A.T.A. 1983)

(*c*) *Assessment of unreported or underpaid tax*
(para. 4 Sch. 7, V.A.T.A. 1983)

(*d*) *Taking of security against possible non-payment of tax*
(para. 5 Sch. 7, V.A.T.A. 1983)

(*e*) *Proceedings for recovery of unpaid tax*
(para. 6 Sch. 7, V.A.T.A. 1983)

(*f*) *Regulations regarding the keeping of records*
(para. 7 Sch. 7, V.A.T.A. 1983)

(*g*) *Regulations as to the provision of information and documents*
(para. 8 Sch. 7, V.A.T.A. 1983; para. 3 Sch. 7, F.A. 1985)

(*h*) *Power to take samples*
(para. 9 Sch. 7, V.A.T.A. 1983)

(*i*) *Power to open gaming machines*
(para. 9A, Sch. 7, V.A.T.A. 1983; para. 4, Sch. 7 F.A. 1985)

(*j*) *Regulations relating to powers of entry and search of premises and persons and access to recorded information* (paras. 10, 10A–10C, Sch. 7, V.A.T.A. 1983; para. 6, Sch. 7, F.A. 1985)

PENALTIES
There are severe penalties for evasion of VAT regulations. The circumstances in which these might apply are summarised hereunder.

(*a*) *Criminal proceedings for evasion* (s. 39, V.A.T.A. 1983; s. 12, F.A. 1985)
  Certain offences can result in criminal proceedings, viz.:
    (i) Fraudent evasion.

(ii) False documents and statements.

(iii) Conduct which must have involved the commission of an offence.

(iv) Connivance at a supplier's evasion.

(v) Failure to provide security.

Such offences can give rise to fines (of up to three times the tax evaded) and custodial sentences of up to six months on summary conviction or 7 years on indictment.

(b) *Civil proceedings for evasion* (s. 13, F.A. 1985)

Where an offence has been committed but there are no criminal proceedings, or no conviction, civil penalties may still apply. The maximum penalty is equal to the whole of the tax evaded. This may be reduced by up to 50% if the tax payer cooperates in the investigation of the true liability.

(c) *Serious misdeclaration* (s. 14, F.A. 1985)

If a person makes a misdeclaration (understated output tax or overstated input tax) this is regarded as "serious" if it amounts to more than 30% of the tax due to or from the person for the period, or the greater of £3,000 or $1\frac{1}{2}$% of the tax due to or from the person for the period. It also has to be shown that the misdeclaration is the third, or subsequent misdeclaration in excess of 15% within the six years to the end of the accounting period concerned. Two of the previous occasions must have occurred within any four year period within the six year limit. The penalty is 30% of the tax misdeclared.

(d) *Failure to notify liability to register and unauthorised issue of invoices* (s. 15, F.A. 1985)

The penalty is £50 (if no tax arises) or £50 plus an amount equal to the tax due in other cases.

(e) *Breach of walking possession* (s. 16, F.A. 1985)

A person who removes goods subject to a distraint is liable to civil penalties.

(f) *Breach of regulatory provisions* (s. 17, F.A. 1985)

Failure to comply with various statutory regulations with regard to notification, records, information, etc, will give rise to a daily penalty which is determined on an increasing scale by reference to the number of previous failures in the preceding two years.

(g) *Interest on tax recovered by assessment* (s. 18, F.A. 1985)

Interest will be charged on tax which is recovered by means of an assessment.

(h) *Default surcharge* (s. 19, F.A. 1985)

Failure to pay by VAT the due date for the period concerned will result in a "default surcharge" the amount of which (up to a maximum of 30%) is determined on an increasing scale by reference to the number of previous occasions of late payment.

ASSESSMENTS (ss. 21, 22, F.A. 1985)

The general time limit for making an assessment is within six years of the end of the prescribed accounting period concerned. However, where there is a conviction for fraud the limit is extended to 20 years (9 years if the individual concerned has died). In any event such an assessment must be made within 3 years after an individual's death.

Penalties, surcharges and interest charges are made by assessment. Similar time limits apply to such assessments. The penalties, interest or surcharge must be made within two years after the tax due is finally determined.

Supplementary assessment can be made at any time within the above time limits.

APPEALS (s. 24, F.A. 1985)
Matters which may be brought on appeal before the tribunal include:
- (i) Estimated assessments.
- (ii) Registration difficulties.
- (iii) Computation difficulties on the amount of input tax which may be deducted.
- (iv) Computation difficulties on the proportion of any supplies which are to be taken as taxable supplies.
- (v) Appeals against any direction made by Customs and Excise regarding the value to be placed on either goods or services.
- (vi) Appeals against any security which a taxable person may be required to deposit as the Customs and Excise regard him as a revenue risk.
- (vii) Appeals against penalties for evasion, serious misdeclaration, failure to notify liability to register and unauthorised use of invoices, breach of walking possession, breach of regulations.
- (viii) Appeals against assessments raised to recover penalties, interest or surcharge.
- (ix) Making an assessment outside the normal time limits.

Appendix 1

RELIEFS, ALLOWANCES AND TAX RATES FOR PREVIOUS YEARS

§ 1.—PERSONAL ALLOWANCES AND RELIEFS FOR THE SIX YEARS BEFORE 1985–86

Personal allowances

Single individual £
1979–80 1,165
1980–81 1,375
1981–82 1,375
1982–83 1,565
1983–84 1,785
1984–85 2,005

Married man
1979–80 . . . . 1,815 (plus wife's earned income—max. £1,165)
1980–81 and
1981–82 . . . . 2,145 (plus wife's earned income—max. £1,375)
1982–83 . . . . 2,445 (plus wife's earned income—max. £1,565)
1983–84 . . . . 2,795 (plus wife's earned income—max. £1,785)
1984–85 . . . . 3,155 (plus wife's earned income—max. £2,005)

Note. The married allowance is reduced by the following amounts for each complete month to the date of marriage:

£
1979–80 . . . . 54.17
1980–81 . . . . 64.17
1981–82 . . . . 64.17
1982–83 . . . . 73.33
1983–84 . . . . 84.17
1984–85 . . . . 95.83

Dependent relative
1978–79 to 1983–84   £100 or £145 but income limit related to basic retirement pension (see text).

Services of son or daughter resident with and maintained by taxpayer
1979–80 to 1984–85   £55

Housekeeper (male or female) or person looking after children
1979–80 to 1984–85   £100

---

* Includes son from 1978–79.

† Female only prior to 1978–79.

Widow(er)s and others entitled to Child Allowance

	£
1979–80	650
1980–81	770
1981–82	770
1982–83	880
1983–84	1,010
1984–85	1,150

Widow's bereavement allowance
1981–82	£770
1982–83	£880 (applies also in year following death)
1983–84	1,010 (applies also in year following death)
1984–85	1,150

Blind persons
1975–76 to 1980–81	£180 less full disability payments (max, £360)
1981–82 to 1984–85	£360 (£720 if both husband and wife blind)

Life assurance relief
1979–80 and 1980–81	$17\frac{1}{2}\%$
1981–82 onwards	15% (deducted from insurance premiums)

withdrawn for policies effected after 13th March 1984

§ 2.—BASIC RATES OF INCOME TAX FOR THE SIX YEARS BEFORE 1982–83

1979–80	30%	(Lower rate of 25% on first £750)
1980–81	30%	
1981–82	30%	
1982–83	30%	
1983–84	30%	
1984–85	30%	

§ 3.—HIGHER RATES
1980–81 and 1981–82

£	%
11,250–13,250	40
13,250–16,750	45
16,750–22,250	50
22,250–27,750	55
Over 27,750	60

1982–83

£	%
12,800–15,100	40
15,100–19,100	45
19,100–25,300	50
25,300–31,500	55
Over 31,500	60

1983–84

£	%
14,600–17,200	40
17,200–21,800	45
21,800–28,900	50
28,900–36,000	55
over 36,000	60

1984–85

£	%
15,400–18,200	40
18,200–23,100	45
23,100–30,600	50
30,600–38,100	55
over 38,100	60

§ 4.—INVESTMENT INCOME SURCHARGE

1979–80:	First £5,000 nil; thereafter 15%
1980–81 and 1981–82:	First £5,500 nil; thereafter 15%
1982–83	First £6,250 nil; thereafter 15%
1983–84	First £7,100 nil; thereafter 15%
1984–85	Nil

§ 5.—AGE ALLOWANCE

	Single £	Married £	Income limit £	Not beneficial	
1979–80.........	1,540	2,455	5,000	5,562	5,960
1980–81.........	1,820	2,895	5,900	6,567	7,025
1981–82.........	1,820	2,895	5,900	6,567	7,025
1982–83.........	2,070	3,295	6,700	7,457	7,975
1983–84.........	2,360	3,755	7,600	8,462	9,040
1984–85.........	2,490	3,955	8,100	8,828	9,300

The allowance is reduced by 2/3 of the excess over the income limit.

Appendix 2

RELIEF FOR INVESTMENT IN NEW CORPORATE TRADES—BUSINESS START-UP RELIEF

BUSINESS START-UP SCHEME (ss. 52–57 and Schedules 11 and 12 F.A. 1981)

APPLICATION (s. 52)

The relief applies for the years 1981–82, 1982–83 and 1983–84 to *qualifying individuals* for *shares* in a new *qualifying company* for the purpose of raising money for a new *qualifying trade* which is carried on by the company or which it intends to carry on within the next twelve months.

The relief is given as a deduction (a personal allowance) against the individual's total income in the year of assessment in which the shares are issued.

A claim for the relief must be made and is not available unless and until the company has carried on the trade for four months. If the company is not carrying on the trade when the shares are issued the relief will be denied unless the trade is commenced within twelve months of the issue date or such further period (up to a maximum of 24 months) as the Board may allow.

The relief is granted after all other personal allowances, although the restriction as to the order of set-off (i.e. earned income first) does not apply.

The conditions as to qualification (see below) must be met throughout the *relevant period* which in general is five years from the date the shares are issued, but shortened to three years as regards qualifying company and qualifying trade. If the conditions are not satisfied the relief is withdrawn (or reduced in the case of sale within the five year relevant period).

RELEVANT PERIOD (s. 52(5))

The relevant period is the period throughout which the various conditions as to qualification must be met from the date shares are issued on which relief is claimed. The period commences with the incorporation of the company (or two years prior to the share issue date if later) and ends five years after the issue of the shares (three years for qualifying company and trade).

RELIEF LIMITATION (s. 53)

The maximum relief available to an individual is as follows:

1981–82	£10,000 (available to carry forward in whole or part to 1982–83 if unutilised)
1982–83	£20,000 (but increased to £30,000 maximum if no relief granted in 1981–82)
1983–84	£20,000

The maximum relief for 1981–82 and 1982–83 is £30,000, but in determining the relief for those two years, the maximum relief for 1981–82 is £10,000.

Example 1

Emma subscribes for the following shares in Delta Ltd:

	£
1981–82	8,000
1982–83	27,000
1983–84	15,000

Assuming that all qualifying conditions are satisfied, relief will be available as follows.

		£
1981–82	....	8,000
1982–83	....	22,000 (£20,000 + £2,000) (unutilised 1981–82: i.e. £10,000 − £8,000)
1983–84	....	15,000

Example 2

Assume that in Example 1 subscription is as follows:

		£
1981–83.	....	15,000
1982–83	....	12,000
1983–84	....	25,000
Relief would be:		
1981–82	....	10,000 (maximum)
1982–83	....	12,000
1983–84	....	20,000 (maximum—N.B. No entitlement to carry forward unutilised relief from earlier years)

No relief is granted if investment in a company is less than £500 (unless investment is made via an approved investment fund).

Example 3

Horse, Bear and Dog subscribe in 1982–83 for shares in Nexos and Paxos Ltd as follows:

	Nexos Ltd	*Paxos Ltd*
Horse	£ 400	£ 300
Bear	2,000	450
Dog	8,000	26,000

Assuming all qualifying conditions are satisfied and that no qualifying investments were made in 1981–82 relief will be granted:

Horse—Nil (since investment in each company is less than £500)
Bear—£2,000 (no relief for investment in Paxos Ltd since less than £500)
Dog—£30,000 (maximum claim available)

Additionally, for full relief to be available the maximum number of shares issued by a company on which relief is claimed is 50%. Where shares issued on which relief is claimed exceed 50% the relief is reduced to allow relief on 50% of the issued shares. This is then pro-rated if claims are made by more than one individual, in proportion to the amounts subscribed, on which claims would be made.

This condition need not be satisfied for shares issued after 5th April 1983 (i.e. to tie in with the new expansion relief).

Example 4

Leaf and Tree subscribe in 1982–83 for shares in Bark Ltd a company qualifying for "start-up relief". The shares issued are as follows:

	%	£
Leaf	....	25	4,000
Tree	....	30	5,000

The maximum relief available is 50% of the share capital. Thus relief on shares
subscribed is $\dfrac{50}{55} \times £9,000 = £8,182$

Relief is therefore available to Leaf and Tree:

Leaf $\dfrac{4,000}{9,000}$ (amount subscribed)
(total amounts on which claims can be made) $\times 8,182 = £3,636$

Tree $\dfrac{5,000}{9,000}$ (————"————)
(————"————) $\times 8,182 = £4,546$

(*n.b.* The 50% limitation will not deny relief to an individual who has subscribed more than
£500 even though the relief may be reduced below that amount).

QUALIFYING CONDITIONS
Relief for investment will not qualify unless the qualifications as to individual,
new company and new trade are satisfied. These are as follows:

(1) INDIVIDUAL SUBSCRIBERS (S. 54)
An individual will only qualify for relief if he is resident and ordinarily resident
in the U.K. in the year the shares are issued *and* he is *not* connected with the
company at any time in the relevant period.
An individual is connected with a company if he *or an associate* of his is:
    (*a*) an employee of the company or an employee of a partner of the
        company
    (*b*) a partner of the company
    (*c*) a director of the company or of a company which is a partner of the
        company, unless no payment is received by the director.
Payment of the following sums to a director are ignored in considering whether
payment is received
    (*a*) any payment or reimbursement of travelling or other expenses wholly,
        exclusively and necessarily incurred by him or his associate in the
        performance of his duties as a director of the company;
    (*b*) any interest which represents no more than a reasonable commercial
        return on money lent to the company;
    (*c*) any dividend or other distribution which does not exceed a normal
        return on the investment;
    (*d*) any payment for the supply of goods which does not exceed their market
        value; and
    (*e*) any reasonable and necessary remuneration which:
        (i) is paid for services rendered to the company in the course of a trade
            or profession (not being secretarial or managerial services or services
            of a kind provided by the company itself); and
        (ii) is taken into account in computing the profits or gains of the trade
            or profession under Case I or II of Schedule D.
An individual is also connected with a company if:
    (i) he directly or indirectly possesses or is entitled to acquire more than 30%
       of:
        (*a*) the issued ordinary share capital of the company; or
        (*b*) the loan capital and issued share capital of the company; or
        (*c*) the voting power in the company.
    (ii) he directly or indirectly possesses or is entitled to acquire such rights
       which would in the event of a winding up of the company entitle him
       to receive more than 30% of the assets available to the equity holders
       (The percentage distribution and equity holders for this purpose are
       determined by reference to paragraphs 1 and 3 of Schedule 12 F.A.
       1973).

(2) NEW QUALIFYING COMPANIES (S. 55)

A company is a *new company* until the end of five years from the date of incorporation or the date of trade commencement if later.

Example 5

Novos Ltd commenced trading on 1st December 1979 having been incorporated on 1st June 1979. Novos will be a new company until 1st December 1984 (i.e.five years from the date of trading).

The requirements to be met for a company to be a *qualifying company* are that throughout the relevant period (in this case "three years"):

    (a) it must be incorporated, and resident in the U.K.;

    (b) it must exist wholly or substantially wholly for the purpose of carrying on one or more *new qualifying trades*;

    (c) its share capital consists only of ordinary shares or fixed interest preference shares;

    (d) its ordinary shares, except for voting rights, carry the same rights;

    (e) all shares are fully paid up;

    (f) it is not controlled by another company or itself controls another company (other than a 100% subsidiary which itself would qualify for relief if available).

[From 5th April 1983 only all or partly paid shares are prohibited and items (c) and (d) are removed.]

A company ceases to be a qualifying company if during the relevant period a winding up commences unless the winding up is for bona fide commercial reasons (and not for tax avoidance purposes) and the assets are distributed before the end of the relevant period or within 3 years from the date of winding up if later.

(3) NEW QUALIFYING TRADES (S. 56)

New trade

A trade is a *new trade* if it is a bona fide new venture, which can include any trade carried on by another person at some time in the five year period before the share issue. This will therefore cover the case where for example a business is transferred to a new company under the capital gains tax provisions of s. 123 C.G.T.A. 1979 (see Chapter 30). A trade is not a *new trade* if:

    (a) a person has a controlling interest in the trade at any time within twelve months from the date the company begins to carry it on and in the same period has a controlling interest in another trade which is carried on at the same time (or which was being carried on more than five years before the share issue) *and*

    (b) the trades are similar (i.e. concerned with similar types of facilities or serving similar outlets or markets).

Qualifying trades

No definition as to a *qualifying trade* is given although the trade must during the relevant period ("3 years") be carried on with a view to profit and on a commercial basis.

If the trade consists substantially of any of the following activities however it will *not* qualify:

    (a) dealing in commodities, shares, securities, land or futures; or

    (b) dealing in goods otherwise than in the course of an ordinary trade of wholesale or retail distribution; or

    (c) banking, insurance, money-lending, debt-factoring, hire-purchase financing or other financial activities; or

    (d) leasing (including letting ships on charter or other assets on hire) or receiving royalties or licence fees; or

    (e) providing legal or accountancy services; or

(*f*) providing services or facilities for any trade carried on by another person which consists to any substantial extent of above activities and in which a controlling interest is held by a person who also has a controlling interest in the trade carried on by the company.

Only an ordinary trade of wholesale or retail distribution is a qualifying trade. A trade of wholesale distribution is one in which the goods are offered for sale and sold to persons for resale by them or for processing and resale by them. A trade of retail distribution is one in which the goods are offered for sale and sold to members of the general public for their use or consumption.

In determining whether a trade is an ordinary trade of wholesale or retail distribution the following factors are relevant:

    (1) The goods are bought by the trader in quantities larger than those in which he sells them.

    (2) The goods are bought and sold by the trader in different markets.

    (3) The trader employs staff and incurs expenses in the trade in addition to the cost of the goods and, in the case of a trade carried on by a company, in addition to any remuneration paid to any person connected with it.

Factors which indicate that an ordinary trade is *not* being carried on are:

    (1) There are purchases or sales from or to persons who are connected with the trader.

    (2) Purchases are matched with forward sales or vice versa.

    (3) The goods are held by the trader for longer than is normal for goods of the kind in question.

    (4) The trade is carried on otherwise than at a place or places commonly used for wholesale or retail trade.

    (5) The trader does not take physical possession of the goods.

REDUCTION WITHDRAWAL OF RELIEF (ss. 57 and 58)

Apart from non-satisfaction of the qualifying criteria set out above, (and the anti-avoidance provisions—see below) relief can also be reduced or withdrawn in the following cases where in the relevant period:

    (*a*) the shares are disposed of *or*

    (*b*) value is received from the company.

(*a*) *Disposed of shares* (N.B. only within the relevant period)

Relief is totally withdrawn if the disposals are not at arm's length. In other cases the relief is reduced by the amount of the disposal proceeds.

Where shares on which relief has been given and other shares are held disposals are deemed to be made from "relief shares" first.

Example

Hamlet acquires the following shares in Shake Ltd:

	Shares	Amount £
1980–81.	2,000	4,000
1981–82 (relief claimed)	3,000	7,000

If Hamlet sells 2,500 shares in Shake Ltd in 1985 (i.e. within the relevant period) for £4,000 in an arm's length transaction, the relief withdrawn will be £4,000 (N.B. The total relief claimed on 2,500 shares is £5,833 = 2,500/3,000 × £7,000.)

(*b*) *Value received from a company* (N.B. only in the relevant period)

Relief is reduced to the extent that value is obtained from the company. Value is received if the company:

AMOUNT OF VALUE

(*a*) repays, redeems or repurchases any of its share capital or securities which belong to the individual or makes any payment to him for giving up his right to any of the company's share capital or any security on its cancellation or extinguishment;

The greater of the shares' market value or the amount received.

(*b*) repays any debt owed to the individual other than a debt which was incurred by the company
   (i) on or after the date on which he subscribed for the shares in respect of which the relief is claimed; and
   (ii) otherwise than in consideration of the extinguishment of a debt incurred before that date;

The greater of the market value of the debt or the amount received.

(*c*) makes to the individual any payment for giving up his right to any debt (other than a debt for travelling or other expenses incurred in the performance of the duties of a director or for professional etc. services rendered or an ordinary trade debt) on its extinguishment.

The greater of the market value of the debt or the amount received.

(*d*) releases or waives any liability of the individual to the company or discharges, or undertakes to discharge, any liability of his to a third person;

The amount of the liability.

(*e*) makes a loan in advance to the individual;

The amount of the loan.

(*f*) provides a benefit or facility for the individual;

The cost of providing the benefit less any amount made good.

(*g*) transfers an asset to the individual for no consideration or for consideration less than its market value or acquires an asset from him for consideration exceeding its market value; or

The market value of the asset less any consideration received.

(*h*) makes to him any other payment except a payment mentioned above as not being treated as a payment to a director (refer Qualifying Conditions above) or a payment in discharge of an ordinary trade debt.

The amount of the payment.

Additionally, value is received where the individual receives any distribution in the course of a winding up (and the winding up in itself does not deny relief: see above).

Relief is withdrawn for earlier share issues first.

Relief will also be reduced if at any time in the relevant period the company redeems or repays any of its share capital which belongs to a shareholder other than an individual claiming the relief. The reduction in the relief is the greater of the amount received the nominal value of the shares redeemed. Where value is received under these circumstances, adjustment is also made to the company's issued share capital for the purposes of calculating future applicability of the 50% and 30% tests.

ANTI-AVOIDANCE (s. 59 F.A. 1981)

Start-up relief will not be granted unless the shares are issued for bona fide commercial reasons and not as part of a scheme or arrangement the main purpose of which is the avoidance of tax. (It is understood that the Commissioners of Inland Revenue do not interpret obtaining relief *per se* as "an arrangement the main . . .")

HUSBAND AND WIFE (s. 60)

A husband and wife living together are treated as one. Subscriptions are accordingly aggregated for limit purposes. Relief is given against the husband's total income (which includes the wife's income) unless an election to separate assessment (s. 38 I.C.T.A. 1970) or separate taxation of the wife's earnings (s. 23 F.A. 1971) applies.

In the case of separate assessment, relief due to the wife is set against her income and any excess set against her husband's income (i.e. as with personal allowances).

In the case of separate taxation, relief is given to the spouse making the payment and set off as with other personal allowances. In both cases where the annual limit is exceeded, relief is apportioned according to the amount subscribed.

Where marriage occurs during the year, husband and wife are treated as separate individuals, so that the limits of £500 and £10,000 are applied separately. Excess relief in the year of marriage where an election under s. 36(7) F.A. 1976 is made can be set against the other's income. The husband can offset any surplus relief against the wife's income, but where the wife has excess relief only that relief applicable to the period after marriage is available for offset.

Where the marriage ends as a result of divorce, or the couple cease to live together or the husband dies, the wife is treated as a separate person from the date the marriage ends and is entitled to her own relief for this period to the end of the year of assessment.

Any assessment withdrawing relief as a result of a disposal by the spouse subscribing for the shares, following the ending of a marriage, is made on that spouse notwithstanding relief may have been granted to the other spouse.

Disposals of shares between spouses does not give rise to a withdrawal of relief and the relevant period is therefore not broken. Where however the shares are sold to a third party following a transfer *and* at that time the marriage has ended, the assessment for withdrawing relief is made on the spouse making the disposal.

CLAIMS AND ASSESSMENTS WITHDRAWING RELIEF (ss. 61 and 62)

Claims for relief cannot be made earlier than the end of the year of assessment in which the shares are issued or if later the end of the first year of the company carrying on the new trade.

The claims to be valid must then be made not later than two years after the earliest date as above.

A claim must be accompanied by a statement by the company that the conditions as to the company and the trade are satisfied up to the date of the claim. The statement must contain a declaration that the information is correct to the best of the company's knowledge and belief. Any fraudulent or negligent statement is liable to a fine not exceeding £250 or £500 in the case of fraud.

Where a claim to be made will result in a partial withdrawal of relief since the 50% limit will be exceeded, the claim must be accompanied by a statement by the individuals to whom relief has already been granted that they consent to the claim being made.

Interest on overdue tax will run notwithstanding relief is subsequently given, but tax not paid (or due and payable later) will for interest purposes be regarded as paid on the date of making the claim.

Assessments for withdrawing relief are made under Case VI of Schedule D in the year in which the relief is granted. The assessment (subject to fraud, wilful default and neglect) can be made up to any time within six years of the end of the year of assessment in which the event giving rise to the withdrawal occurred.

No assessment can however be made for any event occurring after a person's death which would give rise to a relief withdrawal.

The reckonable date for interest purposes depends on the event giving rise to the relief withdrawal. In the case of a disposal the reckonable date is the date of disposal, in the case of value received the reckonable date is the date value is received. For other events it is the date of the event and where relief is not due as a result of tax avoidance it is the date the relief was given.

INFORMATION (s. 63)

Individuals or companies concerned with the start-up relief are required to notify the Inspector if certain events take place. The Inspector is also empowered to obtain information in certain circumstances.

An individual must within 60 days inform the Revenue where events take place which cause relief to be withdrawn, as a result of the following:

    (i) there is a disposal of shares (within the relevant period)

    (ii) the individual ceases to qualify

    (iii) value is received from the company

    (iv) following a spouse transfer and after the marriage ends there is a disposal to a third party.

The company is similarly required to inform the Inspector within 60 days of an event which causes relief to be withdrawn, as a result of the following:

    (i) the company ceases to be a qualifying company or the trade ceases to be a qualifying trade.

    (ii) value is received from the company

    (iii) shares are issued as part of an avoidance scheme (in practice this will be difficult to determine), or shares are redeemed or a shareholder becomes entitled to receive value.

The Inspector is entitled to obtain information either from the individual or the company if he believes a scheme or arrangements is in existence such that:

    (i) the company can become a subsidiary of another company

    (ii) the issue of shares is part of a scheme the main purpose of which is the avoidance of tax.

    (iii) the individual is connected with a company by virtue of any arrangement whereby he subscribes for shares through another person. (see s. 54(9))

The Inspector is furthermore empowered to disclose to a company the number of shares on which relief has been granted notwithstanding an obligation to secrecy that may otherwise apply.

CAPITAL GAINS TAX (s. 64)

The sum deductible in computing any capital gains tax liability is reduced only to the extent a capital loss would otherwise arise (i.e. where cost exceeds proceeds). In this case the cost is reduced by the *lesser* of:

    (i) the whole amount of the relief *or*

    (ii) the difference between cost and proceeds.

Example

In 1982–83 Lear subscribed £12,000 for shares in Othello Ltd and obtained £10,000 of "start-up" relief.

Assuming he sells the shares six years later for:

	£
(a)	15,000
(b)	9,000
(c)	750

the gain will be as follows:

		£
(a) Proceeds		15,000
Cost (no restriction)....................		12,000
		Gain £3,000
(b) Proceeds		9,000
Cost.................................	12,000	
Less (cost excess £12,000 − £9,000)	3,000	9,000
		Gain £ Nil
(c) Proceeds		750
Cost.................................	12,000	
Less Relief granted....................	10,000	2,000
Capital loss		£(1,250)

(In this case the relief granted (£10,000) is less than the difference between proceeds and cost (£11,250) and accordingly is used to reduce the original cost.)

The pooling rules as to shares under s. 65, C.G.T.A. 1979 do not apply to shares on which start-up relief has been granted. The shares are for the purposes of capital gains tax separately identified and where mixed holdings occur, "relief shares" are deemed to be disposed first: earlier acquisitions before later acquisitions.

MISCELLANEOUS

(1) *Subsidiaries* (s. 65)

As noted above, a company will not qualify for relief if it is a 51% subsidiary of another company or itself has 51% subsidiaries. This rule is relaxed so that a company will qualify if it has 100% subsidiaries which themselves would be qualifying companies or acquires a subsidiary during the relevant period which would be a qualifying company (s. 52 F.A. 1982). The subsidiaries will *not* qualify. The relief also applies if the issue of shares was to provide funds for a new qualifying trade to be carried on by a subsidiary (Schedule 12, para. 1, F.A. 1981).

(2) *Nominee Holdings* (s. 66)

Shares subscribed, issued and held by or disposed of for an individual by a nominee are treated for relief purposes as shares of the individual.

(3) *Approved Investment Funds* (s. 66)

Relief is available to an individual who invests through an approved investment fund (approved for start up relief purposes) given the fund merely acts as nominee. Furthermore the £500 *de minimis* limit does not apply where investment is channelled through a fund.

Appendix 3

NATIONAL INSURANCE CONTRIBUTIONS

§ 1.—CLASS 1 EARNINGS (WEEKLY)

		From 6.4.85		From 6.10.85	
Not contracted out:		Employee %	Employer %	Employee %	Employer %
	£				
Less than:	35.50*	—	—	—	—
	55.00			5	5
	90.00			7	7
	130.00	9.00	10.45	9	9
	265.00			9	
Over	265.00	**	**	**	10.45

* Rates apply to all earnings where lower earnings limit exceeded
** Rates apply to a maximum earnings ceiling of £265

		From 6.4.85		From 6.10.85	
Contracted out:		Employee %	Employer %	Employee %	Employer %
	£				
Less than:	35.50	9***	10.45***	—	—
	55.00			2.85	0.90
	90.00			4.85	2.90
	130.00	6.85	6.35	6.85	4.90
	265.00			6.85	6.35
Over:	265.00				
on first	35.50	—	—	9.00	10.45
on balance to	265.00	—	—	6.85	6.35
on excess over	265.00	—	—	—	10.45

*** Where earnings exceed £35.50

§2.—CLASS 2 EARNINGS

	From 6.4.85 Self Employed £	From 6.10.85 Self Employed £
On all earnings where income exceeds £1925 per annum	4.75	3.50

§3.—CLASS 3 VOLUNTARY CONTRIBUTIONS

From 6.4.85 Self Employed £	From 6.10.85 Self Employed £
4.75	3.50

§4.—CLASS 4 (50% income tax deduction for 1985–86 onwards)

Earnings—upper	£13,780
—lower	£4,150
Rate	6.3%
Maximum	£607

Index

References are to chapters and numbered sections within chapters.

Table of Statutes

Table of Cases